FIELD GUIDE TO

BUTTERFLIES

OF SOUTH AFRICA

FIELD GUIDE TO
BUTTERFLIES
OF SOUTH AFRICA

STEVE WOODHALL

Quick colour-coded reference to butterfly subfamilies

PAGES	

36–39

DANAINAE – Monarchs, Friars, Novice, Layman. Medium to large butterflies; slow, sailing flight, distasteful. The African Monarch's orange coloration is a deterrent to predators. Black and white or yellow are also warning colours, as shown by the Novice and Layman.

40–80

SATYRINAE – Browns, Ringlets. Small to medium-sized butterflies (e.g. Dark-webbed Ringlet) with a few larger species (the Beauties and Widows). Characteristic brown colour, often with red or orange patches. Almost all have eye spots on both upper and undersides.

80–101

HELICONIINAE – Bitter Acraeas, Leopards. Bitter Acraeas are small to medium sized with elongated wings and a slow, leisurely flight; distasteful; often with red and yellow or black and white colouring, or transparent wing areas. Leopards are tawny with dark spots.

102–116

CHARAXINAE – Emperors, Queens. Medium to very large, robust, agile, high and fast flying. Do not usually feed at flowers, fonder of rotten fruit, tree sap and animal droppings. Many are orange (e.g. Pearl Emperor); others have blue markings (e.g. Large Blue Emperor), or are black (e.g. Demon Emperor). Queens have rounded, dark wings with paler spots.

116–124

LIMENITINAE – Gliders, Foresters, Nymphs, False Acraeas, Sailers. Small to quite large, showing characteristic gliding flight with few wingbeats. Gliders have angular wings and often settle with flat open wings. Foresters and Nymphs are brightly coloured and fly low. False Acraeas closely resemble Bitter Acraeas, and Sailers are small, black-and-white butterflies.

124

CYRESTINAE – Map Butterfly. Monotypic in Africa; unmistakable. May fly high or low.

124–128

BIBLIDINAE – Tree Nymphs, Jokers, Pipers. Small to medium sized with characteristic expanded forewing veins at base and a flap-glide flight pattern. Tree Nymphs are usually brown (one is brilliant mauve), Jokers orange and Pipers black with white or orange bands.

128–140

NYMPHALINAE – Diadems, Mothers-of-Pearl, Pirate, Commodores, Pansies, Painted Lady, Admirals. Medium to large, colourful and robust, strongly attracted to flowers; flap-glide flight pattern. Diadems are mimics of distasteful species such as the African Monarch. Mothers-of-Pearl are large, pale and iridescent. Pirates, Commodores, Pansies and Admirals are brightly coloured and conspicuous.

140

LIBYTHEINAE – Snout Butterfly. Monotypic in Africa; unmistakable. Small, brown and orange, with low flight.

FAMILY NYMPHALIDAE

LYCAENIDAE

PORITIINAE – Zulus, Buffs, Rocksitters. Small, sedentary, slow flying. Buffs and Zulus are flimsy, yellow to buff with dark markings. Rocksitters have undersides reminiscent of lichen, and bright black-and-orange upper sides.

140-148

MILETINAE – Purples, Woolly Legs, Skollies. Small, dull-coloured butterflies with secretive habits. Purples and Woolly Legs are dull mauve-grey, fast flying around trees and shrubs. Skollies are brown, black or buff, found in small colonies, and with a low flight.

148-164

LYCAENINAE – Sapphires, Hairstreaks, Black-eyes, Proteas, Playboys, High-fliers, Bars, Gems, Scarlets, Arrowheads, Coppers, Opals, Greys, Hairtails, Bronzes, Pies, Blues. Small to medium sized, showing great variety. Common behavioural feature is rubbing of hind wings against one another when resting. Sapphires, Hairstreaks: bright blue, tailed, high flying. Black-eyes, Proteas, Playboys: brown or orange, fast and darting. High-fliers, Bars, Gems: brightly patterned, very fast flying. Scarlets, Arrowheads, Coppers, Opals, Greys: brown or red to copper. Hairtails, Bronzes, Pies, Blues: brown, pied or blue with spots and streaks.

164-317

PIERIDAE

PIERINAE – Zebra White, Vagrants, Tips, Whites, Dotted Borders. Medium to large sized, showy butterflies in colours of white, yellow and orange, strongly attracted to flowers. Vagrants are large, tinged green or blue. Tips are white with red, orange or purple wing tips. Whites and Dotted Borders are pale with black spots and streaks.

318-345

COLIADINAE – Clouded Yellows, Migrant, Grass Yellows. Small to medium sized, yellow or green-white with dark borders.

346-349

PAPILIONIDAE

PAPILIONINAE – Swallowtails, Swordtails. Large to very large with fluttering flight, not always tailed. Swallowtails are larger and more robust than Swordtails. Attracted to flowers and mud puddles.

350-357

HESPERIIDAE

COELIADINAE – Policemen. Comparatively large, fast-flying skippers fond of flowers; often with bold markings.

358-361

PYRGINAE – Flats, Elves, Elfins, Velvet Skippers, Sandmen. Tiny to medium-sized skippers that often sit with wings held flat. Flight very fast and darting. Velvet Skippers are robust and brightly marked. Sandmen are black with white spots.

362-381

HETEROPTERINAE – Sylphs. Small brown skippers, sometimes with bright markings; slow, low flight.

382-388

HESPERIINAE – Rangers, Darts, Nightfighters, Hoppers, Swifts. Small to medium-sized skippers, with darting, skipping flight. Rangers are brown with varying degrees of bright markings. Darts and Hoppers are brown with large white to cream marks. Nightfighters and Swifts are brown with few pale marks; very fast flying.

388-413

Struik Publishers
(a division of New Holland Publishing
(South Africa) (Pty) Ltd)
Cornelis Struik House
80 McKenzie Street
Cape Town 8001

New Holland Publishing is a member of
the Johnnic Publishing Group.

www.struik.co.za

www.imagesofafrica.co.za

IMAGES OF AFRICA
P H O T O   L I B R A R Y

Log on to our photographic website
for an African experience

First published in 2005

10 9 8 7 6 5 4 3 2 1

Copyright © text, 2005: Steve Woodhall
Copyright © maps, 2005: Steve Woodhall
Copyright © photographs, 2005: Steve
    Woodhall, excepting those listed right
Copyright © published edition, 2005:
    Struik Publishers

Publishing manager: Pippa Parker
Managing editor: Lynda Harvey
Consultant: Mark Williams
Editor: Brenda Brickman
Proofreaders: Joanna Ward, Tessa Kennedy
Design director: Janice Evans
Designer: Robin Cox

Reproduction by Hirt & Carter Cape (Pty) Ltd
Printed and bound by Kyodo Printing Co.
    (S'pore) Pte Ltd, Singapore

ISBN 1 86872 724 6 (Standard edition)
ISBN 1 77007 186 5 (Collector's edition)

Picture Credits

Alan Gardiner: p151: **3A**, **3B**, **3C**, **3D**; Alan
Heath: p21; p34: *Chrysoritis zeuxo* egg, *Thestor
rileyi* egg; Alan Weaving: p161: **2A**, **2B**, **2C**,
2D; **3A**, **3B**; André Coetzer: p34: *Amauris
ochlea* egg; p99: **1C**; p127: **1A**; p127: **1B**;
p147: **2A**; p147: **2B**; p227: **3A**; p237: **3A**;
p311: **3B**; p323: **1D**; p425 (action shot);
Andrew Currie: p317: **3A**; Anthony Johnson:
p30: **middle L**; John Joannou: p24: **bottom L**;
p 34: *Pontia helice* egg, *Coeliades pisistratus*
egg, *Phalanta phalantha* pupa; p37: **1C**, **2A**,
2B; p51: **1a**, **1b**; p89: **1A**, **1C**; p95: **1B**; p101:
3A, **3B**; p103: **3A**, **3B**, **3C**; p105: **3A**, **3B**;
p111: **3C**; p113: **1B,1C,1D**; p121: **1C**, **2C**;
p129: **3B**, **3E**; p 130: **2C**; p131: **2C**, **4C**; p169:
2B; p171: **4A**, **4B**, **4C**; p173: **1A**, **1B**, **4A**;
p183: **2B**; p205: **3A**; p213: **1A**; p215: **1A**;
p219: **2A**, **3C**; p221: **3A**, **3B**; p247: **2A**; p257:
4A; p271: **1B**; p275: **5B**; p279: **1B**, **3B**; p307:
2A; p311: **1A**; p323: **3B**; p327: **2A**; p331: **1C**;
p343: **1A**; p353: **2C**; p357: **4B**; p381: **1B**;
p397: **2B**; p399: **1A**, **3A**; p405: **1B**; p413: **1B**;
Jonathan Ball: p105: **1A**; p391: **3A**, **3B**;
Michael Boppré: p20: **bottom**; Mike Picker:
p299: **1C**; p357: **4A**; Robert Paré: p 35: *Cyrestis
camillus* larva; p83: **2E**; p103: **3D**; p109: **1C**;
p119: **1C**; p125: **2B**; p373: **1**; p401: **1C**; Torben
B Larsen: p311: **2A**; Kevin Cockburn: Back
cover portrait

Contents

Acknowledgements

My greatest appreciation is for my dear wife Jayne, who has been unfailingly patient and tolerant of an absent, or uncommunicative, laptop-bound, husband. Thank you darling for your support.

My editor Brenda Brickman† took what I thought was well-planned text and got rid of all the inconsistencies and contradictions. Brenda passed away as she was finishing the book. I am very sad that she never got to see it in print. Helen de Villiers took over to steer the book through correcting, a process which went remarkably smoothly!

Pippa Parker of Struik fought the good fight and kept me motivated and encouraged when it looked as if the book would never see the light of day. Robin Cox was of invaluable help with the distribution maps and the awesome task of shoehorning all those pictures into this book and designing each page.

My employer Scott Bader (Pty) Ltd allowed me to plan my leave and turned a blind eye to my planning of business trips to coincide with butterfly emergence. To Chris Goodall, Peter Hedley and Richard Hesketh, thanks a million.

Prof. Mark Williams made a final check on taxonomic and biological accuracy; Alan Heath, Rolf Oberprieler and Ernest Pringle checked specific areas of text. Alan and Ernest also allowed me previews of taxonomic papers (on *Thestor* and *Chrysoritis*) that helped me avoid last minute re-writes and helped ensure that the book is as up to date as it can be. Dave Edge allowed me to use his recent observations on the genus *Orachrysops*. Any mistakes and omissions are mine only.

Thanks to Bill Steele for persuading me that writing a book is possible, and for help and encouragement along the way.

Over the many years it has taken to compile this book, I have enjoyed the help and companionship of my fellow lepidopterists and their families. Some provided much valued accommodation; others went beyond the call of duty by donating precious specimens for photography, or by allowing me photo opportunities on safari! If I have missed anyone out, I apologise:

Jonathan Ball, Ivan Bampton, Michael Bopprè, Tony Brinkman, Johan Buys, Andrè Claassens, Kevin and Stella Cockburn and family, Jan Coetzee, Bennie and Andrè Coetzer, Isak Coetzer, Steve Collins, Colin Congdon, Alf and Neville Curle, John Daffue, Jeremy and Chris Dobson, Dave Edge, Anthony and Gabriella Elworthy, Gordon Fraser-Grant, Kenneth Gainsford, Alan Gardiner, Owen and Wendy Garvie, Henk Geertsema, Johan Greyling, David Haggett, Alan Heath, Graham and Stephen Henning, Vaughan Jessnitz and family, John and Barbara Joannou, Simon and Tracey Joubert, Douglas Kroon, Martin Kruger, Martin and Dave Kunhardt, Scotty, Diane and Robbie Kyle and family, Torben Larsen, Pierre and Joy le Roux and family, Paul Liversidge, Martin Lunderstedt, Andrew Mayer, Dave and Phil McDermott, Cameron McMaster, Barry Mee, Ian and Sue Mullin, Neil Munnik, John Paul Niehaus, Rolf Oberprieler, Nolan Owen-Johnston, Robt and Claire Parè, Allan and Pam Plowes, Ricky Pott, Mike Prettejohn, Ernest and Anne Pringle, Keith Roos, Pieter Roos, Harold Selb, Peter Sharland, Hermann Staude, Bill and Chris Steele, Richard Stephen, Renier Terblanche, Dave Upshon, Esther and Eugene van der Westhuizen. Simon van Noort, Clive and Conita Walker, Peter Ward, Haydon Warren-Gash, John White and Mark Williams.

Foreword

A television advertisement was contrived to boost the sales of an aerosol insecticide, marketed by an international chemical company. Two chameleons, father and son, are on a branch with a large hairy fly perched nearby. "Yecch, dad – shall I zap him?" asks the son. The father pulls out his can and sprays the ugly fly stone-dead.

This distorted perception of the natural world was probably seen by millions of South Africans, whose revulsion for insects in general, and hairy flies in particular, would have been bolstered by this piece of gross misrepresentation – no doubt many bought the product from the local supermarket as a result. The artistic director from the advertising company had a happy client, and went on to the next job, oblivious to his part in increasing the intolerance of humans towards the little things that share our planet.

It struck me that no creative person in his right mind would have scripted the chameleon to spray a beautiful butterfly stone dead, rather than an ugly fly. To have done so would have outraged the viewers – butterflies, after all, are the epitome of graceful movement and bright colours, living jewels that bring pleasure and joy to gardeners and nature-lovers alike.

In a world where the number and variety of living creatures is in decline, the insects are in dire need of ambassadors who will speak for them, and persuade humankind that every piece of biodiversity is important for the overall health of the earth.

The butterflies are those ambassadors, and this wonderful book by Steve Woodhall is a fine tool with which to awaken the consciousness and compassion of South Africans to the insect world, and the magnificent natural wealth that ranks this country third in the world for its richness of biodiversity.

The bright colours and interesting lifestyles of South Africa's butterflies leap at the reader from the pages of this book. Who could fail to be moved by the sheer beauty of these creatures, and who would not get a thrill from being able to identify the different kinds of butterflies that occur in the different parts of this diverse country?

Butterflies have been popular 'flagships' for conservation, with tracts of land being set aside in South Africa to protect threatened populations of the Roodepoort Copper, the Heidelberg Copper and the Brenton Blue.

If people learn to study and love butterflies, they will become more tolerant of other insects, and more understanding of the need to tread gently on the fragile planet.

This excellent book is a key that can open that green door to a deeper understanding of biodiversity, and our role in conserving it for future generations.

John Ledger

Dr JOHN LEDGER
ENVIRONMENTAL CONSULTANT AND WRITER
ON ENERGY AND THE ENVIRONMENT

Introduction

South Africa is often described as 'a world in one country' because of its spectacularly diverse scenery and vegetation. This diversity extends to the country's wildlife, including its butterflies. There are about 20 000 species of butterfly worldwide, and South Africa is home to more than 660 of these (666 to be exact) – a vast number for a country that lies mostly outside the Tropics.

Generally, the further an area lies from the Equator, the poorer its butterfly fauna. Tropical butterflies are evolutionarily advantaged in that the lush, varied vegetation and warm climatic conditions encourage continuous generations that rapidly fill the region's many environmental niches. South Africa's butterfly richness stems in large part from the many specialist species that have adapted to niches created by our arid and temperate climate and our diverse vegetation types. Many of the butterflies are endemic, being found nowhere else in the world.

Butterflies, like most invertebrates, are sensitive to environmental change and have been recognised as important indicators of terrestrial environmental health. Invertebrates do not disperse as widely as vertebrates, making them more vulnerable to the presence of toxins in the immediate environment; therefore, if there are no butterflies (probably the most visible of the invertebrate species), the environment is unhealthy.

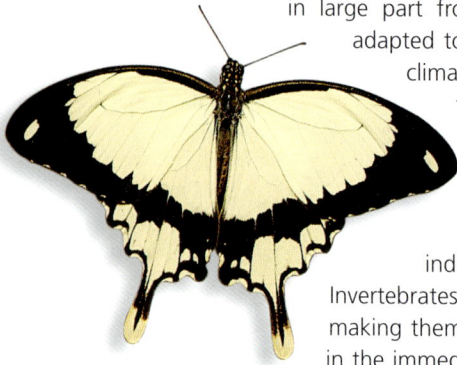

Mocker Swallowtails – male (centre) and two female forms

HOW TO USE THIS BOOK

Photographs/Plates

Butterflies are presented in the form of full-colour photographs and show male ♂ and female ♀ forms (where these differ) and, where possible, both under- and upper sides. Photographs are linked with individual species descriptions (on facing page) by a simple numbering system.

Layout of species accounts

The species accounts are arranged according to family, subfamily, and genus groups. Each genus is described in some detail and covers life history (ova–larvae–pupae) and habits, as these are usually constant within a genus. Each species account is given in a standard format, as shown below, and is accompanied by photographs of the species on the facing page to allow for easy identification and quick reference in the field.

1 African Monarch *Danaus chrysippus aegyptius*
Wingspan: ♂ 50–70 mm ♀ 50–75 mm. **Identification: 1A** ♂ upper side, **1B** ♀ underside (f. *liboria*), **1C** ♂ upper side (f. *transiens*), **1D** ♂ upper side (f. *alcippoides*). Most common colour forms are f. *chrysippus*, with subapical band of large white spots on black wing tip, and similar f. *liboria*, with smaller white spots. Forms *alcippus* and *alcippoides* resemble these two respectively, both with varying amounts of white on upper side of hind wing; in rarer f. *klugii*, wingtips orange, no spots, while f. *transiens* has indistinct spots on orange. Very rare f. *dorippus* resembles f. *klugii*, but wing bases not dark as in other forms. Often seen in numbers feeding on flowers. **Mimic:** ♀ Common Diadem (p. 128) polymorphic mimic of all forms of this butterfly. **Distribution:** Common throughout South Africa in all biomes. **Habitat:** forest edges, parks and gardens, hill tops, flatlands, coast, mountains, wetlands. **Flight period:** Year-round (peak late summer/autumn). **Larval food:** *Asclepias* spp., especially *A. fruticosa*, *Cynanchum obtusifolium*, *Ceropegia*, *Stapelia*, and *Huernia* sp.

1   **Map:** A quick-and-easy guide to the distribution of the species.
2   **Name:** Species' common name, alternative name (where applicable) and scientific name.
3   **Wingspan:** A typical range of sizes, from wing tip to wing tip for ♂ and ♀.
4   **Identification:** Identifies corresponding photographs on the facing page; points out important diagnostic features, and describes behavioural traits particular to the species.
5   **Mimic/Model:** Indicates whether the butterfly is a mimic of another species, or a model for a mimic (see **Coloration – avoiding predators**, p.18).
6   **Distribution:** A detailed description of the species' geographical distribution, including the biome/s in which it is found; to be used in conjunction with the map.
7   **Habitat:** Indicates the terrain in which the butterfly is most likely to be found.
8   **Flight period:** Gives typical and peak flight periods, i.e. when the butterfly is most likely to be seen.
9   **Larval food:** Refers to major larval food sources, usually plants but often (in lycaenids) other insects or insect secretions. A table of butterfly foods is provided on page 415.

Abbreviations

f. = form (morph of polymorphic species; refers to specific colour/pattern); sp = species (plural = spp.); subsp = subspecies; DSF = Dry Season Form; WSF = Wet Season Form; n, s, e, w, c, etc. = north, south, east, west, central, etc.; nr = near (as in an undescribed taxon resembling one already described)

ANATOMY OF A BUTTERFLY

A butterfly's body is made up of three sections – head, thorax and abdomen. The outer shell, or **exoskeleton**, is made of a complex polysaccharide (a carbohydrate made up of sugar molecules) called **chitin**. This is tough and strong, but flexible. It maintains the animal's structural integrity and shape. The muscles are attached to the exoskeleton, which also contains the liquid body contents.

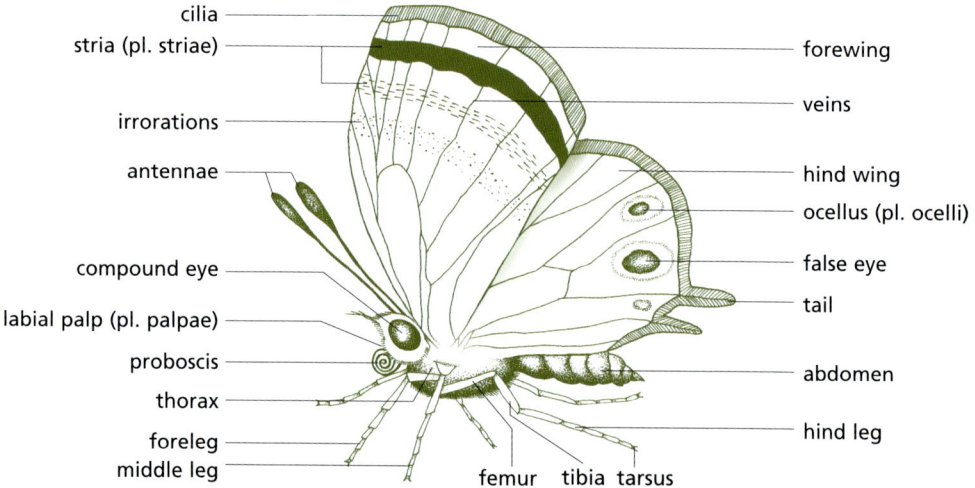

cilia
stria (pl. striae)
forewing
veins
irrorations
antennae
hind wing
ocellus (pl. ocelli)
compound eye
false eye
labial palp (pl. palpae)
tail
proboscis
thorax
abdomen
foreleg
hind leg
middle leg
femur   tibia tarsus

Butterflies have four wings: two forewings and two hind wings. Each is made up of thin skins of chitin held rigid by veins. The larger veins are used to pump blood through the wings to warm them. The pattern of veins on a butterfly's wings differs between species and is of great significance in determining its relationship to other butterflies. Each area of the wing has its own name, used to describe the location of pattern features.

1 = Discocellular vein complete
2 = Discocellular vein poorly developed
S_C = Subcostal vein
R, R_1, R_2, R_3, R_4, R_5 = radial veins
R_S = radial sector
M_1, M_2, M_3 = medial veins
CuA, CuA_1, CuA_2 = anterior cubital veins
CuP = posterior cubital veins
1A, 2A, 3A = anal vein
H = humeral vein
$S_C + R_1$ = composite vein formed from fusion of $S_C + R_1$ of the hind wing

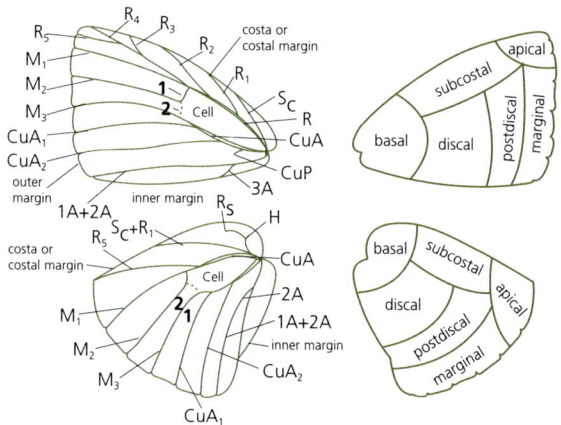

Vein nomenclature and wing parts
forewing (above); hind wing (below)

In flight, the fore- and hind wings are coupled by the overlap where they join the body.

The coloration of the wings, and all the hairs on the body, are made up of minute **scales**. Each scale is made of chitin and is attached to the body or wing by means of a tiny ball-and-socket joint. The patterns are in the form of spots, stripes (known as **striae**), bands, blotches and speckles. Many wings have tiny lines or spots set close to one another and running in one direction – these are known as **irrorations**.

> ## Order Lepidoptera
> The name of the order to which butterflies (and moths) belong – the Lepidoptera – stems from the Greek for wing scales. The word is derived from the Greek words *lepis*, meaning scale, and *pteron*, meaning wing. The patterns that the scales make are distinctive to each species and are important in the identification of butterflies.

TAXONOMY AND NOMENCLATURE

The classification of butterflies

All animals are classified into groups, or phyla. Each of these is made up of creatures with broadly similar anatomy and with certain features in common. The phylum is split up into a hierarchy of subdivisions. This table follows the hierarchy down to the basic unit of nomenclature – the species – using the African Monarch (*Danaus chrysippus*) as an example.

Phylum	Arthropoda	Invertebrate animals with jointed legs and an exoskeleton enclosing the body organs, providing support and shape
Class	Insecta	Insects
Order	Lepidoptera	Butterflies and moths
Superfamily	Papilionoidea	'True' butterflies
Family	Nymphalidae	Brush-footed butterflies
Subfamily	Danainae	
Genus	*Danaus*	Monarchs
Species	*chrysippus*	African Monarch
Subspecies	*aegyptius*	

The naming of butterflies

Carolus Linnaeus (1707–1778), Swedish-born naturalist, was the first to describe southern African butterflies using a binomial. Linnaeus named thousands of organisms in his time, and he, like Roland Trimen, Ken Pennington and Charles Dickson, is credited as 'author' of species he first described.

The purpose of a scientific name is to avoid the ambiguity and confusion that arises from the use of common names, which tend to differ from region to region and country to country. However, the scientific name is standard worldwide.

The first part of the binomial is the **genus** name. This serves to group together closely related species, although in some instances a genus can contain only one species. The second part of the binomial is the **species** (or **specific**) name. Each combination of a genus and species name is unique.

Species may be further subdivided into **subspecies**, which are well-defined local races. Taxonomically, these are identified by a trinomial – genus, species, subspecies – for example, *Danaus chrysippus aegyptius*. If the species and subspecies names are the same, for example, *Danaus chrysippus* **chrysippus**, this is referred to as the **nominate** race, and is the one that was first described to science.

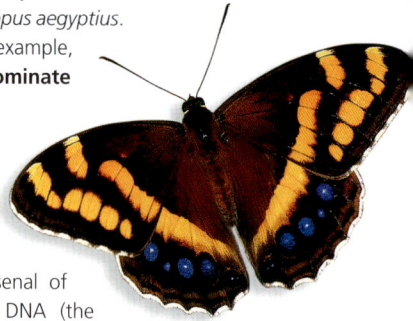

Table Mountain Beauty *Aeropetes tulbaghia* described as *Papilio tulbaghia* by Linnaeus

Name changes

In the early days of taxonomy, biologists classified animals largely on the basis of their external appearance (their **phenotype**). While physical features are still used by modern taxonomists, an increasingly impressive arsenal of other techniques is also used, including analysis of DNA (the **genotype**). Frequently, genetic analyses show that species whose physical appearance is quite similar are only distantly related to one another; the similarity in their phenotypes is merely an evolutionary response to living in the same environment (termed **convergence**). The development of new analytical techniques has plunged modern taxonomy into a state of flux and, frequently, modern taxonomists into a state of acrimonious controversy!

Changes to genus names

A new genus may be erected when, for example, a naturalist who has intensely studied a group of butterflies decides that some are more closely related to each other than they are to the rest of the species in the genus. Conversely, two genera may be so closely related that they are, to all intents and purposes, the same. In instances where two genera need to be merged, the name that was described first in history takes precedence and the more recent name is 'sunk', or synonymised.

Groups of species within a genus that have broadly similar characteristics are known as 'tribes'. Sometimes tribes are reclassified as genera, or they are moved from genus to genus. In neither case, however, does the specific name change.

Rossouw's Skolly *Thestor rossouwi*

Changes to specific names

A biologist may gather enough evidence to prove that one (or more) of a group of subspecies is actually a distinct species. In these cases, the trinomial name is reduced to a binomial, and the original subspecies name becomes the new specific name. This process is known as 'splitting'.

The reverse of this is found where studies show that two or more populations of butterflies that were thought to represent species or subspecies are in fact the same animal. In these cases, as with genera, the older name takes precedence and the newer one is sunk. This process is known as 'lumping'.

New names

New populations are discovered all the time, and sometimes these are sufficiently distinctive to be described as new species or subspecies. To achieve this, the author – the person describing the species or subspecies – must write a paper describing the new species and publish it in a recognised learned publication, for example, the journal of the Lepidopterists' Society of Africa, *Metamorphosis*. Publication implies an acceptance by peers of the new species.

What constitutes a 'species'?

Three features of this book well illustrate the modern taxonomic maelstrom:

- Some species (for example, the *Lepidochrysops* Blues) are so confusingly similar that sometimes the only way to tell specimens apart is to know where they were collected.
- Some species covered by previous works on South African butterflies are absent.
- Some species *not* covered by previous works on South African butterflies are included.

Taxonomic dilemmas stem in part from disagreements among taxonomists themselves as to the definition of a species. Some, for example, maintain that members of different species don't, under normal circumstances, voluntarily mate. But it is a well-documented fact that this is not the case. Is it, therefore, the point at which hybrids are not fertile, as in the horse and ass producing a mule? Recent evidence shows that this is probably not the case. The very distinctive European Mallard and African Yellow-billed Duck successfully hybridise and produce fertile offspring.

For many butterflies, crossing the species line is difficult if not impossible. However, in East Africa two closely related but very distinctive Swallowtail species do sometimes hybridise in the wild but their offspring's fertility is doubtful. The Green Banded Swallowtail *Papilio nireus* and Citrus Swallowtail *P. demodocus* look very different, are not known to mate in the wild, and no hybrids have ever been seen. But what about the high-altitude Oosthuizen's Blue *Lepidochrysops oosthuizeni* and the lower-altitude Koppie Blue *L. ortygia*? These are found not far from one another, behave similarly, and are very difficult to tell apart. To make matters worse, there is another population of Blues in between their ranges with intermediate characters. Could, or would these blues mate if they met? Is the darker colour and smaller size of Oosthuizen's Blue merely an adaptation to cooler and wetter living conditions?

Work by Rand, Heath, Suderman and Pierce on the DNA of some members of the genus *Chrysoritis* provided evidence for groups of species within it actually being single species. Following this study, Heath carried out breeding experiments on *Chrysoritis*. He found *inter alia* that wild adults of the Coetzer's Daisy Copper *Chrysoritis coetzeri* and the Donkey Daisy Copper *C. zonarius* showed consistent differences, but when bred side by side under identical conditions in captivity, the adults appeared identical. The wild populations were identical in most respects – in genitalia, egg and larval structure, and their associated ant species. The only distinguishing feature was

Oosthuizen's Blue *Lepidochrysops oosthuizeni*

Jitterbug Daisy Copper *Chrysoritis zeuxo*

Donkey Daisy Copper *Chrysoritis zonarius*

the wing patterns of the adults, which varied in the wild, but when the climatic variable was removed by captive breeding, the variation disappeared.

In the last 20 years, field workers have discovered many new populations of *Chrysoritis*, collecting specimens from different microclimates and in different seasons. On studying the samples, Heath became convinced that microclimate had such an effect on the appearance of adult *Chrysoritis* that previous workers had mistakenly described separate species that were, in fact, merely climatic forms or variants of the same species. He argued that variations in extent of black wing spotting, blue basal flush, etc., were simply adaptations to local conditions. He also noticed that these putative species shared a common host ant species. He postulated that each 'true' *Chrysoritis* species lives with a particular ant species over a large range, within which microclimatic variations lead to a great number of local forms.

This conclusion led to a revision of the genus, in which several butterflies previously regarded as different species were lumped. One of these was *C. coetzeri*, sunk to the earlier described *C. zonarius*. Another was Cottrell's Daisy Copper *C. cottrelli*, lumped with the Jitterbug Daisy Copper *C. zeuxo*. Several other members of the genus were sunk in this revision, and others are likely to be lumped in future.

Another recently revised genus is the lycaenid genus *Thestor*. Some species have been lumped, but two populations previously identified as the Knysna Skolly *Thestor brachycerus* have been raised to specific status. These are Claassens's Skolly *Thestor claassensi* and the Overberg Skolly *Thestor overbergensis*. Evidence in support of this split included genital microstructure analysis and dissection, physical appearance and differences in the DNA.

BUTTERFLY BIOLOGY

Physiology – how butterflies function

Insect bodies are unlike vertebrates in that the cavity inside the exoskeleton (known as the **haemocoel**) is totally bathed in blood. All the internal organs are directly bathed in this. Insect blood is called **haemolymph** and lacks the corpuscles found in mammal blood; it is usually green, not red. The haemolymph cannot stay still otherwise the various organs would be starved of food and oxygen. A simple 'heart' picks up haemolymph in the abdomen, where food and oxygen are exchanged for waste and carbon dioxide, and pumps it to the head, from where it flows back down the body carrying nutrients.

Butterflies breathe through tiny holes positioned along the sides of the body (two per segment), known as **spiracles**. The holes have muscular walls, which expand to suck up air, and can be closed at will. These divide into progressively smaller branches inside the body until they are microscopic and capable of diffusing gas molecules into the haemocoel. Carbon dioxide is likewise expelled through the spiracles. Although this breathing technique works very well for a small organism, it is less efficient in larger animals, probably explaining why insect bodies are limited in size.

A butterfly's digestive system is simple. Liquid food is sucked up the proboscis into the crop, from where it is passed via a one-way valve into the gullet and stomach for digestion. A partial vacuum is created by muscles in the crop to facilitate the suction. Nutrients are passed directly from the gut to the haemolymph, and then to the organs as needed. The organs pass waste products into the haemolymph. **Malpighian tubules** extract moisture from the waste, and are connected via a network of tubes to the gut and eventually the anus, where the residue is excreted. In larvae the moisture combines with solid faeces, known as **frass**, that have moved through the gut. Adult butterflies excrete only liquid.

Feeding and food – energy for life

As larvae, the vast majority of butterflies feed on plant matter. Choice of larval food is often highly specialised, in some cases restricted to a single plant species. As a result, butterfly distribution patterns are very strongly influenced by the food requirements of the larvae. Leaves are the most common food source, but many larvae feed on seeds or the immature ovules in flowers. Larvae of some of the Lycaenidae use cyanobacteria (previously called blue-green algae) that grow in symbiosis with fungi such as lichens. Others feed on animal matter. For example, *Lepidochrysops* caterpillars enter ant nests and devour the ant brood, and *Thestor* larvae are fed regurgitated food by the ants – just like young birds.

Larval fat deposits stored in the form of waxy sheets in the thoracic cavity and abdomen are vital to the survival of butterfly species that do not feed as adults. Some adults, such as Skollies (*Thestor* species), lack a fully developed proboscis and cannot feed. These butterflies tend to have short, sedentary lives spent near the larval food source.

The high-energy demands of flight require adults to consume sugar-rich foods. They most commonly feed on nectar, but also on fermenting fruit, sap from trees and shrubs, and honeydew from aphids and scale insects.

Some butterflies feed on the juices from carrion. *Charaxes* species are often seen sucking at dead mice, crabs, etc., and *Papilio* species are particularly fond of rotten prawns. Descending the ladder of taste still further, they also feed on the faeces of mammals and birds; these sometimes contain valuable trace nutrients as well as proteins. The faeces of predators – particularly cats – and primates seem to offer the most attractive meals. In hot weather, butterflies need to drink. River and pond banks often swarm with butterflies, which also derive important minerals from puddles of mammal urine.

Species in the *Thestor* genus, such as this skolly seen here, lack a proboscis and cannot feed

Coloration – avoiding predators

Butterflies are attractive prey for many predators, from chameleons to birds and small mammals. In terms of their physical attributes, however, they have few options for escaping such unwanted attention. Exceptions to this include the *Charaxes* species, which are large and extremely fast-flying. The largest ones are capable of outflying even birds as fast as swifts and swallows! Some lycaenids are also extremely rapid and, on the wing, can avoid birds with ease.

Most species, however, rely on cryptic coloration, deception, or camouflage to avoid detection. For example, the undersides of Rocksitters (*Durbania* spp., p. 144) closely resemble the lichen on the rocks that they frequent, rendering them virtually invisible. The Pearl Emperor *Charaxes varanes varanes* (p.102), and African Leaf Butterfly *Junonia tugela* (p.134) resemble dead leaves, while others resemble objects that are unattractive or obviously inedible; in the case of the Buff-tipped Skipper *Netrobalane canopus* (p. 368) it is bird droppings.

Male Ella's Bar, showing hair-like tails

Neita Brown *Neita neita* – a ringlet – showing eyespots

Many lycaenids (for example, Ella's Bar *Cigaritis ella*, p. 186) have hair-like hind-wing tails with eye spots at the base. When the insect is sitting, these look like the head and antennae, a deceit the insect embellishes by moving the tails slowly up and down. The Ella's Bar can lose its tails and part of the hind wing, and still fly with ease. This is preferable to being pecked on the 'real' head, which is likely to prove fatal.

Some Ringlets (Satyrinae, p. 40) have prominent eye spots on the wings, features that fool a bird or lizard into attacking the wings instead of the head. The larger ringlets tend to sit on the ground with closed wings, and then flip them open when disturbed. The suddenly revealed eye spots then give the impression of eyes being opened, which can startle small predators.

Butterflies cannot sting, but many – for example the entire subfamilies Acraeinae and Danainae – are **distasteful**, or even **poisonous** to predators. To advertise the fact that they are unpleasant to eat, these species have evolved bright warning or **aposematic** coloration and markings. Red, black, yellow and white, or some combination of these, are typical aposematic colours.

So how do butterflies become toxic or distasteful? Acraea larvae typically feed on cyanide-containing

The distasteful Fiery Acraea *Acraea acrita acrita*

Pearl-spotted Emperor *Charaxes jahlusa rex* **on baboon dung**

plants, such as *Kiggelaria* species (Wild Peach trees), and can store the poisons in their bodies as extremely bitter-tasting chemicals. The larvae and pupae are conspicuous and aposematic, and are usually avoided by predators (although some birds, such as cuckoos, are immune to the poisons). The poisonous substances remain in the body even as the pupa transforms, although there is evidence that the adults manufacture poisons in their own bodies as well.

Monarch (danaine) larvae also often feed on poisonous plants, such as *Asclepias* (Milkweed), which contains heart muscle toxins. The larvae and pupae are highly conspicuous and, until recently, it was thought that the poisons were transferred to the adults. In fact, Monarch butterflies – males only – can suck up chemicals called pyrrhazolidine alkaloids from certain plants (*see* photograph, p. 20: Blue or Dappled Monarch *Tirumala petiverana* at *Heliotropium*), and use them to synthesise other chemicals in their bodies that make them poisonous. When the butterflies mate, the male transfers alkaloids to the female with his sperm.

When a poisonous butterfly is bitten, the toxins released stimulate a vomiting reflex in the predator that results in immediate release. The chastened predator learns to avoid that particular pattern and colour in future.

There are no business ethics in nature, and 'software piracy' is rife. For every brightly coloured distasteful species, there is usually at least one perfectly palatable species that looks just like it and gains protection from the resemblance. For example, form *hippocoonides* of the palatable female Mocker Swallowtail *Papilio dardanus cerea* (p. 350) **mimics** the distasteful Friar *Amauris niavius dominicanus* (p. 38). The species being mimicked is called the **model**. Mimicry by a palatable species of a distasteful one is termed **Batesian mimicry**.

In **Muellerian mimicry**, distasteful species resemble one another. In this way, the tendency of palatable Batesian mimics to dilute the effect of warning coloration is counteracted. Examples of this are White-barred Acraea *Hyalites encedon encedon* (p. 98), which mimics the African Monarch *Danaus chrysippus* (p. 36), and Eriksson's Copper *Erikssonia acraeina* (a distasteful lycaenid, p. 244), which mimics the Small Orange Acraea *Hyalites eponina* (p. 96).

The lines between Batesian and Muellerian mimicry have recently become blurred, with several species thought to be Batesian mimics proving distasteful in their own right. The theory that *all* brightly marked butterflies are distasteful to some predators is gaining ground.

LIFE HISTORY – THE BREEDING CYCLE

Butterflies are essentially sex machines. The search for a mate and accompanying sexual displays form a major part of butterfly behaviour. A butterfly's time as an adult (or **imago**) is usually short compared to its total life cycle, hence the adult butterfly has only one purpose in life – to reproduce. (See pp. 34–35 for examples of eggs, larvae and/or pupae of different subfamilies.)

Territoriality

Like other animals, male butterflies often occupy and defend territories. However, the butterfly male does not do this to protect food sources, but rather to win the attention of a female with which he can mate. The most common form of territorial behaviour is hill-topping (see p. 32) and related activities. Many butterfly food plants are widely scattered. If the adults kept close to their home plant, they would stand little chance of mating with any female, let alone one descended from different parents. Males of low population density species, such as Hutchinson's High-flyer *Aphnaeus hutchinsoni* (left), tend to congregate at prominent hill tops, around large trees, big rocks on ledges, or bare rocky patches among vegetation. Sometimes, male butterflies endlessly patrol a particular piece of forest edge. This behaviour not only renders the male of the species far more conspicuous than the female, but attracts females to males. When the female visits the male's territory, she is quickly pursued and mated with by the dominant male, who will usually have found a position at the highest point on the hill top. The female then returns to the food plant to lay eggs.

Finding a mate

Butterflies have colour vision and there is no doubt that the **patterns of colour** on their wings play a large part in their recognition of potential mates. Scent also plays a large part in mate identification, although it tends to have a short-range effect, and seems to be used to augment visual cues when the potential partners get close together.

Some male danaines carry scent organs on their wings, which exude pheromones designed to induce the female to copulate. The pheromone is derived from chemicals that the male absorbs by consuming plants containing poisonous pyrrhazolidine alkaloids. The more alkaloids they carry, the stronger the scent. The toxins serve a secondary function, in that they augment chemical defence against predators; in copulation, the male transfers these poisons to the female in his sperm – hence ensuring her survival too.

Sexual behaviour patterns are thought to be of great significance in the evolution of butterflies. Precopulatory

Blue Monarch *Tirumala petiverana* (left) and Friar *Amauris niavius dominicanus* (right) taking alkaloids from *Heliotropium*

behaviour often takes the form of a 'dance', in which the male flits about in an effort to stimulate a response from the female. Although females regularly go in search of males with the specific purpose of mating, they will break off the encounter if they are not correctly stimulated.

Mating and egg-laying

Pairs copulate by joining the sex organs situated at the tips of their abdomens (see p. 337, a pair of mating African Common Whites). At first they may sit side by side, but during the act they face in opposite directions. If disturbed, they may fly united during mating. During mating, the male passes a package of sperm called a **spermatheca** to the female via his **aedeagus** or penis. The female stores the spermatheca in her abdomen and breaks it open to release sperm to fertilise each egg. Mated females of certain Heliconiine nymphalids, such as the genus *Acraea*, carry a 'chastity belt' in the form of a horny covering to the tip of the abdomen called the **sphragis**, which is placed there by the male during copulation, obviously to stop other males from copulating with his chosen mate. However, forced copulation is not unknown in these butterflies.

Once the female is mated, she carries the male's sperm inside her and uses it to fertilise the eggs as she lays them, either in batches or singly, on the appropriate food plant or in the appropriate ant nest. The female shows distinctive behaviour in her search for an oviposition site. Led by scent, a female seeking an oviposition site usually flies slowly, with distinctive quivering wing-beats. On landing, her antennae and 'taste' organs on the legs and feet are brought into play. Usually the correct plant odour is sufficient to induce her to lay, but in the case of ant-associated species, she searches for the correct ant scent-trail as well.

Eggs and larvae

The egg (or ovum) is either attached to the food source by an adhesive excreted by the female, or dropped loose onto the plant. The shape, coloration and patterning of the egg is specific to each butterfly subfamily, and is useful in identification (*see* pp. 34–35). The egg hatches after a period ranging from a few days to months into a larva (the caterpillar). From birth, the larva (generally equipped with rudimentary eyes, smell and taste organs, and strong jaws) eats voraciously.

Larva of the Langeberg Skolly *Thestor pictus* accepting ant regurgitation

Butterflies undergo complete **metamorphosis** (from the Greek for 'change in form'), in which the hatchling is totally different from the adult. The larva undergoes successive moults as it grows, because its chitinous skin is not very flexible and cannot stretch sufficiently to allow for the tremendous growth in size to adulthood (the adult is hundreds of times the size of the newly hatched larva). The stage between each moult is called an **instar**. After four to six instars, the larva is fully grown.

Like ova, larvae are distinctive at family and subfamily level, and sometimes even at genus or species level. Their very distinctive characters (physiological and behavioural) have evolved to protect these soft-bodied, flightless and slow-moving insects from potential predation.

Some green larvae (for example, Sapphires and Swallowtails) are so well camouflaged on their food plants that they are almost impossible to see, while heliconiine and danaiine larvae are often highly brightly coloured (and sometimes bad-smelling), advertising their distastefulness. The heliconiids sometimes gather together in large groups to enhance the effects of coloration and odour. At the other extreme, many satyrine and lycaenid larvae only feed at night in an effort to avoid diurnal predators.

Probably the most important larval survival strategy, at least for the majority of lycaenids, is their association with ants. Certain ant species are attracted, and possibly controlled, by the sweet substance secreted by these larvae. The ants, of course, deter caterpillar predators such as parasitic wasps and flies. Some lycaenid larvae hide inside the ants' nests all the time and are fed by the ants by regurgitation.

When the larva has completed several moults – usually three to five – it stops feeding, often leaves the feeding area, and prepares to pupate. It may look for a sheltered spot, sometimes burrowing underground, or spinning a cocoon in a leaf or debris shelter or in the base of a grass clump, sometimes suspending itself from a suitable support, until its final moult, or pupation.

Pupae and the imago

Members of the Hesperiidae family pupate within a larval shelter. Some spin a silken girdle, and some, such as the Hoppers, genus *Platylesches*, spin a rudimentary cocoon. As with ova and larvae, the stationary pupae are distinctive at subfamily level, and sometimes at genus or species level. Pupae are usually very well camouflaged, some danaids and acraeas being the exception.

The manner in which pupae are attached to the substratum is indicative of the family to which they belong. For example, Nymphalidae (with the exception of some satyrines, which are found loose in grass litter) are suspended from the substrate by the hook-like cremaster on their tail end. Some lycaenids (for example *Iolaus*) are attached tail-end only. Pierid and papilionid pupae are attached at the tail, and held upright by a thin girdle of silk around the thorax and wing case. Some lycaenids also have a girdle.

Within the pupa, the final metamorphosis occurs. The time between pupation and emergence of the adult varies. Some species hibernate or aestivate inside the pupa. During this time, the adult structures develop, and finally the pupal skin becomes transparent, rendering the wings of the adult visible. When this occurs, emergence is only a few hours away. When the time is correct

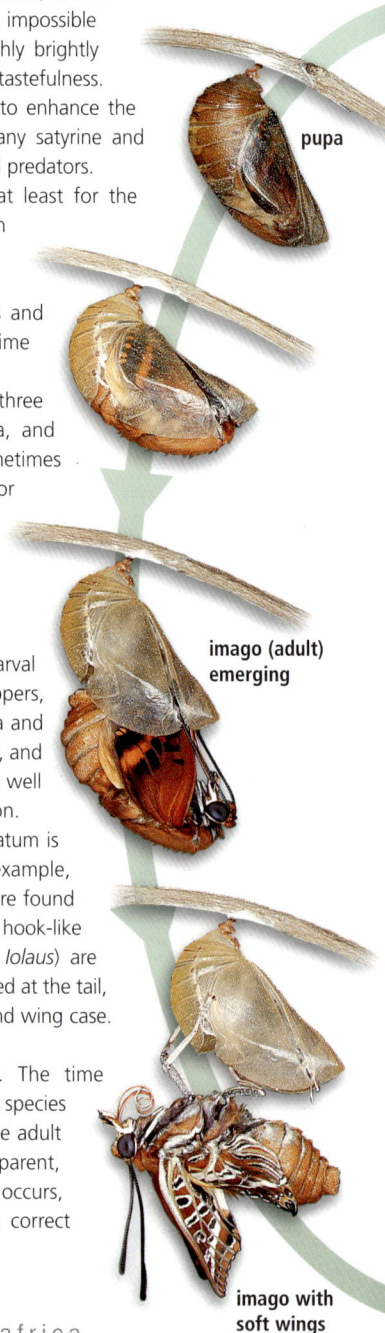

pupa

imago (adult)
emerging

imago with
soft wings

(usually early in the morning), the pupa splits over the thorax and the adult (imago) crawls out as shown by the sequence on these pages. The imago climbs up a nearby twig, rock or leaf, and hangs upside down while the heart pumps haemolymph into the wing veins. These straighten under pressure and 'push' the wings into shape while they are still soft. The wings then harden into their final form.

Flight periods

Adult butterflies appear when the conditions are optimal for oviposition, and flight periods are governed by this need. If there is no food plant available for the larvae, there is no point in the adult emerging. Availability of food plant is largely influenced by climatic factors, the most important being temperature and rain, which govern plant growing seasons, and flowering and seeding times.

Simplistically, South Africa can be split into two climatic zones – winter- and summer-rainfall areas, with an ill-defined transition zone that receives rain year-round.

Winter-rainfall regions

The Western Cape, southern Northern Cape, and western Eastern Cape receive most of their rainfall in winter. The climate is driven by the south Atlantic high-pressure system in summer, and anticyclonic frontal systems in winter. Cold, wet, wintry weather is the norm from May to August, followed by a cool, moist spring from September to early November. The summer is long, hot and dry, from late November to March, becoming cooler during autumn, with some rain alternating with sunny spells.

In the true winter-rainfall zone, plant growth is most vigorous in spring and early summer. Butterfly emergence fits a similar pattern, most species being active in spring and early summer. As summer progresses, and the weather becomes hotter, drier and windier, fewer butterflies are seen, but there is often a second emergence in late summer and autumn. Some, particularly the satyrine genera *Dira* and *Torynesis*, only emerge at this time. Others have larvae that use seeds as food sources, and these are generally more abundant in late summer. The picture is made more complicated by the lycaenids, many of which are capable of flight at the driest times of the year because of their larvae's ability to shelter in ants' nests. Some larvae have even become aphytophagous (non-plant eating), as in the Skollies, whose larvae are fed by ants in a relationship rather like a cuckoo chick in another bird's nest.

imago ready to fly

wings expanding

Sequence of Silver-Barred Emperor, *Charaxes druceanus moerens*, emerging

Summer-rainfall regions

In the eastern part of the Eastern Cape, the north-eastern Free State, KwaZulu-Natal, North West Province, Gauteng, Mpumalanga, Limpopo Province, and the northern parts of Northern Cape, the climate is subtropical. There are still well-defined summer and winter periods, with a short spring after the September/October rains. Early summer, from November to mid-December, is hot and humid, with moist air drawn into the area from the Mozambique Channel, developing into the characteristic afternoon thunderstorms. Late December and January are usually drier, with a second, smaller rainfall peak in February and March. Autumn, from March to May or June in the northern areas, is dry and warm, becoming cooler between June and September. On the highveld, winter is colder and more prolonged.

There is usually a strong butterfly emergence in September and October, especially in high altitude grasslands after the first rains. Many species fly only at this time. However, the great majority of subtropical species fly year-round, with emergence peaks during or after the rains, and a lull in the heat of midsummer. This phenomenon is exaggerated in the forests, where the emergence is often split into two distinct flight periods. The second (late summer/autumn) peak is usually the stronger, when mass emergences or migrations take place; in warmer areas these stretch into the winter months of June and July.

Along the highest peaks of the eastern mountain chain from Lesotho northwards, the warm summer period is restricted to December and January. Butterflies in these areas are best seen in those months.

Pringle's Widow
Torynesis pringlei

Coast Purple Tip
Colotis erone

The transition zone

There is a boundary zone running between the winter- and summer-rainfall zones, where aridity is the norm. Here, Karoo vegetation dominates in the south and semi-desert is prevalent in the north. Moving north and east, the winter rains split into two bands, spring (August to October) and autumn (May to June), with a dry period in between. Summer thunderstorms occur during the hot, dry season from November to April.

This is the home of specialised arid-adapted butterflies – lycaenids that have evolved **myrmecoxenous** (ant-associated) life histories, and satyrines capable of feeding on dry grasses over an extended larval stage. Generally, the best time to see butterflies in this climatic zone is from August to November, but some double-brooded species fly in spring and autumn, and some species fly in midsummer – the hottest, most desiccating time of year.

Ketsi Blue *Lepidochrysops ketsi*

Machacha Brown
Pseudonympha machacha

Movements

South African butterflies are not migratory in the strict sense of the word, i.e. individuals do not make repeated journeys that are predictable in time and space. They do, however, undertake considerable movements, usually in response to food shortages, and in the context of this book, the term **migratory** is used to describe butterflies that disperse over long distances from their natal colonies. The Pierids African Migrant or Common Vagrant *Catopsilia florella* (p. 346) and Brown-veined White *Belenois aurota aurota* (p. 336), for example, are native to the arid west. After good rains, their food plants may burgeon, causing an explosion in their numbers, with several broods raised in quick succession until every plant is covered in larvae. This overcrowding has a knock-on effect; with over-population, large groups are forced to look elsewhere for food and, as if in preparation for this, the emergence of larger, more robust specimens with increased fat reserves is stimulated. In some ways this parallels the pre-migratory fattening of birds. The adults travel eastwards, sometimes over thousands of kilometres, to find new populations of their food plants.

Namaqua Opal
Chrysoritis aridus

African Migrant or Common Vagrant, *Catopsilia florella*

SOUTH AFRICA'S BIOMES

There are six main biomes (vegetation ecosystems) in South Africa – Fynbos, Succulent Karoo, Nama Karoo, savanna (arid and mesic or moist), grassland, and forest (Afromontane, riverine and lowland). Some authorities recognise a seventh – thicket, which is largely confined to the boundary between Karoo and savanna in the south-east. The butterflies found there are usually savanna species, so no special distinction is made here for this biome.

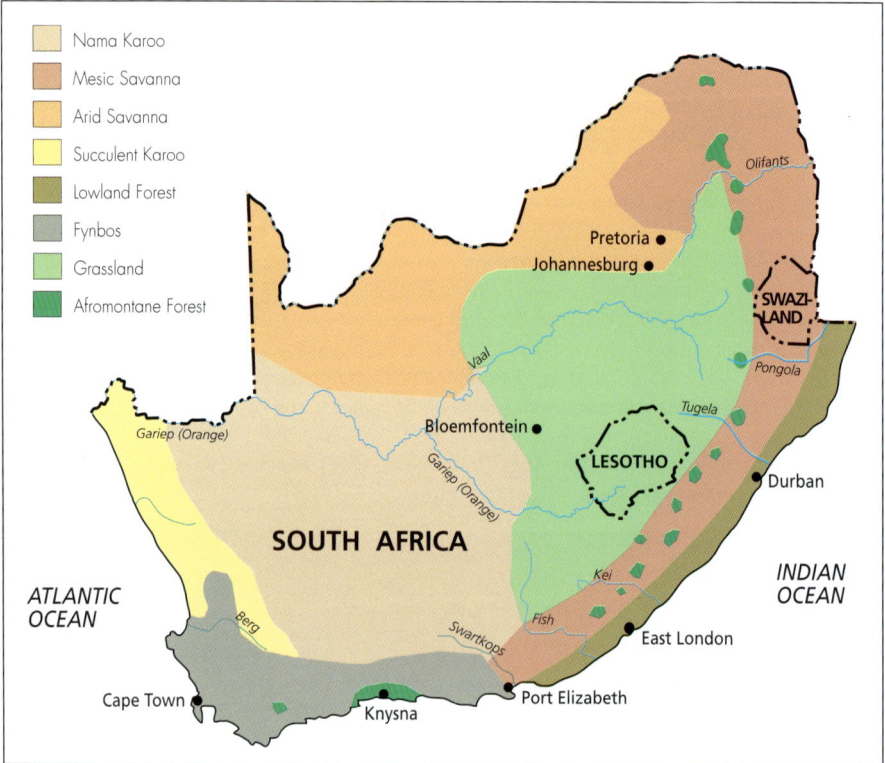

Legend:
- Nama Karoo
- Mesic Savanna
- Arid Savanna
- Succulent Karoo
- Lowland Forest
- Fynbos
- Grassland
- Afromontane Forest

Map labels: Olifants, Pretoria, Johannesburg, SWAZILAND, Pongola, Vaal, Tugela, Gariep (Orange), Bloemfontein, LESOTHO, Durban, SOUTH AFRICA, Kei, INDIAN OCEAN, ATLANTIC OCEAN, Berg, Swartkops, Fish, East London, Cape Town, Knysna, Port Elizabeth

Fynbos

The Fynbos biome, the world's most plant-rich floral kingdom, comprises four dominant plant forms: proteoids, ericoids, restioids and geophytes (bulbs and corms). Fynbos occurs in a narrow coastal band that stretches from the Western Cape as far as the Eastern Cape. As far as butterflies are concerned, Fynbos is very similar to the Karoo, and no butterfly genera are indigenous to Fynbos.

Fynbos

Succulent Karoo

This is a singular vegetation type found along the western seaboard and littoral hills. It is typified by succulent plants, which provide a spectacular blaze of colour each spring. The main area covered by the Succulent Karoo is known as Namaqualand. Most of the butterflies found here are also found in the Nama Karoo, but it is home to some specially adapted species.

Nama Karoo

This vegetation type covers the rain shadow of the Cape mountain chain in the south-central part of South Africa. Overgrazing by livestock (sheep and goats) has degraded large areas. There are two main areas, the Great Karoo and Little Karoo. In the west it intergrades into Succulent Karoo; in the north with grassland and savanna. In the south and east it intergrades with Fynbos, with which it shares many characteristics. The eastern reaches of the Nama Karoo are mosaic-like, and this area is home to many rare and highly localised butterflies. Pockets of karroid scrub occur at the highest altitudes in the Drakensberg, and these harbour butterfly species related to those found in the true Karoo. They have been isolated long enough to form separate species.

Savanna

Savanna covers the regions in South Africa known as Kalahari, bushveld and lowveld, and, being the largest biome, is regarded by many as being the typical vegetation type of this country. Comprising vast stretches of grassy veld, more or less dotted with trees, Savanna may appear uniform; however, there are two quite distinct types of Savanna.

Arid Savanna

Arid Savanna is found in the western areas of South Africa. Sometimes, the gradation into Mesic Savanna is indistinct. To the west, the Arid Savanna region of South Africa intergrades with the semi-desert regions of Namibia, and some specially adapted butterflies are found here.

Mesic Savanna

Typically moist and mostly wooded, this type of Savanna is found across the eastern and northern parts of South Africa. It intergrades with Arid Savanna to the west, Karoo to the south, and grassland to the south and east. Butterflies found here tend to be the same species found in similar vegetation further north in Africa, but some savanna patches in South Africa, cut off in other biomes, house butterflies that have speciated due to their isolation.

Succulent Karoo

Nama Karoo

Arid Savanna

Mesic or Moist Savanna

Grassland

Grassland

True Grassland, as opposed to Savanna, is treeless, and in South Africa is mainly found on the central highveld and in the eastern mountain chain. True highveld Grassland is scarce, as much of it has been planted with pine plantations, maize and other crops. Grassland types are defined by the altitude at which they are found. Isolated Grassland pockets in other biomes are often home to rare species of butterfly.

Forest

Forest is South Africa's scarcest and most fragmented biome. The vast areas covered by alien pine and gum plantations are not considered part of the Forest biome; in fact, they are virtual butterfly deserts. There are three true forest types in South Africa.

Afromontane Forest

Afromontane Forest is found along the eastern escarpment and on isolated inland mountains where the rainfall is sufficient; also at sea level in the Western and Eastern Cape. The total area of this habitat is small, and patches of Afromontane Forest are highly fragmented. These forest patches contain many local butterfly races found nowhere else.

Afromontane Forest

Riverine Forest

Riverine Forest comprises dense woodland usually with Fig and Waterberry trees, which grow on the banks of rivers. These forests are corridors that allow forest-adapted butterflies to penetrate otherwise arid areas, and often the species found in Riverine Forest are totally different from those found in surrounding vegetation.

Riverine Forest

Lowland Forest

An uncommon vegetation type in South Africa, found mostly in tropical lowlands and coastal areas in the north-east. Often, the primary forest has been destroyed and replaced by a tangled secondary growth. Butterflies found here tend to be the same as those found in similar vegetation zones further north in Africa.

Lowland Forest

BUTTERFLY DISTRIBUTION AND CONSERVATION

Butterflies have different needs and as a result live in different populations. Some are highly adaptable and are found in many different habitat types. These are known as **eurytropes**, and include our most familiar species. Some, however, have very specific habitat requirements and live in populations that are concentrated in a small area. The survival of these populations, known as **stenotropes**, depends on the presence of a certain food plant, on a particular ant, or even a specific microclimate. These butterflies are found only where conditions are exactly right. The result is a high population density over a very small area. Stenotropes seldom stray far from where they were born. Some, in fact, are never found outside of their original colonies. In extreme cases, the entire world population of a species is permanently confined to a range the size of a tennis court.

Under wild conditions, several small colonies may be found close together, and colonies may occasionally die if the vegetation in which they live shows rapid changes over a short time. These colonies are usually part of a larger **metapopulation**, within which adults move between populations, allowing gene flow and formation of new colonies in suitable areas.

Some butterflies need only the correct plants and an absence of pesticides to survive. However, many species have extremely specialised food plant and habitat requirements. A great many South African butterflies are confined to such small, specialised habitats where a combination of factors ensures their survival. Many lycaenids, for example, require a combination of ant, plant and microclimate to survive, while a number of satyrines live in tiny areas of type-specific grassland surrounded by hostile forest or Karoo. If any of these essential elements is lost, so too is the butterfly – at least in that area. These specialist species are particularly vulnerable to local extinction by habitat destruction (for example, afforestation) and alteration (for example, agricultural transformation).

In many instances, however, there is no evidence to suggest that the ranges of such species in the past were any larger than they are now. These species are almost certainly naturally rare, rather than having been driven to rarity by habitat destruction. However, they are at risk of natural extinction due to episodic events, such as fire, storms or drought. This condition has been termed the 'rarity trap'. Given the large number of South African butterfly species with extremely restricted ranges, it is highly likely that several such local extinction events have occurred unnoticed.

The collecting of butterflies plays an important role in the insects' conservation. The Lepidopterists' Society of Africa was originally established to study and conserve butterflies in South Africa, and has since expanded to cover the entire continent. The society's aim to protect the habitats of threatened butterflies has resulted in the establishment in South Africa of the Ruimsig Nature Reserve (Gauteng), where the Roodepoort Copper *Aloeides dentatis dentatis* is preserved. Similarly, Brenton-on-Sea in the Western Cape is the now-protected home of the last-known colony of the Brenton Blue *Orachrysops niobe*.

Prospective collectors need to inform themselves of the legalities of collecting in the various provinces of South Africa. To this end they should contact the Lepidopterists' Society of Africa (http://www.lepsoc.org.za) or the nature conservation department in their particular area.

Roodepoort Copper *Aloeides dentatis dentatis*

WATCHING AND IDENTIFYING BUTTERFLIES

The joy of butterfly watching is that you can do it anywhere –
out in the veld or bush, in the mountains, forests, at the coast,
or in a park or garden. The elements necessary for success are
similar to those needed for bird watching. You will need a
comprehensive and easy-to-use field guide, a pair of binoculars
(or a telescope) to bring your quarry into closer view, and a notebook and pencil to record size, shape, special markings, flight patterns
and specific behaviour; patience and perseverance will go a long way too.

Start by familiarising yourself with the characteristics of the main butterfly
families described in your guide and read about butterfly habits so that you have
some knowledge before you set out. If you are looking for a specific butterfly, it is a good idea to
learn the food plants used by the larvae (discussed within each species account). Once you find the
plant, you have a good chance of seeing the butterfly close by. Remember, however, that butterflies
are seasonal in their appearance: some fly almost all year round; others only during very specific times
of year, sometimes for periods as short as a fortnight. Again, the species account will indicate the
best times at which to see each species.

Knowing the type of terrain that butterflies prefer will also help in locating them. Even the most
widespread of butterflies have specific habitat preferences. Information on habitat is provided within
each species account. Terrain preferences may range from parks and gardens to mountain sides,
coastal areas, wetlands, forests or forest edges and hillsides. Some butterflies confine their range to
ridges, ledges or gullies and some to hill tops.

Gardens, forests, mountainsides and hill tops all offer prime butterfly viewing locations

In the field

Most butterflies can be approached closely with stealth. Be sure to avoid jerky movements and don't allow your shadow to fall across them. Always approach gently and quietly; the butterflies will soon become used to your presence and will allow you to get close.

First look at the size and overall shape of the butterfly. Our largest butterflies are in the Papilionidae (Swallowtails), Danainae (Monarchs) and Charaxinae (Emperors) families. Small butterflies are mostly in the families Hesperiidae (Skippers) and Lycaenidae (Blues, Hairstreaks, etc.), and medium-sized butterflies can usually be placed in the Pieridae family (Whites and Yellows), with the majority in the Nymphalidae.

Emperor Swallowtail *Papilio ophidicephalus*

Gaika Blue *Zizula hylax*

Neita Brown *Neita neita*

Size is a useful guide to identification as shown here in life-size examples of a large (Emperor Swallowtail), a medium (Neita Brown) and a small (Gaika Blue) butterfly

Flight behaviour offers many clues to the identity of a butterfly. Swallowtails have a restless, fluttering, dancing flight. The distasteful Acraeas and Danaines have a slow, lazy, floating flight pattern that somehow suggests they are unpalatable. Limenitinae have a characteristic gliding, 'wings-open' flight and Nymphalinae and Charaxinae a typical 'flap-glide' action.

Hill-topping

Hill-topping is a well-known butterfly behaviour, and is usually associated with mate location. Males compete for hill top territories and then perch on prominent features such as twigs and rock pinnacles. Females ascend the hills to seek out the dominant individuals.

Male Ella's Bar perching alertly on a hill top tree

Butterflies are like birds in that the 'jizz', that indefinable combination of body language, posture and behaviour, is almost as important in identification as is size, shape and markings. The live photographs in this book attempt to capture the jizz as closely as possible. The more time you spend observing butterflies, the better acquainted you will become with the jizz of different butterflies and butterfly groups.

Colour is another important clue to identification. Most small blue butterflies fall into the Lycaeninae, a wide group also containing most small orange butterflies. White, orange and yellow butterflies are largely confined to the Pieridae, and brown ones to the Satyrinae. Some groups are easily identified by the markings: the Satyrines show 'ringlet' eye spots and many of the Heliconiines have spotted patterns, which help distinguish them. Note that colours fade with time, even in the lifetime of the insect, and colours of butterflies in the field may vary slightly from those in the photographs featured in the book.

Wing shape is also useful. The heart-shaped hind wings of *Charaxes* are characteristic and help to identify the group. Similarly, the arched anal margin of *Papilio* species or the hair-like tails typical of the genus *Anthene* are useful clues, as are the long, rounded wings of the Bitter Acraeas.

When setting out at first, avoid trying to identify everything you see. Rather concentrate on observing behaviour, recording this and any other points notable about a species you encounter. Flight patterns (described under each species) are especially worth noting and can often help distinguish between like species. Some mimics are much easier to tell from their models by observing flight. For example, the pied form of the female Mocker Swallowtail (*Papilio dardanus cenea*, f. *hippocoonides*) is almost identical in colour and markings to the Friar (*Amauris niavius dominicanus*) but she flies with a typical dancing Swallowtail motion, whereas the Friar shows the slow, floating Monarch-type flight pattern.

Use the Quick Guide (inside front cover) to find the section most likely to contain the butterfly you have just seen. Check distribution maps and photographs, and have a first attempt at identification. Careful recording of the locality where you saw the butterfly will help, as many very similar species do not fly together.

Patience and practice will bring reward and the more time you spend observing, the better equipped you will become in identifying species. If all else fails, catch the butterfly and keep it in a small, smooth-walled container, in the dark. Contact the Lepidopterists' Society of Africa, or your local museum for help. South Africa is still not fully explored butterfly-wise, so there is always the exciting possibility that you've found something totally new!

COLLECTING BUTTERFLIES

Butterfly collecting is an absorbing and rewarding hobby. A common misconception is that collecting leads to butterfly extinction. This is not true. Even small colonies of specialist butterflies are known to withstand regular collecting. Insects are not as vulnerable as are mammals and birds to extirpation by hunting. Females lay from dozens to hundreds of eggs, of which only two have to reach maturity to ensure perpetuation of the species. The life cycle is very fast compared to that of vertebrates, some species having several broods per year and seldom less than one.

A detailed account of butterfly collecting is beyond the scope of this book but the basics of what you will need to start a collection include:

Butterfly net

- **Butterfly net**. Fishermen's landing nets serve well. Replace the open mesh with fine organza or chiffon. You can also make a net using aluminium tubing and soft fabric for the net.
- **Butterfly traps**. These are used to attract high-flying species that seldom visit flowers. These butterflies are attracted to bait such as fermenting fruit. The traps work rather like lobster pots in that the quarry can get in but cannot escape; traps are not lethal and allow unwanted specimens to be released.
- **Cork or plastic foam-lined storage boxes** and cabinet drawers, with insect repellent to keep out pests such as museum beetles.

Butterflies on setting board

- **Setting boards** on which the wings are spread out while the specimen dries out and sets into its mounted position.
- **Setting papers** (tracing paper or celluloid) and glass-headed pins.
- **Entomologists' pins**, 38 mm long, and in several thickness gauges for different sized specimens.
- A means of producing **labels** for attachment to the pin below the specimen (most computers can be used to make these).
- **Glassine envelopes** or plastic 'zip-loc' bags to hold specimens.
- A **field notebook** to collect data on specimens as they are collected.

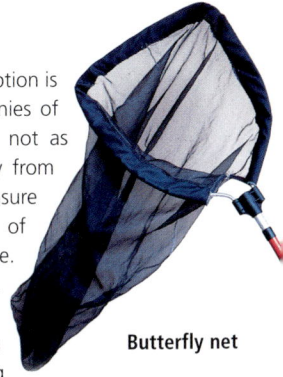

Ethics of Collecting

- Never take more specimens than you need, especially of specialist species.
- Always label specimens accurately with the date of capture, locality data (GPS if possible), and your name.
- Always consult the relevant authorities to find out the legal status of collecting; the legislation is currently under review. Some species are protected by law under various provincial ordinances. Contact your local Nature Conservation Department for a list of these.
- Ask permission of landowners before you collect on their land.
- Contact your local museum and deposit important specimens with the Curator of Lepidoptera.
- Make your collecting and observation data available to conservation bodies, for example, by using the Lepidopterists' Society of Africa's data capture software, Lepibase. This is available to members for a small fee. See www.lepsoc.org.za

Identifying a subfamily in the early stages

The shape, coloration and patterning of the butterfly egg is generally specific to each butterfly *subfamily*, as is the larva and the pupa, and this is useful in identification. The following are examples of species that best typify some of the region's butterfly subfamilies in their early stages.

Danainae *Amauris ochlea ochlea*, egg

Heliconiinae *Acraea acara acara*, eggs

Charaxinae *Charaxes jasius saturnus*, eggs

Limenitinae *Pseudacraea lucretia tarquinia*, egg

Lycaeninae *Chrysoritis zeuxo*, egg

Miletinae *Thestor rileyi*, egg

Pierinae *Pontia helice*, egg

Papilioninae *Papilio constantinus constantinus*, eggs

Coeliadinae *Coeliades pisistratus*, egg

Danainae *Amauris ochlea ochlea*, pupa

Heliconiinae *Phalanta phalantha*, pupa

Charaxinae *Charaxes achaemenes achaemenes*, pupa

Lycaeninae *Iolaus trimeni*, pupa

Papilioninae *Graphium morania*, pupa

Miletinae *Lachnocnema laches*, pupa

Pierinae *Mylothris agathina*, pupa

Biblidinae *Eurytela dryope angulata*, pupa

Hesperiinae *Platylesches neba*, pupa

Danainae *Danaus chrysippus aegyptius*, 5th instar larva

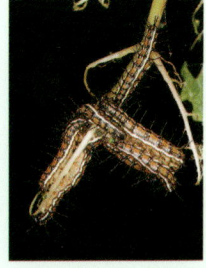

Heliconiinae *Hyalites obeira burni*, 5th instar larva

Satyrinae *Dingana alaedeus*, 5th instar larva

Charaxinae *Charaxes druceanus moerens*, 5th instar larva

Limenitinae *Pseudacraea boisduvalii trimenii*, 5th instar larva

Cyrestinae *Cyrestis camillus*, final instar larva

Nymphalinae *Junonia orithya madagascariensis*, 5th instar larva

Lycaeninae *Iolaus alienus alienus*, 5th instar larva

Lycaeninae *Tuxentius calice calice*, 5th instar larva

Pierinae *Dixeia doxo parva*, 5th instar larva

Lycaeninae *Aphnaeus hutchinsonii*, 4th instar larva

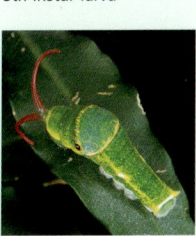

Papilioninae *Papilio nireus lyaeus*, 4th instar larva

Hesperiinae *Moltena fiara*, 5th instar larva

Poritiinae *Durbania limbata*, 5th instar larva

Family NYMPHALIDAE

The second-largest butterfly family worldwide, with 6 000 species in 12 subfamilies, nine of these represented in South Africa. Also known as 'brush-footed butterflies', because the adults' front pairs of legs are atrophied to small brush-like sensory organs, so that they appear to have only four legs instead of the normal six. The front pair of legs serves no walking function.

Subfamily DANAINAE

Distinguished from other subfamilies of Nymphalidae by having forewing vein 3A, which joins vein 2A close to the wing base. Flight is generally slow and sailing. Bright coloration (black patterned with white, yellow, orange, or blue) warns vertebrate predators of their acrid odour and distastefulness. For this reason, danaids are models for many non-distasteful species.

Genus *Danaus*   Monarchs
WORLD 11 SPP., SOUTH AFRICA 1

Large to very large cream to yellow or tawny-orange butterflies, with black veins. Several colour morphs. Sexes similar; ♂ has black sex brands on the hind wing. Single egg, elongated oval, about 20 longitudinal ribs with 25–30 cross-ridges, creamy white. Larva white to cream, ringed with yellow and black, pairs of long black fleshy filaments on the second, fifth and eleventh segments. Pupa translucent white, pale green or turquoise, smooth-skinned with ring of black and gold spots around the abdominal segments; suspended by the tail from a twig.

1 African Monarch   *Danaus chrysippus aegyptius*
Wingspan: ♂ 50–70 mm ♀ 50–75 mm. **Identification: 1A** ♂ upper side, **1B** ♀ underside (f. *liboria*), **1C** ♂ upper side (f. *transiens*), **1D** ♂ upper side (f. *alcippoides*). Most common colour forms are f. *chrysippus*, with subapical band of large white spots on black wing tip, and similar f. *liboria*, with smaller white spots. Forms *alcippus* and *alcippoides* resemble these two respectively, both with varying amounts of white on upper side of hind wing; in rarer f. *klugii*, wingtips orange, no spots, while f. *transiens* has indistinct spots on orange. Very rare f. *dorippus* resembles f. *klugii*, but wing bases not dark as in other forms. Often seen in numbers feeding on flowers. **Mimic:** ♀ Common Diadem (p. 128) polymorphic mimic of all forms of this butterfly. **Distribution:** Common throughout South Africa in all biomes. **Habitat:** Forest edges, parks and gardens, hill tops, flatlands, coast, mountains, wetlands. **Flight period:** Year-round (peak late summer/autumn). **Larval food:** *Asclepias* spp., especially *A. fruticosa, Cynanchum obtusifolium, Ceropegia, Stapelia,* and *Huernia* spp.

Genus *Tirumala*   Dappled Monarchs
WORLD 9 SPP., AFRICA 2, SOUTH AFRICA 1

Large, dark butterflies, wings covered with paler spots. Sexes alike. Flight floating; appears weak, but capable of bursts of speed if disturbed. Early stages similar to *Danaus*; egg oval, with fine longitudinal and transverse ribs, larva black, white and yellow, with similarly placed fleshy filaments; pale pupa with metallic ornamentation.

2 Blue Monarch or Dappled Monarch   *Tirumala petiverana*
Wingspan: 60–75 mm. **Identification: 2A** ♂ upper side, **2B** ♂ underside. ♂ with anal sex brand on hind wing upper side. **Mimics:** ♂ Forest Queen (p. 116), and both sexes of Veined Swordtail (p. 354). Easy to distinguish from mimics on the wing, as flight pattern and habits are similar to *Danaus*. **Distribution:** Very rare vagrant, usually on Afromontane, lowland and Riverine Forest. Only recorded migrants from Polokwane and Chuenespoort (Limpopo Province) and Randburg, Gauteng. **Habitat:** Forest edges, parks and gardens, hill tops, flatlands. **Flight period:** Single-brooded. In Zimbabwe, Feb–May, peak Apr. **Larval food:** *Pergularia daemia* and *Hoya* spp.

A

1B

C

1D

A

2B

Genus *Amauris*   Friar, Novice, Layman, Chief

AFRICA 16 SPP., SOUTH AFRICA 4

Medium-sized to large butterflies, black spotted or blotched with white or cream. Sexes similar, ♂ with dark, shiny scent patch on hind wing anal area. Single egg; elongated oval, about 20 longitudinal ribs with 25–30 cross-ridges, creamy white. Larva shiny black with white or yellow spots, four or five pairs of long fleshy filaments on second, third, fifth (sometimes absent), eleventh and twelfth segments. Pupa buff with shiny golden patches; suspended by tail from twig or branch.

1 Friar   *Amauris niavius dominicanus*

Wingspan: ♂ 80–85 mm ♀ 78–82 mm. **Identification: 1A** ♂ upper side, **1B** ♂ underside. Largest South African *Amauris*; conspicuously marked black and white. ♂ has less white on wings than ♀. ♀ has more rounded wings. Shade-loving; seldom found in the open, except at attractive flowers. Sometimes swarms. **Mimics:** ♀ Mocker Swallowtail (f. *hippocoonides*) (p. 350), both sexes of Variable Diadem (f. *wahlbergi*) (p. 130), and ♀ Forest Queen (p. 116). **Distribution:** More common in north than Novice (below). Coastal and inland Riverine Forest, dense lowland forest. KwaZulu-Natal (Umkomaas), Swaziland, north to Mpumalanga and Limpopo Province. **Habitat:** Forest edges, parks and gardens, flatlands, coast. **Flight period:** Year-round (peak late summer/autumn). **Larval food:** *Cynanchum* and *Tylophora* spp.

2 Novice   *Amauris ochlea ochlea*

Wingspan: ♂ 55–60 mm ♀ 60–65 mm. **Identification: 2A** ♂ upper side, **2B** ♀ upper side, **2C** ♂ underside sucking alkaloids from wilting *Senecio* plants. ♂ has less white on wings than ♀. ♀ has more rounded wings. In ♂, ground colour of hind wing upper side jet black; ♀ grey-brown. Smaller than similar Friar (above), and less active, flying higher. Major differences are: smaller white forewing apical patch, basal forewing white patch *does not reach the anal edge of wing*. Sometimes swarms. **Mimic:** (Possibly) Deceptive Diadem (p. 130). **Distribution:** Scarcer than Friar in the north. Coastal and inland riverine and lowland forests. KwaZulu-Natal south coast, to Limpopo Province lowland forests near Pafuri and Thohoyandou and further north. **Habitat:** Forest edges, flatlands. **Flight period:** Year-round (peak summer/autumn). **Larval food:** *Cynanchum chirindense* and *C. natalitium*, *Tylophora anomala*.

3 Layman   *Amauris albimaculata albimaculata*

Wingspan: ♂ 50–60 mm ♀ 62–68 mm. **Identification: 3A** ♂ upper side, **3B** ♂ underside. Upper side black with *white* forewing spots, hind wing patch pale buff. Slow, floating flight. Male is South Africa's smallest danaid. **Mimics:** ♀ Mocker Swallowtail (f. *acene*) (p. 350), both sexes of Variable Diadem (f. *mima*) (p. 130) and False Chief (p. 120). **Distribution:** More common and widespread than Friar (above) or Novice (above). Coastal, lowland and Riverine Forests, and Savanna. Mbashe River, E Cape, to KwaZulu-Natal, Swaziland, and north to Mpumalanga and Limpopo Province. Vagrant as far west as Gauteng and NW Province. **Habitat:** Forest edges, clearings and tracks, parks and gardens, flatlands. **Flight period:** Year-round (peak summer/autumn). **Larval food:** *Cynanchum chirindense* and *C. natalitium*, *Tylophora anomala*.

4 Chief   *Amauris echeria echeria*

Wingspan: ♂ 55–65 mm ♀ 63–70 mm. **Identification: 4A** ♂ upper side, **4B** ♂ underside. Coloration variable. Distinguished from similar, slightly larger Layman (above) by having forewing spots *always cream to ochre*; hind wing band wider in northern specimens; more frequent in forest than Layman. **Mimics:** ♀ Mocker Swallowtail (f. *cenea*) (p. 350) and some forms of False Chief (p. 120). **Distribution:** Common in lowland, riverine and Afromontane forests. George, W Cape to KwaZulu-Natal, Swaziland, Mpumalanga and Limpopo Province. **Habitat:** Forest edges, flatlands, parks and gardens. **Flight period:** Year-round (peak summer/autumn). **Larval food:** *Cynanchum chirindense* and *Tylophora anomala*.

1A

1B

2A

2B

2C

3B

3A

4A

4B

Subfamily SATYRINAE

Like Danainae and Heliconiinae, Satyrinae are distinguished from the other Nymphalidae by having well-developed discocellular veins in both wings. They lack vein 3A, distinguishing them from Heliconiinae. While not a distinguishing feature of this subfamily, many genera have the forewing subcostal vein swollen at the base. Members of this subfamily are, as the name implies, predominantly brown in ground colour, with patches of red to orange-yellow. Ringlets usually have eye spots (few to many) on the wings. With a few exceptions, satyrines are fairly weak fliers that settle often.

Genus *Melanitis*   Evening Browns   WORLD 12 SPP., AFRICA 3, SOUTH AFRICA 1

Large satyrines, with eye spots on the forewing upper side. The forewing subcostal vein is not swollen at the base. Skulking, reluctant to fly; flight is low and of short duration. Eggs white, spheroidal with flattened base, appearing smooth, but under magnification show fine net-like pattern. Larva cylindrical, tapered at both ends, green with darker longitudinal stripes, bifid tail and two-horned, hairy head capsule. Pupa green, rounded, formed in grass debris.

1 **Evening Brown or Twilight Brown**   *Melanitis leda helena*

Wingspan: ♂ 58–65 mm ♀ 63–72 mm. **Identification: 1A** ♂ upper side, **1B** ♀ upper side (f. *zitenides*), **1C** ♂ underside (f. *helena*). ♀ generally paler than ♂, for all forms. WSF f. *helena* has blunt wingtips, ♂ has small forewing ocelli. DSF f. *zitenides* larger, *both sexes* with large ocelli, undersides very variably coloured and marked. Slow, moth-like flight. Active mainly at dusk or on dull, cloudy days. Fond of fermenting fruits and tree sap. **Distribution:** Widespread in Afromontane, lowland and riverine woodland and forest from W Cape (Cape Town) and E Cape to KwaZulu-Natal, Swaziland, Mpumalanga, and Limpopo and NW provinces. Also in wooded riverine kloofs in fairly arid areas of N Cape. **Habitat:** Forest edges, flatlands, gullies. **Flight period:** Two main overlapping broods: winter (Mar–Aug, when most numerous), spring and summer (Sept–Mar). **Larval food:** Poaceae grasses including *Setaria* and *Cynodon* spp., *Pennisetum clandestinum* and *Saccharum officinarum*.

Genus *Gnophodes*   Evening Browns   AFRICA 3 SPP., SOUTH AFRICA 1

Similar in appearance, habits and life history to *Melanitis*. No eye spots on the upper side. The forewing subcostal vein is *not* swollen at the base. Skulking, reluctant to fly; flight is low and of short duration. Eggs white, spheroidal with flattened base, appearing smooth, but under magnification show fine net-like pattern. Larva cylindrical, tapered at both ends, green with darker longitudinal stripes, bifid tail and two-horned, hairy head capsule. Pupa green, rounded, formed in grass debris.

2 **Yellow-banded Evening Brown**   *Gnophodes betsimena diversa*

Wingspan: ♂ 55–65 mm ♀ 60–70 mm. **Identification: 2A** ♂ upper side, **2B** ♂ underside. Only the DSF found here. ♂ has a conspicuous sex brand on the forewing and the ♀ is paler brown. Similarly sized Evening Brown (above) distinguished by *lack of eye spots*. Active at dusk; hides in dense undergrowth during day. Fond of fermenting fruit. **Distribution:** Rare, localised. Dense coastal and lowland forest and bush, from Port St Johns and other parts of n E Cape coast to Oribi Gorge, and near Ndumu GR, KwaZulu-Natal. Historically found near Durban, but no recent records. **Habitat:** Flatlands, wetlands, gullies. **Flight period:** Probably year-round, but usually Mar–Aug (peak Apr–Jun). **Larval food:** Poaceae grasses, including *Setaria* spp., and *Panicum deustum*. Bred on *Ehrharta erecta*.

A

1C

B

2A

2B

Genus *Bicyclus*   Bush Browns

AFRICA 85 SPP., SOUTH AFRICA 3

Medium-sized, dull brown butterflies. Underside often with numerous large eye spots. Forewing veins strongly swollen at bases. Skulking, shade-loving habits. Fond of fermenting fruit. Egg watery white, flattened sphere almost bun-shaped; fine netting tracery. Larva green or brown, with darker dorsal lines and oblique dorso-lateral lines, flattened oval cross-section, tapered at both ends. Tail bifid. Head capsule carries two bluntly pointed horns. Pupa brown, formed on silken mat on grass or debris.

1 **Common Bush Brown**   *Bicyclus safitza safitza*

Wingspan: ♂ 40–45 mm ♀ 43–48 mm. **Identification: 1A** ♂ upper side, **1B** ♂ underside (f. *safitza*), **1C** ♂ underside (f. *evenus*). ♂ very dark with conspicuous black hair pencil on forewing underside base, large scent patch on forewing base. ♀ paler, with larger ocelli. Both WSFs f. *safitza* and f. *injusta* have enlarged underside ocelli, latter with a yellow ring around the forewing underside ocelli. DSF f. *evenus* also has yellow ring around forewing underside ocelli, but upper side ocelli greatly reduced. Distinctive hopping, bobbing flight along paths; never flies far when flushed. **Distribution:** Abundant. Afromontane, lowland and Riverine Forest and bush in eastern zone of South Africa, from W Cape (Knysna) to Soutpansberg, Limpopo Province. Southern limit of f. *safitza* is Mpumalanga; from here, replaced by f. *injusta* to southern limit of distribution. DSF f. *evenus* throughout the species' range. **Habitat:** Forest edges, flatlands. **Flight period:** Year-round, WSF mainly Oct–Dec (peak Nov), DSF mainly Jan-May (peak Apr). **Larval food:** Poaceae grasses, including *Ehrharta erecta*.

2 **Grizzled Bush Brown**   *Bicyclus ena*

Wingspan: ♂ 38–42 mm ♀ 43–48 mm. **Identification: 2A** ♂ upper side, **2B** ♂ underside (f. *kigonserae*). Sexes similar; ♂ carries conspicuous black hair pencil at forewing base. WSF f. *ena* smaller and darker than DSF f. *kigonserae*, but this *lacks greatly enlarged underside ocelli* of DSFs of other two South African *Bicyclus* spp. Hides in clumps of shrubs and trees. **Distribution:** Rarer than other South African *Bicyclus* spp. Savanna, Riverine Forest from KwaZulu-Natal (Lebombo Mts) to Swaziland, Mpumalanga, Limpopo Province and further north. **Habitat:** Hill tops, steep, wooded hillsides. **Flight period:** Two extended broods: WSF in spring and summer, DSF in autumn and winter. **Larval food:** Probably Poaceae grasses.

3 **Squinting Bush Brown**   *Bicyclus anynana anynana*

Wingspan: ♂ 35–40 mm ♀ 39–45 mm. **Identification: 3A** ♂ upper side, **3B** ♂ underside (f. *anynana*), **3C** ♂ underside (f. *vicaria*). Sexes similar, ♂ with pale, sandy brown outer hair pencil at the forewing base. DSF f. *anynana* has *off-centre pupil* in forewing underside basal ocellus, hence common name. WSF f. *vicaria* darker, underside ocelli enlarged. Often with Common Bush Brown (above) in warmer, lowland areas; similar habits, but warier, more difficult to approach. Well camouflaged on dead leaves. **Distribution:** Wooded kloofs and coastal bush in riverine and lowland forest from Durban, KwaZulu-Natal, to Swaziland, Mpumalanga, Limpopo Province and further north. **Habitat:** Forest edges, flatlands. **Flight period:** Two extended broods: WSF in spring and summer, DSF in autumn and winter. **Larval food:** Poaceae grasses. Bred on *Ehrharta erecta*.

Genus *Henotesia*   Bush Browns

AFRICA 51 SPP. (MOSTLY MADAGASCAR), SOUTH AFRICA 1

Medium-sized, dull brown butterfly. Underside often with numerous large eye spots. Forewing veins strongly swollen at bases. Habits similar to *Bicyclus*, but usually in more open country with patches of long grass; also shade-loving. Flight tends to be more prolonged. Egg almost spherical, with flattened base and fine netting tracery. Larva green or brown, with darker dorsal lines and oblique dorso-lateral lines, flattened oval cross-section, tapered at both ends. Tail bifid. Head capsule carries two bluntly pointed horns. Pupa brown, formed on silken mat on grass or debris.

A

1B

C

2A

2B

3A

3B

3C

1 Eyed Bush Brown or Marsh Patroller   *Henotesia perspicua perspicua*

Wingspan: ♂ 38–43 mm ♀ 42–48 mm. **Identification: 1A** ♂ upper side, **1B** ♂ underside (f. *maevius*), **1C** ♂ underside (f. *perspicua*). Sexes similar, ♂ darker. DSF f. *maevius* has darker upper side and less prominent orange ring around upper side ocelli than WSF f. *perspicua*. Seasonal forms similar on upper side, but WSF has *markedly* more prominent *underside* ocelli. **Distribution:** Common in Grassland, often near low-lying or riverine forest, from Swaziland and Port Shepstone north through savanna of n KwaZulu-Natal to Mpumalanga, Gauteng, and Limpopo and NW provinces. **Habitat:** Flatlands, wetlands. **Flight period:** Year-round. WSF in spring and summer, DSF in autumn and winter. **Larval food:** Poaceae grasses, including *Panicum maximum*. Bred on *Ehrharta erecta* and *Pennisetum clandestinum*.

Genus *Aeropetes*   Mountain Pride   MONOTYPIC, SOUTHERN AFRICA

One of the largest and most spectacular of the satyrines. Dark rich brown with bands of bright orange-yellow spots; forewing subcostal vein not swollen at base. Flight fast, sailing. Egg pale yellow, dome-shaped with a bluntly pointed crown and flattened base, fine netting tracery fading on lower part. Larva a flattened cylinder, bluntly tapered at both ends, with short bifid tail and rounded, hairy head capsule with no horns; green or pale red-brown, with prominent dark dorsal line. Pupa suspended head down from a silken pad; pale dull buff with black spots, wing cases protruding ventrally.

2 Table Mountain Beauty or Mountain Pride   *Aeropetes tulbaghia*

Wingspan: ♂ 70–78 mm ♀ 75–90 mm. **Identification: 2A** ♂ upper side, **2B** ♂ underside. Sexes similar, ♂ darker than ♀; latter has longer, more rounded wings. Settles on shady side of rocks or overhung stream banks. Only known pollinator of Red Disa *Disa uniflora*; fond of red or orange flowers. **Distribution:** Fynbos, Nama Karoo, Grassland, from W Cape (Cape Town) into N Cape (southern Namaqualand), and along southern and eastern mountain ranges into Lesotho, KwaZulu-Natal, Mpumalanga, Gauteng, and Limpopo (Soutpansberg) and NW provinces. **Habitat:** Mountains, rock-strewn hillsides, gullies. **Flight period:** Single-brooded, Nov–Apr (peak Dec–Mar). **Larval food:** Poaceae grasses, including *Hyparrhenia hirta*– and *Ehrharta erecta*. Bred on *Pennisetum clandestinum*.

Genus *Paralethe*   Bush Beauty   SOUTH AFRICA (AND SWAZILAND) 1 SP.

Medium-sized to large satyrine. Forewing subcostal vein not swollen at base. Egg similar to *Aeropetes*; pale yellow, dome-shaped with bluntly pointed crown and flattened base, fine netting tracery fading on lower part. Larva buff to dark red-brown, rounded head capsule and shortly bifid tail, hairy in later stages; darker dorsal stripes and oblique dorso-lateral lines. Pupa blunt, red-brown to black, with rounded abdomen and head; attached, head down, to silken pad spun on grass stem.

3 Bush Beauty or Forest Beauty   *Paralethe dendrophilus*

Wingspan: ♂ 45–60 mm ♀ 48–70 mm. **Identification: 3A** ♂ upper side (nominate), **3B** ♂ underside (f. *alticola* of *P. d. albina*), **3C** ♂ upper side (*P. d. junodi*). Sexes very similar, ♀ slightly paler than ♂. 4 subspp. (*P. d. albina* with 2 forms). Nominate has upper side with *orange* forewing spots, other subspp. have *cream to white* spots. Form *alticola* of *P. d. albina* has mostly white forewing spots, those of *P. d. junodi* are large and totally white. Flight slow and flapping. Often sits on tree boles to hide or feed at sap. **Distribution:** Afromontane and coastal forest fringes. Sometimes in alien pine plantations. Nominate in E Cape from Katberg and Amatolas to Mbashe R; *P. d. albina* from E Cape (Port St Johns) to KwaZulu-Natal along Drakensberg foothills (high-altitude populations are f. *alticola*); *P. d. indosa* in low-altitude forests in KwaZulu-Natal, from south coast to Durban, Eshowe and below Karkloof Falls; *P. d. junodi* along Drakensberg in Mpumalanga and Limpopo Province. **Habitat:** Forest edges, mountains, hillsides. **Flight period:** Single-brooded, late Dec–May. **Larval food:** Poaceae grasses, including *Ehrharta erecta* and *Panicum deustum*.

Genus *Dira*   Widows

SOUTH AFRICA 4 SPP.

Medium to large butterflies; dark brown with numerous eye spots. Forewing subcostal vein not swollen at base. Floating, sailing flight; capable of speed if molested. Usually flies in the earlier, cooler part of the day, later sheltering under a grass clump or rock. Sometimes in swarms of hundreds at the peak of emergence. Egg white to buff, squat, smooth dome with fine netting tracery. Larva fat, bluntly tapered at both ends, rounded head capsule and very short bifid tail. Buff with red-brown stripes in early instars; when fully grown, dark brown to black with paler markings, covered in short dark hairs. Larval stage prolonged. Pupa buff to dark brown, bluntly rounded. Attached to grass stems and debris by the cremaster.

1 Cape Autumn Widow   *Dira clytus*

Wingspan: 45–55 mm. **Identification: 1A** ♂ upper side (nominate), **1B** ♀ upper side, **1C** ♀ underside (*D. c. eurina*). Sexes similar, but ♀ paler. 2 subspp.; *D. c. eurina* is larger and paler than nominate, with more prominent ocelli. ♀ seldom seen because reluctant to take to wing. **Distribution:** Often very common, especially in thick patches of kikuyu. In Fynbos in south-western part of range, and Nama Karoo, Grassland and grassy savanna further north-east. Near sea level in the south, but also at higher altitudes to north and east. Nominate from W Cape (Cape Peninsula, where common in autumn) to E Cape (Humansdorp); *D. c. eurina* from E Cape (Gamtoos R to Great Kei R). **Habitat:** Flatlands, coast, hillsides, parks and gardens. **Flight period:** Single-brooded: nominate late Feb–Apr, *D. c. eurina* late Feb to late March. **Larval food:** Poaceae grasses, including *Ehrharta erecta*, *Pennisetum clandestinum*, *Stipa dregeana* and *Stenotaphrum secundatum*.

2 Pondoland Widow   *Dira oxylus*

Wingspan: ♂ 50–60 mm ♀ 55–65 mm. **Identification: 2A** ♂ upper side (bronze sheen typical of this genus evident), **2B** ♂ underside, **2C** ♀ upper side. Sexes similar, but ♀ duller; ♂ conspicuous against the green hills when swarming. Inner pale marginal forewing line protrudes inwards in area M₃. Generally larger than Cape Autumn Widow (above), but some individuals the same size as *D. c. eurina*; in southern part of range, flight period overlaps with this, but easily distinguished by having *three or four ocelli* in the forewing apex. Flies in the cool of the morning; in heat of day, shelters in shade of large rocks and trees. ♀ far less active. **Distribution:** Grassland. Lower Drakensberg foothills from E Cape (Queenstown, Stutterheim) to KwaZulu-Natal (Kokstad). **Habitat:** Grassy slopes of hillsides, mountains. **Flight period:** Single-brooded, from late Dec to early Mar. **Larval food:** Poaceae grasses, including *Ehrharta erecta*.

3 Swanepoel's Widow   *Dira swanepoeli*

Wingspan: ♂ 58–65 mm ♀ 60–68 mm. **Identification: 3A** ♂ upper side, **3B** ♀ under & upper side. Sexes similar, ♀ with basal suffusion of red-brown on upper side. Huge gap in distribution between this species and its closest relative (Pondoland Widow, above) makes it unmistakable. *Two or three* forewing apical ocelli. Inner pale marginal forewing line protrudes inwards in area CuA₁. 2 subspp.; *D. s. isolata* described as having *extra ocellus* in upper side hind wing marginal row, but individuals of nominate sometimes also exhibit this. Fairly inactive, flight (only in the morning) slow, ponderous. Small groups on ledges between rocky ridges among clumps of suitable tussocky grass; ♂ circles the clumps; ♀ shy and inactive. **Distribution:** Only in Grassland/Afromontane forest ecotone in stunted forest interspersed with grass, on massifs in n Limpopo Province. Nominate on southern slopes of Soutpansberg; *D. s. isolata* on southern slopes of Blouberg. **Habitat:** Mountains, rocky ledges. **Flight period:** Single-brooded, late Feb and early Mar. **Larval food:** Poaceae grasses, including *Eragrostis aspera*. Bred on *Ehrharta erecta* and *Pennisetum clandestinum*.

A

1B

C

2A

A

2B

2C

3B

1 Janse's Widow   *Dira jansei*

Wingspan: ♂ 48–55 mm ♀ 52–58 mm. **Identification: 1A** ♂ upper side, **1B** ♂ underside. Sexes similar, ♀ paler. Marginal row of *five closely spaced small forewing ocelli* distinguish this species. Often found alongside Secucuni Shadefly (p. 60). Only Widow found in its localities, so unmistakable. Usually in groups of three to six, in the shade of trees. Sometimes difficult to flush from the long grass it favours. When flushed, flies fast, easily eluding pursuit in rocky haunts. ♀ less active. **Distribution:** Wooded hillsides in the Savanna/Grassland ecotone in Limpopo Province's Strydpoortberg and Drakensberg, and Makapans Cave (Mokopane) to Mariepskop. **Habitat:** Forest edges, wooded hillsides, rocky ledges, gullies. **Flight period:** Single-brooded, late Feb to mid-Mar. **Larval food:** Poaceae grasses. Bred on *Ehrharta erecta* and *Pennisetum clandestinum*.

Genus *Dingana*   Widows   SOUTH AFRICA AND SWAZILAND 7 SPP.
Medium-sized satyrines, smaller than closely related *Dira* Widows, with certain differences in the ♂ and ♀ genitalia. Forewing subcostal vein not swollen at base. Like *Dira*, they fly in the morning, but tend to be earlier; some species are off the wing by mid-morning. Life history very similar to *Dira*, the main difference in the larva being the final instar setae, pointed in *Dingana* but clubbed in *Dira*. Pupa lacks cremastral hooks, lying loose among the grass roots. This genus was revised by GA & SF Henning in 1996, and these species follow their arrangement.

2 Dingaan's Widow   *Dingana dingana*

Wingspan: ♂ 58–62 mm ♀ 55–60 mm. **Identification: 2A** ♂ upper side, **2B** ♂ underside. Sexes similar, ♀ with stout abdomen, but more elongate wings, and slightly broader postdiscal forewing band of ochreous orange, more or less contiguous blotches. Dark reddish-brown colouring makes this species conspicuous against green spring grass. ♂ patrols patches of hillside, ♀ less active, more often on flowers. **Distribution:** Locally common on rock and boulder-strewn ridges and hillsides in Grassland. KwaZulu-Natal Midlands, from Drakensberg foothills to Mooi River (Estcourt area), as far north as Greytown. **Habitat:** Rocky ledges, hillsides, mountains. **Flight period:** Single-brooded, Sept–Nov (peak Oct). **Larval food:** Probably Poaceae grasses. Bred on *Pennisetum clandestinum*.

3 Narrow-banded Widow   *Dingana angusta*

Wingspan: ♂ 60–65 mm ♀ 56–62 mm. **Identification: 3A** ♂ upper side, **3B** ♂ underside, **3C** ♀ upper side. Sexes similar, ♂ slightly darker than ♀, and with more slender abdomen, shorter wings and slightly narrower ochreous markings on forewing. Ground colour, similar reddish brown to Dingaan's Widow (above). Distinguished by having much *narrower forewing postdiscal ochreous patch broken into interneural spots*, rather than forming a continuous band. Colour of spots varies from creamy yellow to same orange-ochre as in Dingaan's Widow. **Distribution:** Grasslands in eastern highlands, from northern Swaziland to Mpumalanga and Limpopo Province. **Habitat:** Rocky ledges and grassy slopes, hillsides, mountains. **Flight period:** Single-brooded, Sept–Nov (peak Oct). **Larval food:** Probably Poaceae grasses. Bred on *Pennisetum clandestinum*.

4 Wolkberg Widow   *Dingana clara*

Wingspan: ♂ 60–65 mm ♀ 56–62 mm. **Identification: 4A** ♂ upper side, **4B** ♂ underside. Sexes similar, ♀ slightly paler than ♂, and with stout abdomen, more elongate wings and slightly broader white forewing markings. Ground colour *shiny slate brown with golden sheen*, as opposed to red-brown of Dingaan's and Narrow-banded Widows (above); forewing band narrow as in latter, but white. **Distribution:** Steep rock-strewn slopes at high elevation, among *Protea* bushes. Restricted to Wolkberg, Limpopo Province. **Habitat:** Rocky ledges, hillsides, mountains. **Flight period:** Single-brooded, Sept–Nov (peak Oct). **Larval food:** Probably Poaceae grasses. Bred on *Pennisetum clandestinum*.

1 Stoffberg Widow   *Dingana fraterna*

Wingspan: ♂ 56–61 mm ♀ 55–57 mm. **Identification: 1A** ♂ upper side, **1B** ♂ underside. Sexes similar, ♀ slightly paler than ♂, and with stout abdomen, more elongate wings and pale forewing markings slightly broader. Small Widow, more markedly convex outer margin to forewing than *D. clara*, and *slightly yellowish* forewing postdiscal spots. Ground colour shiny slate, with *greenish* gloss. Flies only in the morning from 09h00 to 11h00. **Distribution:** Very rare; only known from one locality – a steep, grassy hillside with *Protea* bushes – to the south-west of Stoffberg, Mpumalanga. **Habitat:** Rocky ledges, hillsides, mountains. **Flight period:** Single-brooded, mid- to late Oct. **Larval food:** Probably Poaceae grasses.

2 Jerine's Widow   *Dingana jerinae*

Wingspan: 65–72 mm. Largest *Dingana*. **Identification: 2A** ♂ upper side, **2B** ♂ underside. Strikingly coloured; ground colour more *matt, blacker brown* than other *Dingana* Widows; forewing with *bright yellow-ochre* postdiscal spots. Sexes similar, ♀ slightly paler than ♂, with stout abdomen, more elongate and rounded wings, and slightly broader pale markings on forewing. Flies early morning, usually off the wing by 11h00. **Distribution:** The most westerly *Dingana* sp. Only known from upper southern scree slopes of the Kransberg, in the Waterberg, Limpopo Province. **Habitat:** Rocky ledges, hillsides, mountains. **Flight period:** Single-brooded, Nov. **Larval food:** Probably Poaceae grasses. Bred on *Pennisetum clandestinum.*

3 Red-banded Widow   *Dingana alticola*

Wingspan: ♂ 57–64 mm ♀ 56–61 mm. **Identification: 3A** ♂ upper side, **3B** ♂ underside. Distinctive deep *orange-red* markings on dark red-brown background. Forewing postdiscal band variable in width, but usually broader than Dingaan's Widow (p. 48), narrower than Wakkerstroom Widow (below). Sexes similar, ♀ slightly paler than ♂, and with stout abdomen, more elongate wings and broader orange-red band on forewing. Larger than Wakkerstroom Widow; smaller than Dingaan's and Narrow-banded Widows (p. 48), wings narrower. **Distribution:** High-altitude Grassland in Steenkampsberg area (near Dullstroom and above Machadodorp), Mpumalanga. **Habitat:** Mountains, rocky ledges/ridges. **Flight period:** Single-brooded, Sept–Nov, peak Oct. **Larval food:** Probably Poaceae grasses.

4 Wakkerstroom Widow   *Dingana alaedeus*

Wingspan: ♂ 51–55 mm ♀ 50–54 mm. Smallest *Dingana*. **Identification: 4A** ♀ underside, **4B** ♂ upper side. Ground colour *silky brown*, with a *very broad*, only slightly convex *red-orange postdiscal patch on forewing*. Sexes similar, ♀ slightly paler than ♂, and with stout abdomen, more elongate wings and red-orange band on forewing broader. **Distribution:** High-altitude Grassland in southern Mpumalanga. Strong colonies on Hele Mt near Wakkerstroom; also, Hlangampisi above Dirkiesdorp, KwaZulu-Natal. **Habitat:** Rocky ledges, hillsides, mountains. **Flight period:** Single brooded, mid-Oct (peak Nov or Dec). **Larval food:** Poaceae grasses. Bred on *Pennisetum clandestinum.*

Genus *Serradinga*   Widows   SOUTH AFRICA, LESOTHO AND SWAZILAND 3 SPP.

Small- to medium-sized browns, split from *Dingana* in revision of that genus by GA & SF Henning, based on certain important differences in the wing venation and genitalia. Most have thin dark submarginal line on underside hind wing. Forewing subcostal vein not swollen at base. Fly in high-altitude grassy areas in midsummer, favouring grassy meadows and gentle slopes, as opposed to the steep, boulder-strewn hillsides preferred by *Dingana*; flight slower and less sustained. Eggs scattered on the wing; a lower dome than *Dira* and *Dingana* Widows. Fat larva bluntly tapered at both ends, rounded head capsule, short bifid tail, markings as in *Dira* and *Dingana*. Pupa bluntly rounded, buff to dark brown, attached to grass stems and debris by the cremaster.

A

1B

2A

2B

3A

3B

4A

4B

1 Bowker's Widow   *Serradinga bowkeri*

Wingspan: ♂ 50–55 mm ♀ 48–54 mm. **Identification: 1A** ♂ upper side, **1B** ♀ upper side, **1C** ♂ underside. Sexes similar, ♀ redder and paler than ♂, with white-ochre postdiscal spots on forewing extending more towards the base. Seldom found far from clumps of coarse *Merxmuellera* grasses. Flight slow. Settles often, diving into the grass if threatened. 2 subspp.; geographically distinct. **Distribution:** Grassland, Nama Karoo. Nominate in Witteberge, E Cape, and Lesotho; *S. b. bella* at Richmond and Cradock (Mountain Zebra NP), E Cape. **Habitat:** Mountains, hillsides. **Flight period:** Single-brooded, Nov–Feb (peak Dec–Jan). **Larval food:** Poaceae grasses, probably *Merxmuellera* spp. Bred on *Pennisetum clandestinum*.

2 Clark's Widow   *Serradinga clarki*

Wingspan: ♂ 45–54 mm ♀ 44–52 mm. **Identification: 2A** ♂ upper side (*S. c. dracomontana*), **2B** ♀ upper side, **2C** ♀ underside (*S. c. amissivallis*). Ground colour *shiny, coppery brown*. ♀ redder and paler than ♂, white-ochre postdiscal spots on forewing extending more towards the base, white markings on underside much broader. Flight slow; sometimes found in huge numbers. 4 subspp., geographically distinct. **Distribution:** Grassland. Nominate in E Cape (Somerset East, and mountains from Cradock to Cathcart); *S. c. dracomontana* lower Drakensberg, from E Cape (Barkly East area) to KwaZulu-Natal, Swaziland and Mpumalanga (Wakkerstroom); *S. c. amissivallis* in Mpumalanga (Verloren Valei); *S. c. ocra* Mpumalanga Drakensberg (Long Tom Pass, Sabie area). **Habitat:** Mountains, grassy hillsides, wetlands, valley marshes. **Flight period:** Single-brooded, Nov–Feb (peak Dec–Jan, later in more northerly populations). **Larval food:** Probably Poaceae grasses. Bred on *Pennisetum clandestinum*.

3 Kammanassie Widow   *Serradinga kammanassiensis*

Wingspan: ♂ 51–60 mm ♀ 52–58 mm. **Identification: 3A** ♂ upper side, **3B** ♂ underside. Sexes similar, ♀ redder and paler than ♂, with coppery sheen and white-ochre postdiscal spots on forewing extending more towards the base. Most similar to Bowker's Widow (*S. b. bella*, above), but with *distinctly angular hind wing shape*, darker ground colour, and *lacks thin dark submarginal hind wing line on underside*. **Distribution:** Most southerly *Serradinga*. Grassland; rarely in macchia-type vegetation. Only known from the slopes of Kammanassie massif near Uniondale, W Cape. **Habitat:** Mountains, hillsides. **Flight period:** Single-brooded, Nov–Jan (peak Dec). **Larval food:** Poaceae grasses, probably *Merxmuellera* spp.

Genus *Torynesis*   Widows   SOUTH AFRICA AND LESOTHO 5 SPP.

Angular patterns of the hind wing underside distinct. Forewing subcostal vein not swollen at base. Short, broad antennal club. Slow, sailing flight, becoming fast and bouncing when molested. ♀ sits and ejects her eggs into a suitable clump of grass. Egg a short dome similar to that of *Dira*, larva similar to *Serradinga* but lacking the diagonal dorso-lateral patches, and with several longitudinal lines. Pupa similar to previous Widows but with more slender thorax.

4 Mintha Widow   *Torynesis mintha*

Wingspan: ♂ 40–45 mm ♀ 45–48 mm. **Identification: 4A** ♀ upper side, **4B** ♀ underside (nominate), **4C** ♂ underside (*T. m. piquetbergensis*). Sexes alike, but ♀ with longer wings and stouter abdomen, markings more distinct. ♀ reluctant to fly, seldom seen. 2 subspp., geographically distinct. **Distribution:** Fynbos, Nama Karoo. In W Cape, in grass patches in Fynbos/Karoo vegetation. Nominate in sw W Cape, from mountains to sea level (Cape Peninsula across the Cape Flats to Riebeek-Kasteel and Sir Lowry's Pass, down to Cape Agulhas); *T. m. piquetbergensis* from Moorreesburg north to Piketberg. **Habitat:** Mountains, rocky hillsides. **Flight period:** Nominate single-brooded, Mar–Apr; *T. m. piquetbergensis* Apr–May. **Larval food:** Poaceae grasses, including *Merxmuellera* spp.

A

1B

1C

A

2B

C

3A

3B

A

4B

4C

1 Hawequas Widow   *Torynesis hawequas*

Wingspan: ♂ 44–50 mm ♀ 47–54 mm. **Identification: 1A** ♂ upper side, **1B** ♀ upper side, **1C** ♂ underside. Sexes alike, but ♀ with longer wings and stouter abdomen, markings more distinct. *Larger* than Mintha Widow (p. 52), with *wider, paler postdiscal band on forewing* and ground colour of hind wing (underside) *deeper brown*; flies at higher altitudes. Some populations found outside the Hawequas Mountains show distinct differences, and may be distinct races or even species. **Distribution:** Fynbos and Nama Karoo in W Cape (mountains from Simonsberg and Franschhoek Pass, north to the Slanghoekberge), and above Nuwekloof and north from Gydoberg to the Cederberg. **Habitat:** Mountains, hillsides. **Flight period:** Single brood in Mar and Apr. **Larval food:** Poaceae grasses, including *Merxmuellera* spp.

2 Large Widow   *Torynesis magna*

Wingspan: ♂ 46–54 mm ♀ 50–60 mm. **Identification: 2A** ♂ upper side, **2B** ♀ upper side, **2C** ♂ underside. Sexes alike, but ♀ with longer wings and stouter abdomen, markings more distinct. The largest *Torynesis* Widow. Sometimes seen in huge numbers around large stands of *Merxmuellera* grass. Differs from Mintha (p. 52) and Hawequas Widows (above) in having the postdiscal spots and band of the forewing (upper side) *broader and white as opposed to ochreous*; the forewing with no more than two apical ocelli, and the dark streak crossing the forewing cell with *no basal fulvous suffusion*. **Distribution:** E Cape, in Grassland and the Grassland/Nama Karoo ecotone on mountains from Lootsberg to Burgersdorp; very common in the Molteno and Steynsburg area. Has been found as far north as Barkly East and as far south as Uniondale. **Habitat:** Mountains, hillsides. **Flight period:** Single-brooded, Feb–Mar. **Larval food:** Poaceae grasses, including *Merxmuellera* spp.

3 Pringle's Widow   *Torynesis pringlei*

Wingspan: ♂ 42–52 mm ♀ 45–55 mm. **Identification: 3A** ♂ upper side, **3B** ♂ underside. Differs from Large Widow (above) in having *darker ground colour, narrower white postdiscal band on forewing*; ♀ has *more rust-red than yellowish* suffusion over the brown in the discal areas of forewing and hind wing on the upper side. Differs from Golden Gate Widow (below) in having *darker* ground colour and *white, not cream,* postdiscal band on forewing. In flight, conspicuous white band, together with dark ground colour, may cause confusion with Bowker's Widow (p. 52), common on same mountainsides but at lower altitude. **Distribution:** Rare. In Lesotho, known only from the mountains near Mokhotlong and Rafolatsanes and above the Sehonghong River valley; one record from the southern Drakensberg near Bushman's Nek (KwaZulu-Natal). **Habitat:** Mountains, hillsides. **Flight period:** Single-brooded, late Jan. **Larval food:** Probably Poaceae grasses (*Merxmuellera* spp.).

4 Golden Gate Widow   *Torynesis orangica*

Wingspan: ♂ 42–52 mm ♀ 45–55 mm. **Identification: 4A** ♂ upper side, **4B** ♂ underside. Most colourful of the otherwise brown *Torynesis* species. ♂ differs from Large Widow (above) in being *smaller*, having *hind wing with darker ground colour* and *creamy, not white* postdiscal band on forewing, and a *greater degree of fulvous-orange* markings on the upper side. **Distribution:** Rare. Only three known localities: the summits of Brandwag Buttress and Mushroom Rocks at Golden Gate Highlands NP, and 'Titanic Rock' near Clarens, Free State. **Habitat:** Mountains, hillsides. **Flight period:** Single-brooded, late Dec to early Feb (peak Jan). **Larval food:** Poaceae grasses, including *Merxmuellera* spp.

Genus *Tarsocera*   Widows

SOUTH AFRICA 7 SPP.

Dark butterflies, with deep rust-red patches and the typical satyrine eye spots. Forewing subcostal vein not swollen at base. Species in this genus are highly similar, and can usually only be accurately distinguished by genital dissection. Flight quite slow, low and controlled unless disturbed, upon which they may disappear rapidly. Egg white to buff, squat, smooth dome with fine netting tracery. Scattered randomly in grass by ♀. Larva fat, bluntly tapered at both ends, rounded head capsule and very short bifid tail. Buff with red-brown stripes in early instars; when fully grown, dark brown to black with paler markings, covered in short dark hairs. Larval stage prolonged. Pupa buff to dark brown, bluntly rounded. Attached to grass stems and debris by the cremaster.

1 Sand-dune Widow   *Tarsocera cassina*

Wingspan: ♂ 35–40 mm ♀ 40–45 mm. **Identification: 1A** ♂ upper side, **1B** ♀ upper side, **1C** ♂ underside. ♂ darker, with much smaller apical ocelli on forewing. ♀ has hind wing (underside) with conspicuous white markings. *Smaller* than its congeners; *much darker* than other *Tarsocera* species, with *smaller apical ocelli on forewing*, and *less extensive* rust-red upper side markings. **Distribution:** Fynbos, Nama Karoo and Succulent Karoo. W Cape, along coast from Lambert's Bay south to Bredasdorp. **Habitat:** Flatlands, coastal sand dunes, low hills. **Flight period:** Single-brooded, Oct–Nov, sometimes as early as Sept. **Larval food:** Poaceae grasses, including *Lolium* spp. and *Brachypodium distachyon*.

2 Spring Widow   *Tarsocera cassus*

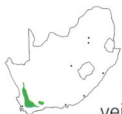

Wingspan: ♂ 42–52 mm ♀ 50–57 mm. **Identification: 2A** ♂ upper side, **2B** ♂ underside. ♀ paler brown, with larger rust-red forewing patch around ocelli. Both sexes have pale discal band on the underside of the hind wing. ♂ has *smaller, less well-defined* rust-red markings than other large *Tarsocera* species; darker brown forewing veins highly conspicuous against brown ground colour. Larger than Sand-dune Widow (above), with which its range occasionally overlaps. 2 subspp., geographically distinct. **Distribution:** Fynbos, Nama Karoo, Succulent Karoo. Nominate from N Cape (Nieuwoudtville) south to sw W Cape (Riversdale); *T. c. outeniqua* in Little Karoo (Calitzdorp, Ladismith and Oudtshoorn), se W Cape. **Habitat:** Slopes or summits of mountains, hillsides. **Flight period:** Single-brooded, Sept–Dec (peak Oct/Nov). **Larval food:** Poaceae grasses, including *Lolium temulentum* and *Hyparrhenia hirta*.

3 Karoo Widow   *Tarsocera fulvina*

Wingspan: ♂ 42–52 mm ♀ 50–57 mm. **Identification: 3A** ♂ upper side, **3B** ♀ upper side, **3C** ♂ underside. ♂ darker than ♀. Has *more distinct orange-fulvous* markings than other *Tarsocera* species. Forewing *more pointed* than Spring Widow (above), and *lacks the pale discal band on the hind wing* (underside). **Distribution:** W Cape from Hex River Mts, across Nama Karoo to Roggeveld escarpment and the Sneeuberg, south to Groot Winterhoekberge, E Cape. **Habitat:** Hillsides. **Flight period:** Single-brooded, Sept–Dec (peak Oct/Nov). **Larval food:** Probably Poaceae grasses.

4 Southey's Widow   *Tarsocera southeyae*

Wingspan: ♂ 42–52 mm ♀ 50–57 mm. **Identification: 4A** ♂ upper side, **4B** ♂ underside, **4C** ♀ upper side. Sexes similar, but ♀ more rounded, with brightly coloured wings and forewing more extensively orange. Very similar to Karoo Widow (above), but subapical orange-fulvous patch on forewing (upper side) *more extensive, paler*, and hind wing markings on underside *duller, flatter*. Fairly fast flight; frequents flowers, especially aloes. **Distribution:** Mid-altitudes from Calvinia, N Cape, across Nama Karoo to Willowmore and Jansenville, E Cape. **Habitat:** Gullies, hillsides, dry riverbeds. **Flight period:** Single brood from Sept–Nov, peak Oct. **Larval food:** Probably Poaceae grasses.

1 Deceptive Widow *Tarsocera imitator*

Wingspan: ♂ 42–52 mm ♀ 50–57 mm. **Identification: 1A** ♂ upper side, **1B** ♂ underside, **1C** ♀ upper side. Similar to Spring Widow (p. 56), but slighter build, with *more brightly coloured* subapical patch (*orange-red*, as opposed to rust-red); also, forewing underside darker in both sexes. ♂ has distinct dark forewing discal band, sometimes present in Spring Widow; ♀ of the 2 spp. are very similar. Overlap in distribution in southern part of this species' range. **Distribution:** Succulent Karoo; Namaqualand from Steinkopf, N Cape, south to Lambert's Bay area, W Cape. **Habitat:** Hillsides, coast, rocky ledges. **Flight period:** Single brood in Sept and Oct. **Larval food:** Probably Poaceae grasses.

2 Dickson's Widow *Tarsocera dicksoni*

Wingspan: ♂ 42–52 mm ♀ 50–57 mm. **Identification: 2A** ♂ upper side, **2B** ♀ upper side, **2C** ♂ underside. ♀ paler, with brighter fulvous markings than ♂. Range overlaps that of the very similar Spring (p. 56) and Namaqua Widows (below); most closely resembles the former, but is *more brightly coloured*. Reliable separation only possible with genital dissection. **Distribution:** Northern and W Cape, over a wide range of karroid veld (including Succulent Karoo, Fynbos and Nama Karoo) from Springbok, N Cape, south and west to Piketberg and east to the Swartberg Pass, W Cape. **Habitat:** Hillsides, mountains, rocky ledges. **Flight period:** Single-brooded, Sept to early Dec (peak Oct/Nov). **Larval food:** Probably Poaceae grasses.

3 Namaqua Widow *Tarsocera namaquensis*

Wingspan: ♂ 38–48 mm ♀ 42–50 mm. **Identification: 3A** ♂ upper side, **3B** ♀ upper side, **3C** ♂ underside. Sexes alike, ♀ paler. Difficult to separate from other *Tarsocera* spp., except by genitalia studies. Very similar to Dickson's Widow (above) but *smaller*, with *larger* apical ocelli on forewing, and *more pointed* forewing apex. **Distribution:** Only in Succulent Karoo, Namaqualand, south to Nieuwoudtville, N Cape. **Habitat:** Rocky hillsides. **Flight period:** Single brood from Aug–Oct, peak Sept. **Larval food:** Not confirmed, but likely to be a member of the Poaceae grasses.

Genus *Coenyra* Shadeflies

SOUTHERN AFRICA 3 SPP.

Small butterflies, brightly coloured for satyrines, and with characteristic irregular stripes of red or orange on the underside. Forewing subcostal vein strongly thickened at base. Flight slow, bouncing. Skulking habits, often under trees, hence the common name, Shadeflies. Egg whitish, barrel-shaped, with 20–25 longitudinal ribs and 15–20 cross-ribs forming rounded depressions. Larva green to buff, slender, tapered both ends with deeply bifid tail segment and two pointed horns on the head capsule. Pupa also slender, with pointed abdomen and bifid head horns; suspended from grass stalk by cremaster.

4 Zulu Shadefly *Coenyra hebe*

Wingspan: ♂ 32–36 mm ♀ 34–38 mm. **Identification: 4A** ♀ upper side, **4B** ♀ underside. Sexes similar, ♀ paler and less active. Small brown butterfly, inconspicuous except for brightly marked underside with deep red bands on shiny buff-brown ground. **Distribution:** Coastal bush and lowland savanna/forest mosaic. KwaZulu-Natal, from Durban (now rare as a result of habitat loss), north along the coastal plain to Maputaland (where fairly common); also Greytown (in Savanna) to Swaziland and Mpumalanga (Blyderivierspoort NR). **Habitat:** Forest edges, flatlands. **Flight period:** Continuously brooded, peak Nov–Jan. **Larval food:** Probably Poaceae grasses. Bred on *Ehrharta erecta*.

A

1B

1C

2A

2B

2C

3A

3B

3C

4A

4B

1 Pondo Shadefly   *Coenyra aurantiaca*

Wingspan: ♂ 35–38 mm ♀ 36–40 mm. **Identification: 1A** ♀ upper side, **1B** ♂ underside. Largest Shadefly, bright *orange-banded* underside distinctive. *Upper side orange bands* unique to this species. Sexes similar, ♀ paler, less active than ♂. **Distribution:** Lowland coastal forest in E Cape, from Alexandria to Wild Coast, as far north as Umdoni Park in s KwaZulu-Natal. Inland to Afromontane forests in the Amatolas and Katberg. **Habitat:** Forest edges, coast. **Flight period:** Continuously brooded from Oct–May, but more common in late summer. **Larval food:** Probably Poaceae grasses. Bred on *Ehrharta erecta*.

2 Secucuni Shadefly   *Coenyra rufiplaga*

Wingspan: ♂ 32–36 mm ♀ 34–38 mm. **Identification: 2A** ♀ upper side, **2B** ♀ underside. Sexes similar, ♀ paler and less active than ♂. Same size as Zulu Shadefly (p. 58), but has greatly extended *red* postdiscal patches on the forewing, and a *darker* underside, with *narrower* darker red bands than the other *Coenyra* species. Found at higher altitudes than Zulu Shadefly (p. 58). **Distribution:** Fairly widespread in Limpopo Province, in wooded, hilly Savanna from the Waterberg (Bela-Bela to Kransberg) and Strydpoortberg to the Wolkberg. **Habitat:** Forest edges, hillsides, mountains. **Flight period:** Continuously brooded Oct–May, but more common late summer. **Larval food:** Probably Poaceae grasses.

Genus *Physcaeneura*   Webbed Ringlets   AFRICA 5 SPP., SOUTH AFRICA 1

Small satyrines, distinguished from others by having white or cream undersides with fine black striae. Forewing subcostal vein strongly thickened at base. Found in wooded savanna. Flight through long grass slow, weak, halting; settles in shade of trees. Egg elliptical, whitish-yellow, with approximately 20 longitudinal ribs crossed by 14–16 transverse ribs, forming indentations that are larger towards the top of the egg. Larva spindle-shaped, with bifid tail and two short, blunt horns on the head capsule. Pupa narrow, green, elongated with no distinct cephalic horns; suspended from cremaster.

3 Dark-webbed Ringlet   *Physcaeneura panda*

Wingspan: ♂ 34–38 mm ♀ 35–39 mm. **Identification: 3A** ♀ upper side, **3B** ♂ underside. Sexes similar, ♀ with more rounded wings than ♂. Beautiful white underside with *fine black striae* and orange ocelli with metallic dark blue-silver centres. Upper side background black-brown, with broad red-ochre bands containing ocelli. Fond of decaying fruit; also sometimes feeds at low-growing flowers. **Distribution:** Common and widespread in hot dry Savanna in KwaZulu-Natal, Swaziland, Mpumalanga, Gauteng, Limpopo Province, NW Province and Swaziland. **Habitat:** Flatlands, hillsides. **Flight period:** Continuously brooded from Sept–May, but more common late summer. **Larval food:** Probably Poaceae grasses. Bred on *Ehrharta erecta* and *Pennisetum clandestinum*.

Genus *Cassionympha*   Browns   SOUTH AFRICA AND SWAZILAND 3 SPP.

Similar to *Melampias* and *Pseudonympha* spp., differing from the former in wing venation and the latter by the gradual club of the antennae. Forewing subcostal vein strongly thickened at base. Found in thick bush or fynbos; fond of flowers. Flight slow. Egg dome-shaped, with numerous indistinct and irregular ribs cross-braced to form small indentations, with a hexagonal network pattern on the top. Larva with bifid tail, and bluntly tapered towards head; rounded head capsule with no horns. Pupa greenish white, elongated, with rounded abdomen; suspended from cremaster.

A

1B

A

2B

A

3B

1 Rainforest Brown   *Cassionympha cassius*

Wingspan: ♂ 34–38 mm ♀ 36–42 mm. **Identification: 1A** ♀ upper side, **1B** ♀ underside. Sexes similar, ♂ with less square-shaped hind wing. Size and number of upper side and underside ocelli variable; as many as 3 on the forewing, and 4 on the hind wing. Fond of shade, but often found feeding on flowers in full sun. **Distribution:** Common in cool, moist forests, coastal or riverine bush and kloofs from W Cape (Cape Peninsula) along eastern seaboard through E Cape to KwaZulu-Natal, eastern slopes of escarpment through Swaziland and Mpumalanga to Limpopo Province (Soutpansberg). **Habitat:** Forest edges, gullies, flatlands. **Flight period:** Year-round, mostly Sept–May. **Larval food:** Poaceae grasses, including *Pentaschistis capensis* and *Juncus capensis*.

2 Cape Brown   *Cassionympha detecta*

Wingspan: ♂ 33–37 mm ♀ 34–38 mm. **Identification: 2A** ♂ upper side, **2B** ♂ underside. Sexes similar, ♀ more brightly coloured, with hind wing slightly squarer. *Smaller, darker* than Rainforest Brown (above), flight faster. **Distribution:** Thick Fynbos and Nama Karoo scrub, in W Cape mountains from Cederberg to Swartberg and down to the coast (Stilbaai). Spreads along south-east coast and hills to E Cape (Uitenhage) and into Great Karoo (Nuweveldberge). **Habitat:** Flatlands, coast, mountains. **Flight period:** Sept–Apr (peaks Oct and Mar). **Larval food:** Sedges, including *Ficina ramossissima* and possibly *F. acuminata*; and restios, possibly *Ischyrolepis* spp. and probably *I. tenuissima*.

3 Camdeboo Brown   *Cassionympha camdeboo*

Wingspan: ♂ 33–37 mm ♀ 34–38 mm. **Identification: 3A** ♂ upper side, **3B** ♂ underside. Sexes similar. Compared to Cape Brown (above) has *completely flat hind wing underside with no ocelli*. Orange patch on forewing (upper side) *lacks any trace of dark ground colour* at end of cell. **Distribution:** Restricted to dry Nama Karoo of Camdeboo Mountains near Aberdeen, E Cape. **Habitat:** Mountains, edges of thick scrub. **Flight period:** Apparently single-brooded, Nov–Dec. **Larval food:** Possibly Poaceae grasses, sedges and/or restios.

Genus *Melampias*   Browns   SOUTH AFRICA 1 SP.

Distinguished from similar *Pseudonympha* by elongated antennal club. Forewing subcostal vein strongly thickened at base. Fairly fast, floating flight over low vegetation, slow flight along ground or along rocky ridges, speeding up if molested; settles often on flowers. Egg laid singly on blade of grass; whitish, elongate dome with many fine longitudinal ribs and cross-braces. Larva pale green, with darker stripes, spindle shaped. Bifid tail; head capsule with two short, blunt horns. Pupa green with broad thorax and small head projections; suspended head-down from cremaster attached to silken pad.

4 Boland Brown   *Melampias huebneri*

Wingspan: ♂ 35–38mm ♀ 33–35mm. **Identification: 4A** ♂ upper side, **4B** ♀ upper side, **4C** ♂ underside (nominate). Sexes similar, ♀ with longer, more rounded wings. The rusty orange-red forewing colouring that surrounds the apical ocellus in ♂ upper side extends into cell and sometimes to wing base in ♀. Sometimes found in huge numbers. 2 subspp., geographically distinct. **Distribution:** Nominate in coastal fynbos and Nama Karoo in W Cape from Clanwilliam, south to Cape Peninsula, east to Gouritz River, at higher altitudes along western edge of Roggeveld escarpment from Nieuwoudtville to Sutherland, and wetter parts of Little Karoo from Oudtshoorn to Calitzdorp; *M. h. steniptera* in Succulent Karoo in Namaqualand hills from Springbok to just south of Garies, N Cape. **Habitat:** Flatlands, coast, mountains, hillsides. **Flight period:** Single-brooded, starting (nominate) Jun (if weather is warm) or (*M. h. steniptera*) Aug, to Oct and sometimes Nov. **Larval food:** Probably Poaceae grasses. Bred on *Ehrharta erecta* and *Avena sativa*.

A

1B

A

2B

A

3B

A

4B

4C

Genus *Neita*   Browns

AFRICA 6 SPP., SOUTH AFRICA 4

Medium-sized Browns. Wing venation differs from *Pseudonympha and Melampias* in that the forewing vein R$_1$ arises from *near the upper angle of the cell, not well before it*, and the antennae have more elongated clubs. Forewing subcostal vein strongly thickened at base. Slow flight from flower to flower, becoming swift and floating when disturbed. Settles in shade. Eggs whitish, laid singly on grass leaves, elongate dome with many fine longitudinal ribs and cross-braces. Larva green, with paler longitudinal stripes; cylindrical, covered in short hairs and with bifid tail; head lacks horns or processes. Pupa has truncated head and elongated wing cases; suspended from cremaster attached to silken pad.

1 Neita Brown   *Neita neita*

Wingspan: ♂ 45–50 mm ♀ 45–58 mm. **Identification: 1A** ♂ upper side, **1B** ♂ underside. Sexes similar, ♀ with more rounded wings and more hind wing upper side ocelli. Distinctive *large yellow-ringed ocelli* on chocolate to slaty brown background, upper side and underside. Geographically very variable; likely that more than one race exists. Settles often on flowers, or on the ground in the shade of large rocks. **Distribution:** Possibly locally common, but colonies few and far between. In Grassland and grassy savanna-covered hillsides from E Cape (Mbashe River) into KwaZulu-Natal (Midlands) and into Swaziland and Mpumalanga (Barberton, Long Tom Pass), Limpopo Province (Bela-Bela) and NW Province (Potchefstroom). **Habitat:** Hillsides. **Flight period:** Single extended brood, Oct–Mar (peak Dec). **Larval food:** Probably Poaceae grasses.

2 Loteni Brown   *Neita lotenia*

Wingspan: ♂ & ♀ 45–48 mm. **Identification: 2A** ♂ upper side shows hind wing margin shredded after attack from a lizard or bird, **2B** ♂ underside. Sexes similar, ♀ larger, with more rounded wings. *Smaller* than Neita Brown (above), *darker* ground colour and *grey*, not yellow, rings around the ocelli. Orange-tawny patch on forewing upper side extends further towards the wing base. ♀ usually found on grassy slopes, ♂ on rocky ledges and cliff bases. **Distribution:** Grassy mountain slopes on high-altitude (2 000 m+) grasslands along s and se KwaZulu-Natal and Lesotho Drakensberg. **Habitat:** Mountains, hillsides, rocky ledges. **Flight period:** Single-brooded, late Nov–Jan. **Larval food:** Probably Poaceae grasses.

3 D'Urban's Brown   *Neita durbani*

Wingspan: ♂ & ♀ 45–48 mm. **Identification: 3A** ♂ upper side, **3B** ♂ underside. Sexes very similar, ♀ with slightly more rounded wings, stouter abdomen; less active than ♂. Upper side resembles Loteni Brown (above). Compared to other *Neita*, hind wing underside ocelli *absent or tiny; strongly contrasting crooked discal transverse lines*. Sometimes occurs in huge numbers. **Distribution:** Scattered populations in E Cape grasslands. Grassy mountain slopes at medium altitude from Camdeboo Mts along escarpment to Bedford, and Stutterheim south to Grahamstown and north to Dordrecht Kloof and Jamestown. **Habitat:** Hillsides. **Flight period:** Single extended brood, Oct–Feb (peak midsummer). **Larval food:** Probably Poaceae grasses; bred on *Ehrharta erecta*.

4 Savanna Brown   *Neita extensa*

Wingspan: ♂ 43–48 mm ♀ 45–50 mm. **Identification: 4A** ♂ upper side, **4B** ♂ underside. Sexes similar, but ♀ with brighter colouring and wings more rounded; ♀ less active. Similar to Neita Brown (above), but slightly smaller; further distinguished by having a *dark line* around the postdiscal upper side forewing orange-red patch. Found at lower altitude in warmer, more wooded country than other *Neita* species. **Distribution:** In bushveld/Savanna from Mpumalanga (Barberton) to Limpopo Province (Polokwane) and further north. **Habitat:** Flatlands. **Flight period:** Single extended brood, late Nov to mid-Apr (peak midsummer). **Larval food:** Probably Poaceae grasses; bred on *Ehrharta erecta*.

1B

2B

3B

4B

Genus *Coenyropsis*   Browns

AFRICA 3 SPP., SOUTH AFRICA 1

Small Ringlets, markings similar to *Neita* and *Paternympha* – brown with orange forewing patches; differs from these in that forewing vein R$_1$ arises from radial stalk well beyond upper angle of cell. Shade-loving; flight slow and bouncing among trees. Early stages unknown.

1 Natal Brown   *Coenyropsis natalii*

Wingspan: ♂ 34–38 mm ♀ 36–38 mm. **Identification: 1A** ♂ upper side, **1B** ♂ underside (nominate). Sexes similar, ♀ brighter than ♂. A small Brown, with *bright orange* forewing upper side patches. 2 subspp., geographically distinct. **Distribution:** Widespread in Savanna. Nominate from N Cape (Kuruman Hills), and north through NW Province and Gauteng (northern foothills of Magaliesberg near Rustenburg and Pienaarsrivier), north of Soutpansberg (Limpopo Province) and south to hills around Polokwane; *C. n. poetulodes* in Limpopo Province (Strydpoortberg and Waterberg). **Habitat:** Rocky ledges, hillsides. **Flight period:** Single extended brood, Oct–May, peak midsummer. **Larval food:** Probably Poaceae grasses.

Genus *Pseudonympha*   Browns

AFRICA 15 SPP., SOUTH AFRICA 13

Differs from similarly marked *Melampias* by having forewing lower discocellular vein approximately *same length* as medial discocellular vein, and from *Stygionympha, Neita* and *Paternympha* by having forewing vein R$_1$ arising from *well before* upper angle of cell. Antennal club broad and spoon-shaped. Single egg laid on grass stem. Whitish, dome-shaped, with numerous longitudinal ribs cross-braced with transverse ribs, irregular near top. Larva green to brown, with darker longitudinal stripes; cylindrical, tapered at both ends. Bifid tail and rounded head capsule, covered in short sparse hairs. Pupa green with truncate blunt head and elongated wing cases.

2 Burchell's Brown   *Pseudonympha hippia*

Wingspan: ♂ 45–48 mm ♀ 46–50 mm. **Identification: 2A** ♂ upper side, **2B** ♂ underside. Sexes similar, ♀ with wings more rounded. Pale grey hind wing underside irrorated with dark brown speckles, more intense (sometimes merging to obscure ground colour) at margin; two dark wavy lines cross the wing at either side of discal area; appears *silvery-white* on wing, ocelli on hind wing underside apex and anal angle *tiny or absent*. Rapid, sustained flight over mountain summits and down gullies, settling infrequently on flowers and the ground; ♀ flight slower. Very difficult to follow, wary and shy. **Distribution:** Cool, high-altitude fynbos-covered hillsides and summits from Cape Peninsula to Hottentots Holland Mts, along Riviersonderend Mts to Groot Swartberg and Outeniquas in W Cape, and E Cape mountain ranges from Kammanassie to Groot Winterhoekberge. **Habitat:** Mountains, hillsides. **Flight period:** Single brood, Dec and Jan, sometimes Feb and Mar. **Larval food:** Poaceae grasses; bred on *Ehrharta erecta, Ischyrolepis capensis* and *Thamnochortus glaber*.

3 Drakensberg Brown   *Pseudonympha poetula*

Wingspan: ♂ 42–44 mm ♀ 43–46 mm. **Identification: 3A** ♀ upper side, **3B** ♀ underside. Sexes similar, ♀ paler, wings more rounded; flies slower. Wings with *fine dark line* inside the upper side margin, unique to this species of *Pseudonympha*. One of the first butterflies to emerge at the end of winter in montane grasslands in Drakensberg. Flies quickly, low over grass; difficult to follow unless resting on the ground or feeding on flowers. **Distribution:** Cool, high-altitude grassy hillsides and summits from E Cape/KwaZulu-Natal border (Kokstad area) along the Little Berg hills, and high altitudes in Free State (Witberg, Vrede). Spreads north along eastern Mpumalanga hills (Dullstroom, Graskop) to Limpopo Province (Mariepskop and Wolkberg). **Habitat:** Mountains, hillsides. **Flight period:** Single-brooded, usually mid-Aug to late Oct. **Larval food:** Probably Poaceae grasses.

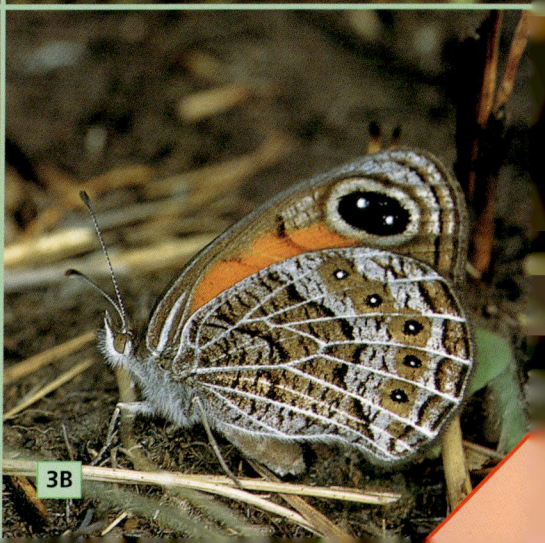

1 Trimen's Brown   *Pseudonympha trimenii*

Wingspan: ♂ 40–52 mm ♀ 44–56 mm. **Identification: 1A** ♀ upper side (nominate), **1B** ♂ underside (*P. t. ruthae*), **1C** ♂ upper side (*P. t. nieuvveldensis*). Sexes similar, ♀ more brightly coloured, wings longer than ♂. Hind wing with *white marginal line* on underside. Similar to Gaika Brown (below), but *duller, paler* and with *more restricted* orange markings. Flight fast and jinking; settles often on the ground or to feed on flowers; ♀ tends to stay hidden in the grass. 4 subspp., geographically distinct. **Distribution:** Found in coarse grassland at high altitudes. Nominate in Fynbos and Nama Karoo from Cape Peninsula and Boland mountains, north to Cederberg in west and Swartberg in east; *P. t. ruthae* in montane grassland, Bedford to Graaff-Reinet and north to Witteberg, E Cape; *P. t. namaquana* in Succulent and Nama Karoo from Kamiesberg, N Cape, to Roggeveld Escarpment and Nieuwoudtville/Calvinia in W Cape; *P. t. nieuvveldensis* in Nama Karoo in Nuweveldberg near Beaufort West, W Cape. **Habitat:** Mountains, hillsides. **Flight period:** Single-brooded, usually early Sept to late Nov. **Larval food:** Poaceae grasses, including *Merxmuellera stricta*, and other coarse, wiry grasses.

2 Gaika Brown   *Pseudonympha gaika*

Wingspan: ♂ 46–48 mm ♀ 48–52 mm. **Identification: 2A** ♀ upper side, **2B** ♀ underside. Sexes similar, ♀ slightly paler, orange in forewing (upper side) more extensive. More brightly coloured than similar Trimen's Brown (above) *P. t. ruthae*, with which it co-occurs, but upper side ground colour *darker brown, ocelli larger, more prominent*, and orange patches *on all wings*. Hind wing underside silvery markings similar to Trimen's Brown, but *grey, not white*; marginal line on underside. Always found fluttering close to patches of coarse grasses, but will fly rapidly if disturbed. **Distribution:** Cool, high-altitude hillsides and summits with ecotone of Nama Karoo and Grassland. E Cape (Gaika's Kop), along the Amatolas, north-east to the Witteberg, and Lesotho to KwaZulu-Natal Drakensberg. **Habitat:** Mountains, hillsides. **Flight period:** Single-brooded, usually Nov–Feb. **Larval food:** Probably Poaceae grasses.

3 Golden Gate Brown   *Pseudonympha paragaika*

Wingspan: ♂ 42–46 mm ♀ 44–47 mm. **Identification: 3A** ♂ upper side, **3B** ♂ underside. Sexes similar, ♀ paler, orange more extensive than ♂. *Smaller* than Gaika Brown (above). Upper side ground colour more *grey-brown* than Gaika Brown, but *darker* than Trimen's Brown (above); *fewer* silvery markings on hind wing underside than both species. Has grey submarginal line, like Gaika Brown. ♀ is reluctant to fly. **Distribution:** Grassland. Rare; only recorded from sandstone buttresses in Golden Gate Highlands NP, Free State. **Habitat:** Mountains. **Flight period:** Single-brooded, Dec–Jan. **Larval food:** Probably Poaceae grasses (e.g. *Merxmuellera* spp.).

4 Silver-bottom Brown   *Pseudonympha magus*

Wingspan: ♂ & ♀ 40–44 mm. **Identification: 4A** ♀ upper side, **4B** ♀ underside. Sexes similar, ♀ paler and more round-winged. Like Burchell's Brown (p. 66), pale silver-grey hind wing underside appears silvery white in flight, but unlike that species, *carries ocelli*, and has a prominent crooked band of brown irroration crossing the discal area. Flies slowly over grass patches, settling on flowers or on the ground; ♀ more reluctant to fly. **Distribution:** Grassy patches in coastal and inland low-altitude Fynbos from W Cape (Melkbosstrand) south to Cape Town (where very common), and along the southern littoral, north to E Cape (Stutterheim). **Habitat:** Flatlands, coast, parks and gardens. **Flight period:** Two overlapping broods, Sept–Apr, peak Oct and Feb. **Larval food:** Poaceae grasses, including *Cynodon dactylon*. Bred on *Ehrharta erecta*.

1 False Silver-bottom Brown   *Pseudonympha magoides*

Wingspan: ♂ 46–48 mm ♀ 44–46 mm. **Identification: 1A** ♀ underside. **1B** ♂ upper side. Sexes very similar, ♀ with wings rounder and abdomen stouter. Similar to Silver-bottom Brown (p. 68), but *larger*. Has *paler, silvery grey-white* hind wing underside with *more prominent, dark brown* irrorated discal band crossing wing. Underside hind wing ocelli *larger*, often 'blind', often pear-shaped. **Distribution:** Low- to high-altitude Grassland. W Cape (Outeniquaberg) to E Cape, along Drakensberg foothills into Lesotho, KwaZulu-Natal, Swaziland, Mpumalanga, and as far north as the Wolkberg (Limpopo Province). Also Free State and Gauteng. **Habitat:** Grassy hillsides. **Flight period:** Two overlapping broods from Sept–May, peak periods varying geographically. **Larval food:** Poaceae grasses; bred on *Ehrharta erecta*.

2 Vári's Brown   *Pseudonympha várii*

Wingspan: ♂ 46–50 mm ♀ 44–48 mm. **Identification: 2A** ♀ upper side, **2B** ♂ upper side, **2C** ♂ underside (KZN midlands form), **2D** ♂ underside (E Cape form). ♀ paler with rounder wings, and more extensive orange markings. Separated from similar False Silver-bottom Brown (above) by having anally more *pointed* hind wing with three submarginal ocelli. Underside hind wing ground colour also silvery grey, but more-or-less covered with *brownish markings*. Coloration variable, from pure silver grey with plain dark marginal border, to having varying amounts of red-brown *striation*. Hind wing underside discal band *red-brown*, prominent to indistinct. Hopping flight deceptively fast; may drop and hide in undergrowth; ♀ flight weak, reluctant to be flushed. **Distribution:** Grassland from E Cape (Groot Winterhoekberge to Amatolas), and Malutis and Drakensberg (Lesotho, KwaZulu-Natal and Free State) to KwaZulu-Natal Midlands (and possibly Mpumalanga; God's Window near Graskop). **Habitat:** Wetlands, gullies. **Flight period:** Double brooded; peaks Nov–Dec and Jan–Mar; single midsummer (Dec and Jan) brood at high altitudes. **Larval food:** Probably Poaceae grasses, or Cyperaceae sedges.

3 Paludis Brown   *Pseudonympha paludis*

Wingspan: ♂ 34–38 mm ♀ 32–36 mm. **Identification: 3A** ♂ upper side, **3B** ♂ underside. ♀ paler, wings more rounded than ♂, stouter abdomen. Underside similar to darker *P. várii* specimens, but variable amount of *pale scaling* along the veins of the hind wing, discal brown band *less distinct*. Upper side dull grey-brown, with *smaller* orange-red markings restricted to wingtips, and *small* ocelli. May fly in huge numbers. Flight bouncing, slow; ♀ reluctant to take wing. **Distribution:** Cool, wet high-altitude Grassland from E Cape (Witteberge to Amatolas), to Lesotho, e Free State (Golden Gate Highland NP), the KwaZulu-Natal Drakensberg, and very high Mpumalanga mountains (e.g. Verloren Valei near Dullstroom). **Habitat:** Mountains, grassy hillsides, wetlands. **Flight period:** Single-brooded, Dec–Jan at very high altitudes; Nov–Apr (peak midsummer) in E Cape hills. **Larval food:** Probably Poaceae grasses.

4 Swanepoel's Brown   *Pseudonympha swanepoeli*

Wingspan: ♂ 46–50 mm ♀ 44–48 mm. **Identification: 4A** ♂ upper side (from Whisky Spruit), **4B** ♂ underside (from Verloren Valei), **4C** ♂ underside (from Whisky Spruit). ♀ smaller, with wings more rounded. Similar in wing shape and habits to Vári's Brown (above), but *only two* ocelli in anal angle of hind wing underside. ♂ underside spectacular, hind wing looks like *beaten pewter*. Crooked discal band crossing wing is more prominent in ♀. Whisky Spruit population may be a distinct race since it lacks brown submarginal line on hind wing underside. **Distribution:** Only known from near Houtbosdorp, Limpopo Province, and Whisky Spruit (Long Tom Pass), Verloren Valei and Mount Sheba, and Pilgrim's Rest, Mpumalanga. **Habitat:** Wetlands, hillsides. **Flight period:** Single-brooded, Feb and Mar in the north, Nov–Feb in south. **Larval food:** Probably Poaceae grasses, or Cyperaceae sedges.

1 Machacha Brown *Pseudonympha machacha*

Wingspan: ♂ 34–35 mm ♀ 32–34 mm. **Identification: 1A** ♂ upper side, **1B** ♀ underside. Sexes similar, ♀ with wings slightly more rounded, colouring paler, underside duller; ♀ flies reluctantly. Small, easily identified by *large forewing patch of unbroken orange-red*, and very attractive, finely marked silvery-grey underside with a *submarginal ocellus between each vein of the hind wing*. Flight fairly fast and hopping, over patches of rough grass. **Distribution:** High-altitude Grassland. Core distribution Lesotho; also in E Cape (Witteberg) and KwaZulu-Natal (Drakensberg). **Habitat:** Mountains, hillsides, grassy slopes, wetlands (vleis) at over 2 400 m. **Flight period:** Single brooded, Dec–Feb. **Larval food:** Probably Poaceae grasses.

2 Pennington's Brown *Pseudonympha penningtoni*

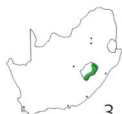

Wingspan: ♂ 30–32 mm ♀ 29–31 mm. **Identification: 2A** ♂ upper side, **2B** ♂ underside. Sexes similar, ♀ slightly paler, underside duller; seldom seen. Could only be confused with Machacha Brown (above), but *smaller, darker* and hind wing underside has beautiful *brocade-like* markings. Highest-flying of *Pseudonympha* species, as high as 3 400 m. Medium-fast, direct flight a few inches above the ground, settling often on flowers or rocks. **Distribution:** Core distribution Lesotho, from 2 700 m to highest summits where Grassland contains Karoo-like shrublets and bare rocks. Also in E Cape at Ben McDhui and summit chain of KwaZulu-Natal Drakensberg. **Habitat:** Mountains, hillsides at over 2 700 m. **Flight period:** Single-brooded, Dec–Feb. **Larval food:** Probably Poaceae grasses.

3 Southey's Brown *Pseudonympha southeyi*

Wingspan: ♂ 46–48 mm ♀ 48–52 mm. **Identification: 3A** ♀ upper side, **3B** ♂ underside (*P. s. wykehami*). Sexes similar, ♂ smaller and darker, orange-red on forewing less extensive, flight faster. Distinctive, *dark brown* hind wing underside irrorated with black, forewing *pointed*. One of the fastest flying *Pseudonymphas*, low, zigzagging flight between small shrubs; almost impossible to follow. 3 subspp., geographically distinct. **Distribution:** Grassland and Nama/Succulent Karoo mountains. Nominate in E Cape, Joubert's Pass and New England (Witteberg); *P. s. wykehami* in W and N Cape, from Ceres area north to Roggeveld escarpment; *P. s. kamiesbergensis* only in Namaqualand's Kamiesberg and Gifberg, N Cape. **Habitat:** Mountains, rocky ledges, steep slopes. **Flight period:** Single-brooded, Sept–Dec, earlier in the south. **Larval food:** Has been observed ovipositing on a Poaceae grass species.

Genus *Paternympha* Browns SOUTH AFRICA 2 SPP.

Small, weak-flying grass Ringlets, similar to *Neita* but ♀ forelegs *not* greatly reduced, and to *Pseudonympha*, but forewing vein R$_1$ arises from *near upper angle of cell, not* well before it. Antennal club broad, more elongate than in *Pseudonympha* and *Stygionympha*. Included in *Pseudonympha* until 1997. Life history not recorded.

4 Spotted-eye Brown or Small Hillside Brown *Paternympha narycia*

Wingspan: ♂ 40–44 mm ♀ 42–47 mm. **Identification: 4A** ♀ upper side, **4B** ♀ underside. Sexes similar, ♀ with more elongated wings; reluctant to fly. Brightly coloured Ringlet, upper side has *golden-brown* ground colour, both surfaces carry small but conspicuous forewing subapical ocelli with *1 to 3* white dots inside, and pure orange forewing patches. Flight slow and low, over hillsides, rough grassland or along rocky ridges; settles often. **Distribution:** Savanna, Grassland, Arid Savanna. Common but localised. From N Cape (Kuruman) north to Vryburg, east Gauteng and NW Province, Limpopo Province, south to Free State, Lesotho, KwaZulu-Natal and into E Cape (Queenstown). **Habitat:** Hillsides, flatlands, rocky ledges. **Flight period:** Double-brooded, Oct–Dec and Jan–Apr. **Larval food:** Probably Poaceae grasses.

A

1B

2A

2B

3A

3B

4B

4A

1 Big-eye Brown   *Paternympha loxophthalma*

Wingspan: ♂ 38–42 mm ♀ 40–45 mm. **Identification: 1A** ♀ upper side, **1B** ♀ underside. Sexes similar, ♀ with more elongated wings; reluctant to fly. Forewing subapical eye spot larger than Spotted-eye Brown (p. 72), and with *4 to 6 or more* white dots inside. Upper side ground colour duller, greyer shade of brown. Slightly *smaller*, wings shorter, squarer, orange forewing patch *longer* and *narrower*, reaching the inner margin but not as far down towards the wing base on the costa. **Distribution:** Savanna and Grassland. In Limpopo Province, Strydpoortberg, Wolkberg and Waterberg (west). **Habitat:** Hillsides, rocky ledges. **Flight period:** Double-brooded, Oct–Dec and Jan–Apr. **Larval food:** Probably Poaceae grasses.

Genus *Stygionympha*   Browns   SOUTH AFRICA 9 SPP.

Small to medium-sized Ringlets, dark. Markings very similar to *Pseudonympha* but, as in *Paternympha*, the forewing vein R₁ arises from *near upper angle of cell, not* well before it. Found in variety of habitats. Flight fairly fast, elusive. Egg domed, whitish, with many longitudinal and transverse ribs creating an indented pattern. Larva green to brown, with darker longitudinal stripes; cylindrical, tapered at both ends. Bifid tail and rounded head capsule, covered in short sparse hairs. Pupa not described.

2 Western Hillside Brown   *Stygionympha vigilans*

Wingspan: 45–48 mm. **Identification: 2A** ♂ upper side, **2B** ♂ underside. ♀ paler, with wings more rounded; more sedentary habits. Upper side deep brown ground colour, with striking, dark russet patches at apex of forewing and anal-postdiscal area of hind wing. Hind wing underside pale fuscous brown, irrorated with tiny darker brown striae and (usually) a *tiny ocellus* at the anal angle. Settles on ground, jerkily opening and closing wings. **Habitat:** Rocky ledges and ridges. **Distribution:** Fynbos, Nama Karoo. Seaward side of mountains, from Cederberg south to the Cape Peninsula, W Cape and along the Drakensberg chain to Grahamstown, E Cape. **Flight period:** Probably multi-brooded, Aug–Apr, peak Oct/Nov and Feb. **Larval food:** Poaceae (*Ehrharta erecta*) in captivity, and Restionaceae (*Ischyrolepis cinncinnata*).

3 Eastern Hillside Brown   *Stygionympha scotina*

Wingspan: 45–48 mm. **Identification: 3A** ♂ upper side, **3B** ♂ underside (nominate). Forewing upper side russet-red patch *wider* and hind wing patch *smaller, more triangular* than Western Hillside Brown (above). Hind wing underside ocelli *always absent*. Dark irroration on the hind wing underside *less diffuse*. Settles on ground, jerkily opening and closing wings. 2 geographically distinct subspp. **Distribution:** Montane grassland. Nominate from Winterberge (east of Cradock, E Cape) to Drakensberg (Lesotho, KwaZulu-Natal) and Malutis (Lesotho, Free State); also Witkoppe, Vrede (Free State). *S. s. coetzeri* along Mpumalanga and Limpopo Province Drakensberg; rare, localised populations in Grassland near forest, from Graskop area to Wolkberg. **Habitat:** Rocky ledges, grassy hillsides. **Flight period:** Probably multi-brooded, Sept–Mar. **Larval food:** Probably Poaceae grasses.

4 Wichgraf's Brown   *Stygionympha wichgrafi*

Wingspan: 40–50 mm. **Identification: 4A** ♀ upper side, **4B** ♂ underside (nominate). Sexes similar, ♀ heavier, with stouter abdomen, and wings more elongated. Wings of both sexes, but especially ♀, more *angular* than *larger* Western or Eastern Hillside Browns (above). *Pale, golden brown* ground colour variable. Hind wing underside sometimes with *large ocelli* in apical and anal areas, underside forewing basal rust-red patch reaches as far as apical ocellus; hind wing underside grey-brown ground colour irrorated with tiny short dark red-brown striae grouped into ill-defined bands. Slow, jinking flight. **Distribution:** Grassland. Nominate in hills of n Free State, Gauteng, Limpopo Province, NW Province and Mpumalanga; *S. w. williami* in KwaZulu-Natal, Free State and Lesotho mountains to E Cape (Witteberge); *S. w. grisea* in low-altitude hinterland of KwaZulu-Natal coast (Oribi Gorge, Margate). **Habitat:** Rocky ledges, hillsides. **Flight period:** Probably multi-brooded, Aug–Mar. **Larval food:** Possibly Poaceae grasses.

1 Curle's Brown   *Stygionympha curlei*

Wingspan: ♂ 43–48 mm ♀ 45–48 mm. **Identification: 1A** ♂ upper side, **1B** ♀ upper side, **1C** ♂ underside. Sexes very similar, ♀ heavier built, with stouter abdomen, and wings more elongated. Similar to Wichgraf's Brown (p. 74); basal rust-red patch on forewing (underside) *darker, does not* reach apical ocellus. Upper side ground colour generally *darker*, underside brown striae *do not form* bands. Slow, jinking flight, in *vleis and marshes* as opposed to rocky areas as in Wichgraf's Brown. **Distribution:** Moist higher altitude (1 500–2 000 m) montane grassland areas probably all along Drakensberg chain. In n KwaZulu-Natal and Mpumalanga (Wakkerstroom area), as far north as Long Tom Pass and Dullstroom area (Verloren Valei). **Habitat:** Mountains, wetlands. **Flight period:** Single-brooded, Dec and Jan. **Larval food:** Probably Poaceae grasses, or Cyperaceae sedges.

2 Robertson's Brown   *Stygionympha robertsoni*

Wingspan: 38–40 mm. **Identification: 2A** ♂ upper side, **2B** ♂ underside. Sexes similar, ♂ with wings more pointed and flight faster. Unlike other *Stygionympha* species, hind wing lacks rust- or orange-red patch on upper side. Always with two small, indistinct hind wing ocelli on underside, one at apex, one at anal angle. **Distribution:** Widespread but not in large numbers. Occasionally in colonies where the grass is lush, seldom more than 6 or 7 individuals at a time. Semi-arid to arid grassy areas within Nama Karoo of N Cape, s Free State, n W Cape and E Cape. **Habitat:** Flatlands, rocky ledges. **Flight period:** Probably multi-brooded, Aug–Mar. **Larval food:** Poaceae grasses; bred on *Ehrharta erecta*.

3 Van Son's Brown   *Stygionympha vansoni*

Wingspan: ♂ 36–38 mm ♀ 38–40 mm. **Identification: 3A** ♂ upper side, **3B** ♂ underside. Sexes similar; ♂ with more pointed wings and faster flight. Like a small Robertson's Brown (above), but with *elongated forewings*, and hind wing with *reddish* patch on upper side. Flight rapid, often straight upwards if disturbed, when the wind may carry it to safety. **Distribution:** Succulent Karoo areas in N Cape, from Kamiesberg to Springbok area. **Habitat:** Rocky ledges, hillsides. **Flight period:** Single-brooded, Aug–Oct. **Larval food:** Probably Poaceae grasses.

4 Karoo Brown   *Stygionympha irrorata*

Wingspan: 32–36 mm. **Identification: 4A** ♂ upper side, **4B** ♂ underside, **4C** ♀ upper side. Sexes very similar, ♂ with wings more pointed. Smallest *Stygionympha*, wings *more rounded* than Robertson's Brown (above), *lacks* hind wing ocelli on underside. Hind wing underside brown, *irrorated with tiny off-white to yellow* speckles; row of *submarginal spots* in same colour. Flight fastest of genus (along with Gerald's Brown (below)); flies close to ground, where small size makes it difficult to follow. **Distribution:** Widespread Nama Karoo areas of N Cape, s Free State, n W Cape and E Cape. **Habitat:** Flatlands, wetlands, dry riverbeds. **Flight period:** Single-brooded, Sept–Nov in winter-rainfall areas. In summer-rainfall areas, possibly double-brooded, Sept–May. **Larval food:** Poaceae grasses.

5 Gerald's Brown   *Stygionympha geraldi*

Wingspan: 32–36 mm. **Identification: 5A** ♂ upper side, **5B** ♀ upper side, **5C** ♂ underside. Sexes very similar, ♂ with wings more pointed. Compared to Karoo Brown (above), forewing upper side apical ocellus *larger and brighter*, wings *more angular*, orange-red patch *much more extensive*. Flight extremely fast, low. **Distribution:** Localised, rare. In grassy areas in Succulent Karoo just inland from N Cape coast (McDougall's Bay to Hondeklip Bay, and probably to the north and south). **Habitat:** Coast. **Flight period:** Single-brooded, Sept and Oct. **Larval food:** Probably Poaceae grasses.

A

1B

1C

A

2B

3A

B

4A

4B

4C

5A

5B

5C

1 Dickson's Brown *Stygionympha dicksoni*

Wingspan: ♂ 34–37 mm ♀ 35–38 mm. **Identification: 1A** ♂ upper side, **1B** ♂ underside. Sexes very similar, ♀ with wings more rounded. Upper side similar to Karoo and Gerald's Browns (p. 76), extent of forewing red patch intermediate between the two. Hind wing underside main difference; unmistakable distinctive *purplish-grey ground colour* and *pale fawn basal to discal patch*. On the wing, difficult to tell apart from similarly sized Boland Brown (p. 62) with which it co-occurs. **Distribution:** Fynbos. Highly localised, rare. Displaced from original habitat at Tygerberg (now extinct here), sw W Cape. Since then only single record from low renosterbos-covered hill near Darling, sw W Cape. **Habitat:** Hillsides. **Flight period:** Single-brooded, Sept and Oct. **Larval food:** Poaceae grasses, including *Tribolium echinatum*.

Genus *Ypthima* Ringlets   WORLD 100+ SPP., SOUTH AFRICA 5

Small, inconspicuous, dull grey Ringlets. Forewing subcostal vein strongly thickened at base. Shy, skulking habits in thick bush and grassy savanna, but can fly fast if disturbed. Single egg laid on grass; pale green, nearly spherical. Head capsule rounded, body thicker in midsection and tapering to bifid tail; buff with short hairs. Pupa green or brown, rounded head, raised wing cases; suspended head-down from cremaster.

2 Bushveld Ringlet *Ypthima impura paupera*

Wingspan: ♂ 32–36 mm ♀ 34–38 mm. **Identification: 2A** ♂ upper side, **2B** ♂ underside. Sexes similar, ♀ with abdomen stouter, habits more sedentary. DSF f. *badhami lacks the hind wing underside ocelli*. **Distribution:** From n KwaZulu-Natal, to Swaziland, Mpumalanga and Limpopo and NW provinces. **Habitat:** Flatlands, hillsides. **Flight period:** Year-round, peak in early summer and autumn. **Larval food:** Poaceae grasses; bred on *Ehrharta erecta*.

3 Granular Ringlet *Ypthima granulosa*

Wingspan: ♂ 32–36 mm ♀ 34–38 mm. **Identification: 3A** ♀ underside, **3B** ♂ upper side, **3C** ♀ upperside. Sexes similar, ♀ with abdomen stouter, habits more sedentary. More *strongly irrorated with grey scales* than other South African *Ypthima* and, unlike other species in the genus, pale patch around forewing ocellus *lacks dark border*. Shy, seldom seen. **Distribution:** Tropical species, only penetrating South Africa in extreme north-east. Well-wooded Savanna in northern KwaZulu-Natal (Emanguzi Forest); single specimen from Blyderivierspoort Nature Reserve, Mpumalanga. **Habitat:** Forest edges, flatlands. **Flight period:** Year-round, peak early summer and autumn. **Larval food:** Probably Poaceae grasses.

4 African Ringlet *Ypthima asterope*

Wingspan: ♂ 30–34 mm ♀ 32–38 mm. **Identification: 4A** ♂ underside (nominate), **4B** ♂ upper side (*Y. a. hereroica*). Sexes similar, ♀ larger, abdomen stouter, habits more sedentary. Has a *single marginal line* on upper side of both wings. 2 subspp. **Distribution:** Most widespread *Ypthima*, found all over drier areas of Africa and into Asia. Nominate in Savanna and low-altitude Grassland of eastern South Africa; *Y. a. hereroica* in drier areas of western South Africa, penetrating Succulent and Nama Karoo areas. **Habitat:** Flatlands, hillsides. **Flight period:** Year-round, peak early summer and autumn. Absent from arid south-western areas in winter. **Larval food:** Poaceae grasses; bred on *Ehrharta erecta*.

5 Condamin's Ringlet *Ypthima condamini condamini*

Wingspan: ♂ 32–36 mm ♀ 34–38 mm. **Identification: 5A** ♂ upper side, **5B** ♂ underside, **5C** ♀ upper side. Sexes similar, ♀ with abdomen stouter, habits more sedentary. Outwardly identical to African Ringlet (above), only distinguished by microscopic examination of the male genitalia. **Habitat:** Flatlands, hillsides. **Distribution:** Wooded Savanna of Limpopo Province; a single confirmed specimen taken near Letaba. **Flight period:** Probably year-round. **Larval food:** Probably Poaceae grasses.

A

1B

2A

B

3A

3B

C

4A

4B

A

5B

5C

1 Clubbed Ringlet *Ypthima antennata antennata*
Wingspan: ♂ 30–34 mm ♀ 32–38 mm. **Identification: 1A** ♂ upper side, **1B** ♀ upper side, **1C** ♀ underside. Sexes similar, ♀ with stouter abdomen, more sedentary. *Large antennal clubs* (other *Ypthima* species have almost no club), otherwise indistinguishable from African Ringlet (p. 78) in the hand. Shy, skulking; shade-loving. **Distribution:** Wooded Savanna in Limpopo Province (Munnik and Letaba). **Habitat:** Flatlands, rocky hillsides with thick shrub cover. **Flight period:** Year-round, peak Sept–May. **Larval food:** Probably Poaceae grasses.

Subfamily HELICONIINAE

Until recently, regarded as a purely New World subfamily of the Nymphalidae. Now includes all species that once comprised Acraeinae with some that were in Nymphalidae. The genera in this subfamily have been subject to three major taxonomic rearrangements in the last 20 years, and in the interests of continuity, this book follows Henning (1992) in recognising the genera *Bematistes* and *Hyalites*. These are familiar and well represented in South Africa.

Genus *Bematistes* Wanderers AFRICA 22 SPP., SOUTH AFRICA 1
Medium-large black or brown butterflies with white, cream, orange or orange-red markings. Sexes similar in markings, but may be dimorphic in colouring. Wings elongated. Flight slow and floating. Eggs laid in batches on Passifloraceae; cylindrical, almost twice as high as broad, evenly domed; cream to yellow. Larva gregarious, white to green, with dark spines and bands, and long fleshy tubercles. Pupa white, yellow or green, with dark markings on wing veins and split lines; also with long filamentous growths. Suspended head down from cremaster attached to a silken pad spun onto a twig or leaf.

2 Common Wanderer *Bematistes aganice aganice*
Wingspan: ♂ 60–65 mm ♀ 70–75 mm. **Identification: 2A** ♂ upper side, **2B** ♀ upper side, **2C** ♀ underside. ♂ with wings narrower than ♀, and *yellow* instead of white wing markings. ♂ strongly territorial; chases off settling intruders. Fond of flowers. **Mimics:** Several, e.g. False Wanderer (p. 120). **Distribution:** Coastal, lowland and riverine bush and forest from E Cape (Port St Johns) to KwaZulu-Natal, and Afromontane Forest of Mpumalanga and Limpopo Province. **Habitat:** Forest edges, parks and gardens, flatlands, coast. **Flight period:** Year-round, more common Oct/Nov–Mar. **Larval food:** *Adenia gummifera, Passiflora edulis* and *P. coerulea.*

Genus *Acraea* Bitter Acraeas WORLD 101 SPP., SOUTH AFRICA 21
Small to medium-large butterflies. Brightly coloured with red, orange and yellow, usually with black spots, and clearly defined hind wing marginal spots on underside. Wings more or less elongated. Flight slow and sailing unless disturbed. Eggs laid in batches; white to yellow, elongated ovals. Larva cylindrical, with six rows of branched spines on all segments except first and last, which have only two spines on each; head rounded, usually smooth; gregarious in early instars, more or less so when fully grown.

3 Garden Acraea *Acraea horta*
Wingspan: ♂ 45–50 mm ♀ 49–53 mm. **Identification: 3A** ♂ upper side, **3B** ♀ upper side, **3C** ♀ underside. ♂ bright brick red, ♀ variable, from dull brick red to tawny buff. Hind wing margin of both sexes a continuous dark band with lunules of ground colour. Popular garden species; visits flowers often. **Distribution:** Usually in large, concentrated colonies. Afromontane Forest fragments from W Cape (Cape Town) along escarpment into E Cape, KwaZulu-Natal, Mpumalanga, Limpopo Province, Gauteng and NW Province, also Riverine Forest. **Habitat:** Parks and gardens, forest edges. **Flight period:** Year-round, more common Oct–Apr. **Larval food:** *Kiggelaria africana, Passiflora coerulea, P. mollisima* and *P. manicata;* absent from *P. edulis.*

1A

1B

1C

A

2B

C

3A

3B

3C

1 Wandering Donkey Acraea   *Acraea neobule neobule*

Wingspan: ♂ 48–55 mm ♀ 50–56 mm. **Identification: 1A** ♀ upper side, **1B** ♂ underside. Closely resembles Garden Acraea (p. 80), but always *paler* red, *more extensive* hyaline wing areas, and *smaller, more regular* spotting. As with Garden Acraea, hind wing margin of both sexes a continuous dark band with lunules of ground colour. ♀ only slightly paler than ♂. Usually found singly or in small numbers, often on hill tops, where ♂ establishes a territory at the highest tree and sails slowly around it, chasing intruders. **Distribution:** Nama Karoo areas of e W Cape and E Cape, Arid Savanna of N Cape, Savanna from E Cape to KwaZulu-Natal and Mpumalanga, and grasslands in Limpopo Province, NW Province and Gauteng. **Habitat:** Hill tops, flatlands. **Flight period:** Year-round, more common Sept–Apr. **Larval food:** *Adenia gummifera*, *Passiflora edulis* and *P. incarnate*.

2 Machequena Acraea   *Acraea machequena*

Wingspan: ♂ 40–45 mm ♀ 45–53 mm. **Identification: 2A** ♂ upper side, **2B** ♂ underside, **2C** ♀ upper side pale morph, **2D** ♀ upper side dark morph, **2E** ♀ underside. ♂ pale brick red, ♀ pale ochre to whitish buff. Similar to Wandering Donkey Acraea (above), but hind wing margins on both surfaces have rows of *black dentate marks with orange marginal bases, discontinuous* bands with spots of ground colour. Distinctive flight, with shallowly fluttering wings. Fond of flowers, particularly Dune Soapberry *Deinbollia oblongifolia*. **Distribution:** Rare tropical species; marginal distribution in South Africa. Savanna in n Limpopo Province (breeding population sometimes established near Polokwane), and north of the Soutpansberg. Lowland Forest in n KwaZulu-Natal (Mandawe near Eshowe, and Kosi Bay, Maputaland). **Habitat:** Hill tops, flatlands, coast. **Flight period:** Late summer and autumn; year-round elsewhere. **Larval food:** No data.

3 Clear-wing Acraea   *Acraea rabbaiae perlucida*

Wingspan: ♂ 45–52 mm ♀ 55–65 mm. **Identification: 3** ♀ upper side. Sexes similar. Almost totally *hyaline wings*, with rainbow sheen if sun shines through them; underside virtually identical to upper side. Slow, high, sailing flight, wings almost motionless; settles on canopy leaves and twigs. May fly lower at forest edges and in windy weather; sometimes seen early in the morning, nectaring at flowers. Roosts communally. **Distribution:** Marginal in South Africa; regular breeding populations in Lowland Forest east of Lebombo Mts (Tembe Elephant Reserve), and coastal forests (Emanguzi, near KwaNgwanase) of Maputaland, KwaZulu-Natal. Occasional stragglers as far south as the Tugela R. **Habitat:** Forest edges, flatlands. **Flight period:** Year-round, mainly Sept–Jun, peak Mar–Jun. **Larval food:** *Schlechterina mitostemmatoides* (Passifloraceae).

4 Rainforest Acraea   *Acraea boopis boopis*

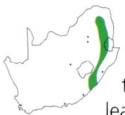

Wingspan: ♂ 45–52 mm ♀ 49–58 mm. **Identification: 4A** ♂ upper side, **4B** ♀ upper side, **4C** ♀ underside. ♂ bright red, ♀ dull brown-buff, sometimes with reddish tinge. Similar to but *smaller* than East Coast Acraea (p. 84). ♂ floats slowly around tree tops of high rainforests. Territorial in forest clearings and edges, perching on a prominent leaf or twig, sallying forth to challenge intruders. ♀ sedentary, seldom away from the food plant. Flowers rarely visited, more often at wet mud along roads and in clearings. **Distribution:** Afromontane and higher Lowland Forest, sparingly at coastal level in E Cape (Port St Johns area). Along escarpment through KwaZulu-Natal; more common in Mpumalanga and Limpopo Province (Woodbush and Legalameetse forests). **Habitat:** Forest edges, gullies. **Flight period:** Year-round, peak Nov–Mar. **Larval food:** Celastraceae, including *Cassine tetragona*, *Maytenus acuminata* and *M. heterophylla*; *Rawsonia lucida*.

A

A

1B

2C

2D

2E

B

3

B

4A

4C

1 East Coast Acraea   *Acraea satis*

Wingspan: ♂ 55–65 mm ♀ 55–70 mm. **Identification: 1A** ♂ upper side, **1B** ♀ upper side, **1C** ♀ underside. ♂ red and black, resembling huge Rainforest Acraea (p. 82); ♀ even larger, with same black and hyaline markings, but red parts replaced with pure white. Largest and most striking *Acraea*. Sailing flight with open wings; flies high in canopy. Flies closer to ground along roads and in clearings. **Distribution:** Tropical forest species; marginal distribution in Lowland Forest in ne KwaZulu-Natal; Lebombo Mountains, Maputaland (Kwaliweni and other forest patches near Ubombo); extremely rare further south. **Habitat:** Forest edges, hillsides. **Flight period:** Multi-brooded, Sept–Apr, peaks Feb and early Mar. **Larval food:** Known to use *Urera hypsilodendron* and *U. trinervis* in East Africa; while *Urera* plants occur within its South African range, to date all attempts to rear larvae on them from eggs laid by local butterflies have failed.

2 Fiery Acraea   *Acraea acrita acrita*

Wingspan: 45–55 mm. **Identification: 2A** ♂ upper side, **2B** ♂ underside (WSF), **2C** ♀ upper side (fresh). Fresh ♂ *almost fluorescent* orange. Coloration varies seasonally; WSF suffused with dark scaling; hind wing may be almost entirely black. ♀ usually darker than ♂. Extreme WSF ♀ upper side almost completely black-brown, only forewing discal area washed with yellowish buff. Conspicuous; sails slowly over green woodland, flees quickly if disturbed. **Distribution:** Open Lowland Forest and wooded Savanna in extreme ne KwaZulu-Natal (Tembe Elephant Park, Emanguzi Forest, Kosi Bay). A few records from Mpumalanga and Limpopo Province. **Habitat:** Forest edges, flatlands. **Flight period:** Year-round, peak Feb–Jun. **Larval food:** Passifloraceae, including *Adenia* spp.

3 Natal Acraea   *Acraea natalica*

Wingspan: 55–65 mm. **Identification: 3A** ♂ upper side (WSF f. *umbrata*), **3B** ♂ upper side (DSF f. *albiventris*), **3C** ♀ upper side, **3D** ♀ underside. Sexes similar, ♂ generally brighter than ♀; more active. Seasonally dimorphic. Nominate form is WSF, hind wing margins wide. There is an extreme WSF, f. *umbrata*, ♂ having dark scaling in discal area of the forewing. DSF f. *albiventris* has reduced black markings, narrow hind wing margins, upper abdomen surface whitish. Form *mesoleuca* is blackish, with white patch in hind wing cell. Large, conspicuous. Joins hordes of other butterflies on *Vernonia* flowers during dry season. **Distribution:** Common and widespread in open, Lowland Forest and Savanna from E Cape (East London) n along KwaZulu-Natal coast and inland through n KwaZulu-Natal, Mpumalanga, Limpopo and NW provinces, and n Gauteng. **Habitat:** Forest edges, flatlands. **Flight period:** Year-round, strong peak late summer. **Larval food:** *Passiflora coerulea*, *Adenia gummifera* and *Tricicleras longipedunculatum*.

4 Black-tipped Acraea   *Acraea caldarena caldarena*

Wingspan: ♂ 40–50 mm ♀ 45–55 mm. **Identification: 4A** ♀ upper side, **4B** ♀ underside. Sexes similar, ♂ slightly darker, wings less rounded. Little seasonal variation; extreme DSFs (e.g. f. *pallida*) with reduced black spotting and black wingtips. Prominent *black forewing tips*. Fiery Acraea (above) and Induna Acraea (p. 96), also with heavy black wingtips, seldom fly with it, and former is far gaudier. Attracted to flowers. **Distribution:** Savanna from n KwaZulu-Natal thorn belt into Mpumalanga, Limpopo and NW provinces, and n Gauteng. **Flight period:** Year-round, most active from Aug–Apr, with a strong peak late summer/autumn. **Habitat:** Flatlands. **Larval food:** Turneraceae including *Tricicleras longipedunculatum*.

1 Suffused Acraea   *Acraea stenobea*

Wingspan: ♂ 48–55 mm ♀ 50–56 mm. **Identification: 1A** ♂ upper side, **1B** ♂ underside. Sexes similar, ♀ with wings more rounded, darker forewing ground colour, and sometimes a whitish suffusion in the hind wing cell. *Whitish abdomen* conspicuous in flight. ♂ can fly very fast, at great height; ♀ more sedentary, flight slower. Both fly slowly near flowers, take fright easily. **Distribution:** Occurs sparsely in Grassland and Savanna from E Cape (King William's Town) and se Free State (Ladybrand to Bloemfontein); locally common in Arid Savanna from N Cape to Limpopo and NW provinces. Occasional migrant to KwaZulu-Natal and Mpumalanga. **Habitat:** Flatlands. **Flight period:** Year-round in warmer areas; peaks Sept, and Mar–May. **Larval food:** No data.

2 Lygus Acraea   *Acraea lygus*

Wingspan: ♂ 48–55 mm ♀ 50–56 mm. **Identification: 2A** ♂ upper side, **2B** ♀ upper side, **2C** ♂ underside. Similar to Suffused Acraea (above); ♂ *paler*, ♀ has *pinker* hind wing (upper side), with a *well-defined white patch*. Basal black suffusion *less evident* in both sexes, and spots on all wings are *smaller and fewer*. The two sometimes fly together in Arid Savanna. Slow flight, usually near flowers. **Distribution:** Rare, marginal distribution in South Africa; Arid Savanna and Savanna from N Cape to Limpopo and NW provinces; occasional migrant to Mpumalanga. **Habitat:** Flatlands. **Flight period:** Year-round, mainly Sept–Jun. **Larval food:** No data.

3 Window Acraea   *Acraea oncaea*

Wingspan: ♂ 40–48 mm ♀ 43–55 mm. **Identification: 3A** ♂ upper side, **3B** ♀ upper side (f. *obscura*), **3C** copulating pair, ♀ underside more visible. ♂ orange-buff, with prominent black interneural lines in forewing apical area of both surfaces. ♀ f. *obscura* has a pinkish-buff ground colour, similar to ♂, but with conspicuous white forewing apical patches on both surfaces. Nominate ♀ form, suffused with grey; rare in South Africa. Flight low and slow, settling often on flowers. **Distribution:** Common. Wooded Savanna and Lowland Forest from KwaZulu-Natal and Swaziland, to Mpumalanga, Limpopo and NW provinces, and Gauteng. **Habitat:** Flatlands, hillsides, forest edges. **Flight period:** Multi-brooded year-round, peak Sept–May. **Larval food:** *Xylotheca kraussiana*, *Tricicleras longipedunculatum* and Passifloraceae, including *Adenia* spp.

A

A

1B

B

2C

3A

B

3C

1 Little Acraea   *Acraea axina*

Wingspan: ♂ 35–40 mm ♀ 36–44 mm. **Identification: 1A** ♂ upper side, **1B** ♀ upper side, **1C** ♀ underside. Sexes similar, ♂ usually a warmer fuscous orange than ♀. Similar to Window Acraea (p. 86), but *duller, more brownish* coloration. Mainly on flatlands and hill slopes, but ♂ often on hill top, perching on a prominent tree. **Distribution:** Widespread in dry Savanna from KwaZulu-Natal (north of Tugela River) to Mpumalanga, Limpopo and NW provinces, and Gauteng. **Habitat:** Hill tops, flatlands, hillsides. **Flight period:** Multi-brooded year-round, peak Sept–May. **Larval food:** No data.

2 Clear-spotted Acraea   *Acraea aglaonice*

Wingspan: ♂ 43–49 mm ♀ 45–55 mm. **Identification: 2A** ♂ upper side, **2B** ♂ underside (WSF f. *albofasciata*), **2C** ♀ upper side (DSF, nominate). Brightly coloured, with distinctive *hyaline spot* in forewing areas M$_2$ and M$_1$; ♀ darker and duller than ♂, wings more rounded. DSF (nominate) ♂ often fluorescent red-orange. DSF ♀ has subapical hyaline forewing patch as ♂, sometimes lacking in darker ♀ WSF f. *latimarginata*. Latter has upper side basal ground colour suffused with grey, and prominent white discal patch on hind wing upper side. Fond of *Vernonia* flowers. **Distribution:** Savanna and Arid Savanna from n KwaZulu-Natal thorn belt to Mpumalanga, and Limpopo and NW provinces. WSF f. *latimarginata* rare. **Flight period:** Multi-brooded year-round, peaks early summer and autumn. **Habitat:** Flatlands. **Larval food:** *Passiflora edulis* and *P. incarnata*.

3 Acara Acraea   *Acraea acara acara*

Wingspan: ♂ 55–66 mm ♀ 60–72 mm. **Identification: 3A** ♂ upper side, **3B** ♂ underside (fresh), **3C** ♀ upper side. Sexes similar, but ♀ duller than ♂, with dark scaling over orange and yellow; wings more rounded. Fresh ♂ a brilliant magenta pink, orange and yellow. Seasonally variable; f. *caffra*: white scaling in hind wing cell area; f. *sufferti*: forewing black discocellular spot merges with the discal black band; f. *barberina*: forewing margin black band wider, completely surrounding orange submarginal spots. Sailing, deceptively fast flight, but may be approached closely on flowers. **Distribution:** May be very common. Lowland Forest, wooded Savanna from extreme n E Cape, to KwaZulu-Natal, Mpumalanga, NW and Limpopo provinces, and further north. **Habitat:** Forest edges, flatlands, hillsides. **Flight period:** Multi-brooded year-round in warmer areas, peak Nov–Mar. **Larval food:** *Passiflora edulis, P. incarnata* and *Adenia glauca*.

1 Trimen's Acraea   *Acraea trimeni*

Wingspan: ♂ 43–49 mm ♀ 45–55 mm. **Identification: 1A** ♂ upper side, **1B** ♂ underside, **1C** ♀ upper side. ♂ resembles a *pale, bright orange* ♂ Barber's Acraea (below), forewing marginal bands narrower, darker, better defined forewing yellow-orange apical patch on upper side. ♀ resembles ♂, paler and duller, *lacks* extensive hyaline areas of Barber's Acraea. Same sailing flight as Acara Acraea (p. 88) and Barber's Acraea. ♂ territorial, patrols hill-top clearings or bushes at the base of hillsides, settles on bare twigs, wings slowly opening and closing. Both sexes feed on *Acacia* and *Ziziphus* nectar. **Distribution:** Uncommon. Only in Arid Savanna in n N Cape and w Free State. **Habitat:** Hillsides, hill tops. **Flight period:** Uncertain whether double-brooded or continuously brooded through summer. Usually Oct–Mar, peak late Oct. **Larval food:** No data.

2 Barber's Acraea   *Acraea barberi*

Wingspan: ♂ 55–66 mm ♀ 60–72 mm. **Identification: 2A** ♂ upper side, **2B** ♂ underside, **2C** ♀ upper side. ♂ bright magenta pink, highly conspicuous against green leaves. ♀ variable, duller, darker ground colour than ♂, more distinct yellow forewing apex on upper side. Forewing transparent to variable degrees. Sailing flight through or over bush as in Acara Acraea (p. 88), with which it occasionally occurs. Fond of flowers, e.g. *Clerodendron glabrum* and *Ozoroa* spp. **Distribution:** Hilly, wooded Savanna in Gauteng, Limpopo (Magaliesberg, Waterberg, Blouberg and surrounding hills) and NW provinces. **Habitat:** Hill tops, hillsides, flatlands. **Flight period:** Continually brooded from Sept–Dec, peaks Oct and Feb. Stragglers may be seen as late as Apr. **Larval food:** *Adenia glauca*.

3 Broad-bordered Acraea   *Acraea anemosa*

Wingspan: ♂ 50–55 mm ♀ 57–64 mm. **Identification: 3A** ♀ upper side, **3B** ♂ underside (f. *anemosa*). Sexes similar, but ♀ tawny-yellow with fuscous wing bases; ♂ bright orange. Both sexes with very distinctive *broad* hind wing black marginal band, *no spots* except in forewing cell. 3 colour morphs: f. *mosana* totally lacks forewing black spots in CuA_1 and M_3, present in f. *anemosa*; f. *arctitincta* has extensive white in the pink hind wing discal band on underside. **Distribution:** Widely distributed in grassy Savanna from n KwaZulu-Natal (Mkuze area), north into Mpumalanga, Limpopo and NW provinces and into Gauteng. **Habitat:** Flatlands, hillsides. **Flight period:** Continuously brooded in warmer areas, peak Sept–May; in cooler areas, only Sept–May. **Larval food:** *Adenia venenata*.

1 Light Red Acraea *Acraea nohara nohara*

Wingspan: ♂ 40–48 mm ♀ 43–50 mm. **Identification: 1A** ♂ upper side, **1B** ♂ underside, **1C** ♀ upper side. Ground colour in ♂ bright orange-pink, in ♀ suffused with brown; contrasts well against green grassy mountain slopes. Similar to Speckled Red Acraea (below) but black markings *variable* in size and extent. WSF f. *junodi* larger and darker, black markings heavy. Small, lightly marked specimens in n Limpopo Province in dry season probably a seasonal variation. **Distribution:** Grassland. Slopes along the high-rainfall areas of the eastern escarpment from E Cape (Port St Johns) to KwaZulu-Natal, Mpumalanga and Limpopo Province. **Habitat:** Hillsides. **Flight period:** Oct–Nov and Jan–Mar, possibly overlapping. **Larval food:** *Basananthe sandersonii* and *Tricicleras longipedunculatum*.

2 Blood-red Acraea *Acraea petraea*

Wingspan: ♂ 45–48 mm ♀ 45–55 mm. **Identification: 2A** ♂ upper side, **2B** ♀ upper side, **2C** ♂ underside. ♂ very conspicuous deep, pure red. ♀ duller, varying from blackish ochre-brown to brown-red, with white forewing upper side subapical patches. Flight slow and fluttering. Popular coastal garden subject. ♂ defends territories at edges of clearings. Both sexes fond of flowers, particularly *Clerodendron glabrum* and *Deinbollia oblongifolia*. **Distribution:** Coastal forest from KwaZulu-Natal (Oribi Gorge) into Mozambique. **Habitat:** Forest edges, parks and gardens, flatlands, coast. **Flight period:** Year-round, peak Nov–Feb. **Larval food:** *Xylotheca kraussiana*.

3 Speckled Red Acraea *Acraea violarum*

Wingspan: ♂ 40–48 mm ♀ 43–55 mm. **Identification: 3A** ♂ upper side, **3B** ♀ upper side, **3C** ♂ underside (WSF f. *assimilis*). ♂ ground colour bright orange-pink with black spots, but unlike similar Light Red Acraea (above) has hind wing margin *squarer, lacks* black scaling along forewing veins, and black spots *more regular*. ♀ f. *violarum* ground colour pale brownish grey, suffused with black; other forms closer to ♂. WSF f. *assimilis* ground colour *paler*, spots *smaller*; DSF f. *gracilis* smaller and *paler*, with *narrower* dark margins, and *even smaller* spots. Flight slow and sailing. Fond of flowers, particularly *Scabious* spp. **Distribution:** Form *violarum* in high-rainfall areas of eastern escarpment, from E Cape (Port St Johns) to KwaZulu-Natal and Mpumalanga. WSF f. *assimilis* and DSF f. *gracilis* in moist Grassland and Savanna in Limpopo and NW provinces. **Habitat:** Flatlands, hillsides. **Flight period:** Year-round, peak Jul–Nov. **Larval food:** *Basananthe sandersonii*.

Genus *Hyalites* Bitter Acraeas

AFRICA 93 SPP., SOUTH AFRICA 11

Small to medium-sized butterflies, similar to *Acraea* species, but with more rounded wings and less well-defined hind wing marginal spots on underside. While some *Hyalites* have black spots on a paler, sometimes transparent ground found in *Acraea* species, the latter do not have the dark background colour with the pale markings of many *Hyalites* butterflies. Flight slow and sailing, unless disturbed. Eggs laid in batches; white to yellow, elongated cylinders, with flat or rounded crown. Larva cylindrical, six rows of branched spines on all segments except first and last, which have only two spines on each; head rounded, usually hairy. Gregarious in early instars, more or less so when fully grown.

1 Dusky-veined Acraea *Hyalites igola*

Wingspan: ♂ 40–45 mm ♀ 45–53 mm. **Identification: 1A** ♂ upper side, **1B** ♀ upper side (f. *igola*), **1C** ♂ underside. Brightly coloured. Hyaline forewing tips with *heavy black scaling along veins and margins* characteristic. ♂ has hind wing upper side and basal area of forewing always red. ♀ f. *igola* pale yellow; f. *maculiventris* as ♂. **Distribution:** E Cape (Port St Johns area), suitable Lowland and Riverine Forest along coast to KwaZulu-Natal; in KwaZulu-Natal localised at Oribi Gorge and the Eshowe area, rare around Durban. **Habitat:** Forest edges, coast. **Flight period:** Year-round, peak Oct–Apr; very scarce in dry months. **Larval food:** *Urera trinervis* and *U. woodii*.

2 Tree-top Acraea *Hyalites cerasa cerasa*

Wingspan: ♂ 32–38 mm ♀ 37–45 mm. **Identification: 2A** ♀ upper side, **2B** ♀ underside. Sexes similar. Similar to Dusky-veined Acraea (above), but with wings *more rounded*, red ground colour *duller*; hyaline forewing tips with *fine* black veins and margin. *Higher flying* than Dusky-veined Acraea. Descends to low-growing food plant in early morning and late afternoon, especially along river courses. **Distribution:** Riverine and coastal forest from E Cape (Port St Johns area), along the coast into KwaZulu-Natal, where it is more widely distributed than Dusky-veined Acraea; found along the foothills of the Midlands escarpment as far as Eshowe. **Habitat:** Forest edges, coast, gullies. **Flight period:** Year-round, peak Oct–Apr. Very scarce in dry months. **Larval food:** *Rawsonia lucida*.

3 Pale-yellow Acraea *Hyalites obeira burni*

Wingspan: ♂ 45–50 mm ♀ 49–53 mm. **Identification: 3A** ♀ upper side, **3B** ♂ underside. Distinctive buff-coloured species. Sexes very similar, ♀ with ground colour slightly paler than ♂, black hind wing spots smaller. No well-defined seasonal forms in South Africa, but dry season specimens paler, appearing faded. Only found near food plants on rocky hillsides and koppies. ♂♂ slowly circle hill-top trees. **Distribution:** Dry Savanna. Locally common in w Mpumalanga and Gauteng; most common in Limpopo Province (Magaliesberg and northern foothills of Waterberg). Scarce in Mooi and Tugela river valleys, KwaZulu-Natal. **Habitat:** Hillsides, hill tops. **Flight period:** Year-round, peak Sept–Apr. **Larval food:** *Laportea peduncularis*, *Obetia tenax* and *Pouzolzia mixta*.

4 Marsh Acraea *Hyalites rahira rahira*

Wingspan: ♂ 35–40 mm ♀ 40–50 mm. **Identification: 4A** ♂ upper side, **4B** ♂ underside. Unmistakable pale buff butterfly. Sexes very similar in markings; ♀ duller orange-buff. Locally common in marshes and vleis, and damp river margins. Flight slow and low, with fairly rapid wing-beats; settles often on plants. **Distribution:** Nama Karoo, Fynbos, Grassland, Savanna and Riverine Forest. From W Cape (as far west as Swellendam and Worcester), along the coast into E Cape and KwaZulu-Natal, where it spreads inland into the warmer areas. Widespread but localised in Mpumalanga, Gauteng and Limpopo and NW provinces. **Habitat:** Wetlands. **Flight period:** Year-round in warmer areas, most active Sept–Apr. In cooler areas, found only in the hot summer months. **Larval food:** *Persicaria attenuata africana* and *Conyza canadensis*.

A

1B

1C

A

2B

A

3B

A

4B

1 Orange Acraea   *Hyalites anacreon*

Wingspan: ♂ 40–50 mm ♀ 45–55 mm. **Identification: 1A** ♂ upper side, **1B** ♂ underside. Brightly coloured, conspicuous against green grass. ♀ paler buff-tawny colour, suffused with yellow (*see* **2**). Basks in the sun, feeds on flowers. Large numbers may fly around food plant. Flight slow, low and fluttering, unless disturbed. **Distribution:** High-altitude Grassland. From E Cape (Amatolas), along Drakensberg into KwaZulu-Natal Midlands, Mpumalanga and Limpopo Province. Also Free State and Gauteng, into NW Province. **Habitat:** Wetlands, gullies, hillsides, marshes, river banks. **Flight period:** Several broods Oct–May, peak Feb; single-brooded (Feb) in high mountains. **Larval food:** *Cliffortia linearifolia.*

2 Long-winged Orange Acraea   *Hyalites alalonga*

Wingspan: ♂ 54–74 mm ♀ 58–74 mm. **Identification:** ♂ (see **1A** ♂ upper side, **1B** ♂ underside) **2** ♀ upper side. Colour and markings, as well as dimorphism, similar to smaller Orange Acraea (above), but *forewings extremely elongated*. Flight in search of food plants fast and gliding, difficult to follow; ♀ flies more randomly. ♂ constantly circles an area about the size of a rugby field. **Distribution:** Montane Grassland from KwaZulu-Natal Drakensberg and Midlands north into Mpumalanga (Stoffberg, Long Tom Pass area) and Limpopo Province (Wolkberg). **Habitat:** Grassy gullies, hillsides. **Flight period:** Two broods, Nov–Jan and Mar–May, peak Dec and Apr respectively. **Larval food:** Fabaceae, including *Aeschynomene* spp.

3 Induna Acraea   *Hyalites induna salmontana*

Wingspan: ♂ 29–54 mm ♀ 54–62 mm. **Identification: 3A** ♂ upper side, **3B** ♀ upper side, **3C** ♀ underside. ♂ more brightly coloured than ♀. Similar to Orange Acraea (above), but *darker* ground colour, black spots on forewing *sparser*, and with prominent *black* forewing tips. Flight sailing, with slow wing-beats, but soars when disturbed. ♂ patrols rocky ridges. ♀ more often on flowers near the food plant. **Distribution:** Confined to montane sourveld on the high ridges of the Soutpansberg (Limpopo Province). **Habitat:** Hill tops, rocky ledges. **Flight period:** Single-brooded, Mar–May. **Larval food:** *Aeschynomene nodulosa.*

4 Small Orange Acraea   *Hyalites eponina*

Wingspan: ♂ 35–40 mm ♀ 36–44 mm. **Identification: 4A** ♂ upper side, **4B** ♂ underside, **4C** ♀ upper side pale form, **4D** ♀ upper side dark form, **4E** ♀ upper side male-like form. Sexes dimorphic. ♂ consistently orange, with characteristic spotted black margins, and black blotch at end of forewing cell on upper side. ♀ very variable (a range is illustrated), from similar to ♂, to greater or lesser suffusion of black, white, buff and brown, to transparent. Often in huge numbers. Roosts communally on long grass stems. Slow, low, fluttering flight. **Distribution:** Common and widespread in wooded Savanna, riverine bush and forest edges north from E Cape (East London) to KwaZulu-Natal, Mpumalanga and Limpopo and NW provinces. Also, more arid areas in w Free State. **Habitat:** Forest edges, parks and gardens, flatlands, coast. **Flight period:** Year-round, more common in the warmer months. **Larval food:** *Hermannia* spp., *Triumfetta rhomboidea, T. annua* and *T. pilosa.*

5 Yellow-banded Acraea   *Hyalites cabira*

Wingspan: ♂ 38–44 mm ♀ 40–45 mm. **Identification: 5A** ♀ upper side, **5B** ♀ underside. Unmistakable. Sexes very similar, ♂ colouring slightly deeper than ♀. Common in thick bush and forest. Fluttering flight low and slow, often visiting flowers. **Distribution:** May be locally common, but usually quite scarce. From E Cape (Port St Johns) to KwaZulu-Natal; throughout Drakensberg forests in Mpumalanga and Limpopo Province (Soutpansberg). **Habitat:** Forest edges. **Flight period:** Year-round, more common in the warmer months. **Larval food:** *Hermannia* spp.; also *Triumfetta tomentosa* and other *Triumfetta* spp.

1 Dusky Acraea   *Hyalites esebria esebria*

Wingspan: ♂ 45–55 mm ♀ 53–60 mm. **Identification: 1A** ♂ upper side, **1B** ♂ underside (f. *protea*), **1C** ♀ underside, **1D** ♀ upper side (f. *esebria*), **1E** ♀ upper side (f. *monteironis*). Distinctive but very variable. Form *esebria* has rich tawny orange basal patches, subapical pale patch ochre in ♂, white in ♀. Both sexes of f. *jacksoni* have subapical band tawny orange, in both sexes of f. *ertli*, broader and white. Form *protea* ♂ (common in South Africa) has ochre basal patches; ♀ has subapical patch white. In f. *monteironis* (both sexes), the patches are all white. Flight slow, easy to approach. Common along forest paths and edges of clearings. **Distribution:** From E Cape (East London) into Afromontane Forest of KwaZulu-Natal and Riverine and Lowland Forest of Mpumalanga and Limpopo Province. **Habitat:** Forest edges. **Flight period:** Year-round, more common in the warmer months. **Larval food:** *Urtica* spp., *Laportea peduncularis*, *Urera trinervis* and *U. hypselodendron*, *Obetia tenax* and *Pouzolzia parasitica*.

2 White-barred Acraea   *Hyalites encedon encedon*

Wingspan: ♂ 40–50 mm ♀ 45–55 mm. **Identification: 2A** ♂ upper side (f. *lycoides*), **2B** ♂ upper side (f. *fumosa*), **2C** ♀ upper side, **2D** pair *in copula* (f. *fulva*). Sexes similar, but several forms. Form *encedon* has ochreous hind wing and forewing basal patch; these areas white in f. *lycoides*; f. *fumosa* similar to f. *encedon*, but with very dark forewing basal patch; f. *fulva* has reddish-brown hind wing and forewing basal patch (resembling a tiny African Monarch, p. 36); f. *infuscatoides* resembles f. *fulva*, but forewing base suffused with dark scaling as f. *fumosa*; f. *daira* resembles pale f. *fulva* with orange-buff suffusion obscuring forewing markings. ♂ patrols forest paths and clearings. **Distribution:** Wooded Savanna and open coastal forests from E Cape (East London) to KwaZulu-Natal, Mpumalanga, and Limpopo and NW provinces, especially along river valleys in Riverine Forest. **Habitat:** Forest edges, parks and gardens, flatlands, coast, hill tops. **Flight period:** Year-round, more common in the warmer months. **Larval food:** *Commelina* spp., including *C. diffusa*.

Genus *Pardopsis*   Polka Dot   MONOTYPIC

Small, buff butterfly, with black spots. Very weak, fluttering flight low over the ground, settling often on grasses and other low-growing plants. Single egg laid on Violaceae. Egg short, barrel-shaped, wider at base with flat crown; pale yellow, with 20 or so vertical ribs joined irregularly to form eight points at the top. Larva thickened in thoracic area; green to grey, with white longitudinal stripes and four rows of branched spines on most segments. The dorsal pair of spines on the first segment are elongated and capable of independent movement. Pupa similar to most *Acraea* pupae, but more slender, suspended head down from the cremaster.

3 Polka Dot   *Pardopsis punctatissima*

Wingspan: ♂ 30–34 mm ♀ 33–36 mm. **Identification: 3A** ♀ upper side, **3B** ♂ underside. Sexes similar. Unique, unmistakable. Favours moist grassy areas; often found at forest edges. **Distribution:** Fynbos, Lowland and Afromontane Forest, and Grassland. From E Cape (Van Staden's Pass) along eastern escarpment foothills into Mpumalanga and Limpopo Province, and further north. **Habitat:** Forest edges, hillsides. **Flight period:** Year-round, peak Oct–Mar. **Larval food:** *Hybanthas capensis*.

Genus *Lachnoptera*   Leopards

AFRICA 2 SPP., SOUTH AFRICA 1

Medium-large forest butterflies. Strong fliers, active and wary. Attracted to flowers and wet mud, as well as fermenting fruit and tree sap. Egg not described. Larva elongated, tapering towards head; three rows of hairy spines on all but first and last segments. Pupa with four long spiny horns on thorax and seven shorter ones on abdomen. Food plants Flacourtiaceae.

1 Blotched Leopard   *Lachnoptera ayresii*

Wingspan: ♂ 45–52 mm ♀ 50–56 mm. **Identification: 1A** ♂ upper side, **1B** ♀ upper side, **1C** ♀ upper side, **1D** ♀ underside. ♂ ground colour orange, with silvery grey sex brand on hind wing upper side costa; ♀ with duller ground colour, black marks more extensive. Similar to *Phalanta* leopards but *larger*, with *squarer* wings. Conspicuous in forests. **Distribution:** Afromontane and Riverine Forest from E Cape (Port St Johns) along the escarpment to KwaZulu-Natal Midlands, Swaziland, Mpumalanga, Limpopo Province (Wolkberg), and further north. **Habitat:** Forest edges, mountains, wetlands, gullies. **Flight period:** Year-round, peak late summer and autumn, Jan–Jun. **Larval food:** *Rawsonia lucida*.

Genus *Phalanta*   Leopards

WORLD 5 SPP., AFRICA 4, SOUTH AFRICA 2

Medium-sized, fast flying and agile butterflies. Restive and wary, they sit with wings constantly moving up and down. Eggs laid singly on shoots or young leaves of Flacourtiaceae, Salicaceae or Celastraceae; barrel shaped, with 25–28 longitudinal ridges, and rows of circular pits in the grooves in between. Larva green, cylindrical, with six rows of branched spines on all segments except first and last, which carry two spines each. Head rounded, without spines. Pupa brightly coloured, green with black markings and dorsal protuberances on thorax and abdomen, which have white or metallic bases and black spines; suspended head down from leaves and twigs.

2 African or Common Leopard   *Phalanta phalantha aethiopica*

Wingspan: ♂ 40–45 mm ♀ 43–48 mm. **Identification: 2A** ♂ upper side, **2B** ♂ underside. Sexes similar. Like a small Blotched Leopard (above), but wings *more rounded*. Woodland species, but penetrates grassland areas where White Poplar *Populus alba* food plant is found. **Distribution:** Savanna and woodland from E Cape (Port Elizabeth, Grahamstown) to KwaZulu-Natal, Swaziland, Mpumalanga, Gauteng and Limpopo and NW provinces, and further north. **Habitat:** Forest edges, flatlands, mountains, hillsides, parks and gardens. **Flight period:** In cooler areas, Oct–Apr; in warm areas, year-round, peak late summer and autumn. **Larval food:** *Trimeria grandifolia*, *Dovyalis caffra*, *Rawsonia indica*, *Populus alba* and *Maytenus* spp.

3 Forest Leopard   *Phalanta eurytis eurytis*

Wingspan: ♂ 40–45 mm ♀ 43–48 mm. **Identification: 3A** ♂ upper side, **3B** ♂ underside, **3C** ♀ upper side. ♀ duller, paler buff-orange than ♂. Extremely similar to African Leopard (above). ♂♂ of the two *Phalanta* spp. are very difficult to tell apart. Forewing marginal line *unbroken by paler interneural spots*, ground colour with *richer orange* hue. ♂ defends territory in the forest canopy. Both sexes attracted to flowers and wet mud. **Distribution:** Restricted to heavy woodland; scarcer than African Leopard. KwaZulu-Natal coastal forest from Port Edward to Mozambique, and inland Afromontane and Riverine Forest from n KwaZulu-Natal to Swaziland, Mpumalanga and Limpopo Province. **Habitat:** Forest edges, coast. **Flight period:** Year-round, peak Jan–Jun. **Larval food:** *Dovyalis caffra* and Salicaceae, including *Populus* spp.

Subfamily CHARAXINAE

Medium-sized to very large, robust, showy, fast-flying butterflies, *Charaxes* usually inhabit the upper canopy of forests or tree tops in Savanna. ♂♂ are strongly territorial, usually found perched on exposed leaves or twigs, frequently darting out to chase intruders. ♀♀ are found closer to food plants. Adults seldom feed on nectar, preferring tree sap (dozens may be seen at 'sucking holes', where beetle larvae have bored into trees), rotten fruit, or dung. ♂♂ are often found drinking from mud.

Genus *Charaxes*   Emperors   WORLD CA. 200 SPP., AFRICA 169, SOUTH AFRICA 23

All South African species (♂ *C. zoolina* being the only exception) have two tails. Generally brightly coloured, in shades of red and orange, or iridescent blue. Sexes are dimorphic in many species, especially those where ♂ has black upper side, and ♀ is easier to distinguish from other ♀ than her mate is from other ♂. Aggressively territorial; capable of pushing other butterflies off food with serrated leading edges of forewings. Eggs laid singly or in small groups. Spheroidal, smooth-sided; flattened top has fine grooves radiating from the centre like wheelspokes. Larvae usually green, medial larval headshield horns longer than lateral ones. Pupae green, sometimes with white stripes or streaks; rounded, with more-or-less pointed head.

1 Pearl Emperor   *Charaxes varanes varanes*

Wingspan: ♂ 65–70 mm ♀ 70–90 mm. **Identification: 1A** ♂ upper side, **1B** ♂ underside. Sexes similar. *Orange and pearly-white* wings conspicuous against foliage. Underside variable, cryptic; usually golden brown, suffused with black markings that sometimes obscure ground colour. Flight slower than other *Charaxes*. **Distribution:** Coastal, Lowland, Afromontane and Riverine Forest, from E Cape (Mossel Bay) to KwaZulu-Natal and Mpumalanga; along rivers in dry n Limpopo and NW provinces. **Habitat:** Forest edges, flatlands, coast. **Flight period:** Year-round in warmer areas, a weak peak Sept–Nov, stronger peak Jan–Jun. In cooler southern part of range (Port Elizabeth to the west), single-brooded midsummer. **Larval food:** *Allophylus africanus*, *A. dregeanus* and *A. natalensis*; also *Cardiospermum halicacabum*.

2 Green-veined Emperor   *Charaxes candiope*

Wingspan: ♂ 65–75 mm ♀ 78–95 mm. **Identification: 2A** ♂ upper side, **2B** ♂ underside. Sexes similar; ♀ with two tails equally long, ♂ with anal tail longer. Forewing *green veins* on underside very conspicuous. Underside markings seasonally variable between two extremes: in wet season specimens, mottled fawn crossed by wavy median and submarginal lines of black and darker brown; in dry season specimens, flat red-ochre with restricted dark lines. **Distribution:** Common and widespread. Coastal, Lowland, Afromontane and Riverine Forest, and wooded Savanna from E Cape (Port St Johns) to KwaZulu-Natal, Mpumalanga, Gauteng and Limpopo and NW provinces. **Habitat:** Forest edges, flatlands, gullies, hillsides, coast. **Flight period:** Year-round; a weak peak Sept–Nov, stronger peak Jan–Jun. **Larval food:** *Croton* spp., including *C. sylvaticus*, *C. gratissimus*.

3 Flame-bordered Emperor   *Charaxes protoclea azota*

Wingspan: ♂ 65–70 mm ♀ 75–95 mm. **Identification: 3A** ♂ upper side, **3B** ♀ upper side, **3C** ♂ underside, **3D** ♀ underside. Sexes strongly dimorphic; ♀ has large patches of *white*; ♂ *appears all black on the wing*, but at close range, orange-red borders visible. In flight, ♀ resembles Pearl Emperor (above), but more conspicuous, striking. **Distribution:** Tropical species, extending marginally into South Africa. Coastal forest and woodland, only in extreme n KwaZulu-Natal (Kosi Bay, Tembe Elephant Park and Emanguzi Forest). **Habitat:** Forest edges, flatlands, coast. **Flight period:** Double-brooded, Oct–Nov, Feb–Jun. **Larval food:** *Afzelia quanzensis*.

1 Protea Emperor   *Charaxes pelias*

Wingspan: ♂ 60–70 mm ♀ 65–75 mm. **Identification: 1A** ♂ upper side, **1B** ♂ underside. Sexes similar. Dark brown upper side ground colour, with tawny orange median band and row of marginal spots; latter whitish at anal corner of hind wing. Underside metallic grey, with white median bands; basal areas patterned in dark red outlined with black-edged white. Not as fond of rotten fruit as other *Charaxes*. **Distribution:** Only *Charaxes* found in true fynbos and Karoo. Montane Fynbos, Nama Karoo and Succulent Karoo from W Cape (Cape Peninsula) to Vanrhynsdorp. Along s W Cape mountain chain and hills surrounding Little Karoo, into E Cape (to Grahamstown). **Habitat:** Hill tops, mountains. **Flight period:** Successive broods Sept–Apr, peak late summer. **Larval food:** *Rafnia amplexicaulis, R. triflora, Hypocalyptus sophoroides* and *Colpoon compressum.* Has been observed ovipositing on *Erythrina* spp.

2 Foxy Emperor   *Charaxes jasius saturnus*

Wingspan: ♂ 65–75 mm ♀ 75–90 mm. **Identification: 2A** ♂ upper side, **2B** ♂ (sucking at wet mud) underside. Sexes similar, ♀ with tails longer than ♂. Similar to Protea Emperor (above), but *larger, paler,* underside basal areas patterned in *ochre-red,* not dark red. **Distribution:** Common, widespread. In Savanna from E Cape (East London), to KwaZulu-Natal thorn belt, and n and w Free State, Gauteng, Mpumalanga, Limpopo and NW provinces and n N Cape. **Habitat:** Forest edges, hill tops, flatlands, hillsides, parks and gardens. **Flight period:** Year-round, but only in warmer months in cooler parts of range. More common late summer to autumn. **Larval food:** *Afzelia quanzensis, Schotia brachypetala, Burkea africana, Bauhinia galpinii, Colophospermum mopane, Xanthocercis zambesiaca, Xeroderris stuhlmannii, Guibourtia conjugata, Maytenus senegalensis, Catha edulis* and *Croton* spp.

3 Giant Emperor   *Charaxes castor flavifasciatus*

Wingspan: ♂ 75–85 mm ♀ 85–105 mm. **Identification: 3A** ♂ upper side, **3B** ♂ underside. South Africa's *largest Charaxes.* Sexes similar, but ♀ with wings less angular, tails longer than ♂. Similar to Foxy Emperor (above), upper side *darker,* with *yellow* not orange-tawny discal band; underside basally grey, red markings darker – as in Protea Emperor (above). More-or-less restricted to wooded savanna and forest, absent from arid and cool areas. ♂ frequents hill tops between 08h00 and 10h00. **Distribution:** Low-altitude Savanna and Forest along the eastern littoral from KwaZulu-Natal (usually north of the Tugela R), into Swaziland and the Mpumalanga and Limpopo Province lowveld. **Habitat:** Hill tops, forest edges, flatlands. **Flight period:** Year-round, more common late summer to autumn. **Larval food:** *Maytenus senegalensis, Afzelia quanzensis, Schotia brachypetala, Senna fistula, Bridelia micrantha* and *Trema orientalis.*

4 White-barred Emperor   *Charaxes brutus natalensis*

Wingspan: ♂ 60–75 mm ♀ 75–90 mm. **Identification: 4A** ♀ upper side, **4B** ♀ underside. Upper side unmistakable *black and white.* Underside similarly marked to Foxy Emperor (above), but ground colour dark tawny orange, deepening to red-ochre basally to white median band; basal patterns *dark grey* with white outlines. Sexes similar, ♂ with wings more angular. Pugnacious and aggressive, chasing all flying creatures entering its domain (even birds). Visits red flowers such as *Spathodea* and *Tecomaria* spp. **Distribution:** Very common. Low-altitude Savanna, Lowland, Riverine and Afromontane Forest along eastern littoral from E Cape (Van Staden's Pass near Port Elizabeth) to KwaZulu-Natal, Swaziland, Mpumalanga and Limpopo Province lowveld. **Habitat:** Forest edges, flatlands, coast. **Flight period:** Year-round, more common late summer to autumn. **Larval food:** *Melia azedarach, Trichilia emetica, T. dregeana, Turraea floribunda, Ekebergia capensis, Khaya nyasica* and *Securinega virosa.*

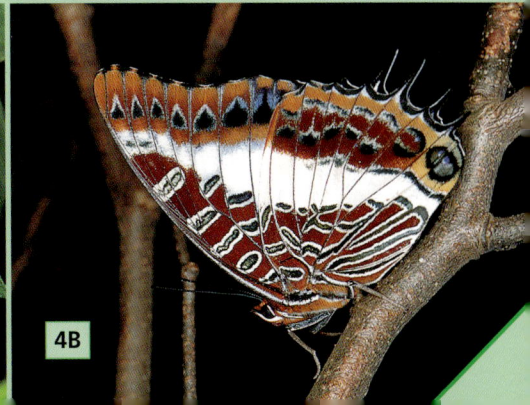

1 Silver-barred Emperor *Charaxes druceanus*

Wingspan: ♂ 55–70 mm ♀ 65–85 mm. **Identification: 1A** ♂ upper side, **1B** ♀ underside (*C. d. moerens*). ♀ similar to ♂ but larger, paler, with less angular wings. Superficially similar to Foxy Emperor (p. 104), but upper side *much darker*, and unmistakable *silvery underside*. 4 subspp. Nominate has paler upper side fulvous markings than other subspp. **Distribution:** Except for nominate, confined to Afromontane Forest. Nominate in coastal forests from Oribi Gorge, north to Eshowe and Ngoye, KwaZulu-Natal. *C. d. entabeni* inhabits moist forests along top and higher southern slopes of Soutpansberg (Limpopo and NW provinces); *C. d. solitarius* an isolated population on Blouberg range, Limpopo Province. *C. d. moerens* from Swaziland, north along Mpumalanga and Limpopo escarpment forests to the Wolkberg. **Habitat:** Forest edges, flatlands, coast, mountains, hillsides. **Flight period:** *C. d. entabeni* and probably *C. d. solitarius* year-round, more common late summer to autumn; *C. d. moerens* and nominate Sept–May, weak peak Oct, stronger peak Mar–Apr. **Larval food:** Myrtaceae spp., including *Syzygium cordatum* and *S. guineense*.
Note: Scarce records from KwaZulu-Natal Midlands Afromontane forests may be of a different race; they are closest to *C. d. moerens*, which inhabits high-altitude forests in Mpumalanga and Limpopo Province (northern limit Woodbush). Further biological and morphological studies are needed to accurately determine whether they are indeed of the race *C. d. moerens*.

2 Forest King Emperor *Charaxes xiphares*

Wingspan: ♂ 65–80 mm ♀ 70–95 mm. **Identification: 2A** ♀ upper side (nominate); **2B** ♂ upper side, **2C** ♀ underside (*C. x. kenwayi*). Sexes strongly dimorphic, ♂ with *royal blue* spots and bands on metallic navy ground, ♀ with *white discal forewing band* (of variable width) sometimes invaded by yellow-ochre. Most have pale yellow hind wing upper side patch, but in some populations, ♀♀ blue-white or pale mauve. Differences between ♀♀ of more value than subtle differences between the ♂♂ in distinguishing races. 9 subspp., geographically distinct. **Distribution:** Common. Pockets of Afromontane Forest along eastern escarpment. Nominate from W Cape (George) to E Cape (Van Staden's Pass); *C. x. occidentalis* in W Cape (Swellendam area); *C. x. thyestes* E Cape, from Amatolas to Port St Johns area; *C. x. penningtoni* KwaZulu-Natal, from low altitude at Kloof to Drakensberg foothills; *C. x. draconis* in eastern Drakensberg foothills, from Swaziland to Mpumalanga and Limpopo Province (Olifants R); *C. x. kenwayi* Limpopo Province (Wolkberg); *C. x. bavenda* on Soutpansberg watershed (Limpopo Province); an isolated population of *C. x. staudei* on Blouberg massif Limpopo Province. **Habitat:** Forest edges, mountains, hillsides. **Flight period:** Nominate and *C. x. occidentalis* singled-brooded Jan–Mar; *C. x. thyestes* single-brooded Feb–Apr; *C. x. penningtoni*, *C. x. draconis* and *C. x. kenwayi* double-brooded, weak peak Oct–Nov, stronger Mar–May; *C. x. bavenda* and *C. x. staudei* year-round, peak late summer. **Larval food:** *Cryptocarya woodii, Scutia myrtina, Rhamnus prinoides* and *Chaetachme aristata*.

3 Large Blue Emperor *Charaxes bohemani*

Wingspan: ♂ 65–75 mm ♀ 80–100 mm. **Identification: 3A** ♂ upper side; **3B** ♀ upper side, **3C** ♀ underside. Sexes dimorphic, ♀ with characteristic white band distal to the forewing basal blue patch. ♂ lacks this, superficially resembling ♀ Demon Emperor (p. 114), but overall *larger*, and body larger in proportion to the wings. **Distribution:** Wooded lowland Savanna in Limpopo Province and Mpumalanga lowveld from Zimbabwe border to Nelspruit. **Habitat:** Hill tops, flatlands. **Flight period:** Year-round, peak Oct and Mar. **Larval food:** *Afzelia quanzensis, Lonchocarpus capassa, Xeroderris stuhlmannii, Dalbergia nitidula, Brachystegia spiciformis* and *Schotia brachypetala*.

1 Violet-spotted Emperor   *Charaxes violetta violetta*

Wingspan: ♂ 65–70 mm ♀ 75–85 mm. **Identification: 1A** ♂ upper side, **1B** ♀ upper side, **1C** ♀ underside. Sexes strongly dimorphic; ♂ blue and navy, ♀ white-banded. Very similar to Blue-spotted Emperor (below), but *smaller* and with a *straight* (not crenellated) white discal stripe on the underside of the hind wing, and having the upper side *more purple* than blue. **Distribution:** Vagrant; only one known specimen, from Dukuduku Forest, near Mtubatuba, KwaZulu-Natal. **Habitat:** Forest edges, flatlands. **Flight period:** Double-brooded (Mozambique and Zimbabwe), Aug–Oct and Apr–Jun. **Larval food:** *Deinbollia oblongifolia* and *Blighia unijugata*.

2 Blue-spotted Emperor   *Charaxes cithaeron cithaeron*

Wingspan: ♂ 70–80 mm ♀ 85–95 mm. **Identification: 2A** ♂ upper side, **2B** ♀ upper side, **2C** ♀ underside. Sexes dimorphic, ♀ a different shape to ♂, and with conspicuous white discal forewing band (on upper side) where ♂ has blue spots. ♀ hind wing upper side band mauvish white, cf. blue with white tinge in ♂. Similar to Violet-spotted Emperor (above), the differences being in *underside markings* and *neutral to green* (not purplish) shade of upper side blue. **Distribution:** Coastal forests from E Cape (East London) to the Mozambique border. Inland along the Limpopo R Valley to the eastern Soutpansberg, Limpopo Province. **Habitat:** Forest edges, flatlands, coast. **Flight period:** Year-round, but more common from Mar–May. **Larval food:** *Chaetachme aristata*, *Trema orientalis*, *Celtis africana*, *Baphia racemosa*, *Afzelia quanzensis*, *Albizia adianthifolia*, *Milletia sutherlandii*, *Maytenus senegalensis*, *Hugonia orientalis* and *Cola natalensis*.

3 Club-tailed Emperor   *Charaxes zoolina zoolina*

Wingspan: ♂ 40–45 mm ♀ 50–58 mm. **Identification: 3A** ♂ upper side (DSF f. *neanthes*), **3B** ♀ upper side, **3C** ♂ underside (WSF f. *zoolina*). The ♂ has wings more triangular than ♀, and *only one* spatulate tail (where the ♀ has two tails). Only South African *Charaxes* with **named** seasonal forms. The whitish WSF f. *zoolina* is unmistakable. In flight, the orange and brown DSF f. *neanthes* is similar to the Pearl-spotted Emperor (below), but markings are *red-brown*, not black. Occasional specimens with colouring intermediate between the two forms have been recorded. The species may swarm in warmer areas. **Distribution:** Rare and local in southern parts of its range. Afromontane, Lowland, Riverine and coastal forests, and Savanna from E Cape (Mbashe R) to Mozambique, inland to Mpumalanga, Gauteng, and Limpopo and NW provinces. **Habitat:** Forest edges, flatlands, gullies. **Flight period:** Year-round; generally f. *zoolina* Oct–Mar, f. *neanthes* Apr–Sept, but depending on timing of rains. Both forms (and intermediates) may fly together during spring and autumn. Numbers gradually peak Sept–Jul, dropping off in dry months. **Larval food:** *Acacia kraussiana*, *A. schweinfurthi* and *A. brevispica*.

4 Pearl-spotted Emperor   *Charaxes jahlusa*

Wingspan: ♂ 42–56 mm ♀ 50–62 mm. **Identification: 4A** ♂ upper side, **4B** ♀ upper side, **4C** ♂ underside (*C. j. rex*). Sexes similar, but ♂ has more triangular wings. Similar to Club-tailed Emperor f. *neanthes* (above), but with *black* spots, not red-brown, and two tails in *both* sexes. 7 subspp., 3 in South Africa. **Distribution:** Widespread. Nominate in Nama Karoo/Savanna transition zone of E Cape, from Little Karoo to Grahamstown; *C. j. rex* in Savanna from n Free State to Gauteng, Limpopo and NW provinces; *C. j. argynnides* in low-altitude Savanna and Lowland Forest, from n KwaZulu-Natal into Mozambique. **Habitat:** Hill tops, flatlands. **Flight period:** Nominate Oct–Mar; *C. j. rex* and *C. j. argynnides* year-round. **Larval food:** *Pappea capensis* and *Dalbergia melanoxylon*.

A

1B

1C

A

2B

C

3A

3B

3C

A

4B

4C

1 Blue-spangled Emperor   *Charaxes guderiana guderiana*

Wingspan: ♂ 50–60 mm ♀ 60–70 mm. **Identification: 1A** ♂ upper side, **1B** ♀ upper side, **1C** ♂ underside. Sexes dimorphic; ♀ very similar to ♀ Bushveld Emperor (below), but orange markings *more extensive, rounder and paler*. ♂ underside superficially resembles that of black *Charaxes* such as Satyr Emperor (p. 112), but more *colourful and variegated*, with *deep brown* submarginal hind wing band. ♂ upper side similar to Scarce Forest Emperor (below), but costal marks *larger, white*, blue spangling *duller, less extensive*; ground colour *duller blue*. **Distribution:** Vagrant; only recently (Nov 2003) described from a single small patch of miombo (*Brachystegia*) woodland at Gundani, north-east of Sibasa, Limpopo Province. **Habitat:** Forest edges, flatlands. **Flight period:** Year-round; in Zimbabwe, peaks spring and autumn. **Larval food:** *Brachystegia spiciformis*, *Dalbergia lactea*, *Julbernardia* spp., including *J. globiflora*.

2 Scarce Forest Emperor   *Charaxes etesipe tavetensis*

Wingspan: ♂ 55–65 mm ♀ 62–72 mm. **Identification: 2A** ♂ upper side, **2B** ♀ upper side, **2C** ♂ underside. Sexes dimorphic. ♂ upper side with *pale blue spangling* over deep metallic-blue ground colour. ♀ with upper side duller, no blue; resembles White-barred Emperor (p. 104), but white median bands often tinged *creamy yellow*. Underside of both sexes superficially similar to Bushveld Emperor (below), but more *colourful and variegated*, with *white flash* along hind wing costa. **Distribution:** Locally common in remote northern Lowland Forest, from n KwaZulu-Natal (Sodwana Bay to Kosi Bay), inland to Tembe Elephant Park, and Limpopo Province (eastern Soutpansberg, near Thohoyandou). **Habitat:** Forest edges, flatlands. **Flight period:** Double-brooded, Aug–Oct, Mar–Jun. **Larval food:** *Afzelia quanzensis*, *Dalbergia nitidula*, *Securidaca longipeduncularis* and *Margaritaria discoidea*.

3 Bushveld Emperor   *Charaxes achaemenes achaemenes*

Wingspan: ♂ 55–60 mm ♀ 60–70 mm. **Identification: 3A** ♂ underside, **3B** ♂ upper side, **3C** ♀ upper and underside. Sexes differ in upper side coloration; ♂ has pure white markings on black ground. ♀ colouring resembles Foxy Emperor (p. 104), but median band broken into individual blotches. Both have discal bands and marginal spots in similar pattern to Foxy Emperor. Underside of both sexes similar to Scarce Forest Emperor (above), but with *grey*, not white, flash on hind wing costa. **Distribution:** Common and widespread. In bushveld and wooded Savanna from n KwaZulu-Natal, to Swaziland, Mpumalanga, and Limpopo and NW provinces. **Habitat:** Hill tops, flatlands. **Flight period:** Year-round, peak Feb–May. **Larval food:** *Pterocarpus rotundifolius*, *P. angolensis*, *Dalbergia nitidula*, *Xanthocercis zambesiaca*, *Piliostigma thonningii* and *Diospyros mespiliformis*.

A

1B

C

2A

B

2C

3A

B

3C

1 Satyr Emperor   *Charaxes ethalion ethalion*

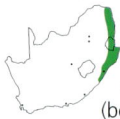

Wingspan: ♂ 45–55 mm ♀ 50–63 mm. **Identification: 1A** ♂ upper side, **1B** ♀ upper side (f. *aurantimaculata*); **1C** ♀ upper side, **1D** ♀ underside (f. *rosae*); **1E** ♀ upper side (nominate). Underside variable shade of brown; ♀ with distinctive white median marks mirroring those on upper side; distinguished from Karkloof Emperor (below) by black discal line intersecting hind wing vein *CuA proximally to the split with M₃* (see arrow in 1D). ♂ difficult to distinguish from other black *Charaxes*; upper side *velvety*, jet black, with dull hind wing marginal band, tiny blue submarginal hind wing spots, and blue costal spot at end of forewing cell. Nominate ♀ form has *whitish* forewing upper side discal band, *blue* in f. *swynnertoni*, *orange tinged, fading basally to white* in f. *aurantimaculata*. Intermediates between latter and nominate are common. Form *rosae* has *curved* (not straight, as in other ♀ forms) band on upper side, always white. Hind wing of all four ♀ forms carries white median band, surrounded by extensive bluish sheen. **Distribution:** Dense forests of coastal lowlands in KwaZulu-Natal, inland to the Midlands, and through Swaziland and lower Afromontane and Riverine Forest in Mpumalanga and Limpopo Province, into Mozambique. **Habitat:** Forest edges, flatlands, coast, mountains. **Flight period:** Year-round, peaks Oct and Mar. **Larval food:** *Albizia adianthifolia*, *Peltephorum africanum*, *Dichrostachys cinerea*, *Acacia ataxacantha* and *Scutia myrtina*.

2 Pondo Emperor   *Charaxes pondoensis*

Wingspan: ♂ 45–55 mm ♀ 48–60 mm. **Identification: 2A** ♂ underside, **2B** ♀ upper side. ♂ distinguished from Satyr (above) and Karkloof (below) Emperors by having *silvery grey*, not brownish, underside, with more marbled appearance. ♂ upper side *more sombre* than Satyr Emperor, forewing costal spot often absent. ♀ resembles Satyr Emperor (above) f. *aurantimaculata*, hind wing has *less extensive* bluish iridescence surrounding white median band. **Distribution:** Rare. Riverine Forest and dense Lowland Forest in coastal lowlands of E Cape (Mazeppa Bay to Embotyi). **Habitat:** Forest edges, coast. **Flight period:** Year-round, peaks Oct/Nov and Mar–May. **Larval food:** *Milletia sutherlandii* and *M. grandis*.

3 Karkloof Emperor   *Charaxes karkloof*

Wingspan: ♂ 45–55 mm ♀ 50–60 mm. **Identification: 3A** ♀ upper side, **3B** ♀ underside, **3C** ♂ underside (*C. k. capensis*). Similar to Marieps Emperor (p. 114), but ♂ with upper side *slightly glossy* black, underside greyish. ♀ underside chestnut brown, as in Marieps Emperor, upper side hind wing median band surrounded by *more extensive* pale blue iridescent sheen than ♀ Satyr Emperor (above). Both sexes with tails *thick* and *blunt-ended*. Underside distinguished from Satyr Emperor individuals with chestnut-brown undersides by black discal line intersecting hind wing vein M₃ distally to its split with CuA₁ (see arrow in 3B). ♂ less fond of fruit baits than other black *Charaxes*. **Distribution:** Afromontane Forest. Nominate from E Cape (Amatolas) to Port St Johns area and KwaZulu-Natal Midlands; *C. k. capensis* from W Cape (Port Elizabeth, Van Staden's Pass) to E Cape (East London); *C. k. trimeni* (rare) Knysna and George, W Cape. **Habitat:** Forest edges, rocky ledges. **Flight period:** Oct–Jun; weak peak Nov, strong peak Mar–May. **Larval food:** *Ochna arborea*, *O. natalitia* and *O. serrulata*.

1 Marieps Emperor   *Charaxes marieps*

Wingspan: ♂ 48–60 mm ♀ 65–70 mm. **Identification: 1A** ♂ upper side, **1B** ♀ upper side, **1C** ♀ underside. Sexes dimorphic. ♂ velvety black, with strong gloss visible from an oblique angle, and *wavy, green* metallic hind wing submarginal band. ♀ upper side *suffused orange* on all wings, deep orange discal bands and strong *purple* gloss overall. Both sexes have *deeper* chestnut-brown underside and *blunter, thicker* tails than similar Karkloof Emperor (p. 112). **Distribution:** Restricted to Afromontane Forest in Mpumalanga, south of Olifants R (centred on Mariepskop) to Sabie (Ceylon Forest). **Habitat:** Forest edges, mountains, rocky ledges. **Flight period:** Double-brooded, Sept–Nov, Mar–May. **Larval food:** *Ochna arborea, O. natalitia, O. holstii* and *O. serrulata*.

2 Demon Emperor   *Charaxes phaeus*

Wingspan: ♂ 48–56 mm ♀ 50–60 mm. **Identification: 2A** ♂ upper side, **2B** ♀ upper side, **2C** ♂ underside. ♂ has shiny black upper side; very similar to Van Son's Emperor (below), slightly greater extent of silvery sheen along costa. Only reliably separable on genital dissection. ♀ distinctive, resembling ♂ Large Blue Emperor (p. 106), but not as large or robust. **Distribution:** Common in Savanna from n KwaZulu-Natal to Swaziland, Mpumalanga, n Gauteng and Limpopo and NW provinces. **Habitat:** Hill tops, flatlands. **Flight period:** Year-round, peak Feb–May, smaller peak spring; scarce Jun–Sept. **Larval food:** *Acacia nigrescens* and *Tamarindus indica*.

3 Van Son's Emperor   *Charaxes vansoni*

Wingspan: ♂ 48–56 mm ♀ 50–60 mm. **Identification: 3A** ♂ upper side, **3B** ♀ upper side, **3C** ♂ underside. ♂ as Demon Emperor (above), with shiny black upper side, hind wing underside usually with silvery sheen *less extensive* on costa beyond the cell; species only reliably separable on genital dissection. ♀ resembles Satyr Emperor (p. 112), but *smaller*, and *more extensive* silvery blue surrounding hind wing white median band. Forewing white discal spots often suffused with peach-pink. ♂ territorial on hill tops. **Distribution:** Savanna from n KwaZulu-Natal to Swaziland, Mpumalanga, n Gauteng, and Limpopo and NW provinces. **Habitat:** Hill tops, flatlands. **Flight period:** Year-round, peak Feb–May, smaller peak spring; scarce Jun–Sept. **Larval food:** *Peltophorum africanum*.

Genus *Euxanthe*   Queens

AFRICA 6 SPP., SOUTH AFRICA 1

Large, tailless butterflies, black with spots of blue or green, or blotches of tan and cream. Abdomen bright yellow. Forest-dwellers. Flight fast, swooping. ♂ often found on hill tops, ♀ near food plants. Single egg laid on Sapindaceae and Fabaceae, kettledrum-shaped, with slightly depressed crown and well-defined ribs radiating from centre; brown, with paler top. Larva green, flattened, very fat in the middle segments, and with pale dorsal markings and lateral margins. Head capsule horned, lateral horns larger than medial horns, and recurved.

1 Forest Queen   *Euxanthe wakefieldi*

Wingspan: ♂ 65–72 mm ♀ 80–90 mm. **Identification: 1A** ♂ upper side, **1B** ♀ upper side, **1C** ♂ underside. Sexes dimorphic. ♂ has pale markings with blue sheen sometimes appearing white. *Bright yellow* abdomen often visible in flight. Strong, soaring flight. **Models:** (♂) Blue Monarch (p. 36); (♀) Friar (p. 38). **Distribution:** Lowland Forest from KwaZulu-Natal (south to Amanzimtoti; rare south of Tugela R) to Swaziland and ne Limpopo Province (Pafuri district). **Habitat:** Hill tops, forest edges. **Flight period:** Year-round, peak Mar–Jun. **Larval food:** *Deinbollia oblongifolia.*

Subfamily LIMENITINAE

The most constant character is floating, sailing flight, from ground level to upper canopies, wings held flat open. *Pseudacraea* species show marked mimicry of other distasteful species.

Genus *Cymothoe*   Gliders

AFRICA 73 SPP., SOUTH AFRICA 2

Flitting, gliding flight; ♂ wary, alert, difficult to approach when perching, easier on mud patches. ♀ low on ground or near flowers and food plants. Eggs laid in clusters on Flacourtiaceae and Bignoniaceae. White to grey. Dome-shaped; covered in deep hexagonal indentations, with short spines at each junction of the edges. Larvae green to yellow or brown, with contrasting longitudinal stripes and four rows of branched processes on segments 2–11. Head capsule rounded, with short hairs. Gregarious in earlier instars. Pupae green to buff, short, broad, with pointed abdomen; paired short horns on head, and prominent dorsal keel.

2 Battling Glider   *Cymothoe alcimeda*

Wingspan: ♂ 40–50 mm ♀ 45–55 mm. **Identification: 2A** ♂ upper side, **2B** ♀ upper side (*C. a. trimeni*), **2C** ♀ upper side, **2D** ♂ underside (*C. a. transvaalica*). ♂ creamy white; both sexes' underside cryptic. In *C. a. transvaalica*, underside cryptic. Darker ♀ with colour of upper side bands variable: white to grey in *C. a. trimeni*, yellow or orange in *C. a. transvaalica*. 5 subspp. **Distribution:** Coastal and moist Afromontane Forest. Nominate from W Cape (Grootvadersbos, Swellendam) to Knysna; *C. a. clarki* in Amatola range of E Cape; *C. a. trimeni* from East London (E Cape), inland along Drakensberg escarpment to KwaZulu-Natal Midlands; *C. a. marieps* south of Olifants R, Mariepskop to Barberton (Mpumalanga); *C. a. transvaalica* Limpopo Province escarpment – Legalameetse, Woodbush, to Duiwelskloof. **Habitat:** Forest edges, mountains. **Flight period:** Year-round, mainly summer from Oct; peak Nov and Feb–Apr. **Larval food:** *Kiggelaria africana.*

3 Blonde Glider   *Cymothoe coranus coranus*

Wingspan: ♂ 50–60 mm ♀ 60–68 mm. **Identification: 3A** ♂ upper side, **3B** ♀ upper side, **3C** ♂ underside. ♂ with upper side similar to Battling Glider (above), but *larger*, wings *more rounded*; underside cryptic; ♀ upper side median band *always white*. More difficult to approach; only comes to mud patches early in the day. **Distribution:** Afromontane, Lowland and Riverine Forest from E Cape (Mbashe R, Port St Johns) to KwaZulu-Natal (Eshowe), north into lower Mpumalanga escarpment forests. Absent from Lowland Forest of Zululand and high Afromontane areas. **Habitat:** Forest edges, coast, flatlands. **Flight period:** Year-round, mainly Feb–Apr, peak Oct–Dec; scarce Jun–Sept. **Larval food:** *Rawsonia lucida.*

Genus *Euryphura*   Nymphs   AFRICA 6 SPP., SOUTH AFRICA 1

Medium-sized forest butterflies, attracted to wet earth and fermenting fruit. Eggs laid singly on leaves of Erythroxylaceae. Green, hemispherical; the pattern of deep hexagonal depressions with bristles at the junctions of the edges is typical of limenitinines. Larvae green, with coloured dorsal stripe and dorso-lateral rows of long, feathery spines. Pupae green, with silvery patches, flattened laterally, tapering sharply towards cremaster; bifid head. Suspended head-down from the cremaster.

1 Mottled-green Nymph   *Euryphura achlys*

Wingspan: ♂ 48–55 mm ♀ 55–65 mm. **Identification: 1A** ♂ upper side, **1B** ♀ upper side, **1C** ♀ underside. ♀ *larger, bluer* than ♂, upper side and underside forewings with *white apical spots*; underside resembles dead leaf. ♂ reddish underside conspicuous as wings flicker in flight. Usually encountered singly. Glides with open wings centimetres above the ground on shady forest paths. **Distribution:** Marginal in South Africa, in Lowland and Riverine Forest of n KwaZulu-Natal (Ngoye Forest to Kosi Bay and Pongola R) and further north. **Habitat:** Forest edges. **Flight period:** Year-round, but usually only seen Mar–Jun. **Larval food:** *Erythroxylum emarginatum.*

Genus *Euphaedra*   Foresters   AFRICA 192 SPP., SOUTH AFRICA 1

Medium-sized to large, gorgeously coloured butterflies. Single egg laid on Sapindaceae. Green, hemispherical; pattern of deep hexagonal depressions with bristles at the junctions of the edges typical of limenitinines. Larva green with coloured dorsal stripe and dorso-lateral rows of long, feathery spines. Pupa green with silvery patches, flattened laterally and very wide at the rear of the thorax, tapering sharply towards cremaster; bifid head. Suspended head down from the cremaster.

2 Gold-banded Forester   *Euphaedra neophron neophron*

Wingspan: ♂ 55–65 mm ♀ 60–78 mm. **Identification: 2A** upper sides, ♀ upper left, ♂ lower right, **2B** undersides, ♀ left, ♂ right. Sexes similar. ♀ rounder-winged than ♂, with underside more marbled, greyer. Brightly coloured, unmistakable. Floating flight along shade-covered forest paths. When approached, glides away open-winged for a few metres, then sits, slowly opening and closing its wings. Attracted to fermenting fruit and wads of chewed sugar cane. **Distribution:** Locally common. Lowland and Riverine Forest in KwaZulu-Natal, from Mtunzini to Maputaland and further north. Historically, occurred near Durban. **Habitat:** Forest edges. **Flight period:** Year-round, peak Feb–Jul. **Larval food:** *Deinbollia oblongifolia* and *Blighia unijugata.*

Genus *Hamanumida*   Guineafowl   MONOTYPIC

Single egg laid on Combretaceae; hemispherical and green, pattern of deep hexagonal depressions with bristles at the junctions of the edges typical of limenitinines. Larva green with coloured dorsal stripe and dorso-lateral rows of long, feathery spines. Pupa green or mauve, tapering sharply at both ends; bifid head. Suspended head-down from the cremaster.

3 Guineafowl   *Hamanumida daedalus*

Wingspan: ♂ 55–65 mm ♀ 60–78 mm. **Identification: 3A** ♀ upper side, **3B** ♂ underside. Sexes similar, ♀ with wings more rounded. Flight floating. Unmistakable. Well-worn specimens may appear dull and unattractive, but freshly emerged butterflies are striking. Some seasonal variation. WSF f. *meleagris* has prominent pattern of underside white spots mirroring upper side black spots. **Distribution:** Common and widespread in Savanna, Arid Savanna and Lowland Forest. From KwaZulu-Natal Midlands to Swaziland, Mpumalanga, Limpopo and NW provinces, and warmer parts of Gauteng. **Habitat:** Flatlands. **Flight period:** Continuously brooded; peaks in midwinter and midsummer. **Larval food:** *Combretum molle* and *Terminalia sericea.*

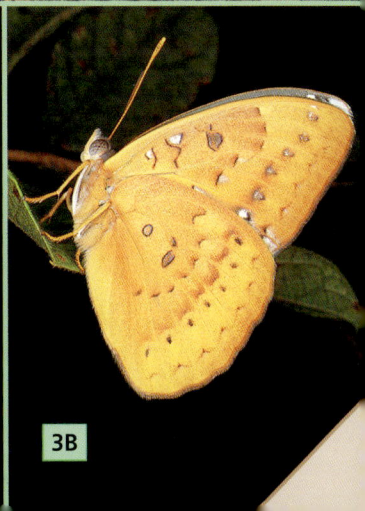

Genus *Pseudacraea*   False Acraeas   AFRICA 16 SPP., SOUTH AFRICA 3

Extremely close mimics of Heliconiinae and Danainae. On close inspection, they are more robust, with a larger thorax holding powerful wing muscles. Typical floating, open-winged limenitinine flight. Eggs laid singly on Sapotaceae, slightly elongated rounded domes with the hexagonal depressions and short spines at the junctions of the edges typical of Limenitinae; whitish to pale green. Larvae cylindrical, thickened at the thorax, with two or four rows of spiny warts or horns on segments 2–11, those on segment 2 sometimes double, and those on the first three and final segment usually much larger. Extremely well camouflaged, as are the pupae, which are usually curved and flattened laterally (resembling a curled leaf), with pointed horns on head. Suspended head down from cremaster.

1 Boisduval's False Acraea   *Pseudacraea boisduvalii trimenii*

Wingspan: ♂ 65–70 mm ♀ 75–88 mm. **Identification: 1A** ♂ upper side, **1B** ♀ upper side (f. *colvillei*), **1C** ♂ underside. Underside and upper side alike. ♀ less brightly coloured than ♂, often with extensive white areas; wings rounder. Almost fluorescent coloration similar to Acara Acraea (p. 88). Form *colvillei lacks* forewing apex buff bar. Flight slow, lazy until chased. ♂ territorial, perching on prominent leaves, chasing intruders. ♀ less active. Both sexes often on flowering trees. **Distribution:** Lowland and Riverine Forest, marginally penetrating Savanna areas. From E Cape (Port St Johns) to Swaziland, KwaZulu-Natal (Kosi Bay), Mpumalanga, Limpopo Province, and further north. **Habitat:** Forest edges, hill tops. **Flight period:** Year-round, peak Jan–May; scarce in winter months. **Larval food:** *Chrysophyllum* spp., *Mimusops obovata* and *M. zeheri, Manilkara discolor, Englerophytum magalismontanum* and *E. natalense*.

2 False Wanderer   *Pseudacraea eurytus imitator*

Wingspan: ♂ 60–68 mm ♀ 65–75 mm. **Identification: 2A** ♂ upper side (f. *eurytus*), **2B** ♀ upper side (f. *chionea*), **2C** ♂ underside (f. *eurytus*). Sexes similar, ♂ with narrower, more angular wings. In flight, almost impossible to distinguish from Common Wanderer (p. 80), but *antennae longer*, and has black spots on *both* surfaces of forewing cell, *lacking* on Common Wanderer forewing underside. Three forms: f. *eurytus* (most often seen) with yellow upper side bands in both sexes; ♀ f. *chionea* has white bands, rare f. *pondo* has orange-red bands. **Model:** Common Wanderer. **Distribution:** Rare, localised. Warm Lowland Forest and riverine bush along coast from E Cape (Port St Johns) north-east to KwaZulu-Natal (Eshowe) and lowland Mpumalanga forests. **Habitat:** Forest edges, coast. **Flight period:** Year-round, mainly Dec–May, strong peak late summer. **Larval food:** *Mimusops obovata, Englerophytum magalismontanum* and *Chrysophyllum viridifolium*.

3 False Chief   *Pseudacraea lucretia*

Wingspan: ♂ 60–72 mm ♀ 65–78 mm. **Identification: 3A** ♂ upper side (f. *lucretia*), **3B** ♂ upper side, **3C** ♂ underside (f. *heliogenes*) (all *P. l. expansa*). Sexes alike, ♀ with markings identical to ♂, but with rounder wings. 2 subspp., *P. l. expansa* with two forms. Forewing marks of *P. l. tarquinia* smaller. In *P. l. tarquinia*, markings vary from white to pale yellow-ochre. In *P. l. expansa*, wing markings white in f. *lucretia*, dark orange in f. *heliogenes*. **Models:** Although the *pattern* of the forewing markings is reminiscent of both the Chief and Layman (p. 38), these two models have colours distinctive to the species. **Distribution:** Common in Lowland Forest and riverine bush; marginally penetrates Savanna. *P. l. tarquinia* from E Cape (Port St Johns) to n KwaZulu-Natal; *P. l. expansa* Mpumalanga and Limpopo Province, along Soutpansberg and Drakensberg foothills. **Habitat:** Forest edges, coast. **Flight period:** Year-round, peak Jan–Jul; scarce in spring and early summer. **Larval food:** *Mimusops obovata, M. zeheri, M. caffra, Chrysophyllum viridifolium* and *Englerophytum magalismontanum*.

A

1B

C

2A

B

2C

A

3B

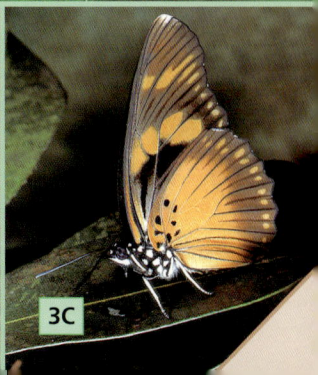

3C

Genus *Neptis* Sailers WORLD 140 SPP., AFRICA 67, SOUTH AFRICA 6

Small to medium-small butterflies with distinctive black-on-white markings and slow, sailing flight; few wing-beats. Eggs laid singly on Fabaceae, Euphorbiaceae and Combretaceae; rounded, thimble-shaped with hexagonal dimples whose rims bear short bristles at the angles. Larvae elongated, thickened at thorax, bristly dorso-lateral fleshy horns on segments 2, 3 (largest), 5 and 11; well camouflaged in brown and green. Fully grown larvae rest with forward part of the body held in a downcurved position. Pupae green, head distinctly bifid; wing cases greatly expanded laterally; slim, pointed abdomen, suspended head down from cremaster.

1 Spotted Sailer *Neptis saclava marpessa*

Wingspan: ♂ 40–45 mm ♀ 45–48 mm. **Identification: 1A** ♂ upper side, **1B** ♂ underside. Sexes similar. Differs from other *Neptis* spp. in having *pale, mottled underside*. ♂ perches on prominent twigs or leaves and sallies forth to inspect intruders. Both sexes attracted to fermenting plant matter and wet earth. **Distribution:** Lowland Forests and dense riverine bush penetrating Savanna. From E Cape (Zuurberg, near Port Elizabeth) to KwaZulu-Natal, Swaziland, Mpumalanga, Limpopo and NW provinces, and Gauteng. **Habitat:** Forest edges, gullies. **Flight period:** Year-round in warmer areas, peak Dec–May. **Larval food:** *Acalypha glabrata*, *Ricinus communis* and *Combretum bracteosum*.

2 Barred Sailer *Neptis trigonophora trigonophora*

Wingspan: ♂ 45–50 mm ♀ 48–55 mm. **Identification: 2A** ♂ upper side, **2B** ♂ underside. Sexes similar. Distinguished from other *Neptis* spp. by having *totally black* forewing upper side cell *and* break in upper side median band (in area M_3 of forewing) with small triangular mark. Flies higher than other Sailers. **Distribution:** Rare; restricted to warm, coastal forests of E Cape (Port St Johns, Ntafufu, Embotyi forests). **Habitat:** Forest edges. **Flight period:** Possibly year-round; peak Mar–Apr. **Larval food:** Unknown in South Africa.

3 Streaked Sailer *Neptis goochii*

Wingspan: ♂ 30–35 mm ♀ 34–38 mm. **Identification: 3A** ♂ upper side, **3B** ♂ underside. Smallest South African *Neptis* sp. Sexes similar. *Broad white streak* in upper side forewing cell diagnostic. Attracted to flowers and wet earth. **Distribution:** Riverine Forest, edges of warm, Lowland Forest; coastal KwaZulu-Natal, scarce at Durban, and more common from Tugela R mouth north into Maputaland forests. Sparse in Mpumalanga and Limpopo Province Lowland and Riverine Forest along base of escarpment. **Habitat:** Forest edges, flatlands, coast. **Flight period:** Year-round, peak Dec–May. **Larval food:** *Acalypha* spp.

4 Common Sailer *Neptis laeta*

Wingspan: ♂ 40–48 mm ♀ 45–52 mm. **Identification: 4A** ♂ upper side, **4B** ♂ underside. Sexes similar. Large, conspicuous and distinctive, with *prominent black veins* in the creamy-white upper side wing bands. ♀ stays close to food plant. **Distribution:** Ubiquitous in warmer forests and bushveld, especially along rivers and streams. From E Cape (Mbashe R) to KwaZulu-Natal, Swaziland, Mpumalanga, and Limpopo and NW provinces. **Habitat:** Forest edges, gullies. **Flight period:** Year-round in warmer areas, peak Dec–May. **Larval food:** *Dalbergia obovata*, *D. armata*, *Albizia adianthifolia* and *Acalypha* spp.

5 Kiriakoff's Sailer *Neptis kiriakoffi*

Wingspan: ♂ 42–48 mm ♀ 45–55 mm. **Identification: 5A** ♂ upper side, **5B** ♂ underside. Very similar to Common Sailer (above), but with a *greater number of white spots* in forewing upper side cell, and a dark line, basal to hind wing underside white discal patch, *crosses* white costal band in this species, *but not* in Common Sailer. **Distribution:** Rare. Only found in Lowland Forest of Tembe Elephant Park, n KwaZulu-Natal. **Habitat:** Forest edges. **Flight period:** Recorded autumn (May–Jun), but probably flies year-round. **Larval food:** Unknown in South Africa.

1 **Jordan's Sailer**   *Neptis jordani*
Wingspan: ♂ 38–42 mm ♀ 40–45 mm. **Identification: 1A** ♂ upper side, **1B** ♂ underside. Sexes alike. *Very broad* white median bands on both wings distinctive. Upper side and underside similar. Usually along streams and in swamps. **Distribution:** Rare. Only records from n KwaZulu-Natal (Emanguzi Forest and streams running towards Kosi Bay). **Habitat:** Forest edges, wetlands. **Flight period:** In South Africa, recorded autumn (May–Jun), but probably flies year-round. **Larval food:** No data.

Subfamily CYRESTINAE

White butterflies with characteristic 'map' pattern of dark lines; flight as Limenitinae.

Genus *Cyrestis*   Map Butterflies   WORLD 26 SPP., SOUTH AFRICA 1

Single egg laid on young leaves and buds of Moraceae; yellow, elliptical, 9–11 longitudinal ribs. Larva with curved head horns, backward-pointing dorsal horn on segment 4, S-shaped backward-pointing anal horn. Colour pattern cryptic, breaks up outline. Pupa similar to *Neptis* but with leaf-like dorsal horns on thorax and abdominal segments.

2 **African Map Butterfly**   *Cyrestis camillus sublineata*
Wingspan: ♂ 42–50 mm ♀ 48–55 mm. **Identification: 2A** ♀ upper side, **2B** ♀ underside. Unmistakable. Sexes alike, ♂ with wings more pointed. Very shy. ♂ drinks from wet mud; sits upside down under leaf with wings outspread. Soars high in canopy. **Distribution:** Rare; n Limpopo Province (Woodbush and Malta forests, Kruger NP (Pafuri area), and the Sibasa area). **Habitat:** Forest edges. **Flight period:** Feb–May, but probably flies year-round. **Larval food:** *Trilepisium madagascariens*, *Ficus sur* and other *Ficus* spp.

Subfamily BIBLIDINAE

Afrotropical and Oriental subfamily; three Afrotropical genera. Small to medium-sized butterflies with rounded wings; many with forewing costal vein expanded as in some satyrines.

Genus *Sevenia*   Tree Nymphs   AFRICA 18 SPP., SOUTH AFRICA 4

Small to medium-sized butterflies, usually brown to orange, some a brilliant metallic mauve. Flight slow, sailing, with infrequent wing-beats; settles often on trees. Single egg laid on Euphorbiaceae; yellow. Larva cylindrical, with five rows of short, branched spines. Head capsule rounded and hairy with a pair of short, branched horns. Slender pupa with two acutely divergent head spines, the thorax keeled dorsally and the wingcases expanded laterally.

3 **Rosa's Tree Nymph**   *Sevenia rosa*
Wingspan: ♂ 50–60 mm ♀ 52–62 mm. **Identification: 3A** ♀ upper side, **3B** ♂ upper side, **3C** ♂ underside. *Lilac* upper side and *orange* underside diagnostic. ♀ darker than ♂, with two black postdiscal forewing bands, larger dark submarginal spots on hind wing upper side. Wary; roosts under leaves. **Distribution:** Rare migrant; erratically from Riverine and Lowland Forest in KwaZulu-Natal. **Habitat:** Forest edges. **Flight period:** Recorded Oct–Jan, but probably flies year-round. **Larval food:** Probably *Maprounea africana*.

4 **Morant's Tree Nymph**   *Sevenia morantii*
Wingspan: ♂ 40–45 mm ♀ 43–50 mm. **Identification: 4A** ♂ upper side, **4B** ♀ upper side, **4C** ♀ underside. *Larger* than Boisduval's Tree Nymph (p.126), and upper side *lacks* submarginal black spots. Upper side plain brown, ♀ with orange marks on black ground along forewing upper side costa. Settles high in trees. **Distribution:** Very rarely encountered. Riverine and Lowland Forest from E Cape (Port St Johns, Embotyi Forest), north along KwaZulu-Natal coastal plain to Lowland Forest in Mpumalanga and Limpopo Province (Malta and the foot of Mariepskop). **Habitat:** Forest edges, flatlands. **Flight period:** Year-round, mainly Dec–May, peak Mar–May. **Larval food:** No data.

A

1B

A

B

3A

3B

3C

4A

B

4C

1 Boisduval's Tree Nymph *Sevenia boisduvali boisduvali*

Wingspan: ♂ 35–40 mm ♀ 38–45 mm. **Identification: 1A** ♂ upper side, **1B** ♀ upper side, **1C** pair *in copula* showing undersides. ♂ flat brown, with *reddish-ringed black submarginal spots on hind wing* on upper side; ♀ apical black patch with orange blotches. Prominent submarginal row of black spots. Underside mottled pale grey and buff, with submarginal row of prominent black spots. *Smallest* and most abundant Tree Nymph. Flight typical of the genus. Sometimes in swarms of thousands (late summer). Strongly attracted to fermenting fruit; may totally fill baited traps. **Distribution:** Coastal Forests from E Cape (Port St Johns, Embotyi Forest), north along KwaZulu-Natal coastal plain to Lowland Forest in Mpumalanga and Limpopo Province (Soutpansberg). **Habitat:** Forest edges, flatlands, coast. **Flight period:** Year-round, peak Dec–May. **Larval food:** *Sapium ellipticum* and *S. integerrimum*.

2 Natal Tree Nymph *Sevenia natalensis*

Wingspan: ♂ & ♀ 40–48 mm. **Identification: 2A** ♂ upper side, **2B** ♀ upper side, **2C** ♂ underside. More *tawny* than Boisduvali's Tree Nymph (above); *larger, paler*, underside flatter, pale grey with submarginal black spots *tiny or absent*. ♂ has vague orange forewing apical spots on a darker tawny background; ♀ larger, with orange marks larger on black ground. Occurs in smaller numbers. Shy, difficult to approach; sits on tree trunks, darting away when disturbed. Comes readily to baited traps. **Distribution:** Common in forests along KwaZulu-Natal coastal plain from Port Edward to Kosi Bay; also in Mpumalanga and Limpopo Province (Lowland Forest to e Soutpansberg). **Habitat:** Forest edges, flatlands, coast. **Flight period:** Year-round, peak Feb–May. **Larval food:** *Sapium integerrimum*.

Genus *Byblia* Jokers

SOUTH AFRICA 2 SPP.

Orange butterflies with black markings, forewing costal vein expanded basally. Flight fairly fast, erratic; frequently alights on vegetation. Sometimes rests with open wings, occasionally slowly opening and closing them. Attracted to fermenting fruit, faeces and mud. Eggs laid singly on young shoots and buds of Euphorbiaceae. White to cream; pointed barrel shape with longitudinal rows of spines, each ending in a long hair. Larvae cylindrical, striped brown and green, with two long spiny cephalic horns, six longitudinal rows of branched spines, and an extra dorsal spine on segments 10 and 11. Pupae slim, two pointed horns on head; expanded wing cases with sinuous edges, a prominent dorsal ridge on the thorax. Suspended head down from the cremaster.

3 Common Joker *Byblia anvatara acheloia*

Wingspan: ♂ 40–45 mm ♀ 43–48 mm. **Identification: 3A** ♂ upper side, **3B** ♂ underside (transitional form). Sexes similar. Considerable seasonal variation; DSF hind wing underside crossed with chocolate-brown bands and yellow-white spots. More common WSF f. *similata* has *yellow-ochre* hind wing on underside, basal spots black, submarginal band black with small white spots. **Distribution:** Abundant in warm Savanna, Grassland, coastal and Lowland Forest from E Cape (East London), to KwaZulu-Natal, lowveld of Swaziland, Mpumalanga and Limpopo Province, and further north. **Habitat:** Flatlands, coast. **Flight period:** Year-round; two main overlapping broods, summer (Nov–Mar) more numerous than winter (May–Aug). **Larval food:** *Tragia glabrata, Dalechampia capensis*.

4 Spotted Joker *Byblia ilithyia*

Wingspan: ♂ 38–43 mm ♀ 40–45 mm. **Identification: 4A** ♂ upper side, **4B** ♂ underside (WSF). Slightly *smaller* than Common Joker (above). Sexes similar. Distinctive DSF f. *badiata* has chocolate brown replacing the underside hind wing orange bands of the WSF. **Distribution:** Widespread. Coastal and inland Savanna and Grassland from E Cape (Port Elizabeth) to KwaZulu-Natal, Free State, Gauteng, Swaziland, Mpumalanga, Limpopo and NW provinces, and parts of N Cape. **Habitat:** Flatlands. **Flight period:** Continuous broods; peak Nov–Mar, smaller peak May–Apr. **Larval food:** *Tragia glabrata, Dalechampia capensis*.

A

1B

1C

A

2B

C

3A

B

4A

4B

Genus *Eurytela*   Pipers
AFRICA 4 SPP., SOUTH AFRICA 2

Medium-sized butterflies. Flight slow; few wing-beats; settles open-winged. Forewing costal vein expanded basally. Eggs white; pointed-barrel shape with longitudinal rows of spines ending in long hairs; laid singly on shoots or leaves of Euphorbiaceae. Larva green or brown, when young cylindrical, striped brown and green, with two long spiny cephalic horns, six longitudinal rows of branched spines, extra dorsal spine on segments 10 and 11. Later instars have longer spiny cephalic horns than *Byblia* larvae, and only dorso-lateral rows of longitudinal spines; those on segment 3 larger, and a larger mid-dorsal process on segments 11 and 12. Pupae slim, two pointed horns on head, greatly expanded, fan-like lateral wing cases; prominent dorso-thoracic ridge. Suspended head down from cremaster.

1 Pied Piper   *Eurytela hiarbas angustata*

Wingspan: ♂ 45–50 mm ♀ 48–55 mm. **Identification: 1A** ♀ upper side, **1B** ♀ underside. Sexes similar. *White* bar on *brown-black* ground conspicuous; rare aberration ab. *flavescens*, seen occasionally in coastal forests, has *yellow-ochre* wing bands on upper side, occasionally in coastal forests. **Distribution:** Common in Afromontane, Lowland and Riverine Forest from W Cape (Wilderness) along the coast to E Cape and KwaZulu-Natal; also along escarpment to Mpumalanga, Limpopo Province, and further north. **Habitat:** Forest edges, coast, mountains. **Flight period:** Continuously brooded; peak Nov–Mar. **Larval food:** *Tragia glabrata*, *Dalechampia capensis* and *Ricinus communis*.

2 Golden Piper   *Eurytela dryope angulata*

Wingspan: ♂ 40–50 mm ♀ 45–55 mm. **Identification: 2A** ♂ upper side, **2B** ♂ underside. Sexes similar. Similar to Pied Piper (above), but wing bands *orange*, not white, on *brown* ground colour. Flight slightly *faster*. **Distribution:** Less common than Pied Piper, more widespread. Afromontane and Lowland Forest from E Cape (Port St Johns) along coast to KwaZulu-Natal; also along escarpment to Mpumalanga, Limpopo Province, and further north, and Riverine Forest in Savanna. **Habitat:** Forest edges. **Flight period:** Year-round, peak Nov–Jun. **Larval food:** *Tragia glabrata*, *Dalechampia capensis* and *Ricinus communis*.

Subfamily NYMPHALINAE

Conspicuous, colourful butterflies, small to quite large. Flight powerful, with characteristic 'flap-glide' action. Fond of fermenting fruit and flowers.

Genus *Hypolimnas*   Diadems
WORLD 30 SPP., AFRICA 15, SOUTH AFRICA 3

Large nymphalines. All danaine mimics. Flight powerful, agile. ♂ territorial on hill tops and in forest clearings. Both sexes found on flowers. Eggs laid singly on Portulacaceae, Acanthaceae and Urticaceae, pale yellow to green, barrel shaped with 10–14 prominent longitudinal ribs, cross-braced with 25–35 very faint transverse ribs. Larvae dark, cylindrical, with seven longitudinal rows of branched spines and long, branched, spiny cephalic horns. Pupae with rounded features, head broadly bifid, two dorsal rows of conical tubercles on abdomen. Suspended head down from cremaster.

3 Common Diadem   *Hypolimnas misippus*

Wingspan: ♂ 60–65 mm ♀ 70–80 mm. **Identification: 3A** ♂ upper side, **3B** ♂ underside, **3C** ♀ upper side, **3D** ♀ underside (f. *inaria*), **3E** ♀ underside (f. *misippus*). Sexes dimorphic; distinctive, ♂ not a mimic. Polymorphic ♀ has *more robust* build, more *powerful flight* than model. **Model:** (♀) African Monarch (p. 36), *Danaus chrysippus aegyptius* f. *chrysippus* (f. *misippus*); f. *alcippus* (f. *alcippoides*); f. *dorippus* (f. *inaria* and f. *dorippoides*, latter with white hind wing of f. *alcippus*). **Distribution:** Common in warmer areas of all biomes; rare in fynbos and Karoo regions. **Habitat:** Forest edges, parks and gardens, hill tops. **Flight period:** Year-round, peak late summer (winter in tropical areas). **Larval food:** *Asystasia gangetica*, *Portulaca* spp. (including *P. foliosa* and *P. oleracea*), *Talinum* spp. and *Ageratum houstonianum*.

1 Deceptive Diadem *Hypolimnas deceptor deceptor*

Wingspan: ♂ 60–65 mm ♀ 70–80 mm. **Identification: 1A** ♂ upper side, **1B** ♂ underside. Sexes similar. Flight high, powerful and direct. ♂ territorial at edge of forest canopy, perching high on a leaf, chasing other butterflies; ♀ usually at flowers high on trees. Roosts under large trees, rocks and in holes. **Model:** Novice (p. 38); mimicry is not very accurate. **Distribution:** Rare. Lowland and Riverine Forest along east coast, from E Cape (East London) to n KwaZulu-Natal (Kosi Bay). One record from Limpopo Province (e Soutpansberg). **Habitat:** Forest edges. **Flight period:** Year-round, peak late summer. **Larval food:** *Laportia peduncularis*.

2 Variable Diadem *Hypolimnas anthedon wahlbergi*

Wingspan: ♂ 75–80 mm ♀ 75–90 mm. **Identification: 2A** ♀ upper side, **2B** ♀ underside (f. *mima*), **2C** ♀ upper side (f. *wahlbergi*). 2 forms; sexes similar in both. Often found along forest streams where there is a break in the canopy. Roosts in holes under tree roots. **Models:** Friar (for f. *wahlbergi*), Layman (p. 38) (for f. *mima*). **Distribution:** Common and widespread from E Cape (East London) to n KwaZulu-Natal coast (Kosi Bay). Lower escarpment Afromontane and Riverine Forest into Swaziland, Mpumalanga and Limpopo Province. **Habitat:** Forest edges, flatlands, gullies, coast. **Flight period:** Year-round, peak late summer. **Larval food:** *Laportia peduncularis*, *Urera cameroonensis* and *U. hypsilodendron*.

Genus *Salamis*   Mothers-of-pearl

AFRICA 9 SPP., SOUTH AFRICA 2

Large butterflies with squared-off wing margins and prominently hooked wingtips. Untidy, flapping flight. Wary, and can move very quickly when molested. Often settles on prominent leaves along forest edges. In summer, found all over the forest. During dry season, concentrated swarms overwinter in riverine bush, well camouflaged under large leaves. Fond of flowers. Eggs laid singly on Acanthaceae; pale green, barrel shaped with 10–14 prominent longitudinal ribs, cross-braced with 25–35 very faint transverse ribs. Larvae with seven longitudinal rows of branched spines, *longer* than *Hypolimnas*, and long, branched, spiny cephalic horns. Pupae with pointed features, head broadly bifid, two dorsal rows of sharp conical tubercles on abdomen; suspended head down from cremaster.

3 Common Mother-of-pearl *Salamis parhassus*

Wingspan: ♂ 65–80 mm ♀ 75–90 mm. **Identification: 3A** ♂ upper side, **3B** ♂ underside (f. *modestus*). Sexes similar. White to pale green, with greenish to gold iridescent sheen, black-edged wings. Black spots and black-centred red ocelli on both surfaces. WSF f. *modestus* smaller, more heavily marked than DSF f. *parhassus*. **Distribution:** Coastal and Lowland Forest from E Cape (Mbashe R) along KwaZulu-Natal coast to Kosi Bay. Also, in Afromontane forests along escarpment (especially deep, wooded kloofs) to Swaziland, Mpumalanga and Limpopo Province. **Habitat:** Forest edges, gullies, coast. **Flight period:** Year-round, peaks late summer and autumn. **Larval food:** *Asystasia gangetica*, *Isoglossa woodii* and *Brilliantasia ulugurica*.

4 Clouded Mother-of-pearl *Salamis anacardii nebulosa*

Wingspan: ♂ 55–68 mm ♀ 65–75 mm. **Identification: 4A** ♂ upper side, **4B** ♂ underside (f. *trimeni*), **4C** ♀ upper side (f. *lurida*). Sexes differ slightly, ♀ with *broader dark margins*, sometimes with a golden sheen as in WSF ♀ f. *lurida*. DSF f. *trimeni* larger, wings more angular than f. *lurida*. Often flies with similar Common Mother-of-pearl (above), but *smaller* and *lacks* green gloss. Follows wooded river valleys into dry savanna, where it feeds on flowers. **Distribution:** Lowland and Riverine Forest, Savanna. E Cape (Port St Johns) along KwaZulu-Natal coast to Kosi Bay, Emanguzi and the Lebombo Mountains. Also along escarpment foothills to Swaziland, Mpumalanga and Limpopo Province. **Habitat:** Forest edges, gullies and deep, wooded kloofs. **Flight period:** Year-round, peak late summer and autumn. **Larval food:** *Asystasia schimperi* and *A. gangetica*.

1B

2C

3A

3B

4B

4C

Genus *Catacroptera*   Pirate

MONOTYPIC

Forewing angled at vein M$_2$, antennal club rounded in cross section. Wary; flight low, fast, settling often on rocks and low vegetation, slowly opening and closing wings. Single egg laid on low-growing Acanthaceae. Pale green, with 12–14 glassy longitudinal ribs and about 48 faint cross-ribs. Larva cylindrical; green-yellow with black transverse bands, nine longitudinal rows of branched spines and prominent, clubbed head horns that are independently mobile. Pupa pale green, bifid head, typical nymphaline shape.

1 Pirate   *Catacroptera cloanthe cloanthe*

Wingspan: ♂ 50–58 mm ♀ 55–62 mm. **Identification: 1A** ♂ upper side (WSF), **1B** ♂ underside (DSF f. *obscurior*). Unmistakable. Sexes similar. DSF f. *obscurior* has a *dark* ground colour and *chocolate-brown* underside; nominate WSF has *golden brown* underside, with more conspicuous submarginal eye spots. Conspicuous; often close to streams and springs. One of the earliest highveld butterflies in spring. ♂ strongly territorial, sitting on prominent patch of bare earth, chasing away intruders. **Distribution:** Common in Grassland and grassy Savanna from W Cape (Mossel Bay) along mountains into E Cape, KwaZulu-Natal, Lesotho, Free State, Gauteng, Limpopo and NW provinces, and Mpumalanga. **Habitat:** Wetlands, hillsides. **Flight period:** Year-round in warmer areas; mainly Sept–Apr in cool zones. **Larval food:** *Justicia protracta, Ruellia cordata* and *Chaetacanthus setiger*.

Genus *Precis*   Commodores

AFRICA 15 SPP., SOUTH AFRICA 4

Robust, medium-sized, brightly coloured nymphalines; similar to *Junonia* but no eye spots, and great differences in colour and markings between WSFs and DSFs. Flight fast, agile; often sits on ground with wings slowly opening and closing. Fond of flowers. Eggs laid singly on Lamiaceae. Bulb-shaped, green to yellow, with 10–16 prominent glassy longitudinal ribs, and (sometimes) 25–40 cross-ridges. Larva dark, sometimes with prominent orange or yellow transverse bands, seven longitudinal rows of branched spines of varying length and head capsule either unadorned or with pair of branched spines. Pupa robust, usually with bifid head, two or more rows of dorsal tubercles on abdomen; suspended head down from cremaster.

2 Gaudy Commodore   *Precis octavia sesamus*

Wingspan: ♂ 50–60 mm ♀ 55–63 mm. **Identification: 2A** ♂ upper side, **2B** ♀ underside (f. *sesamus*); **2C** ♂ upper side, **2D** ♀ underside (f. *natalensis*). Sexes similar. WSF f. *natalensis* bright orange-red, frequents hill tops in Savanna and Grassland. DSF f. *sesamus* blue, found in gardens, forests near montane grassland. Occasional intermediates occur. Form *sesamus* hibernates in deep gullies and under banks and rocks; roosts gregariously. **Distribution:** Widespread in Grassland, Savanna and Afromontane Forest, from E Cape to KwaZulu-Natal, Lesotho, Free State, Gauteng, Swaziland, Mpumalanga, Limpopo and NW provinces, and further north. **Habitat:** Forest edges, parks and gardens, hill tops, hillsides, gullies. **Flight period:** Form *natalensis* mainly Aug–Mar, f. *sesamus* Mar–Aug. **Larval food:** *Plectranthus* spp., including *P. esculentus, Rabdosiella calycina, Pycnostachys reticulata, P. urticifolia*. In captivity, cultivated *Coleus* spp.

3 Darker Commodore   *Precis antilope*

Wingspan: ♂ 40–55 mm ♀ 50–60 mm. **Identification: 3A** ♂ upper side, **3B** ♂ underside (f. *antilope*); **3C** ♂ upper side, **3D** ♂ underside (f. *simia*). Flight slow for a *Precis*; settles often on flowers or rocks. More common DSF f. *antilope* found on hill tops; larger WSF f. *simia* has falcate, leaf-like wings, flies over flatlands. **Distribution:** Scarce and localised. Lowland Forest, Savanna and lowveld areas from KwaZulu-Natal (Eshowe area and Maputaland) to Swaziland, Mpumalanga and Limpopo and NW (as far south as Brits) provinces. **Habitat:** Hill tops, flatlands. **Flight period:** Form *antilope* Dec–Mar, f. *simia* Apr–Aug. **Larval food:** No data.

1 Marsh Commodore *Precis ceryne ceryne*

Wingspan: ♂ 40–45 mm ♀ 42–50 mm. **Identification: 1A** ♂ upper side, **1B** ♂ underside (nominate), **1C** ♀ underside (f. *tukuoa*). DSF f. *tukuoa* less colourful than nominate WSF, wings more angular, forewing tips falcate. DSF *pinkish buff* replacing white median upper side bands of WSF. Sexes similar, ♀ with wings broader. Flight slow; if disturbed, sets off with typical nymphaline flap-glide motion. Found close to water near food plants. Often on flowers. ♂ territorial; sits on grass stems, chasing other butterflies. **Distribution:** Localised. Grassland, Savanna and Lowland Forest, from E Cape to n KwaZulu-Natal, Free State, Mpumalanga, Gauteng, Limpopo and NW provinces, and further north. **Habitat:** Wetlands, hillsides, gullies, marshes, dells and stream banks. **Flight period:** Two broods: WSF Dec–Mar, DSF Apr–Jun, some overlap in autumn. **Larval food:** *Pycnostachys reticulata*, *Plectranthus* spp.

2 Garden Inspector or Garden Commodore *Precis archesia archesia*

Wingspan: ♂ 45–50 mm ♀ 50–60 mm. **Identification: 2A** ♂ upper side, **2B** ♂ upper side, **2C** ♂ underside (f. *pelasgis*), **2D** ♂ underside (f. *archesia*). Most familiar *Precis* in South Africa. Sexes similar, ♀ with wings rounder. Brown, *maroon and blue* DSF f. *archesia* comes to garden flowers, roosts in hollows under banks and rocks. WSF f. *pelasgis* brown, with *cream to buff* postdiscal bands, more often found on hill tops. Intermediates quite common. **Distribution:** Savanna, Grassland and forests from W Cape (Knysna area) to E Cape, KwaZulu-Natal, Free State, Gauteng, Mpumalanga, Limpopo and NW provinces, and further north. **Habitat:** Forest edges, parks and gardens, hill tops, hillsides, rocky slopes, gullies. **Flight period:** Year-round, two main broods: f. *pelasgis* Sept–Mar, f. *archesia* Apr–Aug. **Larval food:** *Plectranthus* spp.

Genus *Junonia* Pansies   WORLD 35+ SPP., AFRICA 18, SOUTH AFRICA 6

Small, brightly coloured nymphalines; very similar to *Precis* but less difference between WSFs and DSFs. Robust butterflies, with fast, agile flight; often sit on ground with wings slowly opening and closing. Fond of flowers. Eggs laid singly on Lamiaceae, Acanthaceae and Scrophulariaceae. Bulb-shaped, green to yellow, with 10–16 prominent glassy longitudinal ribs, and (sometimes) 25–40 cross-ridges. Larva dark, sometimes with prominent orange or yellow longitudinal stripes; seven longitudinal rows of branched spines of varying length; head capsule unadorned. Pupa robust, usually with bifid head, two or more rows of dorsal tubercles on abdomen; suspended head down from cremaster.

3 African Leaf Butterfly *Junonia tugela tugela*

Wingspan: ♂ 55–60 mm ♀ 58–64 mm. **Identification: 3A** ♀ upper side, **3B** ♂ upper side, **3C** ♂ underside (f. *aurorina*). WSF f. *aurorina* smaller than nominate DSF, with both sexes with wingtips *less prominently hooked*. ♂ of both forms has more dramatically hooked wingtips and longer tails than ♀. Dark brown to black ground colour with orange discal bands containing rows of small black spots. One of the finest dead-leaf mimics; no two undersides exactly alike. Flies along lanes and edges of clearings in deep forest. Very wary; heads for the canopy when disturbed. **Distribution:** Afromontane Forest on escarpment from KwaZulu-Natal Midlands (Pietermaritzburg) to Swaziland, Mpumalanga and Limpopo Province. May swarm in Wolkberg in Jun. **Habitat:** Forest edges. **Flight period:** Two main broods: DSF f. *aurorina* Sept–Mar, nominate WSF Apr–Aug; winter brood usually more numerous than summer. **Larval food:** *Plectranthus* spp. and *Englerastrum scandens*.

1B

1C

2C

3A

3C

1 Soldier Pansy   *Junonia terea elgiva*

Wingspan: ♂ 50–55 mm ♀ 52–60 mm. **Identification: 1A** ♂ upper side (DSF), **1B** ♂ underside (WSF). Similar to African Leaf Butterfly (p. 134), but *less robust*, upper side discal bands *paler*, hind wing postdiscal row of ocelli *distal* to discal band, and *lacks spots*; also, flight *slower*. Seasonal forms not named but summer specimens (WSF) have broader, deeper orange discal bands than winter ones (DSF), which have *slate-brown* underside with *yellow* median 'leaf midrib' stripe, as opposed to *buff* with *brown* stripe of WSF. ♂ patrols paths and clearings. Both sexes settle often on low foliage. **Distribution:** Inland Lowland Forest, and along rivers in Riverine Forest at foot of escarpments. Coastal KwaZulu-Natal to Swaziland, Mpumalanga and Limpopo Province. **Habitat:** Forest edges, flatlands. **Flight period:** Two main broods, peaks early summer (Oct and Nov), and autumn to winter (Apr–Jul). **Larval food:** *Ruellia patula, Asystasia gangetica* and *Phaulopsis imbricata*.

2 Brown Pansy   *Junonia natalica natalica*

Wingspan: ♂ 45–50 mm ♀ 48–55 mm. **Identification: 2A** ♀ upper side (f. *natalensis*), **2B** ♂ underside (nominate). Common, wary and easily disturbed. DSF f. *natalensis* has *reduced* underside eye spots. Nominate WSF has underside eye spots *well developed*. Attracted to moisture on roads; fond of flowers, particularly alien mistletoe *Lantana camara*. Sexes similar. **Distribution:** Lowland and Riverine Forest, Savanna in coastal KwaZulu-Natal from Port Edward to Kosi Bay, and Swaziland. Scarce at foot of escarpment in riverine bush of Mpumalanga and Limpopo Province lowveld. **Habitat:** Forest edges, flatlands, coast, parks and gardens. **Flight period:** Year-round, peaks Oct and Nov, and Feb–May. **Larval food:** *Asystasia gangetica* and *Phaulopsis imbricata*.

3 Yellow Pansy   *Junonia hierta cebrene*

Wingspan: ♂ 40–45 mm ♀ 40–50 mm. **Identification: 3A** ♂ upper side, **3B** ♀ upper side, **3C** ♂ underside. ♀ has dark forewing cell bar and black ocelli in yellow postdiscal band on hind wing. Sexes similar. ♂ establishes territories close to patches of open ground. Fond of damp earth and wet sand near streams, and rotting fruit; also flowers. Sometimes found on cultivated *Barleria* spp. in Cape Town gardens. **Distribution:** Common, widespread. From W Cape through warmer, moister Karoo areas into Grassland and Savanna of Free State, Gauteng, KwaZulu-Natal, Swaziland, Mpumalanga, Limpopo and NW provinces, and N Cape. **Habitat:** Parks and gardens, flatlands, hillsides. **Flight period:** Year-round in warmer areas, peaks Oct and Nov, and Feb–May. **Larval food:** *Adhatoda densiflora, Asystasia gangetica, Barleria* spp., including *B. pungens, Chaetacanthus setiger* and *Ruellia cordata*.

4 Blue Pansy   *Junonia oenone oenone*

Wingspan: ♂ 40–50 mm ♀ 48–52 mm. **Identification: 4A** ♂ upper side, **4B** ♀ upper side, **4C** ♂ underside. Sexes similar, ♀ with submarginal red ocelli on hind wing. ♂ establishes territories on hill tops and ridges, sitting on the ground or low vegetation, darting off to chase intruders, flying fast, sometimes soaring in aerial dogfights with larger butterflies such as *Charaxes*. ♀ sedentary near flowers and the food plants. Frequent garden visitor; often found feeding on flowers. **Distribution:** Common, not as widespread as Yellow Pansy (above). Savannas and woodland from E Cape (Grahamstown area) to KwaZulu-Natal, Swaziland, Mpumalanga, Limpopo and NW provinces, Gauteng, Free State and N Cape. **Habitat:** Forest edges, parks and gardens, hill tops, coast. **Flight period:** Year-round in warmer areas, peaks Oct and Nov, and Feb–May. **Larval food:** *Adhatoda densiflora, Asystasia gangetica* and *Mackaya bella*.

A

1B

A

2B

3B

3C

A

4B

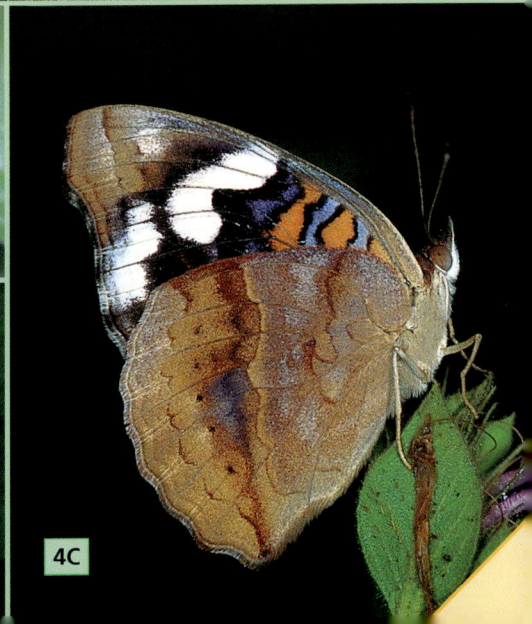

4C

1 Eyed Pansy   *Junonia orithya madagascariensis*

Wingspan: ♂ 35–42 mm ♀ 40–48 mm. **Identification: 1A** ♂ upper side, **1B** ♀ upper side, **1C** ♂ underside. Sexes similar, ♀ with wings more rounded, much *more prominent* upper side ocelli. Underside cryptic. ♂ strongly territorial. **Distribution:** Widespread but uncommon. Mostly inland Savanna and Grassland from E Cape (Port St Johns) to KwaZulu-Natal, Swaziland, Mpumalanga, Limpopo and NW provinces, Gauteng, Free State and N Cape. **Habitat:** Flatlands, hillsides. **Flight period:** Year-round in warmer areas, peaks Aug–Nov, and Feb–May. **Larval food:** *Hygrophila* spp., *Thunbergia alata*, *Plectranthus* spp., *Antirrhinum* spp. and *Graderia subintegra*.

Genus *Vanessa*   Painted Lady

WORLD 14 SPP., AFRICA 2, SOUTH AFRICA 1

Medium-sized butterfly, upper side salmon pink with black markings and white spots on black apical patch; underside hind wing variegated. Typical nymphaline flight. Single egg laid on leaves of many plant families, e.g. Compositae, Malvaceae, Fabaceae and Urticaceae. Barrel-shaped, pale green, with 16–18 conspicuous glassy longitudinal ribs and 21–25 faint cross braces, which fade away on the lower sides of the egg. Larva variable from black to green and buff; nine rows of longitudinal short branched spines and a plain rounded head capsule. Pupa elongated and rounded, with bifid head and rows of dorsal tubercles on thorax and abdomen.

2 Painted Lady   *Vanessa cardui*

Wingspan: ♂ 40–45 mm ♀ 45–50 mm. **Identification: 2A** ♂ upper side, **2B** ♀ underside. Sexes similar. ♂ territorial, defending hill tops and small bare areas among vegetation. Sometimes swarms in Fynbos and Karoo in winter and spring. Often the only active butterfly in cold areas in winter. Strongly migratory. **Distribution:** Common throughout South Africa, particularly in drier areas such as Fynbos/Karoo, Grassland and Savanna. Only absent from true desert. **Habitat:** Forest edges, parks and gardens, hill tops, flatlands, coast, mountains, wetlands. **Flight period:** Year-round; two main peaks, Aug–Oct, and Mar–Jul. **Larval food:** *Carduus* spp., *Arctotheca calendula*, *Arctotis stoechadifolia*, *Gazania* spp., *Berkheya discolor* and *Malva parviflora*.

Genus *Antanartia*   Admirals

AFRICA 6 SPP., SOUTH AFRICA 3

Adults resemble Holarctic Red Admiral but they have short tails. ♂ defends territories along forest edges and paths, sitting on wet mud or on vegetation no more than 1 m above the ground, darting off to challenge intruders with a rapid, whirring flight. ♀ less active, seldom seen except near food plants. Strongly attracted to fermenting fruit and plant juices. Eggs laid singly on Urticaceae, onion to barrel shaped, green with 10–15 prominent glassy longitudinal ribs and many faint cross-ribs. Larva dark, nine rows of short, branched spines and rounded, unadorned head capsule. Pupa with rows of prominent dorsal tubercles and sharply bifid head, and sharp dorsal ridge on thorax.

3 Southern Short-tailed Admiral   *Antanartia hippomene hippomene*

Wingspan: ♂ 40–45 mm ♀ 42–48 mm. **Identification: 3A** ♂ upper side, **3B** ♂ underside. Sexes similar. Very similar to Northern Short-tailed Admiral (p. 140); black upper side ground colour with orange forewing transverse band *tapering to a point* just short of inner margin. Shy and wary; if disturbed, will hide in undergrowth. Occasionally in large numbers. **Distribution:** Quite rare and localised. Moist coastal, and low-altitude Afromontane Forest from W Cape (Knysna), E Cape (Amatolas), n KwaZulu-Natal and Zululand (Eshowe). Absent from warmer Lowland Forest in Maputaland. **Habitat:** Forest edges. **Flight period:** Two or three summer/autumn broods, peaks Apr–May. **Larval food:** *Laportia peduncularis*, *Pouzolzia parasitica* and *Didymodoxa caffra*.

A

1B

2A

C

2B

A

3B

1 Northern Short-tailed Admiral *Antanartia dimorphica dimorphica*
Wingspan: ♂ 42–46 mm ♀ 44–50 mm. **Identification: 1A** ♂ upper side, **1B** ♂ underside. Sexes similar. Similar to Southern Short-tailed Admiral (p. 138), but *darker*; orange forewing transverse band reaches the inner margin *without tapering*. **Distribution:** Afromontane Forest from Mpumalanga (Barberton) along escarpment to Limpopo Province (Wolkberg). **Habitat:** Forest edges. **Flight period:** Year-round, peak Jan–Jun. **Larval food:** *Laportia peduncularis*, *Drogueria* spp. and *Carduus* spp.

2 Long-tailed Admiral *Antanartia schaenia schaenia*
Wingspan: ♂ 40–48 mm ♀ 45–50 mm. **Identification: 2A** ♂ upper side, **2B** ♂ underside. Sexes similar. Tails longer than in other *Antanartia* species; flight stronger. Both sexes very shy and wary, difficult to approach; ♀ seen less often, usually close to food plant. **Distribution:** Afromontane Forest from E Cape (Port St Johns) along escarpment to KwaZulu-Natal Midlands, Swaziland, Mpumalanga and Limpopo Province (Wolkberg). **Habitat:** Forest edges. **Flight period:** Year-round, peak Jan–Jun. **Larval food:** *Laportia peduncularis*, *Boehmeria nivea* and *Pouzolzia parasitica*.

Subfamily LIBYTHEINAE
Monotypic. Consists of only one genus found worldwide in warmer areas; primitive butterflies all with long labial palps; all species have similar markings.

Genus *Libythea* Snouts   WORLD 7 SPP., SOUTH AFRICA 1
The common name of these butterflies refers to the insect's long labial palps. The eggs are skittle shaped, whitish, with 21 longitudinal ribs and 45 cross ribs. They are laid singly on Ulmaceae. The larva is green to brown, smooth skinned, with short, fine hairs. The pupa is smooth, green and elongate, with two blunt thoracic points.

3 African Snout Butterfly *Libythea labdaca laius*
Wingspan: ♂ 40–46 mm ♀ 45–50 mm. **Identification: 3A** ♂ upper side, **3B** ♂ underside (WSF). Sexes similar, ♀ with broader wings. Underside very variable, from blackish through wide range of browns and greys to buff, and mottled with varying numbers of darker markings. WSFs have heavier patterning than dry season individuals. Frequents forest canopy, flying lower to sit on tree branches and wet mud, where it is wary and difficult to approach, flitting off to sit a few metres away. Occasionally encountered in migrating swarms. **Distribution:** Coastal forest from E Cape (East London) and KwaZulu-Natal, inland to Afromontane and Riverine Forest and into Swaziland, Mpumalanga, Limpopo Province, and further north. **Habitat:** Forest edges, flatlands, coast. **Flight period:** Multiple broods in warmer months, Oct–Apr. Jun and Jul winter brood in warmer areas. **Larval food:** *Celtis africana* and *C. mildbraedii*.

Family LYCAENIDAE
The most species-rich and biologically diverse butterfly family, over 6 000 spp. worldwide. Three subfamilies in South Africa. Larvae use high protein foods, some being carnivorous or seed eaters. Many live in restricted ranges and have specialist needs, so the family includes some of our most threatened species.

Subfamily PORITIINAE
Small butterflies, flight weak and halting, settling for long periods on rocks or the end of twigs. Many are distasteful to predators, and are appropriately coloured in 'warning' shades of orange with black spots, or black and white. While some adults do not feed, many ingest the secretions ('honeydew') of Homopterans (sap sucking plant lice). They generally do not move far from their habitat.

Genus *Alaena*   Zulus
AFRICA 23 SPP., SOUTH AFRICA 2

White to buff or orange, veined or netted with black. Found in colonies near suitable algal food. Slow fluttering flight among rocks and grass stems. Eggs laid on rocks or ground; each a truncated cone; rings of indentations around top and sides. Larva hairy, slug-shaped; well camouflaged. Pupa also hairy, hidden in rock crevices and leaf debris.

1 Yellow Zulu   *Alaena amazoula*

Wingspan: ♂ 22–28 mm ♀ 25–32 mm. **Identification: 1A** ♂ upper side, **1B** ♂ underside, **1C** ♀ (top) upper side (*A. a. amazoula*). In both spp., ♂ with dark scaling *heavier* along veins than ♀. In *A. a. ochroma*, both sexes brighter orange-buff, with thinner black veining. **Distribution:** Widespread in Savanna and Grassland. Nominate from E Cape (East London) to n KwaZulu-Natal (Tugela Ferry, Msinga); *A. a. ochroma* from Swaziland to Mpumalanga, Gauteng, parts of Free State, Limpopo and NW provinces. **Habitat:** Hill tops, hillsides. **Flight period:** Single-brooded, Oct–May, peak Dec–Jan. **Larval food:** Cyanobacteria.

2 Wolkberg Zulu   *Alaena margaritacea*

Wingspan: ♂ 24–27 mm ♀ 28–30 mm. **Identification: 2A** ♂ upper side, **2B** ♀ underside. Sexes alike, ♂ with wings more pointed than ♀. Colonies *smaller* and *denser* in numbers than Yellow Zulu (above). **Distribution:** Scarce and localised; colonies on grassy slopes adjoining Afromontane Forest in Haenertsburg area of Limpopo Province (Wolkberg). Under severe threat from alien tree plantations. **Habitat:** Forest edges, hillsides. **Flight period:** Single-brooded, late Dec to early Jan. **Larval food:** Cyanobacteria.

Genus *Pentila*   Buffs
AFRICA 38 SPP., SOUTH AFRICA 1

Small butterflies of shady forest understorey. Weak flight; high in canopy during day, lower in evenings and mornings. May roost congregally on grass stems and creeper tendrils. Ground colour buff to orange, with black speckles or spots. Eggs truncated cones; rings of indentations around the top and sides; laid among Cyanobacteria on tree bark. Larva hairy, slug-shaped, well camouflaged. Pupa hairy, hidden in bark crevices and leaf debris.

3 Spotted Buff   *Pentila tropicalis*

Wingspan: ♂ 29–38 mm ♀ 34–44 mm. **Identification: 3A** ♂ upper side, **3B** ♂ underside (nominate). Sexes similar. Resembles Zulu Buff (p. 146), but *redder, more densely speckled* with black. 2 subspp., geographically distinct. **Distribution:** Nominate in warm coastal bush in KwaZulu-Natal; *P. t. fuscipunctata* in sheltered riverine Lowland Forest of eastern Limpopo Province (Soutpansberg) and further north. **Habitat:** Forest edges, parks and gardens, coast. **Flight period:** Nominate double-brooded, Oct/Nov and Jan–Apr. *P. t. fuscipunctata* continuous broods Nov–Apr. **Larval food:** Cyanobacteria.

Genus *Ornipholidotos*   White Mimics
AFRICA 45 SPP., SOUTH AFRICA 1

Small butterflies, usually white with dark margins and black spots. Flight weak. Eggs laid among Cyanobacteria on tree bark. Larva hairy, slug-shaped, well camouflaged. Pupa also hairy, hidden in bark crevices and leaf debris.

4 White Mimic   *Ornipholidotos peucetia penningtoni*

Wingspan: ♂ & ♀ 35–37 mm. **Identification: 4A** ♂ upper side, **4B** ♂ underside. Sexes similar. Flutters slowly around forest floor, often resting for hours on a grass stem. Usually only seen when disturbed. Easily mistaken for African Wood White (p. 342) but dark borders *broad* and spots *larger*. Usually found singly but sometimes in large congregations. Possibly distasteful; when handled, produces acrid odour similar to that exuded by Acraeas. **Habitat:** Forest edges. **Distribution:** Rare and localised. Warm coastal Lowland Forest in n KwaZulu-Natal (including False Bay, Emanguzi and Kosi Bay). **Flight period:** Single-brooded, Nov–May, peak late summer. **Larval food:** Cyanobacteria.

Genus *Durbania* Rocksitters SOUTH AFRICA AND SWAZILAND 2 SPP.

Small butterflies, upper side brown to black, with bright buff to red markings; underside marbled grey, brown and black. May be aposematic; acrid smell emitted when molested. Settles with wings closed on camouflaging lichen-covered rocks; difficult to flush. When disturbed, may raise forewing to show an orange or red patch on underside. Eggs laid on rocks. A truncated cone with curved base, irregular ribs running from micropyle down the sides, very fine lines running perpendicular to these. The slug-shaped hairy larva feeds on the algal component of lichen. Pupa squat, well camouflaged, with the remains of the larval skin still adhering to the tail.

1 Amakosa Rocksitter *Durbania amakosa*

Wingspan: ♂ 26–35 mm ♀ 29–38 mm. **Identification: 1A** ♂ upper side (*D. a. natalensis*), **1B** ♀ upper side (*D. a. amakosa*), **1C** ♀ upper side (*D. a. ayresi*), **1D** undersides ♀ left, ♂ right (*D. a. natalensis*). ♂ has small red-orange to red spots on jet-black ground colour, ♀ with upper side more orange-red. Southern *D. a. amakosa* has narrow, broken buff-orange bands on the upper side. In northern *D. a. ayresi*, the orange is more extensive, almost covering the upper side. 7 subspp. **Distribution:** Grassland. Nominate in KwaZulu-Natal (Kokstad) and E Cape (Amatolas); *D. a. ayresi* along Drakensberg from Swaziland to Mpumalanga (south of Olifants R); *D. a. sagittata* e Drakensberg and Maluti foothills, Free State; *D. a. natalensis* KwaZulu-Natal Midlands and Drakensberg foothills; *D. a. flavida*, rare and localised in lower KwaZulu-Natal hills (Shongweni to Ngoye Forest); *D. a. albescens* highly localised, from Margate and Port Edward, s KwaZulu-Natal; *D. a. penningtoni* E Cape from Bedford to Grahamstown and Port Elizabeth. **Habitat:** Rocky ledges, hillsides. **Flight period:** Single-brooded, Nov–Jan. **Larval food:** Cyanobacteria.

2 Natal Rocksitter *Durbania limbata*

Wingspan: ♂ 22–27 mm ♀ 24–33 mm. **Identification: 2A** ♂ upper side, **2B** ♂ underside. Sexes similar. *Smaller* than similar Amakosa Rocksitter (above), with forewing red band *closer to margin*. ♂ upper side has *glossy sheen*. Underside cryptic, well camouflaged among pink granite rocks. **Distribution:** Grassland in KwaZulu-Natal Midlands (between Estcourt and Greytown, south to Balgowan), ne Free State (Harrismith) and sw Mpumalanga (Hele Mtn, near Wakkerstroom). **Habitat:** Rocky ledges, hillsides. **Flight period:** Single-brooded, Mar–Apr. **Larval food:** Cyanobacteria.

Genus *Durbaniella* Rocksitters MONOTYPIC; SOUTH AFRICAN ENDEMIC

Very small butterfly, upper side brown to black, with bright buff to orange markings (usually more extensive in ♀), underside marbled grey, brown and black. Settles on rocks with wings closed; difficult to flush or follow in flight. Exudes bitter smell when handled. Eggs laid on rocks. Slug-shaped hairy larva feeds on algal component of lichen. Pupa squat, with the remains of the larval skin still adhering to the tail.

3 Clark's Rocksitter *Durbaniella clarki*

Wingspan: ♂ 18–24 mm ♀ 18–26 mm. **Identification: 3A** ♂ upper side, **3B** ♀ upper side, **3C** ♂ upper side (*D. c. phaea*), **3D** ♂ underside (*D. c. clarki*). Sexes similar in *D. c. clarki*. 4 subspp., varying in markings and colour. **Distribution:** Fynbos, Nama Karoo. Nominate in W Cape from Langeberg (above Riversdale) along Swartberg to Kammanassieberg (above Uniondale), Schoemanspoort, and along Witteberge to Willowmore (E Cape); *D. c. belladonna* (rare) in low-altitude rocky riverbeds near Jansenville, E Cape; *D. c. jenniferae* along Outeniqua range (W Cape), Tsitsikamma and Baviaanskloof ranges to Uitenhage (Port Elizabeth, E Cape); *D. c. phaea* Riviersonderend Mts, hills between Worcester and Montagu, W Cape. **Habitat:** Hill tops, rocky ledges, gullies. **Flight period:** Single-brooded, Sept–Dec. **Larval food:** Cyanobacteria.

1A

1B

C

1D

A

2B

A

3B

C

3D

Genus *Durbaniopsis*   Rocksitters   MONOTYPIC; SOUTH AFRICAN ENDEMIC

Dullest Rocksitter; size variable. Slow, halting flight, but fast if disturbed. Settles with wings closed, on vegetation and sheltered rocks where it is well camouflaged; difficult to flush. Eggs laid on rocks; domed with rounded base, covered with lines of tiny pits. Slug-shaped hairy larvae feed on algae in lichen. Remains of larval skin adheres to tail of squat, rounded pupa.

1 Boland Rocksitter   *Durbaniopsis saga*

Wingspan: ♂ 26–39 mm ♀ 29–40 mm. **Identification: 1A** ♂ upper side, **1B** ♀ upper side, **1C** ♂ underside. Sexes similar. Upper side brown, markings *dull cream* or *buff*, underside *more variegated* than other rocksitters, marbled grey, brown and black coloration resembling lichen and providing camouflage. **Distribution:** In Fynbos, Nama Karoo, and Succulent Karoo over a wide area of inland W Cape and N Cape mountains, from Nieuwoudtville Mts south to Cederberg, Koue Bokkeveld, Hex River and Hawequas Mts. Also low-altitude sites from Lambert's Bay inland to Het Kruis. **Habitat:** Rocky ledges. **Flight period:** Single-brooded, Oct–Dec, as early as Sept at lower altitudes. **Larval food:** Cyanobacteria.

Genus *Teriomima*   Buffs   AFRICA 6 SPP., SOUTH AFRICA 1

Small, bright yellow-buff butterflies with sparse small black spots. Usually deep-forest dwellers, but occasionally seen at forest edge. Flight weak, solitary but may roost communally. Eggs laid on surfaces on which cyanobacteria grow, e.g. tree bark. Larva hairy, slug-shaped, well camouflaged. Pupa also hairy, hidden in bark crevices and leaf debris.

2 Zulu Buff   *Teriomima zuluana*

Wingspan: ♂ 23–28 mm ♀ 24–30 mm. **Identification: 2A** ♂ upper side, **2B** ♂ underside. Sexes similar. Resembles Spotted Buff (p. 142), but *brighter* yellow-buff, *fewer, more well-defined* black spots. Usually flies high in canopy. Settles on twigs where slowly moving wings resemble tiny yellowed leaf waving in the breeze. Occasionally roosts communally in undergrowth. ♀ flies lower searching for oviposition sites on tree trunks. **Distribution:** Rare and localised, in coastal Lowland Forest of n KwaZulu-Natal from False Bay north to Kosi Bay and inland to Makathini Flats and Tembe Elephant Park. **Habitat:** Forest edges. **Flight period:** Double-brooded; main brood Oct and Nov, weaker second brood late summer. **Larval food:** Cyanobacteria.

Genus *Baliochila*   Buffs   AFRICA 21 SPP., SOUTH AFRICA 2

Small buff butterflies of forest or wooded savanna. High, weak flight, often colonial in a single tree. Reluctant to fly; spends hours resting on growing points of creepers or tips of dry twigs, slowly opening and closing wings. Adults feed on secretions of aphids, etc. Eggs bun-shaped, covered in large hexagonal pits; laid among cyanobacteria, e.g. on tree bark. Larvae hairy, slug-shaped, cryptic. Pupae also hairy, hidden in bark crevices and leaf debris.

3 Common Buff   *Baliochila aslanga*

Wingspan: ♂ 23.5–29 mm ♀ 25–31 mm. **Identification: 3A** ♂ upper side, **3B** ♀ upper side, **3C** ♂ underside. Small buff butterfly; ♂ has more dark brown markings along forewing upper side costa and cell, *darker* wingtips and margins than ♀. **Distribution:** Coastal and Riverine Forests of KwaZulu-Natal, inland along Lebombo Mtns into Swaziland, Mpumalanga and further north. **Habitat:** Forest edges. **Flight period:** Single-brooded, Oct–Mar. **Larval food:** Cyanobacteria.

Note: Recently, the Lipara Buff, *Baliochila lipara*, **4A** ♂ upper side, **4B** ♂ underside, was discovered in the Manguzi and Tembe areas of KZN. Its appearance and habits are similar to the Common Buff (above) but the sexes are alike, both resembling a ♀ Common Buff.

Genus *Cnodontes* Buffs
AFRICA 5 SPP., SOUTH AFRICA 1

Small buff-coloured butterflies. Flight high, weak. Difficult to flush. Solitary or in small groups; three to four males slowly circling a tree. Eggs of non-South African spp. laid among Cyanobacteria. Bun-shaped, covered in large hexagonal indentations. Larva hairy, slug-shaped, well camouflaged. Pupa also hairy, hidden in bark crevices and leaf debris.

1 Pennington's Buff *Cnodontes penningtoni*
Wingspan: ♂ 23–27 mm ♀ 24–29 mm. **Identification: 1A** ♀ upper side, **1B** ♀ underside, **1C** ♂ underside. *Sexes similar* on upper side, ♀ underside duller, flatter. Found singly or in small groups, sitting on a dead twig or shaded shrub. **Distribution:** Savannas, Riverine Forest, from KwaZulu-Natal (n Zululand to Mozambique), to Mpumalanga, Limpopo and NW provinces, n Gauteng and N Cape. **Habitat:** Flatlands, hillsides. **Flight period:** Double-brooded, Aug–Oct, Feb–Apr. **Larval food:** Possibly Cyanobacteria.

Genus *Deloneura* Buffs
AFRICA 7 SPP., SOUTH AFRICA 1, POSSIBLY 2*

Small to medium-sized butterflies, upper side cream to buff with brown margins, underside well camouflaged in dry-leaf colours. Secretive, skulking; seldom flies unless disturbed. Gathers in small groups in dense foliage, walking, not flying, and feeding on honeydew secreted by coccids (plant lice). Flight slow, but when flushed, flees with peculiar fast-flapping wing-beats. Larva and pupa hairy, found on tree bark near plant lice colonies.

2 *Mbashe River Buff *D. immaculata* (♀ upper side). This species is classified as *extinct*; however, it may still exist in the densely forested Mbashe River area of the E Cape.

3 Millar's Buff *Deloneura millari millari*
Wingspan: ♂ 32–35 mm ♀ 34–36 mm. **Identification: 3A** ♂ upper side, **3B** ♀ underside (freshly emerged). Sexes similar. Deep buff with *brown-black* wingtip margins and grey-mottled hind wing underside. ♂ has small raised bar of scent scales at base of forewing upper side. Frequents acacias, Mahogany (Trichilia) and Cluster-leaf (Terminalia spp.). **Distribution:** Savanna and open coastal forest from E Cape (East London) along coast to n KwaZulu-Natal (Zululand), where common. **Habitat:** Forest edges. **Flight period:** Double-brooded, Sept/Oct and Mar–May. **Larval food:** Possibly cyanobacteria.

Subfamily MILETINAE
Rather dull butterflies, usually found in isolated colonies. Generally slow fliers, but capable of rapid flight. Adults vary in feeding habits; some feed on the sweet secretions of plant lice. Life history of species in the *Thestor* genus is unique (see p. 152).

Genus *Aslauga* Purples
AFRICA 28 SPP., SOUTH AFRICA 1

Small, grey to blue- or purple-grey butterflies, with a distinctive hook-tipped forewing shape. Secretive. No life history data from South Africa; further north, larvae feed on membracids, coccids and psyllids (Homoptera).

4 Southern Purple *Aslauga australis*
Wingspan: ♂ 22–25 mm ♀ 25–28 mm. **Identification: 4A** ♀ upper side, **4B** ♀ underside. ♂ darker than ♀. Flight slow, moth-like, sometimes hovering; circles shrubs and bushes. **Distribution:** Rare; less than 20 records. Savanna and coastal forest in E Cape (below Amatolas, Port St Johns and Embotyi). Also from Durban, KwaZulu-Natal. **Habitat:** Forest edges. **Flight period:** Uncertain; South African records spring to autumn. **Larval food:** No data.

1A

1B

1C

2

3A

3

4A

4B

Genus *Lachnocnema*   Woolly Legs   AFRICA 36 SPP., SOUTH AFRICA 4

Small, with grey to brown and buff upper side and silvery marks on underside of hind wing. Legs covered with woolly hairs. Flight slow and low in some species; in others, fast and high. Egg flat-topped and pill-shaped, with pattern of minute hexagonal indentations. Laid near colonies of plant lice. Slug-shaped larvae prey on the lice, adults feed on the honeydew produced by them. Larva has specialised true legs, which are long and spiny, allowing it to capture and hold its prey. Pupa rounded, brown with lines of paler dots on abdomen.

1 Common Woolly Legs   *Lachnocnema bibulus*

Wingspan: ♂ 21–27 mm ♀ 21–30.5 mm. **Identification: 1A** ♂ upper side, **1B** ♀ upper side, **1C** ♂ underside, **1D** ♀ underside. ♂ upper side brown-black, ♀ grey-brown, blue-grey discal patches, postcellular white streaks. Dark spot at end of forewing cell. ♂ underside hind wing has more-or-less distinct median band of variable width; when widest and darkest, can only be separated from Southern Pied Woolly Legs (below) by genital dissection. ♀ also variable. ♂ rapidly circles trees and shrubs harbouring larval prey. ♀ sedentary. **Distribution:** Lowland Forest edges and wooded Savanna from E Cape (Port Elizabeth) to KwaZulu-Natal, Swaziland, Mpumalanga, Gauteng, Limpopo and NW provinces. **Habitat:** Forest edges, parks and gardens, flatlands, hillsides. **Flight period:** Year-round in warmer areas, peaks spring and late summer. **Larval food:** Psyllid plant lice (Homoptera).

2 Southern Pied Woolly Legs   *Lachnocnema laches*

Wingspan: ♂ 23–32 mm ♀ 22–32 mm. **Identification: 2A** ♂ upper side, **2B** ♂ underside, **2C** ♀ upper side, **2D** ♀ underside. ♂ upper side brown-black; ♀ distinctly pied; *dark grey with large white* discal patches, limited basal blue-grey. Dark spot at end of forewing cell merges with grey. ♀ underside similar to Common Woolly Legs (above), but *darker*; ♂ with hind wing median band *always dark brown*, width more even than in Common Woolly Legs; *lacks copper sheen*. Similar habits. **Distribution:** Coastal forest from E Cape (Port Elizabeth), along KwaZulu-Natal coast, inland to Swaziland, Mpumalanga, Limpopo and NW provinces along wooded hills and valleys. **Habitat:** Forest edges, parks and gardens, gullies, coast. **Flight period:** Year-round in warmer areas, peaks spring and late summer. **Larval food:** No data.

3 Regular Woolly Legs   *Lachnocnema regularis regularis*

Wingspan: ♂ 28–36 mm ♀ 34–38 mm. **Identification: 3A** ♀ upper side, **3B** ♀ underside, **3C** ♂ upper side, **3D** ♂ underside. Sexes dimorphic; ♂ with upper side brown-black, ♀ grey-brown, as in smaller Common Woolly Legs (above); blue-grey and white markings less well defined. Underside similar to Common Woolly Legs; underside hind wing of both sexes has a *straight, constant width* discal line of silver-edged brown spots. No data on habits. **Distribution:** Only known from single record at 'Limpopo River', Limpopo Province. **Habitat:** Forest edges. **Flight period:** No data. **Larval food:** No data.

4 D'Urban's Woolly Legs   *Lachnocnema durbani*

Wingspan: ♂ 24.5–28 mm ♀ 24.5–30 mm. **Identification: 4A** ♂ upper side, **4B** ♀ upper side, **4C** ♂ underside. Sexes similar, ♂ darker than ♀. Small, plain, *dull brown* butterfly, upper side *lacking* distinctive markings. Always in *grassy areas. Flight low* and slow around grass stems; settles to suck the secretions of scale insects (Homoptera). **Distribution:** Grassland and Savanna from E Cape (Port Elizabeth), along the KwaZulu-Natal coast and inland to Mpumalanga, Gauteng, and Limpopo and NW provinces. **Habitat:** Flatlands, forest edges. **Flight period:** Year-round in warmer areas, peaks spring and late summer. **Larval food:** Coccid and membracid plant lice (Homoptera).

Genus *Thestor*   Skollies

AFRICA 27 SPP., SOUTH AFRICA 27, 26 ENDEMIC

Small, inconspicuous black, buff or dun-coloured butterflies. ♂ ♂ carry a grey-brown trident-shaped androconial patch in areas CuA_1 and CuA_2 of the forewing upper side. Proboscis short; antennae short, thick and blunt, with no obvious club. Usually found in small colonies close to *Anoplolepis* host ants, but some Cape mountain species may number in the hundreds. Flight slow and close to the ground; when disturbed, can put on a considerable turn of speed. ♂ perches on ground or low vegetation, chasing after intruders. ♀ more sedentary, skulking. Egg pill-shaped, with concave top, distinctive bulge to one side of top. Laid in soil or on rocks or vegetation, live or dead, close to ants' nests or trails, or food source of the young larvae. Larva whitish with distinctive dished marks along the sides; pinkish ochre, fat and woodlouse-shaped, with an extensible neck when fully grown. Final instar larva is a fat, buff-white grub. Shelters inside ants' nests feeding on debris or ant brood, or fed by the ants themselves by trophallaxis. The rounded, shiny amber pupa is also found inside ants' nests. Because *Thestor* butterflies are very similar to one another, we have grouped confusing species to aid in identification.

Boland Skolly group

Consists of three yellow-buff Skollies, with light and dark morphs. Upper side marked with black spotting; hind wing underside ground colour whitish to buff heavily irrorated with grey speckles; discal and postdiscal rows of joined, dark-edged darker spots; Boland Skolly, Dryburgh's Skolly, and Rossouw's Skolly.

1 Boland Skolly   *Thestor protumnus*

Wingspan: ♂ 22–37.5 mm ♀ 24–42.5 mm. **Identification: 1A** ♂ upper side, **1B** ♀ upper side, **1C** ♀ underside. 3 subspp., one form. ♂ upper side buff with grey-brown margins and rows of black spots; ♀ brighter buff than ♂, with *rounded* not *pointed* wings. Two colour morphs: cartridge-buff and tawny-buff. *Thestor p. aridus* with upper side buff *more extensive*; *T. p. terblanchei* smaller, *brighter* buff. Nominate has a particularly dark phase. *T. p. aridus* has desert form f. *mijburghi*; very pale buff with black spots restricted to cells in ♀; ♂ also has faint black apical spots. **Distribution:** Widely distributed. Nominate in Fynbos in W Cape (Cape Peninsula n to Tulbagh and Yzerfontein); *T. p. aridus* in Nama and Succulent Karoo in W Cape and N Cape (Burgersdorp to Vanrhynsdorp, Namaqualand, Garies, Steinkopf n to Namibian border), e to N Cape (Kimberley area); *T. p. terblanchei* in Nama Karoo/Grassland ecotone, only at Korannaberg, near Winburg, Free State. **Habitat:** Flatlands, coast. **Flight period:** Single-brooded, Sept–Dec, Aug–Oct in Namaqualand, Jan–Mar for *T. p. terblanchei*; peak varies with locality. **Larval food:** *T. p. aridus* recorded on coccids (Homoptera), but full life history unknown.

2 Dryburgh's Skolly   *Thestor dryburghi*

Wingspan: ♂ 34–37 mm ♀ 36–38 mm. **Identification: 2A** ♂ upper side, **2B** ♀ upper side (pale form); **2C** ♂ upper side, **2D** ♀ upper side (dark form), **2E** ♂ underside. Pale form similar to Boland Skolly (above). Wings *shorter, more rounded*, hind wing upper side apex carries *two small submarginal dark spots*, not a band. Darker form has *fuscous brown* replacing the buff. Underside cryptic. ♀ brighter than ♂. Small colonies on rocky koppie slopes. **Distribution:** Only in n Namaqualand, in Succulent Karoo-covered hills at Kamieskroon to nw of Steinkopf, N Cape. **Habitat:** Hill tops, rocky ledges. **Flight period:** Single-brooded, Aug–Oct. **Larval food:** No data.

A

3

1C

A

2B

2C

D

2E

1 Rossouw's Skolly *Thestor rossouwi*

Wingspan: ♂ 27–32 mm ♀ 30–36 mm. **Identification: 1A** ♂ upper side, **1B** ♂ underside, **1C** ♀ upper side (ovipositing in dry fynbos). Distinctive bright buff colour; occasional specimens darker brown. Unlike others in Boland Skolly group, forewing discal series of black marks extends to basal margin. ♂ darker than ♀; ♀ paler yellow-buff, wings rounded, sparser markings. Sometimes in large numbers. Low limestone ridges in coastal hills, among short vegetation; prefers disturbed ground. **Distribution:** Coastal Fynbos from between Riversdale and Stilbaai, west to Hermanus, Cape Agulhas and Bredasdorp, W Cape. **Habitat:** Coast, rocky ledges. **Flight period:** Sept–Apr, possibly more than one brood. **Larval food:** No data.

Brauns's Skolly group

Consists of three dull buff Skollies marked with dun and black, found in dry riverbeds and on hillsides; underside hind wing has characteristic dark discal mark; Brauns's Skolly, Dickson's Skolly, and Hantamsberg Skolly.

2 Brauns's Skolly *Thestor braunsi*

Wingspan: ♂ 26–28 mm ♀ 27–30 mm. **Identification: 2A** ♂ upper side, **2B** ♂ underside, **2C** ♀ upper side, **2D** ♀ underside. Smallest of group, only one to have light and dark morphs. ♂ much darker than ♀, more pointed wings. Hind wing underside discal dark mark axe or club shaped with white line at lower edge. Often found in *dry riverbeds*. Easily disturbed and flies away rapidly, but often comes back to the same stony patch of ground. **Distribution:** Widespread. W Cape Nama Karoo from Greyton, areas north and south of the Swartberg, east to Willowmore and west to Robertson area. **Habitat:** Flatlands, wetlands, rocky ledges. **Flight period:** Double-brooded, Oct and Mar, Jan at Greyton. **Larval food:** No data.

3 Dickson's Skolly *Thestor dicksoni*

Wingspan: ♂ 34–37.5 mm ♀ 43–45 mm. **Identification: 3A** ♂ upper side, **3B** ♀ upper side, **3C** ♂ underside (*T. d. warreni*). Characteristic *squarish dark hind wing underside discal mark containing hooked white line; sharply* pointed wings in ♂, *longer but rounded wings* in ♀. Flies in areas free of rocky outcrops; settles in stony depressions or in shade of plants. **Distribution:** W Cape. Nominate in montane Fynbos, Dasklip Pass near Porterville to Roodezandsberg near Tulbagh Kloof; *T. d. warreni* in arid strandveld Karoo near Graafwater, between Clanwilliam and Lambertsbaai; *T. d. malagas* (rare) along Atlantic coast, Langebaan peninsula. **Habitat:** Flatlands, hillsides. **Flight period:** Single-brooded, Dec–Apr. **Larval food:** No data.

4 Hantamsberg Skolly *Thestor calviniae*

Wingspan: ♂ 30–34 mm ♀ 38–42 mm. **Identification: 4A** ♂ upper side, **4B** ♀ upper side, **4C** ♂ underside. Extremely similar to Dickson's Skolly (above), but smaller, darker, and ♂ forewing *much more pointed and elongated*. Underside hind wing discal mark large and squarish with *anvil-shaped white patch at lower centre*. Flies in areas free of rocky outcrops; settles in stony depressions or in shade of plants. **Distribution:** Only from montane Fynbos in foothills and at summit of Hantamsberg near Calvinia. **Habitat:** Flatlands, hillsides. **Flight period:** Single-brooded, peaks Dec at lower altitudes, Mar/Apr on summit. **Larval food:** No data.

Mountain Skolly group

Consists of five buff to dun-coloured Skollies found at high altitude; they all have dark and light colour morphs. A common feature is a submarginal row of distinct sagittate marks pointing to the outer margin of the hind wing underside; Mountain Skolly, Langeberg Skolly, Rooiberg Skolly, Van Son's Skolly, and Strutt's Skolly.

A

1B

1C

A

2B

2C

D

3A

3B

C

4A

4B

4C

1 Mountain Skolly   *Thestor montanus*

Wingspan: ♂ 26–28 mm ♀ 27–29 mm. **Identification: 1A** ♂ upper side, **1B** ♂ underside. Sexes similar; ♀ usually paler than ♂. Two distinct colour morphs – yellowish buff and chocolate brown. Many have dark markings elongated into streaks on forewing. Plainer than Rooiberg Skolly (below), colour *more uniform*, forewing *more angulate* (but *less elongated* than Van Son's Skolly, below). Often in groups of three or four. **Distribution:** Fynbos-covered high mountain slopes in sw W Cape, from Caledon to Hottentots Holland, Franschhoek, Hawequas and Riviersonderend Mts. **Habitat:** Mountains, rocky ledges. **Flight period:** Single-brooded, Oct–Feb, peak Nov. **Larval food:** No data.

2 Langeberg Skolly   *Thestor pictus*

Wingspan: ♂ 26–28 mm ♀ 27–29 mm. **Identification: 2A** ♂ upper side, **2B** ♀ upper side, **2C** ♂ underside. Forewing discal area *narrower* than others of the Mountain Skolly species group. *Bright colour* distinctive. ♀ *paler* than ♂. Two slightly different colour morphs – paler and darker buff. Extent of dark upper side markings varies. **Distribution:** Rare and localised. Fynbos-covered mountain slopes above Garcia's Pass, Langeberg (Riversdale, W Cape). **Habitat:** Mountains, rocky ledges. **Flight period:** Single-brooded, end of Sept to Nov, peak Oct. **Larval food:** Larvae and pupae found in Pugnacious Ant *Anoplolepis custodiens* nests, but no data on food.

3 Rooiberg Skolly   *Thestor rooibergensis*

Wingspan: ♂ 26–28 mm ♀ 27–29 mm. **Identification: 3A** ♂ upper side, **3B** ♀ upper side, **3C** ♂ underside. Wings rounder, forewing upper side markings *less angulate, more exaggerated* contrast between light and dark than Mountain Skolly (above); *not as bright* as Langeberg Skolly (above). *Less variable* than Mountain Skolly or Van Son's Skolly (below), but has light and dark morphs. Upper side sexes dimorphic. ♂ upper side shows *prominent dark scaling* along veins. Sexually dimorphic as in *T. pictus*. Underside of both sexes cryptic. **Distribution:** Rare and localised. Fynbos-covered mountain slopes in Rooiberg, above Ladismith, W Cape. **Habitat:** Mountains, rocky ledges. **Flight period:** Single-brooded, Sep–Dec, peak Oct. **Larval food:** No data.

4 Van Son's Skolly   *Thestor vansoni*

Wingspan: ♂ ca. 24–29 mm ♀ ca. 27–34 mm. **Identification: 4A** ♂ upper side, **4B** ♀ upper side, **4C** ♀ underside. Small, dull grey-buff butterfly. Two distinct colour morphs – yellow-buff and mouse brown. ♀ paler, sometimes *much larger* than ♂; both sexes variable in size. Forewing more *acutely angled* than Mountain and Rooiberg Skollies (above). *Duller* than Langeberg Skolly (above). Found on high, (usually) north-facing mountain slopes, in flat, rocky depressions. **Distribution:** Nama Karoo. Just below peaks of Gydoberg, Skurweberg (above Ceres), and Cederberg, W Cape. **Habitat:** Mountains, rocky ledges. **Flight period:** Single-brooded, Sep–Nov, peak Oct. **Larval food:** No data.

5 Strutt's Skolly   *Thestor strutti*

Wingspan: ♂ 25–27 mm ♀ 26–28 mm. **Identification: 5A** ♂ upper side (dark form), **5B** ♂ underside. One of the palest *Thestor* spp. Sexes similar, ♀ larger. Dark form cartridge-buff, pale form ground colour *almost white*. Underside cryptic. **Distribution:** Only in sparse Fynbos on high slopes near north end of Bain's Kloof Pass near Wolseley, W Cape. **Habitat:** Rocky ledges, mountains. **Flight period:** Single-brooded, late Jul, Aug to early Sept. **Larval food:** Pupae found inside Pugnacious Ant *Anoplolepis custodiens* nests, but no data on food.

1A

1B

2A

2B

2C

3A

3B

3C

4A

4B

5C

5A

5B

Compassberg Skolly group

Consists of four buff *Thestor* species; ♂ ♂ have dark brown wings and golden or brassy basal areas: Kaplan's Skolly, Compassberg Skolly, Camdeboo Skolly and Pringle's Skolly.

1 Kaplan's Skolly   *Thestor kaplani*

Wingspan: ♂ 26–28 mm ♀ 27–29 mm. **Identification: 1A** ♂ upper side, **1B** ♀ upper side, **1C** ♀ underside. One of the more handsome members of the genus. ♂ has *golden* wing bases and *black* wingtips. ♀ is more typical buff *Thestor* type, with more pale colouring on wings. Difficult to follow in flight; when settled, superbly camouflaged underside hard to spot. **Distribution:** Only in Fynbos on the slopes of the Riviersonderend Mts above Greyton, W Cape. **Habitat:** Mountains, hillsides. **Flight period:** Single-brooded, Dec–Jan. **Larval food:** No data.

2 Compassberg Skolly   *Thestor compassbergae*

Wingspan: ♂ 26–29 mm ♀ 27–30 mm. **Identification: 2A** ♂ upper side, **2B** ♀ upper side, **2C** ♀ underside. ♂ with dark wingtips similar to Kaplan's (above) and Pringle's (below) Skollies but *not as prominent*. ♀ much paler than ♂. Found in large colonies on stony mountain slopes. Wary if approached, flying off rapidly, usually returning to the same spot. **Distribution:** Grassy inclusions in Nama Karoo on mountain slopes of Kompasberg, above Nieu-Bethesda, E Cape. **Habitat:** Mountains, rocky ledges. **Flight period:** Single-brooded, mid-Dec. **Larval food:** No data.

3 Camdeboo Skolly   *Thestor camdeboo*

Wingspan: ♂ 26–28 mm ♀ 27–29 mm. **Identification: 3A** ♂ upper side, **3B** ♂ underside, **3C** ♀ upper side. Similar to Kaplan's Skolly (above) but ♂ has *less black* on forewing tips. Forewing outer margin straighter, making wings appear *more pointed*. Typical *Thestor* ♂ upper side markings *more visible*, although variable, some specimens as dark as Kaplan's Skolly; ♀ upper side very similar to that of latter. **Distribution:** Grassveld inclusions in Nama Karoo on upper slopes of Camdeboo Mts, north of Aberdeen, E Cape. **Habitat:** Mountains, hillsides, rocky ledges. **Flight period:** Single-brooded, end Nov to mid-Dec. **Larval food:** No data.

4 Pringle's Skolly   *Thestor pringlei*

Wingspan: ♂ 26–28 mm ♀ 27–29 mm. **Identification: 4A** ♂ upper side, **4B** ♀ upper side, **4C** ♂ underside. ♂ *has prominent dark wingtips*. ♀ much paler, but richly coloured. Similar to others of the Compassberg Skolly species group, but with wings *pointed, much more elongated*, and *richer, more golden* basal colour. Flies extremely fast among very low-growing bushes; difficult to follow on the wing and well camouflaged on the ground. **Distribution:** In W Cape, in dry Nama Karoo on Roggeveld escarpment near Sutherland (Swaarweerberg), and near Calvinia (N Cape). **Habitat:** Mountains, hillsides. **Flight period:** Single-brooded, Dec. **Larval food:** No data.

Knysna Skolly group

Consists of eight small brown-black Skollies with pale ♂ forewing sex brands; Knysna Skolly, Overberg Skolly, Claassens' Skolly, Bearded Skolly, Riley's Skolly, Peninsula Skolly, Rock Skolly and Murray's Skolly.

1 Knysna Skolly *Thestor brachycerus*

Wingspan: ♂ 27–36 mm ♀ 29–39 mm. **Identification: 1A** ♂ upper side, **1B** ♂ underside (*T. b. dukei*), **1C** ♀ upper side, **1D** ♀ underside (nominate). ♂ has a *whitish spot* at end of forewing upper side cell. ♀ with *more prominent* forewing white patch on upper side, wings more rounded than ♂. Underside of both sexes cryptic. Flies low among rocky outcrops. 2 subspp. **Distribution:** Nominate (rare) in W Cape, confined to The Heads at Knysna; *T. b. dukei* in Karoo and Fynbos, along Langeberg from Die Koo to Montagu; along Swartberg and Elandsberg to Outeniqua Mts, and along s W Cape coast from Kogelberg to Stanford. **Habitat:** Rocky ledges, hillsides, coast. **Flight period:** Single-brooded, Dec–Jan. **Larval food:** Larvae found inside Pugnacious Ant *Anoplolepis custodiens* nests, but no data on food.

2 Overberg Skolly *Thestor overbergensis*

Wingspan: ♂ 33–38 mm ♀ 44 mm. **Identification: 2A** ♂ upper side, **2B** ♂ underside, **2C** ♀ upper side, **2D** ♀ underside. Largest of Knysna Skolly group; upper side darker than Claassens' Skolly (below), lacking the prominent golden brown markings of that species; cilia prominently chequered. Underside of both sexes cryptic, forewing carries prominent submarginal sagittate marks. Flies low among rocky outcrops on low ridges in coastal hills, among short vegetation. **Distribution:** Coastal Fynbos between Ou Plaas and De Hoop, W Cape. **Habitat:** Rocky ledges. **Flight period:** Nov and Dec. **Larval food:** No data.

3 Claassens' Skolly *Thestor claassensi*

Wingspan: ♂ 27–36 mm ♀ 29–39 mm. **Identification: 3A** ♂ upper side, **3B** ♀ upper side, **3C** ♂ underside. Compared to Knysna Skolly (above), forewing *more pointed*; extent of pale golden brown forewing patch on upper side, especially in ♀, so great as to approach that of a 'yellow' *Thestor*. Flies low among rocky outcrops. **Distribution:** W Cape, coastal rocky outcrops in Fynbos near Stilbaai between Knysna and Cape Town. **Habitat:** Coast. **Flight period:** Single-brooded, Nov to early Dec. **Larval food:** No data.

4 Bearded Skolly *Thestor barbatus*

Wingspan: ♂ 32–38 mm ♀ 36–40 mm. **Identification: 4A** ♂ upper side, **4B** ♀ upper side, **4C** ♂ underside. ♂ with wings more pointed than ♀. Only reliably distinguished from Knysna (above) and Riley's (below) Skollies by genital dissection. Forewing *more elongated* than former; discal band of spots *widened* in areas CuA_1 and M_3, creating an irregular outline. **Distribution:** Rare, localised. W Cape, in Nama Karoo at Paardeberg (nw of Herold), in northern foothills of Outeniqua Mts. **Habitat:** Mountains, rocky ledges. **Flight period:** Single-brooded, Dec. **Larval food:** No data.

5 Riley's Skolly *Thestor rileyi*

Wingspan: ♂ 24–36 mm ♀ 32.5–41 mm. **Identification: 5A** ♂ upper side, **5B** ♀ upper side, **5C** ♀ underside. Very closely resembles Knysna Skolly (*T. b. dukei*, above). ♂ darker than ♀, which lacks forewing upper side sex brand, duller, wings more rounded. Forewing underside mid-cell spot often *double*. Generally lacks *sub-basal spot* Knysna Skolly has in forewing underside cell, but has elongated spot in CuA_1 of forewing underside, *missing* in others of the Knysna Skolly species group. Occupies steeper, higher hillsides than Knysna Skolly. **Distribution:** Fynbos. W Cape, from Helderberg (Somerset West) and Paarl Mountain, to Kouebokkeveldberg, Piketberg and Paardeberg ranges. **Habitat:** Mountains, rocky ledges. **Flight period:** Single-brooded, late Nov to early Jan, peak Dec. **Larval food:** Larvae found inside Pugnacious Ant *Anoplolepis custodiens* nests, but no data on food.

1A

1B

1C

D

2A

2B

2C

D

3A

3B

3C

A

4B

4C

A

5B

5C

1 Peninsula Skolly *Thestor yildizae*

Wingspan: ♂ 25–32 mm ♀ 28–36.5 mm. **Identification: 1A** ♂ upper side, **1B** ♂ underside. Only black *Thestor* on Cape Peninsula. Easily distinguished from Knysna Skolly species group by uniformly darker upper side in both sexes – dark spots *difficult to discern* from background – and *distinctly chequered* cilia. ♂ darker, with squarer wings than ♀, and distinctive forewing sex brand. **Distribution:** Fynbos. Only found high up on slopes of Cape Peninsula mountains, particularly Muizenberg, W Cape. **Habitat:** Mountains, rocky ledges. **Flight period:** Single-brooded, late Nov to early Feb. **Larval food:** Larvae found in Pugnacious Ant *Anoplolepis custodiens* nests, but no data on food.

2 Rock Skolly *Thestor petra*

Wingspan: ♂ 22–28 mm ♀ 26–34 mm. **Identification: 2A** ♂ upper side, **2B** ♀ upper side, **2C** ♂ underside. Very similar to Riley's Skolly (p. 160) , but upper side darker. ♀ darker than ♂, wings more rounded; lacks forewing sex brand. Sometimes found in vast numbers. Flight weak, easy to follow. 2 subspp. **Distribution:** Fynbos and Nama Karoo. Nominate in W Cape, on Gydo, Tierberg, Matroosberg and Skurweberg Mts around Ceres. *T. p. tempe* in W Cape, in Klein Karoo and Great Karoo mountains near Seweweekspoort, Elandsberg and Rooiberg. **Habitat:** Mountains, hillsides, rocky ledges. **Flight period:** Single-brooded, from late Nov to Jan. **Larval food:** No data.

3 Murray's Skolly *Thestor murrayi*

Wingspan: ♂ 26–28 mm ♀ 27–29 mm. **Identification: 3A** ♂ upper side, **3B** ♀ upper side, **3C** ♂ underside. Unique; close to others in Knysna Skolly group but more variable and has two forms: a yellow one resembling Langeberg Skolly (p. 156) and a dull dark brown form resembling Knysna Skolly (p. 160). ♀ has wings more rounded than ♂. **Distribution:** Nama Karoo in W Cape, from Swartberg to Kammanassie, Outeniqua and Tsitsikamma Mts, to Groot Winterhoekberge and Baviaanskloofberge in E Cape. **Habitat:** Mountains, rocky ledges. **Flight period:** Single-brooded, Oct–Jan. **Larval food:** No data.

Stephen's Skolly group

Consists of three dark brown to black Skollies, distinguished by relatively large size, prominent sex brand on ♂ forewing and dark colouring in *both* sexes; Stephen's Skolly; Holmes's Skolly, and Pennington's Skolly.

4 Stephen's Skolly *Thestor stepheni*

Wingspan: ♂ 27–36 mm ♀ 31–40 mm. **Identification: 4A** ♀ upper side, **4B** ♂ upper side, **4C** ♂ underside. Fast-flying black *Thestor. Very dark* upper side colour, sex brand more pronounced than other black *Thestors*. As in Holmes's Skolly (p. 164), black spots in forewing underside submarginal band *extend to basal edge of wing*, but are *much smaller*. ♂ darker, wings much *less rounded* than ♀. ♀ less often encountered; flight slower. **Distribution:** Fynbos. Riviersonderend Mts above Boesmanskloof Pass and Greyton, W Cape. Also on Klipberg. **Habitat:** Mountains, rocky ledges. **Flight period:** Single-brooded, Dec–Jan, peak Dec. **Larval food:** No data.

1A

1B

2A

B

2C

A

3B

3C

A

4B

4C

1 Holmes's Skolly   *Thestor holmesi*
Wingspan: ♂ 26.5–35.5 mm ♀ 30.5–39.5 mm. **Identification: 1A** ♂ upper side, **1B** ♂ underside. ♂ darker than ♀, which has more rounded wings. Distinguished from Stephen's Skolly (p. 162) by having *larger* spots on forewing submarginal band on underside – extended to *basal edge*, unlike Pennington's Skolly (below). **Distribution:** More widely distributed than Stephen's Skolly. Fynbos. W Cape, Hawequas Mts and Jonkershoek (above old road tunnel in Du Toit's Kloof Pass). **Habitat:** Mountains, rocky ledges. **Flight period:** Single-brooded, Dec to early Jan. **Larval food:** No data.

2 Pennington's Skolly   *Thestor penningtoni*
Wingspan: ♂ 26–37 mm ♀ 32–41 mm. **Identification: 2A** ♂ upper side, **2B** ♀ upper side, **2C** ♂ underside, **2D** ♀ underside. ♀♀ often show upper side brown markings; underside, which is often paler, less well marked than that of the ♂. Similar to Holmes's Skolly (above), but lacks *dark discal spots* basal to CuA$_1$ on forewing underside. Submarginal band of dark spots extending to wing base in Holmes's and Stephen's (p. 162) Skollies *stop at CuA$_1$* in this species. **Distribution:** Fynbos. W Cape, from Swartberg Pass along Great Swartberg; Elandsberg north of Seweweekspoort; Keeromsberg and Waboomsberg; Hex River Mountains. **Habitat:** Mountains, rocky ledges. **Flight period:** Single-brooded, late Oct and Nov. **Larval food:** No data.

3 Basuto Skolly or Basuto Magpie   *Thestor basutus*
Wingspan: ♂ 30–39 mm ♀ 35–42 mm. **Identification: 3A** ♂ upper side, **3B** ♀ upper side (nominate); **3C** ♀ upper side, **3D** ♀ underside (*T. b. capeneri*). ♀ with extensive area of black-spotted white on the forewing upper side. Unique and unmistakable; does not fit into any of the Skolly groups. *Brown*, as opposed to buff or grey; build *more robust* than other Skollies and ♀ has distinctive white forewing upperside black and white markings. Usually small groups of three to six, occasionally larger numbers. 2 subspp., geographically distinct. **Distribution:** Most widespread *Thestor*; only species in the genus to be found north of South Africa. Nominate from E Cape (Cathcart), in Grassland and Savanna to Lesotho, KwaZulu-Natal Midlands, Free State, NW Province and N Cape; *T. b. capeneri* from Gauteng, Limpopo Province and Mpumalanga. **Habitat:** Hillsides, flatlands. **Flight period:** Double-brooded, Oct–Nov and Feb–Apr. **Larval food:** Larvae of nominate have been reared to third instar on psyllids (Homoptera), in nests of Pugnacious Ants *Anoplolepis custodiens*. *Thestor b. capeneri* larvae feed on *Pulvinaria iceryi* (Homoptera – Coccidae) until third instar; fourth and final instar larvae live inside nests of Pugnacious Ants, which feed them by trophallaxis; they also consume detritus and ant brood.

Subfamily LYCAENINAE

Large and diverse subfamily. The main distinguishing features of the adults are not constant; for example, the presence of tails on the hind wing. In South Africa, it is safe to say that all tailed lycaenids are Lycaeninae, but not all lycaenines carry tails. The tails, combined with an eye spot at the anal angle of the hind wing, often give the impression of a false head (which fools bird predators into attacking the wrong end of the butterfly!); but then, even if there are no tails, the eye spot is often present. When settled, lycaenines move their hind wings around in a circular motion, so that the tails resemble antennae, creating the effect of a 'false-head'. Adults in this subfamily all feed on nectar.

Genus *Iolaus*   Sapphires

AFRICA 120 SPP., SOUTH AFRICA 14

Spectacular lycaenids, upper side usually sapphire blue with a greater or lesser degree of dark patterning, one notable exception being yellow. Underside in many species white or grey – sometimes patterned with bright red or orange lines. Eyespot and tails at hind wing anal angle. Conspicuous; most ♂ ♂ congregate on hill tops at midday and fly at great speed, chasing one another. Adults feed on nectar. The young larvae eat grooves in the young leaves of food plants; older larvae eat whole leaves or flowers. Eggs are domed, with hexagonal indentations. Laid on growing shoots of parasitic plants of Olacaceae and Loranthaceae. Larva smooth-skinned, slug-shaped, extremely well camouflaged and sometimes outlandishly shaped. Pupa resembles a twig stub or lump of lichen.

1 Bowker's Sapphire   *Iolaus bowkeri*

Wingspan: ♂ 26–32 mm ♀ 29–41 mm. **Identification: 1A** ♂ upper side, **1B** ♂ underside (*I. b. tearei*). Sexes very similar, ♀ *less blue* on the upper side. Underside cryptic. Upper side and underside dark blotches distinctive to this and Dusky Sapphire (below). Flight slower than other sapphires. ♂ perches alert on or in prominent bushes on low rocky ridges, chasing intruders; ♀ more sedentary, usually near food plants. Both sexes attracted to flowers, such as Puzzlebush *Ehretia rigida*, sometimes in numbers. 3 subspp. **Distribution:** Widespread. Nominate in Savanna and Nama Karoo in W Cape and E Cape (Worcester to Leipoldtville), as well as Savanna in KwaZulu-Natal; *I. b. henningi* in Arid Savanna of Free State, and NW Province (Potchefstroom area) and N Cape; *I. b. tearei* from n KwaZulu-Natal to Mpumalanga, Gauteng and Limpopo Province, and moister n NW Province. **Habitat:** Flatlands, rocky ledges. **Flight period:** Continuous broods, Sept–May, peaks Oct and Mar. **Larval food:** Nominate and *I. b. henningi* on *Viscum rotundifolium*; *I. b. tearei* on *Ximenia caffra*, *X. americana*, *Viscum rotundifolium* and *Tapinanthus quinquangulus*.

2 Dusky Sapphire   *Iolaus subinfuscata reynoldsi*

Wingspan: ♂ 25–28 mm ♀ 27–30 mm. **Identification: 2A** ♀ upper side, **2B** ♀ underside. Sexes similar, ♀ with *more* white on upper side. *Smaller* than similar Bowker's Sapphire (above), *heavier black* forewing blotches, upper side blue *deeper, brighter.* Flight slow and fluttering, difficult to approach due to habit of settling on thorn bushes and crawling down a twig into the depths. ♂ ♂ congregate on top of thorn bushes on rocky ridges and red Kalahari sand dunes. Both sexes on flowers and near food plant. **Distribution:** Succulent Karoo and Arid Savanna in N Cape from Garies to Upington and Kuruman, north to Namibia and Botswana. **Habitat:** Flatlands, rocky ledges, hill tops. **Flight period:** Multiple summer broods, peaks Sept and Oct. **Larval food:** *Tapinanthus oleifolius.*

3 White Spotted Sapphire   *Iolaus lulua*

Wingspan: ♂ 26–30 mm ♀ 28–32 mm. **Identification: 3A** ♀ upper side, **3B** ♀ underside. Distinctive; upper side blue has *violet* shade, *broad black margins* and *dark streak across pale area of forewing*. Sexes similar, but ♀ has more white distal to upper side dark transverse streaks of both wings. Underside resembles common Azure Hairstreak (p. 174). Flight slow, settling on low bushes and flowers in thick bush. **Distribution:** Rare; restricted to n KwaZulu-Natal forested coastal dunes and sandy Lowland Forest, from False Bay to Kosi Bay, inland to Ndumu and Lebombo foothills. **Habitat:** Flatlands, coast. **Flight period:** Double brooded, Oct–Dec, and Mar. **Larval food:** *Helixanthera woodii* and other unidentified Loranthaceae.

1B

2B

3B

1 Southern Sapphire   *Iolaus silas*

Wingspan: ♂ 32–37 mm ♀ 34–41 mm. **Identification: 1A** ♂ upper side, **1B** ♀ upper side, **1C** ♂ underside. *Blue colouring* of ♂ intense; ♀ duller blue, *very broad* hind wing upper side red marginal band, and distal part of forewing upper side blue patch *suffused with white*. Both sexes with underside shiny white. ♂ flies around tall forest trees during midday hours, white underside conspicuous in sunlight; ♀ closer to food plant and low flowers. **Distribution:** From Nama Karoo in E Cape, along the eastern littoral from Addo Elephant NP to Somerset East and Bedford, along coastal Savanna and Lowland Forest into KwaZulu-Natal (to Eshowe). **Habitat:** Forest edges, coast. **Flight period:** Year-round in warmer areas. Sept–Jan in cooler, southern part of range. **Larval food:** *Moquinella rubra*, *Erianthemum dregei* and *Loranthus usuiensis*.

2 Straight-line Sapphire   *Iolaus silarus silarus*

Wingspan: ♂ 32–38 mm ♀ 35–40 mm. **Identification: 2A** ♂ upper side, **2B** ♀ upper side, **2C** ♂ underside. Forewings *more pointed* (in both sexes) than Southern Sapphire (above); ♀ has *less extensive* hind wing red marginal band on upper side. Transverse red hind wing line on underside generally but not reliably *straight*, not curved. ♀ often *lacks white* in forewing upper side blue. ♂ often on bushveld hill tops; ♀ on flowers and at food plants. **Distribution:** Warm, wooded savanna in n KwaZulu-Natal (coastal forest in Zululand); Savanna from Swaziland to Mpumalanga, Limpopo and NW provinces, and further north. Afromontane Forest on Wolkberg and n Drakensberg. **Habitat:** Forest edges, hill tops. **Flight period:** Year-round in warmer areas. Sept–Jan in cooler, western part of range. **Larval food:** *Erianthemum dregei*.

3 Trimen's Sapphire   *Iolaus trimeni*

Wingspan: ♂ 34–40 mm ♀ 36–42 mm. **Identification: 3A** ♂ upper side, **3B** ♀ upper side, **3C** ♀ underside. Superficially very similar to Straight-line Sapphire (above) but not closely related; early stages, genitalia very different. In adult, wings *more angular* than Straight-line Sapphire. ♂ brilliant blue, ♀ duller, powder blue. Hind wing underside transverse stripe *thin*, often *broken, black* not *red*, seldom extends as far as costa. ♂ exuberant hill topper, superb sight among *Protea* bushes on which most common food plant grows; ♀ seldom found far from food plant. **Distribution:** Grassland, Savanna, Arid Savanna from n KwaZulu-Natal (Hluhluwe) to Swaziland, Mpumalanga, Gauteng (common on Witwatersrand and Magaliesberg), and NW Province. **Habitat:** Hill tops, hillsides. **Flight period:** Year-round in warmer areas, peak Sept–Jan in cooler, western part of range. **Larval food:** *Tapinanthus oleifolius*, *T. quinquangulus*, *T. rubromarginatus* and *T. subulatus*.

4 Saffron Sapphire   *Iolaus pallene*

Wingspan: ♂ 30–35 mm ♀ 34–38 mm. **Identification: 4A** ♂ upper side, **4B** ♀ underside. Resembles a yellow-buff Pierid in flight, so common name is contradictory. Sexes similar. *Weaker, slower* flight than other *Iolaus* spp. ♂ defends territories in bush clearings, patrolling slowly as opposed to high speed of most *Iolaus* spp. ♀ near flowers and food plant. Seldom seen in numbers. **Distribution:** Widespread in wooded Savanna from thorn belt of KwaZulu-Natal (Estcourt to Weenen area, north to Tongaland), Swaziland to Mpumalanga, Gauteng (near Pretoria in Magaliesberg), Limpopo and NW provinces. **Habitat:** Forest edges, flatlands, hillsides. **Flight period:** Year-round in warmer areas, peaks spring and late summer; Sept–Feb in the cooler, south-western part of range. **Larval food:** *Ximenia caffra* and *X. americana*.

1A

1B

1C

2A

2B

2C

3A

3B

3C

4A

4B

1 Red-line Sapphire *Iolaus sidus*

Wingspan: ♂ 28–31 mm ♀ 29–32.5 mm. **Identification: 1A** ♂ upper side, **1B** ♀ upper side, **1C** ♂ underside. Easily identified *bright red underside lines*. ♂ *bright, metallic blue* with conspicuous *sex brand*. ♀ has white scaling surrounding blue, *less metallic* than ♂, dark submarginal lunules on hind wing upper side. ♂ on tall shrubs with shiny leaves at hill tops. ♀ on flowers and close to food plants. **Distribution:** Coastal woodland from E Cape (East London), through Savanna and thorn belt to Tongaland and Bedford, KwaZulu-Natal thorn belt (Estcourt to Weenen area) to Swaziland and Mpumalanga (Nelspruit area). **Habitat:** Forest edges, coast, hill tops. **Flight period:** Year-round, peaks in summer. **Larval food:** *Moquinella rubra, Tieghemia quinquenervia, Tapinanthus oleifolius, T. kraussianus, T. brunneus* and *T. subulatus*.

2 Mimosa Sapphire *Iolaus mimosae*

Wingspan: ♂ 26–31 mm ♀ 30–32 mm. **Identification: 2A** ♂ underside, **2B** ♂ upper side (*I. m. rhodosense*). Sexes similar, ♂ with wings more angular. Similar to Red-line Sapphire (above), powder blue, not metallic upper side. *I. m. rhodosense* has *paler, shinier upper side blue* and *paler grey* underside than nominate. Slow flight, similar to Bowker's Sapphire (p. 166). ♂ perches alert on or inside prominent bushes, chasing intruders; ♀ more sedentary, usually near food plants. Both sexes attracted to flowers. **Distribution:** Nominate in Nama Karoo and Arid Savanna from Little Karoo (Oudtshoorn) to Port Elizabeth and inland Savanna zone, Bedford to East London, E Cape; *I. m. rhodosense* widespread in Savanna across KwaZulu-Natal, to Mpumalanga, Gauteng (Magaliesberg), Limpopo and NW provinces, and N Cape. **Habitat:** Flatlands, rocky ledges, hill tops. **Flight period:** One or more broods, Sept–Mar, peak Oct–Nov. **Larval food:** *Moquinella rubra, Plicosepalus kalachariensis* and *Tapinanthus dicrous*.

3 Yellow-banded Sapphire *Iolaus aphnaeoides*

Wingspan: ♂ 26–28 mm ♀ 27–29 mm. **Identification: 3A** ♂ upper side, **3B** ♀ upper side, **3C** ♀ underside. ♀ with wings more rounded, and white edge to forewing upper side blue; area distal to hind wing upper side postdiscal transverse dark stripe *white*, not *blue* as in ♂. Upper-canopy dweller, ♂ adults seldom seen unless bred from larvae, but latter not difficult to find. ♀ usually flies near food plant. **Distribution:** Rare, restricted to Afromontane Forest of E Cape, along southern foothills of Winterberge, Bedford to Stutterheim, and low-altitude forests north of Port St Johns. **Habitat:** Forest edges. **Flight period:** Single-brooded, Oct–Jan. **Larval food:** *Tapinanthus kraussianus*.

4 Zimbabwe Yellow-banded Sapphire *Iolaus nasisii*

Wingspan: ♂ 26–28 mm ♀ 27–29 mm. **Identification: 4A** ♂ upper side, **4B** ♀ upper side, **4C** ♀ underside. *Broader* underside yellow bands than Yellow-banded Sapphire (above); *little or no* black edging. Sexes differ; ♂ hind wing upper side postdiscal transverse dark stripe *only penetrates top half of hind wing*, fully developed in ♀; white areas distal to dark stripe. ♂ around tall treetops and shrubs. **Distribution:** Forest and Savanna in far n Limpopo Province (Buffelsberg near Munnik and Musina area), north into Zimbabwe. **Habitat:** Forest edges, flatlands, rocky ledges. **Flight period:** Single-brooded, Oct–Mar in South Africa. **Larval food:** *Tapinanthus quinquangulus, T. brunneus, T. subulatus, T. dichrous, T. nyasicus, T. ceciliae* and *Oliverella rubroviridis*.

1 Natal Yellow-banded Sapphire   *Iolaus diametra natalica*
Wingspan: ♂ 26–28 mm ♀ 27–29 mm. **Identification: 1A** ♂ upper/underside, **1B** ♀ upper side, **1C** ♀ underside. Very similar to Yellow-banded Sapphire (p. 170), but paler yellow underside streaks, *double* (not single) *very narrow black line* running up hind wing underside anal edge from anal spot. Compared to other Sapphires, flight slow; may fly close to ground. Flies away rapidly if disturbed. ♀ closer to food plant. Both sexes fond of flowers. **Distribution:** Uncommon and rare, but most widespread of Yellow-banded Sapphires. Lowland Forest and thickly wooded Savanna in n KwaZulu-Natal (Richards Bay to Kosi Bay and further north), inland to Muden and Estcourt. **Habitat:** Forest edges, flatlands, rocky ledges, hill tops. **Flight period:** Single-brooded, Jul–Dec, peak Oct. **Larval food:** *Actinanthella wylliei.*

2 Brown-line Sapphire   *Iolaus alienus alienus*
Wingspan: ♂ 33–37 mm ♀ 35–40 mm. **Identification: 2A** ♂ upper side, **2B** ♀ upper side, **2C** ♀ underside. Sexes similar, ♀ outer edge of blue patches *suffused with white*, hind wing upper side has *dark submarginal stripe.* Distinctive *grey-mottled* underside. ♂ on prominent hill tops (usually seen after 14h00), settling on exposed twigs; chases intruders. ♀ also visits hill tops in search of a mate (as late as 17h00); more likely to be found around food plant. **Distribution:** Widespread, locally common in Savanna from n KwaZulu-Natal to Swaziland, Mpumalanga, Gauteng, and Limpopo and NW provinces. **Habitat:** Hill tops. **Flight period:** Double-brooded. Mainly Aug–Nov, peak Sept. Sometimes Apr–May. **Larval food:** *Tapinanthus brunneus, T. subulatus, Oliverella rubroviridis* and *Helixanthera kirkii.*

3 Short-barred Sapphire   *Iolaus aemulus*
Wingspan: ♂ 25.5–29.5 mm ♀ 26–29 mm. **Identification: 3A** ♂ upper side, **3B** ♀ upper side, **3C** ♂ underside. Underside white with *red* bands broken into *spots.* ♂ upper side resembles Red-line Sapphire (p. 170). ♀ upper side blue, suffused with white; hind wing upper side has dark transverse and submarginal stripes. ♂ flies around prominent bushes and trees at the summit of dunes, usually only after 13h00. **Distribution:** Wooded hills and dunes, along E Cape coast (East London) to KwaZulu-Natal (Burman Bush, Durban), and as far as Ndumu in Zululand. **Habitat:** Forest edges, coast. **Flight period:** Year-round, mainly Sept–May, peaks Nov and Feb/Mar. **Larval food:** *Tieghemia quinquenervia.*

Genus *Hypolycaena*   Hairstreaks   WORLD 46 SPP., AFRICA 31, SOUTH AFRICA 4
South African species generally not as brightly coloured and tails shorter than those found further north in Africa. More sedentary than *Iolaus* sapphires. Underside usually white to grey with distinctive pattern of lines. Flight slow. Found in thick bush and forests, along paths and in clearings, often on flowers. ♂ perches on prominent twigs on bushes. Fond of mud patches, particularly when urine-soaked. Egg a flat-topped dome with hexagonal indentations. Laid on growing shoots of food plant. Smooth-skinned, slug-like larva is well camouflaged. Pupa squat, rounded and usually green.

4 Purple-brown Hairstreak   *Hypolycaena philippus philippus*
Wingspan: ♂ 22–28 mm ♀ 23.5–31 mm. **Identification: 4A** ♂ upper side, **4B** ♀ upper side, **4C** ♀ underside. Hind wing tails conspicuous. ♀ *lacks* purple sheen of ♂, and has *two* white hind wing upper side submarginal white bands, *larger* anal lunules, tails longer. **Distribution:** Common and widespread in Savanna, Lowland and Riverine Forest from E Cape (East London), along coast and inland to Swaziland, Mpumalanga, Gauteng, and Limpopo and NW provinces, and beyond. **Habitat:** Forest edges, parks and gardens, flatlands, coast. **Flight period:** Year-round in warmer areas, peaks Nov and Mar/Apr. **Larval food:** *Clerodendrum glabrum, Ximenia caffra* and *X. americana, Deinbollia oblongifolia, Vangueria* spp. and *Maytenus senegalensis.*

1 Coastal Hairstreak *Hypolycaena lochmophila*

Wingspan: ♂ 22–28 mm ♀ 23.5–31 mm. **Identification: 1A** ♂ upper side, **1B** ♂ underside, **1C** ♀ upper side, **1D** ♀ underside. Upper side *darker* and underside *paler* grey than in Purple-brown Hairstreak (p. 172). Forewing underside postdiscal stripe *bends towards submarginal stripe* in areas CuA$_1$ and CuA$_2$, unlike Purple-brown Hairstreak, in which it is *parallel* to submarginal stripe. ♀ has greater tendency to *pale* forewing upper side discal area than ♀ Purple-brown Hairstreak. Shyer than latter, seldom far away from thick bush. **Distribution:** Rare; only in Lowland Forest in n KwaZulu-Natal (Hluhluwe/False Bay area to Kosi Bay and further north, inland to Makhathini Flats). **Habitat:** Forest edges, coast. **Flight period:** Year-round, peaks Nov and Mar/Apr. **Larval food:** *Deinbollia oblongifolia.*

2 Buxton's Hairstreak *Hypolycaena buxtoni buxtoni*

Wingspan: ♂ 25–30 mm ♀ 28–33 mm. **Identification: 2A** ♂ upper side, **2B** ♀ upper side, **2C** ♂ underside. Resembles tropical *Hypolycaena*, with *very long tails.* Sexes dimorphic. ♂ upper side iridescent *steel blue*, ♀ upper side *white discal bands* on grey-black ground. *Bright white* underside of both sexes conspicuous in flight. Fairly slow flight along forest edge, settling frequently on shrubs. **Distribution:** Lowland and Riverine Forest from Kei River to Kosi Bay (KwaZulu-Natal) and north. **Habitat:** Forest edges. **Flight period:** Double-brooded, Sept–May, peak Oct/Nov, and Feb–May, peak Mar/Apr. **Larval food:** No data from South Africa.

3 Azure Hairstreak *Hypolycaena caeculus caeculus*

Wingspan: ♂ 30–35 mm ♀ 34–38 mm. **Identification: 3A** ♂ upper side, **3B** ♀ upper side (f. *caeculus*), **3C** ♀ underside (f. *dolores*). Only South African *Hypolycaena* sp. with *iridescent blue* upper side. ♂ *deeper, brighter blue* than ♀, wings *more angular.* DSF f. *dolores* with underside *darker* than WSF f. *caeculus*, stripes *narrower*, upper side blue *less extensive.* May swarm under correct conditions in Nov. Found around thick bush clearings, woodland edges and hill tops. Fond of mud puddles. **Distribution:** Dry wooded Savanna from Swaziland and Mpumalanga across Limpopo and NW provinces. Follows riverine bush into Arid Savanna. **Habitat:** Forest edges, hill tops, flatlands, rocky ledges. **Flight period:** Year-round, with prominent peaks after rains. Form *caeculus* Nov–Apr, f. *dolores* May–Oct. **Larval food:** *Olax dissitiflora* and *O. obtusifolia.*

Genus *Leptomyrina* Black-eyes   AFRICA 9 SPP., SOUTH AFRICA 4

Characteristic white-ringed black eye at the forewing upper side tornus. Flight fairly slow, in small clearings in low vegetation and between large rocks. Egg laid on the surface of leaves of Crassulaceae. Domed with hexagonal indentations. Green, slug-shaped larva lives inside the leaves of these succulents. Pupa squat, rounded, green to brown, formed in food plant debris.

4 Tailed Black-eye *Leptomyrina hirundo*

Wingspan: ♂ 19–24 mm ♀ 19.5–26 mm. **Identification: 4A** ♀ upper side, **4B** ♀ underside. Unmistakable; *long white tails.* Sexes almost identical. Can be common near food plant, but inconspicuous. Flutters slowly close to the ground, settles often on low leaves, not easily flushed. **Distribution:** Localised. Warm wooded Savanna from E Cape (Uitenhage) to coastal KwaZulu-Natal, and inland in Riverine Forest to Swaziland, Mpumalanga and Limpopo Province; lowveld to high up in warm mountains (Soutpansberg). One high-altitude record from Lesotho. **Habitat:** Forest edges, flatlands, gullies. **Flight period:** Year-round in warmer areas, peaks Nov and Mar. **Larval food:** *Kalanchoe, Crassula* and *Cotyledon* spp.

1 Cape Black-eye *Leptomyrina lara*

Wingspan: ♂ 20–29 mm ♀ 23–31 mm. **Identification: 1A** ♂ upper side, **1B** ♂ underside. Sexes similar, ♀ with wings more rounded. Distinctive bright *bronze-brown* upper side; easy to confuse with other small brown lycaenids frequenting rocky Karoo and fynbos scrublands. ♂ chases intruders. Fond of rocky slopes and low ridges from sea level to high mountain peaks. Low, zigzagging flight. **Distribution:** Fynbos, Nama Karoo and Succulent Karoo throughout W Cape to E Cape, e Free State and Lesotho mountains, and N Cape. **Habitat:** Hill tops, rocky ledges, mountains. **Flight period:** Several broods in spring and summer, Aug–Apr. **Larval food:** *Kalanchoe lugardii* and *Cotyledon orbiculata*.

2 Henning's Black-eye *Leptomyrina henningi*

Wingspan: ♂ 18.5–29 mm ♀ 25–32 mm. **Identification: 2A** ♂ upper side, **2B** ♀ underside. *Larger* than Cape Black-eye (above), with more *angular* wings. Unlike Common Black-eye (below), *dull* basal colouring but with some shiny scaling in ♂. ♀ similar, but lacks shiny basal wing scaling; wings more rounded. Found near food plants. **Distribution:** Savanna, Arid Savanna, Grassland from Free State to Gauteng, Limpopo and NW provinces and further west. **Habitat:** Hill tops, rocky ledges, mountains. **Flight period:** Year-round, peaks Nov and Mar. **Larval food:** *Cotyledon orbiculata* and *Crassula alba*.

3 Common Black-eye *Leptomyrina gorgias gorgias*

Wingspan: ♂ 18.5–29 mm ♀ 25–32 mm. **Identification: 3A** ♂ upper side, **3B** ♂ underside. Closest to Henning's Black-eye (above) in appearance (underside very similar), but *extensive mauve-grey* basal scaling on ♂ upper side. Underside very similar to previous species. Sexes similar. **Distribution:** Savanna, Arid Savanna, Grassland from E Cape to KwaZulu-Natal, Mpumalanga and w Limpopo Province. **Habitat:** Hill tops, rocky ledges, mountains. **Flight period:** Year-round, peaks Nov and Mar. **Larval food:** *Kalanchoe, Crassula* and *Cotyledon* spp.

Genus *Capys* Proteas

AFRICA 15 SPP., SOUTH AFRICA 3

Medium to large lycaenids, fast-flying and robust. Upper side grey-brown to bronze, orange or red; underside cryptically marked. ♂ forms territories at hill tops, chasing intruders. ♀ larger, heavier build; slower, more stately flight. Usually only seen near food plants. Egg laid singly on side of unopened immature flower buds of Proteaceae. Bun-shaped, with fine tracery of ribs and concentric lines; prominent micropyle. Larva bores into side of the bud, where it eats the immature seeds in the ovary. It grows large and grub-like, and eventually enlarges a hole at the base of the bud. Brown, rounded pupa formed inside the bud.

4 Orange-banded Protea or Protea Scarlet *Capys alphaeus*

Wingspan: ♂ 31–40 mm ♀ 32–47 mm. **Identification: 4A** ♂ upper side, **4B** ♀ upper side, **4C** ♂ underside (*C. a. extentus*). Unmistakable *broad red bands* in both sexes; underside also colourful. Most brightly coloured *Capys*. ♂ familiar, glorious sight buzzing along mountain and hill tops. Small numbers found at all times except midwinter. Endemic to South Africa; 2 subspp. **Distribution:** Nominate in Fynbos, Nama and Succulent Karoo from Cape Peninsula to Kouebokkeveld Mts and s Namaqualand, W Cape, to E Cape (Port Elizabeth area); *C. a. extentus* in Grassland from E Cape (Amatolas) along mountains to e Free State and KwaZulu-Natal Drakensberg, Swaziland, Mpumalanga and Limpopo Province. **Habitat:** Hill tops, mountains. **Flight period:** Two main broods: Aug–Nov and Feb–Apr. **Larval food:** Flower buds of *Protea* spp., including *P. cynaroides, P. roupelliae, P. subvestita, P. repens* and *P. grandiceps*.

1B

2B

3B

4B

4C

1 Pennington's Protea *Capys penningtoni*
Wingspan: ♂ 32–40 mm ♀ 34–47 mm. **Identification: 1A** ♂ upper side, **1B** ♂ underside. Upper side solid bronze with narrow dark margins. Sexes similar, ♂ deeper red-bronze than ♀, wings more angular. Flies with Orange-banded Protea *C. alphaeus extentus* (p. 176), which usually outnumbers it. Rarely seen, despite abundant food plant. **Distribution:** Rare; restricted to KwaZulu-Natal Drakensberg foothills (Bulwer Mountain, and high ridges such as Lundy's Hill) near Umkomaas River valley in Grassland. **Habitat:** Hill tops, mountains. **Flight period:** Single-brooded, mid-Sept to early Nov. **Larval food:** Flower buds of *Protea caffra*.

2 Russet Protea *Capys disjunctus disjunctus*
Wingspan: ♂ 31–37 mm ♀ 31.5–38 mm. **Identification: 2A** ♂ upper side, **2B** ♀ upper side, **2C** ♂ underside. Most widespread Protea butterfly in South Africa, only one to show dimorphism in sexes. ♂ upper side resembles Pennington's Protea (above) but *smaller, brighter bronze-red* with *wider* dark margins; underside also similar to Pennington's. ♀ upper side *dove-grey* above with russet edges, sometimes a buff forewing apical streak. **Distribution:** Grassland and Savanna from E Cape (Amatolas) to KwaZulu-Natal (close to sea level), inland to Swaziland, Mpumalanga, Gauteng (Witwatersrand and Magaliesberg) and Limpopo Province. **Habitat:** Hill tops, mountains, hillsides. **Flight period:** Double-brooded, Aug–Oct and Jan–Mar, sometimes as late as Apr. **Larval food:** Flower buds of *Protea caffra, P. welwitschii, P. angolensis, P. gazensis* and *P. petiolaris*.

Genus *Deudorix* Playboys
WORLD CA. 120 SPP., AFRICA 91, SOUTH AFRICA 7
Small butterflies, with short, single hind wing tails. Flight fast and buzzing, ♂ found at hill tops and on prominent shrubs at forest edges. Both sexes very fond of flowers. In South African species, upper side is brown, grey or orange-red, underside cryptically marked. Further north, species have brilliant blue upper sides. Egg bun-shaped, with fine tracery of ribs and concentric lines; prominent micropyle. Laid singly on the side of seed pods and stem galls, where the slug-shaped, sparsely haired larva feeds internally until fully grown; brown, rounded pupa formed inside the empty shell.

3 Orange-barred Playboy *Deudorix diocles*
Wingspan: ♂ 26–36 mm ♀ 29–41 mm. **Identification: 3A** ♂ upper side, **3B** ♀ upper side, **3C** ♂ underside. Bright *orange-and-black* ♂ upper side, purple shot. ♀ dull, blue-grey. Underside cryptic in both sexes. ♂ conspicuous when chasing other butterflies; usually returns to same perch on high forest edge leaves. ♀ on flowers and close to food plant. **Distribution:** Common and widespread. Lowland and Riverine Forest along east coast from E Cape (Port St Johns) to KwaZulu-Natal, to Lebombos, north along foothills of escarpment to Mpumalanga, Limpopo Province and Zimbabwe. **Habitat:** Forest edges, coast. **Flight period:** Year-round, peaks Sept and Mar. **Larval food:** Fruits and seeds of *Bauhinia galpinii, Milletia grandis, M. sutherlandii, Caesalpinia pulcherrima* and *Baphia racemosa;* also peaches, plums and *Prunus* spp.

4 Black-and-orange Playboy *Deudorix dariaves*
Wingspan: ♂ 23–25 mm ♀ 28–33 mm. **Identification: 4A** ♂ upper side, **4B** ♂ underside, **4C** ♀ upper side. ♂ upper side forewing black shot with purple, *no* orange patch. ♀ much duller. ♂ spends midday whirling around tree tops; seen usually early morning or late afternoon with ♀ on flowers. **Distribution:** Rarer, more localised than Orange-barred Playboy (above). Lowland and Riverine Forest along KwaZulu-Natal coast, from Durban to sand forests of Kosi Bay, where it is quite common. Also north along escarpment foothill forests into Mpumalanga, Limpopo Province and Zimbabwe. **Habitat:** Forest edges, coast, gullies. **Flight period:** Year-round, peaks Sept and Apr–Jun. **Larval food:** Fruit of *Deinbollia oblongifolia* and *Hyperacanthus amoenus*.

A

1B

2A

B

2C

3A

B

3C

4A

B

4C

1 Orange Playboy *Deudorix dinomenes*

Wingspan: ♂ 24–30 mm ♀ 26–32 mm. **Identification: 1A** ♂ upper side, **1B** ♀ upper side, **1C** ♂ underside. Sexually dimorphic, ♂ upper side spectacular *flame-orange* shot with yellow-gold, purple androconial spot on hind wing underside costa, *narrow black margin* at forewing apex. ♀ upper side dull blue-grey. Underside of both sexes has bright red spots and lines. Wary, easily disturbed; usually keeps to canopy, seldom seen. Occasionally in numbers on flowers of *Deinbollia* and Lamiaceae. **Distribution:** Lowland Forest along KwaZulu-Natal coast. Sparse south of the Tugela, but quite numerous in Tongaland sand forests. **Habitat:** Forest edges, coast. **Flight period:** Year-round, peak Apr–Jul. **Larval food:** Probably fruits of *Deinbollia* spp.

2 Apricot Playboy *Deudorix dinochares*

Wingspan: ♂ 24–30 mm ♀ 26–32 mm. **Identification: 2A** ♂ upper side, **2B** ♀ upper side, **2C** ♂ underside. ♂ with upper side conspicuous orange, but less fiery than Orange Playboy (above); *grey-brown margins spread to forewing anal angle.* ♀ upper side brown to grey. Underside of both sexes cryptic. ♂ on hill tops and koppies; rapid, whirring flight. ♀ flies slowly. Both sexes found on flowers near food plants. **Distribution:** Common and widespread in Savanna and Lowland Forest, from n KwaZulu-Natal to Swaziland, Mpumalanga, Limpopo and NW provinces and Gauteng. **Habitat:** Hill tops, rocky ledges. **Flight period:** Year-round, peaks Sept–Oct and Mar–May. Sometimes common in midwinter in n Limpopo Province. **Larval food:** Fruits of *Combretum zeyheri, Burkea africana, Syzygium cordatum, Gardenia volkensii* and *Pseudolachnostylis maprouneifolia.*

3 Brown Playboy *Deudorix antalus*

Wingspan: ♂ 22–34 mm ♀ 22–40 mm. **Identification: 3A** ♂ upper side, **3B** ♀ upper side, **3C** ♀ underside. ♀ an attractive *pale blue-grey;* ♂ *dull brown,* with shifting purple sheen over upper side. Size extremely variable, depending on size of larval food seeds. ♀ usually on flowers. ♂ strongly territorial, on hill tops, prominent trees and shrubs, or rocks. **Distribution:** Most widespread and common *Deudorix* sp. Throughout South Africa in all biomes; absent only from the highest mountains. **Habitat:** Forest edges, parks and gardens, hill tops, flatlands, coast, rocky ledges. **Flight period:** Year-round, peaks Sept–Oct and Mar–May. **Larval food:** Fruits of *Haplocoelum gallense, Schotia afra, Faidherbia albida, Syzygium guineense* and *Ximenia caffra.*

4 Van Son's Playboy *Deudorix vansoni*

Wingspan: ♂ 20–23 mm ♀ 20–26 mm. **Identification: 4A** ♂ upper side, **4B** ♀ upper side, **4C** ♂ underside. Resembles *small, dark* Brown Playboy (above). ♂ *dark brown,* ♀ *grey-blue.* Rarely seen because it keeps to the tree tops, occasionally at hill tops. **Distribution:** Lowland Forest and Savanna from n KwaZulu-Natal to Swaziland, along Lebombo foothills to s Mpumalanga and further north. **Habitat:** Forest edges, hill tops. **Flight period:** Year-round, peak Sept–Oct. **Larval food:** Stem galls on twigs of *Acacia burkei.*

5 Pennington's Playboy *Deudorix penningtoni*

Wingspan: ♂ 20–23 mm ♀ 20–26 mm. **Identification: 5** ♂ upper side. Appearance and habits very similar to Van Son's Playboy (above). ♀ indistinguishable from that butterfly. Only difference between the ♂♂ is that this species has forewing upper side *red triangular patch.* **Distribution:** Wooded Savanna of n KwaZulu-Natal and s Mpumalanga; along Lebombo foothills, and s Limpopo Province (Waterberg and east to Leolo Mtns). **Habitat:** Hill tops, forest edges. **Flight period:** Sparingly all year, peak Sept–Oct; in Limpopo Province, main brood Apr–Jun. **Larval food:** Stem galls on twigs of *Acacia burkei.*

A

1B

1C

A

2B

2C

A

3B

C

4A

4B

C

5

Genus *Myrina*   Fig-tree blues   AFRICA 5 SPP., SOUTH AFRICA 2

Medium-sized lycaenids, characterised by long, thick tails and brilliantly iridescent blue upper side markings. Underside is dead-leaf mimic. Flight quick, jerky, around tops of trees and shrubs on hill tops and prominent clearings in bush. Eggs laid singly on fresh growth or young fruit of Moraceae trees and shrubs; domed, with hexagonal indentations. Larva slug-shaped, cryptically marked in green, brown and white, attended by ants on the food plant (larvae do not enter the nests). Pupa squat, rounded, marked in green and brown; formed among leaf debris or in bark crevices.

1 Common Fig-tree Blue   *Myrina silenus*

Wingspan: ♂ 26.5–34.0 mm ♀ 33–41 mm. **Identification: 1A** ♀ upper side, **1B** ♀ underside (*M. s. ficedula*). Sexes similar, ♂ with forewing upper side apical chestnut patch smaller, blue more mirror-like. Underside cryptic. Found wherever food plants grow. ♂ hill tops at midday, also along rocky ridges. In woodland, both sexes settle often on trees. **Distribution:** Common and widespread in Succulent Karoo, Lowland Forest and Savanna. *Myrina silenus ficedula* from W Cape (Mossel Bay, Knysna), to KwaZulu-Natal, Free State, Mpumalanga, Gauteng and Limpopo and NW provinces; *M. s. penningtoni* from Clanwilliam (W Cape) to Springbok (N Cape). **Habitat:** Forest edges, parks and gardens, rocky ledges, hill tops. **Flight period:** Year-round, peaks Sept–Oct and (in eastern areas) Apr–Jun. **Larval food:** *Ficus* spp., including *F. cordata* (*M. s. penningtoni*), *F. sur, F. pumila* and *F. ingens*.

2 Lesser or Scarce Fig-tree Blue   *Myrina dermaptera dermaptera*

Wingspan: ♂ 26–32 mm ♀ 30–38 mm. **Identification: 2A** ♂ upper side, **2B** ♀ upper side, **2C** ♂ underside. ♂ *intensely iridescent blue*. Extent of blue variable, sometimes reduced to none in late summer specimens. ♀ may have hardly any blue; what there is, is *powder blue*. Underside cryptic. Flies with Common Fig-tree Blue (above) along forest edges and on hill tops, sometimes emerging in swarms near food plant. **Distribution:** Lowland Forest from E Cape (East London) along coast to Kosi Bay, KwaZulu-Natal and along Mpumalanga/Limpopo Province escarpment foothills to Soutpansberg. **Habitat:** Forest edges, hill tops, rocky ledges. **Flight period:** Year-round, strong peaks Nov and Apr–Jun. **Larval food:** *Ficus sur, F. thonningii* and *F. natalensis.*

Genus *Aphnaeus*   High-fliers   AFRICA 22 SPP., SOUTH AFRICA 1

Large lycaenids, ♀ heavier than ♂. Underside often spectacularly marked with pearly spots, upper side an iridescent blue. Forewings triangular; narrow hind wings carry two small tails at anal angle. ♂ territorial; flight rapid, direct, usually around hill tops, ridges or prominent trees. ♀ usually found around food plants. Eggs laid singly on twigs and young shoots of trees of Fabaceae. Bun-shaped, with prominent pattern of criss-cross ribs forming hexagons divided into triangles. Young larvae live on leaves and twigs but, after third instar, move into holes inhabited by *Crematogaster* ants, from which they emerge at night to feed. Larvae flattened dorsally, with lateral hairs and mottled grey-brown appearance. Pupa brown, elongated abdomen, rounded thorax and head.

3 Hutchinson's High-flier   *Aphnaeus hutchinsonii*

Wingspan: ♂ 29.5–33.0 mm ♀ 32–43 mm. **Identification: 3A** ♂ upper side, **3B** ♀ underside. *Silver spots on underside* conspicuous. Sexes similar, but ♀ has tiny white streak in distal edge of forewing blue of area CuA$_2$, *absent in ♂*. ♂ perches on prominent hill top bushes. ♀ less often seen except near food plant. **Distribution:** Savanna from n KwaZulu-Natal (Estcourt through thorn country to Lebombo foothills) to Gauteng, Mpumalanga and Limpopo Province (Magaliesberg and Daspoortrant). **Habitat:** Hill tops. **Flight period:** Single brood Sept–Jan, peak Oct–Nov. **Larval food:** *Acacia robusta, Burkea africana, Loranthus* and *Viscum* spp.

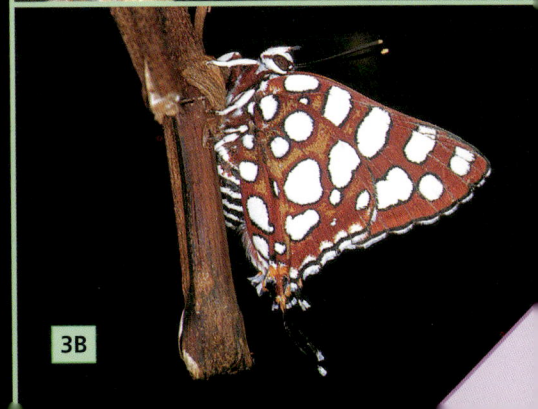

Genus *Cigaritis* Bars

WORLD CA. 40 SPP., AFRICA 36, SOUTH AFRICA 5

Small, active butterflies with more convex forewing outer margin than *Aphnaeus*; sexes similar, ♀ heavier build. Upper side characterised by dark bars on a paler background orange, often with blue reflective scaling at the wing bases. Underside with dark bars on a paler ground, usually with silvery sheen or spots. Two short hind wing tails (one is stunted or absent in some species). ♂ has rapid, whirring, direct flight; found on hill tops and rocky ridges. Egg bun-shaped, with prominent pattern of criss-cross ribs forming hexagons divided into triangles; laid singly on shoots of wide variety of host plants; larva flattened dorsally, with lateral hairs and mottled grey-brown appearance, sheltering in holes occupied by *Crematogaster* or *Pheidole* ants. Pupa brown, rounded head and thorax, elongated abdomen.

1 Natal Bar   *Cigaritis natalensis*

Wingspan: ♂ 25–32.5 mm ♀ 26.5–34 mm. **Identification: 1A** ♂ upper side, **1B** ♂ underside, **1C** ♀ upper side. Sexes similar, ♀ with more white in forewing cell on upper side. In KwaZulu-Natal and E Cape, f. *obscurus* has forewing apex on upper side covered with blackish scaling. ♂ often settles upside down, with half-open wings. Both sexes found on flowers and at mud puddles. **Distribution:** Widespread and common, but densities usually low. Wooded Savanna and wooded hill tops in Grassland from E Cape (Port Elizabeth) along coast to KwaZulu-Natal (Kosi Bay), to Swaziland, Free State, Mpumalanga, Gauteng, Limpopo and NW provinces, and parts of the N Cape. **Habitat:** Hill tops, rocky ledges. **Flight period:** Year-round, peaks Sept–Oct and Mar–May. **Larval food:** *Canthium inerme, Clerodendron glabrum* and *Ximenia caffra.*

2 Mozambique Bar   *Cigaritis mozambica*

Wingspan: ♂ 22–25 mm ♀ 25–28 mm. **Identification: 2A** ♀ upper side, **2B** ♂ underside. Darker than other *Cigaritis* spp.; underside has *deep orange* bars on cream ground. Sexes similar, ♀ with wings more rounded. Unlike other butterflies in the genus, found in *concentrated colonies* on hillsides and at base of hills. ♂ flies rapidly around grassy hillside territories, never far from food plant. Both sexes attracted strongly to flowers. **Distribution:** Widespread but localised. Grassland, and grassy Savanna, from KwaZulu-Natal coast to Drakensberg, to Swaziland, Free State, Gauteng, Mpumalanga, Limpopo and NW provinces. **Habitat:** Hillsides, flatlands. **Flight period:** Year-round, but more common Sept–May; peaks late summer. **Larval food:** *Sphenostylis angustifolia.*

3 Silvery Bar   *Cigaritis phanes*

Wingspan: ♂ 24–27 mm ♀ 26–30 mm. **Identification: 3A** ♂ upper side, **3B** ♀ upper side, **3C** ♂ underside. Sexes dimorphic; ♂ upper side deep steel to violet blue with royal blue iridescent sheen; orange apical patches carry typical *Cigaritis* dark bars. ♀ upper side orange-buff with dark bars covering whole surface; silvery blue colour confined to wing bases; *lacks* blue upper side flush of ♂. Underside of both sexes *pale chestnut*, with *wavy silver-white* bars (width variable). ♂ territorial on flat ground or hillsides, perching on low thorny bushes and shrubs. Sometimes swarms with pierids around *Vernonia* flowers in winter. **Distribution:** Widespread in Savanna and Arid Savanna from nw KwaZulu-Natal to n Free State, Gauteng, Mpumalanga, Limpopo and NW provinces and N Cape to north of the Orange R. **Habitat:** Flatlands, hillsides, rocky ledges. **Flight period:** Year-round, peaks Sept–Nov and Mar–Jun. **Larval food:** *Acacia mellifera* and *Ximenia caffra.*

A

1B

E

2A

B

3A

B

3C

1 Namaqua Bar   *Cigaritis namaquus*

Wingspan: ♂ 22–25 mm ♀ 24–28 mm. **Identification: 1A** ♂ upper side, **1B** ♀ upper side, **1C** ♀ underside. Similar to Silvery Bar (p. 184), but *smaller* and *darker,* underside silvery hind wing bars broken into spots, not wavy bars. ♂ upper side orange apical patch *almost obscured* by purple-blue basal colour. ♀ upper side *lacks* whitish-blue wing base scaling on the upper side. Rapid flight around low, dry bushes on lower slopes of hills. Fond of flowering mesembs. **Distribution:** Restricted to Succulent Karoo, from extreme N Cape (Namibian border) to n W Cape (Namaqualand). **Habitat:** Hillsides. **Flight period:** Single-brooded, Sept–Dec, peak Oct. **Larval food:** Possibly *Zygophyllum* spp.

2 Ella's Bar   *Cigaritis ella*

Wingspan: ♂ 21–24 mm ♀ 25–30 mm. **Identification: 2A** ♂ upper side, **2B** ♀ upper side (f. *ella*), **2C** ♂ underside (DSF f. *junodi*). Small *Cigaritis,* forewing submarginal dark bar running from the apex to base, *not* stopping halfway or zigzagging. Sexes similar, ♀ paler. DSF f. *junodi* has underside ground colour *buff,* with *poorly defined* brownish stripes. WSF f. *ella* has ground colour similar to Natal Bar (p. 184). ♂ extremely pugnacious hill-topper. **Distribution:** Wooded Savanna, and wooded hill tops in Grassland from E Cape (Port Elizabeth) along coast to KwaZulu-Natal (Kosi Bay), inland to Swaziland, Free State, Mpumalanga, Gauteng, Limpopo and NW provinces, and N Cape. **Habitat:** Hill tops, rocky ledges. **Flight period:** Year-round, peaks Aug–Oct and Mar–Jul. Often only butterfly seen in highveld midwinters. **Larval food:** *Ximenia caffra.* Larvae hide in crevices and under the bark.

Genus *Chloroselas*   Gems   AFRICA 13 SPP., SOUTH AFRICA 2

Tiny butterflies, flight *direct, rapid*; easily overlooked. Dark upper side with shifting iridescent lustre only visible when viewed from certain angles. Underside cryptic; pale ground colour spotted with darker marks and silvery scaling. Both sexes often found on flowers. Egg laid on Fabaceae (*Acacia* and *Brachystegia*); bun-shaped; with prominent pattern of criss-cross ribs forming hexagons divided into triangles. Larva brown, flattened dorsally and carrying short bristles. Pupa brown, rounded head and thorax, elongated abdomen.

3 Brilliant Gem   *Chloroselas pseudozeritis pseudozeritis*

Wingspan: ♂ & ♀ 20–24 mm. **Identification: 3A** ♂ upper side, **3B** ♀ upper side, **3C** ♂ underside. Shifting *blue iridescence* of ♂ upper side very beautiful, but only visible when viewed from the correct angle. ♀ has same gold-spotted underside, *dull brown* above, sometimes with buff patch in middle of forewing on upper side. Occasionally in strong colonies, but more often in groups of 6–8. **Distribution:** Wooded Savanna from E Cape (Grahamstown area) to KwaZulu-Natal (Kosi Bay), inland across thorn country to Estcourt, Mpumalanga, and Limpopo and NW provinces. **Habitat:** Hill tops. **Flight period:** Year-round, peaks Sept–Nov and Mar–May. **Larval food:** Unknown in South Africa; possibly young shoots of *Acacia* spp. Further north, larvae live in tunnels in twigs of *Julbernardia globiflora.*

4 Purple Gem   *Chloroselas mazoensis*

Wingspan: ♂ 20–24 mm ♀ 22–25 mm. **Identification: 4A** ♂ upper side, **4B** ♀ upper side, **4C** ♂ underside. Underside similar to Brilliant Gem (above), but *lacks* gold spotting. Iridescence *purple, less shiny* than blue of Brilliant Gem; covers *more* of ♂ upper side. ♀ upper side *flat* dull brown to black. **Distribution:** Rarer, more localised than Brilliant Gem. Wooded Savanna in n KwaZulu-Natal (Lebombo foothills and Makhatini Flats), Mpumalanga, and Limpopo and NW provinces. **Habitat:** Hill tops. **Flight period:** Main brood Sept–Dec, small May/Jun emergence in n KwaZulu-Natal. **Larval food:** Possibly young shoots of *Acacia* spp.

A

1B

1C

A

2B

2C

A

3B

3C

A

4B

4C

Genus *Axiocerses*   Scarlets   AFRICA 20 SPP., SOUTH AFRICA 4

Small butterflies, upper side characteristically red with black markings. Rapid, darting flight, ♂ often at hill tops, settling on bare twigs with wings open. Both sexes found on flowers. Eggs laid on fresh growth of food plant; bun-shaped, with prominent pattern of criss-cross ribs forming hexagons divided into triangles. Larva dorsally flattened, slug-shaped, green or brown with darker markings; feeds on fresh growth, hides during daylight hours in shelters made from folded leaves, or under loose bark or stones, attended by *Crematogaster* and *Pheidole* ants. Pupa brown, mottled with darker brown or black; rounded head and thorax, elongated abdomen.

1 Common Scarlet   *Axiocerses tjoane tjoane*

Wingspan: ♂ 24–32 mm ♀ 25–34 mm. **Identification: 1A** ♂ upper side, **1B** ♀ underside (ovipositing on *Acacia*), **1C** ♂ underside. ♂ upper side red with black markings. ♀ with rounder wings, and usually *paler*, with pattern of *black spots*. Underside of both sexes cryptic. ♀ usually found close to the food plants. **Distribution:** Widespread and abundant. Grassland and wooded Savanna from E Cape (Grahamstown area) to KwaZulu-Natal, Mpumalanga, Gauteng, and Limpopo and NW provinces. **Habitat:** Hill tops, flatlands, hillsides. **Flight period:** Year-round, peaks Sept–Nov and Mar–May. **Larval food:** *Acacia polyacantha, A. karroo* and *A. sieberana*.

2 Dark-banded Scarlet   *Axiocerses croesus*

Wingspan: ♂ 24–32 mm ♀ 25–34 mm. **Identification: 2A** ♂ upper side, **2B** ♀ upper side, **2C** ♂ underside. Sexes dimorphic as in Common Scarlet (above); ♂ with *more extensive* dark markings than Common Scarlet; dark hind wing *submarginal band of lunular spots* on upper side. ♀ has similar band, where Common Scarlet has spots. **Distribution:** Flies with Common Scarlet in southern part of range, but usually in less arid areas. Wooded Savanna and Riverine Forest in E Cape as far west as Port Elizabeth, spreading into s KwaZulu-Natal. **Habitat:** Hill tops, hillsides, flatlands. **Flight period:** Year-round in the north, peaks Sept–Oct and Feb–May; double-brooded in the south, Sept–Oct and Feb–May. **Larval food:** *Acacia* spp.

3 Black-tipped Scarlet   *Axiocerses coalescens*

Wingspan: ♂ 24–32 mm ♀ 25–34 mm. **Identification: 3A** ♂ upper side, **3B** ♂ underside, **3C** ♀ upper side. ♂ forewing *almost totally black* on upper side, with orange-red patch at basal edge. ♀ resembles Common and Dark-banded Scarlets (above), difficult to tell apart. Underside of both sexes cryptic. **Distribution:** Wooded Savanna in Gauteng, Mpumalanga, and Limpopo and NW provinces, and further north. **Habitat:** Hill tops, hillsides, flatlands. **Flight period:** Year-round, peaks Oct–Nov and Mar–Apr. **Larval food:** *Acacia* spp.

4 Bush Scarlet   *Axiocerses amanga amanga*

Wingspan: ♂ 24–28 mm ♀ 25–30 mm. **Identification: 4A** ♂ upper side, **4B** ♂ underside. Sexes *similar, dark veins* in orange on forewing of upper side, has *broad* pearl-white basal streak on forewing costa on underside, *large* basal white spots with *little or no* black border. ♀ has rounder wings, upper side paler orange. *Colonial* breeder, never far from food plants. ♂ defends small territories around grassy clearings, settling on low bushes and herbs. Feeds on flowers; sometimes also on tree sap. **Distribution:** Wooded Savanna and Lowland Forest from KwaZulu-Natal to Mpumalanga, Gauteng, and Limpopo and NW provinces, and further north. **Habitat:** Flatlands, hillsides. **Flight period:** Year-round, peaks Sept–Nov and Mar–May. **Larval food:** *Ximenia caffra* and *X. americana*.

Genus *Phasis*   Arrowheads

4 SPP., ALL ENDEMIC TO SOUTH AFRICA

Medium-sized to large lycaenids. Restless, wary, difficult to approach closely, capable of a considerable turn of speed if molested. Colonial breeder. Both sexes feed on flowers. Upper side brown to black with chequered markings of copper-orange. Upper side of sexes similar, ♂ darker than ♀. Cryptic underside. Hind wing has silver or white discal marks – distinctive to each species. Eggs laid singly on shoots of the food plant. Bun-shaped, with prominent micropyle depression; very fine pattern of ribs forming triangular cells, with tiny bulges where the ribs meet. Larva flattened dorsally; brown to green with short bristles and prominent tubercles on penultimate segment. It lives in hollowed-out twigs of the food plants (Anacardiaceae and Melianthaceae), attended by *Crematogaster* ants, or in carton nests of the ants themselves. Pupa dark brown, elongated with rounded head and thorax.

1 Silver Arrowhead   *Phasis thero*

Wingspan: ♂ 31–46 mm ♀ 38–47 mm. **Identification: 1A** ♀ upper side, **1B** ♂ underside. Sexes similar, ♀ *larger, paler* than ♂. Underside pale discal mark has *flat* edge towards costa, another pale mark basal to it. One of the larger Fynbos and Karoo lycaenids. 2 subspp. **Distribution:** Fynbos, Nama Karoo in W Cape. Nominate in Fynbos from Cape Peninsula (where common), north along coast to Lambert's Bay, east to Knysna; *P. t. cedarbergae* from Cederberg, and Gifberg near Vanrhynsdorp. **Habitat:** Flatlands, coast, rocky ledges. **Flight period:** Nominate double-brooded, Sept–Nov and Mar–May; *P. t. cedarbergae* Oct–Nov, probably also autumn brood. **Larval food:** *Rhus undulata* and *Melianthus major.* Larvae found inside hollow stems of plants, and carton nests of *Crematogaster peringueyi* ants at base of stems.

2 Namaqua Arrowhead   *Phasis clavum*

Wingspan: ♂ 29–39.5 mm ♀ 35–44 mm. **Identification: 2A** ♂ upper side (nominate), **2B** ♂ underside (*P. c. erythema*). *Single* hind wing tails, wing margins *smooth*, hind wing upper side *lacks* submarginal orange band found in other Arrowheads; underside discal mark *T-shaped*. Sexes similar, ♀ paler, more extensively orange. Feeds on flowers of food plants as well as mesembryanthemums. 2 subspp. **Distribution:** Nominate in montane Fynbos in W Cape from Worcester to Het Kruis, Succulent Karoo and Nama Karoo through Namaqualand to Steinkopf (N Cape), east to Roggeveld Escarpment; *P. c. erythema* in Nama Karoo high on Roggeveld near Sutherland. **Habitat:** Rocky ledges, mountains, hill tops. **Flight period:** Single-brooded, Sept–Nov, sometimes into Jan. **Larval food:** *Rhus* spp.

3 Brauer's Arrowhead   *Phasis braueri*

Wingspan: ♂ 32–42 mm ♀ 36–45 mm. **Identification: 3A** ♂ upper side, **3B** ♀ upper side, **3C** ♂ underside. Similar to Silver Arrowhead (above), but with *more extensive* orange upper side marking, *smaller, rounder, single* silver streak on underside. Wary and agile, easily flushed; flight fast, undulating. Close to food plant on rocky ridges and hill tops in mountainous country. **Distribution:** Nama Karoo from Little Karoo (Oudtshoorn) in W Cape to Queenstown (E Cape); may be common in Cradock district. **Habitat:** Rocky ledges, mountains, hill tops. **Flight period:** Single-brooded, Sept–Jan, peak Nov. **Larval food:** *Rhus longispina.*

4 Pringle's Arrowhead   *Phasis pringlei*

Wingspan: ♂ 32–38 mm ♀ 36–43 mm. **Identification: 4A** ♀ underside, **4B** ♂ upper side, **4C** ♀ upper side. Upper side resembles Silver Arrowhead (above). Underside ground colour distinctive *fawn brown*, hind wing discal silvery markings small. Close to large rocks and cliff bases, near food plant. **Distribution:** Nama Karoo. Restricted to Roggeveld escarpment (Sutherland, Verlatekloof and Voelfontein area), N Cape. **Habitat:** Mountains, rocky ledges. **Flight period:** Single-brooded, Sept–Dec, peak Nov. **Larval food:** *Melianthus* spp.

Genus *Tylopaedia*   King Copper   MONOTYPIC; ENDEMIC TO SOUTH AFRICA

Medium to large-sized, robust and fast flying. ♂ on hill tops or rocky ridges; territorial. Wary, difficult to approach; flutters rapidly around small bushes. ♀ usually found on flowers. Both sexes fond of wet mud. Eggs laid on shoots of the food plant. Bun-shaped, with prominent micropyle depression; very fine pattern of ribs forming triangular cells, with tiny bulges where the ribs meet. Larvae flattened dorsally; brown to green with short bristles and prominent tubercles on penultimate segment. Larva shelters under stones adjacent to the food plants (Anacardiaceae, Rhamnaceae and Fabaceae); attended by *Crematogaster* ants. Pupa brown, elongated with rounded head and thorax, also under stones.

1 King Copper   *Tylopaedia sardonyx*

Wingspan: ♂ 32–40 mm ♀ 35–50 mm. **Identification: 1A** ♂ upper side, **1B** ♀ underside (nominate), **1C** ♂ underside (*T. s. peringueyi*). Sexes similar. Black markings on upper side usually extensive; in very arid areas, reduced to a few forewing costal spots. Nominate has white discal hind wing stripe on underside; *T. s. peringueyi* has only faint dark line. **Distribution:** Nominate in Nama Karoo, Succulent Karoo and Arid Savanna from e W Cape north to Namaqualand and near Kuruman, N Cape, n into Botswana, east to E Cape and Free State (Springfontein area); *T. s. peringueyi* in Fynbos and Succulent Karoo on low hills north of Piketberg, Het Kruis to Klawer, W Cape. **Habitat:** Hill tops, rocky ledges. **Flight period:** Two broods: Aug–Dec and Jan–Apr. **Larval food:** *Aspalathus spinosa* and *Phylica olaefolia* (*T. s. peringueyi*); also *Euclea undulata*.

Genus *Argyraspodes*   Warrior Silver-spotted Copper   MONOTYPIC; ENDEMIC TO SOUTH AFRICA

Striking Karoo lycaenid, very closely related to *Trimenia*. Large, robust and fast. Flight rapid and powerful, fairly close to the ground and usually circling widely back to the original perch from which it was flushed. ♂ ascends to the tops of koppies and rocky ridges, and defends territories there. Life history unknown.

2 Warrior Silver-spotted Copper   *Argyraspodes argyraspis*

Wingspan: ♂ 32–38 mm ♀ 35–45 mm. **Identification: 2A** ♀ upper side, **2B** ♂ underside. *Silver spots* on brown hind wing underside. Larger ♀ wings broader, rounder than ♂, visits hill tops in late afternoon. Both sexes frequent flowers on lower ground. **Distribution:** Widespread and abundant. Fynbos, Nama Karoo and Succulent Karoo in W Cape, E Cape, s Free State and N Cape. **Habitat:** Hill tops, rocky ledges. **Flight period:** Aug–Mar (sometimes Jul–Apr). **Larval food:** No data.

Genus *Trimenia*   Silver-spotted Coppers   SOUTH AFRICA 5 SPP.

Usually has orange-red upper side with black markings and margins; underside hind wing with metallic (shiny) spots or cursive streaks. Fast and low flight, ♂ perching on rocks or low vegetation and setting off to chase other insects. Colonial breeder, sometimes in very small numbers. Does not fly far from colony. Life history little known. Egg bun-shaped, pale blue or grey to whitish-yellow, covered in tiny polygonal depressions. Larvae flattened dorsally; brown to green with short bristles and prominent tubercles on penultimate segment.

3 Wallengren's Silver-spotted Copper   *Trimenia wallengrenii*

Wingspan: ♂ 24–35 mm ♀ 29–42 mm. **Identification: 3A** ♂ upper side, **3B** ♀ upper side, **3C** ♂ underside (*T. w. gonnemoi*). Magnificent underside has *cursive* silvery marks. Sexes similar, ♀ orange markings *paler*, wings *rounder*, hind wing margin *more scalloped*. Occurs in huge numbers under good conditions. **Distribution:** Very rare and localised. Nominate only in Fynbos on hills near Darling, W Cape; several strong colonies of *T. w. gonnemoi* confined to upper slopes of Piketberg, W Cape. **Habitat:** Rocky ledges. **Flight period:** Single-brooded, Nov–Dec. **Larval food:** No data.

1 Large Silver-spotted Copper *Trimenia argyroplaga*
Wingspan: ♂ 25–34 mm ♀ 29–41 mm. **Identification: 1A** ♂ upper side, **1B** ♂ underside (*T. a. cardouwae*), **1C** ♀ upper side (nominate). Resembles Wallengren's Silver-spotted Copper (p. 192), but underside markings *rounded spots.* Sexes similar, ♀ with wing margins *more scalloped,* orange markings *paler.* **Distribution:** Widespread and abundant. Nominate in Nama and Succulent Karoo; in Great Karoo and Little Karoo from W Cape to E Cape; grassy savanna near Grahamstown; also in N Cape (Namaqualand); *T. a. cardouwae* Olifantsrivierberge above Porterville, W Cape. **Habitat:** Hill tops, rocky ledges. **Flight period:** Single-brooded, Nov–Dec. **Larval food:** No data.

2 Wykeham's Silver-spotted Copper *Trimenia wykehami*
Wingspan: ♂ 24–32 mm ♀ 27–39 mm. **Identification: 2A** ♂ upper side, **2B** ♀ upper side, **2C** ♀ underside. Similar to Large Silver-spotted Copper (above), but upper side orange area suffused with *more dark scaling.* Generally darker; silver hind wing underside spots more *uniformly sized;* outer wing margin *straighter* on forewing. **Distribution:** Nama Karoo. Great Karoo mountains from Beaufort West (Nuweveldberge) to Roggeveld escarpment, W Cape. **Habitat:** Hill tops, rocky ledges. **Flight period:** Single-brooded, Nov–Dec. **Larval food:** No data.

3 McMaster's Silver-spotted Copper *Trimenia macmasteri*
Wingspan: ♂ 24–32 mm ♀ 27–39 mm. **Identification: 3A** ♂ upper side, **3B** ♂ underside (*T. m. mijburghi*). ♀ with orange upper side markings *much paler* than ♂. Hind wing underside silver spotting *bold and unelaborate.* Frequents dry riverbeds. 2 subspp. **Distribution:** Widespread in Fynbos, Nama Karoo, and Succulent Karoo. Nominate in W Cape from Great Karoo along coastal hills in Little Karoo to E Cape (Queenstown, Uitenhage and Port Elizabeth); *T. m. mijburghi* in Namaqualand and Bushmanland, N Cape, and northwards. **Habitat:** Rocky ledges, flatlands, wetlands. **Flight period:** Single-brooded, Sept–Jan, peak Oct–Dec. **Larval food:** No data.

4 Scarce Mountain Copper *Trimenia malagrida*
Wingspan: ♂ 24–29 mm ♀ 29–33 mm. **Identification: 4A** ♂ upper side, **4B** ♀ underside (*T. m. maryae* brown form), **4C** ♂ underside (*T. m. paarlensis* red form). *Wings rounder* than in other *Trimenia* spp. ♀ with upper side ground colour *paler orange,* wings *rounder* than ♂. Underside hind wing ground colour brown to red. 4 subspp., all rare, with limited ranges. **Distribution:** W Cape Fynbos; nominate in Cape Peninsula; *T. m. paarlensis* Paarl Mountain and Paardeberg; *T. m. cedrusmontana* Cederberg and Skurweberg; *T. m. maryae* in coastal dune fynbos from De Hoop to Witsand. **Habitat:** Rocky ledges, coast, hillsides. **Flight period:** Single-brooded, late Jan–Mar. **Larval food:** Larvae of *T. m. maryae* attended by *Anoplolepis custodiens* ants; no data on food.

Genus *Aloeides* Coppers
AFRICA 57 SPP., SOUTH AFRICA 49

Small butterflies, upper side usually brown to orange or copper, with dark borders. Underside ground colour variable, hind wing cryptic. Flight low, jinking to escape pursuit. ♂ defends territories on bare patches of ground and rocky ledges, settling on ground, low vegetation or prominent rocks. ♀ near food plants, less easily flushed, more wandering flight. Colonial. Eggs laid on low-growing food plants of Fabaceae, Zygophyllaceae, Sterculiaceae and Malvaceae, sometimes in or on the earth close by. Pale pink to cream or pale yellow, flattened domes to bun-shaped; covered in fine reticulated patterns of ribs. Larva flattened dorsally, bluntly tapered at both ends, whitish green to blue or buff, striped or lined diagonally with reddish brown to green. Pupa green to yellow or brown, rounded at both ends. Associated with *Lepisiota* and *Pheidole* ants, usually sheltering with them during the day and emerging to feed on plants at night, but sometimes fed by ants, or predacious on ant brood. *Aloeides* are very similar to one another, so we have grouped confusing species to aid in identification.

Roodepoort Copper group

Upper side bright orange to red-orange with medium to wide dark margins. Medium to large Coppers. Hind wing underside discoidal fascia and submarginal row of dentate spots large as in Transvaal Copper group but *continuous and complete*. Red Copper; Roodepoort Copper; Rossouw's Copper; Riley's Copper; Wakkerstroom Copper; Giant Copper; Pringle's Copper; Brauer's Copper; Kaplan's Copper; Mbulu Copper.

1 Red Copper   *Aloeides thyra*

Wingspan: ♂ 22–26 mm ♀ 24–28 mm. **Identification: 1A** ♂ upper side, **1B** ♂ underside, **1C** ♀ underside. Sexes similar, ♀ with wings rounder, orange marks penetrate post-cell area of forewing upper side. Markings variable – upper side dark veins sometimes reduced, hind wing ground colour varies from grey-brown through red-brown, to purplish crimson on underside. Hind wing underside discal spots large and partly joined into roughly X-shaped discoidal fascia. The outer edge of this is uneven and not parallel to the outer margin. Submarginal serrated row of spots present but broken and discontinuous. **Distribution:** Abundant in coastal Fynbos. Nominate from Cape Peninsula, north-west to Lambert's Bay and east to Matjiesfontein; *A. t. orientis* Stilbaai to Knysna, W Cape. **Habitat:** Flatlands, coast, mountains, rocky ledges **Flight period:** Several broods through warmer months; Jul–Apr, peaks Oct and Feb. **Larval food:** *Aspalathus acuminata, A. laricifolia,* and *A. cymbiformis*. Larvae associate with *Lepisiota capensis* ants.

2 Roodepoort Copper   *Aloeides dentatis*

Wingspan: ♂ 22–26 mm ♀ 24–28 mm. **Identification: 2A** ♂ upper side, **2B** ♂ underside. Sexes similar, ♀ paler than ♂, with rounder wings. Underside ground colour from fawn to red-brown and bright crimson. Serrated discal fascia well marked; lines of basal spots and distinct scalloped submarginal line of merged spots all *silver, distally edged black*. Found in disturbed areas in Grassland. **Distribution:** Rare and localised Grassland species. Nominate in sandy grassveld in Gauteng – Ruimsig, Roodepoort, where a reserve has been established to protect the species, and Suikerbosrand NR near Heidelberg; *A. d. maseruna* in scattered colonies in sandy grassveld of Free State and NW Province. **Habitat:** Flatlands, mountains. **Flight period:** Double-brooded, Aug–Nov and Feb–Mar. **Larval food:** *Hermannia depressa* and *Lotononis eriantha* (nominate); *Hermannia jacobeifolia* (*A. d. maseruna*). Larvae associate with *Lepisiota capensis* ants.

3 Rossouw's Copper   *Aloeides rossouwi*

Wingspan: ♂ 22–26 mm ♀ 24–28 mm. **Identification: 3A** ♂ upper side, **3B** ♀ upper side, **3C** ♂ underside. Underside silver markings *narrower, more regular, less* distal black shading; upper side resembles Transvaal Copper (p. 202). Usually a few orange spots in forewing upper side black apical patch. Often with crimson ground colour on underside, but some more brownish. ♀ larger and with rounder wings than ♂. **Distribution:** Rare. Grassland on sandy highveld. Mpumalanga south of Stoffberg; possibly also from De Berg and Verloren Valei near Dullstroom, and high above Waterval Boven. **Habitat:** Mountains, rocky ledges. **Flight period:** Double-brooded, Sept–Nov and Feb–Mar. **Larval food:** No data.

4 Riley's Copper   *Aloeides rileyi*

Wingspan: ♂ 24–28 mm ♀ 26–30 mm. **Identification: 4A** ♂ upper side, **4B** ♂ underside. Resembles large Oreas Copper (p. 210); cilia *chequered grey and black*, forewing upper side orange patch pointed at apex where it joins black apical patch. Underside hind wing *olive- to grey-brown;* toothed discoidal marking forms *dark silver-grey band distally edged black.* ♀ paler, rounder wings, more sedentary habits than ♂. Found on rocky ledges in montane grassland. **Distribution:** Grassland. Sour montane grassveld in Lesotho, and e Free State (Golden Gate Highlands NP). **Habitat:** Hillsides, mountains. **Flight period:** Single-brooded, Nov–Feb. **Larval food:** No data.

1 Wakkerstroom Copper   *Aloeides merces*

Wingspan: ♂ 24–28 mm ♀ 26–30 mm. **Identification: 1A** ♂ upper side, **1B** ♀ upper side, **1C** ♀ underside. Sexes similar, ♀ *paler,* with wings rounder than ♂. Similar to Riley's Copper (p. 196). Forewing apex orange patch on upper side *more rounded.* Hind wing underside warmer colour, sometimes bright red, *less well-defined* markings; *lacks* black marginal spots. Colonial breeder on mountain peaks. **Distribution:** Rare. Sour montane grassveld in KwaZulu-Natal (Amajuba) and Mpumalanga (Hele Mtn near Wakkerstroom, and Hlangampisi, near Dirkiesdorp). **Habitat:** Hill tops, hillsides, rocky ledges. **Flight period:** Single-brooded, Oct–Nov. **Larval food:** No data.

2 Giant Copper   *Aloeides pallida*

Wingspan: ♂ 30–39 mm ♀ 34–45 mm. **Identification: 2A** ♂ upper side, **2B** ♂ underside (nominate), **2C** ♀ underside (*A. p. grandis*, brown form), **2D** ♀ underside (*A. p. littoralis*, red form). Sexes similarly marked, but ♀ more heavily built than ♂; among largest of *Aloeides*. *Bright orange* upper side, underside coloration varies from fawn to crimson with *well-defined* basal, discal and submarginal rows of dentate spots merged to form silver-grey bands edged black. ♂ territorial on rocky outcrops and ledges; ♀ found at random on hillsides below where ♂♂ congregate. **Distribution:** Widespread but localised. Nominate in Grassland and Nama Karoo from W Cape (Matjiesfontein) to E Cape (Graaff-Reinet), north to Free State (Springfontein); *A. p. grandis* in montane Fynbos from mountain's above Paarl and Franschhoek north to Gydo Mtn and east to Garcia's Pass; *A. p. littoralis* in coastal Fynbos from Hermanus to Knysna, W Cape; *A. p. juno* in Fynbos in E Cape (Nature's Valley and Kareedouw); *A. p. jonathani* in montane Fynbos in Kammanassie Mtns, W Cape; *A. p. liversidgei* in E Cape Baviaanskloof Mtns. **Habitat:** Hill tops, rocky ledges, coast, mountains. **Flight period:** Single-brooded: nominate as early as Aug, other subspecies Oct to early Jan. **Larval food:** Nominate and *A. p. jonathani* on *Aspalathus* spp; *A. p. grandis* fed by trophallaxis by *Lepisiota capensis* ants, as well as feeding on its eggs.

3 Pringle's Copper   *Aloeides pringlei*

Wingspan: ♂ 30–34 mm ♀ 32–36 mm. **Identification: 3A** ♂ upper side, **3B** ♀ upper side, **3C** ♀ underside. Sexual size difference similar to *A. pallida*. Upper side *black* wing margins *narrower*, hind wing ground colour *darker* on underside, *less robust* build than Giant Copper (above). Very similar to Mbulu Copper (p. 200), but black and silver-grey dentate markings on hind wing underside *narrower, more finely etched.* Both sexes found around bare patches of rocky ground among grass. **Distribution:** Confined to a few localities in Grassland of E Cape, Great Winterberg. **Habitat:** Mountains, rocky ledges. **Flight period:** Single-brooded, Nov–Dec. **Larval food:** No data.

4 Brauer's Copper   *Aloeides braueri*

Wingspan: ♂ 26–28 mm ♀ 28–32 mm. **Identification: 4A** ♂ upper side, **4B** ♀ upper side, **4C** ♂ underside. Sexes similar, ♀ paler than ♂ with wings rounder. *Pale orange* with *grey-brown*, as opposed to black, upper side markings; *narrow, even,* dark margins. Underside fawn to red-brown; silver discal 'tooth' markings appear *faded;* less well defined than Mbulu Copper (p. 200) or Pringle's Copper (above). Found on rough, rocky hill slopes where they fly rapidly up- and downhill. **Distribution:** Highland hillsides covered in sour grassveld in E Cape (Queenstown, and Cathcart area). Single record from Nsututse Pass, s Lesotho. **Habitat:** Hillsides. **Flight period:** Double-brooded, Oct–Nov and Jan–Feb. **Larval food:** No data.

1A

1B

1C

A

2B

2C

D

3A

3B

C

4A

B

4C

1 Kaplan's Copper   *Aloeides kaplani*

Wingspan: ♂ 28–32 mm ♀ 30–40 mm. **Identification: 1A** ♂ upper side, **1B** ♀ upper side, **1C** ♂ underside. Size variable, sexes similar. *Broad* upper side black margins. Underside ground from pale sandy brown to pink, discoidal fascia *restricted to wing centre.* Habits as Giant Copper (p. 198). **Distribution:** W Cape, bare patches of ground in arid Nama Karoo (mountain renosterveld); Roggeveld escarpment to Matjiesfontein, Nuweveldberge near Beaufort West. **Habitat:** Mountains, rocky ledges, hillsides. **Flight period:** Single-brooded, Sept–Dec, peak Oct. **Larval food:** No data.

2 Mbulu Copper   *Aloeides mbuluensis*

Wingspan: ♂ 26–32 mm ♀ 29–37 mm. **Identification: 2A** ♂ upper side, **2B** ♀ upper side, **2C** ♂ underside. Sexes similar. Resembles Brauer's Copper (p. 198), *deeper* upper side orange. Upper side generally *duskier* than larger Giant or Pringle's Coppers (p. 198). Underside as Pringle's Copper but dentate markings *broader, more diffuse.* **Distribution:** Bare patches of ground in highland sour grassveld in Mbulu area, E Cape, and near Loteni, KwaZulu-Natal. **Habitat:** Hillsides, rocky ledges. **Flight period:** Single-brooded, Nov–Jan. **Larval food:** No data.

Dune Copper group

Upper side pale copper-orange to deep orange with distinctive *narrow* dark margins; underside has discoidal fascia and dentate submarginal spots similar to Transvaal Copper group. Dune Copper, Bampton's Copper, Nolloth's Copper, Van Son's Copper.

3 Dune Copper   *Aloeides simplex*

Wingspan: ♂ 26–32 mm ♀ 29–34 mm. **Identification: 3A** ♂ upper side, **3B** ♀ underside. Sexes similar, ♀ with wings rounder. Upper side attractive *bright golden orange.* Underside ground colour chestnut to *sandy brown; well-defined* basal spots, strongly *zigzagged* discal series, *not fused,* and *bright white* submarginal marks. ♂ flight rapid, jinking and low, difficult to follow; only returns to original perch after some time. ♀ less active, flight wandering. **Distribution:** Sandy areas in Kalahari Arid Savanna, red dunes from Kuruman, Hotazel and further west (N Cape). **Habitat:** Flatlands. **Flight period:** Double-brooded, Aug–Nov and Jan–Mar, depending on rains. **Larval food:** No data.

4 Bampton's Copper   *Aloeides bamptoni*

Wingspan: ♂ 20–24 mm ♀ 22–26 mm. **Identification: 4A** ♂ upper side, **4B** ♀ upper side, **4C** ♀ underside. Sexes similar, ♂ more pointed wings. Resembles Dune Copper (above), but *smaller;* orange on upper side *deeper, duller; wider* black margins *extending down forewing costa.* Hind wing *darker, dingier* brown, spotting *hardly visible* on underside. **Distribution:** Succulent Karoo (Namaqualand broken veld) in N Cape (Steinkopf, Springbok to Komaggas Hills and north to Richtersveld). **Habitat:** Rocky ledges, flatlands. **Flight period:** Single-brooded, Aug–Dec; possible second brood in late-summer (Mar–Apr). **Larval food:** No data.

5 Nolloth's Copper   *Aloeides nollothi*

Wingspan: ♂ 19–22 mm ♀ 20–24 mm. **Identification: 5A** ♂ upper side, **5B** ♂ underside. Sexes similar, ♀ with wings rounder, flight slower. Similar to Bampton's Copper (above), but *smaller, paler – underside spots visible through orange of upper side.* Cilia more *strongly chequered, wider* dark forewing border extends *halfway along costa* on upper side. Forewing *angled* ('rétroussé') halfway along costa, clearly visible. Hind wing underside *darker* than Dune Copper (above), spotting *better defined* than Bampton's Copper. ♂ has more pointed apex than ♀. **Habitat:** Coast. **Distribution:** Coastal dunes and flats in Succulent Karoo (west coast strandveld) in N Cape (Port Nolloth to Hondeklip Bay), and a few kilometres inland, south along coast almost to Lambert's Bay. **Flight period:** Single-brooded, Aug–Dec; possible second brood in late-summer (Mar–Apr). **Larval food:** No data.

A

1B

1C

A

2B

2C

A

3B

4A

B

4C

A

5B

1 Van Son's Copper   *Aloeides vansoni*

Wingspan: ♂ 27–32 mm ♀ 29–35 mm. **Identification: 1A** ♂ upper side, **1B** ♀ upper side, **1C** ♂ underside. Sexes similar, ♀ with rounder wings. Robust butterfly. Wings *more pointed* than others of Dune Copper group, upper side black borders *broader*. Underside deep, rich *brown to red tone*, large, *very diffuse* markings. ♂ on hill tops and rocky ledges at midday; flight rapid, close to ground. Settles abruptly on or below rocks with closed wings. ♀ on flat areas below the rocks where ♂ flies. **Distribution:** Widely distributed in W Cape Nama Karoo, across Great Karoo and Roggeveld escarpment, south along north side of Swartberg and neighbouring mountains to E Cape. **Habitat:** Hill tops, rocky ledges, mountains. **Flight period:** Single spring and midsummer brood, Sept–Jan, peak Dec. **Larval food:** No data.

Transvaal Copper group

Both surfaces similar to Red Copper (p. 196), but bright orange to orange-red upper side has veins that are *not* darkened and the hind wing upper side costa is *not* extensively dark. Hind wing underside discal spots as in Red Copper – large and partly joined into discoidal fascia. The outer edge of this is uneven and not parallel to the outer margin. Submarginal row of dentate spots present but broken and discontinuous. Transvaal Copper, Pennington's Copper, Tite's Copper, Dickson's Copper, Border Copper, Juana Copper, Caledon Copper, Cederberg Copper, Worcester Copper, Carolynn's Copper, Marguerite's Copper, Pointed Copper and Depicta Copper.

2 Transvaal Copper   *Aloeides dryas*

Wingspan: ♂ 26–31 mm ♀ 28–34 mm. **Identification: 2A** ♀ upper side, **2B** ♂ underside, **2C** ♀ underside. Sexes similar, ♀ with wings rounder, upper side *paler orange* than ♂. Medium-sized, *brightly coloured* Copper; forewing upper side dark borders of *even width*, cilia *uniformly coloured*. Underside hind wing red-brown to scarlet with *well-defined* serrated silver discoidal fascia and submarginal band of dentate spots. **Distribution:** Grassland, Riverine Forest, Afromontane Forest from Swaziland to n KwaZulu-Natal (often close to Afromontane Forest) and Mpumalanga (Barberton); along Drakensberg and Wolkberg to Polokwane and Tzaneen, and Soutpansberg (Limpopo Province). **Habitat:** Hillsides, hill tops, mountains, forest edges. **Flight period:** Several broods through warmer months, Sept to as late as Jun, peaks Nov and Feb. **Larval food:** *Lotononis* spp.

3 Pennington's Copper   *Aloeides penningtoni*

Wingspan: ♂ 26–31 mm ♀ 28–34 mm. **Identification: 3A** ♂ upper side, **3B** ♂ underside. Sexes similar, ♂ with more pointed wings. Similar to Transvaal Copper (above). Upper side orange *paler*, cilia *chequered*. Wings less *square*, forewing apical patch on upper side *triangular*. Hind wing underside red-brown to scarlet, *greyish-silver* bands of marks, *no dark edges*. Colonies on hill tops and ridges. **Distribution:** Grassland of n E Cape and Drakensberg foothills (Kokstad), to KwaZulu-Natal Midlands and Ngoye and Enseleni forests in the north. **Habitat:** Hillsides, rocky ledges, hill tops, mountains. **Flight period:** Several broods through warmer months, Aug–Jun, peaks Nov and Feb. **Larval food:** No data.

4 Tite's Copper   *Aloeides titei*

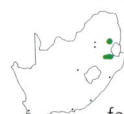

Wingspan: ♂ 25–30 mm ♀ 26–33 mm. **Identification: 4A** ♂ upper side, **4B** ♀ upper side, **4C** ♂ underside (red form), **4D** ♀ underside (brown form). ♀ with wings rounder. Upper side similar to Pennington's Copper (above), wings more elongated. Paler hind wing underside ground colour. *Very well-defined* silver serrated discoidal fascia, basal spots and submarginal series, *with dark edges*. Two main underside colour phases, red and brown. ♀ flies with ♂ in colonies on hill tops and ridges. **Distribution:** Grassland from n KwaZulu-Natal Drakensberg foothills (Amajuba), to s Mpumalanga hills near Wakkerstroom, Dirkiesdorp and Piet Retief. **Habitat:** Hillsides, rocky ledges, hill tops, mountains. **Flight period:** Single-brooded, Nov–Feb. **Larval food:** No data.

1 Dickson's Copper *Aloeides dicksoni*

Wingspan: ♂ 25–30 mm ♀ 26–33 mm. **Identification: 1A** ♀ upper side, **1B** ♀ underside. Sexes similar. Similar to Pennington's Copper (p. 202). Antennae *brown*, not black; hind wing underside colour *paler*, silvery grey marking *less well defined*, cilia *more chequered*. Flies at high altitude but not on peaks. **Distribution:** Grassland, Nama Karoo. E Cape Drakensberg, from Winterberge to Gaika's Kop. **Habitat:** Rocky ledges, mountains. **Flight period:** Single-brooded, Oct–Dec. **Larval food:** No data.

2 Border Copper *Aloeides caffrariae*

Wingspan: ♂ 25–30 mm ♀ 26–33 mm. **Identification: 2A** ♂ upper side, **2B** ♀ upper side, **2C** ♀ underside. *Pale antennae and upper side orange* as Dickson's Copper (above), but *narrower* black forewing upper side borders; *dark* underside hind wing with *prominent silver marks* as Pennington's Copper (p. 202). Smaller than both. ♀ paler, with wings rounder than ♂. ♂ sits on bare patches of ground and flies off after other ♂ ♂, soon returning to original site. ♀ more sedentary. **Distribution:** Coastal Grassland in E Cape, from East London to Alexandria. **Habitat:** Coast. **Flight period:** Two or more broods in summer, from Oct–Mar. **Larval food:** No data.

3 Juana Copper *Aloeides juana*

Wingspan: ♂ 29–34 mm ♀ 30–38 mm. **Identification: 3A** ♂ upper side, **3B** ♂ underside. Similar to Van Son's Copper (p. 202), but *larger*, more robust; *more richly coloured*, black upper side borders *narrower*, forewing upper side orange *invades apical patch*, costal black edging *broader* at end of cell. Sexes similar, ♀ with wings rounder than ♂. **Distribution:** W Cape in Nama Karoo, from Little Karoo to southern side of Swartberg (where it flies with Van Son's Copper); in ne W Cape, in mountains in Fynbos, nw into Succulent Karoo of Namaqualand, to Steinkopf area (N Cape). **Habitat:** Hill tops, rocky ledges, mountains. **Flight period:** Double-brooded, Sept–Dec and Feb–Apr. **Larval food:** No data.

4 Caledon Copper *Aloeides caledoni*

Wingspan: ♂ 35–39 mm ♀ 38–45 mm. **Identification: 4A** ♂ upper side, **4B** ♀ upper side, **4C** ♂ underside. Large, *brightly coloured*. Sexes similar, ♀ with wings more rounded, orange upper side *paler* but still very bright. Upper side superficially resembles Depicta Copper (p. 208), but brighter orange, and black of costa does not extend to forewing base. Hind wing underside red-brown to pinkish rose, discal markings *very small* but distinct, few submarginal or basal marks. **Distribution:** Rare and localised over a wide range. Fynbos, Nama Karoo, Grassland in the W Cape from Caledon area (Shaw's Mountain Pass); also Touws River, Matjiesfontein and Lootsberg Pass. **Habitat:** Hill tops, rocky ledges. **Flight period:** Single-brooded, Aug–Nov. **Larval food:** No data.

5 Cederberg Copper *Aloeides monticola*

Wingspan: ♂ 35–39 mm ♀ 38–45 mm. **Identification: 5A** ♂ upper side, **5B** ♀ upper side, **5C** ♂ underside. Similar to Caledon Copper (above), but upper side ground colour *deeper red-orange*, with more *extensive, intense* black borders, apical patches and costa; black scaling extends closer to wing base. Underside marking with pale marks more *well defined*; submarginal silver band *present*. Sexes similar, ♀ wings more rounded. **Distribution:** Fynbos macchia in W Cape (high slopes of the Cederberg). **Habitat:** Mountains, rocky ledges. **Flight period:** Single-brooded, Aug–Nov. **Larval food:** No data.

1A

1B

A

2B

2C

A

3B

A

4B

4C

A

5B

5C

1 Worcester Copper *Aloeides lutescens*

Wingspan: ♂ 25–28 mm ♀ 27–33 mm. **Identification: 1A** ♂ upper side, **1B** ♀ underside. Orange upper side *very pale*, dark borders more *grey* than black. Underside hind wing ground colour *pale, sandy* (sometimes reddish), serrated discal band and basal spots *grey, edged distally with black*; paler submarginal patch halfway along the hind wing margin on underside. ♂ usually on slight hills, from which he pursues other butterflies; ♀ on flowers, flight more random. **Distribution:** Rare. Fynbos, Nama Karoo. In sandy flats along the Breede River, Nama Karoo in Worcester area (Brandvlei Dam) and Robertson Karoo in W Cape. **Habitat:** Coast, flatlands. **Flight period:** Double-brooded, Sept–Dec and Jan–Mar, possibly with some overlap. **Larval food:** Probably *Aspalathus* spp.

2 Carolynn's Copper *Aloeides carolynnae*

Wingspan: ♂ 23–28 mm ♀ 25–33 mm. **Identification: 2A** ♂ upper side, **2B** ♂ underside, **2C** ♀ upper side, **2D** ♀ underside (nominate). Very similar to Worcester Copper (above) but black upper side margins *broader; deeper orange* upper side ground colour. Hind wing ground colour on underside *brown to red*, pale postdiscal patch *reduced or absent*. Sexes similar, ♂ darker than ♀. Usually found in scrub at the base of hillsides. 2 subspp., both rare. **Distribution:** Nominate in Fynbos macchia in W Cape, Slanghoek Valley, near Goudini; *A. c. aurata* in Fynbos on limestone ridges near De Hoop NR, sandy ground near Witsand. **Habitat:** Coast, rocky ledges. **Flight period:** Two broods; spring (Sept–Nov), and summer (Jan–Mar), with some overlap. **Larval food:** Probably *Aspalathus* spp.

3 Marguerite's Copper *Aloeides margaretae*

Wingspan: ♂ 25–30 mm ♀ 26–33 mm. **Identification: 3A** ♂ upper side, **3B** ♀ upper side, **3C** ♀ underside. Distinctive underside; ground colour warm red-brown to bright magenta; serrated silver-grey hind wing fascia confined to discal area, *fused with two of the basal spots to form X-shaped mark*. Few other markings apart from some small basal spots and faint submarginal row of silvery dentate spots. Sexes similar, ♀ *paler*, wings rounder, hind wing outer margin on upper side more scalloped than ♂. Colonies found in bare rocky areas and on low ledges. **Distribution:** Widespread. West coast in Fynbos and Nama Karoo from Moorreesburg to Lambert's Bay; also along south coast at Hermanus and Struisbaai, W Cape. **Habitat:** Flatlands, coast, rocky ledges. **Flight period:** Several broods, Sept–May. **Larval food:** *Aspalathus spinosa*; larvae shelter under stones near the stem, where they are tended by ants.

4 Pointed Copper *Aloeides apicalis*

Wingspan: ♂ 23–27 mm ♀ 25–30 mm. **Identification: 4A** ♂ upper side, **4B** ♀ upper side, **4C** ♂ underside. Very similar to Marguerite's Copper (above), but *smaller*, forewing apex *more pointed*. Hind wing ground colour *darker on underside*, same X-shaped discoidal fascia, but *suffused with brown*; not as well defined, but variable. Sexes similar, ♀ paler, wings more rounded (but no more pointed apically than other ♀ *Aloeides*). **Distribution:** W Cape and N Cape in Succulent and Nama Karoo, from Piketberg along Namaqualand hills to Springbok, east along Hantamsberg and Roggeveld escarpment and arid western foothills of the Swartberg in the Laingsburg area. **Habitat:** Hill tops, rocky ledges. **Flight period:** Several broods, Sept–May. **Larval food:** Associates with *Monomorium fridae* ants, but no data on food.

1B

2B

2D

3B

3C

4B

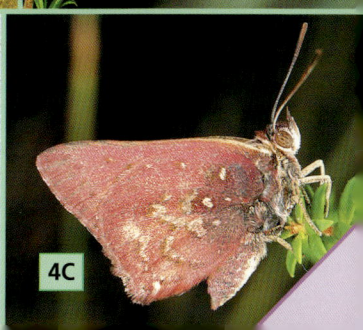

4C

1 Depicta Copper *Aloeides depicta*

Wingspan: ♂ 26–29 mm ♀ 29–35 mm. **Identification: 1A** ♂ upper side, **1B** ♀ upper side, **1C** ♀ underside. Very variable, upper side ground colour orange, *wide grey-black border* similar to other *Aloeides*. Hind wing underside ground colour *sandy to buff-brown*, occasionally reddish. Spots and serrated discoidal fascia well developed, *slightly silvery wash* over ground colour outlined in brown, creating marbled effect. Sexes similar, ♀ paler, wings rounder. **Distribution:** Fynbos, Nama Karoo along mountain chains from Matjiesfontein to Gydo Mtn, and E Cape (Port Elizabeth). **Habitat:** Hillsides, rocky ledges. **Flight period:** Continuous broods through warmer months, Sept–Jun. **Larval food:** *Aspalathus* spp.; larvae shelter under rocks close to the food plant.

Red Hill Copper group

Smaller than Red Copper and Transvaal Copper groups. Bright orange to red-orange upper side with dark margins. Underside carries large discal spots joined into fascia but the outer edge of this is *evenly sinuous and runs parallel to the outer margin*. Quickelberge's Copper, Red Hill Copper, Cloud Copper, Oreas Copper, Coega Copper, Gowan's Copper and Arid Copper.

2 Quickelberge's Copper *Aloeides quickelbergei*

Wingspan: ♂ 24–26 mm ♀ 25–28 mm. **Identification: 2A** ♂ upper side, **2B** ♂ underside. Resembles a dark Depicta Copper (above). Upper side *deep, dark* orange with black borders, hind wing underside also dark, *maroon to sepia*. Indistinct discoidal markings and basal spots dark. ♀ with upper side paler orange, wings rounder. **Distribution:** Fynbos-covered mountain slopes in s W Cape, from Swellendam and Langeberg to Kammanassie and Outeniqua Mtns. **Habitat:** Rocky ledges, mountains. **Flight period:** Single-brooded, Nov–Jan. **Larval food:** No data.

3 Red Hill Copper *Aloeides egerides*

Wingspan: ♂ 21–24 mm ♀ 22–26 mm. **Identification: 3A** ♂ upper side, **3B** ♂ underside. Resembles Carolynn's Copper (p. 206), but *smaller*, cilia *more chequered*, orange colour *brighter, paler*. Underside hind wing richly coloured, mid-brown to red-brown, never straw coloured; large, *bright silvery-white* discoidal fascia marks may be fused as in Red Copper (p. 196); appearance generally marbled. Sexes similar, ♀ paler, wings rounder. **Distribution:** Rare and localised. Coastal Fynbos macchia in W Cape; Red Hill (Simon's Town) on Cape Peninsula, north to Pella Mission (near Mamre), Piketberg and Lambert's Bay. Also at Karwyderskraal near Hermanus on south coast. **Habitat:** Flatlands, hillsides, coast. **Flight period:** Two main broods, Oct–Dec (peak Nov) and Jan–Apr (peak Mar). **Larval food:** No data.

4 Cloud Copper *Aloeides nubilus*

Wingspan: ♂ 21–24 mm ♀ 22–26 mm. **Identification: 4A** ♂ upper side, **4B** ♀ underside. Upper side orange *bright*, forewing tips *blunt*. Underside, hind wing ground colour deep *red-brown to purple-red*, silvery markings in centre of wing fused into *solid discal patch interspersed with ground colour*, with well-defined *submarginal pale band* and distal row of spots. Sexes similar, ♀ wings rounder. **Distribution:** Rare. Afromontane Forest, Grassland. Low rocky ridges in mistbelt grassland interspersed with Afromontane forest in Mpumalanga Drakensberg (including Robbers' Pass above Pilgrim's Rest, and other high areas). **Habitat:** Forest edges, rocky ledges, mountains. **Flight period:** Single-brooded, Sept–Nov. **Larval food:** No data.

1A

1B

1C

A

2B

A

3B

A

4B

1 Oreas Copper   *Aloeides oreas*

Wingspan: ♂ 21–24 mm ♀ 22–26 mm. **Identification: 1A** ♂ upper side, **1B** ♂ underside. Forewing *pointed*, upper side ground colour extensive deep orange. Hind wing underside *brown to purple-red*, discoidal fascia variable, not well marked, silvery wash over ground colour with darker distal shading; short submarginal bands. Found on bare patches of ground among grassland. Sexes similar, ♀ larger, paler, rounder wings. **Distribution:** Highland sourveld Grassland from E Cape (Amatolas) to KwaZulu-Natal Drakensberg (ne to Amajuba), Free State (near Vrede), and peaks of Mpumalanga near Wakkerstroom. **Habitat:** Rocky ledges, mountains. **Flight period:** Double-brooded, Sept–Dec (peak Oct) and Jan–Apr (peak Jan), with some overlap. **Larval food:** No data.

2 Coega Copper   *Aloeides clarki*

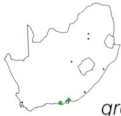

Wingspan: ♂ 25–28 mm ♀ 25–29 mm. **Identification: 2A** ♂ upper side, **2B** ♀ upper side, **2C** ♀ underside. Sexes similar, ♀ paler, wings rounder than ♂. Cilia *strongly chequered*, upper side and underside *much paler* than Oreas Copper (above). Hind wing margin strongly scalloped in both sexes. Hind wing underside ground colour *grey-buff* marbled with paler discoidal fascia, submarginal spots *well defined, black edged*. **Distribution:** Rare. Low slopes and ridges in scrubby coastal Karoo flats of E Cape, also flat rocky land further inland (Langkloof, Sundays River), in valley bushveld. **Habitat:** Flatlands, rocky ledges. **Flight period:** Continuous broods, from Oct–Apr. **Larval food:** *Aspalathus* spp.

3 Gowan's Copper   *Aloeides gowani*

Wingspan: ♂ 25–29 mm ♀ 28–30 mm. **Identification: 3A** ♂ upper side, **3B** ♂ underside. Similar to Coega Copper (above). Upper side and underside *paler*, hind wing underside *sandy grey*, markings broken up, *poorly defined*, edged with *slightly darker grey*. Sexes similar, ♀ *paler*, wings rounder than ♂. Flies in sandy flat ground with sparse arid vegetation; well camouflaged. ♂ territories on slightly raised sandy areas. **Distribution:** Nama Karoo in W Cape (Colesberg), E Cape (Molteno), over a wide area to N Cape (Kimberley, Hotazel). **Habitat:** Flatlands. **Flight period:** Continuous midsummer broods, Oct–Apr, peak Dec–Feb. **Larval food:** *Aspalathus* spp.

4 Arid Copper   *Aloeides arida*

Wingspan: ♂ 26–32 mm ♀ 29–35 mm. **Identification: 4A** ♂ upper side, **4B** ♀ upper side, **4C** ♂ underside. *Larger*, upper side orange *more extensive, narrower* black borders, cilia even more *prominently chequered* than Coega Copper (above). Hind wing underside same broken pattern as Gowan's Copper (above), but ground colour richer, sometimes with *orange hue*. Sexes similar, ♀ *paler*, wings rounder than ♂. Colonies on flat rocky areas on hillsides or flats. **Distribution:** Namaqualand broken veld and strandveld from n W Cape (Lambert's Bay) east to Hantamsberg, north to Springbok and Steinkopf (N Cape). **Habitat:** Flatlands, rocky ledges. **Flight period:** Continuous midsummer broods, Sept–Apr, peak Dec–Feb. **Larval food:** No data.

1 Aranda Copper   *Aloeides aranda*

Wingspan: ♂ 20–29 mm ♀ 27–31 mm. **Identification: 1A** ♂ upper and underside, **1B** ♀ upper side, **1C** ♀ underside, **1D** ♂ underside. Unique; in its own species group. Has *tail-like projection* at hind wing anal angle. Upperside *brighter* orange than most *Aloeides*. Several forms; extent of marginal and apical black varies. Underside hind wing from sandy buff to warm brown to vivid magenta. *Faint* bands of small spots similar to Almeida Copper group. Sexes similar, ♀ wings rounder. ♂ perches on low vegetation or rocks and chases other butterflies, ♀ more sedentary. **Distribution:** Widespread. Throughout South Africa in all biomes except in high montane forests and arid western areas. **Habitat:** Forest edges, hill tops, flatlands, coast, mountains, gullies, hillsides, rocky ledges. **Flight period:** Sept–Apr in warm areas, peaks Oct and Feb. Double-brooded (Oct and Feb) in cooler areas. **Larval food:** *Aspalathus* spp. Larvae associated with *Pheidole capensis* ants.

Almeida Copper group

Underside spots very small, upper side dark markings extensive on deep red-orange ground, hind wing not tailed. Almeida Copper, McMaster's Copper, Susan's Copper, Henning's Copper and Stevenson's Copper.

2 Almeida Copper   *Aloeides almeida*

Wingspan: ♂ 25–29 mm ♀ 28–30 mm. **Identification: 2A** ♂ upper side, **2B** ♀ underside. Closely related to next four species. ♂ forewing apex *less pointed*. Extent of upper side dark marking variable, veins sometimes with black scaling. Hind wing underside ground colour grey to buff or mid-brown, to bright magenta red. Small but well-defined basal and discal series of spots. ♀ paler than ♂, orange ground colour more often penetrating apical area. ♂ settles on flat rocks on hillsides; chases other butterflies. ♀ more sedentary. **Distribution:** Fynbos, Nama Karoo. From W Cape, Cape Peninsula and main Cape fold mountains, north to Ceres, east along Langeberg, Swartberg and parallel ranges such as Kammanassie and Tsitsikamma, to E Cape, Baviaanskloof. **Habitat:** Flatlands, hillsides. **Flight period:** Two main broods, Sept–Nov and Feb–Apr. **Larval food:** No data.

3 McMaster's Copper   *Aloeides macmasteri*

Wingspan: ♂ 28–32 mm ♀ 30–35 mm. **Identification: 3A** ♂ upper side, **3B** ♀ underside, **3C** ♀ upper side. Largest of Almeida Copper group. Distal half of upper side forewing often *totally covered in black* in ♂, with small orange spots in apical area. Upper side ground colour usually *deep tawny red*. Underside hind wing *grey-brown to red-brown*, spotting similar to Almeida Copper (above). ♀ paler, *greyish brown* where ♂ is black. **Distribution:** Widespread but localised. Nama Karoo in W Cape (Ladismith to Colesberg), across Great Karoo to arid areas of Little Namaqualand in Succulent Karoo. Also valley bushveld near Coega, to Grassland in E Cape (Dordrecht area). **Habitat:** Hillsides, rocky ledges. **Flight period:** Two main broods, Sept–Nov and Feb–Apr, sometimes overlapping. **Larval food:** No data.

4 Susan's Copper   *Aloeides susanae*

Wingspan: ♂ 21–24 mm ♀ 22–26 mm. **Identification: 4A** ♂ upper side, **4B** ♂ underside. Similar to Henning's Copper (p. 214), but wings *shorter, rounder*. Orange-red upper side ground colour of ♂ *heavily suffused with dark brown*; may appear black, with only hind wing submarginal band red. Cilia *long, paler* than upper side dark colour, *not chequered*. Underside hind wing mid-brown to dark red-brown. Basal spots separated, discal and submarginal series *fused to form thin, wavy bands*. ♀ orange forewing ground colour *much brighter*, and *penetrates apical area*, leaving square black patch at end of cell. In small, *highly concentrated* colonies. **Distribution:** Grassland in KwaZulu-Natal Midlands, to Free State (Witkoppe, Vrede) and e E Cape (Kokstad area). **Habitat:** Rocky ledges, hillsides. **Flight period:** One, possibly two broods, Sept–Jan. **Larval food:** No data.

1 Henning's Copper   *Aloeides henningi*

Wingspan: ♂ 23–26 mm ♀ 24–26 mm. **Identification: 1A** ♂ upper side, **1B** ♂ underside, **1C** ♀ upperside, **1D** ♀ underside. *Larger* than Susan's Copper (p. 212), forewing *more pointed*. Forewing outer margin *straighter* than Almeida Copper (p. 212), ♂ upper side ground colour *brighter* orange-red, with black margins and apical patch of varying extent. ♀ orange forewing ground colour *brighter*, and *penetrates apical area*, leaving square dark patch at end of cell, dark margins and apical colouring grey-brown. Hind wing underside ground colour grey to brown to red, spots small but well defined. **Distribution:** Widespread in Grassland from n E Cape (Barkly East) to Lesotho, w KwaZulu-Natal, e Free State, Mpumalanga, Limpopo Province (Waterberg) and Gauteng (common on Witwatersrand). **Habitat:** Rocky ledges, hillsides. **Flight period:** In cooler areas single-brooded, Sept–Nov; in warm areas, second brood, Jan–Feb. **Larval food:** No data.

2 Stevenson's Copper   *Aloeides stevensoni*

Wingspan: ♂ 23–26 mm ♀ 24–26 mm. **Identification: 2A** ♂ upper side, **2B** ♂ underside. Sexes alike. Small, dark, with *squarish wings*. Upper side of both sexes almost entirely *velvety dark brown with very small paler markings*. Upper side fuscous coloration restricted to *submarginal band* of small buff lunules, in ♂ forewing apex and ♀ hind wing. Underside darker than Susan's Copper (p. 212), but spot pattern similar. In small, *highly concentrated* colonies on hillsides. **Distribution:** Restricted to montane sourveld Grassland in Wolkberg near Haenertsburg. **Habitat:** Hillsides. **Flight period:** Single-brooded, Nov–Dec, but later summer emergence is likely. **Larval food:** No data.

Dull Copper group

Wing shape narrow and angular, underside spots not as small as in Almeida group, upper side **grey-brown to charcoal** with **greater or lesser degree of** *dull orange* **markings. Discal area ochreous. Dull Copper, Maluti Copper, Swanepoel's Copper, Trimen's Copper and Damara Copper.**

3 Dull Copper   *Aloeides pierus*

Wingspan: 25–30 mm. **Identification: 3A** ♂ upper side, **3B** ♀ upper side, **3C** ♂ underside. ♂ upper side usually *tawny-red*, dark borders *very wide*, veins *black*. Some specimens totally dark brown upper side, orange only in hind wing submarginal area. ♀ paler, upper side orange *more extensive*, penetrating forewing apical area. Underside hind wing ground colour pale sand to dusky pink, or many shades of grey-brown, with large black-edged spots. Break in discal series of spots *at vein M₂*. Settles on bare rocks or sand, ♂ chasing intruders but soon returning. ♀ more wandering flight. **Distribution:** Common and widespread in Fynbos in W Cape (Cape Peninsula) to Succulent Karoo in N Cape (Namaqualand); wide range of Nama Karoo localities over N Cape, W Cape and E Cape, Grassland in Free State. **Habitat:** Flatlands, coast, hillsides, rocky ledges. **Flight period:** Several broods; Sept–Apr, peaks Oct and Feb. **Larval food:** *Aspalathus* spp. Larvae shelter in nests of *Lepisiota capensis* ants during the day, emerging at night to feed.

1A

1B

1C

1D

2A

2B

3A

3B

3C

1 Maluti Copper   *Aloeides maluti*

Wingspan: ♂ 21–26 mm ♀ 23–27 mm. **Identification: 1A** ♂ upper side, **1B** ♀ upper side, **1C** ♀ underside. Resembles Dull Copper (p. 214), but wings *smaller, rounder*. Sexes similar, ♀ more brightly coloured than ♂. Upper side orange *more extensive, duskier* than Dull Copper. Underside hind wing ground colour *darker*, less marbled, *no break* in median series at vein M$_2$. Found on bare rocky patches on hillsides. **Distribution:** Centred in high-altitude alpine Grassland of Lesotho; penetrates surrounding hills in Golden Gate Highlands NP in Free State, Barkly East in E Cape. **Habitat:** Mountains, rocky ledges. **Flight period:** Single-brooded, Dec–Feb. **Larval food:** No data.

2 Swanepoel's Copper   *Aloeides swanepoeli*

Wingspan: ♂ 25–29 mm ♀ 28–30 mm. **Identification: 2A** ♀ upper side, **2B** ♀ underside. Brighter orange than Dull Copper (p. 214). Sexes similar, ♀ upper side dark marking less extensive, orange *paler* than ♂. Underside hind wing ground colour *buff to red-brown*, median and basal series of small dark spots in *regular curved rows running parallel to margin*. Inhabits rocky outcrops among grass; usually several in one small colony. **Distribution:** Grassland and grassy Savanna, from coastal KwaZulu-Natal, through Midlands to Drakensberg, along foothills of Lebombos and north into Mpumalanga and Limpopo Province (to Makhado). **Habitat:** Rocky ledges. **Flight period:** Double-brooded, Sept–Nov and Jan–Feb. **Larval food:** No data.

3 Trimen's Copper   *Aloeides trimeni*

Wingspan: ♂ 22–33 mm ♀ 24–35 mm. **Identification: 3A** ♂ upper side, **3B** ♀ upper side, **3C** ♀ underside. Sexes similar, ♀ has greater extent of orange. Upper side variable; tawny-orange with *wide black-brown borders*, orange marked and suffused with greater or lesser amount of dark colour. Apical patch usually orange, bases tawny buff, *dark band* crossing *forewing centre*. Some specimens, notably *A. t. southeyae*, show hardly any orange. Underside hind wing ground colour *buff to red-brown*. Spots slightly darker than ground colour, submarginal series forming neat lines as in Swanepoel's Copper (above), median and basal spots *discrete, more scattered*. 2 subspp., geographically distinct. **Distribution:** Nominate from Nama Karoo in E Cape (Port Elizabeth), inland to montane Grassland and Nama Karoo in Free State, Gauteng and Mpumalanga; *A. t. southeyae* in grassy Fynbos near Mossel Bay (W Cape). **Habitat:** Flatlands. **Flight period:** Two broods, Sept–Dec (peak Oct), and Jan–Apr (peak Feb), some overlap in summer. **Larval food:** *Aspalathus* spp. and *Hermannia depressa*.

4 Damara Copper   *Aloeides damarensis*

Wingspan: ♂ 25–32 mm ♀ 28–36 mm. **Identification: 4A** ♀ upper side, **4B** ♂ underside (nominate). Sexes similar, ♀ *paler*, wings rounder than ♂, almost totally orange in very arid areas. *Bright pale orange*, variable; *narrow* upper side dark borders, *no dark suffusion* of middle of wing. Orange penetrates apical patch to create dark blotch at end of forewing cell. Some specimens have tawny-brown basal suffusion. Underside similar to Dull Copper (p. 214). 2 subspp., geographically distinct. **Distribution:** Nominate in Nama Karoo, Succulent Karoo and Arid Savanna of W Cape, N Cape, E Cape and sw Free State; *A. d. mashona* in Savanna from n KwaZulu-Natal to Mpumalanga, Gauteng, Limpopo and NW provinces, and further north. **Habitat:** Flatlands, hillsides. **Flight period:** Continuous broods, Sept–Apr in southern areas. Year-round in arid north. **Larval food:** *Aspalathus* spp.

1 Molomo Copper   *Aloeides molomo*

Wingspan: ♂ 22–33 mm ♀ 24–35 mm. **Identification: 1A** ♂ upper side, **1B** ♂ underside, **1C** ♀ upper side. Unmistakable, in its own species group with upper side *bright orange* borders wide and dark, ground colour penetrating forewing apex, creating *dark square blotch* on costa at end of cell. Cilia *conspicuously chequered*, margins *strongly scalloped*. Underside hind wing ground colour buff, *cloudy dark band* distal to median series of spots. Sexes similar, ♀ larger, *more convex* outer margin on forewing. ♂ sits on bare ground, wary and easily flushed, chases other butterflies and returns to original perch. ♀ has more wandering flight. 2 subspp., geographically distinct. **Distribution:** Nominate in Nama Karoo in E Cape, Free State and e N Cape, and Grassland, Arid Savanna, thornveld and bushveld in Gauteng, Mpumalanga and Limpopo and NW provinces (also n KwaZulu-Natal); *A. m. krooni* in Arid Savanna in n N Cape, to Namibia and Botswana. **Habitat:** Hillsides, rocky ledges, flatlands. **Flight period:** Double-brooded, Aug–Dec, Mar–Apr. **Larval food:** *Sida ovata* (*A. m. krooni*).

Dusky Copper group

Two small dull grey-brown 'Coppers' with more-or-less prominent upper side pale submarginal bands; underside median and submarginal series of paler spots in more-or-less regular curves. Dusky Copper, Barbara's Copper.

2 Dusky Copper   *Aloeides taikosama*

Wingspan: ♂ 22–27 mm ♀ 27–33 mm. **Identification: 2A** ♀ upper side, **2B** ♀ underside. Compared to other *Aloeides* with brown upper sides, forewing margin *more convex*, orange *arrow-shaped* submarginal upper side markings. Hind wing margins *strongly scalloped*, veins CuA_1 and CuA_2 may form small tails. Underside hind wing dirty grey to yellow or red-brown. Sexes similar, ♂ with *smaller and duller* orange forewing markings. In small colonies; settles on bare earth. Easily flushed, seldom flying far from colony. **Distribution:** Grassland, grassy areas in Nama Karoo, and thorny Savanna from e W Cape to E Cape, Free State, n KwaZulu-Natal, Gauteng, Mpumalanga, Limpopo and NW provinces, and e N Cape. **Habitat:** Flatlands, hillsides. **Flight period:** Continuous broods, Aug–Apr, peaks Nov and Mar. **Larval food:** No data.

3 Barbara's Copper   *Aloeides barbarae*

Wingspan: ♂ 22–24 mm ♀ 24–26 mm. **Identification: 3A** ♂ upper side, **3B** ♀ upper side, **3C** ♂ underside. Sexes similar, ♂ upper side orange marks *fainter* than ♀. Very similar to Dusky Copper (above), but upper side *olivaceous* shade of grey-brown; costal spot of forewing underside submarginal series *displaced towards apex* (see arrow). Hind wing underside ground colour more often *grey-brown* (but reddish individuals, as illustrated, are found); spots have centres whitish as opposed to same as ground colour. ♂ territorial, flies very close to ground in grassy areas; ♀ more wandering flight. **Distribution:** Very rare and highly localised. Only record in montane Grassland on one small hill top between Fairview and Sheba Mines, Barberton (Mpumalanga). **Habitat:** Mountains. **Flight period:** Single-brooded, Oct–Nov; may fly over a longer period. **Larval food:** No data.

4 Barkly's Copper   *Aloeides barklyi*

Wingspan: ♂ 30–34 mm ♀ 32–36 mm. **Identification: 4A** ♂ upper side, **4B** ♀ upper side, **4C** ♀ underside. Unique, in its own species group; *metallic silver-grey* upper side conspicuous on the wing. Underside markings similar to Almeida Copper group (pp. 212–214) but spots much larger, ground colour suffused with orange. ♀ with *prominent orange apical patch* on upper side. Colonial. ♂ wary, easily disturbed. ♂ flight fast, more sustained than most *Aloeides*; ♀ has more wandering flight. **Distribution:** Succulent Karoo from Port Nolloth/Steinkopf in N Cape, south to W Cape, Cederberg and Nama Karoo at Matjiesfontein. **Habitat:** Rocky ledges, hillsides. **Flight period:** Double-brooded, Aug–Oct and Mar–May. **Larval food:** No data.

A

1B

A

2B

A

3B

3C

A

4B

4C

Genus *Chrysoritis*   Coppers, Opals   42 SPP., ENDEMIC TO SOUTH AFRICA AND LESOTHO

Small butterflies, upper side bronze to orange or copper, borders usually dark. Many have basal portion of upper side opalescent silvery blue, suffused with a greater or lesser degree of intense electric lustre, green to blue or violet. Underside forewing orange with dark borders, and black spots sometimes with silver centres. Underside hind wing distinctively marked with cryptic patterns. Rapid, buzzing flight; ♂ territorial on hill tops, small prominences, ridges, chasing other butterflies from perches on rocks or twigs. ♀ near food plants, both sexes on flowers. Egg white to pale green or cream, mostly bun-shaped domes with depressions in honeycomb pattern. Some have involuted whorls of fine cross-ribs, forming a pattern of triangular depressions. Larva onisciform, white to green or buff, longitudinal darker stripes and lines, broadest along middle. Usually shelters under rocks or in ants' carton nests, emerging to feed at night, sometimes fed by ants. Rounded pupa brown to black, formed in debris near ants' nests. *Chrysoritis* butterflies are similar to one another so we have broadly grouped confusing species to aid in identification.

1 Dickson's Strandveld Copper   *Chrysoritis dicksoni*

Wingspan: ♂ 26–35 mm ♀ 33–40 mm. **Identification: 1A** ♀ upper side, **1B** ♀ underside. Sexes alike. Upper side *dark copper*, with large square black 'spots' and 'hoary' appearance. Underside cryptic. Flight vigorous, but not sustained; usually returns to small bush from which flushed. ♀ more sedentary. Colonies may be concentrated in very small area, usually low prominences. **Distribution:** Extremely rare. Only found inland from Witsand in a single spot in Fynbos. Previously found north of Cape Town, W Cape, in Melkbosstrand and Atlantis areas; some have been wiped out by agricultural and urban development. **Habitat:** Flatlands, coast. **Flight period:** Single-brooded, late Jul to mid-Sept. **Larval food:** Trophallaxis from *Crematogaster peringueyi* ants. Other food sources unknown.

Daisy Copper group

Small Coppers with variegated underside hind wings and rounded wings; copper colour somewhat brassy in tone. Drakensberg Daisy Copper, Karoo Daisy Copper, Jitterbug Daisy Copper and Donkey Daisy Copper. While Dickson's Strandveld Copper (above) belongs in this group, it is noticeably larger.

2 Drakensberg Daisy Copper   *Chrysoritis oreas*

Wingspan: ♂ 21–23 mm ♀ 22–24 mm. **Identification: 2A** ♀ upper side, **2B** ♂ underside. Underside with complicated pattern of saggitate brown marks on a silvery white ground. Extent of upper side spotting *variable*, sometimes only single spots in forewing and hind wing cells. Sexes similar, ♀ with less extensive dark upper side markings. Flight of flushed ♂ slow, jinking; soon returns to original perch. May dive into a tuft of grass in high winds. ♀ flight more random. **Distribution:** Rare. Montane Grassland in e KwaZulu-Natal Drakensberg foothills, 1 800–2 200 m, Bulwer to Loteni, south to Sani Pass and Bushman's Nek. **Habitat:** Mountains, hillsides. **Flight period:** Single brooded, late Sept to mid-Nov. **Larval food:** *Thesium* spp. Larvae associated with *Myrmicaria* nr *nigra* ants.

3 Karoo Daisy Copper   *Chrysoritis chrysantas*

Wingspan: ♂ 22–25 mm ♀ 27–30 mm. **3A** ♀ upper side, **3B** ♀ underside. Upper side *bright pale orange*, cilia *heavily chequered* black and white. Hind wing underside *marbled grey, black and white*. Sexes similar, ♀ with wings rounder. Well camouflaged in natural habitat. Flight rapid, evasive and sustained. Fond of pink mesembs. **Distribution:** Succulent Karoo of N Cape (Richtersveld and Namaqualand), to Nama Karoo in W Cape (Matjiesfontein) and Little Karoo (Ladismith, Oudtshoorn). **Habitat:** Rocky slopes. **Flight period:** Double-brooded, Aug–Nov and Mar–May. **Larval food:** No data.

1 Jitterbug Daisy Copper *Chrysoritis zeuxo*

Wingspan: ♂ 22–25 mm ♀ 24–28 mm. **Identification: 1A** ♀ upper side, **1B** ♂ underside. Upper side *bright, deep metallic copper*, broad black margins, well-defined square black 'spots', cilia *not chequered*. Underside cryptic. Sexes similar, ♀ forewing outer margin more convex. Specimens from east of range have ground colour much darker on both surfaces, reduced hind wing upper side black markings, scalloped margins, more falcate forewing tips. Usually close to food plant. **Distribution:** Coastal Fynbos in W Cape, from Cape Peninsula to Knysna area; also Nama Karoo from Seweweekspoort to Calitzdorp and Oudtshoorn. **Habitat:** Coast, flatlands, rocky slopes. **Flight period:** Single-brooded, Sept–Jan, peak Oct–Nov. **Larval food:** *Chrysanthemoides monilifera*. Larvae associated with *Crematogaster* nr *liengmei* ants.

2 Donkey Daisy Copper *Chrysoritis zonarius*

Wingspan: ♂ 18–22 mm ♀ 20–24 mm. **Identification: 2A** ♂ upper side, **2B** ♂ underside. *Smaller*, upper side *darker*, copper *less metallic* than Jitterbug Daisy Copper (above), but pattern of square black spots similar. Upper side wing margins darker, *broader*; flight slower. Underside cryptic. Sexes similar. Never far from food plant; settles soon after disturbance. **Distribution:** In Fynbos, Nama Karoo and Succulent Karoo along coast and inland from Cape Peninsula north-west to Paleisheuwel and Lambert's Bay, and along hills to Nieuwoudtville area, W Cape. **Habitat:** Flatlands, coast, sandy dunes, rocky slopes. **Flight period:** Single-brooded, Sept–Nov. **Larval food:** *Chrysanthemoides incana*. Larvae associated with *Crematogaster peringueyi* ants.

Burnished Opal group

Nine small Coppers with underside hind wings sparsely marked; upper sides glittering, red-copper to bronze; wings pointed but forewing apex tapers gently. Feltham's Opal, Sand-dune Opal, Lydenburg Opal, Mooi River Opal, Tsomo River Opal, Heidelberg Copper, Burnished Opal, Natal Opal and Midas Opal. Although similar to others in this group, Scarce Scarlet has distinctive upper side dark markings.

3 Feltham's Opal *Chrysoritis felthami*

Wingspan: ♂ 22–27 mm ♀ 23–33 mm. **Identification: 3A** ♂ upper side, **3B** ♂ underside (*C. f. dukei*). Wing margins *smooth*, upper side dark marginal band has orange *marginal lunules*. Sexes similar, but ♀ has wings rounder, markings *heavier*. 2 subspp.: nominate has upper side black spotting *more extensive* than *C. f. dukei*, and dark hind wing underside markings less variegated. **Distribution:** Nominate in coastal Fynbos in W Cape (excluding Cape Peninsula), along west coast and coastal flats in Succulent Karoo to Hondeklip Bay, and south coast to Stilbaai area; scarce in Nama Karoo. *C. f. dukei* in Succulent Karoo hills in Steinkopf area (N Cape), south-east to Worcester, Roggeveld escarpment and Little Karoo (W Cape). **Habitat:** Coast, flatlands, gullies, dry riverbeds. **Flight period:** Several broods, Aug–Apr, peaks Oct and Feb. **Larval food:** *Zygophyllum flexuosum, Z. sessilifolium*. Larvae associated with *Crematogaster peringueyi* ants.

4 Sand-dune Opal *Chrysoritis pyroeis*

Wingspan: ♂ 22–31 mm ♀ 25–38 mm. **Identification: 4A** ♂ upper side (*C. p. hersaleki*), **4B** ♂ underside (nominate). Similar to ♀ Feltham's Opal (above), but upper side has *basal blue scaling* and shifting *blue-violet sheen over copper areas*. ♂ darker than ♀. 2 subspp.: nominate upper side *paler*, blue iridescence *less obvious* than *C. p. hersaleki*. Underside of both subspp. cryptic. In colonies on sand dunes and rocky hillsides. **Distribution:** Nominate in Fynbos in W Cape, from Cape Peninsula north into Hawequas and Du Toit's Kloof Mountains, west coast Succulent Karoo to Hondeklip Bay (N Cape); also along south coast as far as Stilbaai; *C. p. hersaleki* (rare) in Fynbos in coastal hills near Port Elizabeth, E Cape. **Habitat:** Coast, mountains, rocky slopes. **Flight period:** Several broods, Aug–Apr; peaks Sept–Oct and Feb; in the west, Dec and Jan. **Larval food:** *Zygophyllum flexuosum* and *Thesium* spp. Larvae associated with *Myrmecaria nigra* ants.

A

1B

A

2B

A

3B

A

4B

1 Lydenburg Opal *Chrysoritis aethon*

Wingspan: ♂ 24–28 mm ♀ 28–32 mm. **Identification: 1A** ♂ upper side, **1B** ♀ underside. Sparkling *red-copper* upper side, *gold to green* iridescence at certain angles. Sometimes confused with Mooi River Opal (below), but *larger*, red-orange *deeper*, well-defined rows of *discal spots* on upper side, *both wings*. ♀ orange *less metallic* than ♂, wings rounder. Underside cryptic. Colonies, including territorial males, occur in rocky outcrops because the larval food plant only grows among these rocks. Both sexes feed on nectar. **Distribution:** Montane Grassland and edges of Afromontane Forest from n KwaZulu-Natal (Utrecht) to Mpumalanga (Wakkerstroom hills and Vaalkop, near Morgenzon); along Drakensberg escarpment to Mariepskop (Limpopo Province), further west in high mountains near Dullstroom, Lydenburg and Machadodorp (Mpumalanga). **Habitat:** Mountains, rocky slopes, hillsides, forest edges. **Flight period:** Several broods, Sept–Apr, peaks Nov and Feb. **Larval food:** *Rhus zeyheri*. Vaalkop population feeds on a *Diospyros* sp. Larvae and pupae associated with *Crematogaster* nr *liengmei* ants.

2 Mooi River Opal *Chrysoritis lycegenes*

Wingspan: ♂ 21–24 mm ♀ 23–26 mm. **Identification: 2A** ♂ upper side, **2B** ♂ underside. Similar to Lydenburg Opal (above), but *smaller*, shade of orange ground colour *less red, fewer* black spots on forewing, *none* on hind wing. Underside cryptic. Sexes similar, ♀ paler orange, forewing outer margin *more rounded*. Colonies close to food plants. ♂ perches on low vegetation, chasing other butterflies. ♀ more sedentary, usually on flowers. **Distribution:** Montane Grassland in n KwaZulu-Natal Midlands, along Drakensberg foothills to Mpumalanga (Wakkerstroom). **Habitat:** Rocky slopes, hillsides. **Flight period:** Double-brooded, Sept–Oct and Dec–Jan. **Larval food:** *Diospyros austro-africana, D. lycioides, Myrsine africana, Rhus* spp., and *Chrysanthemoides monilifera*. Larvae associated with *Crematogaster* nr *liengmei* ants.

3 Tsomo River Opal *Chrysoritis lyncurium*

Wingspan: ♂ 21–24 mm ♀ 23–26 mm. **Identification: 3A** ♂ upper side, **3B** ♂ underside, **3C** ♀ underside. Upper side more red-orange than Mooi River Opal (above), black margins *wider, dark scaling* at hind wing upper side costa and base. Underside cryptic. Sexes similar, ♀ with *greenish hue* on hind wing underside. **Distribution:** Rare and localised. Montane Grassland from n E Cape (Tsomo River area, Mbulu) to s KwaZulu-Natal (Bushman's Nek, Kokstad). Threats include livestock grazing and alien plantations. **Habitat:** Rocky slopes, hillsides. **Flight period:** Usually midsummer (Dec and Jan) but possible earlier brood. **Larval food:** *Myrsine* spp. and *Diospyros* spp. Larvae associated with *Crematogaster* ants.

4 Heidelberg Copper or Golden Opal *Chrysoritis aureus*

Wingspan: ♂ 24–28 mm ♀ 28–32 mm. **Identification: 4A** ♂ upper side, **4B** ♂ underside. Upper side *paler*, orange shade *more golden* than Lydenburg Opal (above). Forewing underside has *elongated spot* (see arrow) in postdiscal series in CuA_2. ♂ perches on ground or on low vegetation, periodically patrolling territory, always near clumps of food plant. Sometimes four or five seen circling together. ♀ more sedentary, also near food plant. Both sexes on flowers. **Distribution:** Rare. Montane Grassland in Gauteng (Suikerbosrand near Heidelberg), and Mpumalanga, near Balfour and Greylingstad. **Habitat:** Mountains, rocky slopes, hillsides. **Flight period:** Year-round, peaks Dec and Mar. **Larval food:** *Clutia pulchella*. Larvae and pupae associated with *Crematogaster* nr *liengmei* ants.

1 Burnished Opal *Chrysoritis chrysaor*

Wingspan: ♂ 22–27 mm ♀ 23–30 mm. **Identification: 1A** ♂ upper side, **1B** (typical) ♂ underside. Specimens from south-eastern part of range have more pronounced anal lobes, so may be confused with Natal Opal (below), but upper side black spots smaller and sparser and tail absent. Hind wing anal lobe pronounced, but less so than in Natal Opal. Extent of black spotting on upper side varies from colony to colony; sometimes no spots except for those in cells. Underside hind wing ground colour varies from reddish brown to brownish buff with basal, discal and submarginal rows of faint darker spots; those at apex larger and joined to form a blotch of darker colour. Sexes similar, ♀ with wings more rounded. **Distribution:** Widespread, mainly in e South Africa. In Fynbos up the west coast of W Cape, in Nama Karoo of W Cape and E Cape (also in valley bushveld near Port Alfred), montane grassland of KwaZulu-Natal, Free State, s Mpumalanga, and Gauteng. **Habitat:** Coast, flatlands, mountains, hillsides, rocky slopes. **Flight period:** Year-round at the coast; peaks Nov and Feb at high altitude. **Larval food:** *Tylecodon paniculatus, Cotyledon orbiculata, Zygophyllum sessilifolium* and *Z. retrofractum, Acacia karroo* and *Rhus* spp. Larvae associated with *Crematogaster* nr *liengmei* ants.

2 Natal Opal *Chrysoritis natalensis*

Wingspan: ♂ 24–30 mm ♀ 28–34 mm. **Identification: 2A** ♂ upper side, **2B** ♀ upper side, **2C** ♂ underside. The only *Chrysoritis* found on KwaZulu-Natal coast. Similar to Burnished Opal (above), but upper side black spots larger, and more pronounced hind wing anal lobe carries a short tail. Sexes similar, ♀ with rounder wings, less brilliant copper. Always close to food plant. **Distribution:** Grasslands, Savanna from E Cape (East London) along KwaZulu-Natal coast and inland to Zululand and Midlands. **Habitat:** Coast, rocky slopes. **Flight period:** Year-round, peaks Nov and Feb. **Larval food:** *Chrysanthemoides monilifera* and *Cotyledon orbiculata.*

3 Midas Opal *Chrysoritis midas*

Wingspan: ♂ 24–28 mm ♀ 25–30 mm. **Identification: 3A** ♂ upper side, **3B** ♀ upper side, **3C** ♂ underside. Resembles *small* Burnished Opal (above), but copper upper side has *deeper* red tone, underside hind wing *dark, almost unmarked*. Sexes similar, ♀ *larger*, wings *rounder*, hind wing underside sometimes with large green patch. Often found in numbers around food plant. **Distribution:** High hills in Nama Karoo. Roggeveld escarpment to Nuweveldberge near Beaufort West (W Cape). **Habitat:** Mountains, rocky slopes. **Flight period:** Single-brooded, Sept–Nov. **Larval food:** *Diospyros austro-africana* var. *microphylla.* Larvae associated with *Crematogaster* nr *liengmei* ants.

4 Scarce Scarlet or Golden Flash *Chrysoritis phosphor*

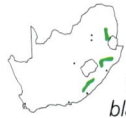

Wingspan: ♂ 24–28 mm ♀ 26–31 mm. **Identification: 4A** ♂ upper side, **4B** ♀ upper side (*C. p. borealis*), **4C** ♀ underside (nominate). Upper side *glittering golden orange*; wing tips large, black, forewing cell with conspicuous black spot. Underside hind wing buff to red-brown, with basal, discal and submarginal series of *gold-centred black spots*. Sexes similar, ♀ duller orange and with more well-developed dark submarginal hind wing band on upper side. Extremely wary; elusive canopy dweller, seldom seen except through binoculars. Both sexes on flowers in early morning, ♂ also on wet mud. 2 subspp., geographically distinct. **Distribution:** Rare. Afromontane Forest. Nominate in E Cape, Amatolas, Katberg, north-east to Mbashe River; *C. p. borealis* from KwaZulu-Natal Midlands (Karkloof area to Eshowe) and Mpumalanga (Shiyalongcubo Forest near Barberton, Kowyn's Pass near Graskop). **Habitat:** Forest edges. **Flight period:** Year-round, mainly Nov and Apr. **Larval food:** No data.

A

1B

A

2B

2C

A

3B

3C

A

4B

4C

Common Opal group

Common features are variegated hind wing underside and subapical indentation in angular forewing margin. Most have variable degree of basal opalescent blue covering the base of the wings. Namaqua Opal, Turner's Opal, Waaihoek Opal, Water Opal (the preceding 4 spp. all lack the basal blue), Common Opal, Azure Opal, Riley's Opal, Plutus Opal, Trimen's Opal, Perseus Opal, Pan Opal, Beulah's Opal, Irene's Opal, Swanepoel's Opal, Daphne's Opal, Endymion Opal, Violet Opal, Beaufort Opal, Pyramus Opal, Brauer's Opal, Machacha Opal, Pennington's Opal, Eastern Opal, Brooks's Opal, Dark Opal, Uranus Opal and Adonis Opal.

1 Namaqua Opal   *Chrysoritis aridus*

Wingspan: ♂ 22–26 mm ♀ 28–34 mm. **Identification: 1A** ♂ upper side, **1B** ♂ underside. No upper side basal blue; underside flat sandy buff; southern specimens may show variegation, small upper side black spots and paler orange upper side ground colour. Sexes similar, ♀ slightly larger, forewing margin more convex. Whirling flight around bushes among rocks. **Distribution:** Succulent Karoo in N Cape (Steinkopf, Springbok, Kamiesberg, Bitterfontein, south to Hantamsberg). **Habitat:** Flatlands, rocky slopes. **Flight period:** Single-brooded, Sept–Nov. **Larval food:** *Chrysanthemoides incana*, and *Zygophyllum* spp. in captivity.

2 Turner's Opal   *Chrysoritis turneri*

Wingspan: ♂ 22–26 mm ♀ 33–40 mm. **Identification: 2A** ♂ upper side (*C. t. amatola*), **2B** ♀ underside (nominate). Upper side markings *more extensive* than Namaqua Opal (above); *narrower* dark margins. *Darker* orange than Waaihoek Opal (below). Upper side dark margins and spots, underside hind wing pattern variable. Found on rocks or bushes below small ridges or cliffs. Sexes similar, ♀ slightly larger, forewing margin more convex. 2 subspp. **Distribution:** Widespread. Nominate in W Cape Succulent Karoo, s Namaqualand (Hantamsberg), Nama Karoo, Hex River Pass, Roggeveld escarpment, Nuweveldberg, Swartberg, Matjiesfontein, Little Karoo, *C. t. amatola* – hills of E Cape escarpment, Amatolas, n to Winterberg and Lesotho, in karroid areas near summits. **Habitat:** Mountains, rocky slopes. **Flight period:** Sept–Apr, peaks Oct, Feb (nominate) and Dec (*C. t. amatola*). **Larval food:** *Zygophyllum* spp., *Dimorphotheca cuneata*, *Osteospermum* spp. Larvae associated with *Crematogaster* nr *liengmei* ants.

3 Waaihoek Opal   *Chrysoritis blencathrae*

Wingspan: ♂ 26–36 mm ♀ 30–37 mm. **Identification: 3A** ♂ upper side, **3B** ♀ upper side, **3C** ♂ underside. Upper side *pale yellow-orange*, forewing upper side dark margin *wide, merged with submarginal black spots*. Prominently chequered cilia. Underside hind wing similar to Endymion Opal (p. 236). Sexes similar, ♀ wings rounder. High mountain slopes (over 1 600 m). ♂ territorial; perches on rocks and low vegetation. ♀ usually on flowers. **Distribution:** Fynbos. Peaks of Waaihoek and Sybasberg, Waaihoekberge, between Ceres and Worcester, W Cape. **Habitat:** Mountains, rocky slopes. **Flight period:** Single-brooded, Dec–Feb. **Larval food:** *Dimorphotheca venusta*. Larvae associated with *Crematogaster* ants.

4 Water Opal   *Chrysoritis palmus*

Wingspan: ♂ 21–29 mm ♀ 25–31 mm. **Identification: 4A** ♂ upper side, **4B** ♂ underside (nominate). *Deep copper-orange*. Underside heavily marked, *dark*. Sexes similar, ♀ larger, wings rounder. Occurs in large numbers in small areas. Both sexes fond of yellow *Compositae* flowers; settle often on bracken. Fast flight not sustained. 2 subspp. **Distribution:** Fynbos. Nominate in W Cape, from Cape Peninsula to Tygerberg Hills, and mountains from Bain's Kloof to Du Toit's Kloof, east to Riviersonderendberge and Langeberg; *C. p. margueritae* from southern slopes of Outeniquas, W Cape, to Tsitsikamma Mtns and Vanstadensberg (west of Port Elizabeth), E Cape. **Habitat:** Wetlands, gullies, hillsides. **Flight period:** Several broods: nominate Sept–Apr, peak Dec; *C. p. margueritae* peak Jan–Mar. **Larval food:** *Aspalathus sarcantha* and *A. carnosa*, *Chrysanthemoides monilifera*, *Berzelia intermedia*, *B. lanuginosa* and *B. abrotanoides*. Larvae associated with *Crematogaster peringueyi* ants.

A

1B

A

2B

A

3B

3C

A

4B

1 Common Opal   *Chrysoritis thysbe*

Wingspan: ♂ 24–32 mm ♀ 23–35 mm. **Identification: 1A** ♂ upper side, **1B** ♀ upper side (*C. t. thysbe*); **1C** ♂ underside (*C. t. schloszae*); **1D** ♂ underside (*C. t. thysbe* f. *thysbe*); **1E** ♂ underside (*C. t. thysbe* f. *osbecki*). Spectacular; copper wings with *blue bases* and *electric opalescent lustre*. Amount of blue on upper side varies, in some subspecies almost covering forewing. ♀ with rounder wings, upper side blue restricted to basal 25% of wings, no opalescent sheen. Two forms north of Cape Town; f. *thysbe* has variegated underside hind wing (as in *C. t. schloszae*); in f. *osbecki*, flat, sandy to reddish tan. ♂ intensively territorial on hill tops or sand dunes; ♀ found at random on flowers. 6 subspp. **Distribution:** Fynbos-covered hills and dunes, and Succulent Karoo: nominate from Cape Peninsula to Mossel Bay (W Cape), north to Lambert's Bay, inland to Piketberg and Citrusdal; *C. t. schloszae* Moorreesburg area, W Cape; *C. t. psyche* from Bitterfontein south to Nardouwsberg (north of Clanwilliam), W Cape; *C. t. bamptoni* Hondeklipbaai area, inland to Wallekraal (N Cape); *C. t. mithras* Stilbaai to Brenton-on-Sea, W Cape; *C. t. whitei* E Cape, near Port Elizabeth. **Habitat:** Hill tops, flatlands, mountains, coast. **Flight period:** Year-round, peaks Oct and Mar. **Larval food:** *Chrysanthemoides incana* and *C. monilifera*, *Osteospermum polygaloides*, *Lebeckia plukenetiana*, *Aspalathus* spp., *Thesium* spp. and *Zygophyllum* spp. Larvae associated with *Crematogaster peringueyi* ants.

2 Azure Opal   *Chrysoritis azurius*

Wingspan: ♂ 32–36 mm ♀ 35–40 mm. **Identification: 2A** ♂ upper side, **2B** ♀ upper side, **2C** ♂ underside. Large for a *Chrysoritis* butterfly, upper side ground colour *deep orange*, ♂ silvery blue *extensive*, sometimes covering all the orange. *Deep blue* opalescence spreads over most of hind wing upper side, and to forewing apex in some specimens. Hind wing underside of both sexes somewhat like Pan Opal (p. 232) – pale buff with patches of rich red-brown, *appearing 'streaky'*; cilia conspicuously chequered. ♀ upper side resembles Beaufort Opal (p. 236). **Distribution:** Succulent Karoo and Nama Karoo. In N Cape, along Roggeveld escarpment from Sutherland (Swaarweerberg) to Quaggafontein; also in hills near Nieuwoudtville (W Cape). **Habitat:** Gullies, mountains, dry riverbeds. **Flight period:** Single extended brood, Oct–Dec. **Larval food:** No data.

3 Riley's Opal   *Chrysoritis rileyi*

Wingspan: ♂ 30–35 mm ♀ 32–38 mm. **Identification: 3A** ♂ upper side, **3B** ♀ upper side, **3C** ♀ underside. Larger, wings *squarer* than Common Opal (above), cilia more *distinctly chequered*, upper side *paler*, blue sheen *more metallic*. Hind wing upper side usually *lacks postdiscal black spots*, blue sheen *covers discal spots*. Underside of both sexes cryptic. ♀ *paler* than ♂, upper side blue *much reduced*, no iridescent sheen. ♂ active, ♀ more sedentary. **Distribution:** Succulent Karoo. Only from low hill slopes and river flats at east end of Brandvlei Dam, Worcester, W Cape. **Habitat:** Flatlands, hillsides. **Flight period:** Sept–Apr, peaks Oct/Nov and Mar. **Larval food:** *Thesium* spp., *Zygophyllum* spp. Larvae associated with *Crematogaster peringueyi* ants.

A

B

1C

1D

E

2A

2B

C

3A

B

3C

1 Plutus Opal   *Chrysoritis plutus*

Wingspan: ♂ 24–28 mm ♀ 26–35 mm. **Identification: 1A** ♂ upper side, **1B** ♀ upper side, **1C** ♂ underside. Markings similar to Pan Opal (below), but overall *darker, more richly coloured*. Forewing upper side with *much wider* dark borders; in ♂ may merge with submarginal black spots. Underside hind wing variegated, less variably so than Pan Opal. ♀ with *very little* upper side basal blue, and larger black spots than ♂. Colonies found on steep rocky slopes. **Distribution:** Nama Karoo. W Cape, from Hex River Pass, south to Montagu, along Groot Swartberg (Swartberg Pass, Teeberg) to Willowmore, E Cape. **Habitat:** Rocky ledges, mountains. **Flight period:** Two extended broods, Aug–Dec and Jan–Apr. **Larval food:** *Thesium* spp. Larvae associated with *Crematogaster peringueyi* ants.

2 Trimen's Opal   *Chrysoritis trimeni*

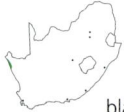

Wingspan: ♂ 26–30 mm ♀ 28–34 mm. **Identification: 2A** ♂ upper side, **2B** ♀ upper side, **2C** ♀ underside. Similar to Pan Opal (below). *Slightly larger*, forewing apex *more pointed*. Upper side with very *narrow, smooth* dark margins, ♂ cilia black with *small white interneural spots* (more strongly chequered in ♀), and *few, well-defined* black spots on *pale orange* ground colour. Underside variegated and cryptic. ♀ has less upper side blue than ♂, silvery, *no opalescent sheen*. ♂ territories in sand dunes; very fast flight close to ground. ♀ found on flowers. **Distribution:** N Cape, on coastal dunes with Succulent Karoo in Port Nolloth/McDougall's Bay area, south to Kleinsee. **Habitat:** Coast, flatlands. **Flight period:** More than two broods, Aug–Mar, peak Nov. **Larval food:** *Zygophyllum* spp. Larvae associated with *Crematogaster* ants.

3 Perseus Opal   *Chrysoritis perseus*

Wingspan: ♂ 24–28 mm ♀ 26–30 mm. **Identification: 3A** ♂ upper side, **3B** ♀ upper side, **3C** ♂ underside. Range overlaps with Pan Opal (below). Both sexes with hind wing upper side silver-blue *more extensive*; variable amount and extent of black forewing spotting and dark marginal borders. Underside cryptic. ♀ basal blue *less extensive* and *darker* than ♂, wings rounder, ground colour *paler orange*. **Distribution:** N Cape, on coastal dunes with Succulent Karoo in Hondeklip Bay/Groenriviermond area, inland to Wallekraal. **Habitat:** Coast, flatlands, hillsides. **Flight period:** More than two broods, Aug–Mar, peak Nov. **Larval food:** *Zygophyllum* spp. and *Thesium* spp. Larvae associated with *Crematogaster melanogaster* ants.

4 Pan Opal   *Chrysoritis pan*

Wingspan: ♂ 20–28 mm ♀ 22–32 mm. **Identification: 4A** ♂ upper side, **4B** ♀ upper side, **4C** ♂ underside. Smaller than Common Opal (p. 230), habits more colonial. ♂ upper side opal-blue covers *smaller* area of wing, but variable – some spring specimens very dark. Hind wing underside variable, pale buff to almost black, darker spots vary from indistinct to streaky marbling of russet brown with brassy sagittate streaks. ♀ upper side *lacks* opal sheen, basal blue *restricted* to basal 25% of wings. **Distribution:** Widespread in Fynbos, Nama Karoo, Succulent Karoo. In W Cape, from Tygerberg to Yzerfontein, Het Kruis and Lambert's Bay to N Cape (Hondeklip Bay, inland to Kamiesberg foothills). From Sutherland (N Cape), east along Nuweveld escarpment to Beaufort West, north to Hamtamsberg (near Calvinia). Along W Cape south coast to Struisbaai and from Matjiesfontein along Klein Swartberg to Langeberg and Little Karoo (Huis River Pass to Garcia's Pass); east as far as Willowmore, E Cape. Colonies near Cape Town under threat from alien vegetation. **Habitat:** Coast, flatlands, hillsides, gullies, dry riverbeds. **Flight period:** Several broods Aug–May, peaks Oct/Nov and Feb/Mar. **Larval food:** *Osteospermum* spp., *Chrysanthemoides incana* and *Zygophyllum retrofractum*. Larvae associated with *Crematogaster* nr *liengmei* ants.

A

1B

1C

A

2B

2C

A

3B

3C

A

4B

4C

1 Beulah's Opal   *Chrysoritis beulah*

Wingspan: ♂ 21–25 mm ♀ 23–32 mm. **Identification: 1A** ♂ upper side, **1B** ♀ upper side, **1C** ♂ underside. Upper side resembles Irene's Opal (below), but forewing basal blue *less extensive*; hind wing basal blue *more extensive; broad orange* hind wing postdiscal area with *sparse or absent* black spotting. Underside hind wing markings *flat* rather than variegated, base colour *pale buff*, with darker tan basal marks and marginal area than Irene's Opal, brassy saggitate streaks *faint or absent*. ♀ with wings rounder than ♂, larger black spotting, *no* iridescent lustre. Flight fast along dry stream beds. Both sexes fond of flowers, including *Acacia karroo*. **Distribution:** E Cape, in arid Nama Karoo on lower slopes of Klein Winterhoekberge and Grootrivierberge hills between Steytlerville and Willowmore, to Jansenville and across the Plains of Camdeboo to Witmos and Graaff-Reinet. **Habitat:** Gullies, hillsides. **Flight period:** Multiple broods, Oct–Feb, peak Nov. **Larval food:** No data.

2 Irene's Opal   *Chrysoritis irene*

Wingspan: ♂ 30–32 mm ♀ 32–34 mm. **Identification: 2A** ♂ upper side, **2B** ♀ upper side, **2C** ♂ underside. Superficially resembles Beulah's Opal (above), forewing upper side dark margin *broader*, usually *touches* basal blue patch; postdiscal black spots *closer to margin*. ♂ forewing basal blue patch *broader*, blue hind wing basal patch *less extensive, few* if any hind wing upper side spots, orange covered with *shifting pinkish lustre* almost to margin. Hind wing underside similar to Beulah's Opal; even less variegated, appearing *flat buff*. ♀ with almost *no basal blue*, hind wing upper side postdiscal black spots *small*. Found at top of steep rocky talus slopes below huge mountain cliffs. **Distribution:** Rare. In Fynbos on Du Toit's Kloof mountains and Riviersonderendberge near Greyton, W Cape. **Habitat:** Rocky slopes, mountains. **Flight period:** Multiple broods, Oct–Apr, peaks Nov and Mar. **Larval food:** Probably *Dimorphotheca* spp.

3 Swanepoel's Opal   *Chrysoritis swanepoeli*

Wingspan: ♂ 23–26 mm ♀ 24–34 mm. **Identification: 3A** ♂ upper side, **3B** ♀ upper side, **3C** ♂ underside. Bright orange Opal, ♂ upper side blue wing patches *small*, hind wing upper side markings *dark*, variable forewing dark borders, specimens from higher altitudes have *more extensive* dark markings. Both sexes have chequered cilia. Underside cryptic. ♀ has *little or no* basal blue, similar black spotting to other ♀ *Chrysoritis* spp., and rounded wings. Colonies in gullies and dry riverbeds from base to summits of high mountains. **Distribution:** Fynbos, Nama Karoo in W Cape. Swartberg Pass and Schoemanskloof (near Cango Caves), Groot Swartberg, and Huis Rivier Pass, Gamkaskloof. **Habitat:** Gullies, mountains, rocky ledges. **Flight period:** Single extended brood, Oct–Jan. **Larval food:** *Thesium* spp. and *Tylecodon paniculata*. Larvae associated with *Crematogaster* nr *liengmei* ants.

4 Daphne's Opal   *Chrysoritis daphne*

Wingspan: ♂ 25–29 mm ♀ 29–31 mm. **Identification: 4A** ♂ upper side, **4B** ♀ upper side, **4C** ♂ underside. Upper side ground colour deep red-orange as in Pyramus Opal (p. 236), ♂ basal blue *not as extensive*; some orange at end of cell. Upper side dark margins broad, merging with submarginal forewing spots. Underside cryptic. ♀ has *less blue, no* shifting lustre, wings *rounder* than ♂. Large, sparse colonies high up steep rocky gullies above big cliffs; difficult to follow. **Distribution:** W Cape, in Fynbos high on southern slopes of Kammanassie Mtns. **Habitat:** Mountains, gullies, rocky ledges. **Flight period:** Single extended brood Nov–Feb, peak Dec. **Larval food:** *Thesium* spp. Larvae associated with *Crematogaster* nr *liengmei* ants.

A

1B

1C

A

2B

2C

A

3B

3C

A

4B

4C

1 Endymion Opal   *Chrysoritis endymion*

Wingspan: ♂ 30–34 mm ♀ 30–38 mm. **Identification: 1A** ♂ upper side, **1B** ♀ upper side, **1C** ♂ underside. Large *Chrysoritis*, upper side orange ground colour *bright* in both sexes, *basal blue patches small* as in Swanepoel's Opal (p. 234), but ♀ has more basal blue, albeit very small patches. Underside hind wing more *brightly marked* than Swanepoel's Opal. Both sexes fly at summits or ridges of huge mountains, ♀ sometimes found higher up than ♂. **Distribution:** W Cape, in high Fynbos on Du Toit's Kloof mountains and Mont Rochelle above Franschhoek, and Jonah's Kop and Die Galg in Riviersonderendberge. Protected in W Cape. **Habitat:** Hill tops, mountains. **Flight period:** Single extended brood, Nov–Jan, possibly continuing later in summer. **Larval food:** *Thesium* spp. and *Thesidium* spp. Larvae associated with *Crematogaster peringueyi* ants.

2 Violet Opal   *Chrysoritis violescens*

Wingspan: ♂ 26–30 mm ♀ 28–32 mm. **Identification: 2A** ♂ upper side, **2B** ♀ upper side, **2C** ♂ underside. Smaller than Beaufort Opal (below), with which it is often found, ♂ silvery blue restricted to *basal third* of upper side. Silvery blue has *violet cast; electric violet* iridescence over upper side orange ground colour. Underside distinctive, with dark basal area and postdiscal band. Sexes dimorphic; ♀ very difficult to distinguish from Turner's Opal (p. 228). Found along rocky ridges on upper slopes of escarpment. **Distribution:** Nama Karoo, restricted to Roggeveld escarpment w of Sutherland (N Cape). **Habitat:** Mountains, rocky ledges. **Flight period:** Aug–Dec, but possibly more than one brood. **Larval food:** *Dimorphotheca cuneata*. Larvae live in shelters attended by *Crematogaster peringueyi* ants.

3 Beaufort Opal   *Chrysoritis beaufortius*

Wingspan: ♂ 32–36 mm ♀ 32–38 mm. **Identification: 3A** ♂ upper side, **3B** ♀ upper side, **3C** ♂ underside. Closely resembles Pyramus Opal (below), upper side dark borders and hind wing spotting *more variable* in extent. ♂ shiny opalescence *paler, more greenish*. Forewing dark borders vary from narrow to so broad as to cover one-third of the wing. Underside hind wing *pale sandy* colour with darker postdiscal band in both sexes; *few* silver saggitate marks. Specimens from higher rainfall areas have darker basal markings. Sexes dimorphic; ♀ with basal blue *limited*, in some specimens only a few scales. Sometimes seen in huge numbers, all over the Karoo, showing no preference for any particular type of habitat, swarming on pink mesembs. **Distribution:** Nama Karoo, Succulent Karoo from W Cape to N Cape on Nuweveldberge and Roggeveld escarpment, and on Hantamsberg and Kamiesberg, Namaqualand. **Habitat:** Mountains, flatlands, hill tops, hillsides, rocky ledges. **Flight period:** Single extended brood, Aug–Feb depending on locality. **Larval food:** *Dimorphotheca cuneata*. Larvae associated with *Crematogaster peringueyi* ants.

4 Pyramus Opal   *Chrysoritis pyramus*

Wingspan: ♂ 32–36 mm ♀ 32–38 mm. **Identification: 4A** ♂ upper side, **4B** ♀ upper side, **4C** ♂ underside. *Deeper red-orange* upper side ground colour than Beaufort Opal (above), ♂ basal silvery blue covered by *electric blue sheen* stretching at forewing base as far as margin. *Broad, black* marginal borders, merging with submarginal spots in some specimens, so that shifting blue lustre prominent. Cilia strongly chequered with white. Underside hind wing *deep red- or ochre-brown*, with *conspicuous* brassy saggitate markings. Sexes dimorphic; ♀ has typical *Chrysoritis* markings, noticeably *deep, rich colouring*. Frequents bare rocky ribs on fynbos-covered hillsides. **Distribution:** Fynbos, Nama Karoo in W Cape, high up northern slopes of Swartberg at Swartberg Pass and surrounding mountains, above Seweweekspoort; also Kammanassie Mts, and Langeberg, above Grootvadersbosch. **Habitat:** Mountains, rocky ledges, hill tops. **Flight period:** Single extended brood, Oct–Jan, peak Nov. **Larval food:** *Thesium* spp., *Osteospermum asperulum* and *Dimorphotheca montana*. Larvae associated with *Crematogaster peringueyi* ants.

A

1B

1C

A

2B

2C

A

3B

3C

A

4B

4C

1 Brauer's Opal   *Chrysoritis braueri*

Wingspan: ♂ 20–24 mm ♀ 21–26 mm. **Identification: 1A** ♂ upper side, **1B** ♀ upper side, **1C** ♂ underside. Upper side margins very *broad and dark*, cilia *strongly chequered* orange and white. Hind wing anal angle *extended to form small tail*. Forewing outer margin strongly angled outwards just below apex, more so than others of the Common Opal group except Brook's (p. 240), Dark (p. 240) and Adonis (p. 242) Opals; ♂ hind wing basal blue blends with postdiscal black spots on upper side, the black forming a border around blue. Sexes very different. ♂ orange markings restricted to forewing upper side apex and hind wing submarginal band, ♀ orange ground colour extensive, basal blue patches small but bright. Underside of both sexes cryptic. Found along ledges of rocky outcrops on grassy hills, often near remnant patches of Afromontane Forest. **Distribution:** Grassland and Savanna in E Cape, from Mbashe River, along Drakensberg foothills to Cala and Queenstown (Long Hill), Winterberg foothills to Bedford and Amatolas. Commercial forestry has destroyed many colonies. **Habitat:** Mountains, rocky ledges, forest edges. **Flight period:** Two extended broods, Aug–Nov and Feb–Apr. **Larval food:** *Zygophyllum* spp. and *Myrsine africana*. Larvae associated with *Crematogaster* spp. ants.

2 Machacha Opal   *Chrysoritis pelion*

Wingspan: ♂ 20–24 mm ♀ 22–30 mm. **Identification: 2A** ♂ upper side, **2B** ♀ upper side, **2C** ♂ underside. Highest flying *Chrysoritis*, 3 000 m and higher. *Bright brick-orange* upper side ground colour similar to Eastern Opal (below), but both sexes with *blue restricted to basal 30% of wing*. Sexes similar, ♀ upper side spots *larger, more well defined*; basal blue *less extensive* than ♂. Underside cryptic. **Distribution:** Mainly in Drakensberg Grassland; E Cape (Ben MacDhui and above Lundean's Nek), Lesotho, KwaZulu-Natal (Langalibalele Pass), Free State (Generaalkop, Golden Gate Highlands NP, Clarens). In Nama Karoo-type vegetation above the grasslands. **Habitat:** Mountains, rocky slopes, hill tops. **Flight period:** Single extended brood, Nov–Feb, peaks Dec. **Larval food:** No data.

3 Pennington's Opal   *Chrysoritis penningtoni*

Wingspan: ♂ 18–22 mm ♀ 20–24 mm. **Identification: 3A** ♂ upper side, **3B** ♀ upper side, **3C** ♂ underside. Similar to Eastern Opal (below), ♂ upper side black borders *narrower*; hind wing postdiscal spots *smaller or absent; pinkish opalescent sheen* distal to blue patches. Sexes similar; both with basal blue more extensive than Eastern Opal. Underside cryptic. Small colonies (3–6 individuals) around rocky outcrops overgrown with bushes. **Distribution:** Rare. Grassland in E Cape, on high slopes of Amatolas (Gaika's Kop, Elandsberg and Hogsback). **Habitat:** Mountains, rocky ledges. **Flight period:** Multi-brooded, Oct–Mar, peak Dec. **Larval food:** No data.

4 Eastern Opal   *Chrysoritis orientalis*

Wingspan: ♂ 18–22 mm ♀ 20–24 mm. **Identification: 4A** ♂ upper side, **4B** ♀ upper side, **4C** ♀ underside. Similar to Brauer's Opal (above), but *smaller*, upper side *brighter, redder orange*; both sexes have *restricted* basal blue, ♂ blue deep and iridescent, ♀ less conspicuous. Upper side forewing margins *broad*, cilia *deeply chequered*, less extensive apical black patches than Brauer's Opal, discal spots *smaller*. Underside cryptic. E Cape specimens more like Machacha Opal (above). Found on ledges of rocky outcrops, congregating where the ledge widens or a gully crosses it. **Distribution:** Grassland in s Drakensberg (above Bushman's Nek), KwaZulu-Natal. **Habitat:** Mountains, rocky ledges, gullies. **Flight period:** Single-brooded, Oct–Jan, peak Dec. **Larval food:** *Thesium* spp. Larvae associated with *Crematogaster* nr *liengmei* ants.

A

1B

1C

A

2B

2C

A

3B

3C

A

4B

4C

1 Brooks's Opal *Chrysoritis brooksi*

Wingspan: ♂ 26–30 mm ♀ 28–32 mm. **Identification: 1A** ♂ upper side, **1B** ♂ underside (*C. b. tearei*), **1C** ♀ upper side (nominate). Distinctive; cilia strongly chequered *black and white*, upper side margins *broad and dark*, forewing apex *squared off*. Underside hind wing has dark lines along veins in marginal area. ♀ upper side paler, blue less extensive than ♂. Nominate upper side paler than *C. b. tearei*, upper side margins *brown*, not black, underside less variegated. **Distribution:** Fynbos, Succulent Karoo. Nominate in W Cape from near Cape Town (but not to the Peninsula) to Brandvlei and Hex River Mountain foothills near Worcester, north to Langebaan; *C. b. tearei* (rare) in W Cape, from Bredasdorp and Riversdale areas. **Habitat:** Flatlands, hillsides. **Flight period:** Sept–Apr, occasionally as late as Jun. Peaks Oct/Nov and Feb. **Larval food:** *Thesium* spp., *Zygophyllum* spp. Larvae associated with *Crematogaster peringueyi* ants.

2 Dark Opal *Chrysoritis nigricans*

Wingspan: ♂ 22–33 mm ♀ 23–38 mm. **Identification: 2A** ♂ upper side, **2B** ♀ upper side, **2C** ♂ underside. Very angular wing shape as in Brauer's (p. 238), Brooks's (above) and Adonis (p. 242) Opals. ♂ upper side forewing apex *black*, sometimes with orange-red spots, hind wing orange-red *restricted to submarginal lunules*. Silvery blue covers basal half of ♂ upper side forewing and much of hind wing; suffused with *electric royal blue to blue-green* opalescent glow. Strongly chequered cilia. Sexes dimorphic; ♀ with rounder wings, *deep orange ground colour, little* basal blue, *heavy* black spots and *wide dark margins*. Both sexes have underside hind wing variegated with silver-gold sagittate streaks. Settles on rocks or flowers. 2 subspp., geographically distinct. **Distribution:** Fynbos. Nominate from Cape Peninsula, to high in Hawequas, Waaihoek, Riviersonderendberge, at sea level Hermanus to Cape Infanta, W Cape; *C. n. zwartbergae* in the Groot Swartberg, from Seweeksport to Swartberg Pass, W Cape. **Habitat:** Mountains, hillsides, coast. **Flight period:** Multi-brooded; longer flight period at lower altitudes, Sept–Apr, peaks Dec and Mar. **Larval food:** *Thesium* spp., *Osteospermum polygaloides* and *Zygophyllum* spp. Larvae associated with *Crematogaster* ants.

3 Uranus Opal *Chrysoritis uranus*

Wingspan: ♂ 24–30 mm ♀ 25–32 mm. **Identification: 3A** ♂ upper side, **3B** ♀ upper side, **3C** ♂ underside. Markings similar to Dark Opal (above), but wings *less angular*; shape similar to Common Opal (p. 230). ♂ forewing *silvery blue more extensive* than Dark Opal; shifting electric blue even *more extensive, more* apical red-orange marks. Underside hind wing *less* finely marked, more ochreous in colour. Sexes dimorphic, ♀ markings similar to Dark Opal. ♂♂ on hill tops and ridge summits, whirling around tall rocks, settling often on the ground but wary. ♀ slower flight, below where ♂♂ fly. Two subspecies. **Distribution:** Fynbos, Succulent Karoo. Nominate – on sw W Cape mountain tops (not to the peninsula); Du Toit's Kloof east to Hex River, north to Waaihoek, Waboomsberge, Gydoberg, Skurweberg, and Witzenberg; south to Riviersonderend area. *C. u. schoemani* Gifberg and Koebee Mt near Vanrhynsdorp, W Cape. **Habitat:** Mountains, hill tops, rocky ledges. **Flight period:** Several broods, Oct–Apr. **Larval food:** *Centella* spp., *Aspalathus* spp. and *Zygophyllum* spp. Larvae associated with *Crematogaster* nr *liengmei* ants.

1A

1B

1C

2A

2B

2C

3A

3B

3C

1 Adonis Opal   *Chrysoritis adonis*

Wingspan: ♂ 29–36 mm ♀ 30–37 mm. **Identification: 1A** ♂ upper side, **1B** ♀ upper side, **1C** ♂ underside. Probably the most spectacular butterfly of the genus. Wing shape angular as in Dark Opal (p. 240), ♂ forewing upper side markings also similar, basal blue *less extensive*. ♂ upper side has electric blue opalescent sheen, penetrating black forewing apex as in Dark Opal, but hind wing upper side orange-red postdiscal band *much broader*, dark wing base *covered with silvery blue*. Sexes dimorphic; ♀ similar to Uranus Opal (p. 240), black postdiscal hind wing upper side spots placed *more basally*, leaving wider orange submarginal area free from spotting; underside hind wing redder. ♂ usually in dry riverbeds and gullies at medium altitude, below ridges where Uranus Opal flies; Elandskloof population ♂♂ found on prominences. ♀ away from ♂ territory, often on flowers with ♀♀ of Uranus Opal. **Distribution:** Rare. W Cape, in Fynbos on northern slopes of Gydoberg, Skurweberg, Baviaanskloofberg and Waboomberg (north of Ceres); Elandskloof near Seweeweekspoort. **Habitat:** Mountains, gullies. **Flight period:** Multiple broods, Oct–Mar, peaks Nov and Jan. **Larval food:** *Thesium* spp. and *Zygophyllum* spp. Larvae associated with *Crematogaster* nr *liengmei* ants.

Genus *Crudaria*   Greys   3 SPP., ENDEMIC TO SOUTH AFRICA, LESOTHO AND SWAZILAND

Small lycaenids, dull grey upper side, underside similar to *Aloeides* but hind wing pale grey with dark mottling. Flight fast and low, not sustained, settling often on the ground, on small rocks, flowers or low branches of shrubs. If disturbed, returns soon to original perch. Found in colonies. Egg laid singly on shoots of Fabaceae and Zygophyllaceae; domed, with finely reticulate pattern of ribs. Larva flattened dorsally with lateral hairs; colour whitish green to pale grey-brown, with fine lines of darker grey, green and red. Shelters under rocks near food plant, attended by *Anaplolepis* ants. Pupa brown, rounded head and thorax, elongated abdomen.

2 Silver-spotted Grey   *Crudaria leroma*

Wingspan: ♂ 20–32 mm ♀ 25–34 mm. **Identification: 2A** ♂ upper side, **2B** ♀ underside. Very variable, especially underside, whose ground colour varies from pale sandy buff to grey-brown; series of spots on both wings vary from strongly outlined in black to being almost invisible. Series of postdiscal spots on forewing underside in zigzag pattern. Upper side varies from pale grey to olive-brown. There is possibly more than 1 subsp. within the range. Sexes similar, ♀ larger, wings rounder. Hind wing carries short tail. Singular resting posture, wings open and forewings held proud. Usually in bare rocky areas; also fond of flowers. **Distribution:** Widespread in Nama Karoo, Savanna, from W Cape (Great Karoo) to E Cape, KwaZulu-Natal, Free State, Mpumalanga, Limpopo and NW provinces, Gauteng and N Cape. **Habitat:** Flatlands, hillsides, rocky slopes. **Flight period:** Year-round in warmer areas, Oct–Mar in cooler areas. **Larval food:** *Acacia karroo, A. sieberana, Elephantorrhiza burkei*.

3 Cape Grey   *Crudaria capensis*

Wingspan: ♂ 20–32 mm ♀ 25–34 mm. **Identification: 3A** ♂ upper side, **3B** ♀ upper side, **3C** ♀ underside. Very similar to Silver-spotted Grey (above). A series of forewing postdiscal spots on underside form a definite oblique line. Underside greyer, with *less metallic spotting* than Silver-spotted Grey. Forewing margin *more convex*. Sexes similar, ♀ with wings rounder than ♂. **Distribution:** In Nama Karoo, from W Cape and E Cape (Calitzdorp to Cookhouse and Witmos); also at Kenhardt in N Cape. **Habitat:** Flatlands, hillsides, rocky slopes. **Flight period:** Single-brooded, Oct–Dec. **Larval food:** Probably *Zygophyllum retrofractum*.

1 Wykeham's Grey   *Crudaria wykehami*

Wingspan: ♂ 20–32 mm ♀ 25–34 mm. **Identification: 1A** ♂ upper side, **1B** ♀ upper side, **1C** ♂ underside. ♂ *darker* than ♀, wings more pointed. Very similar to Silver-spotted Grey (p. 242) but tail *absent*; series of forewing postdiscal spots on underside form a *line parallel to the outer margin*. Flies in open ground between thorn trees. **Distribution:** So far only from farm Huntly Glen north of Bedford, N Cape, in Nama Karoo/Savanna ecotone, but probably found more widely in that area. **Habitat:** Hillsides, rocky slopes. **Flight period:** Probably year-round; found in Nov, Jan and Feb. **Larval food:** Probably *Acacia karroo*.

Genus *Erikssonia*   Coppers   AFRICA 3 SPP., SOUTH AFRICA 1

Small orange butterflies; colonial breeders, low flight, territorial. Egg laid on food plant or on ground near it; dome-shaped with irregular raised convolutions, yellow ochre darkening to grey. Larva flattened dorsally, pinkish grey with maroon dorsal line, bluish-green dorso-lateral stripes, and rows of reddish-brown marks. Pupa squat, deep ochre with rounded head and abdomen. Probably unpalatable; emits bitter smell when handled.

2 Eriksson's Copper   *Erikssonia acraeina*

Wingspan: ♂ 32–40 mm ♀ 34–45 mm. **Identification: 2A** ♂ upper side, **2B** ♂ underside. Cannot be mistaken for any other lycaenid. Superficially resembles ♂ Small Orange Acraea (p. 96); probably a Muellerian mimic. *Bright orange colour* on both surfaces, conspicuous in flight. Slow, low, fluttering flight; ♀ flight more random, found on flowers and near food plant. **Distribution:** *Vulnerable*. Only known from one colony in South Africa, in grassy Savanna dotted with *Burkea africana* near Trichardt's Pass, Waterberg, Limpopo Province. **Habitat:** Flatlands. **Flight period:** Single extended brood, Nov–Feb. **Larval food:** *Gnidia kraussiana*. Larvae shelter during day in nests of *Lepisiota* ants.

Genus *Lycaena*   Sorrel Coppers   WORLD 40 SPP., AFRICA 3, SOUTH AFRICA 2

Small, bright copper butterflies with grey-mottled hind wing underside. Feed on Polygonaceae plants. Flight low, slow, settling often on rocks or low plants. Sometimes occurs in large numbers. Egg laid singly on a shoot of the food plant; white to pale yellow flattened dome, with tracery of ribs forming irregular polygons. Slug-shaped, green larva crawls down to root level of the food plant and shelters there, feeding on the lower leaves. Pupa also smooth and green, concealed below food plant in leaf debris.

3 Western Sorrel Copper   *Lycaena orus*

Wingspan: ♂ 19–25 mm ♀ 21–29 mm. **Identification: 3A** ♂ upper side, **3B** ♀ upper side, **3C** ♀ underside. Brilliant red-orange upper side conspicuous against greenery of habitat. Sexes similar; ♂ darker and shinier than ♀, with shifting *blue-purple iridescence* over the copper, and wings more *angular*. Underside cryptic. **Distribution:** Fynbos. W Cape, from Cape Peninsula east along coast and lower mountain ranges as far as E Cape (Port Elizabeth). **Habitat:** Flatlands, coast, hillsides, wetlands. **Flight period:** Year-round, peak in summer. **Larval food:** *Polygonum undulatum, Rumex lanceolatus*.

4 Eastern Sorrel Copper   *Lycaena clarki*

Wingspan: ♂ 21–27 mm ♀ 22–30 mm. **Identification: 4A** ♂ upper side, **4B** ♀ upper side, **4C** ♀ underside. Has *pale rings* around dark spots on underside. ♂ upper side has *purplish iridescence* over the copper, lacking in paler ♀. Usually found in vleis and along watercourses where food plant grows. Congregates in damp spots along streams even in the driest Karoo and Savanna. **Distribution:** Widespread in Nama Karoo, Grassland, Savanna. From W Cape to E Cape, Free State, KwaZulu-Natal, Limpopo and NW provinces, Gauteng and through Great Karoo to N Cape. **Habitat:** Wetlands, gullies. **Flight period:** Year-round in warmer areas, peak in summer. **Larval food:** *Rumex lanceolatus*.

Genus *Anthene* Hairtails WORLD CA. 144 SPP., AFRICA 137, SOUTH AFRICA 14

Small, fast-flying, active butterflies. Upper side usually blue or shiny brown, underside mottled grey, hind wing veins CuA_1, CuA_2, 1A+2A *extend beyond the margin as* small hairlike tufts, hence the common name, Hairtail. Fond of flowers, on which they can often be approached closely. Eggs laid singly on the food plant; white to pale blue or green, flat-topped or slightly domed discs, criss-crossed with geometric pattern of lines, a small knob at each point where lines cross. Larva slug-shaped and green, often with diagonal dorso-lateral stripes, patterning providing camouflage against Acacia leaves. It feeds on leaves; sometimes attended by ants, but no close association. Most are not difficult to distinguish, except for the Otacilia Hairtail group (p. 250).

1 Common Hairtail *Anthene definita definita*

Wingspan: ♂ 21–27 mm ♀ 24–29 mm. **Identification: 1A** ♂ upper side, **1B** ♀ upper side, **1C** ♂ underside. Sexes dimorphic; ♂ has pointed wings, upper side deep *steel blue*, and underside *dove grey*, with rows of slightly darker grey spots. ♀ upper side *pale blue* with grey borders; underside ground colour *whitish*, with *dark spots* where ♂ is spotted grey. **Distribution:** Widespread and common in the north and around the coast. **Habitat:** Forest edges, parks and gardens, coast, hillsides. **Flight period:** Year-round in warmer areas, peak in summer. **Larval food:** *Allophyllus africanus, Pappea capensis, Mangifera indica, Myrica sericea, Acacia karroo, A. saligna, Paraserianthus lophanta, Schotia* sp., *Bersama* sp. and *Kalanchoe* spp.

2 Large Hairtail *Anthene lemnos lemnos*

Wingspan: ♂ 27–30 mm ♀ 27–31 mm. **Identification: 2A** ♂ upper side, **2B** ♀ upper side, **2C** ♂ underside. Sexes dimorphic. ♂ upper side resembles Common Hairtail (above), underside with *whitish-edged grey bands* on *fawn-grey* background. ♀ upper side extensively *violet-blue*, grey underside ground colour suffused with white. Flight slow compared to other Hairtails, along edges of forest, settling often on leaves. Fond of flowers, particularly *Deinbollia*. **Distribution:** Lowland Forest in KwaZulu-Natal, from Durban to Kosi Bay and further north. **Habitat:** Forest edges, coast. **Flight period:** Year-round, peaks late summer/autumn. **Larval food:** *Erythrococca berberidea, E. polyandra.*

3 Liodes Hairtail *Anthene liodes*

Wingspan: ♂ 21–25 mm ♀ 21–27 mm. **Identification: 3A** ♂ upper side, **3B** ♀ upper side, **3C** ♀ underside. Prominent *whitish underside.* ♂ has upper side *pale metallic blue,* ♀ upper side blue *duller, restricted,* sometimes tinged *whitish.* Found along forest edges and around treetops. **Distribution:** Rare in South Africa. Lowland and Riverine Forest from KwaZulu-Natal (Pongola River below Jozini Dam) to Swaziland, Mpumalanga (Komati River, Malelane) and Limpopo Province (Pafuri), and further north. **Habitat:** Forest edges. **Flight period:** Year-round, peak in summer. **Larval food:** *Mangifera indica, Combretum* sp., *Myrica* sp. and *Allophyllus* spp.

A

1B

C

2A

B

2C

3A

B

3C

1 Black-striped Hairtail   *Anthene amarah amarah*

Wingspan: ♂ 21–26 mm ♀ 23–29 mm. **Identification: 1A** ♂ upper side, **1B** ♀ upper side, **1C** ♂ underside. ♂ upper side a darker olive-brown than ♀, with a distinctive *brassy sheen*. Unique *black streak* at forewing base on underside of both sexes. Very fond of *Acacia* blossoms. **Distribution:** Widespread and common throughout South Africa excluding the western parts and the highest mountains. **Habitat:** Flatlands, hillsides. **Flight period:** Year-round, peak in summer. **Larval food:** *Acacia* spp., especially *A. karroo, A. sieberana* and *A. gerrardii.*

2 Kersten's Hairtail   *Anthene kersteni*

Wingspan: ♂ 26–28 mm ♀ 23–29 mm. **Identification: 2A** ♂ upper side, **2B** ♀ upper side, **2C** ♂ underside. Often found with Large Hairtail (p. 246), ♂ with similar dark *steel-blue* upper side. ♀ upper side dark *grey to black*, whitish *submarginal lunules* on both wings, usually with some white scaling at basal margin of forewing. Both sexes with striking underside pattern of white-edged dark grey bands on paler grey ground. **Distribution:** Coastal Lowland Forest in KwaZulu-Natal, from south coast to Kosi Bay, inland across the Makathini Flats, and north into Mozambique and Zimbabwe. **Habitat:** Forest edges. **Flight period:** Year-round, peak in summer. **Larval food:** *Acacia kraussiana* and *Albizia adianthifolia.*

3 Pale Hairtail   *Anthene butleri livida*

Wingspan: ♂ 23–28 mm ♀ 25–32 mm. **Identification: 3A** ♂ upper side, **3B** ♀ upper side, **3C** ♀ underside. Sexes similar, ♀ with wings *rounder*, upper side usually *brighter blue* than ♂, underside *flat grey*. ♂ a common midday hill-topper in rocky, hilly country. **Distribution:** Widespread in Savanna and Grassland in N Cape, E Cape, KwaZulu-Natal, Free State, Gauteng, Mpumalanga, Limpopo and NW provinces, and further north. **Habitat:** Hill tops, hillsides. **Flight period:** Year-round, peak in warmer months. **Larval food:** *Kalanchoe crenata, K. lugardii* and *Cotyledon* spp., including *C. orbiculata.*

4 Millar's Hairtail   *Anthene millari*

Wingspan: ♂ 21–24 mm ♀ 22–28 mm. **Identification: 4A** ♂ upper side, **4B** ♂ underside. Resembles small Pale Hairtail (above), ♂ with upper side a more *conspicuous blue*. ♀ with wings *more elongated* than ♂. Underside of both sexes grey. May be overlooked because ♂ flies high in trees and ♀ is secretive. **Distribution:** Most often found in Savanna and Grassland in thorn belt of E Cape (Cookhouse and Fort Beaufort), KwaZulu-Natal Midlands, Gauteng (Magaliesberg), Mpumalanga (hills near Lydenburg) and Limpopo Province (Letaba). **Habitat:** Hill tops, hillsides. **Flight period:** Single extended brood, Oct–Jan, peak Nov. **Larval food:** Probably *Kalanchoe* and *Cotyledon* spp.

A

1B

1C

A

2B

2C

A

3B

3C

A

4B

1 Cupreous Hairtail   *Anthene princeps princeps*

Wingspan: ♂ 22–27 mm ♀ 24–29 mm. **Identification: 1A** ♂ upper side, **1B** ♀ upper side, **1C** ♂ underside. Similar to Pale Hairtail (p. 248), underside grey irrorations *more well defined*, ♂ upper side *metallic pinkish grey*. ♀ upper side resembles dull ♀ Pale Hairtail. ♂ flies around hill tops at midday, ♀ found lower down, often on wet mud at stream banks. Sometimes in gardens in Durban. **Distribution:** Lowland Forest, Riverine Forest, Savanna. Mostly in coastal woodland and lowland savanna; most common in KwaZulu-Natal coastal areas, inland to Swaziland, and lowlands of Mpumalanga. One record from Nooitgedacht, near Parys, Free State. **Habitat:** Forest edges, parks and gardens, coast, wetlands. **Flight period:** Year-round, mainly Nov–Feb. **Larval food:** Probably *Albizia gummifera*.

2 Juanita's Hairtail   *Anthene juanitae*

Wingspan: ♂ 25 mm ♀ 27–29 mm. **Identification: 2A** ♂ upper side, **2B** ♀ upper side, **2C** ♀ underside. ♂ upper side *purplish blue*, narrow dark outer marginal line. ♀ upper side dark grey-brown with white submarginal lunules and *bright blue suffusion* on both wings. Underside (both sexes) resembles Kersten's Hairtail (p. 248) but *paler, with narrower dark grey bands*. **Distribution:** Extremely rare. Only in Riverine Forest at Olifants River, Limpopo Province near Abel Erasmus Pass, sucking at wet mud; pupae found nearby under a stone. Locality has been destroyed by development, and discovery of other colonies is desirable. **Habitat:** Forest edges. **Flight period:** Only found Nov, but probably year-round. **Larval food:** No data.

Otacilia Hairtail group

This complex comprises five very similar species: Otacilia Hairtail, Mashuna Hairtail, Talbot's Hairtail, Little Hairtail and Linda's Hairtail. The ♂ ♂ in this group are visually discernible by individual upper side coloration, but the ♀ ♀ are extremely difficult to tell apart. However, the ♂ ♂ tend not to mix with other species, so identification of the ♂ should indicate the species to which the ♀ belongs. Generally, ♀ ♀ have grey to grey-brown ground colour, hind wing upper side anal spots well defined, sometimes whitish postdiscal streaks on hind wing upper side, variable amounts of basal blue.

3 Otacilia Hairtail   *Anthene otacilia otacilia*

Wingspan: ♂ 22–23 mm ♀ 23–24 mm. **Identification: 3A** ♂ upper side, **3B** ♀ upper side (broad basal blue), **3C** ♀ upper side (little basal blue), **3D** ♂ underside. Sexes dimorphic. ♀ almost impossible to distinguish from others of Otacilia Hairtail group. ♂ upper side mid-blue to pale violet-blue *visible at all angles*, unlike Mashuna or Talbot's Hairtails (p. 252), on a grey-brown ground. Blue covers hind wing to *submarginal area*, forewing from *inner margin to cell* and in areas *1A + 2A, CuA₁ and CuA₂*. ♀ has blue (*paler, less brassy* than the ♂) on forewing varying from none to a strong basal patch. Underside (both sexes) cryptic. Rapid flight, small size makes it difficult to follow. Whirls around tree tops with other small lycaenids; also around low-growing flowers. **Distribution:** Savanna, Lowland Forest and coastal bush from W Cape (Mossel Bay) to E Cape, KwaZulu-Natal, Swaziland, Mpumalanga, Limpopo and NW provinces, and further north. **Habitat:** Coast, flatlands, hillsides. **Flight period:** Sept–May, peaks Nov and Mar. **Larval food:** *Acacia* spp., including *A. karroo*.

1B

C

2A

B

2C

3A

B

3C

3D

1 Mashuna Hairtail *Anthene contrastata mashuna*

Wingspan: ♂ 19–23 mm ♀ 21–24 mm. **Identification: 1A** ♂ upper side, with violet-blue visible, **1B** ♂ upper side, violet-blue not visible, **1C** ♀ upper side, with basal blue, **1D** ♀ upper side, no basal blue, **1E** ♂ underside, **1F** ♀ underside. ♂ identified by upper side brassy violet-blue forewing patch, only visible from certain angles. It covers inner margin and basal part of cell, areas 1A + 2A and CuA$_1$, *but not* CuA$_2$. ♀ upperside almost impossible to distinguish from other ♀♀ of Otacilia Hairtail group. As with Otacilia (p. 250) and Talbot's (below) Hairtails, amount of upper side basal blue varies, as shown. Underside (both sexes) cryptic. **Distribution:** Nama Karoo, Savanna, Arid Savanna. From W Cape (Robertson, Beaufort West), through thorn savanna of KwaZulu-Natal Midlands to Free State, Gauteng, Mpumalanga, Limpopo and NW provinces; also N Cape. **Habitat:** Flatlands, hillsides. **Flight period:** Sept–Jun, peaks Nov and Mar/Apr. **Larval food:** *Acacia* spp., including *A. karroo* and *A. tortilis*.

2 Talbot's Hairtail *Anthene talboti*

Wingspan: ♂ 20–24 mm ♀ 22–25 mm. **Identification: 2A** ♂ upper side, **2B** ♀ upper side, **2C** ♀ underside. ♂ like Mashuna Hairtail (above) in that upper side brassy violet-blue is only visible from certain angles, but its extent is different; it only covers inner margin and basal part of cell, area 1A + 2A *to outer margin*, and *not* CuA$_1$ or CuA$_2$. ♀ almost impossible to distinguish from other ♀♀ of Otacilia Hairtail group. Underside (both sexes) cryptic. **Distribution:** Thorny Savanna in KwaZulu-Natal Midlands, through Free State, Gauteng, Mpumalanga, Limpopo and NW provinces; also Arid Savanna in N Cape. **Habitat:** Flatlands, hillsides. **Flight period:** Sept–Jun, peaks Nov and Mar/Apr. **Larval food:** *Acacia* spp., including *A. karroo* and *A. tortilis*.

3 Little Hairtail *Anthene minima*

Wingspan: ♂ 18–22 mm ♀ 19–23 mm. **Identification: 3A** ♂ upper side, **3B** ♂ underside. *Very small*, dark, *no* upper side blue in either sex. Sexes similar; ♂ ground colour coppery brown, ♀ similar to other ♀♀ of Otacilia Hairtail group, but smaller. Underside (both sexes) cryptic. Forewing outer margin convex. May have been overlooked due to small size and habit of congregating with dozens of other tiny lycaenids on tree tops. **Distribution:** Thorny Savanna in ne KwaZulu-Natal, Hluhluwe and Mkuze area; scattered records from Durban area, and Savanna of n Limpopo Province and Mpumalanga. **Habitat:** Flatlands, hillsides. **Flight period:** Sept–Apr. **Larval food:** Probably *Acacia* spp.

1 Linda's Hairtail *Anthene lindae*

Wingspan: ♂ 19 mm ♀ 22 mm. **Identification: 1A** ♂ upper side, **1B** ♀ underside, **1C** ♂ underside. Similar in size, appearance and habits to Little Hairtail (p. 252); ♂ upper side *darker bronze-brown*, with dark brown marginal border. ♀ upper side as Little Hairtail. ♂ hind wing underside has *pale white* basal suffusion almost obscuring grey ground colour. ♀ hind wing underside pale white-grey, with conspicuous *dark spots* in typical *Anthene* pattern, *outlined in white*. Feeds on blossoms of *Acacia erioloba* and *Grewia flava*. **Distribution:** Only known from a few localities in Arid Savanna near Witsand, N Cape, near the Langeberge. **Habitat:** Flatlands. **Flight period:** Single-brooded, Sept–Dec, emergence probably depends on timing of rains; may fly all summer. **Larval food:** No data, but possibly *Acacia erioloba*.

Genus *Uranothauma* Black Heart

AFRICA 14 SPP., SOUTH AFRICA 1

Small lycaenids, upper side brown, suffused with iridescent purple-bronze. Fond of flowers and wet mud; active, fast fliers. Both sexes fly rapidly around Acacia trees, settling often on blossoms. Eggs laid singly on young shoots of food plants (Fabaceae). Slug-shaped green larva feeds on shoots and leaves; smooth, rounded green pupa concealed under a leaf or in crevices in bark.

2 Black Heart *Uranothauma nubifer nubifer*

Wingspan: ♂ 22–26 mm ♀ 24–28 mm. **Identification: 2A** ♂ upper side, **2B** ♀ upper side, **2C** ♂ underside. Common name refers to black scent patch in centre of ♂ forewing on upper side, absent in ♀. ♀ has series of *small discal black spots* on the forewing. Underside (both sexes) dull dun-brown with darker brown basal, discal and submarginal bands outlined with white irroration, cryptic when sitting on the ground. Sometimes occurs in large numbers. **Distribution:** Widespread but rather localised. Grassland and thorny Savanna of KwaZulu-Natal Midlands, Free State, Gauteng, Mpumalanga, Limpopo and NW provinces, and Arid Savanna in N Cape. Also in savanna enclaves in Grassland. **Habitat:** Flatlands, hillsides. **Flight period:** Year-round, peak Nov–Feb. **Larval food:** *Acacia* spp., including *A. karroo*.

Genus *Cacyreus* Bronzes

AFRICA 9 SPP., SOUTH AFRICA 5

Small, low-flying butterflies, underside ground colour dun-brown, irrorated with white, forewing with joined series of darker brown spots edged with white. Hind wing underside marbled with brown, white and black. Upper side blue or shiny brown. Favours stream banks, wooded kloofs, and gardens. Egg laid singly on shoots and flowers of food plants (Lamiaceae and Geraniaceae). Pill-shaped, with concave top and reticulate pattern of ribs in involuted curves radiating from the micropyle, forming triangles and quadrangles, rather like the centre of a daisy. Small knobs at the points where the ribs cross. Larva slug-shaped, green or pale pink, marked with darker green or dull red in longitudinal stripes or diagonal lines. Feeds on shoots and flowers; not ant associated. Pupa more or less hairy, rounded, whitish to green or grey, speckled with darker colour. Concealed in debris below the food plant.

3 Bush Bronze *Cacyreus lingeus*

Wingspan: ♂ 22–27 mm ♀ 22–28 mm. **Identification: 3A** ♂ upper side, **3B** ♀ upper side, **3C** ♂ underside. Very similar to Mocker Bronze (p. 256); only certain distinguishing feature the orientation of the inner edge of a blotch on hind wing costa of underside (see arrow), which points *towards* the body. ♂ upper side *soft metallic blue*, ♀ *variegated grey* with *blue and white* marks. Cilia chequered in both sexes. **Distribution:** Afromontane, Lowland and Riverine Forest from W Cape (Cape Peninsula), along wet side of mountains to E Cape, KwaZulu-Natal, Swaziland, Mpumalanga, Free State and Limpopo Province. **Habitat:** Forest edges, parks and gardens, gullies, wetlands. **Flight period:** Year-round, peak Oct–Feb; seldom in winter months in cooler areas. **Larval food:** Flowers of various Lamiaceae including *Plectranthus*, *Salvia*, *Calamintha*, *Lavandula*, *Mentha* and *Hemizygia* spp.

A

1B

1C

A

2B

C

3A

B

3C

1 Mocker Bronze or Mocker Blue *Cacyreus virilis*

Wingspan: ♂ 24–26 mm ♀ 24–27 mm. **Identification: 1A** ♂ upper side, **1B** ♀ upper side, **1C** ♂ underside. Extremely similar to Bush Bronze (p. 254), upper side almost identical: ♂ cilia *more evenly chequered*, ♀ white *less extensive*, lacks dark grey forewing discal mark. On underside, the inner edge of small white-edged grey blotch on hind wing costa points *away from* the body (see arrow – in Bush Bronze it points *towards it*). **Distribution:** Not as widespread as Bush Bronze. In thorny and grassy Savanna areas of KwaZulu-Natal, Mpumalanga, Gauteng, Limpopo and NW provinces, and further north. **Habitat:** Rocky ledges, hillsides, gullies. **Flight period:** Year-round, peak Nov–Feb. **Larval food:** Flowers of various Lamiaceae including *Coleus, Salvia, Calamintha* and *Lavandula* spp.

2 Water Bronze or Water Blue *Cacyreus tespis tespis*

Wingspan: ♂ 15–25 mm ♀ 17–25 mm. **Identification: 2A** ♂ upper side, **2B** ♂ underside (f. *ecaudata*, latter on *Geranium incanum* flower). Sexes similar, ♂ uniform *coppery violet* sheen over brown upper side, ♀ *shiny brown* with basal *violet-blue* patches. Underside cryptic. Populations described as f. *ecaudata* along eastern hills of Free State and from Lesotho often *lack hind wing tail*. Found in small colonies. **Distribution:** Widespread, locally common in Grassland. From W Cape (Cape Peninsula) along coast to E Cape; at varying altitudes (up to 3 000 m) along Drakensberg chain into KwaZulu-Natal, Lesotho, Free State, Mpumalanga, and Limpopo Province. **Habitat:** Wetlands, mountains, gullies, coast. **Flight period:** Year-round in warmer areas, usually Aug–May; at highest altitudes, only Dec and Jan. **Larval food:** Buds and green seeds of *Geranium* and *Pelargonium* spp.

3 Geranium Bronze *Cacyreus marshalli*

Wingspan: ♂ 15–23 mm ♀ 18–27 mm. **Identification: 3A** ♂ upper side, **3B** ♂ underside. Range overlaps with Water Bronze (above), with which it may be confused if only underside visible; upper side *totally lacks violet or violet-blue sheen*. Sexes similar, ♀ *larger* wings more *rounded*. **Distribution:** Very widespread due to adaptation to cultivated pelargoniums; probably originally only in sw South Africa, but has spread to the rest of the country and even to Europe (pest in Spain, has reached UK). In Forest, Savanna and Grassland from W Cape (Cape Peninsula) along coast to E Cape; at varying altitudes along Drakensberg chain into KwaZulu-Natal, Lesotho, Free State, Gauteng, Mpumalanga, and Limpopo and NW provinces. **Habitat:** Parks and gardens, gullies, mountains, coast, hillsides, wetlands, flatlands. **Flight period:** Year-round in warmer areas, usually Aug–May; at highest altitudes only Dec and Jan. **Larval food:** Buds, flowers and green seeds of *Geranium* and *Pelargonium* spp.

4 Dickson's Geranium Bronze *Cacyreus dicksoni*

Wingspan: ♂ 16–24 mm ♀ 19–25 mm. **Identification: 4A** ♂ upper side, **4B** ♂ underside. *Smaller* than Geranium Bronze (above), upper side *deeper, more metallic bronze* in both sexes, cilia *heavily* chequered. Underside hind wing carries *more* basal white marbling than Geranium Bronze, inverted V-shaped postdiscal mark blended into marbling in that species, *conspicuous* in Dickson's Geranium Bronze. Sometimes on hill tops and ridges, flying in the shelter of small shrubs. **Distribution:** Fynbos, Nama Karoo, Succulent Karoo, from W Cape (Cape Peninsula) along west coast to N Cape (Namaqualand), over a wide range of altitudes. **Habitat:** Coast, hillsides, hill tops, rocky ledges, mountains. **Flight period:** Aug–Mar. **Larval food:** Buds, flowers and green seeds of *Geranium* and *Pelargonium* spp.

A

1B

1C

A

2B

A

3B

A

4B

Genus *Zintha*   Hintza Blue

A small, active blue butterfly with underside chequered white and black. ♂ forms territories and perches on twigs of prominent shrubs, chasing intruders; flight fast, whirling. ♀ more sedentary. Both sexes often found sucking at wet mud, also fond of flowers. Egg laid singly on young leaves of Rhamnaceae; pill-shaped, covered in tiny polygonal indentations formed by a double whorled pattern of ribs. Larva shaped like flattened slug; green, with fringe of short hairs and longitudinal pattern of darker lines. Eats surface of leaf only, leaving troughs or a whole skeletal leaf skin. Pupa slightly hairy, white to cream or grey, spotted and speckled with black. Concealed under a leaf or in loose debris.

1 Hintza Blue   *Zintha hintza hintza*

Wingspan: ♂ 24–28 mm ♀ 24–27 mm. **Identification: 1A** ♂ upper side, **1B** ♀ upper side, **1C** ♂ underside. One of South Africa's most striking small Blues. ♂ with *blue more extensive* than ♀. In flight, difficult to separate from *Tuxentius* spp. Found wherever food plant grows. **Distribution:** Uncommon. Savanna, Arid Savanna in e and c South Africa, from E Cape coastal areas, to KwaZulu-Natal, Free State, Gauteng, Mpumalanga, Limpopo and NW provinces and N Cape. **Habitat:** Flatlands, hillsides, hill tops. **Flight period:** Sept–Apr. **Larval food:** *Ziziphus* spp., including *Z. zeheriana* and *Z. mucronata*.

Genus *Tuxentius*   Pies

Tiny lycaenids; underside black spotted white. Upper side white or buff with black markings. Flits around trees, feeding on flowers, and often sucks damp mud. May be found in numbers near the food plant. ♂ visits hill tops in the mornings. Egg laid singly on young leaves of Rhamnaceae; white, pill-shaped, covered in tiny polygonal indentations formed by a double whorled pattern of ribs. Larva shaped like flattened slug; green, with fringe of short hairs and longitudinal pattern of darker lines. Eats surface of leaf only, leaving troughs or a whole skeletal leaf skin. Pupa slightly hairy, white to cream or grey, spotted and speckled with black; concealed under a leaf or in loose debris.

2 White Pie   *Tuxentius calice calice*

Wingspan: ♂ 21–24 mm ♀ 21–25 mm. **Identification: 2A** ♂ upper side, **2B** ♂ underside. Sexes alike; black and white on both upper side and underside. More localised than very similar Black Pie (below). **Distribution:** Savanna in e and c South Africa, from KwaZulu-Natal Midlands thorn areas, to Gauteng, Mpumalanga, and Limpopo and NW provinces. **Habitat:** Hill tops, flatlands, hillsides. **Flight period:** Year-round, most common Oct–Mar. **Larval food:** *Ziziphus mucronata* and probably other *Ziziphus* spp.

3 Black Pie   *Tuxentius melaena*

Wingspan: ♂ 19–24 mm ♀ 21–25 mm. **Identification: 3A** ♂ upper side (*T. m. griqua*), **3B** ♂ upper side, **3C** ♂ underside (nominate). Similar to White Pie (above); distinguished by underside markings. *A wide gap* (see arrow) divides distal three black dots from the rest along hind wing costa. In *T. calice*, they are *evenly spaced*. Upper side of *T. m. griqua* sometimes suffused with grey-brown. Sexes similar. 2 subspp., geographically distinct. **Distribution:** Savanna, Arid Savanna, Riverine Forest, Lowland Forest. Spp. as follows: nominate in woodland and savanna from E Cape to KwaZulu-Natal coast, through thorn areas, into Gauteng, Mpumalanga and Limpopo and NW provinces; *T. m. griqua* (rare) in Arid Savanna and riverine bush in N Cape, along Vaal River from Windsorton to Barkly West, and north-west to Kuruman and Witsand area. **Habitat:** Coast, hill tops, flatlands, hillsides. **Flight period:** Year-round, most common Oct–Mar. **Larval food:** *Ziziphus mucronata*, probably other *Ziziphus* spp.

A

1B

C

2A

B

3A

B

3C

1 **Western Pie**   *Tuxentius hesperis*
Wingspan: ♂ 18–22 mm ♀ 20–23 mm. **Identification: 1A** ♂ upper side, **1B** ♀ upper side, **1C** ♂ underside. Upper side *darker* than other two South African *Tuxentius* spp.; underside *creamy buff*, not white, with *very small* black spots. Sexes similar, ♀ upper side more brown-grey than ♂. Usually found high around trees; sometimes on low-growing flowers. **Distribution:** Riverine Forest, Arid Savanna. Only at Groblershoop and Vioolsdrif and along banks of Orange River, N Cape. **Habitat:** Wetlands. **Flight period:** Year-round, most common Oct–Dec. **Larval food:** *Ziziphus mucronata*.

Genus *Leptotes*   Blues

WORLD CA. 20 SPP., AFRICA 13, SOUTH AFRICA 5

Small blue lycaenids, all very similar in appearance.

Common Blue group

Common Blue, Short-toothed Blue, Jeannel's Blue, and Babault's Blue are impossible to tell apart in the hand, let alone in the field, genital dissection being the only sure method of identification. They tend not to mix, so once one is identified its companions are usually the same species. Attracted to wet mud; with other small Blues, whirls around trees. Single egg laid on shoots and flower buds of Fabaceae; a flat-topped pill shape, with fine reticulate pattern of double whorled ribs. Larva slug-shaped, white to green or buff, with darker marks of brown, red or black, dorsal stripe and strongly marked diagonal lateral stripes. Pupa rounded, white to cream or pale grey, speckled or spotted with black or brown. Concealed in debris or empty seed pods.

2 **Common Blue**   *Leptotes pirithous pirithous*
Wingspan: ♂ 21–29 mm ♀ 24–30 mm. **Identification: 2A** ♂ upper side, **2B** ♀ upper side, **2C** ♀ underside. Only distinguishable from others of Common Blue group by genital dissection. ♂ upper side plain blue, ♀ with wide grey-brown margins, blue crossed by white-edged grey-brown bands. Underside ground colour pale grey with darker grey bands and blotches, outlined in white. **Distribution:** Common and widespread. Throughout South Africa in all biomes; only absent from highest mountains. **Habitat:** Parks and gardens, hill tops, flatlands, hillsides, rocky ledges, coast, forest edges. **Flight period:** Year-round in warmer areas, Oct–Mar in cooler areas. **Larval food:** Flowers and immature seeds of *Plumbago auriculata*, also *Indigofera, Rhynchosia, Vigna, Burkea, Mundulea, Melilotus* and *Crataegus* spp., and *Medicago sativa*.

3 **Short-toothed Blue**   *Leptotes brevidentatus*
Wingspan: ♂ 22–29 mm ♀ 26–30 mm. **Identification: 3A** ♂ upper side, **3B** ♀ upper side, **3C** ♂ underside. Only reliably distinguished from others of Common Blue group by genital dissection. **Distribution:** In all biomes except arid ne W Cape and N Cape, from W Cape (Cape Town), along coast to E Cape and KwaZulu-Natal, inland to Mpumalanga and Limpopo Province and further north. **Habitat:** Parks and gardens, hill tops, flatlands, hillsides, rocky ledges, coast, forest edges. **Flight period:** Year-round in warmer areas, Oct–Mar in cooler areas. **Larval food:** Flowers and immature seeds of *Plumbago auriculata*; probably also *Indigofera, Rhynchosia, Vigna, Burkea, Mundulea, Melilotus* and *Crataegus* spp., and *Medicago sativa*.

4 **Jeannel's Blue**   *Leptotes jeanneli*
Wingspan: ♂ 22–29 mm ♀ 26–30 mm. **Identification: 4A** ♂ upper side, **4B** ♀ upper side, **4C** ♂ underside. Only distinguishable from others of Common Blue group by genital dissection. ♂ upper side plain blue, ♀ with wide grey-brown margins, blue crossed by white-edged grey-brown bands. Underside ground colour pale grey with darker grey bands and blotches, outlined in white. **Distribution:** Savanna, Grassland and Forest in Mpumalanga and Limpopo Province lowveld and escarpment, and further north. **Habitat:** Hill tops, hillsides, flatlands, rocky ledges, forest edges. **Flight period:** Year-round, peak Nov–Apr. **Larval food:** No data.

A

1B

1C

A

2B

C

3A

B

3C

A

4B

4C

1 Babault's Blue   *Leptotes babaulti*

Wingspan: ♂ 22–29 mm ♀ 26–30 mm. **Identification: 1A** ♂ upper side, **1B** ♀ upper side, **1C** ♂ underside. Only reliably distinguished from others of Common Blue group by genital dissection, but underside grey tends to be darker than others of group. **Distribution:** Savanna, Afromontane, Riverine and Lowland Forest, Grassland. Mpumalanga and Limpopo Province lowveld and escarpment, and further north. **Habitat:** Hill tops, hillsides, flatlands, rocky ledges, forest edges. **Flight period:** Year-round, peak Nov–Apr. **Larval food:** No data.

2 Sesbania Blue   *Leptotes pulchra*

Wingspan: ♂ 18–24 mm ♀ 18–26 mm. **Identification: 2A** ♂ upper side, **2B** ♀ upper side, **2C** ♂ underside. Easily distinguished from Common Blue group by smaller size, paler but brighter upper side blue in both sexes. ♂ upper side hind wing has white scaling around anal area. Underside white lines thinner and more well defined. Ground colour more brown-grey; pale hind wing submarginal markings merge to form pale band. Usually found in colonies close to food plant. Flight slow, fluttering. **Distribution:** Riverine and Lowland Forest, Grassland. Only from KwaZulu-Natal: lowlands near Richards Bay, Makane's Drift near Ndumu GR, and at higher altitude at Merthley's Lake, near Greytown. **Habitat:** Forest edges, wetlands. **Flight period:** Year-round, peak Nov–May further north, probably only the warmer months in South Africa. **Larval food:** *Sesbania sesban*.

Genus *Lampides*   Long-Tailed Blue   MONOTYPIC

Common and widespread all over the Old World and Africa. Flight fast and uneven, ♂ a familiar hill top sight, whirling around high points and prominent shrubs, settling on leaves and twigs. ♂ also founds territories in forest clearings and broad parts of rocky ledges. Both sexes may be found on flowers. Egg laid singly on flowers and seed pods of Fabaceae; pale blue-green, flat-topped pill shape, with fine reticulate pattern of double whorled ribs. Slug-shaped, humpbacked pale green larva with darker green or pale reddish dorsal and diagonal lateral stripes. Feeds on seeds, lives concealed in seed pods. Smooth white to cream or grey pupa speckled with grey or black, concealed in dry seed pod.

3 Long-Tailed Blue   *Lampides boeticus*

Wingspan: ♂ 24–32 mm ♀ 24–34 mm. **Identification: 3A** ♂ upper side, **3B** ♀ upper side, **3C** ♂ underside. Sexes dimorphic; ♂ upper side blue with *deeper mauve-blue wing bases* visible in flight; ♀ upper side has broader grey-brown borders on both wings. Underside (both sexes) with distinctive *white lines on fawn ground colour*. ♀ more sedentary habits than ♂. **Distribution:** Throughout South Africa in all biomes. **Habitat:** Hill tops, parks and gardens, flatlands, hillsides, mountains, rocky ledges, coast, forest edges. **Flight period:** Year-round, peak Nov–Mar in warmer areas; only Nov–Mar in cold areas. **Larval food:** Flowers, seeds and pods of many Fabaceae including *Medicago, Crotolaria, Polygala, Sutherlandia, Dolichos, Cytisus, Spartium* and *Lathyrus* spp.

Genus *Tarucus*   Blues   WORLD CA. 23 SPP., AFRICA 12, SOUTH AFRICA 3

Small, brilliant blue lycaenids. Underside white or grey with dark mottling or spotting. ♀ blue less extensive, limited by dark markings and white areas. Flight flitting, and usually only around food plants. Egg laid singly on shoots of food plant; white, cup-shaped, with double whorled reticulate pattern of ribs forming polygons, and tiny elongated protuberances where the ribs cross. Larva flattened, slug-like, triangular in cross-section; green or white to grey, with faint pattern of longitudinal or diagonal darker lines. Eats surface of leaf. Pupa white to cream or pale grey, speckled with black or dark red. Concealed below leaf or in debris below plant.

A

1B

1C

A

2B

C

3A

B

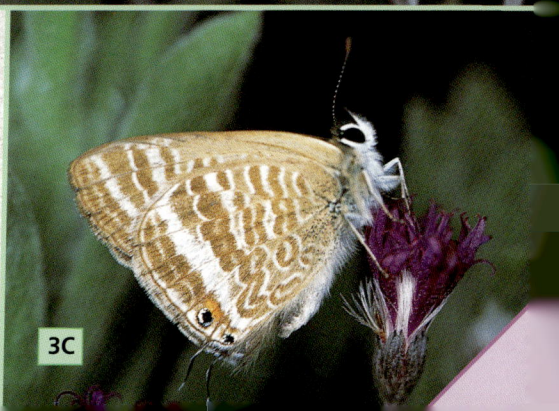

3C

1 Dotted Blue   *Tarucus sybaris*

Wingspan: ♂ 22–26 mm ♀ 20–27 mm. **Identification: 1A** ♂ upper side (*T. s. linearis*), **1B** ♀ upper side, **1C** ♀ underside (nominate). Only member of *Tarucus* genus in South Africa to carry a hind wing tail. Sexes dimorphic; ♂ upper side brilliant sky-blue, ♀ dark grey-brown with *white discal areas* spotted with grey-brown, *only blue at wing bases*. Underside (both sexes) white, *polka-dotted* with black. Flight slow, close to food plant. 2 subspp., geographically distinct. **Distribution:** Common in grassy Savanna and Grassland. Nominate in E Cape, KwaZulu-Natal, e Free State, Gauteng, Mpumalanga and Limpopo and NW provinces. *Tarucus s. linearis* in Arid Savanna in N Cape and w Free State. **Habitat:** Flatlands, hillsides, wetlands. **Flight period:** Year-round, peak Nov–Mar. **Larval food:** *Ziziphus* spp., including *Z. zeyheriana* and *Z. mucronata*.

2 Fynbos or Vivid Blue   *Tarucus thespis*

Wingspan: ♂ 20–25 mm ♀ 20–27 mm. **Identification: 2A** ♂ upper side, **2B** ♀ upper side, **2C** ♂ underside. ♂ upper side deeper, more *sapphire blue* than Dotted Blue (above), ♀ upper side pale markings *squarer* than Dotted Blue. Cilia of both sexes *strongly chequered black and white*. Underside forewing has white chequering on dark grey ground; hind wing marbled grey-buff and brown with discal and costal series of squared-off white spots. Sometimes extremely numerous, hundreds fluttering slowly through the fynbos. **Distribution:** Succulent Karoo in N Cape (Namaqualand) south to Fynbos in the W Cape, and east to the Amatolas (E Cape). **Habitat:** Flatlands, hillsides, coast. **Flight period:** Year-round, peaks Sept–Nov and Feb/Mar. **Larval food:** *Phylica imberbis* and *Saxifraga* spp.

3 Bowker's Blue   *Tarucus bowkeri*

Wingspan: ♂ 23–27 mm ♀ 26–29 mm. **Identification: 3A** ♂ upper side, **3B** ♀ upper side (both *T. b. transvaalensis*), **3C** ♂ underside. Upper side similar to Fynbos Blue (above), deep sapphire blue with conspicuous black-and-white chequered cilia. Underside ground colour *creamy white*, regular pattern of squarish *black spots with buff to brown centres*. 2 subspp., geographically distinct; a separate population found high on Blouberg Mts, n Limpopo Province, possibly a distinct subspecies. **Distribution:** Uncommon and localised; Afromontane Forest/montane Grassland ecotone. Nominate from E Cape (Port St Johns) along escarpment into KwaZulu-Natal and along Drakensberg foothills; *T. b. transvaalensis* from Mpumalanga and Limpopo Province, along Drakensberg escarpment (e.g. Kowyn's Pass near Graskop and The Bonnet near Pilgrim's Rest). **Habitat:** Rocky ledges, forest edges, mountains, hillsides. **Flight period:** Multi-brooded, Oct–Mar, most often early summer, sometimes winter. **Larval food:** *Phylica paniculata*.

Genus *Harpendyreus*   Blues

AFRICA 15 SPP., SOUTH AFRICA 3

Small dull lycaenids, brown or blue upper side, buff to grey underside, with delicate markings. Flight not fast or sustained, near ground. Egg laid singly on seed pods and flowers of low-growing Lamiaceae and Rosaceae. White, bun-shaped; pattern of ribs radiating in straight lines from micropyle, crossed by concentric ribs, forming a polygonal pattern with elongated protuberances where the ribs cross. Larva slug-shaped, pale green to cream, marked with darker green or reddish dorsal lines and rows of diagonal stripes. Eats the flowers, seed ovules and pods. Pupa pale green to cream or buff, slightly hairy, speckled with black or red-brown; formed in leaf debris at base of plant.

A

1B

C

2A

B

2C

A

3B

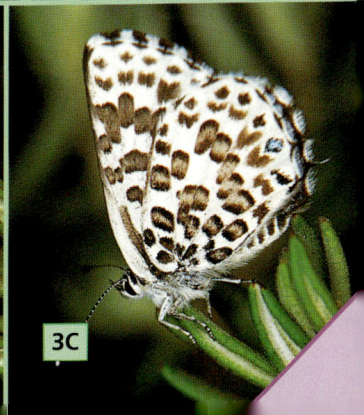

3C

1 Salvia Blue   *Harpendyreus notoba*

Wingspan: ♂ 26–27 mm ♀ 27–29 mm. **Identification: 1A** ♂ upper side, **1B** ♀ upper side, **1C** ♀ underside. Sexes dimorphic; ♂ upper side *dull violet-blue*, ♀ *grey-brown* with *mauve* basal colouring. Both sexes have chequered cilia. Underside of both sexes pale brown, with series of joined spots of same colour, edged in white. Found in scattered colonies, wherever food plant grows. May be locally numerous. ♀ never strays far from food plant except to mate. ♂ defends territories on nearby koppies. **Distribution:** Nama Karoo, Savanna, Arid Savanna, Grassland. From n E Cape (Cradock area), through central Karoo and s Free State, to s Gauteng, s NW Province and further north; also in N Cape. **Habitat:** Flatlands, hill tops. **Flight period:** Aug–May, peak Sept/Oct. **Larval food:** Flowers and immature seeds of *Salvia* spp., especially *S. radula*.

2 Tsomo Blue   *Harpendyreus tsomo*

Wingspan: ♂ 17–22 mm ♀ 18–23 mm. **Identification: 2A** ♂ upper side, **2B** ♀ underside. Inconspicuous; *both sexes brown, cilia plain cream*. ♀ sometimes has some *upper side mauve scaling*. Underside of both sexes warm pale brown, with series of joined spots of same colour, faintly edged in white. Flight weak and fluttering, only centimetres from the ground. **Distribution:** Grassland. Core distribution Lesotho; also to south and east at high altitude in Free State and E Cape, as far south as the Amatolas and as far west as the Camdeboo Mountains. **Habitat:** Wetlands, mountains, gullies, hillsides. **Flight period:** Oct–Mar, peak Nov/Dec. **Larval food:** Young leaves, flowers and seeds of *Mentha* spp.

3 Marsh Blue   *Harpendyreus noquasa*

Wingspan: ♂ 17–23 mm ♀ 18–24 mm. **Identification: 3A** ♂ upper side, **3B** ♀ upper side, **3C** ♂ underside. Until recently, thought to be a subspecies of Tsomo Blue (above). *Sexes dimorphic*, ♂ upper side *lavender blue* with grey-brown forewing apex; hind wing with *black anal spot*. ♀ *grey-brown* on upper side, with varying amount of *basal powder blue*. Underside similar to Tsomo Blue, but hind wing submarginal band *paler*. **Distribution:** Grassland from KwaZulu-Natal Drakensberg, north along escarpment to Mpumalanga (Long Tom Pass and Verloren Valei near Dullstroom). **Habitat:** Wetlands, mountains, gullies, hillsides. **Flight period:** Sept–Mar; two main broods, in spring (Sept–Nov) and again in late summer (Mar), but may be numerous in midsummer as well. **Larval food:** *Alchemilla capensis*.

Genus *Pseudonacaduba*   Dusky Blues   AFRICA 2 SPP., SOUTH AFRICA 1

Small genus of dull blue lycaenids, fluttering flight around thorn tree tops like so many of the closely related genera. Both sexes feed at flowers; ♂ perches on high twigs and circles rapidly around them. Often found on wet mud along streams. Full life history not known. Egg pill-shaped with concave top, with reticulate pattern of ribs in involuted curves radiating from the micropyle, forming triangles and quadrangles, rather like the centre of a daisy. There are also small knobs at the points where the ribs cross. Reticulated pattern on sides stops short of base.

4 Dusky Blue   *Pseudonacaduba sichela sichela*

Wingspan: ♂ 25–28 mm ♀ 25–27 mm. **Identification: 4A** ♂ upper side, **4B** ♀ upper side, **4C** ♂ underside. Small Blue. Sexes dimorphic; ♂ upper side *deep steel blue*, ♀ upper side *grey-brown*, with *powder blue* forewing basal/discal patch and hind wing with blue suffusion. Underside of both sexes *slate grey*, with *fine white* striations. **Distribution:** Lowland Forest and wooded Savanna from E Cape (East London), along KwaZulu-Natal coast and inland to Mpumalanga, Gauteng, Limpopo and NW provinces, and further north. **Habitat:** Hillsides, flatlands, coast. **Flight period:** Continuous broods, Oct–May, winter emergence on KwaZulu-Natal coast. **Larval food:** Probably *Mundulea sericea*.

A

1B

1C

A

2B

A

3B

C

4A

B

4C

Genus *Lepidochrysops*   Ant Blues   AFRICA 130+ SPP., SOUTH AFRICA, LESOTHO, SWAZILAND 48*

Small to medium-sized lycaenids. Some species low density, widespread: others colonial. Flight fast. ♂ upper side more or less uniform blue or shiny brown, ♀ has darker markings in the form of discal spots and/or much wider dark margins and basal areas. Underside ground colour grey or white, with varying amount of black spotting and saggitate markings. Single pill-shaped egg, convex sides and concave top, with reticulate double-whorled patterns of lines in geometric shapes radiating from the micropyle. Laid on flower bud or ovary of food plant, where host ant *Camponotus* spp. is active. Young larva usually bores into plant ovary, eating the ovules. One, *L. dukei*, feeds on galls. At third instar, emerges from shelter and emits chemicals mimicking the ant's brood pheromone, stimulating an ant finding the larva into carrying it into its nest. Larva then preys on ant brood, growing fat, creamy-white and grub-like. Cream to brown, smooth rounded pupa formed inside ant nest. Adult emerges in nest and crawls, wings unexpanded, through the tunnels to escape, whence it climbs up a grass stem or similar and expands its wings. This large genus has many similar species that are difficult to distinguish. Most (37 of the 48 spp.) fall into convenient species groups, noted here to aid identification. *See Note on p. 280.

Monkey Blue group

15 spp., all but one with upper sides brown, cilia chequered. Brown underside with discal and submarginal series of white-edged darker brown spots, often joined. Hind wing has white-edged basal black spots. Postdiscal hind wing series of sagittate white marks varies in prominence between species. Monkey Blue, Variable Blue, Ketsi Blue, Victor's Blue, Loewenstein's Blue, Robertson's Blue, Duke's Blue, Wineland Blue, Mouse Blue, Badham's Blue, Southey's Blue, Pennington's Blue, McGregor's Blue, James's Blue and Lesotho Blue.

1 Monkey Blue   *Lepidochrysops methymna*

Wingspan: ♂ 35–40 mm ♀ 33–42 mm. **Identification: 1A** ♂ upper side, **1B** ♂ underside. Large, *dark brown* species; rare *L. m. dicksoni* 'Dickson's Monkey Blue' has extensive blue scaling. Sexes similar, ♀ forewing upper side has faint blue-edged dark discal marks. Underside typical of brown *Lepidochrysops*; dark spots large and well defined on both wings; hind wing postdiscal sagittate marks large but slender. ♂♂ territorial on mountain tops, circling around, chasing other Blues and perching on low vegetation. ♀♀ scarcer, found near food plant. **Distribution:** Nominate on fynbos-covered hills in Cape Peninsula (W Cape) and from Groot Winterhoek along Hottentots Holland range to Langeberg and Helderberg; *L. m. dicksoni* only Tygerberg Hills, Bellville (W Cape). **Habitat:** Hill tops, hillsides, mountains, coast. **Flight period:** Single-brooded Sept–Jan, most common Nov and Dec. **Larval food:** *Selago fruticosa*, *S. serrata* and *S. spuria*. From third instar, brood of *Camponotus maculatus* ants.

2 Variable Blue   *Lepidochrysops variabilis*

Wingspan: ♂ 28–35 mm ♀ 34–37 mm. **Identification: 2A** ♂ upper side, **2B** ♂ underside. Brown 'Blue' with variable markings. Sexes similar. Underside pattern similar to Monkey Blue (above) but more variable, esp. on forewing where series of white-edged brown marks varies from *one cell spot* to *full postdiscal series*. Postdiscal saggitate marks vary from discrete spots to unbroken band. Upper side colour paler than Monkey Blue; KwaZulu-Natal specimens may show light blue suffusion. ♂♂ ascend hill tops in morning and stay most of the day, perching on low rocks or plants and chasing other butterflies. ♀ more sedentary, less often seen; flies more randomly, lower down. **Distribution:** Widespread in Fynbos, Nama Karoo, Succulent Karoo and Grassland. From Cape Peninsula (W Cape), inland along western mountains to s Namaqualand, along eastern Drakensberg to E Cape, KwaZulu-Natal, Free State, Lesotho, Mpumalanga and s Limpopo Province; from here, west to central Limpopo Province, NW Province and Gauteng hills. **Habitat:** Hill tops, hillsides, mountains. **Flight period:** Double-brooded, Sept–Feb, peaks Oct and Jan. Single-brooded at high altitude (Dec/Jan). **Larval food:** *Selago* spp., including *S. corymbosa*, *Becium* spp. and *Salvia* spp. From third instar, brood of *Camponotus niveosetus* ants.

1A

1B

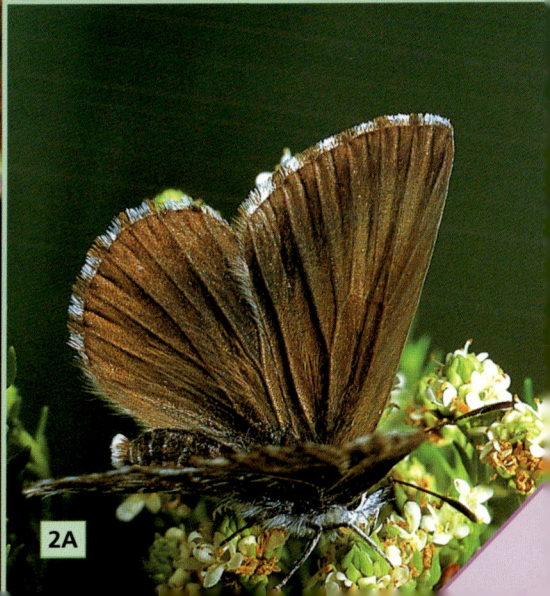

2A

1 Ketsi Blue   *Lepidochrysops ketsi*

Wingspan: ♂ 32–35 mm ♀ 32–33 mm. **Identification: 1A** ♀ upper side (laying on *Selago geniculata*), **1B** ♂ upper side, **1C** ♂ underside. Sexes similar. Upper side more *grey-brown* than Variable Blue (p. 268), underside paler, white markings *more restricted*. ♂ does not hill-top; sexes fly together. Colonial in restricted areas at foothills, on flat ground or in vleis, always near food plants. 2 subspp. **Distribution:** Nominate from W Cape (Caledon and Riviersonderend Mts) in Fynbos, to Nama Karoo Rooiberg and Camdeboo Mtns, along E Cape mountain chain, coastal Karoo/Grassland to Lesotho, Free State, KwaZulu-Natal hills, and highveld in Gauteng, Mpumalanga and NW Province; *L. k. leucomacula* in coastal grassland and savanna, E Cape (Port St Johns), KwaZulu-Natal (Margate and Port Edward). **Habitat:** Flatlands, wetlands, coast, mountains, gullies. **Flight period:** Double-brooded, Oct–Mar, broods overlap; peak Nov and Jan. **Larval food:** *Selago* spp., including *S. corymbosa* and *S. geniculata*, and *Salvia* spp.

2 Victor's Blue   *Lepidochrysops victori*

Wingspan: ♂ 31–35 mm ♀ 32–36 mm. **Identification: 2A** ♂ upper side, **2B** ♀ upper side, **2C** ♂ underside. Underside resembles Ketsi Blue (above), but upper side *darker grey-brown*, margin *more rounded*, resembling Loewenstein's Blue (below). As in the latter species, cilia *less obviously chequered*; upper side forewing costa base dusted with yellow. Found in colonies. ♂ flies rapidly but erratically over hillsides in restricted areas. More sedentary ♀ flies in the same limited territory. **Distribution:** Rare and localised; only known from four small areas high up on the Groot Winterberg near Bedford, E Cape (Nama Karoo). **Habitat:** Mountains, hillsides. **Flight period:** Single-brooded, mid-Feb to end Mar. **Larval food:** *Selago corymbosa*.

3 Loewenstein's Blue   *Lepidochrysops loewensteini*

Wingspan: ♂ 32–35 mm ♀ 32–33 mm. **Identification: 3A** ♂ upper side, **3B** ♂ underside. High-altitude species; *smaller*, underside *paler* than Lesotho Blue (p. 274); upper side *less glossy, cilia chequered*. Upper side *dark grey-brown*, underside ground colour distinctive *tan brown*; markings faint except for *prominent creamy-white, squarish* saggitate hind wing postdiscal marks, base colour with *ashy tint*. Sexes similar, ♀ upper side darker than ♂. Flight medium fast, erratic, along hillsides. Usually flies with large numbers of other mountain Blues, so difficult to spot. **Distribution:** Grassland. Core distribution Lesotho; in South Africa, only on high slopes above Dulcie's Nek (Barkly East area), E Cape. **Habitat:** Mountains, hillsides. **Flight period:** Single-brooded, Jan–Feb. **Larval food:** No data.

4 Robertson's Blue   *Lepidochrysops robertsoni*

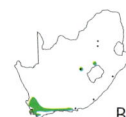

Wingspan: ♂ 28–32 mm ♀ 29–33 mm. **Identification: 4A** ♂ upper side, **4B** ♂ underside, **4C** ♀ upper side. Dark upper side similar to Monkey Blue (p. 268), but *much smaller*; ♀ *lacks blue edges* to forewing upper side dark marks. Upper side ground colour *dark grey-brown*, underside with white-edged dark markings similar to Monkey Blue (p. 268) but *less extensive*. Fairly slow and wandering flight. ♂ ascends to hill tops but sometimes found at low altitude in flat country. ♀ lower on slopes. **Distribution:** Common in Fynbos, Nama Karoo, Grassland. From W Cape to E Cape in hills from Riviersonderendberge to Van Stadensberg, and north to Vanrhynsdorp along Groot Winterhoek and Cederberg ranges, low altitudes near Mamre and Strandfontein. Also Free State (Bethlehem, Bloemfontein) and (dubious record) Springs in Gauteng. **Habitat:** Mountains, hill tops, hillsides. **Flight period:** Single extended brood, Nov–Feb. **Larval food:** *Selago* spp., including *S. serrata*. From third instar, brood of *Camponotus niveosetus* ants.

1 Duke's Blue   *Lepidochrysops dukei*

Wingspan: 28–29 mm. **Identification: 1A** ♂ upper side, **1B** ♀ underside. Sexes very similar. *Smaller* than Robertson's Blue (p. 270); upper side ground colour *very dark*, forewing tip *rounded*, underside with *large, distinct dark spots*. Flight weak; reluctant to flush. ♂ does not hill-top, found at random over habitat, sometimes in large numbers. **Distribution:** Widespread. In Fynbos, Nama Karoo and Succulent Karoo from W Cape (between Worcester and Robertson), on Gydo Pass, Cederberg and Piketberg in the west, and Swartberg, Langkloofberg and other Little Karoo ranges to the east. **Habitat:** Flatlands, hillsides, mountains. **Flight period:** Single extended brood, late Aug to Oct at low altitude, mid-Nov to Jan at high altitude. **Larval food:** Weevil galls on flowers of *Selago fruticosa*.

2 Wineland Blue   *Lepidochrysops bacchus*

Wingspan: ♂ 22–29 mm ♀ 24–30 mm. **Identification: 2A** ♀ upper side, **2B** ♀ underside. Similar to Pennington's Blue (p. 274); upper side brown has *no golden shine*. Sexes similar. Colonies scattered, isolated. Sometimes abundant under favourable conditions. Sexes fly together. Flight medium-fast, low and erratic, settling often on low bushes and the ground. **Distribution:** Rare; scarce and localised. Fynbos in W Cape, from Piketberg and Gydo Pass, near Malmesbury, Koedoesberg near Matjiesfontein, to E Cape at Coega, Uitenhage and Cookhouse in Nama Karoo. **Habitat:** Flatlands, hillsides. **Flight period:** Single-brooded, Sept–Jan, later in the east. **Larval food:** *Selago fruticosa* and *S. geniculata*.

3 Mouse Blue   *Lepidochrysops puncticilia*

Wingspan: ♂ 27–29 mm ♀ 27–30 mm. **Identification: 3A** ♀ upper side, **3B** ♀ underside. Sexes similar. Distinctive, dark species, *conspicuously white-spotted* cilia. Underside also dark, white markings *diffuse and less well defined* than other 'brown' *Lepidochrysops*. Colonies scattered, may be locally plentiful. Flight slow and low, circling and wandering around low vegetation and rocks. Found from low hills to tops of large mountains. ♂♂ ascend to the tops in morning and remain through the day. **Distribution:** Fynbos in W Cape, near Mamre and Malmesbury, Riebeek-Kasteel, Piketberg, mountains from Michell's Pass, Du Toit's Kloof, Mont Rochelle above Franschhoek, to Shaw's Mountain Pass and hills behind Hermanus. Also Gifberg near Vanrhynsdorp. **Habitat:** Hill tops, hillsides, mountains. **Flight period:** Single Sept–Oct brood at low elevations, Oct–Dec on high mountains. **Larval food:** *Selago fruticosa* and *Dichisma* spp.

4 Badham's Blue   *Lepidochrysops badhami*

Wingspan: ♂ 28–32 mm ♀ 29–34 mm. **Identification: 4A** ♂ upper side, **4B** ♂ underside. Sexes similar, ♀ larger with stouter abdomen. Upper side *dark brown*, cilia *inconspicuously chequered*. Underside hind wing has *well-developed basal white-edged black spots* and *conspicuous white submarginal sagittate markings*. Fast, dodging flight around bushes at the bases of hills. Settles on low bushes; flies up suddenly when approached and disappears rapidly. **Distribution:** Rare. Succulent Karoo to east of Springbok, N Cape. Single record from south-east of Mamre, W Cape. **Habitat:** Flatlands. **Flight period:** Single-brooded, Sept–Oct. **Larval food:** *Pelargonium dasyphyllum*.

5 Southey's Blue   *Lepidochrysops southeyae*

Wingspan: ♂ 27–30 mm ♀ 28–32 mm. **Identification: 5A** ♂ upper side, **5B** ♀ upper side, **5C** ♀ underside. Sexes similar, ♀ slightly darker. Superficially resembles Wineland Blue (above), but *larger*, upper side *bronzy coloured*. Forewing upper side has *no discocellular spot*. Underside has large hind wing basal black spots and *elongated* postdiscal white saggitate marks. Large colonies in flat country; flight low among bushes. **Distribution:** Nama Karoo in E Cape, between Grahamstown, Steynsburg, Tarkastad and Bedford, in hills east of Graaff-Reinet. **Habitat:** Flatlands, hillsides. **Flight period:** One or more broods between Sept and Mar, depending on rains. **Larval food:** No data.

1 Pennington's Blue   *Lepidochrysops penningtoni*
Wingspan: ♂ 28–34 mm ♀ 34–36 mm. **Identification: 1A** ♂ upper side, **1B** ♂ underside. Closely resembles Wineland Blue (p. 272); slightly larger, upper side more *golden bronze brown*; pale mark (not always present) above the dark spot at the hind wing on underside tornus *dull orange*, not whitish. Sexes similar. Scarce, seldom seen, found in colonies. Flight low and undulating, difficult to follow among low bushes in a high wind. Sexes fly together. **Distribution:** Rare. In Succulent Karoo of N Cape, north of Steinkopf; also in Kamieskroon and Garies areas. **Habitat:** Flatlands, hillsides. **Flight period:** Single-brooded, Aug–Oct, emerging only after good rains. **Larval food:** No data.

2 McGregor's Blue   *Lepidochrysops macgregori*
Wingspan: ♂ 28–32 mm ♀ 30–33 mm. **Identification: 2A** ♂ upper side, **2B** ♂ underside. Sexes similar. Brown upper side has *bright coppery-golden sheen*. Underside similar to Pennington's Blue (above), but postdiscal sagittate marks *larger*. Well camouflaged against dun-coloured vegetation. Colonies large, widely dispersed. Sexes fly together. Flight similar to related species; low, fast and erratic among bushes, difficult to follow. **Distribution:** In Succulent Karoo of N Cape, south of Nieuwoudtville, and Nama Karoo in Voëlfontein area of Roggeveld escarpment. **Habitat:** Flatlands. **Flight period:** Single-brooded, late Aug to early Oct. **Larval food:** No data.

3 James's Blue   *Lepidochrysops jamesi*
Wingspan: 30–36 mm. **Identification: 3A** ♂ upper side, **3B** ♂ underside. Larger than McGregor's Blue (above), upper side copper sheen *darker*, spot at hind wing upper side anal angle *more pronounced*. Sexes similar, ♀ has *more brassy sheen than* ♂. Underside hind wing white markings *extensive*; in *L. j. claassensi*, the white may obscure the brown ground colour. Usually solitary; sometimes in small colonies on hillsides on high slopes of arid mountains covered in thick Karoo bush. Flight very fast and direct, difficult to follow. Settles on ground between bushes. 2 subspp. **Distribution:** Nominate on hillsides in Nama Karoo of N Cape, Koedoesberg and Swaarweerberg on Roggeveld escarpment; *L. j. claassensi* on Hantamsberg near Calvinia, N Cape. **Habitat:** Hillsides, mountains. **Flight period:** Single-brooded, Sept to early Nov, depending on locality. **Larval food:** No data.

4 Lesotho Blue   *Lepidochrysops lerothodi*
Wingspan: ♂ 32–36 mm ♀ 33–38 mm. **Identification: 4A** ♀ upper side, **4B** ♂ underside. Upper side dark *velvety brown* with *strong gloss*, underside *fawn*. Cilia shiny grey-brown, not chequered. Sexes similar, ♀ paler, upper side colouring *more golden*. Wary and easily disturbed. Flight rapid; ♂ patrols base of steep mountain slopes, settling on low vegetation. **Distribution:** Grassland. Core distribution Lesotho; in South Africa, only on high mountain peaks of Golden Gate Highlands NP, Limpopo Province, Free State, and E Cape (Barkly East area). **Habitat:** Mountains, hillsides. **Flight period:** Single-brooded, Jan–Feb. **Larval food:** *Selago flanaganii*.

5 Free State Blue   *Lepidochrysops letsea*
Wingspan: ♂ 33–35 mm ♀ 32–33 mm. **Identification: 5A** ♂ upper side, **5B** ♂ underside. Upper side *brown-grey*, hind wing anal lunule prominent *black and orange-yellow*. Cilia *whitish*. Underside similar to Patrician Blue (p. 294). Sexes similar. Found in scattered colonies in flat country. Flight rapid, erratic, close to ground. Often feeds at flowers. **Distribution:** Grassland and Savanna in E Cape, e Free State and Gauteng. **Habitat:** Flatlands. **Flight period:** Single extended brood from Oct–Jan. **Larval food:** *Hemizygia pretoriae*.

A

1B

A

2B

A

3B

A

4B

A

5B

1 Zulu Blue   *Lepidochrysops ignota*
Wingspan: ♂ 27–29 mm ♀ 27–30 mm. **Identification: 1A** ♂ upper side, **1B** ♂ underside. Sexes very similar, ♀ slightly paler than ♂. Small brown species, upper side grey-brown; underside paler grey, with *small blackish spots*. Found in colonies. Both sexes fly together on grassy hillsides near food plant. Flight rapid and jinking close to the ground, difficult to follow. Settles on bare earth or on flowers, often those of food plant. **Distribution:** Widespread in Grassland and Savanna from KwaZulu-Natal Midlands (Estcourt, Mooi River area), to Swaziland, Mpumalanga (Barberton hills), and Limpopo Province (Haenertsburg and other Wolkberg localities); also Gauteng (Ruimsig, Roodepoort). **Habitat:** Hillsides. **Flight period:** Single-brooded, Oct–Nov. **Larval food:** *Becium* spp. From third instar, brood of *Camponotus niveosetus* ants.

2 Irving's Blue   *Lepidochrysops irvingi*
Wingspan: ♂ 32–36 mm ♀ 33–38 mm. **Identification: 2A** ♂ upper side, **2B** ♂ underside. Similar to Zulu Blue (above) but *larger*, upper side *shiny bronze-brown*, sometimes with *greeny-blue iridescence*. Underside *dull fawn-grey*, spots and markings ill-defined, hind wing basal spots small, sometimes absent. Sexes similar, ♀ *paler*, upper side more golden shade than ♂. Two or more ♂ ♂ found in territories around large rocks or bushes. Flight fast, erratic, circling; settles often on the ground or on food plant. Colonies found where food plant grows in profusion. **Distribution:** Restricted to montane Grassland in Swaziland and Mpumalanga (Sabie, Graskop, Nelshoogte near Barberton). **Habitat:** Hillsides. **Flight period:** Single-brooded, Sept–Nov. **Larval food:** *Becium* spp., including *B. grandiflorum*.

3 Estcourt Blue   *Lepidochrysops pephredo*
Wingspan: ♂ 32–38 mm ♀ 36–40 mm. **Identification: 3A** ♂ upper side, **3B** ♂ underside. Similar to Zulu Blue (above), but with unmistakable *broad white band on underside hind wing*, which flickers in flight. Upper side cilia *conspicuously white*. Sexes similar, ♀ *paler* than ♂. Rare and localised; less than five or six specimens seen at one time. Flight fast, low and erratic. ♂ hill-tops at midday with other Blues; ♀ on lower slopes of hills, feeding on flowers, often on the food plant. **Distribution:** Grassy hills of KwaZulu-Natal Midlands – from below Amphitheatre in uKhahlamba Drakensberg Park to Bulwer in the south, centred on Mooi River/Howick area. **Habitat:** Hillsides, hill tops. **Flight period:** Single-brooded, Oct–Nov. **Larval food:** *Becium grandiflorum*. From third instar, brood of *Camponotus niveosetus* ants.

4 Graham's Blue   *Lepidochrysops grahami*
Wingspan: ♂ 32–36 mm ♀ 34–38 mm. **Identification: 4A** ♂ upper side, **4B** ♀ upper side, **4C** ♂ underside. White underside band flickers in flight as Estcourt Blue (above). Upper side resembles King Blue (p. 280); *blue* in ♂, *brown with basal blue* in ♀. ♂ flight rapid, sustained, up and down steep, rocky hillsides; very difficult to follow, settling seldom. ♀ usually found on flowers. **Distribution:** Localised and restricted range. Grassland in hills of ne E Cape, Dordrecht area, Stormberge and Baviaans River ranges, Windvoël Mountains above Cathcart, and Long Hill above Queenstown. **Habitat:** Hillsides. **Flight period:** Single extended brood from early Nov to Jan. **Larval food:** *Becium* spp.

1 Swanepoel's Blue *Lepidochrysops swanepoeli*

Wingspan: ♂ 36–40 mm ♀ 38–42 mm. **Identification: 1A** ♂ upper side, **1B** ♀ upper side, **1C** ♂ underside. Underside white band even more conspicuous than Estcourt and Graham's Blues (p. 276). ♂ upper side has shifting *blue lustre* over *grey* base colour; ♀ *brighter blue* with *grey* marginal borders. Both sexes have conspicuous *orange-and-black lunules* at hind wing anal angle. ♂ rapid flight around hill tops and ridges, from 09h00 to as late as 17h00. ♀ slightly lower, near patches of the food plant; also visits summits in search of ♂. **Distribution:** Rare; montane Grassland in hills above Fairview and Sheba Mines, Barberton, Mpumalanga; single record from Mt Ngwibi, n KwaZulu-Natal. **Habitat:** Hill tops, hillsides. **Flight period:** Single extended brood, Sept to early Dec, peak Nov. **Larval food:** *Becium grandiflorum*.

2 Potchefstroom Blue *Lepidochrysops procera*

Wingspan: ♂ 28–34 mm ♀ 29–36 mm. **Identification: 2A** ♂ upper side, **2B** ♀ upper side, **2C** ♂ underside. Small *Blue* species. Sexes similar, ♀ with wings *rounder* than ♂, marginal borders *broader, grey*. Underside dun-grey, with pale-ringed darker grey discal and submarginal spots; black basal hind wing spots. Colonial in scattered localities. Flight fast, low and erratic but not sustained; settles often on flowers or low vegetation. **Distribution:** Widespread but rare in Grassland and grassy Savanna from KwaZulu-Natal Midlands (Estcourt) to Mpumalanga (Gladdespruit, near Carolina), Gauteng (Walkerville, Carletonville and Wonderboom), Limpopo Province (Nylsvley) and NW Province (Potchefstroom). **Habitat:** Hillsides, flatlands. **Flight period:** Single-brooded, Sept–Nov. **Larval food:** *Becium grandiflorum* and *Ocimum canum*.

3 Van Son's Blue *Lepidochrysops vansoni*

Wingspan: ♂ 28–34 mm ♀ 29–36 mm. **Identification: 3A** ♂ upper side, **3B** ♀ upper side, **3C** ♂ underside. Similar to Potchefstroom Blue (above), upper side *paler blue*, marginal hind wing lunules *better defined*. Underside ground colour *whitish*, not dun-grey, spots *darker*, outlined with *paler scaling*. Sexes similar, ♀ with wings *rounder* than ♂, and grey marginal borders *broader*. Colonial in scattered localities. Flight fast, low and erratic but not sustained; settles often on flowers or low vegetation. **Distribution:** Savanna. Limpopo Province, in several localities north and west of the Soutpansberg, and north to Botswana and Zimbabwe. **Habitat:** Flatlands. **Flight period:** Single summer brood (Dec–Mar), only after good rains. **Larval food:** *Lantana rugosa, Becium grandiflorum* and *Ocimum canum*.

1 King Blue *Lepidochrysops tantalus*

Wingspan: ♂ 30–38 mm ♀ 34–40 mm. **Identification: 1A** ♂ upper side, **1B** ♀ upper side, **1C** ♂ underside. Difficult to follow and identify on the wing due to extremely rapid and sustained flight and dark colour. Underside *warm grey* with *dark spots*, easily recognisable when sitting. Sexes dimorphic; ♂ upper side *steel blue*, ♀ *dark brown-grey*; darker forewing discal spots, *basal blue flush*. Specimens from Limpopo Province *brighter blue*, wings *shorter, more pointed*. ♂ patrols hillsides, visiting summits. ♀ lower on slopes, usually on flowers of food plant. **Distribution:** Grassland. From Drakensberg foothills (Mbashe River), E Cape, to KwaZulu-Natal Midlands, Swaziland, along escarpment hills to Mpumalanga (Volksrust, Verloren Valei, Barberton hills), Gauteng (Suikerbosrand NR). Also, Limpopo Province (Wolkberg near Haenertsburg and Soekmekaar, and Soutpansberg). **Habitat:** Hillsides, hill tops. **Flight period:** Single-brooded, Sept–Nov. **Larval food:** *Becium grandiflorum*.

2 Jeffery's Blue *Lepidochrysops jefferyi*

Wingspan: ♂ 38–44 mm ♀ 42–46 mm. **Identification: 2A** ♂ upper side, **2B** ♀ upper side, **2C** ♂ underside. Sexes dimorphic; ♂ upper side *brown with strong violet sheen*, ♀ *bright violet-blue*, with broad grey-brown marginal borders. Underside of both sexes grey, with very faint pale-outlined grey spots and small black basal hind wing spots. Territorial ♂ ascends hill tops and sits on low vegetation or rocks, taking off and chasing other ♂ ♂. ♀ flight random, lower on slopes near food plant; ascends hills late in afternoon in search of ♂. **Distribution:** Rare. In Grassland dotted with bush on hills above Ulundi, Fairview and Sheba Mines, Barberton, Mpumalanga. **Habitat:** Hillsides, hill tops. **Flight period:** Single-brooded, Oct–Nov. **Larval food:** *Becium grandiflorum*.

3 Highveld Blue *Lepidochrysops praeterita*

Wingspan: ♂ 36–42 mm ♀ 38–44 mm. **Identification: 3A** ♂ upper side, **3B** ♀ upper side, **3C** ♀ underside. Sexes dimorphic; ♂ upper side *dark blue*, ♀ *dark grey-brown* with darker discal spotting and *blue basal and discal areas* on all wings. Underside of both sexes fawn-grey with slightly darker pale-edged discal and submarginal spots, and black hind wing basal spots. Easily flushed. Flight very rapid and sustained; seldom settles. ♂ ♂ in territories near prominent trees, circling and chasing other specimens. ♀ flight random, usually near food plant. **Distribution:** Rare and localised in highveld Grassland with trees, between Potchefstroom (NW Province) and Walkerville (Gauteng), south to Sasolburg (Free State). **Habitat:** Flatlands, hillsides. **Flight period:** Single-brooded, early Sept–Nov. Emergence very sparse or fails in year of poor rainfall. **Larval food:** *Becium grandiflorum*.

Note: A male specimen of *extinct* Morant's Blue *L. hypopolia* is housed in the SA Museum, labelled Potchefstroom, Transvaal, 1879 (**4A** upper side, **4B** underside). The only other specimens known (in the British Museum) were found at Blue Bank, near Ladysmith (KwaZulu-Natal), where the species may yet be rediscovered. The specimen is in very good condition and its underside is different to the Highveld Blue; pale whitish brown with a 'hoary' appearance. The forewing outer margin is very convex, exactly as in the Ladysmith specimens. Females are unknown.

A

1B

1C

A

2B

2C

A

3B

C

4A

4B

1 Lotana Blue *Lepidochrysops lotana*

Wingspan: ♂ 42–44 mm ♀ 42–46 mm. **Identification: 1A** ♂ upper side, **1B** ♀ upper side, **1C** ♂ underside. Appearance and habits, sexual dimorphism similar to Highveld Blue (p. 280) but *larger*, wings *squarer*. ♂ upper side *dark blue* with *large, prominent hind wing anal black-and-orange lunule*, ♀ *dark grey-brown* with darker discal spotting and *blue basal and discal areas* on all wings. Underside of both sexes *pale fawn-grey* with slightly darker pale-edged discal and submarginal spots, and tiny black hind wing basal spots. **Distribution:** Savanna/Grassland. Only known from two localities in Limpopo Province: Rietvlei farm, on western slope of Ysterberg (30 km south of Polokwane), and on road from Moria (east of Polokwane) to Serala Forest in Wolkberg. **Habitat:** Flatlands, hillsides. **Flight period:** Single-brooded, Sept to early Nov. **Larval food:** Not confirmed, but specimens are usually found close to clumps of *Becium grandiflorum*.

Koppie Blue group

15 spp., similar in shape and markings to Monkey Blue group, but upper sides *blue*. Cilia chequered. Undersides black to grey-brown, both wings with discal and submarginal series of darker black or brown spots, often joined, white-edged. Hind wing carries basal black spots, also edged with white. Postdiscal hind wing series of sagittate white marks varies in prominence between species. Koppie Blue, Southern Blue, Gydo Blue, Tite's Blue, Swartberg Blue, Outeniqua Blue, Oosthuizen's Blue, Coastal Blue, Baviaanskloof Blue, Ball's Blue, Wykeham's Blue, Peninsula Blue, Pringle's Blue, Quickelberge's Blue and Brauer's Blue.

2 Koppie Blue *Lepidochrysops ortygia*

Wingspan: ♂ 35–40 mm ♀ 33–42 mm. **Identification: 2A** ♂ upper side, **2B** ♀ upper side, **2C** ♂ underside. Underside dull fawn-grey, with well-defined white-edged darker grey series of joined spots, black basal spots and white postdiscal sagittate marks; cilia *strongly chequered*. ♂ upper side *dull violet-blue*, ♀ upper side *dark grey-brown* with darker forewing discal spots, *basal blue on all four wings*, blue hind wing submarginal lunules. ♂ ascends koppies and ridges at midday. ♀ among food plant at lower altitude, ascends heights in afternoon looking for a mate. **Distribution:** Widespread. Nama Karoo from E Cape hills (Steynsburg/Bedford area), in Grassland north through lower parts of Lesotho to greater part of Free State, s Mpumalanga and Gauteng (World's View on Witwatersrand, Krugersdorp). **Habitat:** Flatlands, hill tops, hillsides. **Flight period:** Possibly multi-brooded, Oct–Apr, peaks Dec or Mar, depending on rainfall patterns. **Larval food:** *Selago geniculata*.

A

1B

C

2A

B

2C

1 Southern Blue   *Lepidochrysops australis*
Wingspan: ♂ 32–36 mm ♀ 33–40 mm. **Identification: 1A** ♂ upper side, **1B** ♀ upper side, **1C** ♂ underside. ♀ resembles Koppie Blue (p. 282), but blue flush *deeper, often more extensive.* ♂ upper side *darker and bluer;* marginal borders *wider,* underside ground colour darker grey with *more prominent white markings, especially the postdiscal saggitate series.* Found on fynbos-covered hillsides, ♂ on peaks at midday. Flight fast and erratic, circling hill tops, settling on prominent rocks or shrubs. **Distribution:** From hills above Greyton (Riviersonderendberge) and Caledon, along coastal ranges to E Cape (Vanstadensberg, west of Port Elizabeth). **Habitat:** Hillsides, mountains, hill tops. **Flight period:** Single- or double-brooded from Nov–Mar. **Larval food:** *Selago* spp.

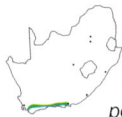

2 Gydo Blue   *Lepidochrysops gydoae*
Wingspan: ♂ 41–45 mm ♀ 43–46 mm. **Identification: 2A** ♂ upper side, **2B** ♀ upper side, **2C** ♀ underside. Largest of the Koppie Blue group. Underside similar to Southern Blue (above). ♂ upper side blue *purer hue;* ♀ has upper side *brighter blue,* over *darker* ground colour. ♂ upper side has *narrower, dark borders.* May fly in numbers. ♂ on hill tops and ridges, also rocky ledges between large crags, below main peaks. ♀ lower down slopes at base of rocky escarpment. Fast, patrolling flight, seldom settling, easily disturbed. **Distribution:** Restricted to Fynbos on northern slopes of Gydo Mountain and Theronsberg, north of Ceres, W Cape. **Habitat:** Mountains, rocky ledges, hillsides, hill tops. **Flight period:** Single-brooded, Nov–Jan. **Larval food:** Not confirmed, but ♀ is often found on *Selago* spp.

3 Tite's Blue   *Lepidochrysops titei*
Wingspan: ♂ 30–34 mm ♀ 31–36 mm. **Identification: 3A** ♂ upper side, **3B** ♀ upper side, **3C** ♂ underside. Brighter, shinier blue upper side than Southern Blue (above), but ♂ with same broad dark borders; ♀ as Southern Blue, but with more extensive dark markings. Underside similar to Southern Blue, but more conspicuous white markings, a more prominent 'lacy' effect. Forewing apex more acute, hind wing more rounded, larger in proportion to forewing. ♂♂ congregate on hill tops and ridges, ♀ flight random, lower down the slopes; seen less often. **Distribution:** W Cape, in Fynbos on low hills in Malmesbury and Moorreesburg, below Riebeek-Kasteel and the Porseleinberg. Also on hills in Vanrhynsdorp area (Gifberg). **Habitat:** Mountains, hill tops, hillsides. **Flight period:** Single-brooded, Sept–Nov. **Larval food:** *Selago* spp.

1A

1B

1C

2A

2B

2C

3A

3B

3C

1 Swartberg Blue   *Lepidochrysops swartbergensis*

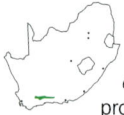

Wingspan: ♂ 32–36 mm ♀ 34–38 mm. **Identification: 1A** ♂ upper side, **1B** ♀ upper side, **1C** ♂ underside. Very similar to Southern Blue (p. 284). Upper side of both sexes *deeper, purer blue colour*, dark margins *wider*, appearing darker. ♀ has *more extensive* upper side blue than Southern Blue, making dark markings appear more prominent. Underside of both sexes *paler*; white marks *more extensive*, especially the postdiscal sagittate series. ♂ flight fast along high ridges and hill tops, but not at the highest summits; ♀ found lower down the slopes. **Distribution:** Fynbos on Swartberg range from E Cape (Toorwater) to Seweweekspoort and Klein Swartberg in W Cape to the W, also Rooiberg. **Habitat:** Mountains, hill tops, hillsides. **Flight period:** Single extended brood, Nov–Feb. **Larval food:** No data.

2 Outeniqua Blue   *Lepidochrysops outeniqua*

Wingspan: ♂ 32–36 mm ♀ 34–38 mm. **Identification: 2A** ♂ upper side, **2B** ♀ upper side, **2C** ♂ underside. Distinctive *dark blue* species, in both sexes black markings heavier than other Blues in this group; underside ground colour *darker brown*, with distinctive *deeply saggitate* white submarginal marks. ♂ flies rapidly around mountain tops, seldom staying in one place for long. ♀ flight random; found lower down the slopes or on the food plant. **Distribution:** Fynbos on Outeniqua range (W Cape) above Avontuur. **Habitat:** Hill tops, hillsides, mountains. **Flight period:** Single-brooded, Nov–Dec. **Larval food:** No data.

3 Oosthuizen's Blue   *Lepidochrysops oosthuizeni*

Wingspan: ♂ 33–37 mm ♀ 34–38 mm. **Identification: 3A** ♂ upper side, **3B** ♀ upper side, **3C** ♂ underside. Similar to Koppie Blue (p. 282), but upper side *deeper, violet-blue*; ♂ as in Southern Blue (p. 284), dark margins vary from very broad to quite narrow. Many ♂♂ have dark forewing *postmedian spots* similar to ♀ but smaller. ♀ upper side similar to Southern Blue. Main difference is underside: hind wing ground colour *browner, reduced white* around the dark spots, sagittate marks *smaller*. **Distribution:** High-altitude Grassland and Nama Karoo in Witteberg (above Lundean's Nek), E Cape, Maluti Mountains of Lesotho and e Free State (Golden Gate Highlands NP). **Habitat:** Hill tops, hillsides, mountains. **Flight period:** Single-brooded, Dec–Jan. **Larval food:** *Selago galpinii*.

1A

1B

C

2A

B

2C

A

3B

3C

1 Coastal Blue *Lepidochrysops littoralis*
Wingspan: ♂ 34–36 mm ♀ 36–38 mm. **Identification: 1A** ♂ upper side, **1B** ♀ upper side, **1C** ♂ underside. Similar to Southern Blue (p. 284), upper side *deeper, purer blue*, forewing upper side marginal border *broader*, but hind wing border *narrower, more pointed* forewing apex. *Paler* underside ground colour; *broader* submarginal row of white sagittate marks on hind wing. ♂ flies fast over coastal sand dunes; territories around large clumps of shrubs, dune peaks and clearings in dense vegetation. ♀ flight random; usually found on flowers. **Distribution:** Coastal fynbos-covered dunes from Cape Agulhas to Mossel Bay, W Cape. **Habitat:** Coast, flatlands. **Flight period:** Extended brood, from late Aug–Dec. **Larval food:** No data.

2 Baviaanskloof Blue *Lepidochrysops poseidon*
Wingspan: ♂ 34–40 mm ♀ 40–44 mm. **Identification: 2A** ♂ upper side, **2B** ♀ upper side, **2C** ♂ underside. Upper side base colour *deep blue without any violet*, a rather iridescent shade of *aquamarine*, close to powdery blue of Brauer's Blue (p. 292). Underside ground colour more *greyish* than Outeniqua Blue (p. 286), sagittate hind wing underside submarginal marks *much shallower*. ♂ on highest points of mountains; ♀ flight random, below peaks on slopes. **Distribution:** Rare. E Cape, on highest points of Baviaanskloof Mtns between Willowmore and Patensie in Fynbos. **Habitat:** Mountains, hill tops. **Flight period:** Single-brooded, late Nov to Feb. **Larval food:** No data.

3 Ball's Blue *Lepidochrysops balli*
Wingspan: ♂ 32–34 mm ♀ 34–36 mm. **Identification: 3A** ♂ upper side, **3B** ♀ upper side, **3C** ♂ underside. Smaller than Brauer's Blue (p. 292), *lacks* silvery, powdery hue; ground colour *more violet*, marginal borders *broader*. ♀ ground colour *darker*. Both sexes with forewing apex *more rounded*. ♂ sometimes has *dark postmedian spots* as in Oosthuizen's Blue (p. 286). Underside hind wing has *very large* white-edged dark spots almost obscuring ground colour, *wide* band of postdiscal sagittate spots. ♂ ♂ congregate around rocky crags and ridges in warmer hours, rapidly circling and patrolling area in company of other Blues. ♀ flight more random; sometimes visits crags in search of mate. **Distribution:** In Fynbos on highest points of Kammanassie Mtns between Uniondale and Oudtshoorn, W Cape. **Habitat:** Mountains, hill tops. **Flight period:** Single-brooded, late Nov to Feb. **Larval food:** No data.

A

1B

1C

A

2B

E

3A

B

3C

1 Wykeham's Blue   *Lepidochrysops wykehami*

Wingspan: ♂ 36–44 mm ♀ 42–46 mm. **Identification: 1A** ♂ upper side, **1B** ♀ upper side, **1C** ♂ underside. Only Blue of the Koppie Blue group to have a *blue* ♂ and *black* ♀. ♂ upper side resembles dark Peninsula Blue (below), but with *broader* wing margins. ♀ resembles ♀ Monkey Blue (p. 268). Underside *darker* than others of the group. ♂ ascends low ridges and koppies at midday, flight fast, circling. ♀ flight slow; skulks around in thick vegetation at the base of hills, visiting flowers. **Distribution:** Succulent Karoo in hills in Kamieskroon area, Namaqualand (N Cape). **Habitat:** Mountains, hill tops. **Flight period:** Single-brooded, late Aug to Oct. **Larval food:** *Selago* spp.

2 Peninsula Blue   *Lepidochrysops oreas*

Wingspan: ♂ 24–38 mm ♀ 27–38 mm. **Identification: 2A** ♂ upper side (*L. o. junae*), **2B** ♀ upper side, **2C** ♂ underside (nominate). Smaller butterfly, upper side *brighter blue* than most of the Koppie Blue group. Underside of both sexes *conspicuous pale grey ground colour*. ♂ ascends at midday to higher mountain slopes and summits with other lycaenids. ♀ found lower down the slopes, usually near food plant. 2 subspp. **Distribution:** Fynbos in W Cape. Nominate rare, on upper slopes of Cape Peninsula mountains; *L. o. junae* in mountains east of Cape Flats, from Du Toit's Kloof and Franschhoek to Langeberg in the east, and Hermanus in the south. **Habitat:** Mountains, hillsides, hill tops. **Flight period:** Single-brooded, Oct–Feb. **Larval food:** *Selago* spp., including *S. serrata*. From third instar, brood of *Camponotus* ants.

3 Pringle's Blue   *Lepidochrysops pringlei*

Wingspan: ♂ 30–34 mm ♀ 36–38 mm. **Identification: 3A** ♂ upper side, **3B** ♀ upper side, **3C** ♂ underside. Similar to Peninsula Blue (above), ♂ a *deeper, richer* blue on upper side. ♀ upper side dark marks *reduced or absent*. Underside of both sexes *darker* than Peninsula Blue. ♂ flight very restless, appearing at hill tops but soon moving to others, very hard to follow. ♀ lower down the slopes and on flowers. **Distribution:** Fynbos. Restricted to rocky peaks of Swartberg between Towerwater (E Cape) and Seweweekspoort (W Cape). **Habitat:** Mountains, hill tops. **Flight period:** Single-brooded, early Oct to late Nov. **Larval food:** No data.

A

1B

C

2A

2B

C

3A

B

3C

1 Quickelberge's Blue *Lepidochrysops quickelbergei*

Wingspan: ♂ 32–36 mm ♀ 36–38 mm. **Identification: 1A** ♂ upper side, **1B** ♀ upper side, **1C** ♂ underside. Very similar to Peninsula Blue (p. 290), especially underside, but upper side *pale silvery blue.* ♀ upper side has attractive tracery of *pale blue* on *dark slate grey.* ♂ flies around large crags on the mountainside, but not at the high summits; fast, circling flight. ♀ found below the crags, usually on flowers. **Distribution:** In Fynbos on northern slopes of Gydo Mtn and Waboomsberg, north of Ceres (W Cape). **Habitat:** Mountains, hill tops, hillsides. **Flight period:** Single-brooded, Oct to late Dec. **Larval food:** No data.

2 Brauer's Blue *Lepidochrysops braueri*

Wingspan: ♂ 33–37 mm ♀ 34–38 mm. **Identification: 2A** ♂ upper side, **2B** ♀ upper side, **2C** ♀ underside. Both sexes have similar markings to Ball's Blue (p. 288), but blue is distinctive *pale mauve,* appearing powdery. Underside forewing submarginal markings *parallel with wing edge,* not incurved or angled as in Ball's Blue. ♂ hill tops with other *Lepidochrysops* spp. over a range of altitudes from 600–1 200 m. ♀ flight random; found lower down the hills. **Distribution:** Fynbos. From Kougaberge, Langkloofberge, Kammanassie and Outeniqua Mountains in W Cape, to Baviaanskloof Mountains in E Cape. **Habitat:** Mountains, hill tops, hillsides. **Flight period:** Single-brooded, Nov–Jan. **Larval food:** No data.

Twin-spot Blue group

4 large species with small hind wing tails, iridescent blue upper sides and grey undersides carrying well-defined rows of white-edged, darker grey spots and basal hind wing black spots. Twin-spot Blue, Patrician Blue, Silvery Blue, and Rossouw's Blue.

3 Twin-spot Blue *Lepidochrysops plebeia plebeia*

Wingspan: ♂ 35–43 mm ♀ 38–45 mm. **Identification: 3A** ♂ upper side, **3B** ♀ upper side, **3C** pair *in copula* ♂ above, ♀ below. Sexes dimorphic; ♂ upper side *flat grey*, ♀ upper side *violet-blue*, resembling Patrician Blue (p. 294). ♂ patrols high points in veld, settling on grass stems and low bushes. Compared to others of group, *extra hind wing underside black spot* at base of area CuA$_2$, white edges to spots *more extensive.* ♀ flight random, often found on flowers. **Distribution:** Common Savanna species. Northern E Cape and KwaZulu-Natal, nw Free State, Gauteng, Mpumalanga and Limpopo and NW provinces; also N Cape. **Habitat:** Hill tops, flatlands. **Flight period:** Two broods, Sept–Dec and Jan–Apr, with some overlap. **Larval food:** *Lantana rugosa.* From third instar, brood of *Camponotus* nr *niveosetus* ants.

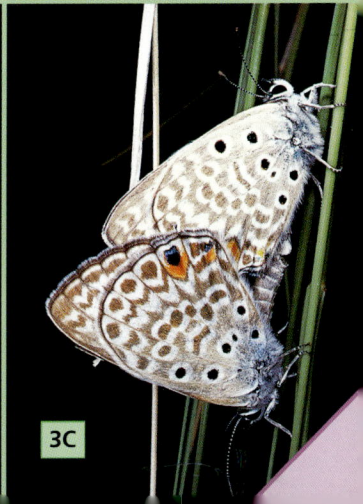

1 Patrician Blue *Lepidochrysops patricia*

Wingspan: ♂ 35–44 mm ♀ 36–46 mm. **Identification: 1A** ♂ upper side, **1B** ♀ upper side, **1C** ♂ underside. Sexes dimorphic; ♂ upper side *pearlescent mauve-blue*. ♀ upper side has variable basal and discal *mauve-blue* on *brown-grey* ground, *whitish* saggitate hind wing submarginal marks. Underside of both sexes fawn-grey, with well-defined rows of white-edged, darker grey spots and basal hind wing black spots. Most fly rapidly and randomly over grassland or bushveld, colonies not concentrated, ♂♂ congregating near prominent trees. Where food plant is *Salvia*, colonial behaviour, high density in small areas. **Distribution:** Common and widespread in Nama Karoo from W Cape (Oudtshoorn) to E Cape, through Grassland, Savanna, Arid Savanna and lowland woodland to KwaZulu-Natal, Free State, Gauteng, Mpumalanga and Limpopo and NW provinces, and N Cape. **Habitat:** Hillsides, flatlands. **Flight period:** Two broods, Sept–Dec and Jan–Apr, with some overlap. **Larval food:** *Salvia* spp., *Lantana rugosa* and *L. camara*. From third instar, brood of *Camponotus maculatus* ants.

2 Silvery Blue *Lepidochrysops glauca glauca*

Wingspan: ♂ 35–40 mm ♀ 38–48 mm. **Identification: 2A** ♂ upper side, **2B** ♂ upper side, **2C** ♂ underside. Both sexes similar to Patrician Blue (above), upper side *pale, silvery green-blue*, not *mauve-blue*. Some specimens are a purer sky blue. Underside of both sexes as Patrician Blue, usually *paler* ground colour. Rapid flight across open bushveld, settling occasionally on flowers. ♂ may hill-top. Some populations exhibit high density, colonial behaviour, usually where *Ocimum canum* is food plant. **Distribution:** Savanna and Arid Savanna over Limpopo and NW provinces, and part of Gauteng. **Habitat:** Hillsides, hill tops, flatlands. **Flight period:** Two broods, Sept–Dec and Jan–Apr, with some overlap. **Larval food:** *Ocimum canum* and *Lantana rugosa*.

3 Rossouw's Blue *Lepidochrysops rossouwi*

Wingspan: ♂ 33–43 mm ♀ 42–50 mm. **Identification: 3A** ♂ upper side, **3B** ♀ upper side, **3C** ♂ underside. When stationary, ♂ upper side appears *grey shot with blue-green*. On the wing, the most brilliant and glittering of the Twin-spot Blue group. Sexes dimorphic; ♀ larger, upper side blue markings better defined than ♂, *whitish-blue* submarginal row of spots and pale postdiscal row of sagittate marks following those on underside. Underside of both sexes as Patrician Blue (above), usually *paler* ground colour. At midday, ♂ ascends high grassy ridges, territories near prominent features such as isolated trees. ♀ found lower down the slopes near food plant. **Distribution:** Restricted to grassy escarpments near Stoffberg, Dullstroom and Lydenburg (Mpumalanga). **Habitat:** Hillsides, hill tops. **Flight period:** Two broods, Oct–Dec and Jan–Mar, with some overlap. **Larval food:** *Lantana rugosa*. From third instar, brood of *Camponotus maculatus* ants.

1B

C

2A

B

2C

A

3B

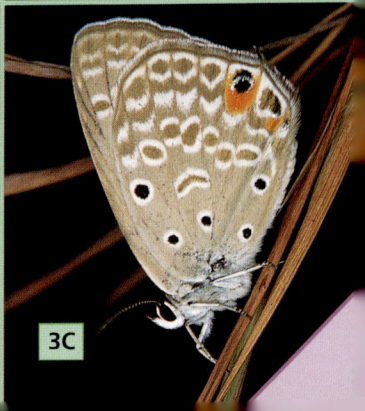

3C

1 Star Blue or Brilliant Blue *Lepidochrysops asteris*

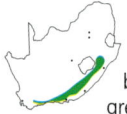

Wingspan: ♂ 32–40 mm ♀ 27–44 mm. **Identification: 1A** ♂ upper side, **1B** ♀ upper side, **1C** ♂ underside. Sexes dimorphic; ♀ upper side resembles ♀ Patrician Blue (p. 294), but *brighter, deeper blue*. ♂ upper side *iridescent azure*. Underside of both sexes *boldly patterned*, dove grey ground with white rings around *very large* darker grey markings. ♂♂ – a dozen or more – ascend hills at midday but seldom to summits, circling prominent trees or rocks. Also in flat country near prominent trees and shrubs. Flight rapid, jinking and erratic. ♀ flight more random; usually on flowers. **Distribution:** Fynbos from W Cape, along Riviersonderendberge above Greyton, and Roodeberg near Worcester, along coastal ranges to E Cape (Vanstadensberg) and Grassland in KwaZulu-Natal Midlands. **Habitat:** Hillsides, mountains, flatlands. **Flight period:** Two broods from Port Elizabeth northwards, Sept–Nov and Feb–Mar, some overlap. Southern populations single-brooded, Nov–Dec. **Larval food:** *Selago* spp., including *S. serrata, Becium burchellianum* and *Plectranthus grandidentatus*.

2 Trimen's Blue *Lepidochrysops trimeni*

Wingspan: ♂ 37–40 mm ♀ 35–42 mm. **Identification: 2A** ♂ upper side, **2B** ♀ upper side, **2C** ♂ underside. Similar to Star Blue (above), ♂ upper side *deeper, more sombre blue*. Underside *darker*, with series of blackish-grey spots so large that their white edges give the impression of white lace on a black background. ♀ resembles a dark ♀ Star Blue. Inhabits steep, rough slopes, ♂ patrolling contours, ♀ found on flowers. Flight rapid and erratic, difficult to follow. **Distribution:** Fynbos in W Cape; Cape Peninsula mountains above Camps Bay and Simon's Town, low hills near Melkbosstrand, mountains near Franschhoek and Du Toit's Kloof; low hills Hermanus and Kleinmond. **Habitat:** Hillsides, mountains. **Flight period:** Single extended brood from Sept–Jan and sometimes Feb, peak depending on rainfall, but usually Oct–Nov. **Larval food:** *Selago* spp., including *S. serrata*, and *Aspalathus sarcantha*. From third instar, brood of *Camponotus maculatus* ants.

Genus *Orachrysops* Blues 11 SPP., ALL ENDEMIC TO SOUTH AFRICA, LESOTHO AND SWAZILAND

Similar to *Lepidochrysops*, small bronze-brown or violet-blue butterflies with underside in varying shades of grey. ♀ *Orachrysops* always have variable amount of upper side blue, from almost none to a maximum extent that varies from species to species. Distinguishing feature is curved row of white or grey marks on hind wing underside forming a pale postdiscal band running parallel to the margin. Species are often confusingly similar, and variable in size and markings within populations. In colonies, sometimes in large numbers over quite large areas. ♂ generally patrols hillside on a beat along a contour. ♀ more sedentary; found near food plant. Egg laid singly or in pairs on young shoots and stems of food plant. Whitish blue to pale green. Pill-shaped, with convex sides and concave top; reticulate double-whorled patterns of lines in geometric shapes radiating from the micropyle, small protruberances wherever the lines cross. Larva slug-like, white to green or pink, with brown lateral and dorsal lines, covered in short bristles and carries tubercles on the penultimate segment. Larva feeds on *Indigofera* (Fabaceae) leaves and young shoots at least in early instars; later instar larva of one species is known to eat the woody rootstock of the food plant; association with *Camponotus* ants known in some species, nature of relationship is probably facultative. Pupa cream to brown, smooth and rounded.

1 Brenton Blue *Orachrysops niobe*

Wingspan: ♂ 24–38 mm ♀ 22–42 mm. **Identification: 1A** ♂ upper side, **1B** ♀ upper side, **1C** ♂ underside. Sexes dimorphic. ♂ upper side dull violet-blue, marginal borders *broad, grey-brown*; dark hind wing upper side subtornal lunule. ♀ borders much wider, blue variable in extent, brighter, *less violet* than ♂. Underside of both sexes flat grey, postmedian series of black spots in forewing *circular to slightly oval*, small spots in discal area of hind wing, and *indistinct* pale hind wing band. Size variable, autumn brood often has dwarfs. **Distribution:** Only at Brenton-on-Sea (W Cape) in Fynbos. **Habitat:** Hillsides, coast. **Flight period:** Two broods, Oct–Nov and Feb–Mar; occasional stragglers in summer. **Larval food:** Leaves in first two instars and (in later instars) rootstock of *Indigofera erecta*. Larvae found at base of host plants in holes, attended by the ant *Camponotus baynei*.

2 Brinkman's Blue *Orachrysops brinkmani*

Wingspan: ♂ 24–38 mm ♀ 28–39 mm. **Identification: 2A** ♂ upper side, **2B** ♀ upper side, **2C** ♂ underside. Upper side of both sexes similar to Brenton Blue (above), hind wing subtornal lunule *absent*. Forewing underside postmedian series of black spots *much more oval*, and in area M_3, *elongated to a streak*. Flight low and slow for an *Orachrysops*. Both sexes feed on flowers of food plant. **Distribution:** Rare. In Fynbos in W Cape. Intermediate plateau below main peaks of Kammanassie Mts at ±1 500 m. **Habitat:** Flatlands, mountains. **Flight period:** Only recorded Oct–Nov. **Larval food:** Oviposition observed on *Indigofera declinata*.

3 Karkloof Blue *Orachrysops ariadne*

Wingspan: 26–40 mm. **Identification: 3A** ♂ upper side, **3B** ♀ upper side, **3C** ♀ underside. Unmistakable. Sexes dimorphic. ♂ upper side purplish-blue, brown-grey marginal borders *narrow*, cilia *white*. ♀ upper side brown with *blue pearlescent sheen*, *broad* marginal borders, hind wing submarginal and postmedian rows of *blue lunules*. Underside (both sexes) *dark grey-brown*, with *clear postmedian bands* of white marks on both wings. Forewing postmedian series of dark spots *broadly outlined with white*. Colonial in steep-sided grassy gullies near Afromontane Forest. ♂ patrols the gully, stopping to feed at flowers in thick vegetation, where ♀ is found. **Distribution:** Only known from a few localities (e.g. Wahroonga, near Midmar Dam, and The Start above Karkloof Falls) in Grassland in KwaZulu-Natal Midlands. **Habitat:** Hillsides, gullies, forest edges. **Flight period:** Single-brooded, Mar–Apr. **Larval food:** *Indigofera woodii* var. *laxa*.

1 Restless Blue *Orachrysops lacrimosa*
Wingspan: ♂ 32–44 mm ♀ 32–40 mm. **Identification: 1A** ♂ upper side, **1B** ♀ upper side, **1C** ♂ underside. Sexes dimorphic. ♂ upper side dark mauve to purplish blue, with *broad* black-brown marginal borders (but not as broad as Brenton or Brinkman's Blues (p. 298)). ♀ upper side forewing dark brown, with *variable extent* of bright blue scaling below cell from base only to covering discal area. Underside of both sexes *pale brownish grey, small* dark brown spots in hind wing discal area and forewing postmedian series. ♂ flight fast, direct, up and down steep grassy slopes. ♀ lower down, sedentary, on flowers, often of food plant. **Distribution:** Widespread in Grassland on high hills from KwaZulu-Natal Midlands (Newcastle area), to e Free State and Mpumalanga. **Habitat:** Hillsides, mountains. **Flight period:** Single-brooded, Oct–Dec, timing dependent on spring rains. **Larval food:** *Indigofera* spp.

2 Grizzled Blue *Orachrysops subravus*
Wingspan: ♂ 30–36 mm ♀ 22–36 mm. **Identification: 2A** ♂ upper side, **2B** ♀ upper side, **2C** ♂ underside. ♂ upper side similar to Restless Blue (above) but *less pinkish* sheen, ♀ upper side darker brown, basal blue scaling *never as extensive*. When worn, ♀ appears identical to Restless Blue, genital dissection being required to distinguish them where they fly together. Underside of both sexes *darker grey*, with *small, indistinct black spots* in hind wing discal area and forewing postmedial area; white postmedial bands have *indistinct edges*. Variable, northerly specimens have *paler* underside with *more distinct* spotting; southerly specimens with spotting *almost absent*. **Distribution:** Montane Grassland from E Cape (Kokstad, Mbotyi, Amatolas) to Bulwer, southern Drakensberg foothills, and KwaZulu-Natal Midlands (Karkloof, Midmar area). **Habitat:** Hillsides, mountains, gullies. **Flight period:** Single-brooded, Oct–Jan, depending on spring rains; flies later in south of range. **Larval food:** *Indigofera woodii* var. *woodii*.

3 Royal Blue *Orachrysops regalis*
Wingspan: ♂ 34–40 mm ♀ 30–42 mm. **Identification: 3A** ♂ upper side, **3B** ♀ upper side, **3C** ♀ underside. Habits and appearance similar to Karkloof Blue (p. 298), generally a *paler insect*; both sexes' upper side blue *brighter*, ♀ has more *well-defined* submarginal row of white-blue lunules. Underside of both sexes *pale dove grey*, hind wing discal and forewing postmedial black spots *well defined*. Flight rapid and direct; ♂ patrols steep rocky slopes, ♀ sedentary, found lower on slopes. **Distribution:** Localised; grassy savanna-covered hillsides from Mpumalanga (Lydenburg, Watervalsrivierpas) to Strydpoortberge south-west of Haenertsburg (Limpopo Province) and Letsitele Kop. **Habitat:** Mountains, hillsides. **Flight period:** Single-brooded, Oct–Dec, depending on spring rains. **Larval food:** *Indigofera* spp.

4 Violescent Blue *Orachrysops violescens*
Wingspan: ♂ 23–36 mm ♀ 36–38 mm. **Identification: 4A** ♂ upper side, **4B** ♀ upper side, **4C** ♂ underside. Forewing apex *more rounded* than other *Orachrysops* spp. ♂ upper side has *strong violet sheen*, ♀ upper side grey-brown, with paler, *more violet basal blue* than Restless Blue (above). Underside of both sexes *very pale* brown-grey with black spots. **Distribution:** Grassland near Afromontane Forest, from Mpumalanga (Hendriksdal) to Limpopo Province (Mariepskop); also near Mac-Mac Pools and Kowyn's Pass near Graskop, and Khandwe Mountain in s Kruger National Park. **Habitat:** Hillsides, forest edges. **Flight period:** Single-brooded, Sept–Dec, depending on spring rains. **Larval food:** *Indigofera* spp.

A

1B

1C

A

2B

2C

A

3B

3C

A

4B

4C

1 Mijburgh's Blue *Orachrysops mijburghi*

Wingspan: ♂ 31–39 mm ♀ 32–38 mm. **Identification: 1A** ♂ upper side, **1B** ♀ upper side, **1C** ♂ underside. Similar to Restless Blue (p. 300), but both sexes *paler on both surfaces* and hind wing upper side submarginal lunular marks *better defined.* ♂ dark marginal border *narrower*, ♀ blue *more extensive.* Underside *pale grey*, forewing and hind wing dark spots *with black centres, very conspicuous.* In colonies; ♂ flight fast, zigzagging and evasive. ♀ slower, more sedentary; usually on flowers. **Distribution:** Highly localised. Highveld Grassland in Free State at Heilbron and Petrus Steyn. **Habitat:** Flatlands, hillsides, wetlands. **Flight period:** Two broods, Oct–Dec and Jan–Mar, with some overlap. **Larval food:** *Indigofera evansiana.*

2 Golden Gate Blue *Orachrysops montanus*

Wingspan: ♂ 28–36 mm ♀ 24–30 mm. **Identification: 2A** ♂ upper side, **2B** ♀ upper side, **2C** ♂ underside. ♂ upper side *darker, more transparent purplish blue* than Nosy Blue (below); ♀ upper side *golden to bronze-brown*, basal blue *very restricted or absent.* Underside similar to Karkloof Blue (p. 298), *paler brown-grey*, well-defined black spots *narrowly* outlined with *cream.* ♂ fast, elusive flight up and down steep mountainside between gullies. ♀ flight slower, feeds on flowers. **Distribution:** Only known from montane Grassland of Golden Gate Highlands NP, below Brandwag Buttress (Free State). **Habitat:** Hillsides, gullies, wetlands, mountains. **Flight period:** Single-brooded, Dec–Jan. **Larval food:** *Indigofera* spp.

3 Nosy Blue *Orachrysops nasutus*

Wingspan: ♂ 30–38 mm ♀ 25–39 mm. **Identification: 3A** ♂ upper side, **3B** ♀ upper side, **3C** ♂ underside. Very similar to Grizzled Blue (p. 300), but ♂ has a more *pinkish-bronze* sheen on upper side. ♀ has paler brown ground colour, more extensive basal blue scaling. Underside of both sexes *slightly darker* with *less well-defined* black spots, but where they fly together, as in Lesotho, the Grizzled Blue is in the southern part of its range, where the underside is darker than on northern specimens. Worn ♀♀ only reliably distinguished by genital dissection. 2 subspp., geographically distinct. **Distribution:** Nominate in high-altitude montane Grassland in Amatolas and southern Drakensberg (Barkly East area) of E Cape; *O. n. remus* – north-east of Senqu R in Lesotho, to se KwaZulu-Natal Drakensberg. **Habitat:** Hillsides, gullies, mountains. **Flight period:** Single-brooded, Dec–Jan. **Larval food:** *Indigofera cuneifolia.*

4 Warren's Blue *Orachrysops warreni*

Wingspan: ♂ 32–36 mm ♀ 32–40 mm. **Identification: 4A** ♂ upper side, **4B** ♀ upper side, **4C** ♂ underside. ♂ upper side *darker purplish blue* than Golden Gate Blue (above), ♀ upper side *dark bronze-brown, almost no* blue scaling. Underside *darker brown-grey*, dark markings *better defined*, discal spots outlined with *grey-white.* **Distribution:** Only known from one hillside in Verloren Valei NR, Mpumalanga, at 2 100 m in Grassland. **Habitat:** Hillsides, wetlands. **Flight period:** Single-brooded, Dec–Jan. **Larval food:** *Indigofera* spp.

Genus *Euchrysops*   Smoky Blues   AFRICA 26 SPP., SOUTH AFRICA 5

Small to very small blue butterflies, like *Lepidochrysops*, found in open country but species whose life histories are known do not show obligate association with ants. Single egg, pill-shaped with convex sides and concave top, with reticulate double-whorled patterns of lines in geometric shapes radiating from the micropyle (except that of *E. barkeri* which is smooth and rounded). Larva slug-shaped, pale green with darker green or reddish dorsal and lateral stripes, and diagonal lateral lines. Pupa rounded, smooth skinned and green to cream or pale grey. Food plants Fabaceae, Bignoniaceae, Lamiaceae.

1 Osiris Smoky Blue   *Euchrysops osiris*

Wingspan: ♂ 22–29 mm ♀ 25–30 mm. **Identification: 1A & 1B** ♂ upper side, **1C** ♀ upper side (tails missing), **1D** ♂ underside. ♂ upper side *pinkish mauve*, ♀ upper side striking, *dark grey*, forewing basal and discal areas *deep blue*, and *double row* of *white sagittate lunules* on hind wing. Both sexes have conspicuous *double black spots* on both wing surfaces, with *large double orange lunules* at hind wing anal angle, with short tails. Underside of both sexes a pale fawn-grey ground colour, with paler-edged, slightly darker *squarish* spots in cells and postdiscal and marginal series, submarginal series of white sagittate marks and 3 to 5 basal white-edged black spots. Flight brisk but low and erratic; settles often. ♂ hill-tops at midday. Both sexes suck wet mud near streams. **Distribution:** Edges of wooded, thorny Savanna from KwaZulu-Natal coast to Mpumalanga, Gauteng and Limpopo Province. **Habitat:** Coast, flatlands, hill tops. **Flight period:** Two main broods, Sept–Nov and Feb–Apr, but may be found at other times of year. **Larval food:** *Rhynchosia totta, Vigna tenuis* and *V. unguiculata.*

2 Barker's Smoky Blue   *Euchrysops barkeri*

Wingspan: ♂ 26–32 mm ♀ 27–33 mm. **Identification: 2A** ♂ upper side, **2B** ♀ upper side, **2C** ♀ underside. Very similar to Osiris Smoky Blue (above), slightly *larger*, only a *single* black spot and orange lunule at tailed hind wing anal angle, both wing surfaces. Sexes dimorphic as in Osiris Smoky Blue (above), both surfaces *paler* in both sexes; ♂ upper side *powder blue*, not pinkish mauve, *broader* grey marginal borders. ♀ blue *powder blue*, not sky blue. Underside as Osiris Smoky Blue but paler. Slow, fluttering flight close to ground, settling often on flowers. ♀ seen more often than ♂. **Distribution:** Edges of wooded coastal Savanna from E Cape (Port St Johns) along KwaZulu-Natal coast to Mozambique; also in Limpopo Province north of Polokwane. **Habitat:** Coast, flatlands, hillsides. **Flight period:** Continuous broods; DSF Apr–Sept, WSF Oct–Mar. Most often seen Nov–Jul. **Larval food:** *Crotolaria* spp., *Rhynchosia* spp. and *Vigna unguiculata.*

3 Common Smoky Blue   *Euchrysops malathana*

Wingspan: ♂ 22–30 mm ♀ 23–31 mm. **Identification: 3A** ♂ upper side, **3B** ♀ upper side, **3C** ♀ underside (laying on food plant). Sexes dimorphic, ♂ upper side *plain flat grey* with *double row* of paler hind wing submarginal lunules, *single black and orange lunule* at anal angle. ♀ resembles small Osiris Smoky Blue (above), but *tailless*, and only a *single* orange and black anal lunule. Unobtrusive; slow, fluttering flight low among grasses, settling often on flowers or on the ground. Both sexes fond of wet mud. **Distribution:** Savanna and Arid Savanna from n E Cape (inland of East London) to KwaZulu-Natal, e Free State, Mpumalanga, Gauteng, and Limpopo and NW provinces. **Habitat:** Flatlands, hillsides, coast. **Flight period:** Year-round, peak Dec–May. **Larval food:** *Sphenostylis angustifolia, Canavalia* spp. and *Vigna* spp., including *V. unguiculata.*

1 Sabi Smoky Blue   *Euchrysops dolorosa*

Wingspan: ♂ 22–26 mm ♀ 23–29 mm. **Identification: 1A** ♂ upper side, **1B** ♀ upper side, **1C** ♂ underside. Could be mistaken for a small, dull blue *Lepidochrysops*. Sexes dimorphic; ♂ upper side *dull steel blue*, ♀ upper side *grey-brown*, basal and discal areas blue; hind wing with *submarginal blue lunules*. Underside of both sexes fawn-brown, with paler-edged, slightly darker *rounded* spots in cells and postdiscal and marginal series; submarginal series of white sagittate marks and five basal white-edged dark brown spots. Flight very low, weak and erratic, settling on flowers or the ground. **Distribution:** Grassy areas in Savanna from E Cape (Mbashe R) to KwaZulu-Natal, e Free State, Mpumalanga, Gauteng, and Limpopo and NW provinces. **Habitat:** Flatlands, hillsides. **Flight period:** Several broods, Aug–Mar, depending on spring rains; later in n KwaZulu-Natal. Peaks Oct and Feb. **Larval food:** *Salvia* spp. and *Becium* spp.

2 Ashen Smoky Blue   *Euchrysops subpallida*

Wingspan: ♂ 23–25 mm ♀ 24–28 mm. **Identification: 2A** ♂ upper side, **2B** ♀ upper side, **2C** ♀ underside. Very similar to Sabi Smoky Blue (above), wings *more angular*; upper side hind wing submarginal lunules *better defined*. Underside ground colour *paler*, hind wing discal spots *black instead of brown, more distinct* pale colour outlining underside spotting. Flight very low, weak and erratic, settling on flowers or the ground. **Distribution:** Rare in South Africa; in Savanna and on grassy hillsides in n Limpopo Province (Soutpansberg, Waterberg, and Madikwe Game Reserve) and n KwaZulu-Natal. **Habitat:** Hillsides, flatlands. **Flight period:** Single-brooded, Sept–Feb, depending on rains. **Larval food:** Not confirmed, but often found near *Becium* spp.

Genus *Eicochrysops*   Blues

AFRICA 15 SPP., SOUTH AFRICA 2

Tiny blue or brown butterflies, sedentary habits. Flight usually low, weak, but sustained if disturbed. Egg laid singly on food plant, Santalaceae or Polygonaceae; pill-shaped with convex sides, double-whorled pattern of ribs forming polygons with tiny protuberances where the ribs cross. Larva slug-shaped, green with darker green or reddish dorsal and lateral lines. Pupa rounded, green to whitish, marked with reddish or dark grey, covered in fine hairs.

3 Cupreous Blue   *Eicochrysops messapus*

Wingspan: ♂ 17–22 mm ♀ 17–24 mm. **Identification: 3A & 3B** ♂ upper side, **3C** ♀ upper side, **3D** ♀ underside. Sexes dimorphic. ♂ *E. m. mahallakoeana* has *variable* (see illustrations) *pinkish-copper blush, absent* in nominate; ♀ upper side *black*, hind wing has *black and orange* anal lunule varying in size. Underside of both sexes and both subspp. grey with black spots. Flight slow among grass and low vegetation; settles often on flowers and stems. **Distribution:** Nominate in Fynbos from W Cape (common in Cape Peninsula) north into Nama Karoo and east along coast and mountain chain to Free State (Springfontein); *E. m. mahallakoeana* in Savanna and Grassland from n E Cape to KwaZulu-Natal, n Free State, Mpumalanga, Gauteng, and Limpopo and NW provinces. **Habitat:** Hillsides, flatlands, mountains. **Flight period:** Year-round in warmer areas, peaks Oct and Mar, absent from cooler areas Apr–Sept. **Larval food:** *Thesium* spp.

1 White-tipped Blue   *Eicochrysops hippocrates*

Wingspan: ♂ 18–23 mm ♀ 20–24 mm. **Identification: 1A** ♂ upper side, **1B** ♀ upper side, **1C** ♂ underside. Sexes dimorphic. ♂ upper side *black-brown* with bold *white forewing apical tip*; ♀ with wings *rounder*, upper side much *brighter pale metallic blue*, marginal borders *broad, grey-brown*. Underside of both sexes grey with black spots. Flight unhurried. Found in wet, marshy areas, especially where animals have stirred up mud at the water's edge; seldom strays far from water. **Distribution:** Lowland forest, Riverine Forest, Savanna. Local but common along streams in Riverine Forest and in marshes in Savanna and Lowland Forest, from E Cape (Port St Johns) along KwaZulu-Natal coast, to Swaziland, Mpumalanga and Limpopo Province, and further north. **Habitat:** Forest edges, wetlands, gullies. **Flight period:** Two broods, Sept–Nov and Jan–Jun. **Larval food:** *Polygonum* spp. and *Rumex* spp.

Genus *Cupidopsis*   Meadow Blues   AFRICA 3 SPP., SOUTH AFRICA 2

Small blue lycaenids, found in Grassland and Savanna. Flight low, wandering and erratic, but capable of fast evasive action if disturbed. Both sexes usually found close to food plants, often feeding on flower nectar. Egg laid singly on Fabaceae; domed or pill-shaped, with pattern of double whorls of ribs with tiny protuberances where they cross. Larva green to straw or buff-pink with darker green or reddish series of longitudinal or diagonal lines, slug-shaped. Pupa white to green, with tiny black dots; sparsely covered with fine hairs.

2 Common Meadow Blue   *Cupidopsis cissus cissus*

Wingspan: ♂ 22–34 mm ♀ 23–36 mm (variable). **Identification: 2A** ♂ upper side (slightly aberrant specimen, left hind wing orange lunules elongate), **2B** ♀ upper side, **2C** ♀ underside. ♂ upper side *deep clear blue*, dark margins *narrow*, ♀ upper side blue *suffused distally with white*, marginal borders *wide*. Both sexes have conspicuous *bright orange hind wing anal lunules*; both *tailless*. Underside dove grey fading to white towards the outer margin, with series of prominent white-edged black spots. Usually found *singly or in small groups* in open grassland. **Distribution:** Common and widespread in Grassland from sea level to over 2 000 m, along east coast from W Cape (Knysna) to E Cape and KwaZulu-Natal, inland along Drakensberg foothills across highveld to Gauteng and NW Province; also mountain chains in Mpumalanga, NW and Limpopo provinces. **Habitat:** Flatlands, hillsides, mountains. **Flight period:** Sept–Apr and May, sometimes Jun and Jul in subtropical areas. **Larval food:** Flowers of *Eriosema* spp. and *Vigna* spp.

3 Tailed Meadow Blue   *Cupidopsis jobates jobates*

Wingspan: ♂ 23–30 mm ♀ 26–33 mm. **Identification: 3A** ♂ upper side, **3B** ♀ upper side, **3C** ♂ underside. Not as common as Common Meadow Blue (above), habitat similar but prefers *damper areas*. *Paler*, on average *smaller* than Common Meadow Blue, ♂ upper side has *broader grey marginal borders*, so sexual dimorphism *less obvious*, but ♀ still distinguished by *white distal suffusion*. Hind wing carries *short anal tail*; orange lunules spread along margin *forming a band*. ♀ very similar to ♀ Common Meadow Blue. **Distribution:** Grassland and Savanna from sea level to 2 000 m, along east coast from E Cape (Port Elizabeth) and KwaZulu-Natal, inland along Drakensberg foothills and across highveld to Gauteng and NW Province, and along mountain chains in Mpumalanga, NW Province and Limpopo Province. **Habitat:** Flatlands, hillsides, mountains, wetlands. **Flight period:** Sept–Apr and May, sometimes to Jun or Jul in the subtropical areas. **Larval food:** Flowers of low-growing grassland Fabaceae, e.g. *Rhynchosia puberula* and other Fabaceae species.

Genus *Actizera* Blues
AFRICA 3 SPP., SOUTH AFRICA 2

Tiny, slow-flying butterflies, sedentary habits, found in Grassland. Egg laid singly on Oxalidaceae and Fabaceae; pill-shaped, double whorls of ribs forming a reticulated pattern of geometric cells. Larva flattened, slug-shaped, green or straw coloured with dorsal stripe. Pupa dirty grey or brown, rounded, formed in leaf litter.

1 Rayed Blue *Actizera lucida*

Wingspan: ♂ 15–23 mm ♀ 17–25 mm. **Identification: 1A** ♂ upper side, **1B & 1C** ♀ upper side, **1D** ♂ underside. Distinguished from other small Blues by having *bright white diagonal streak* on underside hind wing. On upper side, ♂ *dull blue*, ♀ *brown* with variable amount of basal blue (as illustrated). Usually found singly or in small groups. **Distribution:** Widespread from W Cape (Hermanus area) and grassy edges of Karoo, to Grassland, Forest and Savanna in Free State, KwaZulu-Natal, Gauteng, Mpumalanga, and Limpopo and NW provinces. **Habitat:** Flatlands, hillsides, forest edges, parks and gardens, coast. **Flight period:** Year-round, more numerous in summer. **Larval food:** *Oxalis* spp., *Argyrolobium* sp., *Rhynchosia* spp. and *Crotolaria lanceolata*.

2 Red-clover Blue *Actizera stellata*

Wingspan: ♂ 13–18 mm ♀ 15–19 mm. **Identification: 2A** ♂ upper side, **2B** ♂ underside. Sexes similar, ♀ slightly larger than ♂. *Smaller* than Rayed Blue (above). Upper side black-brown with pattern of *tiny white arcuate marks*; underside lacks white diagonal streak. Inconspicuous; circles slowly close to food plant. **Distribution:** E Cape, hilly Grassland/Nama Karoo ecotone centred on Dordrecht. Colonies at Stormberg, Burgersdorp, near Bedford and Kompasberg, near Nieu-Bethesda, and near Springfontein in s Free State. **Habitat:** Mountains, wetlands, gullies. **Flight period:** Single extended brood, Jan–May, peaks Jan and Feb. **Larval food:** *Trifolium africanum*.

Genus *Zizeeria* Blues
AFRICA 2 SPP., SOUTH AFRICA 1

Tiny and widespread common butterfly. Flight low, quite fast, circling and erratic. Egg very pale green, laid singly on wide range of food plant families; pill-shaped with depressed top, double involuted lines of ribs forming a fine pattern of geometric cells with tiny protuberances where they cross. Larva woodlouse-shaped, green with darker dorsal and diagonal lateral lines. Pupa whitish to green, rounded with dark marks.

3 Sooty Blue *Zizeeria knysna*

Wingspan: ♂ 18–23 mm ♀ 21–26 mm. **Identification: 3A** ♂ upper side, **3B** ♀ upper side, **3C** ♂ underside. ♂ upper side *dull violet-blue*, ♀ upper side *black-brown* with variable amount of *brighter basal blue*. Underside *dark grey*, wings *only slightly elongated*, abdomen *shorter* in comparison to the hind wing. Most common small Blue, most often on suburban lawns infested with its food plant, a common weed. **Distribution:** Throughout South Africa, from sea level to highest mountains and wet forests to Arid Savanna. **Habitat:** Parks and gardens, flatlands, wetlands, forest edges, mountains, hillsides, coast. **Flight period:** Year-round, peaks Oct–Dec and Feb–Apr. **Larval food:** *Tribulus terrestris, Amaranthus deflexus* and *A. viridis, Oxalis corniculata, Medicago sativa* and *Zornia* spp.

Genus *Zizina* Blues

WORLD 3 SPP., AFRICA INCL SOUTH AFRICA 1

Small blue butterfly resembling *Zizeeria* with similar weak, low flight. Life history very similar to *Zizeeria*. Egg laid singly on Fabaceae; white, pill-shaped with depressed top, double involuted lines of ribs forming a fine pattern of geometric cells with tiny protuberances where they cross. Larva woodlouse-shaped, green with dorsal and lateral darker, parallel lines. Pupa green, lines of dark marks on abdomen, rounded.

1 Clover Blue *Zizina antanossa*

Wingspan: ♂ 20–24 mm ♀ 21–28 mm. **Identification: 1A** ♀ upper side, **1B** ♂ underside. Upper side *steel blue* with *broad grey-brown marginal borders* in both sexes. ♂ blue *more extensive* than ♀. Underside hind wing discal row of spots *'elbowed' basally just below the costa*. Seldom found far from the food plant. **Distribution:** Grassland near forests along coast from E Cape (Cintsa, near East London) spreading into Savanna of KwaZulu-Natal, Mpumalanga, Limpopo Province and further north. **Habitat:** Coast, flatlands, hillsides, forest edges. **Flight period:** Year-round in warm areas, peaks Oct–Nov and Mar–Apr; double brooded at those times in cooler areas. **Larval food:** *Desmodium incanum*, *Indigofera* sp.

Genus *Brephidium* Blues

WORLD 3 SPP., AFRICA INCL SOUTH AFRICA 1

Very small brown butterfly. Flight low, erratic, weak; flits around low bushes. Egg laid singly on Chenopodiaceae; pill-shaped with convex sides, double-whorled pattern of ribs. Larva whitish, double row of dorsal serrations. Pupa also whitish, rounded.

2 Tinktinkie Blue *Brephidium metophis*

Wingspan: ♂ 16–20 mm ♀ 17–21 mm. **Identification: 2A** ♂ upper side, **2B** ♂ underside. Sexes very similar, both sepia on upper side with dark hind wing submarginal spots mirroring those on underside. Underside grey-brown, with spots of same colour ringed in white; prominent black hind wing submarginal spots, containing metallic marks. Can be very common in small areas where the food plant grows in dense masses. Usually found at low altitudes in arid veld. **Distribution:** Locally common in Nama Karoo, Succulent Karoo, Grassland, Savanna from W Cape (Montagu, Molteno Pass), north to Namaqualand, N Cape, east to E Cape, KwaZulu-Natal and w Free State. **Habitat:** Coast, flatlands, hillsides. **Flight period:** Continuous broods, depending on rainfall. May be as early as Aug in Namaqualand, through spring and summer to Apr. **Larval food:** *Exomis axyrioides*.

Genus *Oraidium* Dwarf Blue

MONOTYPIC

Tiny brown butterfly. Flight weak, low – only a few centimetres above the ground. Life history not recorded.

3 Dwarf Blue *Oraidium barberae*

Wingspan: ♂ 10–15 mm ♀ 12–18 mm. **Identification: 3A** ♂ upper side, **3B** ♀ underside. South Africa's smallest butterfly. Best distinguished from Tinktinkie Blue (above) by genital dissection, but generally upper side *darker* in both sexes; underside hind wing submarginal spots *not visible on upper side*. Underside hind wing markings differ – spots also enclosed by white rings, but *darker than ground colour and hind wing white marks faint or absent*. **Distribution:** Locally common in Fynbos and Nama Karoo from W Cape (Yzerfontein), north into Succulent Karoo in Namaqualand, Savanna and Grassland in N Cape, and east to E Cape and Free State; Lowland Forest in n KwaZulu-Natal. **Habitat:** Coast, flatlands, hillsides. **Flight period:** Continuous broods, depending on rains; peaks usually Sept–Nov and Feb–Apr. **Larval food:** Probably *Exomis axyrioides*.

A

1B

A

2B

A

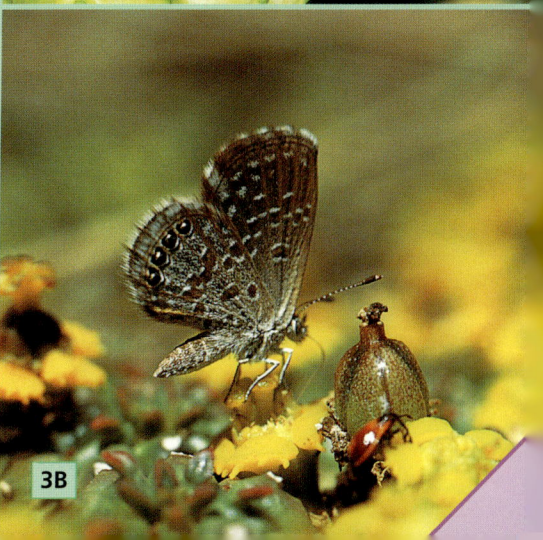

3B

Genus *Azanus*   Blues

Small blue butterflies, widespread in Savanna areas. ♂ ♂ with upper sides iridescent blue, ♀ ♀ brown with variable (between species) amount of white. Undersides pale grey to white, with black or brown bands or series of spots, and hind wing lunules. May fly in huge numbers. Flight rapid and whirling, around the sides and tops of trees. Also fond of mud puddles. Egg laid singly on Fabaceae; pill-shaped, flat-topped, pattern of double involuted sets of ribs crossing to form geometric shapes and sometimes prominent protuberances where they cross. Larva woodlouse-shaped with ridged 'hogsback' dorsal serrations, cryptically marked. Pupa rounded, whitish to green.

1 Velvet-spotted Blue   *Azanus ubaldus*

Wingspan: ♂ 16–23 mm ♀ 18–21 mm. **Identification: 1A** ♂ upper side, **1B** ♀ upper side, **1C** ♂ underside. Sexes dimorphic; ♀ upper side *uniform dark brown*. ♂ has narrow, pointed forewing and forewing upper side *velvety blue patch*. Underside more *finely marked* than other *Azanus* spp. Flight slow; flies with other *Azanus* spp. and other small lycaenids. **Distribution:** Nama Karoo with acacias from W Cape (Robertson) to E Cape; Savanna in KwaZulu-Natal, Mpumalanga, Free State, Gauteng and Limpopo Province, and Arid Savanna in NW Province and N Cape. **Habitat:** Flatlands, hillsides. **Flight period:** Continuous broods, Sept–Apr. **Larval food:** *Acacia* spp., including *A. karroo*.

2 Topaz-spotted Blue   *Azanus jesous jesous*

Wingspan: ♂ 17–26 mm ♀ 22–28 mm. **Identification: 2A** ♂ upper side, **2B** ♀ upper side, **2C** ♂ underside. Sexes dimorphic. ♂ upper side *shiny pinkish blue*, marginal borders *black*, cilia *prominent white*. ♀ upper side *brown*, paler basal areas *suffused with blue*, variable white discal forewing patch, *conspicuous brown spot* at end of forewing cell. Some specimens have overall suffusion of pinkish-mauve iridescence. Underside typical *Azanus* pattern but has *broad, straight, white-edged forewing apical bands;* hind wing carries prominent series of postdiscal white-edged brown spots, and squarish submarginal series of white spots. **Distribution:** Most common South African *Azanus*. Widespread over almost all of South Africa. **Habitat:** Flatlands, hillsides, parks and gardens, forest edges, coast. **Flight period:** Continuous broods from Sept–May in cooler areas; in warmer areas, year-round, peak late summer. **Larval food:** Flowers, buds and fresh shoots and stem galls of *Acacia* spp., including *A. karroo*, and *Adenopodia spicata*. Probably also *Acacia cyclops* and other exotic Australian *Acacia* spp., because it is found near Cape Town where no other Acacias grow.

3 Natal Spotted Blue   *Azanus natalensis*

Wingspan: ♂ 23–27 mm ♀ 24–30 mm. **Identification: 3A** ♂ upper side, **3B** ♀ upper side, **3C** ♂ underside. Largest *Azanus*, underside resembles Thorn-tree Blue (p. 316) but spots in *areas M_1 and M_2 closer to margin than the spot in Rs* (see arrow) – in Thorn-tree Blue (and Mirza Blue, p. 316) it is the other way around – the spot in Rs *is closer* to margin than those in areas M_1 and M_2. *Two broad black bands* in white forewing cilia give wing edges a wavy appearance. Forewing underside postdiscal band of spots *squarer* than Thorn-tree and Mirza Blues, and *not* white edged. Sexes dimorphic, ♂ upper side *brilliant blue*, but *less pink* than Topaz-spotted Blue (above). ♀ upper side has *much more white* than other *Azanus* spp., with its dark square spots and blue wing bases closely resembling ♀ *Hintza Blue* (p. 258). **Distribution:** Savanna from E Cape (East London) north-east along coast to KwaZulu-Natal, to thorn belt and edges of Lowland Forest, and to Mpumalanga and Limpopo Province lowveld. **Habitat:** Flatlands, hillsides, coast. **Flight period:** Continuous broods all year, mainly Sept–May. **Larval food:** Flowers, buds and fresh shoots of *Acacia* spp., including *A. karroo*.

A

1B

C

2A

B

2C

A

3B

3C

1 Thorn-tree Blue *Azanus moriqua*

Wingspan: ♂ 19–24 mm ♀ 19–25 mm. **Identification: 1A** ♂ upper side, **1B** ♀ upper side, **1C** ♂ underside. Duller colour than Topaz-spotted Blue (p. 314). ♂ upper side *dull violet-blue* with *black-brown* margins. ♀ upper side white *less extensive*. White-edged underside forewing dark markings on pale grey ground. Hind wing pattern similar to Natal Spotted Blue (p. 314) but positioning of spots in areas M$_1$, M$_2$ and R$_s$ different. **Distribution:** All over South Africa, absent from high mountains and Fynbos/Karoo areas. **Habitat:** Flatlands, hillsides, parks and gardens, forest edges, coast. **Flight period:** Continuous broods all year, mainly Sept–May. **Larval food:** Flowers, buds and fresh shoots of *Acacia* spp., including *A. karroo*.

2 Mirza Blue *Azanus mirza*

Wingspan: ♂ 20–25 mm ♀ 21–25 mm. **Identification: 2A** ♂ upper side, **2B** ♀ upper side, **2C** ♂ underside. ♂ upper side *brighter* than Thorn-tree Blue (above), margins *narrower*; ♀ upper side white patches *larger*. Underside as Thorn-tree Blue, with *yellow-orange spot* above black lunule in area CuA$_2$ of hind wing. **Distribution:** Savanna and open forest from KwaZulu-Natal (Durban) north to lowveld of Mpumalanga and Limpopo Province. **Habitat:** Flatlands, hillsides, coast. **Flight period:** All year, but mainly Sept–Mar. **Larval food:** Flowers, buds and fresh shoots of *Acacia* spp. and *Allophylus* spp.

Genus *Chilades* Jewel Blues   WORLD 15 SPP., AFRICA 9, SOUTH AFRICA 1

Tiny brown butterflies. Flight slow and halting, low among vegetation. Generally solitary in grassy areas, in vleis and marshes sometimes in numbers. Single egg on Fabaceae and Boraginaceae; flat-topped bun shape, criss-crossed with involuted double whorls of ribs. Larva slug-shaped, pink or green with dorsal and lateral stripes and faint dorso-lateral oblique lines. Pupa green to pale brown, formed in leaf litter.

3 Grass Jewel Blue *Chilades trochylus*

Wingspan: ♂ 15–19 mm ♀ 16–20 mm. **Identification: 3A** ♂ upper side, **3B** ♂ underside. Small dark brown butterfly, with *conspicuous orange hind wing anal patch*. Settles often on small flowers. Sexes similar. **Distribution:** Savanna, Nama Karoo, Grassland, Lowland Forest. All over e South Africa, most westerly records from Swellendam (W Cape); absent from high mountains. **Habitat:** Wetlands, flatlands, hillsides, parks and gardens, forest edges. **Flight period:** In warmer areas, continuous broods all year, mainly Oct–May. In cooler areas only found Oct–May. **Larval food:** *Indigofera cryptantha* and *Heliotropium* spp.

Genus *Zizula* Blues   WORLD 2 SPP., SOUTH AFRICA 1

Small blue butterfly. Flight weak. May be common in Riverine and coastal forests. Single egg on Acanthaceae and Oxalidaceae; white, pill-shaped; double involuted lines of ribs form fine pattern of geometric cells. Larva cylindrical, green or pink, darker dorsal and lateral stripes. Pupa more elongated than other small Blues, pale green, dark dorsal lines on abdomen.

4 Gaika Blue *Zizula hylax*

Wingspan: ♂ 17–21 mm ♀ 18–25 mm. **Identification: 4A** ♂ upper side, **4B** ♀ upper side, **4C** ♂ underside. *Delicate*; abdomen *protrudes beyond hind wings*. Sexes dimorphic, the *powder blue* ♂ smaller than *brown-black* ♀. Underside *has tiny black spots* on pale grey ground colour. Frequents shady spots, often under forest canopy. **Distribution:** Savanna, Grassland, Lowland, Afromontane and Riverine Forest, Nama Karoo, Fynbos. From W Cape (Cape Peninsula), along south coast to E Cape, inland through KwaZulu-Natal to Free State, Gauteng, Mpumalanga, Limpopo and NW provinces. **Habitat:** Flatlands, hillsides, parks and gardens, forest edges. **Flight period:** In warmer areas, continuous broods all year, peaks Sept–Nov and Mar–Jun. In cooler areas double brooded at those times. **Larval food:** *Phaulopsis imbricata*, *Ruellia* spp., *Justicia* spp., *Chaetacanthus setiger*, *Dyschoriste* spp. and *Oxalis corniculata*.

Family PIERIDAE

A large family of about 1 000 species worldwide. They form a very well-defined group, and are easily distinguished. Base colour generally white or yellow, with distinctive red, orange, purple or black markings. There are few dark pierids – only one found in South Africa. Of the four subfamilies of the Pieridae, two are found in South Africa.

Subfamily PIERINAE

A widespread group with many members in South Africa. Flight pattern varies from slow and halting to fast and direct. Distinguished from other pierids mainly by wing venation (hind wing S_c+R_1 running freely to margin) and food plant preferences (Brassicaceae, Capparaceae, Loranthaceae and Santalaceae). Some show pearlescent or iridescent effects, and some have strong wing patterns only visible in ultraviolet light.

Genus *Pinacopteryx*   Zebra White   MONOTYPIC

Only South African pierid with largely dark upper side. Flight rapid and direct, usually found near food plants and feeding at flowers. Typical pierid egg, spindle-shaped, laid in batches on Capparaceae, larva cryptically coloured with fringes of hairs along the sides which aid in preventing the larva from throwing a shadow. Pupa also very cryptic, resembling a dried, curled up leaf. Monotypic genus, unique in the Pierinae.

1 **Zebra White**   *Pinacopteryx eriphia eriphia*
Wingspan: ♂ 40–55 mm ♀ 42–47 mm. **Identification: 1A** ♂ upper side, **1B** ♂ underside (f. *eriphia*). Upper side black or brown-black, with conspicuous white to cream-yellow zebra stripes and spots. Sexes similar, but seasonally dimorphic; DSF f. *nyassae* has paler upper side bands; underside more uniform, paler pinkish grey than f. *eriphia*, which has pale patches mirroring the upper side stripes. **Distribution:** Throughout South Africa; absent from Fynbos and Succulent Karoo areas, and highest mountains. **Habitat:** Flatlands, hillsides, forest edges, parks and gardens. **Flight period:** Year-round in warmer areas, Oct–Apr in cooler areas; WSF Sept–Apr, DSF Mar–Oct, depending on rainfall. Peak usually late summer. **Larval food:** *Maerua cafra, Boscia albitrunca* and *B. oleoides*.

Genus *Eronia*   Vagrants   AFRICA INCL. SOUTH AFRICA 2 SPP.

Brightly coloured. Fast, wandering flight along the edge of bush, stopping often to feed on flowers. Single egg laid on Capparaceae; elongate, tapering at top, 9–10 longitudinal ribs cross-braced with about 24 ribs. Larva broadest at third segment, tapering to shortly bifid tail; mossy green with longitudinal pale lateral stripe. Pupa green or buff, laterally compressed, very prominent wing cases bulging ventrally; short, acute head spike.

2 **Vine-leaf Vagrant**   *Eronia cleodora cleodora*
Wingspan: ♂ 45–60 mm ♀ 50–62 mm. **Identification: 2A** ♀ upper side, **2B** ♀ underside (DSF). Sexes very similar. White upper side with *bold black marginal borders*, underside hind wing in *dead-leaf* pattern. WSF larger, broad continuous borders on upper side. DSF smaller, borders narrower, breaking into dots. **Distribution:** Fairly common in wooded Savanna and Riverine Forest from E Cape (Port Elizabeth), along coast and inland through KwaZulu-Natal to Swaziland; also Mpumalanga and Limpopo Province in escarpment forests and Riverine Forest penetrating Savanna. **Habitat:** Forest edges, parks and gardens, flatlands, coast, hillsides. **Flight period:** Year-round, depending on rainfall. Generally two peaks, spring and late summer. **Larval food:** *Capparis fascicularis*.

A

B

A

2B

1 Autumn-leaf Vagrant or Orange-and-Lemon Butterfly   *Eronia leda*

Wingspan: ♂ 50–55 mm ♀ 48–56 mm. **Identification: 1A** ♂ upper side, **1B** ♂ underside, **1C** ♀ upper side (intermediate f. *pupillaris*). ♂ upper side unspotted orange forewing tips on yellow ground. Fond of flowers, especially red ones. ♀ upper side forewing tips carry small black spots, but WSF f. *leda* ♀♀ upper side forewing tips have *no orange*. Forewing tips develop more orange as conditions get drier. Intermediate ♀ f. *pupillaris* has a trace of forewing tip orange, small silvery underside spots. In Jun, f. *trimeni* prevails, forewings tip orange as ♂. Both sexes with dark underside hind wing spots that become larger and silver-centred as dry season progresses. Shy, elusive. **Distribution:** Wooded Savanna and Lowland Forest from E Cape (Port St Johns) along coast and inland to Swaziland, through thorn belt in KwaZulu-Natal and dry savanna forests along base of escarpment, and edges of riverine bush in Mpumalanga and Limpopo Province. **Habitat:** Forest edges, flatlands, coast, hillsides. **Flight period:** Year-round, depending on rainfall. Peaks late summer and autumn. **Larval food:** *Capparis tomentosa*.

Genus *Nepheronia*   Vagrants   AFRICA 4 SPP., SOUTH AFRICA 3

Medium to very large pierids. Flight rapid and direct, settling often on flowers. Usually white to green with bright yellow or orange and dark markings. Egg white to cream or yellow; laid singly on leaves of food plant. Elongate, tapered at both ends, ca. 24 vertical ribs cross-braced with many transverse ribs; not all vertical ribs reach the top – those that do end in a small bulbous projection. Larva broadest at third segment, tapering to *tail more deeply bifid than Eronia*; mossy green with longitudinal pale lateral stripe. Pupa green or buff, laterally compressed, very prominent wing cases bulging ventrally; short, acute head spike. Food plants Celastraceae, Rhizophoraceae and Oleaceae in addition to those used by *Eronia*.

2 Large Vagrant   *Nepheronia argia*

Wingspan: ♂ 50–65 mm ♀ 48–70 mm. **Identification:** (all *N. a. variegata*): **2A** ♂ upper side, **2B** ♂ underside, **2C** ♀ upper side, **2D** ♀ underside (both ♀ f. *aurora*). South Africa's largest pierid. 2 subspp. ♂ appearance constant across seasons and subspp., *size of black forewing tip* main variable character. Many ♀ forms. WSF ♀ larger, marginal upper side dark spots larger, hind wing upper side *white*. Variable extent of basal orange-red on upper side forewing. DSF ♀ smaller, hind wing upper side varies from white, to patches of orange-yellow, to yellow and deep yellow-orange. Yellow hind wing forms rare at coast. F. *aurora* most typical ♀ form. Both sexes attracted to red blooms or any bright red object. **Distribution:** *N. a. varia* in Lowland Forest from E Cape (Port St Johns) along coast, inland along Riverine Forest into KwaZulu-Natal to Oribi Gorge; *N. a. variegata* from KwaZulu-Natal (Umzumbe River), Swaziland, Mpumalanga and Limpopo Province in Riverine Forest along base of escarpment, and lower edges of Afromontane Forest. **Habitat:** Forest edges, flatlands, coast, hillsides. **Flight period:** Year-round, depending on rainfall; peaks late summer and autumn. **Larval food:** *Hippocratea longipetiolata*.

3 Buquet's Vagrant or Green-eyed Monster   *Nepheronia buquetii*

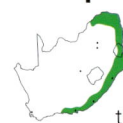

Wingspan: ♂ 45–50 mm ♀ 48–56 mm. **Identification: 3A** ♂ upper side, **3B** ♂ underside. Forewing *pointed and falcate*, dark *discocellular spot* on underside hind wing. Other *Nepheronia* species have green compound eyes but those of the Green-eyed Monster are particularly brilliant. Sexes similar, ♀ upper side forewing tips *paler* than ♂; DSF has dark upper side forewing tips reduced; in f. *capensis* (predominates from KwaZulu-Natal southwards), dark tips absent or reduced to a thin black line around the margin of the apex. **Distribution:** Found in more arid areas than its congeners. Savanna and woodland from Knysna, W Cape (sometimes as far west as Cape Town), along coast, inland to Swaziland, along riverine bush in thorn belt of KwaZulu-Natal, north to Mpumalanga, Limpopo and NW provinces. Stragglers reach Gauteng in years that mass migrations of Brown-veined White (p. 336) occur. **Habitat:** Forest edges, flatlands, coast, hillsides. **Flight period:** Year-round, depending on rainfall; f. *capensis* usually only seen in the dry season, and summer in the W Cape. More common in winter months in warmer areas. **Larval food:** *Azima tetracantha* and *Salvadora persica*.

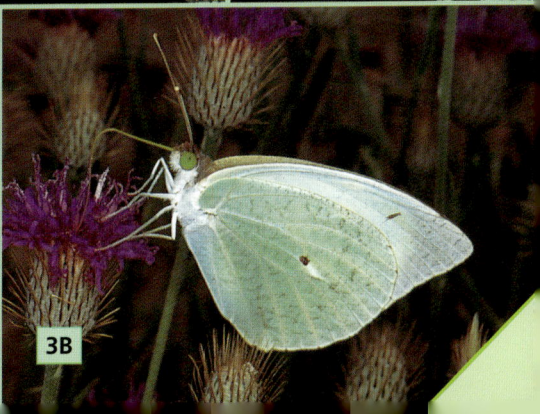

1 Cambridge Vagrant   *Nepheronia thalassina sinalata*

Wingspan: ♂ 50–55 mm ♀ 55–60 mm. **Identification: 1A** ♂ upper side, **1B** ♀ upper side (f. *thalassina*), **1C** ♀ upper side (f. *sinalata*), **1D** mating pair, ♂ upper, ♀ lower. ♂ upper side unmistakable, *pale blue*; both sexes with dark forewing upper side margins and hind wing marginal spots. Underside of both sexes has distinctive '*watered silk*' appearance, with colouring mirroring upper side. Two ♀ forms: f. *thalassina* with white hind wing upper side, f. *sinalata* yellow. **Distribution:** Found in thicker forest than its congeners, seldom venturing into Savanna. Lowland and Riverine Forest, and lower Afromontane Forest, from n KwaZulu-Natal (Tongaland) to Swaziland, Mpumalanga and Limpopo Province along escarpment. **Habitat:** Forest edges, gullies. **Flight period:** Year-round, peak Feb–May. **Larval food:** *Jasminium* spp. and *Hippocratea africana*.

Genus *Colotis*   Tips   WORLD CA. 60 SPP., AFRICA 45, SOUTH AFRICA 18

Very large genus of small to quite large pierids, many of which have orange or purple forewing tips. Flight weak in smaller species, strong and persistent in larger species. In the northern areas of South Africa, in the dry season, thousands may be seen together with *Belenois* butterflies on roadside flowers. Egg (usually single but Topaz Arab (below) lays batches) laid on Capparaceae and Salvadoraceae; white to cream, elongated, tapered towards top with 10–24 longitudinal ribs cross-braced by many transverse ribs. Larva elongated, cylindrical, tapering slightly to a slightly bifid tail; green with longitudinal lateral or dorsal pale stripes, sometimes broken into lines of spots, covered in short hairs which may exude noxious oils derived from the food plant. Pupa variable, laterally compressed, conical head spike, wing cases slender or protruding, green to buff or tan in colour.

2 Topaz Tip or Topaz Arab   *Colotis amata calais*

Wingspan: ♂ 32–35 mm ♀ 34–38 mm. **Identification: 2A** ♂ upper side, **2B** ♀ upper side, **2C** ♂ underside (all f. *calais*). Upper side ground colour *salmon pink*, ♀ with postdiscal *cream-yellow bands*, absent in ♂. Seasonal dimorphism mostly evident on underside; hind wing green-yellow in WSF f. *calais*, in DSF f. *dynamene*, pinkish cream. Flight slow, weak, close to ground; settles often. **Distribution:** Savannas and woodland from Swaziland, north-east along coast to KwaZulu-Natal (only in northern thorn country), Mpumalanga, and Limpopo and NW provinces. **Habitat:** Flatlands, hillsides. **Flight period:** Year-round, depending on rainfall; peak Feb–May. **Larval food:** *Salvadora persica*.

3 Doubleday's Orange or Doubleday's Tip   *Colotis doubledayi flavulus*

Wingspan: ♂ 33–35 mm ♀ 34–38 mm. **Identification: 3A** ♂ upper side, **3B** ♀ upper side, **3C** ♂ underside. Superficially resembles Veined Orange (p. 324), but dark discal band on hind wing upper side *very faint*. Very distinct *dark stripes* along hind wing upper side veins; interneural pale marginal spots larger than Veined Orange, giving hind wing a 'rayed' appearance. ♀ resembles extreme DSF ♀ Veined Orange, hind wing upper side has *streaky appearance*. In both sexes, hind wing underside much more faintly marked than upper side. Only found in sheltered semi-desert gullies near food plant. **Distribution:** In South Africa, only from Arid Savanna in stony valleys of Orange R tributaries in Richtersveld, N Cape. **Habitat:** Hillsides, gullies. **Flight period:** Double-brooded, Sept–Oct and Apr–May; occasionally other times of year. **Larval food:** *Maerua schinzii*.

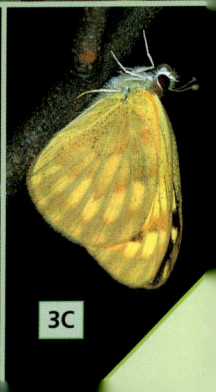

1 Veined Orange or Veined Tip   *Colotis vesta argillaceus*

Wingspan: ♂ 32–40 mm ♀ 34–45 mm. **Identification: 1A** ♂ upper side, **1B** mating pair, ♂ at top (f. *pluvius*). Similar to Doubleday's Orange (p. 322), but hind wing upper side discal dark band *prominent in both sexes*, hind wing underside dark pattern *well defined*. Seasonally dimorphic; WSF f. *pluvius* larger, more richly coloured than DSF f. *argillaceus*, underside hind wing ground colour *green-yellow*, not pink to orange-buff. Sexes similar, ♀ upper side dark markings heavier, little or no silvery white basal scaling. Some ♀♀ with upper side ground colour pale lemon yellow. **Distribution:** Widespread in Savanna and open woodland from Durban through thorn belt of n KwaZulu-Natal to Swaziland, Mpumalanga, n Gauteng and Limpopo Province (lowveld north of Soutpansberg) to NW Province. **Habitat:** Hillsides, flatlands. **Flight period:** Year-round, depending on rainfall; peaks late summer and autumn. **Larval food:** *Maerua angolensis.*

2 Lilac Tip   *Colotis celimene amina*

Wingspan: ♂ 32–40 mm ♀ 34–40 mm. **Identification: 2A** ♂ upper side, **2B** ♀ upper side, **2C** ♂ underside. Distinctive, *broad deep lilac-purple* apical half of ♂ upper side forewing. ♀ very different to ♂, with black and white upper side forewing tip. ♂ sexual behaviour unique: hovers in circles, 2–4 m up, close to a prominent tree, seldom settles, only moving away to mate or chase off other ♂♂. At other times flies across veld as do other Tips. Both sexes found on flowers. **Distribution:** Localised, uncommon in Arid Savanna in KwaZulu-Natal thorn belt (Weenen and parts of Umvoti, Umgeni and Bushman's River valleys), Limpopo Province from Sekhukhuneland north in rain shadow of Drakensberg to Zimbabwe and north of the Soutpansberg. **Habitat:** Hillsides, flatlands. **Flight period:** Year-round, peak Mar–May. **Larval food:** *Boscia albitrunca* and *Capparis* spp.

3 Coast Purple Tip   *Colotis erone*

Wingspan: ♂ 40–45 mm ♀ 45–50 mm. **Identification: 3A** ♂ upper side, **3B** ♂ underside (f. *erone*), **3C** ♀ upper side (f. *natalensis*), **3D** ♀ upper side, **3E** ♀ underside (f. *jobina*). Very similar to Bushveld Purple Tip (p. 326). ♂ upper side always white; black forewing apical tip with *three* discrete metallic purple cells and *no* grey scaling in the black border. Some specimens have a tiny extra spot of purple on costal edge of tip, *never four full-sized spots* as in Bushveld Purple Tip. Also, purple *less obviously shiny* and iridescent. Two seasonal ♂ forms: WSF f. *erone* has black veins, DSF f. *jobina* lacks black veins. Four ♀ forms, two orange-tipped, two dark-tipped, DSF and WSF for each. Most common WSF f. *natalensis* has upper side with *heavy black markings on forewing tips and margins*. Corresponding DSF f. *jobina* has marginal black reduced to spots. Both have *three pale spots* (compared with four to five in dark-tipped forms of ♀ Bushveld Purple Tip). Orange-tipped forms less common. WSF f. *erone* and DSF f. *millari* both have *four dark spots* in the orange, compared to *five* in ♀ f. *ione* orange-tipped forms. Underside varies from pinkish white in all DSFs, to deep yellow in WSFs; distinctive dark markings remain the same. **Distribution:** Coastal Lowland Forest and wooded Savanna from E Cape (Port St Johns) along coast to Durban and n, possibly as far as Mozambique. **Habitat:** Coast. **Flight period:** Year-round, with two peaks: WSF Dec–Jan, DSF Mar–Jul. **Larval food:** *Maerua racemulosa.*

1 Bushveld Purple Tip or Common Purple Tip   *Colotis ione*

Wingspan: ♂ 45–50 mm ♀ 48–52 mm. **Identification: 1A** ♂ upper side, **1B** ♂ underside, **1C** ♀ upper side, **1D** ♀ underside (all f. *ione*), **1E** ♀ upper side (f. *woodi*). Three ♂ forms; southern WSF f. *ione* has heavy black veins on hind wing upper side; to north, WSF f. *phlegyas* has *less distinct* veins. ♂ DSF is f. *jalone*, with thin or absent dark veins. Several ♀ forms, like Coast Purple Tip (p. 324), orange-tipped and dark-tipped groups, WSF and DSF. Common WSFs are f. *ione*, orange-tipped, and f. *woodi*, dark-tipped. Common DSF is orange-tipped f. *jalone*. Dark-tipped (brown-edged) DSF f. *erubescens* rare. Several rarer variants of ♀ forms, some with yellow ground colour, too many to describe here. All can be told from Coast Purple Tip by number of purple cells in ♂ forewing – *four*, not *three*, with grey scales in black margin. ♀ orange-tipped forms have *five* dark spots in tip, not *four*, dark-tipped forms have *five*, not *four*, pale spots in tip. Undersides of WSFs yellow to cream, DSFs pinkish white, but generally *dingier* than Coast Purple Tip, tinged with grey. **Distribution:** Common and widespread in open woodland and Savanna from KwaZulu-Natal thorn belt to Maputaland, north to Mpumalanga, Gauteng and Limpopo and NW provinces, stragglers reach Arid Savanna in N Cape. **Habitat:** Hillsides, flatlands. **Flight period:** Year-round, depending on rainfall. WSF mainly Oct–Mar, DSF mainly Feb–Nov. Peaks late summer and autumn. **Larval food:** *Boscia* spp., including *B. albitrunca*, and *Capparis* spp.

2 Queen Purple Tip   *Colotis regina*

Wingspan: ♂ 45–60 mm ♀ 48–62 mm; variation in size of seasonal forms. **Identification: 2A** ♂ upper side (f. *regina*), **2B** ♀ upper side (f. *regina*), **2C** ♂ underside (f. *regina*), **2D** ♂ underside (f. *anax*). Forewing apical tips cover *almost half the wing*. Seasonally dimorphic, *no* orange-tipped ♀ forms as in Coast (p. 324) and Bushveld (above) Purple Tips. DSF f. *regina* ♂ forewing upper side tip has *five or six* purple cells in black background with *green or blue iridescence*, upper side black veins *faint or absent*; ♀ upper side purple tip plain, crossed with *black band*, dark veins *absent*. Hind wing underside of both sexes pink-tinged. WSF f. *anax* ♂ upper side tip *deeper purple, heavy black veins* ending in spots at hind wing margin. ♀ upper side forewing tips black, with one or two rows of white spots, some purple or tinged with it. Hind wing veins black, ending in black marginal spots. Underside of both sexes white to pale brown, hind wing sometimes bright yellow. Rare ♀ f. *louisa* has yellow upper side ground colour. ♂ visits hill tops, seldom lingers. Easy to approach on flowers. **Distribution:** Widespread but sparse in open woodland and Savanna from KwaZulu-Natal thorn belt to Maputaland, north to Mpumalanga, Gauteng and Limpopo and NW provinces, and Arid Savanna in N Cape. **Habitat:** Hillsides, flatlands, hill tops. **Flight period:** Year-round, depending on rainfall. WSF Oct–Mar, DSF Feb–Nov. Peaks towards late summer and autumn. **Larval food:** *Boscia* spp., including *B. albitrunca*, and *Capparis* spp.

3 Scarlet Tip   *Colotis danae annae*

Wingspan: 35–55 mm; variation in size of seasonal forms. **Identification: 3A** ♂ upper side, **3B** ♀ upper side WSF, **3C** mating pair, ♂ underside visible – another ♂ dances attendance while pair mate – a common pierid behavioural trait (all f. *annae*). Sexually and seasonally dimorphic. All forms have ♂ upper side forewing tips broad, brilliant red. Underside of both sexes, all forms, has discal row of *brown-centred black spots on both wings*. WSF f. *annae* ♂ upper side has *broad* black hind wing margins and basal edge to red forewing tip. ♀ upper side ground colour white with very heavy black basal patches, discal spotting and marginal borders, sometimes appearing marbled. Forewing apical tip either a red patch crossed with black spots, or black, with a series of pale salmon-pink or buff spots. DSF f. *wallengrenii* ♂ smaller, black margins reduced to spots, apical patch paler red with narrower black edge. ♀ basal patches white to grey, reduced discal spots and dark margins. ♀ forms occasionally with yellow, not white, ground colour. Where food plant is abundant, may swarm in large numbers. **Distribution:** Open to wooded Savanna from E Cape (King William's Town area), to KwaZulu-Natal, Maputaland, north to Mpumalanga, and Limpopo and NW provinces. **Habitat:** Hillsides, flatlands, forest edges. **Flight period:** Year-round, depending on rainfall. WSF Oct–Mar, DSF Feb–Nov. Peaks towards late summer and autumn. **Larval food:** *Cadaba termitaria*, *C. natalensis* and *Maerua angolensis*.

A

1B

1C

D

1E

2A

2C

2D

B

3A

B

3C

1 Sulphur Orange Tip   *Colotis auxo*

Wingspan: 35–40 mm. **Identification: 1A** ♂ upper side, **1B** ♀ upper side (f. *auxo*), **1C** ♂ underside (f. *topha*). Sexually and seasonally dimorphic. Ground colour distinctive *pale yellow*. WSF f. *auxo* ♂ orange forewing upper side apex black bordered, black hind wing upper side marginal spots. ♀ similar to yellow form ♀ Scarlet Tip f. *wallengrenii* (p. 326), tips *orange*, not red or salmon pink. Underside flat yellow, with black spots in ♀. DSF f. *topha* ♂ orange apical patch has little or no black edging. ♀ upper side black spotting reduced, orange tip sometimes missing. Ground colour sometimes creamy white. Underside hind wing suffused with brown, giving dead-leaf effect. Found close to food plant, together with Scarlet Tip. **Distribution:** Riverine and Lowland Forest, Savanna from E Cape (Port Elizabeth/Grahamstown area) to KwaZulu-Natal, Maputaland, north to Mpumalanga, Limpopo and NW provinces. Stragglers may reach n Gauteng. **Habitat:** Hillsides, flatlands, forest edges, gullies, coast. **Flight period:** Year-round, depending on rainfall. WSF Oct–Mar, DSF Feb–Nov. Peaks towards late summer and autumn. **Larval food:** *Cadaba termitaria* and *C. natalensis*.

2 Red Tip   *Colotis antevippe gavisa*

Wingspan: 40–45 mm. **Identification: 2A** ♂ upper side (f. *hero*), **2B** ♀ upper side, **2C** ♂ underside (f. *gavisa*). Sexes dimorphic, seasonally polymorphic. Generally, ♂ apical third of forewing upper side *vermilion edged with black*, black marginal hind wing border or spots, *black 'moustache'* mark formed by black basal edge of forewing and hind wing costal edge. ♀ forewing upper side apical patch red to orange-yellow, with black veins, edged with black, black band proximal to patch or crossing it. Variable black basal forewing patch and black marginal borders on both wings, angled hind wing black discal band. WSF f. *gavisa* has heavy black markings in both sexes, black hind wing underside veining. F. *hero* is more common WSF, *no black veins*. ♀ WSF hind wing discal band fuses with marginal band. Both sexes with underside variably tinged with yellow. DSF f. *zera* has reduced upper side black, 'moustache' reduced to basal dark scaling in ♂, present in ♀. Extreme DSF f. *harmonides* has even less extensive black. Pinkish hind wing underside in both these forms. Intermediate forms common. ♂ usually follows a 'beat' around a selected patch of bush. Usually seen on flowers. **Distribution:** Common in Nama Karoo from W Cape (Wilderness and Little Karoo), Savanna of E Cape, and open woodland, coastal forest and Savanna from KwaZulu-Natal, Maputaland, Free State, Mpumalanga, Gauteng, and Limpopo and NW provinces, and Arid Savanna in N Cape. **Habitat:** Hillsides, flatlands, forest edges, coast. **Flight period:** Year-round, depending on rainfall. WSF Oct–Apr, DSF Feb–Nov. Peaks towards late summer and autumn. **Larval food:** *Boscia albitrunca, B. oleoides* (Shepherd's Trees), *Capparis sepiaria* (Wild Caper bush), *Maerua cafra* and *M. juncea* (Bush Cherries).

3 Common Orange Tip   *Colotis evenina evenina*

Wingspan: ♂ 38–45 mm ♀ 35–42 mm. **Identification: 3A** ♂ upper side, **3B** ♂ underside, **3C** ♀ underside (f. *evenina*), **3D** ♀ upper side (f. *deidamoides*). Sexually and seasonally dimorphic, upper side resembles small Red Tip (above), ♂ with orange tips *paler*, ♀ with distal edge of forewing basal patch on both surfaces forming *three square blocks*, both sexes *lacking black spot at end of cell* on upper side of forewing. Underside hind wing has *white-edged dark diagonal stripe* running from base to middle of margin. WSF f. *evenina* similarly marked to Red Tip, except above difference. Underside hind wing white to yellow, faint diagonal stripe and orange patches in extreme WSF; veining never dark. DSF f. *deidamoides* lacks dark scaling, underside pinkish white speckled with grey. Specimens from driest areas have almost no dark markings, e.g. f. *lerichei*. **Distribution:** Succulent Karoo from N Cape coast (northern Namaqualand) east across Arid Savanna and Nama Karoo to Swaziland, Free State, Gauteng, Limpopo and NW provinces, Mpumalanga (absent from highveld grassland), and n KwaZulu-Natal (Maputaland, dry valleys in Muden area). **Habitat:** Hillsides, flatlands, forest edges. **Flight period:** Year-round, depending on rainfall. WSF Oct–Apr in bushveld, year-round on east coast; DSF Feb–Nov in bushveld, in arid areas after rains. Peaks towards late summer and autumn. **Larval food:** *Boscia albitrunca* and *Capparis* spp.

1 Smoky Orange Tip   *Colotis euippe omphale*

Wingspan: 35–45 mm. **Identification: 1A** ♂ upper side, **1B** ♀ upper side, **1C** ♂ underside (all f. *omphale*). WSF f. *omphale* most common in eastern parts of South Africa. Sexes similar, white ground colour, heavily black-edged red-orange forewing tips on upper side, *zebra-striped* series of black forewing basal and hind wing costal and postdiscal bands. Underside hind wing white, with orange marks speckled with black, and *dark postdiscal band parallel to costa*, corresponding with that of upper side. In winter in drier areas, DSF f. *theogone* has similar upper side to Red Tip (p. 328) f. *zera*. F. *omphalioides* intermediate. Rare DSF f. *ochreoleucus* occasionally found in KwaZulu-Natal. DSFs have pink hind wing underside speckled with black. **Distribution:** Widespead throughout South Africa except moist fynbos, mountains and highveld grassland areas. **Habitat:** Hillsides, flatlands, forest edges, coast. **Flight period:** Year-round, depending on rainfall: f. *omphale* Oct–Apr in the east, year-round in north-east; f. *omphalioides* Mar–Jun; f. *theogone* Feb–Nov in warmer areas. Peaks towards late summer and autumn. **Larval food:** *Maerua rosmarinoides, M. cafra, M. juncea, Capparis sepiaria, Cadaba aphylla* and *Boscia oleoides*.

2 Bushveld Orange Tip   *Colotis pallene*

Wingspan: 28–35 mm. **Identification: 2A** ♂ upper side, **2B** ♂ underside, **2C** ♀ upper side, **2D** ♀ underside (WSF f. *halyattes*), **2E** ♀ underside (WSF f. *absurda*). ♂ upper side resembles small Red Tip (p. 328), wings *more rounded*, orange forewing tips *duller*. Forewing of both sexes always has distinct *black spot at end of cell*. WSFs have 'moustache' as in Red Tip; in DSFs, reduced to basal dark patch. ♀ basic pattern is white ground colour with dark upper side wing tip carrying an orange patch variable from absent to large, and a 'moustache' that is heavy in WSFs and weak, but still present, in DSFs. Hind wing has dark marginal and submarginal bands, latter angled outwards at cell. The forewing underside apical patch carries *no deep orange areas*. There are a large number of named seasonal forms. ♀ WSFs have heavy upper side dark markings and pale underside hind wing, DSFs with lighter upper side markings, pink hind wing underside with black scaling, dark postdiscal spots. These can be told apart from the very similar ♀ DSF Small Orange Tip (p. 332) by the *lack of underside forewing orange tip*, and the patch distal to the hind wing underside cell, which is *paler* in *C. evagore*, but *same grey-irrorated pink or buff* as rest of hind wing in *C. pallene*. In many intermediates, forewing upper side apical patch varies from broad orange cells to none at all as in f. *absurda*. **Distribution:** Savanna from n KwaZulu-Natal (Maputaland and thorn belt), through Swaziland and Mpumalanga, Limpopo Province and into Arid Savanna in NW Province. **Habitat:** Flatlands, hillsides. **Flight period:** Year-round, depending on rainfall. WSF Oct–Mar and DSF Apr–Sept. Peaks towards late summer and autumn. **Larval food:** *Capparis* spp.

3 Kalahari Orange Tip   *Colotis lais*

Wingspan: 30–38 mm. **Identification: 3A** ♂ upper side, **3B** ♀ upper side, **3C** ♀ underside (all f. *lais*). Seasonally and sexually dimorphic; both sexes resemble forms of Bushveld Orange Tip (above) but apical orange has *brownish* tinge, ♂ always lacks 'moustache', ♀ apical orange patch *not broken into cells*. WSF f. *lais* has heavier dark markings in both sexes than DSF f. *felthami*. Underside similar to Bushveld Orange Tip in all forms. Flight usually slow and close to ground, may move rapidly when disturbed. Uncommon, seldom seen in numbers. **Distribution:** Arid Savanna in N Cape from Richtersveld to Windsorton and Vryburg, north into Kalahari region and Botswana; also NW Province near Carletonville, and Limpopo Province on northern side of Waterberg from Thabazimbi to Marken. **Habitat:** Hillsides, flatlands. **Flight period:** Year-round, depending on rainfall. WSF Oct–Mar. Scarcer DSF Apr–Sept. **Larval food:** Probably Capparaceae.

A

1B

C

2A

B

2C

2D

E

3A

B

3C

1 Speckled Sulphur Tip   *Colotis agoye*

Wingspan: ♂ 30–40 mm ♀ 32–45 mm. **Identification: 1A** ♂ upper side, **1B** ♀ upper side, **1C** ♀ underside (all nominate). Nominate larger than *C. a. bowkeri*, ♂ with *upper side dusting of black scales* and black veins. Upper side forewing tip golden yellow *edged basally with black*. Even fresh ♀ specimens have worn appearance: upper side forewing tip *grey-brown with dull orange centre*. *C. a. bowkeri* has *more elongated wings*, lacks dusting of black scales. Upper side forewing tip dark basal edge *broadened below costa*. Underside white, but brown in dry season specimens of nominate. **Distribution:** Nominate in Savanna from Swaziland and n KwaZulu-Natal (Maputaland) to Mpumalanga and Limpopo Province lowveld; *C. a. bowkeri* in N Cape in Arid Savanna from Citrusdal/Clanwilliam to Namaqualand (Soebatsfontein), Richtersveld to Windsorton and Vryburg, into Kalahari and s Botswana. *C. a. bowkeri* may be found hundreds of kilometres from home range during pierid migrations. **Habitat:** Hillsides, flatlands. **Flight period:** Year-round, peak Dec–Apr. **Larval food:** *Boscia* spp., including *B. albitrunca*, and *Cadaba* spp.

2 Small Orange Tip   *Colotis evagore antigone*

Wingspan: ♂ 28–35 mm ♀ 28–38 mm. **Identification: 2A** ♂ upper side (f. *delphine*), **2B** ♀ upper side (f. *galathinus*), **2C** ♀ underside (f. *delphine*). Seasonally polymorphic. All forms of ♂ have black edge of forewing apical tip *only reaching one-third of the way from margin to costa*. Where this ends it *bends towards apex, forming an elbow penetrating the orange*. DSF ♂ f. *delphine* lacks *upper side 'moustache'* of WSF, upper side margins spotted with black, not solid. DSF sexes dimorphic. Very many DSF ♀ forms; many resemble DSF ♀ Bushveld Orange Tip (p. 330), upper side varying from full 'moustache' to dark wing bases only; forewing apical patch dark markings varying in extent; tip colour varies from bright orange to buff and pale yellow; ground colour from white to pale yellow. **2C** shows in ♀ underside, pale patch distal to hind wing cell and orange forewing patch shows difference to DSF ♀ Bushveld Orange Tip. Sexes similar in WSFs (e.g. common f. *phlegetonia*, f. *emini*); upper side margins and forewing basal marginal bands *broad, black*, as are hind wing upper side costal and anal margins. Underside hind wing creamy yellow, with orange-black postdiscal hind wing bar. **Distribution:** Nama Karoo and dry coastal forest from W Cape (Wilderness) along coast and valley bushveld of E Cape, coast and Savanna in KwaZulu-Natal, inland to Savanna of Swaziland, n Free State, Mpumalanga, Gauteng, and Limpopo and NW provinces; also in Arid Savanna in extreme n N Cape. **Habitat:** Hillsides, flatlands. **Flight period:** Year-round, depending on rainfall. WSF (main emergence in southern part of range) Oct–Mar. DSF Apr–Sept, may be common May–Jun in arid areas after good rains. **Larval food:** *Capparis sepiaria*, *Cadaba aphylla*. *Maerua cafra* and *M. juncea*.

3 Banded Gold Tip   *Colotis eris eris*

Wingspan: 40–45 mm. **Identification: 3A** ♂ upper side (f. *fatma*), **3B** ♀ upper side, **3C** ♂ underside (f. *eris*). ♂ upper side has *glossy black forewing upper side basal band* joining broad marginal border in WSF, golden yellow wingtip has *flame-like blue iridescence*. In ♂♂ of some DSFs (e.g. f. *fatma*), black markings *more restricted*, sometimes with *pale markings* in marginal black; hind wing underside *pink*. In WSF f. *eris*, ♀ markings similar to ♂, *more extensive* hind wing upper side costal black, marginal forewing band carries *no pale marks*. ♀ may have pale yellow ground colour as in f. *abyssinicus*. ♀ DSFs paler than WSFs, with varying amount of marginal dark marking on white forewing upper side background. Fast flying, elusive. **Distribution:** Widely distributed in Lowland and Riverine Forest and Savanna, valley bushveld, Succulent and Nama Karoo. From W Cape (Great and Little Karoo as far south as Oudtshoorn) to E Cape, n KwaZulu-Natal, w Free State, Mpumalanga and Limpopo Province; also N Cape (northern Namaqualand). **Habitat:** Hillsides, flatlands. **Flight period:** Year-round in warmer areas, peak Mar–Jun, seasonal forms at variable times depending on rainfall and locality. **Larval food:** *Boscia oleoides* and *B. albitrunca*.

A

1B

C

2A

2B

E

3A

B

3C

1 Lemon Traveller or Lemon Tip *Colotis subfasciatus subfasciatus*

Wingspan: ♂ 45–52 mm ♀ 48–55 mm. **Identification: 1A** ♂ upper side, **1B** ♀ upper side, **1C** ♂ underside (all f. *subfasciatus*). Upper side pale yellow, forewings pointed. WSF f. *subfasciatus* ♂ has grey-black tip with four or five yellow cells with flame-like blue sheen; deep black mark runs along basal edge towards margin. ♀ paler yellow, with wingtip brown where ♂ is black or grey, apical patch burnt-orange. DSF f. *ganymedes* paler than WSF, dark apical markings (except for ♂ costal black band in tip) *less developed*. Underside *pale green finely striated with pale grey-brown*; white-edged darker line *crosses hind wing*. ♂ patrols with rapid, sustained flight, settling seldom. ♀ more sedentary, less often seen. **Distribution:** Rare in thorn belt and Maputaland of n KwaZulu-Natal; commoner in Savanna of Swaziland, Mpumalanga, Limpopo and NW provinces, Arid Savanna in N Cape and Savanna/Grassland ecotone of Gauteng and ne Free State. **Habitat:** Flatlands, hillsides. **Flight period:** Year-round in warmer areas; WSF Oct–Mar, with peaks Dec–Feb; DSF Apr–Sept. **Larval food:** *Boscia albitrunca*.

Genus *Belenois* Whites

AFRICA 30 SPP., SOUTH AFRICA 5

Pearly white to yellow or orange butterflies, with dark markings. Fast flying, often strongly migratory, fond of flowers. Eggs laid on Capparaceae, singly or in batches; elongated, tapering towards top, ca. 12 vertical ribs, numerous transverse smaller cross-ribs. Larva plain green to strongly longitudinally striped, usually broad at head, tapering to tail end, covered in short hairs. Green to cream or buff pupa plain or ornate, angular dorso-lateral horns project outwards from base of abdomen; sometimes with curved head horns.

2 False Dotted Border *Belenois thysa thysa*

Wingspan: ♂ 45–60 mm ♀ 48–62 mm, varying with seasonal forms. **Identification: 2A** ♂ upper side (DSF), **2B** ♀ underside (WSF), **2C** ♀ upper side (WSF). WSF ♂ upper side white, double row of marginal and submarginal black spots; *black forewing tip*. Underside hind wing *canary yellow*, black spots corresponding with upper side; white forewing has yellow tip, orange base. DSF ♂ markings similar, black spotting *reduced*, submarginal series can be absent. WSF ♀ variable; upper side black spots much larger than ♂, forewing bases may be pinkish and hind wing bases salmon; sometimes dusted with black. DSF ♀ more consistent colour, apricot-yellow to salmon above with pink forewing base, orange hind wing base, black spotting less. WSF ♀ underside hind wing same as ♂, forewing underside same canary yellow as hind wing, large basal orange patch. ♂ flies fast, high along forest edges, occasionally settles on flowers; ♀ slower, settles more often. **Distribution:** Edges of coastal Lowland and Riverine Forest, from E Cape (Port St Johns) into KwaZulu-Natal and Mozambique. **Habitat:** Flatlands, coast. **Flight period:** Year-round in warmer areas; WSF Oct–Mar (peak Dec–Jan), DSF Apr–Sept (peak Apr–May). **Larval food:** *Capparis* spp. and *Maerua racemulosa*.

3 Forest White *Belenois zochalia zochalia*

Wingspan: 40–50 mm. **Identification: 3A** ♂ upper side, **3B** ♀ upper side, **3C** ♂ underside. Sexes similar. ♂ upper side ground colour shiny white with pearlescent bases. ♀ upper side black markings heavier, both wings often white, but sometimes hind wing cream to yellow, or cream on forewing and hind wing deep yellow-ochre. Dumbbell-shaped mark at distal end of forewing cell. Forewing upper side black tip encloses varying number of white marks extending down outer margin; tip broad, touches tornus in wet season specimens. Hind wing upper side always has marginal black spots, more extensive in wet season, which have wavy submarginal line joining the tops of the spots, creating diamond-shaped white or yellow spots on black background. Underside hind wing ground white to greyish cream, delicate tracery of black veins and transverse submarginal lines. Fast-flying. **Distribution:** Edges of coastal Lowland and Riverine Forest, along rivers from Knysna, W Cape, to KwaZulu-Natal, Afromontane Forest patches (Amatolas to Soutpansberg) and suitable woodland in Limpopo Province, NW Province and Gauteng. **Habitat:** Hillsides, gullies, coast. **Flight period:** Year-round in warmer areas, peak Nov–Feb. **Larval food:** *Maerua racemulosa*, *M. cafra* and *Capparis* spp.

1 Brown-veined White   *Belenois aurota aurota*

Wingspan: ♂ 40–45 mm ♀ 42–50 mm. **Identification: 1A** ♂ upper side, **1B** ♀ upper side, **1C** ♂ underside. The familiar white butterfly that migrates across the country in vast numbers almost every year. Sexes similar, ♀ dark markings *brown, black* in ♂. ♀ with dark marginal borders much broader than ♂, containing *no white marks*, dumbell-shaped dark mark at distal end of forewing upper side cell larger, merges with costal stripe. DSFs have less extensive dark markings. Flight medium fast, direct, stopping often to feed on flowers. ♂ fond of wet mud. **Distribution:** Arid Savanna and Savanna in n N Cape, arid areas of Limpopo and NW provinces, and n Gauteng. Found almost everywhere during migrations, late summer. **Habitat:** Hillsides, flatlands, parks and gardens, forest edges, coast, mountains. **Flight period:** Year-round in home areas, numbers grow until overcrowding triggers lemming-type migration, usually Dec–Feb, in southerly and easterly direction. Large numbers may be seen in Limpopo Province, late summer and autumn. **Larval food:** *Boscia albitrunca, B. oleoides, Maerua angolensis, M. cafra*, and *Capparis* spp., including *C. sepiaria*.

2 African Common White   *Belenois creona severina*

Wingspan: 40–45 mm. **Identification: 2A** ♂ upper side, **2B** ♀ upper side (nominate form), **2C** underside (mating pair, ♀ left ♂ right), **2D** ♀ upper side (f. *infida*). Often in same migrating swarms as Brown-veined White (above). ♂ upper side resembles Brown-veined White, but *forewing has spot in upper side cell instead of a bar*, hind wing underside *yellow*, black veining distinctive. Sexes dimorphic; ♀ upper side has very broad dark marginal borders on both surfaces of both wings. DSF upper side ground colour creamy white, lemon-yellow in wet season, when marginal borders are broadest and darkest in f. *infida*, on whose underside forewing a discocellular bar replaces the spot. **Distribution:** From wetter side of Nama Karoo near Mossel Bay (W Cape), east in forests along rivers, escarpment and coast into KwaZulu-Natal, thorn belt savanna, across Swaziland, Mpumalanga, n Gauteng (absent from highveld grassland, but has penetrated Johannesburg's wooded environment) and Limpopo and NW provinces; also in extreme e N Cape. **Habitat:** Hillsides, flatlands, parks and gardens, forest edges, coast. **Flight period:** Year-round, peak Nov–Mar. Scarce in midwinter except along KwaZulu-Natal coast. **Larval food:** *Boscia albitrunca, B. oleoides, Maerua angolensis, M. cafra, M. racemulosa, Capparis sepiaria, C. fascicularis* and *C. tomentosa*.

3 African Veined White   *Belenois gidica abyssinica*

Wingspan: ♂ 40–55 mm ♀ 40–53 mm, varying with seasonal form. **Identification: 3A** ♂ upper side, **3B** ♀ upper side, **3C** ♂ underside (all f. *doubledayi*). Strongly seasonally and sexually dimorphic. Two WSFs: f. *westwoodi* with *white* ground colour, and f. *doubledayi* buff-yellow. Upper side f. *doubledayi* ♂ resembles ♂ Brown-veined White (above), forewing *more falcate and pointed.* ♀ similar to Brown-veined White, upper side *more heavily marked* with brown-black. Two ♀ DSFs: f. *abyssinica* with pale lemon upper side, and f. *masculina*, as sparsely marked as the ♂ WSF. DSF hind wing underside pale coffee-brown, streaked with darker brown, with *white-edged brown streak from base through the cell to margin.* DSF f. *abyssinica* ♂ smaller than WSF, dark upper side markings *sparser.* **Distribution:** Woodland from near Mossel Bay (W Cape), east in Savanna and valley bushveld along rivers and coast into KwaZulu-Natal, Maputaland, Swaziland, and lowveld of Mpumalanga and Limpopo Province north of Soutpansberg in Savanna. **Habitat:** Hillsides, flatlands, forest edges, coast. **Flight period:** Year-round, more common in late summer and autumn (Jan–May); seasonal forms depending on rainfall: WSF Sept–Apr, DSF Mar–Oct. **Larval food:** *Capparis sepiaria* and *C. tomentosa*.

Genus *Dixeia*   Small Whites   AFRICA 10 SPP., SOUTH AFRICA 4

Small, sparsely marked white to yellow or orange butterflies. Found along woodland edges; fairly fast flight not sustained. Eggs laid singly or in clusters on Capparaceae; spindle-shaped, tapering towards top, ca. 12 vertical ribs with numerous transverse smaller cross-ribs. Larva cylindrical, tapered at both ends, green to fawn, with longitudinal rows of dots or blotches of contrasting colour; covered in short hairs. Pupa green or fawn, with one angular dorso-lateral horn projecting outwards at base of abdomen.

1 African Small White   *Dixeia charina charina*

Wingspan: ♂ 34–40 mm ♀ 36–42 mm. **Identification: 1A** ♂ upper side, **1B** ♀ upper side, **1C** ♂ underside (f. *anactoriae*), **1D** ♂ underside (f. *charina*). Sexes dimorphic; ♂ upper side pure white, forewing apex with *fine black border*. ♀ has variable number of upper side dark postdiscal black spots. WSF f. *charina* dark markings heavier than DSF f. *anactoriae*. WSF has underside hind wing more grey-green, irrorated, spotted. Extreme DSF hind wing underside same clear white as forewing underside. Flutters erratically but rapidly around forest edges and undergrowth, settling on flowers and low vegetation. **Distribution:** Common in wooded Savanna on E of South Africa from near Mossel Bay (W Cape), along coast and inland in Riverine Forest as far as the Drakensberg foothills, into Swaziland lowveld, KwaZulu-Natal (Maputaland), Barberton district of Mpumalanga. **Habitat:** Hillsides, flatlands, forest edges, coast. **Flight period:** Year-round, more common in midsummer and autumn (Dec–Apr). Seasonal forms depending on rainfall: WSF Sept–Apr, DSF Mar–Oct. **Larval food:** *Capparis sepiaria*.

2 Black-veined White   *Dixeia doxo parva*

Wingspan: ♂ 34–40 mm ♀ 36–42 mm. **Identification: 2A** ♂ upper side, **2B** ♀ upper side, **2C** ♀ underside (f. *parva*). Upper side very similar to African Small White (above), but usually (especially in the ♂) has *fine but prominent black veins*. Sexual dimorphism as in African Small White; WSF f. *parva* ♂ upper side has well-defined black veining, ♀ less so, dark colour confined to *distal ends of veins*. ♂ underside white with faint dark veins. In DSF f. *inspersa* ♂, dark veining less intense, absent in ♀, which has less extensive spotting than WSF. DSF underside hind wing more-or-less heavily dusted with dark brown, giving faded dead-leaf effect. Usually found around food plant. **Distribution:** Wooded Savanna and Lowland Forest from Swaziland to KwaZulu-Natal (Maputaland), through Mozambique to Limpopo Province lowveld. **Habitat:** Hillsides, flatlands, forest edges. **Flight period:** Year-round, more common in late summer and autumn (Dec–May). **Larval food:** *Capparis* spp.

3 Ant-heap Small White   *Dixeia pigea*

Wingspan: ♂ 40–48 mm ♀ 40–52 mm. **Identification: 3A** ♂ upper side, **3B** ♀ upper side (f. *alba*), **3C** ♀ upper side (f. *luteola*), **3D** ♀ underside (f. *pigea*). Sexes dimorphic; ♀ with prominent rows of *postdiscal dark spots on* upper side, ♂ *plain white* with black margin at wingtips. Unlike other white *Dixeia* spp., hind wing costal edge carries *yellow streak*. Underside resembles upper side, dark markings smaller or absent. Seasonally dimorphic; WSF f. *pigea* markings darker, more prominent than DSF f. *alba*. ♀ has a variable amount of upper side and underside hind wing yellow. Two other ♀ forms: f. *rubrobasalis* has upper side creamy yellow, underside resembling small ♀ False Dotted Border (p. 334); rare f. *luteola* deep apricot, varying amount of dark marking in dry and wet season forms. Flight fairly slow. Large numbers may be found in riverine bush. **Distribution:** Common in wooded Savanna, Riverine and Lowland Forest from E Cape (Port St Johns) to Swaziland, along KwaZulu-Natal coast to Maputaland, Mpumalanga and Limpopo Province lowveld as far as Soutpansberg, following rivers into dry savanna areas. **Habitat:** Hillsides, flatlands, forest edges, coast. **Flight period:** Year-round, more common in late summer and autumn (Dec–May). **Larval food:** *Capparis sepiaria, C. tomentosa*.

1 Spiller's Sulphur Yellow or Spiller's Canary White   *Dixeia spilleri*

Wingspan: ♂ 33–40 mm ♀ 35–42 mm. **Identification: 1A** ♂ upper side, **1B** ♂ underside, **1C** ♀ upper side white form, **1D** ♀ upper side yellow form. Unique, *sulphur-yellow Dixeia*. ♂ upper side and underside always same colour, upper side forewing tip margin *black*. ♀ polymorphic, varying from same colour as ♂ to pale yellow or creamy white. Forewing upper side marginal border broader, brown-black; extends further down margin, almost to tornus; hind wing underside has postdiscal row of dark smudges. Seasonally dimorphic, WSF f. *spilleri larger*, underside hind wing *paler* than DSF f. *gallenga*, which may have a more buff-coloured hind wing underside; ♀ occasionally has orange underside wing bases. May fly in huge numbers. **Distribution:** Wooded Savanna, Riverine and Lowland Forest from KwaZulu-Natal (as far south as Margate and along coast to Maputaland), Swaziland, Mpumalanga and Limpopo Province lowveld to Soutpansberg, following rivers into dry savanna. **Habitat:** Hillsides, flatlands, forest edges, coast. **Flight period:** Year round; WSF peak Jan–Apr; scarcer DSF Jun–Aug. **Larval food:** *Capparis* spp., including *C. sepiaria*.

Genus *Appias*   Whites   WORLD 34 SPP., AFRICA 6, SOUTH AFRICA 2

Medium-sized, fast flying forest pierids. ♂ ♂ white with black margins; ♀ ♀ more brightly coloured, with orange or yellow markings. Egg laid singly on Capparaceae or Euphorbiaceae; spindle-shaped, tapering towards top, ca. 12 vertical ribs with numerous transverse smaller cross-ribs. Larva cylindrical, tapered at both ends, green to fawn, with longitudinal rows of paler dots; covered in short hairs. Pupa pale green or fawn, with one angular dorso-lateral horn projecting outwards at base of abdomen and back-curved head horn.

2 Albatross White   *Appias sabina phoebe*

Wingspan: ♂ 44–55 mm ♀ 44–53 mm. **Identification: 2A** ♂ upper side, **2B** ♀ upper side, **2C** ♀ underside (f. *gertrudae*). Sexes dimorphic, ♂ with *brilliant white* upper side, dark forewing marginal border *broken into spots at vein ends*; black spots at hind wing vein ends. Underside hind wing white with *yellow costal edge*. More common ♀ f. *gertrudae* has forewing tips *diffuse black*, veins black at wing edges, forewing basal patch orange, variable extent of hind wing yellow; underside *similar to upper side*. Rarer f. *phoebe* has both surfaces of hind wing *deep yellow*, upper side with heavy marginal saggitate black marks along veins, forewing upper side tip black with yellow streaks between veins. **Distribution:** Scarce, but may be locally common. Lowland Forest at E Cape (Port St Johns), n KwaZulu-Natal (Eshowe and Maputaland – Manguzi and Kosi Bay area), Riverine Forest in eastern foothills of Mpumalanga and Limpopo Province Drakensberg (such as Lekgalameetse), lower Afromontane Forest at Woodbush in Magoebaskloof. **Habitat:** Gullies, forest edges. **Flight period:** Occurs sparingly year-round; main emergence Mar–May. **Larval food:** *Drypetes gerrardi*.

3 Diverse White   *Appias epaphia contracta*

Wingspan: 40–50 mm. **Identification: 3A** ♂ upper side, **3B** ♂ underside, **3C** ♀ underside, **3D** ♀ upper side (f. *contracta*), **3E** ♀ underside (f. *albida*). WSF f. *albida* ♂ like a smaller Albatross White (above); black upper side marginal spots *more diffuse*, hind wing underside yellow costal streak *absent*. DSF *contracta* lacks hind wing marginal spots. ♀ black marginal borders *much broader*, always continuous; upper side forewing apical tip contains *white cells*. WSF f. *contracta* dark wing bases merge with dark forewing cell (transitional DSF f. *malatha* has dark forewing costal patch, none in DSF; these forms have progressively narrower marginal borders). F. *limbophora* has pale yellow ground colour. Underside markings mirror upper side, dark markings pale grey, basal patch yellow. **Distribution:** More widespread and less localised than Albatross White. E Cape coastal forest, Mbashe River north to KwaZulu-Natal, Lowland and Riverine Forest in eastern foothills of Mpumalanga and Limpopo Province Drakensberg, as far north as Soutpansberg. Invades nearby Savanna, sometimes in wooded parts of Gauteng. **Habitat:** Hillsides, flatlands, forest edges, coast. **Flight period:** Year-round, mainly Mar–May. **Larval food:** *Capparis* spp., including *C. sepiaria*, and *Maerua racemulosa*, *Boscia albitrunca*.

Genus *Pontia* Whites
WORLD 10 SPP., AFRICA 4, SOUTH AFRICA 1

Small- to medium-sized pierids, slow flying, fond of flowers. Egg laid singly on Brassicaceae or Resedaceae; pale yellow, elongate, tapering at top, with 12–13 vertical ribs and 30–35 cross-ridges. Larva whitish, striped grey, green and yellow, mottled with black or grey. Pupa whitish grey to green, elongated and slender, with pointed thorax.

1 Meadow White   *Pontia helice helice*

Wingspan: ♂ 35–40 mm ♀ 37–43 mm. **Identification: 1A** ♂ upper side, **1B** ♀ upper side, **1C** ♂ underside. Both sexes' forewings have *large square black discocellular mark*; black apex enclosing *white cells*. ♀ upper side more *heavily marked* with brownish black; submarginal spot just above forewing tornus. ♀ hind wing has *broader brown-black marginal band with white interneural spots*. Underside forewing dark marks follow upper side but dusted with yellow; hind wing has pattern of yellow-white spots on black ground dusted with yellow, veins yellow. Dry season specimens more sparsely marked. **Distribution:** Common and widespread, often in old farmlands. Throughout South Africa, from high mountains to Arid Savanna. **Habitat:** Forest edges, parks and gardens, flatlands, coast, mountains, wetlands, hillsides. **Flight period:** Year-round, peaks Sept–Nov and Mar. **Larval food:** *Heliophila* spp., including *H. linearis*, and *Lobularia maritima, Lepidum capense, Rapistrum rugosum, Reseda odorata.*

Genus *Pieris* Whites
WORLD 14 SPP., AFRICA 4, SOUTH AFRICA 1

Only South African representative an introduced alien Palaearctic species, first seen in 1994. Now established. Common autumn garden butterfly near Cape Town. Medium sized, sustained flight, usually white to cream with dark spots. Eggs laid in batches on Brassicaceae or Resedaceae; pale yellow, elongate, tapering at top, with 12–13 vertical ribs and 30–35 cross-ridges. Larva whitish with darker grey, green and yellow stripes, mottled with black or grey. Pupa whitish grey to green, elongated and slender, with pointed thorax.

2 Large White or Cabbage White   *Pieris brassicae*

Wingspan: 50–55 mm. **Identification: 2A** ♂ upper side, **2B** ♂ underside. Sexes dimorphic; ♂ upper side white, black marginal band apically sprinkled with grey scales, small black spot at end of hind wing costa. ♀ has *two large upper side spots*, one below the other, in lower middle forewing, where ♂ only has underside spots. Late summer and winter specimens have more grey scaling in black forewing apical band. Low flight, settles often on flowers, fond of nectar. **Distribution:** Parks, gardens and farmland in Cape Peninsula and immediate vicinity, Bellville and Somerset West, spreading to E Cape. **Habitat:** Parks and gardens, flatlands, coast. **Flight period:** Year-round, peaks Aug–Nov and Mar–May. **Larval food:** *Tropaeolum majus, Brassica* spp., *Lobularia maritima* and *Rapistrum rugosum.*

Genus *Leptosia* Wood Whites
WORLD 8 SPP., AFRICA 7, SOUTH AFRICA 1

Small forest butterflies, very slim-bodied with tissue-thin wings. Flight slow and halting, settles briefly and often on tiny flowers. Usually white with dark forewing cell spot and greater or lesser degree of greenish irroration on hind wing underside. Egg laid singly on Capparaceae; elongated. Larva and pupa green, very small and slender.

3 African Wood White   *Leptosia alcesta inalcesta*

Wingspan: ♂ 30–40 mm ♀ 35–42 mm. **Identification: 3A** ♂ upper side, **3B** ♂ underside. Similar to lycaenid White Mimic (p. 142), but *no yellow on body*. Sexes similar. Degree of dark striae on underside varies; appears green, illusion caused by a mix of tiny black and yellow scales. Only South African pierid found in deep forest, favours shady spots in undergrowth. **Distribution:** From coastal Lowland Forest of KwaZulu-Natal north of Durban, through Swaziland, to Mpumalanga and Limpopo Province, along Riverine and Afromontane Forest on wet side of Drakensberg and Soutpansberg escarpments. **Habitat:** Forest edges, gullies, hillsides. **Flight period:** Year-round, peak Mar–May. **Larval food:** *Capparis brassii* and *C. fascicularis.*

Genus *Mylothris*   Dotted Borders

AFRICA 69 SPP., SOUTH AFRICA 3

These have more gentle, sailing flight than most other pierids. Usually found close to the food plant slowly floating through the foliage of trees. Fond of flowers. White to yellow and orange, sometimes very brightly coloured. Eggs laid in large batches on Loranthaceae and Santalaceae. Cylindrical, elongated, but more barrel-shaped than other Pierinae; tapered towards blunt top, with numerous vertical ribs and many fine cross-ridges. Larva gregarious; green to brown or black, shiny, with short hairs and small raised pale dots. Pupa ornate, brightly coloured in white, yellow or green marked with black; several protruding knobs on dorsal surface of thorax; three or four curved dorso-lateral horns projecting outwards at base of abdomen; back-curved head horn.

1 Twin Dotted Border   *Mylothris rueppellii haemus*

Wingspan: ♂ 48–55 mm ♀ 50–56 mm. **Identification: 1A** ♂ upper side, **1B** ♀ upper side, **1C** ♀ underside. Attractive species, deep orange basal forewing flush on *both surfaces of wings*. As common name implies, wing edges have black spots at the end of veins – variable in appearance, less prominent in dry season specimens. Sexes dimorphic, ♀ orange paler than ♂, covering at least the basal half of both wings. **Distribution:** Wooded Savanna, coastal Lowland and Riverine Forest from George (W Cape), King William's Town (E Cape) to Swaziland, KwaZulu-Natal, Limpopo Province, Mpumalanga, NW Province and n Gauteng (Magaliesberg and Witwatersrand – Krugersdorp). **Habitat:** Forest edges, flatlands, coast, hillsides, gullies. **Flight period:** Year-round, peaks Oct and late Feb–Apr. **Larval food:** *Tapinanthus oleifolius* and *T. rubromarginatus.*

2 Common Dotted Border   *Mylothris agathina agathina*

Wingspan: ♂ 50–60 mm ♀ 52–65 mm. **Identification: 2A** ♂ upper side, **2B** ♀ upper side (f. *agathina*), **2C** ♂ underside. Superficially similar to False Dotted Border (p. 334) but only has marginal hind wing spots; *lacks submarginal spots*. Sexes dimorphic; ♂ upper side white, ♀ creamy yellow, rarely white (f. *leucoma*) or deep ochre-apricot (f. *ochrascens*). Wet season specimens have larger, more prominent marginal dots at end of veins. Often found in open country; frequent garden visitor. **Distribution:** Common, widespread throughout s and e South Africa, from W Cape Fynbos and Nama Karoo to E Cape, along coastal forests and in suitably wooded country to Swaziland, KwaZulu-Natal, Free State, Gauteng, Mpumalanga, lowland Lesotho, Limpopo and NW provinces, and wooded parts of Savanna and Grassland. **Habitat:** Forest edges, parks and gardens, flatlands, coast, hillsides. **Flight period:** Year-round, peaks Oct and Feb–Apr. **Larval food:** *Tapinanthus oleifolius, T. rubromarginatus, Erianthemum dregei, Tieghemia quinquenervia, Ximenia caffra, Osyris lanceolata* and *Colpoon compressum.*

3 Trimen's Dotted Border   *Mylothris trimenia*

Wingspan: 45–50 mm. **Identification: 3A** ♂ upper side, **3B** ♂ underside. Only South African Dotted Border with *white forewing* and *yellow hind wing* on *both wing surfaces*. Sexes similar, ♀ hind wing warmer yellow than that of ♂. Faster flight than other *Mylothris* spp.; may float high over forest canopy. Visits red flowers. **Distribution:** Only in moist Afromontane and Riverine Forest; wet side of Winterberg escarpment from E Cape (Bedford area), along riverine bush to coast (East London to Port St Johns), KwaZulu-Natal (Umzumbe, Umdoni Park to Umhlanga Rocks, inland to Eshowe and Kranskop). Absent from higher altitude KwaZulu-Natal and Mpumalanga forests, but found in Mariepskop and Woodbush forests of Limpopo Province. **Habitat:** Forest edges, coast, mountains, hillsides. **Flight period:** Year-round in warmer areas, peak Oct–Apr; only Oct–Apr in cooler areas. **Larval food:** *Tapinanthus oleifolius* and *T. kraussianus.*

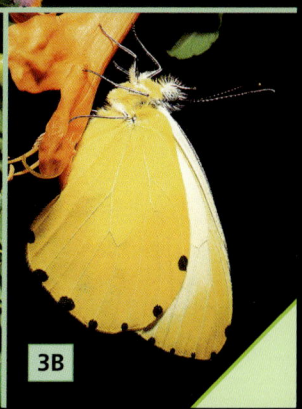

Subfamily COLIADINAE

Butterflies sometimes white, but more often cream to sulphur yellow.

Genus *Colias*   Clouded Yellows

WORLD 80 SPP., AFRICA 3, SOUTH AFRICA 1

Northern hemisphere genus, greatest number found in tundra and montane areas. Sole South African member is a species that has dispersed over the aeons down the East African mountain chain, and although found in warmer areas, most common in cool montane regions. Adults are very fond of flowers. Egg laid singly on Fabaceae; elongated, oval, yellow to pink, 12–30 longitudinal ribs and many fine transverse cross-ridges. Larva green, with longitudinal darker green stripes edged with yellow-green, speckled with minute dark spots. Pupa pale green, counter-shaded in darker green, head and thorax bluntly pointed, wing cases keeled at the junction.

1 African Clouded Yellow or Lucerne Butterfly   *Colias electo electo*

Wingspan: ♂ 35–40 mm ♀ 32–40 mm. **Identification: 1A** ♂ upper side, **1B** ♂ underside, **1C** ♀ upper side (f. *electo*). Sexes dimorphic, ♂ upper side *bright orange* with black marginal borders and spot at end of forewing cell. Underside hind wing of both sexes green, forewing underside green where upper side is black. ♀ f. *electo* has ground colour pale orange-yellow with dark marginal borders, within which are pale yellow spots; f. *aurivillius* has yellow replaced with *grey-white* on upper side and underside. Low, fluttering flight, usually close to food plants, never far from flowers. **Distribution:** Throughout South Africa in all biomes. **Habitat:** Forest edges, parks and gardens, flatlands, coast, mountains, wetlands. **Flight period:** Continuous broods, year-round; peak Apr–Aug. **Larval food:** *Medicago sativa*, *Trifolium* spp., *Vicia* spp., *Robinia pseudoacacia*.

Genus *Catopsilia*   Migrants

WORLD 6 SPP., AFRICA 3, SOUTH AFRICA 1

A genus of large, robust butterflies, usually strong migrants with powerful flight. Egg laid singly on Fabaceae (usually *Senna*); white to cream, spindle shaped, 12–15 longitudinal ribs and many transverse cross-braces. Larva cylindrical, tapering at both ends with longitudinal stripes and finely granulate skin. Pupa green or buff, resembling curled up leaf. Adult male's inner underside forewing margin has *long, silky hairs*. These make contact with a patch of scent scales along the upper side upper margin of hind wing, releasing pheromones to attract the ♀.

2 African Migrant or Common Vagrant   *Catopsilia florella*

Wingspan: ♂ 54–60 mm ♀ 56–66 mm. **Identification: 2A** ♂ upper side, **2B** ♀ underside (f. *florella*), **2C** ♀ underside (f. *pyrene*) ovipositing on *Senna*. Rivals Brown-veined White (p. 336) as South Africa's most familiar migratory butterfly. ♂ pale greenish white on both surfaces. ♀ f. *florella deep yellow*, with brown marginal lunular spots; f. *hyblaea* paler yellow, with smaller marginal spots; f. *pyrene* same colour as ♂, with grey marginal spots. Flight rapid, sustained and direct; stops at flowers or to oviposit. **Distribution:** Throughout South Africa; core distribution in Arid Savanna in north-west. **Habitat:** Forest edges, parks and gardens, flatlands, coast, mountains, wetlands. **Flight period:** Continuous broods, year-round. Migrations usually occur from summer to autumn (Nov–Jun, most often Feb and Mar), flying in a north-easterly direction. **Larval food:** *Senna occidentalis*, *S. septentrionalis*, *S. petersiana*, *S. italica*.

A

1B

C

2A

B

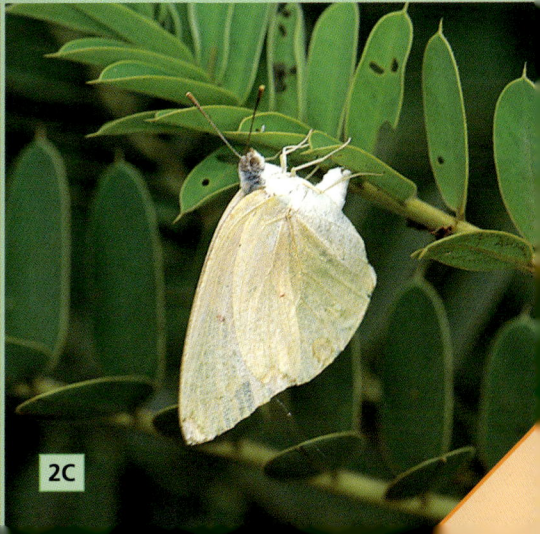

2C

Genus *Eurema*   Grass Yellows

WORLD CA. 70 SPP., AFRICA 9, SOUTH AFRICA 3

Small- to medium-sized pierids, found all over the tropics. In Africa, usually yellow or cream, but on other continents may be orange. Weak, fluttering flight, never more than one or two metres above the ground. Egg laid singly on Clusiaceae or Fabaceae; white to cream, slender, spindle-shaped, with many transverse and longitudinal ribs. Larva cylindrical, tapered at both ends with reddish longitudinal stripes edged with paler yellow; slightly hairy. Pupa slender, laterally compressed, acutely pointed at both ends and with wing covers keeled convexly.

1 Common Grass Yellow   *Eurema hecabe solifera*

Wingspan: ♂ 32–41 mm ♀ 34–42 mm. **Identification: 1A** ♂ upper side, **1B** ♂ underside (f. *bisinuata*). Black forewing upper side marginal band *scalloped*. Sexes similar, ♀ *paler yellow* than ♂, grey scaling at upper side wing bases. DSF f. *bisinuata* smaller than WSFs; f. *hecabe* has black upper side borders *narrower*, on the hind wing reduced to a row of spots. Forewing underside carries *dark brown apical patch*. Another, unnamed WSF is found in n KwaZulu-Natal, resembles f. *bisinuata*, but lacks the underside forewing apical patch. **Distribution:** Savanna, open woodland, Riverine and Lowland Forest, from E Cape (Mbashe River) along eastern lowlands through KwaZulu-Natal, Swaziland, Mpumalanga, and Limpopo Province. **Habitat:** Flatlands, coast, hillsides. **Flight period:** Continuous broods, year-round, depending on rainfall. WSF Sept–May, DSF Mar–Oct. Peaks in late summer. **Larval food:** *Hypericum aethiopicum* and *Chamaecrista mimosoides*.

2 Broad-bordered Grass Yellow   *Eurema brigitta brigitta*

Wingspan: 30–35 mm. **Identification: 2A** ♂ upper side, **2B** ♀ upper side, **2C** ♀ underside (all f. *zoe*). Sexes similar, ♂ *deeper, brighter yellow* than ♀, lacks basal dusting of grey scales. Seasonally dimorphic, WSF f. *zoe* brighter yellow, broader marginal upper side black borders than the DSF f. *brigitta*; underside of latter usually suffused with pink, while in f. *zoe* it is yellow, heavily suffused with grey. **Distribution:** More common and widespread than other *Eurema* species; tolerates drier conditions and frost-prone grassland. Found over nearly all of South Africa, absent from Namaqualand and the more arid Karoo. **Habitat:** Flatlands, coast, hillsides. **Flight period:** Continuous broods, all year – appearance of forms depends on rainfall. WSF from Sept–May, DSF Mar–Oct. Peaks in late summer. **Larval food:** *Hypericum aethiopicum* and *Chamaecrista mimosoides*.

3 Angled Grass Yellow   *Eurema desjardinsii marshalli*

Wingspan: ♂ 35–38 mm ♀ 37–40 mm. **Identification: 3A** ♂ upper side, **3B** ♂ underside (all f. *marshalli*). Hind wing outer margin *sharply angled*. Sexes similar, ♀ *paler, more greenish yellow* than ♂, with grey scaling at wing bases. Seasonally dimorphic; WSF f. *pseudoregularis* has much broader black wing margins on upper side than DSF f. *marshalli*; latter has hind wing margin broken into a series of black spots. In extreme DSF, only tiny edge of black at apical margin of forewing on upper side. Inhabits more heavily wooded country than other *Eurema* spp. **Distribution:** Wooded Savanna and Lowland Forest from W Cape (Plettenberg Bay), along coast and inland along Riverine Forest penetrating Savanna in Swaziland, KwaZulu-Natal, Mpumalanga and Limpopo Province. **Habitat:** Flatlands, coast, hillsides, forest edges. **Flight period:** Continuous broods, year-round, depending on rainfall. Two peaks: WSF Sept–May, DSF Mar–Oct. **Larval food:** *Chamaecrista mimosoides* and probably *Hypericum aethiopicum*.

A

1B

A

2B

2C

A

3B

Family PAPILIONIDAE

Generally large, showy butterflies. conspicuous when on the wing. Three subfamilies; only Papilioninae – by far the largest – found in South Africa.

Subfamily PAPILIONINAE

Well represented in Africa. The sexes are usually similar. Male Swallowtails in the genus *Papilio* have shiny scent scales on the submarginal area of the forewing. Male *Graphium* have scented hairs that are concealed in the anal fold of the hind wing. These are revealed during mating.

Genus *Papilio*   Swallowtails   WORLD CA. 220 SPP., AFRICA 90, SOUTH AFRICA 7

Papilio is the largest genus in the family, with species all over the world, including some of the most spectacular butterflies. Large to very large butterflies, with fast, agile, swooping and dancing flight. Despite their common names, Swallowtails are often tailless. Hover over flowers with quivering wings; do not settle. ♂ ♂ are often found drinking at mud puddles, particularly where animals have urinated. Eggs laid singly, mainly on Rutaceae and Lauraceae; large, almost spherical. Larva green or yellow with camouflage markings, thickened behind the head, often with eye spots that give the impression of a small snake. Pupa cryptic, green or various shades of brown, suspended by a girdle from bark, a twig or rock.

1 Citrus Swallowtail   *Papilio demodocus demodocus*

Wingspan: ♂ 100–120 mm ♀ 110–130 mm. **Identification: 1A & 1B** ♂ upper side, **1C** ♀ underside. Sexes very similar. Pale crescent, distal to hind wing costal upper side eye spot, *yellow* on ♂, *suffused with red* on ♀. Common garden butterfly, ♂ also circles hill tops, seldom perching. **Distribution:** Common and widespread throughout South Africa, particularly in wooded areas and gardens; absent from extremely arid areas. **Habitat:** Forest edges, parks and gardens, hill tops, flatlands. **Flight period:** Continuous broods year-round, mainly Sept–May. **Larval food:** Cultivated *Citrus* spp.; considered a pest. Also *Calodendron capense, Clausena anisata, Zanthoxylum capense, Vepris lanceolata, Teclea natalensis, Oricia swynnertonii, Toddalia asiatica, Ptaeroxylon obliquum, Hippobromus pauciflorus*. In Fynbos and Karoo – *Foeniculum vulgare, Peucedanum galbanum, P. gummiferum, Deverra burchelliae*.

2 Mocker Swallowtail   *Papilio dardanus cenea*

Wingspan: ♂ 80–100 mm ♀ 90–110 mm. **Identification: 2A** ♂ upper side, **2B** ♂ underside (f. *cenea*). ♀ upper sides: **2C** (f. *hippocoonides*), **2D** (f. *natalica*), **2E** (f. *trophonius*), **2F** (f. *cephonius*), **2G** (f. *cenea*), **2H** (f. *aikeni*). Sexes dimorphic. ♂ upper side ground colour always pale sulphur-yellow with black marginal borders varying in width – broad in WSF f. *tibullus* and *discopunctatus* (latter has black spot at end of cell), narrower in DSF f. *cenea*. On hind wing, these always contain submarginal patches of ground colour; in rare f. *maculatus* the forewing has them also. Underside yellow-ochre where upper side is black. Several ♀ forms, a selection of which are illustrated; basic ground colour black, with pale markings of varying extent, colours from white through yellow and buff to salmon pink and orange-ochre. ♂ found on flowers or mud puddles; ♀ shy, only near food plant. **Models:** Friar (p. 38) (for ♀ f. *hippocoonides*); African Monarch (p. 36) (for ♀ f. *aikeni* and ♀ f. *trophonius*); Chief (p. 38) (for ♀ f. *cephonius*, although buff patch at inner forewing margin is larger); Layman (p. 38) (for ♀ f. *cenea*). **Distribution:** Many sspp. in tropical Africa; *P. d. cenea* is the one found south of the Limpopo River. Common, widespread. Afromontane Forest, along coast from W Cape (George, Knysna) and mountain chain, into Lowland Forest of E Cape and KwaZulu-Natal, Riverine and montane forests in Mpumalanga, and Limpopo Province. **Habitat:** Forest edges, parks and gardens. **Flight period:** Year-round in northern areas; absent from southern forests in winter. **Larval food:** *Xymalos monospora, Oricia swynnertonii, Teclea natalensis, T. nobilis, Clausena anisata, Vepris lanceolata, Toddalia asiatica*.

1 Constantine's Swallowtail   *Papilio constantinus constantinus*

Wingspan: ♂ 70–90 mm ♀ 80–95 mm. **Identification: 1A** ♀ upper side, **1B** ♀ underside. Sexes similar; ground colour dark brown to black, with pale sulphur-yellow median bands, a large spot at the end of the cell and rows of submarginal spots in both sexes. ♂ has *shiny black scent-carrying scale patches* distal to median cream band on forewing on upper side. Underside markings as upper side, but dark areas suffused with yellow ochre. ♂ more often on mud puddles than flowers; ♀ seldom seen except near food plant. **Distribution:** Most often in Riverine Forest of savanna areas, seldom far from river courses. Also in Afromontane Forest. From n KwaZulu-Natal (particularly Tugela and Mooi River valleys), eastern Wolkberg and Drakensberg foothills into Mpumalanga and Limpopo Province (Blouberg, Soutpansberg, Wolkberg), NW Province and n Gauteng (Magaliesberg). **Habitat:** Forest edges, wetlands, gullies. **Flight period:** Continuous broods during warmer months, peak Nov–Feb. **Larval food:** *Vepris reflexa* and *V. lanceolata.*

2 White-banded Swallowtail   *Papilio echerioides echerioides*

Wingspan: 65–75 mm. **Identification: 2A** ♂ upper side, **2B** ♀ upper side, **2C** ♀ underside. Medium-sized *tailless* Swallowtail; distinctive *low fluttering flight* along paths, and edges of clearings. ♂ often on flowers of *Impatiens*. ♀ near food plants, seen less often. Sexes dimorphic; ♂ *upper side* with *white median bands* on black ground colour. **Models:** Chief (p. 38) (♀ upper side); Common Wanderer (p. 80) (underside, ♂ and ♀). **Distribution:** Only in suitable Afromontane Forest areas from E Cape (Stutterheim area, Port St Johns) into KwaZulu-Natal Midlands, Mpumalanga along Drakensberg and Wolkberg chains, Limpopo Province on Soutpansberg/Blouberg massifs. **Habitat:** Forest edges. **Flight period:** Double-brooded, Jan–Mar and Sept–Nov. **Larval food:** *Clausena anisata, Vepris lanceolata, Zanthoxylum capense.*

3 Bush Kite or Forest Swallowtail   *Papilio euphranor*

Wingspan: ♂ 80–100 mm ♀ 90–110 mm. **Identification: 3A** ♂ upper side, **3B** ♀ upper side, **3C** ♂ underside. Only *Papilio* endemic to South Africa. Superficially similar to Constantine's Swallowtail (above), but *upper side spots deeper yellow, no spot in cell;* underside unmistakable *chestnut to sepia brown ground colour*, deeper in ♂, with pale markings following those of upper side. Sexes similar. ♂ *lacks row of forewing postdiscal yellow spots;* only *single* row on hind wing, where ♀ has *double* row. Characteristic *high, sailing flight* in gaps in forest canopy, wings open; ♂ settles on tree tops, defending territory, ♀ only near food plant. Visits flowers in morning, particularly red ones. Attracted to brightly coloured shiny objects such as cars. **Distribution:** Confined to Afromontane Forest areas from E Cape (Stutterheim area, Port St Johns) to KwaZulu-Natal Midlands, Mpumalanga, and Limpopo Province along Drakensberg chain. **Habitat:** Forest edges. **Flight period:** Double-brooded, Jan–Apr and Sept–Dec. **Larval food:** *Cryptocarya woodii.*

4 Green-banded Swallowtail   *Papilio nireus lyaeus*

Wingspan: ♂ 75–90 mm ♀ 85–95 mm. **Identification: 4A** ♂ upper side, **4B** ♀ underside (recently emerged on empty pupal case). ♂ upper side with *bright silvery green-blue* markings on black background, ♀ *duller, greener* shade. ♀ underside silvery-white suffusion over rich chocolate-brown ground colour; ♂ lacks silvery suffusion, has well-defined submarginal rows of *shiny cream-white spots* on dark brown background. ♂♂ often in numbers on mud. **Distribution:** Common, widespread in wooded areas from W Cape (Mossel Bay), to E Cape (Stutterheim, East London, Wild Coast), KwaZulu-Natal, Mpumalanga, Limpopo and NW provinces, and Free State (rare). Has invaded suburban gardens in Gauteng feeding on *Citrus* spp. **Habitat:** Forest edges, parks and gardens, flatlands. **Flight period:** Year-round in warmer areas, peaks Nov and Feb. **Larval food:** Cultivated *Citrus, Calodendron capense, Clausena anisata, Vepris lanceolata, Teclea natalensis, Toddalia asiatica, Oricia swynnertonii* and *Zanthoxylum capense.*

1B

2A

B

2C

A

3B

4A

C

4B

1 Emperor Swallowtail   *Papilio ophidicephalus*

Wingspan: ♂ 90–110 mm ♀ 100–120 mm. **Identification: 1A** ♂ upper side (*P. o. transvaalensis*), **1B** ♂ underside (*P. o. ayresi*). Largest South African butterfly. Sexes similar, ♂ has *shiny scent scales* on forewing between postdiscal and submarginal yellow spots. Flies high; may stoop low to investigate flowers. Follows gullies in thick forest. ♂ often on mud and flowers; ♀ on flowers and food plants. **Distribution:** Afromontane and Riverine Forest in warmer areas as follows: *P. o. entabeni* in Soutpansberg, Limpopo Province; *P. o. transvaalensis* in Drakensberg and Wolkberg north of Olifants River, Mpumalanga and Limpopo Province; *P. o. ayresi* from nw KwaZulu-Natal to sw Mpumalanga; *P. o. zuluensis* in forests in Eshowe district, KwaZulu-Natal; *P. o. phalusco* from Amatola Mountains (E Cape) through KwaZulu-Natal Midlands to Tugela R. **Habitat:** Forest edges, gullies. **Flight period:** Double-brooded; spring brood (Aug–Dec) less abundant and smaller specimens than summer brood (Jan–Apr). Broods may overlap in summer. **Larval food:** *Clausena anisata, Zanthoxylum capense* and *Calodendron capense*.

Genus *Graphium*   Ladies, Swordtails   WORLD CA. 94 SPP., AFRICA 39, SOUTH AFRICA 7

Medium to large butterflies, similar to *Papilio*, more delicately built; wings narrower, more elongate. Not all have tails despite common name. ♂ has pouch of scented hairs in anal fold on hind wing. Flight fast and dashing, hovers at flowers. ♂ ♂ sometimes in hundreds at mud puddles. Single, almost spherical, egg on Annonaceae. Larva cigar-shaped; cryptically coloured in greens, yellows and browns. Pupa also cryptic, blunter at the head than *Papilio*.

2 Angola White Lady   *Graphium angolanus angolanus*

Wingspan: ♂ 65–70 mm ♀ 70–75 mm. **Identification: 2A** ♂ upper side, **2B** ♀ underside. Tailless. Sexes alike. Upper side ground colour black, with white spots and discal patches; underside suffused yellow-ochre with red at wing bases. Similar to White Lady (below), but has *three large white spots* in forewing cell. Fast-flying, often rapidly traverses country. Found on wet mud and flowers; ♂ also found on hill tops, where he seldom settles. **Distribution:** Warm wooded Savanna from lowveld of n KwaZulu-Natal, spreading further west in the north, into Mpumalanga, Limpopo and NW provinces. **Habitat:** Hill tops, flatlands. **Flight period:** Year-round in warmer months, peaks Nov and Feb. **Larval food:** *Annona senegalensis* and *Sphedamnocarpus pruriens*.

3 White Lady   *Graphium morania*

Wingspan: ♂ 50–55 mm ♀ 55–60 mm. **Identification: 3A** ♂ upper side, **3B** ♂ underside. Sexes alike. Smaller than similar Angola White Lady (above), with only *two large white spots* in forewing cell. **Distribution:** Coastal Lowland Forest in KwaZulu-Natal s to Umzimkulu. Warm Savanna in lowveld of n KwaZulu-Natal, into Mpumalanga, Limpopo and NW provinces, rarely in Gauteng (Magaliesberg). **Habitat:** Hill tops, flatlands, coast. **Flight period:** Continuous broods in warmer months, Sept–May. **Larval food:** *Annona senegalensis, Hexalobus monopetala, Uvaria caffra* and *Artabotrys brachypetalus*.

4 Veined Swordtail   *Graphium leonidas leonidas*

Wingspan: ♂ 75–80 mm ♀ 75–85 mm. **Identification: 4A** ♀ upper side (f. *leonidas*), **4B** ♀ upper side, **4C** ♀ underside (f. *brasidas*). Regularly visits hill tops and forest edges. Sexes similar. Upper side ground black with green-white to blue spots. Underside red-brown, pale spots following those of upper side. Two forms: f. *brasidas* has *smaller, sparser green-white spots* than f. *leonidas*. **Model:** Blue Monarch (p. 36). **Distribution:** Common in coastal Lowland and Riverine Forest in KwaZulu-Natal and E Cape as far as East London, and warm wooded Savanna in lowveld of n KwaZulu-Natal, into Mpumalanga, Limpopo Province. F. *leonidas* in northern part of range, f. *brasidas* further south, but may fly together. **Habitat:** Hill tops, flatlands, forest edges. **Flight period:** Continuous broods, peaks in warmer months from Oct–Apr; flies midwinter in subtropical areas. **Larval food:** *Annona senegalensis, Monanthotaxis caffra, Uvaria caffra, Friesodielsia obovata* and *Artabotrys brachypetalus*.

A

1B

A

2B

3A

B

4A

B

4C

1 Large Striped Swordtail *Graphium antheus*

Wingspan: ♂ 65–70 mm ♀ 70–75 mm. **Identification: 1A** ♂ upper side (on wet mud with two Angola White Ladies), **1B** ♂ underside. Large and conspicuous, brilliant *turquoise and black* swordtail. Sexes similar. Upper side ground colour black with turquoise bands and spots; transverse bands in forewing cell *wavy*; underside similarly marked, but grey-brown and pale green. Flight high and rapid. Both sexes visit flowers, ♂♂ may be found in hundreds on wet mud. **Distribution:** Coastal Lowland Forest from E Cape (Port St Johns area), spreading into Savanna in KwaZulu-Natal, Mpumalanga, and Limpopo Province. **Habitat:** Forest edges, flatlands. **Flight period:** Continuous broods in warmer months, peak Nov–Dec; may fly as late as May. **Larval food:** *Hexalobus monopetala, Uvaria caffra, Cleistochlamys kirkii, Artabotrys monteiroae* and *A. brachypetalus.*

2 Small Striped Swordtail *Graphium policenes policenes*

Wingspan: ♂ 55–60 mm ♀ 60–65 mm. **Identification: 2A** ♂ upper side, **2B** ♂ underside. Sexes similar. *Smaller* than Large Striped Swordtail (above), black ground; markings a *greener* shade of turquoise, shading to *moss green* at forewing base; transverse stripes in forewing cell *straight*, not wavy. Visits flowers, often in the canopy so difficult to approach closely. ♂ on mud puddles. Very fast and elusive flight over tree tops. **Distribution:** Coastal wooded Savanna and Lowland Forest from E Cape (Port St Johns area), and southern to central KwaZulu-Natal (rare in Maputaland). **Habitat:** Forest edges, flatlands, coast. **Flight period:** Continuous broods in warmer months; commoner earlier in the season but often seen as late as May. **Larval food:** *Uvaria caffra* and *Artabotrys monteiroae.*

3 Cream Striped Swordtail *Graphium porthaon porthaon*

Wingspan: ♂ 55–60 mm ♀ 60–65 mm. **Identification: 3A** ♀ upper side, **3B** ♀ underside. Wavy forewing transverse stripes in cell as in Large Striped Swordtail (above), but upper side markings *pale lemon-cream*, and *thinner*, making black background appear *darker*. Sexes similar. ♀ has extra, *pink* inner submarginal lunule in CuA$_1$. ♂ less fond of mud puddles than other Swordtails, but attracted to pools of urine. Particularly fond of *Albizia* flowers. Only in numbers under exceptionally favourable conditions. **Distribution:** Uncommon and localised. Thick Riverine and Lowland Forest in central to n KwaZulu-Natal (may be common in Maputaland), and e Mpumalanga to Limpopo Province (Soutpansberg). **Habitat:** Forest edges, flatlands, gullies. **Flight period:** Continuous broods in warmer months; peak Oct–Jan, sometimes as late as May. **Larval food:** *Monodora junodii, Friesodielsia obovata* and *Artabotrys monteiroae.*

4 Mamba or Black Swordtail *Graphium colonna*

Wingspan: ♂ 55–60 mm ♀ 60–65 mm. **Identification: 4A** ♂ upper side, **4B** ♂ underside. Sexes alike. Upper side ground colour black with fine, straight peppermint-green blotches and stripes. Discal area of hind wing upper side *lacks* banding and spotting of other Swordtails. Underside ground red-brown, with pale markings following those of upper side, but pale green, with red and black discal marks. Flies low, prefers shady places. Flutters quite slowly through undergrowth of thick coastal bush and forest, its *white tail tips* very conspicuous. Visits muddy places in the forest, and low-growing flowers. **Distribution:** Uncommon and localised. Thick coastal Lowland Forest in KwaZulu-Natal (Maputaland) from Richards Bay to Mozambique. **Habitat:** Forest edges, flatlands, coast. **Flight period:** Continuous broods in warmer months, Oct–Apr. **Larval food:** *Uvaria caffra* and *Artabotrys monteiroae.*

A

1B

A

2B

A

3B

A

4B

Family HESPERIIDAE

The 'Skippers' differ from other butterflies in their wide-set antennae, and often moth-like robust and hairy bodies. They tend not to rest with wings folded vertically like most Butterflies; resting postures vary between subfamilies, from wings held completely open flat, to partially closed wings. The larvae make leaf shelters and live, and often pupate, in these.

Subfamily COELIADINAE

About 75 species, all from Old World tropics. Distinguished by long, slender third segment of labial palpi, protruding forward at right angles to second segment. Large, muscular and hairy, many are strong migrants. Mostly diurnal; some crepuscular or nocturnal.

Genus *Coeliades* Policemen   AFRICA 17 SPP., SOUTH AFRICA 6

Large Skippers, swift, darting flight. Alert and shy; found at flowers and, occasionally, mud puddles. ♂ territorial. Usually brown, varying degree of paler hind wing markings. Single-domed, ribbed egg laid on young leaf of food plant from a wide variety of dicotyledons. Larva has alternate rings of dark and pale hues, resembling a distasteful danaine larva. Pupa whitish, covered in white powder, hidden in leaves bound with silken threads.

1 One-pip Policeman   *Coeliades anchises anchises*

Wingspan: ♂ 55–70 mm ♀ 65–72 mm. **Identification: 1A** ♂ upper side, **1B** ♂ underside. Sexes similar, ♀ with wings more rounded, abdomen heavier. Upper side dark grey, underside hind wing white patch *relatively small*, with *single black spot*. ♂ frequents hill tops, ♀ seldom seen. Occasionally migrates in swarms, more usually found singly. **Distribution:** Rare. Scattered records from Swaziland, and KwaZulu-Natal coast, in Riverine Forest to Midlands and Maputaland; also Mpumalanga (Nelspruit) and Limpopo Province (Mokopane and hills north and east of Polokwane, Mariepskop, Blyderivierspoort) Savanna. **Habitat:** Hill tops, hillsides, flatlands. **Flight period:** Likely to be found in warmer months, Oct–May. **Larval food:** *Triaspis glaucophylla* and *Dregea angolensis.*

2 Spotless Policeman   *Coeliades libeon*

Wingspan: ♂ 45–52 mm ♀ 50–55 mm. **Identification: 2A** ♂ upper side, **2B** ♂ underside. Sexes similar, ♀ wings more rounded, abdomen heavier. *Lacks pale markings* of other *Coeliades* spp. *Largest and darkest* diurnal all-brown Skipper (Strelizia and Palm-tree Night-fighters (p. 398), which have *pale antennae*, are crepuscular). **Distribution:** Uncommon migrant to South Africa. Scattered records from E Cape (Port St Johns), along coast and coastal rivers to Swaziland and KwaZulu-Natal (coast, Midlands, Maputaland), lowveld Savanna of Mpumalanga, Limpopo Province (also Waterberg) and further north. **Habitat:** Hillsides, flatlands, coast. **Flight period:** Likely to be found in all warmer months, mainly Oct–May, winter in subtropical areas. **Larval food:** *Drypetes gerrardii.*

3 Striped Policeman   *Coeliades forestan*

Wingspan: ♂ 42–55 mm ♀ 55–64 mm. **Identification: 3A** ♀ underside, **3B** ♂ upper and underside. Sexes similar, ♀ with wings more rounded, abdomen heavier than ♂. Upper side brown; hind wing carries basal-discal pale yellow-ochre patch, anal lobe black with orange cilia. Underside brown, with white hind wing band, with *no black spots*. **Distribution:** Abundant and widespread in Lowland and Riverine Forest and Savanna from E Cape (Port Elizabeth) to Swaziland, KwaZulu-Natal, w Free State, Mpumalanga, Limpopo and NW provinces, and nw N Cape. **Habitat:** Hill tops, hillsides, flatlands, coast. **Flight period:** Continuous broods, all year in warmer areas; peak Sept–Apr. **Larval food:** *Parinari curatellifolia*, *Combretum bracteosum*, *C. apiculatum*, *Solanum mauritianum* (Bugweed), *Milletia sutherlandii*, *Robinia pseudacacia*, *Lonchocarpus capassa*, and *Sphedamnocarpus pruriens.*

1 Two-pip Policeman   *Coeliades pisistratus*

Wingspan: ♂ 55–65 mm ♀ 63–70 mm. **Identification: 1A** ♂ upper side, **1B** ♂ underside. Sexes similar, ♀ with wings more rounded, abdomen heavier than ♂. Upper side brown; hind wing carries basal-discal pale yellow-ochre patch, anal lobe black with orange cilia. Underside brown, with white hind wing band carrying twin *black postdiscal spots*, and fused double spot inside anal margin. **Distribution:** Abundant and widespread in Lowland and Riverine Forest and Savanna from Swaziland through KwaZulu-Natal (Durban) into w Free State, Mpumalanga, and Limpopo and NW provinces. **Habitat:** Hill tops, hillsides, flatlands, coast. **Flight period:** Continuous broods, all year in warmer areas; peak Sept–Apr. **Larval food:** *Sphedamnocarpus pruriens, Triaspis macropteron, Acridocarpus* spp., *Indigofera* spp., *Dregea* spp. and *Combretum* spp.

2 Red-tab Policeman   *Coeliades keithloa keithloa*

Wingspan: ♂ 58–64 mm ♀ 61–66 mm. **Identification: 2A** ♂ upper side, **2B** ♂ underside. Sexes similar, ♀ larger and heavier bodied, wings more rounded than ♂. *Almost identical* to Lorenzo Red-tab Policeman (below). Red underside hind wing patch *may not be as extensive*, but this character is variable; only reliably separated on ♂ genital dissection, or when bred from the distinctively different larvae. **Distribution:** Lowland and Riverine Forest from E Cape (Port Elizabeth area), where rare; Port St Johns, and up KwaZulu-Natal coast to Eshowe and the Tugela River valley, lowveld of e Mpumalanga, Riverine Forest along flanks of mountain chains to Soutpansberg (Mpaphuli), Limpopo Province. **Habitat:** Hillsides, flatlands, coast. **Flight period:** Continuous broods, year-round in warmer areas, more numerous in late summer and autumn. **Larval food:** *Barringtonia racemosa, Acridocarpus natalitius, A. zanzibaricus, A. glaucescens, Dregea* spp., *Combretum* spp. and *Byrsocarpus* spp.

3 Lorenzo Red-tab Policeman   *Coeliades lorenzo*

Wingspan: ♂ 58–64 mm ♀ 61–66 mm. **Identification: 3A** ♂ upper side, **3B** ♂ underside. Sexes similar, ♀ larger and heavier bodied, with more rounded wings. Until recently, regarded as a subspecies of almost identical Red-tab Policeman (above). Red-orange hind wing underside patches *may be more extensive*; only reliable separation by ♂ genital dissection, or when bred from the distinctively different larvae. **Distribution:** Maputaland forests of n KwaZulu-Natal, north into Mozambique. **Habitat:** Hillsides, flatlands, coast. **Flight period:** Continuous broods, year-round; more numerous in late summer and autumn. **Larval food:** *Acridocarpus natalitius.*

1A

1B

2A

B

3A

3B

Subfamily PYRGINAE

Second largest subfamily of Hesperiidae. A somewhat weakly defined grouping, certain secondary sexual characteristics being used to distinguish them, such as the costal fold on the ♂ forewing, which carries androconial scales. This is not, however, present in all genera. Generally, they tend to rest with wings held flat open, often on the underside of a leaf. Size and physical appearance varies, but most have fairly robust bodies and are accomplished fliers. Eggs – laid on dicotyledons such as Tiliaceae, Malvaceae and Acanthaceae – are variable, usually domed, with or without ribs. Larvae are diverse in appearance. Many have green bodies, sometimes with coloured markings, and dark heads covered in long white hairs; others may have shiny bodies, sometimes garishly coloured. Like many other hesperiids, the rounded pupae are formed inside shelters made of leaves stitched together with silken threads.

Genus *Celaenorrhinus*   Flats   WORLD 90+ SPP., AFRICA 38, SOUTH AFRICA 1

Medium-sized, broad-winged Skippers, bright markings on darker ground. Forest understorey dwelling. Flight flitting and dancing, alighting on leaves (sometimes on underside of leaf) with wings open. Single white egg laid on Acanthaceae; domed and ribbed. Larva green, with darker longitudinal stripes. Pupa greenish, covered with white powder, concealed in leaves held together with silk.

1 Large Sprite, Large Flat or Christmas Forester   *Celaenorrhinus mokeezi*

Wingspan: ♂ 40–48 mm ♀ 45–51 mm. **Identification: 1A** ♂ upper side, **1B** ♀ upper side (*C. m. separata*). Sexes similar, ♀ slightly *larger and paler*; forewing apex *rounder*, upper side hind wing submarginal row of pale spots *more developed* than ♂. Underside very similar to upper side. Usually found around shady spots at edges of forest clearings, glades and paths, especially wetter areas. 2 subspp., geographically distinct. **Distribution:** Nominate in cool coastal and Afromontane Forest and along rivers from E Cape (Amatolas and East London) to s KwaZulu-Natal coast and Midlands (Balgowan, Greytown area); *C. m. separata* in Afromontane Forest from Eshowe, Lebombo Mtns of Maputaland, through Swaziland and along Drakensberg foothills of Mpumalanga and Limpopo Province (to Soutpansberg). **Habitat:** Hillsides, gullies. **Flight period:** Nominate double-brooded, Dec and (larger brood) Feb–Apr; *C. m. separata* single-brooded, Feb–May, sometimes as late as Jul. **Larval food:** *Isoglossa woodii*.

Genus *Tagiades*   Flats   WORLD 17 SPP., AFRICA 3, SOUTH AFRICA 1

Medium to large, broad-winged Skippers. Flitting, darting flight under forest canopy and in clearings. White underside conspicuous in flight and at rest when wings held flat. Single cream to pale yellow egg laid on Dioscoreaceae; domed, ribbed. Larva red to brown, shiny; stout, with conspicuous blunt bifid head capsule. Pupa brown with white markings, dusted with white powder, concealed in leaves held together with silk.

2 Clouded Flat, Clouded Forester or Clouded Skipper   *Tagiades flesus*

Wingspan: ♂ 35–47 mm ♀ 43–49 mm. **Identification: 2A** ♀ upper side, **2B** ♀ underside (f. *flesus*). WSF f. *flesus* hind wing upper side suffused with grey and spotted with black; DSF f. *ophelia* upper side more brownish, markings sparser. ♂ defends territories around forest clearings. Several may circle around the same spot. May settle precipitately on underside of leaves, apparently disappearing into thin air. Also on flowers, particularly *Deinbollia*. **Distribution:** Coastal Lowland and Riverine Forest from E Cape (Somerset East) to KwaZulu-Natal, spreading into Afromontane Forest and heavily wooded Savanna in Swaziland, Mpumalanga and Limpopo Province, and further north. **Habitat:** Hillsides, gullies, flatlands, coast. **Flight period:** Year-round, more numerous in late summer and autumn. **Larval food:** *Dioscorea cotinifolia*.

Genus *Eagris* Flats, Elfins

AFRICA 9 SPP., SOUTH AFRICA 1

Small to medium-sized Skippers, rapid dodging flight along roads and forest margins, settling suddenly underneath leaves. Similar to *Tagiades*, but hind wing vein M$_2$, absent in that genus, is present in *Eagris*. Single egg, domed, white to pale green with 12–13 ribs. Larva red-brown in early instars, becoming green with red-brown head. Pupa yellow-brown, mottled with dark brown and white; white wing cases.

1 Rufous-winged Flat or Rufous-winged Elfin *Eagris nottoana*

Wingspan: ♂ 35–42 mm ♀ 39–43 mm. **Identification: 1A** ♂ upper side, **1B** ♂ underside. Underside very similar to upper side, but never has white patches. ♂ always *has brown underside hind wing*. ♀ *E. n. nottoana* has white underside hind wing; difficult to separate from Clouded Flat (p. 362) except by *smaller size* and *larger hyaline forewing spot* in area CuA$_2$. ♀ *E. n. knysna* has dark hind wing underside. **Distribution:** Nominate in coastal Lowland and Riverine Forest, from E Cape (Port St Johns) to Swaziland, KwaZulu-Natal (Maputaland), Mpumalanga and Limpopo Province lowveld, including the Wolkberg and Soutpansberg foothills along heavily wooded river valleys. *E. n. knysna* in coastal Afromontane Forest from W Cape (Knysna) to E Cape (East London). **Habitat:** Hillsides, gullies, flatlands, coast. **Flight period:** Year-round, more numerous in summer and autumn (Oct–May). **Larval food:** *Grewia occidentalis, Dombeya cymosa, Rinorea arborea* and *Scutia myrtina*.

Genus *Calleagris* Flats

AFRICA 6 SPP., SOUTH AFRICA 2

Small genus of medium-sized, broad-winged Skippers, light to dark brown (both South African species dark brown), sometimes with white markings. Habits very similar to *Celaenorrhinus*. Early stages of the South African spp. unrecorded.

2 Mrs Raven's Flat or Mrs Raven's Skipper *Calleagris kobela*

Wingspan: ♂ 42–44 mm ♀ 43–45 mm. **Identification: 2** ♂ upper side. In flight, *dark, appearing almost black*. Sexes similar, ♀ ground colour slightly paler, forewing hyaline spots *more developed*. Upper side brown with black spots and *postdiscal ochreous irroration* visible on closer examination. Underside very similar to upper side. Often flies with Large Sprite (p. 362). **Distribution:** Afromontane Forest from E Cape (Somerset East), along Amatolas and coastal forests at Port St Johns and the Mbashe River, into KwaZulu-Natal as far as Midlands (Karkloof area). **Habitat:** Hillsides, gullies. **Flight period:** Single late summer brood, peak Feb–Mar. **Larval food:** No data.

3 Kroon's Flat or Kroon's Skipper *Calleagris krooni*

Wingspan: ♂ 43–45 mm ♀ 47–51 mm. **Identification: 3A** ♂ upper side, **3B** ♀ upper side. Similar to Mrs Raven's Flat (above), but forewing with *hyaline spots more developed*, forewing upper side and hind wing underside with *less brown-ochreous irroration*. Sexes similar, ♀ larger with paler brown colour and forewing hyaline spots *better developed* than ♂. **Distribution:** Confined to Afromontane Forest of Mpumalanga (Barberton to Mariepskop). **Habitat:** Hillsides, gullies. **Flight period:** Single late summer brood, peak Feb–Apr. **Larval food:** No data.

Genus *Eretis* Elves

AFRICA 11 SPP., SOUTH AFRICA 2

Small, broad-winged brown Skippers. Flight slow, low; flits over grass or in forest understorey. Settles frequently, on low vegetation, the ground and on flowers, with wings held flat. Egg laid on Acanthaceae; domed, with well-developed ribs. Larva green to brown, living in shelter of leaves bound with silk. Pupa greenish, formed in larval shelter; proboscis tube extends beyond end of abdomen.

1 Marbled Elf   *Eretis djaelaelae*

Wingspan: ♂ 31–35 mm ♀ 34–36 mm. **Identification: 1A** ♂ upper side, **1B** ♂ underside. Small dark Skipper. Sexes similar, ♀ abdomen larger, stouter. Upper side dark brown with black and ochre marbling, underside reddish ochre, bands of darker brown. Forelegs *bright white*. **Distribution:** Lowland, Riverine and Afromontane Forest from E Cape (Port Elizabeth, Amatolas) coastal bush to Swaziland, KwaZulu-Natal (Maputaland and Lebombos), Mpumalanga and Limpopo Province lowveld, Drakensberg, Wolkberg and Soutpansberg, wooded Savanna in Waterberg and Magaliesberg (Gauteng). **Habitat:** Hillsides, gullies, flatlands, coast. **Flight period:** Year-round, commoner in warmer areas and during Sept–Mar. **Larval food:** *Phaulopsis imbricata, Chaetacanthus setiger, Dyschoriste* spp., *Justicia* spp., including *J. protracta*.

2 Small Marbled Elf   *Eretis umbra umbra*

Wingspan: ♂ 30–32 mm ♀ 32–37 mm. **Identification: 2** ♀ upper side. Sexes similar, ♂ abdomen slimmer. Wing markings as larger Marbled Elf (above), underside *slightly darker* red-brown. Forelegs *dark brown*. Found in grassy areas, settling on flowers or low vegetation, mud or fresh cow dung. **Distribution:** Grassland and wooded Savanna, often at edges of thick forest, also in open highveld grassland, grassy areas and along coast from W Cape (Mossel Bay) to E Cape (East London), Swaziland, KwaZulu-Natal, Free State, Limpopo and NW provinces, Mpumalanga, Gauteng, and e N Cape. **Habitat:** Hillsides, gullies, flatlands, coast, mountains. **Flight period:** Year-round in warmer areas, Aug–May in cooler areas. **Larval food:** *Phaulopsis* spp., *Chaetacanthus setiger, Dyschoriste* spp., *Justicia* spp. and *Asystasia schimperi*.

Genus *Sarangesa*   Elfins   WORLD 25 SPP., AFRICA 23, SOUTH AFRICA 4

Medium-sized, grey to blackish and dull brown, darker mottlings and hyaline spots. Always settles with wings held flat. Shade-loving; skulking habits. ♂ territorial; perches, wings open, on plants on edge of small clearings and chases away other ♂ ♂. ♀ usually on flowers. Flight low, fast and darting. Fond of roosting on walls of animal burrows and small caves. Single egg laid on Acanthaceae; domed with well-developed ribs. Larva buff to green, with light and dark longitudinal stripes; lives in shelter of leaves stitched together with silk. Pupa whitish to green, blunt ended, with proboscis tube extending as far as mid-abdomen.

3 Small Elfin   *Sarangesa phidyle*

Wingspan: 26–38 mm. **Identification: 3A** ♂ upper side (f. *phidyle*), **3B** ♂ upper side, **3C** ♂ underside (f. *varia*). Characteristic *bright yellow-ochre underside*, mottled with brown. Sexes similar, ♀ has larger, stouter abdomen. DSF f. *varia* paler than WSF f. *phidyle*, forewing upper side dark patches *more contrasting*, forewing hyaline spots *smaller*. **Distribution:** Common and widespread. In wooded Savanna and Lowland Forest, edges of Riverine Forest, from E Cape (Port Elizabeth) to Swaziland, KwaZulu-Natal (Maputaland), Mpumalanga and Limpopo Province (to Waterberg), NW Province and Gauteng (Magaliesberg). **Habitat:** Forest edges, hillsides, gullies, flatlands. **Flight period:** Year-round, scarcer in winter and dry season. **Larval food:** *Peristrophe hensii* and *Barleria* spp.

4 Dark Elfin   *Sarangesa seineri*

Wingspan: ♂ 36–38 mm ♀ 38–40 mm. **Identification: 4A** ♂ upper side (nominate), **4B** ♂ upper side, **4C** ♂ underside (*S. s. durbana*). Sexes similar, ♀ has larger, stouter abdomen. Upper side *more mottled* than Small Elfin (above), underside *duller ochre-yellow to brown*. White flash below antenna club. 2 subspp., geographically distinct. **Distribution:** Nominate in wooded Savanna and Arid Savanna from north of Soutpansberg, Limpopo Province, to n Gauteng and n Mpumalanga; *S. s. durbana* in wooded Savanna, Riverine and Lowland Forest in thorn belt and lowveld of Swaziland, KwaZulu-Natal (Durban to Maputaland), and Mpumalanga. **Habitat:** Forest edges, hillsides, gullies, flatlands. **Flight period:** Year-round, scarcer in winter and dry season. **Larval food:** *Peristrophe hensii*.

1 Forest Elfin *Sarangesa motozi*

Wingspan: ♂ 36–38 mm ♀ 38–40 mm. **Identification: 1A** ♂ upper side, **1B** ♂ underside (WSF f. *motosi*). Sexes similar, ♀ has larger, stouter abdomen. Well-marked, dark underside hind wing has *contrasting deep yellow-ochre chequering*, forewing hyaline spots *larger* than *Dark Elfin* (p. 366). Has *large hyaline spot at end of hind wing cell*. DSF f. *pertusa*, like most DSF *Sarangesa* Skippers, has *reduced hyaline spots*, dark and light areas of upper side *more variegated*. **Distribution:** Heavily wooded areas, Lowland Forest and lower altitude Afromontane and Riverine Forest, from E Cape (Port Elizabeth), to Swaziland, and KwaZulu-Natal along coastal forest belt to Maputaland, lowveld of Mpumalanga and Limpopo Province (woodland of Soutpansberg, Wolkberg and Waterberg). **Habitat:** Forest edges, hillsides, gullies, coast. **Flight period:** Year-round, scarcer in dry season. **Larval food:** *Peristrophe hensii*.

2 Ruona Elfin *Sarangesa ruona*

Wingspan: ♂ 32–42 mm ♀ 40–43 mm. **Identification: 2A** ♂ upper side, **2B** ♂ underside. Sexes similar, ♀ has larger, stouter abdomen. Upper side closely resembles Forest Elfin (above), hyaline spot in hind wing cell *replaced by squared-off pale spot*. Underside *less contrasting*. Occasionally in numbers in hot dry savanna. **Distribution:** Marginal in South Africa. Only in thickly wooded Savanna and Lowland Forest in Maputaland area of KwaZulu-Natal, and north-western parts of Limpopo Province lowveld east of Wolkberg, north and east of Soutpansberg. **Habitat:** Forest edges, hillsides, gullies, flatlands. **Flight period:** Several broods, Sept–May. **Larval food:** No data.

Genus *Netrobalane* Buff-tipped Skipper   MONOTYPIC

Rests wings open, resembling a bird dropping. Single pale yellow egg laid on Tiliaceae, Sterculiaceae and Malvaceae, domed with slight ribs. Larva green with short white hairs, dark head with long filamentous hairs. Pupa white, with dark marks and dark bifid head spine.

3 Buff-tipped Skipper *Netrobalane canopus*

Wingspan: ♂ 26–44 mm ♀ 42–45 mm. **Identification: 3** ♂ upper side. Sexes similar, ♀ larger, wings more elongated, abdomen stouter. *Upper side mottled buff-brown, white, with prominent discal hyaline bands*. Underside similar, dark markings fewer, *prominent black dot at hind wing anal angle*. Usually found singly. Flight medium fast, dancing. ♂ selects a prominent twig or leaf perch, patrols forest edge or hill top. When courting, ♂ flight has buzzing, clicking sound. Both sexes found at flowers. **Distribution:** Thick woodland, bush and Lowland Forest, from E Cape (East London, King William's Town) coastal and riverine bush to KwaZulu-Natal (Maputaland), warmer Savanna in Swaziland, lowveld of Mpumalanga, and Limpopo Province (Soutpansberg and Wolkberg). **Habitat:** Hill tops, forest edges, hillsides, flatlands, coast. **Flight period:** Year-round, peaks Sept–Nov and Feb–May. **Larval food:** *Grewia* spp., including *G. occidentalis*, *G. similis* and *G. flavescens*, *Dombeya cymosa* and *D. calantha*, and *Pavonia burchelli*.

Genus *Caprona* Skippers   WORLD 6 SPP., AFRICA 3, SOUTH AFRICA 1

Small genus of narrow-winged Skippers, grey and buff wings with hyaline spots; wings held flat at rest. Fast, darting flight. Inhabits Savanna, sometimes Arid Savanna. Egg laid on Tiliaceae and Sterculiaceae; not described. Larva green-white, short hairs on body, dark head with longer hairs. Pupa white, formed in larval shelter of leaves held together with silk.

A

1B

A

2B

B

1 Ragged Skipper *Caprona pillaana*

Wingspan: ♂ 30–37 mm ♀ 35–44 mm. **Identification: 1A** ♂ upper side, **1B** ♀ upper side (DSF), **1C** ♂ underside. Sexes similar; underside as upper side. ♂ hill-topper, chases other butterflies; perches on prominent forest edge trees. Both sexes often on flowers. DSF ♀♀ paler and smaller than WSF ♀♀. **Distribution:** Widespread but local. Savanna and Arid Savanna, lowland woodland and rivers from Swaziland through thorn belt and Maputaland areas of KwaZulu-Natal; extreme w Free State, Mpumalanga, Limpopo and NW provinces, n Gauteng, and e N Cape. **Habitat:** Hill tops, forest edges, hillsides. **Flight period:** Year-round, peaks Sept–Nov and Mar–May. **Larval food:** *Grewia flava, G. monticola, Dombeya rotundifolia, D. burgessiae* and *Sterculia quinqueloba*.

Genus *Leucochitonea* Skippers AFRICA 3 SPP., SOUTH AFRICA 1

White Skippers with black markings, closely related to *Caprona* and *Abantis*. Flight fast, darting and skipping. Early stages unrecorded, but known to feed on Tiliaceae.

2 White-cloaked Skipper *Leucochitonea levubu*

Wingspan: ♂ 30–40 mm ♀ 35–45 mm. **Identification: 2A** ♂ upper side, **2B** ♂ underside. Beautiful, conspicuous, easily recognised. Sexes similar, ♀ more elongated wings, stouter abdomen. Conspicuous white wings veined and banded with black; yellow-ochre body hair on underparts. ♂ prominent hill-topper, pursuing intruders; perches on bare twigs with forelegs raised. Both sexes on flowers. **Distribution:** Savanna and Arid Savanna, from Maputaland area of KwaZulu-Natal to extreme w Free State, lowveld of Mpumalanga, Limpopo and NW provinces, Gauteng, and e N Cape. **Habitat:** Hill tops, hillsides. **Flight period:** Single extended brood, Nov–Apr, peak Jan–Feb. **Larval food:** *Grewia flava*.

Genus *Abantis* Paradise Skippers AFRICA 22 SPP., SOUTH AFRICA 4

Medium-sized, narrow-winged, colourful Skippers. Extremely fast, high, darting flight, settling wings open or half-closed. ♂ territorial, perches on prominent hill-top trees, chases away intruders. ♀ seldom seen; flight slower near flowers and food plants. ♂ sometimes on wet mud. Single egg laid on shoots of plants from several families; white to pale yellow, finely ribbed, domed. Larva pale-bodied, varying degree of rows of dark subdorsal spots. Pupa brown to white, with forked head horn; formed inside larval shelter of leaves spun with silk.

3 Spotted Velvet Skipper *Abantis tettensis*

Wingspan: ♂ 35–40 mm ♀ 35–45 mm. **Identification: 3A** ♂ upper side, **3B** ♂ underside. Sexes alike, ♀ more elongated wings, stouter abdomen. Upper side black with forewing rows of white blotches; hind wing has white centre spotted with black. Underside forewing yellow-ochre, pink basally, pale markings following upper side. Underside hind wing pink, black spots and black marginal band containing white spots. **Model:** Underside hind wing resembles that of *Acraea* spp. (p. 80). **Distribution:** Savanna and Arid Savanna, from Maputaland area of KwaZulu-Natal, extreme w Free State, lowveld in Mpumalanga, Limpopo and NW provinces, n Gauteng, and extreme e N Cape. **Habitat:** Hill tops, hillsides. **Flight period:** Single extended brood, Sept–Apr, peak Oct–Nov. **Larval food:** *Grewia flava* and *G. monticola*.

4 Bicoloured Skipper *Abantis bicolor*

Wingspan: ♂ 36–41 mm ♀ 35–45 mm. **Identification: 4A** ♂ upper side, **4B** ♂ underside. *Striking deep golden yellow* with *black forewing upper side blotches and marginal bands* on both wings. Sexes similar; ♀ larger than ♂, wings more elongated, yellow ground colour *duller*, abdomen stouter. Large emergences occur very rarely, with both sexes common on flowers close to forests. **Distribution:** Restricted to Lowland Forest from E Cape – East London (single record); Mt Thesiger at Port St Johns to KwaZulu-Natal south coast (Durban area and Ngoye Forest near Eshowe). **Habitat:** Hill tops, hillsides, forest edges. **Flight period:** Double-brooded; spring peak Oct–Nov, stronger autumn peak Mar–Jun. **Larval food:** No data.

1 Paradise Skipper   *Abantis paradisea*

Wingspan: ♂ 40–45 mm ♀ 43–55 mm. **Identification: 1** ♂ upper side. Sexes alike, ♀ more elongated wings, stouter abdomen. *Cream- and white-spotted black wings* contrast with *brightly coloured body*. Upper side as underside, hind wing discal patch *white*, not cream. **Distribution:** Widespread but local. Lowland Forest from KwaZulu-Natal south coast (Umkomaas) to Maputaland, lowveld Savanna of Swaziland, Mpumalanga, Limpopo Province and n Gauteng. **Habitat:** Hill tops, forest edges, hillsides, flatlands. **Flight period:** Year-round, peaks autumn (Apr–Jun) and spring (Aug–Nov). **Larval food:** *Hibiscus tiliaceus, Cola natalensis, Annona* spp., *Bridelia cathartica, B. micrantha, Pseudolachnostylis maprouneifolia, Lonchocarpus capassa* and *Lecaniodiscus fraxinifolius.*

2 Veined Skipper   *Abantis venosa*

Wingspan: ♂ 36–41 mm ♀ 35–45 mm. **Identification: 2A** ♂ upper side (f. *umvulensis*), **2B** ♀ upper side, **2C** ♂ underside (f. *venosa*). Sexes alike, ♀ more elongated wings, stouter abdomen. *Black-veined ochre-yellow* upper side. Seasonal forms: WSF f. *venosa* has *prominent* black veining; *white* underside hind wing with *broad* black margin. DSF f. *umvulensis* paler, veins *less well defined*, buff hind wing underside with *narrow* black margin. **Distribution:** Lowland Forest and Savanna from Swaziland, to KwaZulu-Natal (Maputaland), Mpumalanga, e Limpopo Province and further north. **Habitat:** Hill tops, forest edges, hillsides, flatlands. **Flight period:** Year-round, peaks late summer (Feb–Apr) and spring (Aug–Nov). **Larval food:** *Pterocarpus rotundifolius* and *P. brenanii.*

Genus *Spialia*   Sandmen   WORLD 27 SPP., AFRICA 20, SOUTH AFRICA 14

Small to tiny dark Skippers, chequerboard-like white upper side pattern distinctive to species, but differences in underside hind wing patterns easier to discern in the field. Sexes similar, ♀ with abdomen stouter, forewing rounder. Flight generally fast, low, skipping and hopping, very fast, buzzing wing-beats – may be mistaken for flies. ♂ patrols territory with rapid wing-beats and slow flight, except when chasing intruders. Single egg laid on Sterculiaceae, Tiliaceae and Malvaceae; white to pale blue or green; domed, with fine, sometimes sinuate ribs. Stout larva variable in colour; dark head; short hairs on body and longer hairs on head and back. Pupa brown to grey-black, formed inside larval shelter.

3 Dwarf Sandman   *Spialia nanus*

Wingspan: ♂ 18–24 mm ♀ 23–27 mm. **Identification: 3A** ♂ upper side, **3B** ♂ underside. Upper side dark brown with white spots, none in R_1, R_2 of forewing or at base. Underside hind wing pale brown to ochre, with *wavy cream-white median band*; only South African *Spialia* sp. with this character. ♂ perches on low vegetation or rocks on the ground, usually on rocky ledges or bare patches between bushes. ♀ seen less frequently, usually on flowers. **Distribution:** Fynbos and Nama Karoo all over W Cape and w Free State, s NW Province, and Succulent Karoo in N Cape; absent from arid Kalahari region. **Habitat:** Hillsides, rocky ledges, flatlands. **Flight period:** Double-brooded, peaks Mar/Apr and Sept/Oct, occasionally in summer between broods. **Larval food:** *Hermannia diffusa, H. incana, H. comosa, H. cuneifolia* and *H. pulverata*, and *Hibiscus aethiopicus.*

4 Delagoa Sandman   *Spialia delagoae*

Wingspan: ♂ 21–24 mm ♀ 24–28 mm. **Identification: 4A** ♂ upper side, **4B** ♂ underside. Similar to Dwarf Sandman (above), but underside hind wing median band *straight*. Constant in width. ♂ establishes territories on small rocky prominences. Also on flowers, wet mud, and fresh animal droppings. **Distribution:** Savanna, Lowland Forest, and thorn veld from Swaziland, KwaZulu-Natal (Maputaland area), Mpumalanga lowveld, n Gauteng and Limpopo and n NW provinces. **Habitat:** Hill tops, hillsides, rocky ledges, flatlands. **Flight period:** Double-brooded, peaks Feb/Mar and Aug/Sept, occasionally seen between broods. **Larval food:** No data.

1

2A

2B

2C

3A

3B

4A

4B

1 Boland Sandman   *Spialia sataspes*

Wingspan: ♂ 21–26 mm ♀ 24–28 mm. **Identification: 1A** ♂ underside, **1B** ♀ underside. Resembles Delagoa Sandman (p. 372) but hind wing underside submarginal spots *absent*. Whitish median band wider at costa, hind wing underside basal area more distinctly pale, creating darker band basal to median band. Range and behaviour very different, but field identification difficult because extremely difficult to approach. Found in small colonies near food plant, where ♂ perches on low vegetation, patrolling the immediate area. ♀ seen less frequently, usually on flowers or food plant. **Distribution:** Fynbos of W Cape, along mountain chains N Cape, along coast to E Cape (Port Elizabeth) and inland to Bedford and Grahamstown. **Habitat:** Hillsides, mountains, coast. **Flight period:** Single extended brood, peak Nov–Jan. **Larval food:** *Hermannia* spp., *Pavonia burchellii* and *Hibiscus aethiopicus.*

2 Wandering Sandman   *Spialia depauperata australis*

Wingspan: ♂ 23–28 mm ♀ 31–33 mm. **Identification: 2A** ♀ upper side, **2B** ♀ underside. Very similar to Common Sandman (p. 378), but *no basal forewing cell spots* on both wing surfaces, forewing area 1 *has only one* forewing upper side outer median spot, not two; pale hind wing underside submarginal band *straight*, not curved towards costa. Found in colonies near food plant; ♂ seen more frequently than ♀, although sometimes found together. ♂ patrols the vicinity from a spot on the ground or grass stem. Both sexes found on wet mud. **Distribution:** Dry montane Grassland along Drakensberg from n KwaZulu-Natal, Swaziland and Mpumalanga, spreading across Savanna bushveld in Limpopo Province. **Habitat:** Hillsides, mountains, flatlands. **Flight period:** Year-round in warmer areas; peaks Sept–Dec and Jan–Mar. **Larval food:** *Melhania* spp.

3 Star Sandman   *Spialia asterodia*

Wingspan: ♂ 21–26 mm ♀ 26–29 mm. **Identification: 3A** ♂ upper side, **3B** ♂ underside. Forewing upper side central cell spot *closer to discocellular spot* than basal spot. Underside hind wing pale median band *irregular but complete*, runs parallel to series of pale basal spots, creating two jagged, black-edged ochreous-brown bands. ♂ hill-tops, more often on grassy hillsides, and patrols the area. Both sexes fond of flowers, seldom on mud. ♂ often sitting on the ground, ♀ scarcer, most often near food plants. **Distribution:** Savanna and Grassland. Grassy hillsides and mountains in Fynbos from W Cape (but not the extreme south) to s N Cape, across E Cape, Lesotho (up to 3 000 m), Free State, Swaziland, w KwaZulu-Natal, greater part of Mpumalanga, Limpopo Province and e NW Province, and Gauteng. **Habitat:** Hillsides, mountains, rocky ledges. **Flight period:** Several broods, Aug–Mar, peaks midsummer. **Larval food:** *Hermannia diffusa, H. incana, Pavonia burchellii* and *Hibiscus* spp.

4 Grassveld Sandman   *Spialia agylla*

Wingspan: ♂ 20–22 mm ♀ 22–24 mm. **Identification: 4A** ♂ upper side, **4B** ♂ underside (nominate). Similar to Star Sandman (above), upper side and underside *more heavily marked with white*. Irregular hind wing underside white median band, unlike Star Sandman, *not parallel* to basal spots. Hind wing underside median band connected to large submarginal spot by *thin white line* in cell. ♂ more often on ledges and ridges than hill tops, ♀ near food plants. Both sexes fond of flowers, particularly *Mesembryanthemum* vygies. 2 subspp., geographically distinct. **Distribution:** Nominate on grassy hillsides in Nama Karoo, from W Cape (but not extreme south) to s N Cape, across w E Cape, Grassland of Free State, e Lesotho, s Gauteng, sw Mpumalanga, Arid Savanna in NW Province; *S. a. bamptoni* in Succulent Karoo around coastal border of W Cape and N Cape in Namaqualand, Lambert's Bay, Hondeklip Bay and inland to Kamiesberg. **Habitat:** Hillsides, mountains, flatlands. **Flight period:** Several broods, Aug–Apr, peaks midsummer. **Larval food:** *Hermannia* spp. and *Pavonia burchellii.*

A

1B

2A

2B

3A

3B

A

4B

1 Bushveld Sandman *Spialia colotes transvaaliae*

Wingspan: ♂ 21–24 mm ♀ 26–28 mm. **Identification: 1A** ♂ upper side, **1B** ♂ underside. Forewing apex *markedly pointed*, hind wing underside *distinctly spotted*. Hind wing submarginal spots at M$_1$ and M$_2$ *do not form a smooth line with the rest of series*, they are placed more basally. Hind wing underside spots mirror those on upper side, *large, white, rounded* and separated on brown-grey background. ♂ patrols territory among thorn trees, often on low, shaded vegetation in flat country or on lower slopes of hills. ♀♀ found with ♂♂, flying randomly in search of nectar or food plant. **Distribution:** Dry to Arid Savanna from n Swaziland, to Mpumalanga lowveld, all of Limpopo Province and further north. **Habitat:** Hillsides, flatlands. **Flight period:** Single extended brood from Dec–May, peak Feb–Apr. **Larval food:** *Hibiscus fuscus*.

2 Confusing Sandman *Spialia confusa confusa*

Wingspan: ♂ 19–23 mm ♀ 23–25 mm. **Identification: 2A** ♀ upper side, **2B** ♀ underside. Tiny; in flight, easily mistaken for a small fly. Only South African *Spialia* besides Bushveld Sandman (above) to have *hind wing submarginal spots in M$_1$ and M$_2$ out of line, shifted basally*. Forewing apex *short and blunt*, hind wing underside median band *straight, contiguous*. ♂ found on sandy patches at edge of bush, among low grass and herbs, often along paths. Usually in flat country although found on hill tops and hillsides further north. Both sexes on flowers, but ♀ very seldom seen. **Distribution:** Rare and localised. Lowland Forest and Savanna in e Swaziland, Maputaland (KwaZulu-Natal), and Kaapmuiden/Barberton area (Mpumalanga). Single record from Musina, Limpopo Province. **Habitat:** Flatlands, hillsides, forest edges. **Flight period:** Year-round, peak Oct–Mar. **Larval food:** Probably *Melhania* spp. and *Triumfetta* spp.

3 Mafa Sandman *Spialia mafa mafa*

Wingspan: ♂ 22–25 mm ♀ 23–26 mm. **Identification: 3A** ♂ upper side, **3B** ♂ underside. Separated from other *Spialia* spp. by hind wing underside median band *being broken into a series of three spots*, character shared with Mountain Sandman (p. 378) only. Compared to latter, upper side *lacks smaller markings*, has *no spot* at base of forewing costa. Hind wing underside ground colour varies from *creamy buff to reddish brown*. Always in grassy areas, even in middle of Fynbos or Karoo, usually on slopes of koppies and sand dunes. ♂ sits on patches of bare ground among low vegetation, circling back to the original spot if disturbed. ♀ flies at random looking for food plants. **Distribution:** Widespread but localised. From W Cape Fynbos to Succulent Karoo of Namaqualand, across Grassland and Savanna of e N Cape, to Free State, Lesotho (up to 3 000 m), Swaziland, w KwaZulu-Natal, Mpumalanga, Gauteng, and Limpopo and NW provinces. **Habitat:** Flatlands, hillsides, hill tops, mountains, coast. **Flight period:** Year-round, peaks spring and summer (Sept–Apr); in cooler areas, only these months. **Larval food:** *Hermannia depressa*, *Hibiscus aethiopicus* and *Pavonia* spp.

4 Mite Sandman *Spialia paula*

Wingspan: ♂ 20–24 mm ♀ 23–27 mm. **Identification: 4A** ♂ upper side, **4B** ♂ underside. *Hind wing with large silvery white spots in underside cell and area M$_1$/M$_2$*. ♂ hill-tops, but usually not at main summit. Also in flat country. Favours patches of stony ground among low vegetation. ♂ circles these areas with low, rapid flight, fast wing-beats. ♀ sometimes near the ♂♂, more usually looking for food plants. Both sexes feed on flowers. **Distribution:** Rare and localised in Arid Savanna and grassy areas of Savanna, from extreme w N Cape (Windsorton area) to NW Province, w Gauteng, and central Limpopo Province (Waterberg, Strydpoortberg, Wolkberg). **Habitat:** Flatlands, hillsides, hill tops. **Flight period:** Continuous brood, Aug–Apr, mainly Aug–Oct. **Larval food:** No data.

1A

1B

2A

2B

3A

3B

4A

4B

1 Wolkberg Sandman *Spialia secessus*

Wingspan: ♂ 27–31 mm ♀ 30–32 mm. **Identification: 1A** ♀ upper side, **1B** ♀ underside (f. *secessus*), **1C** ♂ underside (f. *trimeni*). Sexes similar, ♀ with abdomen stouter. Cilia *plain cream*, prominent *cream-white marginal and submarginal spots* on upper side hind wing and forewing. Underside hind wing median band *broad, straight*, outer edge finely dentate, contrasts with dark ground colour. Only seasonally dimorphic South African *Spialia*: DSF f. *secessus* hind wing underside basal spots and median band *cream-buff on ochre-brown ground*; in WSF f. *trimeni, white on red-brown ground*. ♂ hill-tops at midday; patrols paths and roads from perches on dry grass stems. Seldom in numbers. **Distribution:** Uncommon. High Savanna, montane Grassland from Swaziland to n KwaZulu-Natal, e Limpopo Province (Soutpansberg, Wolkberg and Drakensberg escarpments), and Mpumalanga (Barberton mines). **Habitat:** Hillsides, hill tops, mountains. **Flight period:** Continuous broods, Jul–Mar, peaks Sept–Nov (WSF) and Feb (DSF). **Larval food:** No data.

2 Forest Sandman or Large Grizzled Skipper *Spialia dromus*

Wingspan: ♂ 23–29 mm ♀ 29–32 mm. **Identification: 2A** ♂ upper side, **2B** ♂ underside. Common in woodland edges and clearings, grassy hillsides and hill tops. Similar to Confusing Sandman (p. 376), upper side white markings *larger*, especially *kidney-shaped hind wing central spot*; hind wing underside median band *curved*. Low flight, rapid wing-beats, but not as fast or sustained as Confusing Sandman. ♀ usually found with ♂, but settles more frequently. **Distribution:** Lowland and Riverine Forest along E Cape coast from East London, to KwaZulu-Natal (to Maputaland), grassy areas near forests in Lebombos, into Swaziland. Wooded Savanna and at forest edges of Mpumalanga and Limpopo Province lowveld (e Drakensberg and Wolkberg slopes, Waterberg and Magaliesberg) into n Gauteng and extreme nw NW Province. **Habitat:** Forest edges, coast, flatlands, hillsides, hill tops. **Flight period:** Year-round, more common in warmer months. **Larval food:** *Triumfetta tomentosa* and *T. rhomboidea, Melhania* spp. and *Waltheria* spp.

3 Common Sandman *Spialia diomus ferax*

Wingspan: ♂ 27–31 mm ♀ 29–33 mm. **Identification: 3A** ♂ upper side, **3B** ♀ underside. Superficially resembles Wandering Sandman (p. 374), but has *three* white spots in forewing cell not *two*, hind wing underside pale bands *distinctly curved outwards towards margin*. ♂ patrols territories on hill tops, ridges or any small rocky prominence, especially on bare patches of ground, fresh animal droppings and wet mud. ♀ found usually on flowers and food plant. **Distribution:** Most common and most widespread South Africa *Spialia*. Throughout South Africa, scarcer in arid Karoo and wet rainforests. **Habitat:** Forest edges, parks and gardens, hill tops, hillsides, flatlands, coast, mountains. **Flight period:** Year-round in warmer areas; more common in warmer months. In cool areas, Aug–Apr, usually one of the first spring butterflies. **Larval food:** *Hermannia diffusa, H. incana, H. comosa, H. depressa, H. cuneifolia, Waltheria* spp., *Hibiscus aethiopicus, Pavonia burchellii* and *Sida* spp.

4 Mountain Sandman *Spialia spio*

Wingspan: ♂ 22–29 mm ♀ 28–31 mm. **Identification: 4A** ♀ upper side, **4B** ♀ underside. Markings very similar to Mafa Sandman (p. 376), white upper side spots *larger, more rounded*; upper side forewing costa has *pale spot* at base. Hind wing underside white discocellular spot *larger and more rounded*, white inner spot in S_c+R_1 larger, *edges smoother*. ♂ hill tops, lower on slopes or in flat country near food plant. Fond of animal faeces; often on wet mud. **Distribution:** All over e side of South Africa but absent from aridest Karoo and Savanna, commonest Cape Peninsula *Spialia*. **Habitat:** Forest edges, parks and gardens, hill tops, hillsides, flatlands, coast, mountains. **Flight period:** Continuous broods; year-round in warmer areas, more common in warmer months. In cool areas, Aug–Apr; in W Cape Fynbos mainly Aug–Oct. **Larval food:** *Hermannia diffusa, H. incana, H. comosa, H. coccocarpa, H. cuneifolia, Hibiscus aethiopicus, H. pusillus, Pavonia burchellii, P. columella, Lavatera arborea, Sida* spp., *Triumfetta* spp.

1A

1B

1C

2A

2B

3A

3B

4A

4B

Genus *Gomalia*   Sandmen   WORLD 2 SPP., SOUTH AFRICA 1

Small Skipper with distinct markings. Single pale yellow-brown egg, with wavy ribs, laid on Malvaceae. Larva green-white with hairy black head. Pupa grey-white with powdery white coating, head rounded.

1 Green-marbled Sandman   *Gomalia elma elma*

Wingspan: ♂ 26–31 mm ♀ 29–36 mm. **Identification: 1A** ♂ upper side, **1B** ♀ underside. Common name descriptive of forewing upper side; hind wing upper side has white discal band. Underside markings mirror upper side. Sexes alike. *Roosting posture* distinctive, wings folded downwards, moth-like, abdomen curled upwards towards thorax. Seldom found on hill tops. Low flight skipping and circling, not very fast. ♂ patrols territory, settling momentarily on vantage points with open wings. Both sexes found on flowers and wet mud. **Distribution:** Widespread but uncommon. On E side of South Africa, in woodland clearings and rides, open grassy bush, vleis and riverine bush, coast and wooded hillsides from W Cape and N Cape, to E Cape, Swaziland, KwaZulu-Natal, Free State, Mpumalanga, Gauteng, and Limpopo and NW provinces, and further north. **Habitat:** Forest edges, parks and gardens, flatlands, coast, wetlands. **Flight period:** Year-round in warmer areas, mainly Aug–Apr. Only Aug–Apr in cooler areas. **Larval food:** *Abutilon grandiflorum, A. someratianum* and *A. grantii.*

Genus *Alenia*   Dancers or Sandmen   2 SPP., ENDEMIC TO SOUTH AFRICAN KAROO BIOME

♂ establishes territory in patches of bare stony ground in gullies or on rocky ledges. Quick, low-circling flight with fast wing-beats, wary and difficult to approach when not feeding. Settles often on open ground or prominent rocks, where underside markings afford excellent camouflage. Seldom found far from colonies on food plants. Fond of flowers, particularly *Mesembryanthemum* spp. Egg laid on Acanthaceae; yellow elongated dome with flattened top and finely fluted ribs. Larva white to grey, with paler dorso-lateral stripes, and head black with paler hairs. Pupa white with fine dusting of black, appearing grey; formed in larval shelter.

2 Karoo Dancer or Karoo Sandman   *Alenia sandaster*

Wingspan: ♂ 22–27 mm ♀ 26–28 mm. **Identification: 2A** ♀ upper side, **2B** ♂ underside. Sexes similar, ♀ with stouter abdomen. Upper side dark brown; forewing has small white basal and postdiscal spots; indistinct grey smudge at end of cell. Hind wing upper side carries faint postdiscal white spots, sometimes absent. Hind wing underside has *two white bands* separated by a dark brown median fascia, *thin white striae* at base and submarginal areas. **Distribution:** Arid Nama Karoo in e W Cape and central N Cape, and w E Cape. **Habitat:** Hillsides, flatlands, rocky ledges, gullies. **Flight period:** Single extended brood, Aug–Jan, peak Sept–Nov. **Larval food:** *Blepharis capensis* and *Barleria* spp.

3 Namaqua Dancer or Namaqua Sandman   *Alenia namaqua*

Wingspan: ♂ 21–26 mm ♀ 26–29 mm. **Identification: 3A** ♂ upper side, **3B** ♂ underside. Very similar to Karoo Dancer (above), hind wing underside with *greater degree of white irroration, covering the median fascia.* Upper side ground colour *more charcoal grey*; upper side forewing markings *sharper and whiter.* Has a *pale mark* at the end of the cell, where Karoo Dancer has indistinct grey smudges. Sexes similar, ♀ with abdomen stouter. **Distribution:** Only in montane Succulent Karoo of N Cape Namaqualand, from Calvinia north through Kamiesberg and surrounding hills into Namibia. **Habitat:** Hillsides, flatlands, rocky ledges, gullies. **Flight period:** Single-brooded, Sept–Nov. **Larval food:** *Blepharis capensis.*

1A

1B

2A

2B

A

3B

Subfamily HETEROPTERINAE

Small Skippers, with broad wings and slender bodies, usually sombre coloured, some with yellow spots. Flight generally quite weak; seldom found far from food plants (Poaceae grasses).

Genus *Metisella*   Sylphs

AFRICA 22 SPP., SOUTH AFRICA 6

Small to medium-sized Skippers, some brilliantly coloured; black to brown with paler spots and streaks. Underside hind wing markings useful in identifying species. Flight skipping and hopping, sometimes fast and darting. Sexes similar. Single egg, white to pale blue, on Poaceae grasses; domed, not ribbed. Larva green, elongated, lives in shelter of folded grass leaf stitched with silk. Pupa elongated, both ends tapered, in larval shelter.

1 Mountain Sylph   *Metisella aegipan aegipan*

Wingspan: ♂ 28–34 mm ♀ 28–36 mm. **Identification: 1A** ♀ upper side, **1B** ♂ underside. ♀ upper side *brown* with *yellow forewing upper side subapical spots*; sometimes with *faint yellow patch* at end of cell. ♂ upper side *deeper sepia-brown*, with *three small yellow subapical spots*. Underside hind wing of both sexes shiny *grey-buff to yellow-brown*, forewing darker, apical margin strongly sprinkled with yellow scales; subapical yellow spot as upper side. Cilia yellow. ♂ territorial on east-facing marshy hillside patches, perching on grass stems, flying just above the grass with slow, skipping flight. ♀ seen less frequently. Both sexes on flowers. **Distribution:** High montane Grassland along e Drakensberg slopes from Barkly East area (E Cape), to Lesotho, nw KwaZulu-Natal, e Free State, Mpumalanga, Limpopo Province (into Strydpoortberg and Waterberg), west to extreme e NW Province. **Habitat:** Mountains, wetlands, gullies. **Flight period:** Single-brooded, early Dec–Feb. **Larval food:** Probably Poaceae grasses.

2 Grassveld Sylph   *Metisella malgacha*

Wingspan: ♂ 25–29 mm ♀ 27–31 mm. **Identification: 2A** ♂ upper side (*M. m. orina*), **2B** ♀ underside (nominate). Small yellow-spotted dark brown Skipper. Sexes similar, ♀ with stouter abdomen, smaller submarginal yellow spots on upper side of both wings. Fond of flowers and wet mud. Slow flight, skipping above the grass, settling often with wings closed; sunbathes with wings held open. ♂ establishes territories in grassy dells, perching on a grass stem, sallying forth on short flights. ♀ usually near food plant. 2 subspp., geographically distinct. **Distribution:** Nominate in Nama Karoo, grassy areas in Fynbos and mountains of W Cape (frequents gardens in Cape Town), to s N Cape, across c E Cape to Kokstad, Free State, nw KwaZulu-Natal, s Gauteng, and e NW Province; *M. m. orina* in high montane grassland in Lesotho, KwaZulu-Natal Drakensberg and se Mpumalanga (Sterkspruit), up to 3 000 m. **Habitat:** Parks and gardens, hillsides, flatlands, coast, mountains. **Flight period:** Several broods, Aug–May, most common in summer months. Only Dec–Jan at highest elevations. **Larval food:** *Ehrharta erecta*.

3 Gold Spotted Sylph   *Metisella metis*

Wingspan: ♂ 26–34 mm ♀ 30–33 mm. **Identification: 3A** ♂ upper side, **3B** ♂ underside (nominate). *Much brighter* than Grassveld Sylph (above), upper side *spots brilliant golden-yellow on dark brown-black ground*. Sexes differ slightly; yellow spot at CuA_1 is single in ♀, double in ♂. ♂ underside hind wing *flat brown-black*, ♀ underside has upper side pattern of yellow spots *repeated in red-brown* on brown-black ground. Very conspicuous. Slow, hopping flight around low vegetation, settling often, wings open. ♂ and ♀ fly together. 2 subspp., geographically distinct. **Distribution:** Nominate along streams and patches of Afromontane Forest in W Cape (frequents gardens in Cape Town), as far east as Swellendam; *M. m. paris* in Afromontane and Lowland Forest from W Cape (George), along E Cape (Amatolas) and KwaZulu-Natal coast to Durban, inland to Midlands and Swaziland, in forests on southern and eastern slopes of Drakensberg, to Mpumalanga and Limpopo Province (Wolkberg and Soutpansberg). **Habitat:** Forest edges, parks and gardens. **Flight period:** Year-round, peaks Sept–Nov and Feb–Mar; scarce in dry season in cool areas. **Larval food:** *Stenotaphrum secundatum, S. glabrum, S. dimidiatum, Panicum deustum, Ehrharta erecta, Stipa dregeana* and *Setaria megaphylla*.

1A

1B

2A

2B

3A

3B

1 Netted Sylph *Metisella willemi*

Wingspan: 30–32 mm. **Identification: 1A** ♂ upper side, **1B** ♂ underside. Sexes similar, ♀ has stouter abdomen. Upper side *black-brown with pale cream markings*. Cream-white hind wing underside with black-brown veins *crossed by thin black bands*, appearing 'netted'. Found in groups of 5 to 20 individuals in shade along streams and rivers, at the base of hills or patches of trees on hillsides and flat country. Both sexes on flowers, ♂ on wet mud. Flight slow, skipping and zigzagging just above the ground. ♂♂ form territories in shade of trees, perching on grass stems or leaves, periodically making short, fairly fast flights to chase intruders. **Distribution:** Savanna and dry woodland, and river valleys from Barberton area of Mpumalanga, north along western side of Drakensberg and Wolkberg hills into Limpopo Province, Gauteng (except the highveld grassland areas) and NW Province to Groot Marico. **Habitat:** Hillsides, flatlands, wetlands, gullies. **Flight period:** Single extended brood, Dec–May, peak Feb–Mar. **Larval food:** *Setaria* spp.

2 Marsh Sylph *Metisella meninx*

Wingspan: ♂ 26–28 mm ♀ 27–29 mm. **Identification: 2A** ♂ upper side, **2B** ♀ showing upper side apical spots, **2C** ♂ underside. ♀ has stouter abdomen. Upper side similar to Mountain Sylph (p. 382), but with *strong bronzy sheen*; only ♀ has three buff forewing upper side subapical spots. Underside of both sexes dark brown with yellow marginal spots and discal streaks of yellow on both wings; hind wing with bright white streaks at anal fold and area M_2/M_3. Flight low, darting and skipping, of short duration unless disturbed. ♂ territorial around prominent clumps of marsh grass, ♀ seen less frequently. Both sexes on flowers. **Distribution:** Restricted to wet vleis of highveld Grassland in n KwaZulu-Natal (Newcastle area), Mpumalanga (from western border with Swaziland) to Gauteng, n Free State and extreme e NW Province. Lost from many Johannesburg localities due to building developments. **Habitat:** Flatlands, wetlands. **Flight period:** Single extended brood, Dec–Mar, peak Jan–Feb. **Larval food:** Poaceae marsh grasses.

3 Bamboo Sylph *Metisella syrinx*

Wingspan: ♂ 32–34 mm ♀ 32–37 mm. **Identification: 3A** ♂ upper side, **3B** ♂ underside. Upper side resembles Grassveld Sylph (p. 382), but ground colour *duller brown*, markings *pale buff, not yellow*. Underside *distinctive golden brown*, hind wing with *ray of cream-white* from base through cell along vein M_2 to margin; white streak at anal fold. Sexes similar, ♀ with stouter abdomen. ♂ territorial among clumps of food plant. ♀ less frequently seen in the same places, ovipositing, feeding on flowers. Flight darting and zigzagging, faster than other *Metisella* spp., difficult to follow. **Distribution:** Rare, highly localised; protected in E Cape. Only near clumps of mountain bamboo among large rocks at or near summits of Grassland mountains from E Cape (Amatolas) through s Lesotho to extreme s KwaZulu-Natal (Mzimkulu Wilderness and Drakensberg Gardens). **Habitat:** Mountains, hill tops. **Flight period:** Single-brooded, Jan–Feb. **Larval food:** *Thamnocalamnus tessellatus*.

1A

1B

2A

2B

2C

3B

3A

Genus *Tsitana*   Sylphs   4 SPP., ENDEMIC TO SOUTH AFRICA, LESOTHO AND SWAZILAND

Small to medium-sized Skippers; unmarked brown upper side, distinctively streaked or striped hind wing underside. Flight slow, skipping and zigzagging, low among grass stems, frequently settling on grass or feeding on flowers. Never far from food plant. Single egg on Poaceae; domed, not ribbed. Larva pale brown or green, elongated, cylindrical, anal segment spade-shaped; lives in shelter of grass leaves stitched with silk. Pupa elongated, cylindrical, white with darker ends, in larval shelter.

1 Dismal Sylph   *Tsitana tsita*

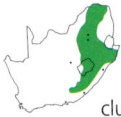

Wingspan: ♂ 30–38 mm ♀ 32–38 mm. **Identification: 1A** ♂ upper side, **1B** ♂ underside. Upper side *plain shiny sepia-brown*. Only *Tsitana* sp. lacking hind wing underside white streaks; suffused with white towards the tornus. Sexes similar, ♀ paler, wings rounder, abdomen stouter. ♂ territorial, sometimes on hill tops but always near clumps of the food plant. **Distribution:** Widespread in Grassland; common but colonies localised and scattered. From Winterberg and Amatolas (E Cape), along Drakensberg into Lesotho and KwaZulu-Natal, to sea level from Durban across Midlands to the Tugela; highveld of Free State, e NW Province and Gauteng (Witwatersrand and Magaliesberg), into Limpopo Province (Waterberg, Strydpoortberg, Soutpansberg and Wolkberg). **Habitat:** Mountains, hillsides, hill tops. **Flight period:** Single-brooded, Dec–Mar, peak in Jan. **Larval food:** *Stipa dregeana*.

2 Uitenhage Sylph   *Tsitana uitenhaga*

Wingspan: ♂ 30–35 mm ♀ 31–36 mm. **Identification: 2A** ♂ upper side, **2B** ♀ underside. Hind wing underside has *central cream streak* from base through cell along vein M$_2$, and *faint streak along vein 3A*. Streak runs *all the way to the wing margin*. Upper side brown. ♀ similar to ♂, *paler brown*, abdomen stouter, wings more rounded. Usually in dry riverbeds near food plant, difficult to follow among dense thorns. **Distribution:** Rare, localised. Dry grassy scrubland in Nama Karoo from W Cape (Seweweekspoort, Heidelberg) to E Cape (Bedford/Grahamstown area). **Habitat:** Flatlands, hillsides, gullies. **Flight period:** Single extended brood, Sept–Mar, peak Oct–Nov. **Larval food:** *Stipa dregeana*.

3 Tulbagh Sylph   *Tsitana tulbagha*

Wingspan: ♂ 30–40 mm ♀ 40–41 mm. **Identification: 3A** ♀ upper side (*T. t. kaplani*), **3B** ♀ underside (nominate). Sexes similar, ♀ with stouter abdomen. Underside hind wing ground colour *fawn to brown suffused with white towards the anal angle*. Hind wing underside central rayed streak *does not reach margin*. Found on rough hillsides; *fast, jerky, sustained flight* through patches of food plant; seldom seen at flowers. Difficult to flush in windy conditions. ♂ territorial in food plant patches, perching on rocks or prominent grass stems, periodically patrolling. ♀ usually near food plant. Two subspecies. **Distribution:** Nominate in grassy inclusions in Fynbos and Nama Karoo from w W Cape mountains (Tulbagh, Piketberg) to s N Cape (Vanrhynsdorp area); *T. t. kaplani* in similar habitats in s and e W Cape mountains from Worcester area, Hex River Valley to Montagu and Swellendam, along Swartberg to Uitenhage, E Cape. **Habitat:** Hillsides, gullies, mountains. **Flight period:** Single-brooded, Sept–Dec, peak Oct–Nov. **Larval food:** Probably *Merxmuellera* spp.

4 Dickson's Sylph   *Tsitana dicksoni*

Wingspan: ♂ 35–37 mm ♀ 40–42 mm. **Identification: 4A** ♂ upper side, **4B** ♂ underside. Similar flight pattern, habits to Tulbagh Sylph (above). Has *ochreous-brown hind wing underside with little white scaling*. Upper side *darker*. Sexes similar, ♀ with wings more rounded, abdomen stouter than ♂. **Distribution:** Rare; protected in the W Cape. Steep, high mountainsides with mix of grass and fynbos shrubs, W Cape above Franschhoek Pass and Klein Drakenstein mountains; also Garcia's and Robinson passes, and probably at inaccessible spots in the mountains in between. **Habitat:** Hillsides, mountains. **Flight period:** Single-brooded, Nov–Dec. **Larval food:** Probably *Pseudopentameris macrantha*.

1A

1B

2A

2B

3B

3A

4A

4B

Genus *Astictopterus*   Sylphs

WORLD 8 SPP., AFRICA 7, SOUTH AFRICA 1

Small dull brown Skippers with broad wings. Flight slow, hopping in marshy grassy areas. Sexes similar. Early stages unrecorded. Food plant Poaceae.

1 Modest Sylph   *Astictopterus inornatus*

Wingspan: ♂ 24–29 mm ♀ 27–29 mm. **Identification: 1A** ♂ upper side, **1B** ♂ underside. Unlike Dismal Sylph (p. 386), underside rust-brown, postdiscal series of small cream spots. Sexes similar, ♀ paler than ♂, abdomen stouter. ♂ territorial among Tamboekie grass, perches on prominent stem, patrols with slow, zigzagging flight, darts after intruders. ♀ seen less frequently. **Distribution:** Afromontane Forest from E Cape (Somerset East and Amatolas), e along Drakensberg foothills to KwaZulu-Natal Midlands, coastal Lowland Forest between Port St Johns, Durban and Tugela Mouth, and coastal rivers. **Habitat:** Forest edges, wetlands. **Flight period:** Several broods, Sept–Apr; peak Jan. **Larval food:** *Imperata cylindrica*.

Subfamily HESPERIINAE

Distiguished by wing veins; forewing vein M$_2$ curving basally to M$_3$, well marked in some genera, indistinct in others. Resting posture with hind wings horizontal, forewings half-open.

Genus *Kedestes*   Rangers

AFRICA 24 SPP., SOUTH AFRICA 11

Small to medium-sized, wings narrow. Upper side brown, with paler spots. Species' distinct underside patterns range from golden yellow to brown, spotted and streaked with darker colours. Flight very fast, low over grassy areas. Single egg on Poaceae; white to cream, domed. Larva lives in shelter made from silk-bound grass leaves; green, elongated, tail segment flattened. Headshield ornate, yellow to cream, dark spots or lines. Elongated dark brown pupa in larval shelter.

2 Fulvous Ranger or Harlequin Skipper   *Kedestes mohozutza*

Wingspan: ♂ 27–31 mm ♀ 33–42 mm. **Identification: 2A** ♂ upper side, **2B** ♂ underside. Forewing has *no white spots* in areas M$_1$ and M$_2$. ♀ hind wing upper side has more yellow streaks than ♂, bigger yellow-ochre submarginal spots on both wings. Variegated underside; both wings have *unbroken black marginal line*; orange hind wing has *single* black-edged cream-white discal band. Found in wet hillside vleis; ♂ territorial around patches of short grass, perching on tall grass stems. ♀ seldom seen. Fond of flowers, particularly white Scabious. **Distribution:** Widespread. Moist montane Grassland, often near Afromontane Forest, southern and eastern slopes of Drakensberg foothills from E Cape (Somerset East and Amatolas, coast near Port St Johns), inland through KwaZulu-Natal Midlands and Mpumalanga, s Gauteng, adjoining area of e NW Province. **Habitat:** Hillsides, forest edges, wetlands. **Flight period:** Single-brooded, Nov–Mar, depending on altitude and latitude; peaks Nov–Dec. **Larval food:** No data.

3 Shaka's Ranger or Shaka's Skipper   *Kedestes chaca*

Wingspan: ♂ 36–38 mm ♀ 38–44 mm. **Identification: 3A** ♀ upper side, **3B** ♀ underside. Larger than Fulvous Ranger (above). Sexes dimorphic. ♀ upper side forewing discal spots *cream* (white in ♂); ♀ has *full series* of orange-buff submarginal spots – faint, red-orange, and only on forewing in ♂. Both have *pale spots present* in areas M$_1$ and M$_2$. Underside with *two* cream bands submedian and discal, on orange hind wing, both outlined by rows of elongated black 'dots' separated by cream veins. Marginal black line on both wings broken into dots. ♂ territorial on grassy hill tops or ridges. ♀ further down the slopes, in wet gullies with long grass. Flight not as rapid or sustained as Fulvous Ranger. **Distribution:** Widespread. Moist montane Grassland, often near Afromontane Forest, along southern and eastern slopes of Drakensberg foothills from E Cape (Grahamstown and Amatolas) through Kokstad area into KwaZulu-Natal near Bushman's Nek, in uKhahlamba Drakensberg Park in n KwaZulu-Natal. **Habitat:** Hillsides, forest edges, wetlands, gullies, hill tops. **Flight period:** Single-brooded, Oct–Apr, depending on altitude and latitude; generally peaks Dec–Jan. **Larval food:** No data.

1A

1B

2A

2B

3A

3B

1 Scarce Ranger or Scarce Skipper *Kedestes nerva nerva*

Wingspan: ♂ 27–31 mm ♀ 33–36 mm. **Identification: 1A** ♂ upper side, **1B** ♀ upper side, **1C** ♂ underside. Sexes dimorphic. ♀ upper side forewing discal spots *cream* (white in ♂); ♀ has *full series* of buff submarginal spots – in ♂, faint, red-orange, only on forewing. Both have *pale spots* in areas M_1 and M_2. Resembles small Shaka's Ranger (p. 388), underside ground *yellow, not orange*; submedian hind wing pale band *absent*. White discal underside hind wing band not as elongated, black-edged white spot in cell, two sub-basal black dots in S_c+R_1 and one in 1A+2A. **Distribution:** Scarce, local. Savanna, Grassland and open woodland, from ne KwaZulu-Natal across e Mpumalanga to extreme s Limpopo Province (Waterberg), Gauteng and adjoining areas of e NW Province. **Habitat:** Hill tops, hillsides, gullies. **Flight period:** Double-brooded; weak brood Oct–Nov, stronger brood Feb–Apr. **Larval food:** Unknown.

2 Barber's Ranger *Kedestes barberae*

Wingspan: ♂ 26–33 mm ♀ 29–38 mm. **Identification: 2A** ♂ upper side (*K. b. bonsa*), **2B** ♀ underside (nominate). Dark species with chequered cilia, grey to brown underside has *arrowhead-shaped* glossy white streak in area M_1 of hind wing, forms broken line with elongated submedian white mark of cell. Also white streak in CuA_1 of hind wing underside. Underside colour and extent of streaks varies between subspecies. Sexes similar, ♀ paler, wings more elongated, abdomen stouter. Flight low, circling and zigzagging over grass, settling on vegetation or ground. **Distribution:** Nominate in open Grassland and grassy Savanna from E Cape coast (Port Elizabeth), hills of c E Cape, Lesotho, w KwaZulu-Natal, e Free State, Gauteng, w Mpumalanga, se part of Waterberg (Limpopo Province); *K. b. bonsa* in dry Grassland of nw E Cape and se N Cape; *K. b. bunta* (rare – habitat under threat) in Fynbos on coastal dunes in Cape Peninsula and Cape Flats, near Retreat and Strandfontein, W Cape. **Flight period:** *K. b. bunta* single-brooded, Sept; other subspp. double-brooded, mainly Oct–Nov, weaker summer brood, Feb–Apr. **Larval food:** *Imperata cylindrica*.

3 Sarah's Ranger *Kedestes sarahae*

Wingspan: ♂ 31–34 mm ♀ 54–63 mm. **Identification: 3A** ♂ upper side, **3B** ♂ underside. Similar to Barber's Ranger (above), but cilia *grey, not black and white* chequered, wings *more rounded*. Underside hind wing *flat grey-brown (no grey mottling)*, crossed by white streaks *without the arrowhead shape* to the streak in M_1. Sexes similar, ♀ much larger, largest South African *Kedestes*, more elongated wings and pale streak in hind wing upper side area M_1. Rapid flight around stands of tall grass on rough mountain slopes, difficult to follow. **Distribution:** Only known from one location, at ca. 1 500 m in Cederberg of W Cape, in patches of *Merxmuellera* grass in montane Fynbos. **Habitat:** Hillsides, mountains. **Flight period:** Only found late Sept. **Larval food:** Probably *Merxmuellera* grasses.

4 Dark Ranger or Dark Skipper *Kedestes niveostriga*

Wingspan: ♂ 31–35 mm ♀ 33–36 mm. **Identification: 4A** ♂ upper side, **4B** ♂ underside. Upper side similar to Wallengren's Ranger (p. 392), underside similar colour to Unique Ranger (p. 392), with *white streak on anal fold*, pale streak along vein M_2 *better developed*, veins *paler*. Sexes similar, ♀ paler, with more elongated but rounded wings. ♂ occupies territories in clumps of Tamboekie grass. Numbers never large. Flight fast and jerky, difficult to approach or follow. ♀ usually near clumps of grass. Both sexes attracted to flowers. 2 subspp., geographically distinct. **Distribution:** Nominate in Grassland at edges of Afromontane Forest and streams on southern and eastern slopes of E Cape mountain foothills from Somerset East along Amatolas to coastal forests, Port St Johns to Port Edward, se Lesotho, and KwaZulu-Natal Midlands to Greytown and Eshowe; *K. n. schloszi* in thick stands of grass in fynbos at foot of Riviersonderend Mountains in W Cape near Greyton. **Habitat:** Forest edges, wetlands. **Flight period:** Nominate double-brooded, Sept–Nov and Feb–Apr, with some overlap; *K. n. schloszi* Dec–Apr. **Larval food:** *Imperata cylindrica* and *Pennisetum macrourum*.

1A

1B

1C

2A

2B

3A

3B

4A

4B

1 Unique Ranger   *Kedestes lenis*

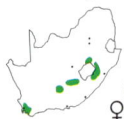

Wingspan: ♂ 26–31 mm ♀ 29–35 mm. **Identification: 1A** ♂ upper side, **1B** ♀ upper side, **1C** ♀ underside (*K. l. alba*). Upper side *darker* than Dark Ranger (p. 390), forewing cell, discal and subapical spots *reduced or absent*. Underside hind wing *darker*, same white streak in anal fold but pale streak along vein M$_2$ *less developed*. Sexes similar, ♀ larger and paler than ♂, rounder, more elongated wings, abdomen stouter, forewing upper side spots *better developed*. ♂ does not hill-top, stays close to food plants, perching and patrolling, chasing away any other ♂. Flight fast and skipping. ♀ slower, among food plants, seldom on flowers. 2 subspp., geographically distinct. **Distribution:** Nominate in grassy areas in Fynbos, at Strandfontein east of Muizenberg, W Cape; *K. l. alba* in montane Grassland on mountains in n E Cape, Free State (at ca. 1 800 m, Golden Gate Highlands NP), and along south-eastern foothills of KwaZulu-Natal Drakensberg. **Habitat:** Hillsides, mountains, wetlands, gullies. **Flight period:** Single-brooded, Oct–Mar; nominate peaks spring, *K. l. alba* midsummer. **Larval food:** *Imperata cylindrica.*

2 Wallengren's Ranger or Skipper   *Kedestes wallengrenii wallengrenii*

Wingspan: ♂ 27–31 mm ♀ 30–35 mm. **Identification: 2A** ♂ upper side, **2B** ♂ underside. Upper side similar to Dark Ranger (p. 390), but white spot at end of cell *double, not single*. Underside with *prominent white streak along vein M$_2$*, sometimes also fainter streak along CuA$_2$. ♂ not on hill tops, territorial; perches and patrols area near food plant. Sexes similar, ♀ paler than ♂, rounder, more elongated wings, abdomen stouter, forewing upper side spots *more developed*. Very fast flight, wary; if disturbed, disappears, not to be seen for a time. ♀ in same area; more sedentary, searching for oviposition sites. **Distribution:** Grassland and wooded Savanna from KwaZulu-Natal Drakensberg foothills near Kokstad, Midlands and thorn belt to hills of c Mpumalanga, e Limpopo Province and s Gauteng. **Habitat:** Forest edges, wetlands. **Flight period:** Double-brooded; spring brood Aug–Nov, summer Feb–Apr, sometimes overlapping. **Larval food:** Probably *Imperata cylindrica.*

3 Chequered Ranger or Chequered Skipper   *Kedestes lepenula*

Wingspan: ♂ 27–29 mm ♀ 30–33 mm. **Identification: 3A** ♀ upper side, **3B** ♀ underside. Sexes similar, ♀ with wings rounder, abdomen stouter than ♂. Upper side similar to Macomo Ranger (below), *paler brown ground colour, larger, pure orange markings, fused into bands*. Underside *yellow*, with *no hind wing spots*. ♂ hill-tops on koppies and ridges at midday, perching on prominent stones, rocks or vegetation, fast and whirling flight, returning to the same perch. ♀ sedentary, seldom seen, usually seeking oviposition sites and feeding on flowers. **Distribution:** Dry Grassland and Savanna from central E Cape (Uitenhage), through w Free State, e NW Province, into drier western reaches of Limpopo Province, as far east as Polokwane. **Habitat:** Hill tops, hillsides. **Flight period:** Several broods; scarce Sept, more common through summer, peak Feb–Apr. **Larval food:** *Imperata cylindrica.*

4 Macomo Ranger   *Kedestes macomo*

Wingspan: ♂ 28–32 mm ♀ 33–35 mm. **Identification: 4A** ♂ upper side, **4B** underside (pair *in copula*, ♀ at top). Sexes similar, ♀ with wings rounder, abdomen stouter than ♂. Separable from Chequered Ranger (above) by having upper side spots *square, orange-yellow, separated, not fused into bands*. Underside yellow with *small black spots* on hind wing, forewing veins black at margin. ♂ does not hill-top, territorial in long grass in shade of trees. ♀ more sedentary, seldom seen, at random in the veld, seeking oviposition sites and feeding on flowers. **Distribution:** Grassy bush, Lowland Forest and Savanna from E Cape (Addo, Port Elizabeth area) to Swaziland, and along coast and hinterland into KwaZulu-Natal, Mpumalanga, nw Gauteng, and e Limpopo Province. **Habitat:** Flatlands, hillsides, forest edges. **Flight period:** Continuous broods; scarce in winter, peaks late summer and autumn. **Larval food:** *Imperata cylindrica.*

1A

1B

1C

2A

2B

3A

4A

3B

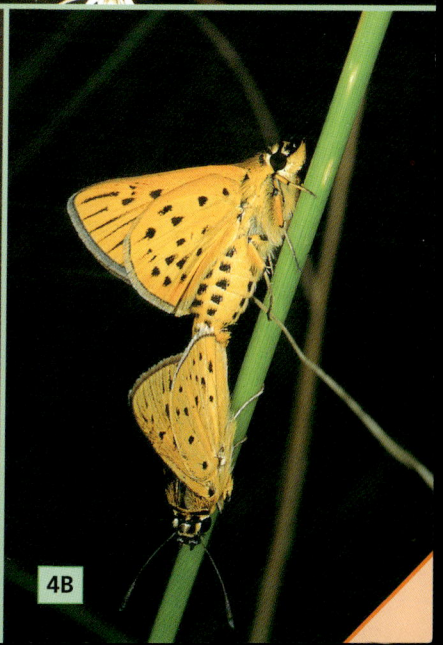

4B

1 Pale Ranger *Kedestes callicles*

Wingspan: ♂ 27–29 mm ♀ 31–33 mm. **Identification: 1A** ♂ upper side, **1B** ♀ underside. Sexes similar, ♀ paler, wings rounder, abdomen stouter than ♂. Upper side resembles Macomo Ranger (p. 392), but spots rounded and *yellow-buff*, not square and orange-yellow. Underside striking; *black-ringed cream spots* on golden-yellow ground, distal parts of veins fine black lines. Flight skipping, in shade of trees. ♂ territorial, often around edges of thick patches of bush; ♀ seldom encountered. **Distribution:** Thick bush, Lowland Forest and Savanna from Swaziland to KwaZulu-Natal (Durban and along coast to Maputaland), to e and n Mpumalanga, extreme n Gauteng and across Limpopo Province to Ellisras and Thabazimbi in west. **Habitat:** Flatlands, hillsides, forest edges. **Flight period:** Single extended brood, Nov–Apr, peaks Feb–Mar. **Larval food:** No data.

Genus *Acada*   Oranges or Skippers   AFRICA 2 SPP., SOUTH AFRICA 1

Adults with narrow wings resembling *Kedestes*. Low, skipping flight in forest understorey, perching often on vegetation. Food plant Fabaceae. Life history unknown.

2 Axehead Orange or Axehead Skipper *Acada biseriata*

Wingspan: ♂ 25–30 mm ♀ 25–35 mm. **Identification: 2A** ♂ upper side, **2B** ♀ underside. Sexes similar, ♀ larger, wings more rounded. Upper side with orange markings on dark brown ground as Morant's Orange (below), but forewing upper side orange cell spot *merged with postdiscal orange band*. Underside orange-yellow; forewing has *black spot at end of cell*, hind wing has *two distinct rows of black marginal spots*. **Distribution:** Only found in shady areas of small patches of *Brachystegia* (miombo) woodland at eastern end of Soutpansberg, Limpopo Province, where recently discovered. Common in forested areas of Zimbabwe and Mozambique. **Habitat:** Forest edges, hillsides, wetlands. **Flight period:** Year-round, peak late summer/autumn in Zimbabwe and Mozambique, so far only in Dec in South Africa. **Larval food:** *Brachystegia spiciformis*.

Genus *Parosmodes*   Oranges or Skippers   MONOTYPIC

Adults with narrow wings resembling *Kedestes*. Flight fast, low. Single flattened, domed egg with ribs, laid on Combretaceae, Euphorbiaceae and Myrtaceae. Larva long and flattened dorsally, with large and velvety headshield. Lives in shelters made from leaves joined with silk. Pupa short, blunt ended, brown and cream.

3 Morant's Orange or Morant's Skipper *Parosmodes morantii*

Wingspan: ♂ 28–31 mm ♀ 33–35 mm. **Identification: 3A** ♂ upper side, **3B** ♂ underside. Sexes similar, ♀ with more elongated, rounded wings. Upper side, as in Axehead Orange (above); orange markings on dark brown ground, but forewing cell spot separated from other orange markings. Hind wing *discal orange patch situated more basally*. Underside orange-yellow, with *no* black spot at end of cell; hind wing spots *sparse, single* submarginal row. Flight fast and skipping along forest edges and prominent hill tops where ♂ establishes territory. ♀ less often seen, sedentary, near food plants. Rarely on flowers. **Distribution:** Wooded Savanna and Lowland Forest from Swaziland, KwaZulu-Natal (Port Edward and along coast to Maputaland), across Mpumalanga, n Gauteng, and c Limpopo Province. **Habitat:** Forest edges, hill tops. **Flight period:** Double-brooded; spring brood early Jul to early Oct, stronger summer brood Dec–May, peak Feb–Mar (some overlap midsummer). **Larval food:** *Terminalia* spp., *Quisqualis* spp., *Combretum molle*, *Bridelia micrantha* and *Syzygium cordatum*.

1A

1B

2A

2B

3A

3B

Genus *Acleros* Darts

AFRICA 8 SPP., SOUTH AFRICA 1

Small Skippers with finely webbed brown and cream underside and black upper side. Body dark, with white tip to abdomen. Shade-loving; flight skipping and hopping about forest floor, can put on speed if disturbed. Single egg laid on Anacardiaceae and Malpighiaceae; brown-red, domed with finely sculpted ribs. Larva broad in middle segments, tapering at ends with green, leaf-shaped markings on pale background. Headshield ornate. Pupa also with green leaf markings; short and blunt, formed in larval shelter of leaves joined with silk threads.

1 Macken's Dart *Acleros mackenii*

Wingspan: ♂ 27–32 mm ♀ 29–33 mm. **Identification: 1A** ♀ upper side, **1B** mating pair underside (♀ to R) (nominate). ♂ upper side plain, ♀ has white spots. Seasonally dimorphic; WSF f. *denia* darker than nominate DSF, larger ♀ forewing upper side spots; wider white hind wing upper side margin. ♂ territorial along forest edges and paths, skipping around, settling for long periods on low vegetation. If disturbed, usually returns to original perch. ♀ seen less frequently. Both sexes visit flowers, and also feed on bird droppings; seldom observed feeding. **Distribution:** Thick Afromontane Forest and coastal Lowland Forest from E Cape (Port St Johns) to Swaziland, KwaZulu-Natal coast and Midlands forest belt to Maputaland, Mpumalanga and Limpopo Province; heavier riverine bush along Drakensberg, Wolkberg and Soutpansberg foothills. **Habitat:** Forest edges, wetlands, gullies. **Flight period:** Year-round, more common in late summer, autumn and winter than in hotter midsummer months. **Larval food:** *Rhus corarius* and *Acridocarpus smeathmanni*.

Genus *Andronymus* Darts

AFRICA 10 SPP., SOUTH AFRICA 2

Medium to large Skippers, with narrow brown wings carrying creamy white markings, and large hyaline spots on both wings, which distinguish this genus from all other hesperiids. Flight very fast. Found in woodland and forest. Domed creamy-white egg laid on Caesalpiniodeae and Sapindaceae. Larva elongated with patterned, coloured head. Pupa green to brown, elongated to the rear with rounded head; formed in larval shelter of silk-bound leaves. Migratory.

2 Common Dart or Nomad Dart *Andronymus neander neander*

Wingspan: ♂ 38–46 mm ♀ 42–48 mm. **Identification: 2A** ♂ upper side, **2B** ♂ underside. Lacks white hind wing underside markings found in very similar White Dart (below). Sexes similar, ♀ paler than ♂, wings more elongated, abdomen stouter. Flight fast, bouncing, 1–2 m above the ground. Fond of flowers but shy and wary. **Distribution:** Savanna, and Lowland and Riverine Forest. Resident in extreme ne Limpopo Province, at eastern end of the Soutpansberg in Levubu, Thohoyandou and Pafuri area. Population replenished by migrants from Zimbabwe, which may be found as far as Mpumalanga, Gauteng and KwaZulu-Natal. **Habitat:** Forest edges, wetlands, flatlands, gullies. **Flight period:** In South Africa, Sept–Apr; continuous broods year-round further north **Larval food:** Possibly *Brachystegia spiciformis*.

3 White Dart *Andronymus caesar philander*

Wingspan: 38–44 mm. **Identification: 3A** ♂ upper side, **3B** ♂ underside. Distinguished from Common Dart (above) by having *extensive white discal and basal hind wing underside patches*. Sexes similar, ♀ paler than ♂, wings more elongated, abdomen stouter. Usually seen in undergrowth. Fairly slow, skipping flight, rapid wing-beats, settling with wings erect on low flowers and vegetation. If disturbed will fly away quickly. **Distribution:** Savanna and Riverine Forest. Marginal species recorded from extreme north-eastern Kruger National Park and Waterpoort (Soutpansberg), Limpopo Province; single record from Blyderivierspoort (Mpumalanga). **Habitat:** Forest edges, flatlands. **Flight period:** Year-round; in South Africa, mainly Nov–Apr. **Larval food:** *Deinbollia* spp., *Blighia unijugata*.

1A

1B

2A

2B

3A

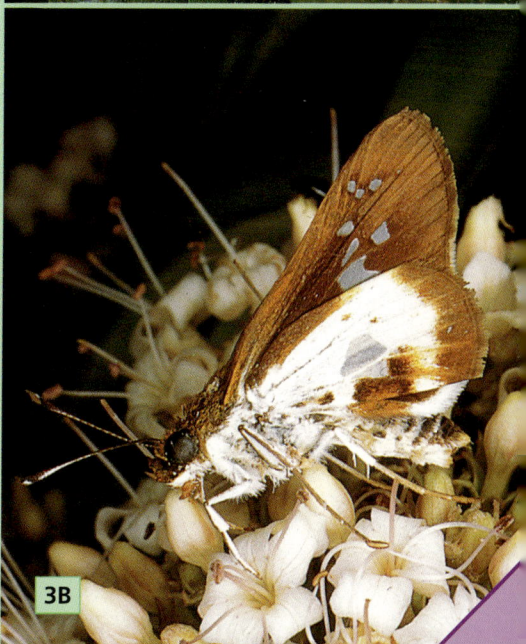

3B

Genus *Moltena*   Banana-tree Night-fighter   MONOTYPIC

Very large, robust-bodied plain brown Skipper. Crepuscular; if seen in daylight hours only in overcast weather, attracted to lights. Egg laid singly on Strelitziaceae; yellow-green, domed, with finely sculpted ribs. Larva fat, green and orange, internal organs visible through transparent skin; ornate head. Shelters in folded-over corner of leaf, anchored with silken threads. Pupa brown, thickened at head, not elongated; formed in folded leaf.

1   Strelitzia Night-fighter or Banana-tree Night-fighter   *Moltena fiara*

Wingspan: ♂ 54–57 mm ♀ 58–64 mm. **Identification: 1A** ♂ upper side, **1B** ♂ underside. White antennae conspicuous as it flies at dusk. ♂ territorial around food plant at forest edges, chasing away intruders. Sexes similar, ♀ wings more rounded, abdomen stouter. Flight rapid and noisy, wings buzzing like a Hawk Moth (Sphingidae), with which it is sometimes confused. ♂ and ♀ fly together. **Distribution:** Coastal Lowland and Riverine Forest from E Cape (Port Alfred) along KwaZulu-Natal coast to Maputaland and further north to Maputo, Mozambique. **Habitat:** Forest edges, parks and gardens, coast. **Flight period:** Double-brooded, Aug–Oct and Feb–Apr. **Larval food:** *Strelitzia nicolae.*

Genus *Zophopetes*   Palm-tree Night-fighter   MONOTYPIC

Large, dull brown Skipper, with hyaline spots on forewing. Single, domed, white-brown egg, laid on Arecaceae. Larva elongated, flattened dorsally, green with darker dorsal stripe, head brown lined with black. In shelter formed from leaves held together with silk. Pupa brown, thickened at head, abdomen more elongated than *Moltena*; formed in larval shelter.

2   Palm-tree Night-fighter   *Zophopetes dysmephila*

Wingspan: ♂ 40–49 mm ♀ 45–52 mm. **Identification: 2A** ♂ upper side, **2B** ♀ upper side, **2C** ♀ underside. *Antennae only white at club*; forewing with *three discal hyaline spots*. Sexes similar, ♀ with wings rounder, underside hind wing with *white streak* along length of vein M_1, *lacking* in ♂. ♂ territorial near food plants, fast buzzing flight at dusk or in dull cloudy weather. ♀ seen less frequently. **Distribution:** Coastal Lowland and Riverine Forest from E Cape (Port Elizabeth) to Swaziland, KwaZulu-Natal (along coast to Maputaland), and in lowveld savanna Mpumalanga and Limpopo Province. Migrant; has also penetrated areas such as Cape Town, where food plant is grown as a park and garden subject. **Habitat:** Forest edges, coast, parks and gardens. **Flight period:** Year-round, peak Nov–May. **Larval food:** *Phoenix reclinata, P. dactylifera, P. canariensis, Cocos* sp., *Borassus* sp., *Raphia* sp., *Chrysalidocarpus lutescens.*

Genus *Artitropa*   Night-fighters   AFRICA 9 SPP., SOUTH AFRICA 1

Large, ornately marked; upper side forewing has white or hyaline spots; hind wing orange or yellow marks. Single egg on Dracaenaceae; grey-white, becoming pink-brown; domed. Pale green, elongated larva; head yellow with black spots. Larva cuts a slot in the leaf, folds over a section anchored with silken threads to form shelter. Pupa cream, covered with white powder; proboscis tube protrudes beyond tip of abdomen. Formed in larval shelter.

3   Bush Night-fighter   *Artitropa erinnys erinnys*

Wingspan: ♂ 53–57 mm ♀ 59–63 mm. **Identification: 3A** ♂ upper side, **3B** ♀ underside. Large crepuscular Skipper, brightly and attractively marked. Upper side forewing *chocolate brown, with series of hyaline median and apical spots*. Hind wing brown-black, with thin orange *discal band*. Underside unmistakable. Sexes alike, ♀ has longer, more rounded wings. ♂ territorial near food plants, ♀ flight random. **Distribution:** Coastal Lowland and Riverine Forest from E Cape (East London), KwaZulu-Natal coast to Maputaland, spreading to Riverine Forest and lower Afromontane Forest along eastern Drakensberg and Wolkberg foothills, to Soutpansberg, Limpopo Province. **Habitat:** Forest edges, coast, parks and gardens. **Flight period:** Year-round; scarce May–Aug. **Larval food:** *Dracaena hookeriana, D. afromontana, D. angustifolia, D. fragrans* and *D. steudneri.*

1A

1B

2A

2B

2C

3A

3B

Genus *Fresna*   Acraea Hoppers   AFRICA 5 SPP., SOUTH AFRICA 1

Medium-sized Skippers, upper side brown with white spots resembling *Platylesches*; underside markings *Acraea*-like. Flight very fast, elusive in woodland. Egg domed, pale rose pink, laid singly on Caesalpinioideae. Young larva red with black head, final instar white with black marks and ornate, black-spotted yellow head. Brown, blunt-ended pupa formed in larval shelter of leaves held together with silk threads.

1 Variegated Acraea Hopper   *Fresna nyassae*

Wingspan: ♂ 34–38 mm ♀ 39–42 mm. **Identification: 1A** ♂ upper side, **1B** ♂ underside, **1C** ♀ underside. Sexes alike, larger ♀ has longer wings. Upper side similar to *Platylesches* hoppers; brown, spotted white, but forewing *lacks subapical spots along the costa*. Underside forewing marked as upper side, but with brown-pink apex veined in black; hind wing yellow to dark gold or rust-pink, carrying black discal and submarginal spots. ♂ does not hill-top; establishes territories along edges of thick bush and forest, perching high on a prominent twig or leaf, chasing away other butterflies. Fond of flowers. Flight fairly slow, skipping, hopping. Shy and wary; if disturbed, flies off rapidly, seldom returning. **Model:** Resembles a generic *Acraea* (p. 80); hind wing underside carries spots in a generally similar pattern to these, on a similar ground colour. **Distribution:** Lowland Forest, Savanna. Scarce and seldom seen. Only in Maputaland area of KwaZulu-Natal, mostly near Tembe Elephant Park, and Mpaphuli NR, Limpopo Province. More widespread further north in Africa. **Habitat:** Forest edges, flatlands. **Flight period:** Year-round, mainly late summer and autumn in South Africa. **Larval food:** Unknown in South Africa; *Julbernardia globiflora* in Zimbabwe.

Genus *Platylesches*   Hoppers   AFRICA 20 SPP., SOUTH AFRICA 8

Small- to medium-sized, robust-bodied Skippers, wings short, narrow, pointed. Fast, erratic, buzzing flight in Savanna, woodland and forest. ♂ highly territorial. Egg unrecorded. Larva on Chrysobalanaceae in shelters made from leaves stitched together, or cut and folded. Stitching pattern distinct to each species. Larva green or brown to red, dark head ornately marked with white or cream. Brown pupa formed in larval shelter, in loose cocoon.

2 White-tail Hopper   *Platylesches galesa*

Wingspan: ♂ 33–37 mm ♀ 36–40 mm. **Identification: 2A** ♂ upper side, **2B** undersides, ♂ on R, ♀ on L. ♂ white abdomen tip *always visible in flight, unique to this species* (usually absent in ♀). Underside hind wing has *pattern of whitish spots* in a discal series on a dark brown ground. ♀ can be identified with wings closed because of white irroration covering hind wing discal area. ♀ wings slightly longer, more rounded than ♂, abdomen stouter. Frequents forest clearings, streams and paths, ♂ perching 2–3 m above ground on prominent leaves or twigs. Several may be seen darting around, chasing one another. **Distribution:** Lowland and Riverine Forest along eastern foothills of Drakensberg in Mpumalanga (Mariepskop north to Woodbush below Wolkberg, eastern Soutpansberg), and north into Zimbabwe. **Habitat:** Forest edges, flatlands, hillsides. **Flight period:** Year-round, mainly late summer and autumn in South Africa. **Larval food:** *Parinari curatellifolia*.

3 Peppered Hopper   *Platylesches ayresii*

Wingspan: ♂ 27–32 mm ♀ 35–38 mm. **Identification: 3A** ♂ upper side, **3B** ♂ underside. Underside hind wing *evenly striated*. Sexes similar, ♀ with stouter abdomen. ♂♂ hill-top, perching on rocks and low vegetation, circling around territory, chasing one another at high speed. Difficult to approach; flees rapidly if disturbed, returning soon to same perch. ♀ more sedentary, found near food plant or on flowers. **Distribution:** Grassy hills and ridges in Grassland and Savanna of Swaziland and extreme n KwaZulu-Natal, through n NW Province, all of Gauteng, and most of Mpumalanga. **Habitat:** Hill tops, hillsides. **Flight period:** Continuous broods Jul–Apr, peaks Sept and Jan. **Larval food:** *Parinari capensis*.

1A

1B

1C

2A

2B

3A

3B

1 Flower-girl Hopper *Platylesches neba*
Wingspan: ♂ 29–34 mm ♀ 31–35 mm. **Identification: 1A** ♀ upper side, **1B** ♀ underside. Similar to Honey Hopper (below) with which it often flies. Forewing underside apical area has *pale lilac scaling*, hind wing underside *suffused with pale colouring*. Frequents grassy woodland clearings and edges where food plant grows. ♂ does not hill-top; territories at edge of bush; perches on low shrubs or grass stems near the food plant, chasing intruders. ♀ sedentary, found around food plant. Both sexes found on flowers and wet mud. **Distribution:** Lowland Forest and wooded Savanna from Swaziland and KwaZulu-Natal (Maputaland), into grassy Savanna of Gauteng, and foothills of Wolkberg, Drakensberg and Soutpansberg in Mpumalanga and Limpopo Province. **Habitat:** Hillsides, flatlands, forest edges. **Flight period:** Year-round, peaks Sept–Oct and Feb–Apr. **Larval food:** *Parinari capensis.*

2 Hilltop Hopper *Platylesches dolomitica*
Wingspan: ♂ 32–35 mm ♀ 33–37 mm. **Identification: 2A** ♂ upper side, **2B** ♂ underside. Underside hind wing similar to Peppered Hopper (p. 400), but striations *more widely spaced*, upper side resembles Honey Hopper (below), with upper side forewing spots *larger* than Peppered Hopper. Sexes similar, ♀ slightly larger, wings longer, more rounded, abdomen stouter than ♂. ♂ territorial on low ridges and koppies, perching on rocks or low vegetation. Fastest *Platylesches*, very wary and shy. ♀ also fast-flying, on flowers close to the ♂♂. Flies with Peppered Hopper, but scarcer. Unlike latter, when disturbed seldom returns. **Distribution:** Probably overlooked; colonies recorded only on dolomite ridges near Steelpoort, Mpumalanga, Horn's Nek near Pretoria, and Carletonville, Gauteng; in Savanna, Grassland areas. **Habitat:** Hill tops, rocky ledges. **Flight period:** Single-brooded, Aug–Sept. **Larval food:** Probably *Parinari capensis.*

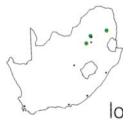

3 Robust Hopper *Platylesches robustus robustus*
Wingspan: ♂ 34–42 mm ♀ 36–44 mm. **Identification: 3A & 3B** ♂ upper side, **3C** ♀ underside. *Strong contrast* between upper side *yellow* markings on hind wing, and *whitish* or hyaline spots on forewing. Underside similar to smaller Flower-girl Hopper (above), but hind wing has *strong violaceous sheen*. ♂ territorial on hill tops or forest edges, from early in the day to late afternoon; also frequents stands of Tamboekie grass at forest edges. ♀ found in same areas, but more sedentary. **Distribution:** Uncommon. Thickly wooded Savanna and Riverine Forest from Swaziland to KwaZulu-Natal (Maputaland), lowveld of Mpumalanga and Limpopo Province to Limpopo R, and north to Maputo, Mozambique. **Habitat:** Forest edges, hill tops. **Flight period:** Double-brooded, Aug–Oct and Mar–Apr; occasionally midsummer. **Larval food:** Probably *Parinari curatellifolia.*

4 Honey Hopper *Platylesches moritili*
Wingspan: ♂ 31–33 mm ♀ 33–35 mm. **Identification: 4A** ♂ upper side, **4B** ♂ underside. Resembles Flower-girl Hopper (above), underside ground colour *darker*, with *violet sheen; no pale scaling* on forewing underside apical area. Flight not terribly fast, hopping and skipping, but rapid if molested. ♂ does not hill-top, territories on edges of bush and grassy clearings, perching on grass tops or low shrubs. ♀ closer to food plants. Both sexes may congregate on flowers, particularly *Deinbollia oblongifolia*. ♂ also often seen on wet mud. **Distribution:** Most common and most widespread South African *Platylesches*. Swaziland and Lowland and Riverine Forest in KwaZulu-Natal, north along coast and hinterland to Maputaland, from Mpumalanga to n Gauteng, wooded Savanna of c Limpopo Province and Lowland Forest to Pafuri. **Habitat:** Forest edges, flatlands, hillsides. **Flight period:** Year-round, more common Mar–May and Oct–Dec. **Larval food:** *Parinari curatellifolia.*

1A

1B

2A

2B

3A

3B

3C

4A

4B

1 Small Hopper *Platylesches tina*

Wingspan: ♂ 25–27 mm ♀ 27–29 mm. **Identification: 1A** ♂ upper side, **1B** ♂ underside. Forewing *markedly pointed*, upper side *dark*, with *restricted hyaline spots*. Underside like a small Honey Hopper (p. 402). ♀ slightly more robust than ♂. Rarely seen, probably due to small size and high-flying behaviour. ♂ territorial around trees, whirling in aerial 'combat' with other Skippers, resembling small flies on the wing. Also on flowering canopy trees, and in Riverine Forest on wet mud and bird droppings. ♀ on flowers, usually low-growing or coppiced specimens of the food plant. **Distribution:** Dense Riverine Forest at eastern end of Soutpansberg, and vicinity of Thohoyandou hospital, Limpopo Province. One specimen from near Hazyview, Mpumalanga. **Habitat:** Forest edges, gullies, flatlands, hillsides. **Flight period:** Double-brooded, Sept–Oct and Jan–Apr. **Larval food:** *Parinari curatellifolia*.

2 Banded Hopper *Platylesches picanini*

Wingspan: ♂ 30–37 mm ♀ 38–40 mm. **Identification: 2A** ♂ upper side, **2B** ♂ underside, **2C** ♀ upper side. Hind wing underside has single *broad, well-defined white or cream* median band. Sexes similar, ♀ with wings more elongated. ♂ territorial in canopy of tall (over 6 m) trees, perching on prominent twigs. Feeds on flowers, occasionally bird droppings, in early morning and late afternoon at forest edge. Extremely wary, difficult to approach, fleeing into forest canopy at slightest disturbance. ♀ feeds at flowers or seeks food plants all through the day. **Distribution:** Thick Riverine Forest below foothills of Mpumalanga Drakensberg, and Wolkberg and Soutpansberg of Limpopo Province. **Habitat:** Forest edges, gullies, hillsides. **Flight period:** Double-brooded, Jan–May and Jun–Aug. **Larval food:** *Parinari curatellifolia*.

Genus *Zenonia* Orange-spotted Hopper   MONOTYPIC

Fast-flying inhabitant of mist forests, similar to *Kedestes* with orange-spotted brown wings. Early stages not recorded.

3 Orange-spotted Hopper or Orange-spotted Skipper *Zenonia zeno*

Wingspan: ♂ 34–39 mm ♀ 36–41 mm. **Identification: 3A** ♂ upper side, **3B** ♂ underside. Upper side brightly marked; orange basal spots and bands of postdiscal spots on black-brown ground. Underside yellow marks mirror upper side orange, on mottled yellow–brown ground. ♂ territorial at edge of forest, along roads, paths or streams, chasing intruding males. Flight rapid, but settles often on low shrubs, grass stems or rocks; fairly easy to approach. ♀ more sedentary, around flowers. **Distribution:** Afromontane Forest from E Cape (Mbashe River) to KwaZulu-Natal Midlands (and coastal hinterland in wetter places and riverine bush) into escarpment foothills of Swaziland, Mpumalanga and Limpopo Province. **Habitat:** Forest edges, gullies. **Flight period:** Year-round, peaks early spring after the rains. **Larval food:** *Zea mays* and Poaceae grasses.

Genus *Pelopidas* Swifts   WORLD 9 SPP., SOUTH AFRICA 2

Medium-sized, dull brown Skippers; forewing narrow, elongated. ♂ has conspicuous diagonal sex brands in discal area of forewing upper side. Found in Savanna and forest edges. ♂ territorial on hill tops, may stay there all daylight hours. From a prominent perch, chases away all other butterflies. ♀ more sedentary. Flight rapid, both sexes fond of flowers and wet mud; can be approached closely when feeding. Egg laid singly on Poaceae; yellow to green-white; flattened, domed. Larva elongated, cream to green, headshield edged with darker colouring. Pupa pale green, elongated, narrow, with long, pointed head spike; formed in larval shelter of grass leaves held together by silk.

1A

1B

2A

2B

2C

3A

3B

1 Black-banded Swift   *Pelopidas mathias*

Wingspan: ♂ 36–38 mm ♀ 38–41 mm. **Identification: 1A** ♂ upper side, **1B** ♂ underside, **1C** ♀ upper side. Upper side ground colour brown, ♂ sex brands *black*. Underside medium brown, suffused with white; *five small white discal spots* on hind wing. ♀ *lacks sex brand*; larger than ♂, wings more elongated, forewing upper side has *hyaline discal spot* in CuA$_2$, *white spot* in CuA$_1$. **Distribution:** Common and widespread in coastal Lowland and Riverine Forest, wooded Savanna and river valleys from E Cape (East London), KwaZulu-Natal, Swaziland to Mpumalanga, Gauteng (absent from highveld); all of Limpopo Province. **Habitat:** Forest edges, gullies, flatlands, coast, hill tops. **Flight period:** Year-round, scarcer in winter. **Larval food:** *Zea mays, Ehrharta erecta, Panicum* spp. and *Andropogon* spp.

2 White-banded Swift   *Pelopidas thrax inconspicua*

Wingspan: ♂ 42–46 mm ♀ 49–51 mm. **Identification: 2A** ♂ upper side, **2B** ♂ underside, **2C** ♀ upper side. ♂ *white* upper side forewing sex brands more prominent than *black* brands of Black-banded Swift (above). ♀ has more elongated wings, *lacks sex brand*; upper side similar to Black-banded Swift but has *hyaline discal spot* in CuA$_2$ of forewing; white spot in CuA$_1$. Underside olive-green with white discal spots as in Black-banded Swift. **Distribution:** Very widespread. Afromontane, Lowland and Riverine Forest, wooded Savanna and Grassland from W Cape (Somerset West) to Swaziland, KwaZulu-Natal, Gauteng, Mpumalanga, Limpopo Province, e NW Province, and further north. **Habitat:** Forest edges, gullies, flatlands, coast, hill tops, parks and gardens. **Flight period:** Year-round, scarcer in winter. **Larval food:** *Zea mays, Imperata cylindrica, Pennisetum clandestinum* and other Poaceae grasses.

Genus *Borbo*   Swifts

WORLD 21 SPP., AFRICA 18, SOUTH AFRICA 9

Small- to medium-sized Skippers, various shades of brown with pale spots on upper side forewing, hind wing underside with species-specific pale markings on brown or grey ground. ♂ lacks forewing upper side sex brands of similar *Pelopidas* spp. Fast, darting flight over forest floor and at forest edges, usually returning to same perch. ♂ establishes territory on hill tops, at edges of forests, clearings or marshes, perching on a low leaf and chasing intruders. ♀ flies with ♂, but flight more random. Egg laid singly on Poaceae; white to pale green, domed, finely ribbed. Larva green, cylindrical, broader towards head; headshield in final instar white with dark margins. Pupa narrow, elongated, green, pointed at both ends.

3 Lesser-horned Swift or Lesser-horned Skipper   *Borbo lugens*

Wingspan: ♂ 30–35 mm ♀ 36–38 mm. **Identification: 3A** ♀ upper side, **3B** ♂ underside. One of only two South African Skippers with all-black upper side and *dark chocolate underside*, appearing black on the wing, with *curved discal row of slightly paler hind wing spots*. ♀ larger and paler, with faint white discal and subapical spots on upper side. Flight slower than other *Borbo* spp., unless disturbed. **Distribution:** Thick coastal Lowland Forest in KwaZulu-Natal, from Durban to Maputaland, further north through Mozambique. **Habitat:** Forest edges, coast. **Flight period:** Year-round, more common Oct–May. **Larval food:** *Ehrharta erecta, Panicum deustum, Stipa* spp., *Setaria megaphylla* and *Pennisetum* spp.

4 Long-horned Swift or Long-horned Skipper   *Borbo fatuellus fatuellus*

Wingspan: ♂ 33–42 mm ♀ 40–43 mm. **Identification: 4A** ♂ upper side, **4B** ♀ underside, **4C** ♀ upper side. Unlike other *Borbo* spp., *lacks white or hyaline spots* in forewing cell on upper side, but has *three* subapical costal spots. Hind wing underside has *white spots* in areas CuA$_1$, M$_3$ and R$_s$. Sexes similar, ♀ has larger paler markings; wings more elongated. DSF f. *cinerea* has pale grey scaling in hind wing underside discal area. **Distribution:** Widespread and common in coastal Lowland Forest and wooded Savanna from E Cape (East London) to Swaziland and along coast to n KwaZulu-Natal, Mpumalanga and Limpopo Province lowveld, and further n. **Habitat:** Forest edges, coast. **Flight period:** Year-round, peaks Nov–Feb; f. *cinerea* peak Jun–Aug. **Larval food:** *Ehrharta erecta* and *Setaria megaphylla*.

1A

1B

1C

2A

2B

2C

3A

3B

4A

4B

4C

1 False Swift   *Borbo fallax*

Wingspan: ♂ 36–43 mm ♀ 41–44 mm. **Identification: 1A** ♂ upper side, **1B** ♂ underside, **1C** ♀ underside. Resembles Long-horned Swift (p. 406), but with *double hyaline spot* at end of forewing cell. Upper side hind wing with many *pale discal spots*. Hind wing underside same colour as Long-horned Swift, but with less regular series of discal spots: usually a spot in R_s and an irregular series in M_1–CuA_1, but sometimes only in M_1 and M_2. ♀ more elongated, rounder wings. **Distribution:** Swaziland, coastal KwaZulu-Natal Lowland and Riverine Forest (from Oribi Gorge to Maputaland), into Savanna of Mpumalanga, n Gauteng and Limpopo Province, to extreme ne NW Province. **Habitat:** Forest edges, flatlands, coast, hill tops, parks and gardens. **Flight period:** Year-round, scarcer in winter. **Larval food:** *Ehrharta erecta, Saccharum* spp. and other Poaceae grasses.

2 Rusty Swift   *Borbo detecta*

Wingspan: ♂ 34–36 mm ♀ 36–38 mm. **Identification: 2A** ♂ upper side, **2B & 2C** ♂ underside. Underside similar to Long-horned Swift (p. 406), variable shade of olive-green. Hind wing spots *usually larger and more elongated*. Upper side forewing has *radiating basal rust-ochre streaks* and hind wing suffusion of same colour. ♀ paler, with markings similar to ♂, but hind wing markings more distinct; wings rounder, more elongated. **Distribution:** Swaziland, and KwaZulu-Natal Lowland and Riverine Forest and Savanna hinterland, from Durban to Greytown, Maputaland and Pongola, into se Mpumalanga (De Kaap area). **Habitat:** Forest edges, flatlands, coast, hill tops. **Flight period:** Year-round, scarcer in winter. **Larval food:** *Ehrharta erecta* and other Poaceae grasses.

3 Marsh Swift   *Borbo micans*

Wingspan: ♂ 32–36 mm ♀ 36–40 mm. **Identification: 3A** ♂ upper side, **3B** ♀ upper side, **3C** ♂ underside. Upper side *golden-brown with yellow-ochre spots*. Underside *golden orange-ochre*. ♀ has *larger, paler, better developed spots* than ♂, forewing discal series *hyaline*. Found in swamps; both sexes on flowers in or close to swamp. ♂ territorial at edges of open patches of water or shorter vegetation. ♀ flight random in the same areas. **Distribution:** Scarce; restricted to KwaZulu-Natal Riverine and Lowland Forest, swampy areas close to Manguzi Forest, Pongola River, and Kosi Bay, Maputaland. More common further north in Africa. **Habitat:** Wetlands. **Flight period:** Probably continuous broods, year-round; most specimens seen autumn and winter. **Larval food:** Probably Poaceae swamp grasses.

4 Ferrous Swift or Ferrous Skipper   *Borbo ferruginea dondo*

Wingspan: ♂ 36–39 mm ♀ 42–45 mm. **Identification: 4A** ♂ upper side, **4B** ♂ underside. ♂ upper side *dark brown*, with faint white forewing discal and subapical spots. ♀ upper side similar, suffused with paler scaling, forewing spots *more developed*. Underside *dark rusty brown*, forewing spots as upper side, small discal series of hind wing spots. Elusive forest canopy dweller, descending at edges to feed at flowers. Shy and wary; if disturbed will disappear and rarely return. **Distribution:** Lowland Forest in KwaZulu-Natal, from Richards Bay to Maputaland and north to s Mozambique. **Habitat:** Forest edges, flatlands. **Flight period:** Probably continuous broods, year-round; most specimens seen Oct–May. **Larval food:** No data.

1A

1B

1C

2A

2B

2C

3A

3B

3C

4A

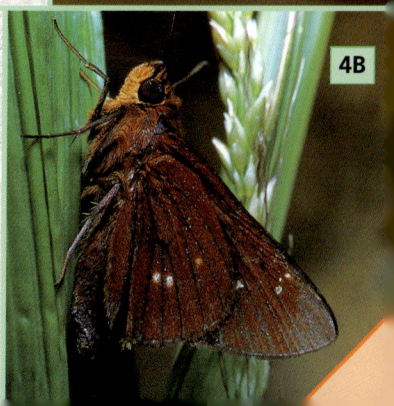

4B

1 Olive-haired Swift *Borbo borbonica borbonica*

Wingspan: ♂ 40–44 mm ♀ 41–45 mm. **Identification: 1A** ♂ upper side, **1B** ♂ underside. Sexes similar, ♀ paler. Forewing *elongated, pointed*. Upper side forewing *pale along inner margin and at base*, similar to Rusty Swift (p. 408), but *pale brown*, not golden ochre. Underside hind wing and forewing apical area ochre-yellow, 3–4 *black-ringed hyaline hind wing spots* in areas R_s–M_2. **Distribution:** Uncommon but widespread. Lowland and Riverine Forest and wooded Savanna, especially near rivers, from E Cape (Port Elizabeth) along coast to KwaZulu-Natal (Maputaland), and Swaziland, Mpumalanga, Limpopo Province, and extreme n Gauteng. Migratory; vagrant to inland E Cape and Free State. **Habitat:** Forest edges, flatlands, wetlands, coast. **Flight period:** Year-round, peaks Mar–May and Aug–Nov. **Larval food:** Grasses including *Ehrharta erecta*, *Oryza* spp., *Pennisetum* spp. and *Zea mays*.

2 Twin Swift *Borbo gemella*

Wingspan: ♂ 35–37 mm ♀ 40–42 mm. **Identification: 2A** ♂ upper side, **2B** ♀ upper side, **3C** ♂ underside. Sexes similar, ♀ paler. Like Olive-haired Swift (above), has rays of upper side paler scaling, but forewing *less pointed*. Underside *grey*, hind wing white spots *plain*, in areas R_s, M_3 and CuA_1. **Distribution:** Lowland and Riverine Forest and wooded Savanna, especially near rivers, from E Cape (Port St Johns) to Swaziland, KwaZulu-Natal (Maputaland), Mpumalanga, and Limpopo Province to Thabazimbi area. **Habitat:** Forest edges, flatlands, coast, hill tops. **Flight period:** Year-round, peak Mar–May. **Larval food:** Grasses including *Triticum sativum* (wheat), *Ehrharta erecta*, *Saccharum* spp. and *Zea mays*.

3 Variable Swift *Borbo holtzi*

Wingspan: 36–41 mm. **Identification: 3A** ♂ upper side, **3B** ♀ upper side, **3C** ♀ underside. Dull, easily overlooked. Upper side dark, forewing subapical spots indistinct, no spot in forewing area CuA_2 in the ♂. ♀ similar to ♂, more developed forewing spots, rounder wings. Both sexes have variable amount of paler scaling on the hind wing and forewing inner margin and base. Hind wing underside flat grey-brown, with up to 5 small black discal spots; on wet season specimens these may have hyaline centres, as in Olive-haired Swift (above). **Distribution:** Uncommon. Lowland Forest, wooded savanna and lowveld savanna from Swaziland to KwaZulu-Natal (Maputaland), Mpumalanga, and Limpopo Province. **Habitat:** Forest edges, flatlands, coast, hill tops. **Flight period:** Year-round, peaks Mar–Jun and Nov–Feb. **Larval food:** No data.

Genus *Parnara* Skippers

WORLD 4 SPP., AFRICA 2, SOUTH AFRICA 1

Small- to medium-sized Skippers, grey to brown upper side with pale or hyaline markings; underside yellow to grey-buff, with faint dark marks. Skipping, hopping flight around edges of woodland or near water (in marshes and along wet river banks). ♂ establishes territory among the water plants, darting off with rapid wing-beats to chase intruders. ♀ flight more random in the same areas. Egg laid singly on Poaceae; a flattened yellow dome. Larva cylindrical, green with headshield in final instar orange-buff with dark markings. Pupa brown, short and stubby; formed in larval shelter of grass leaves held together with silk.

4 Water Watchman or Water Skipper *Parnara monasi*

Wingspan: ♂ 30–33 mm ♀ 32–34 mm. **Identification: 4A** ♂ upper side, **4B** ♂ underside. Similar on the wing to other marsh Skippers, e.g. Marsh Swift (p. 408). Sexes similar, ♀ with larger pale markings. Upper side warm grey-brown, with square hyaline discal series of spots on forewing; hind wing has straight series of whitish discal spots in areas M_2 to CuA_2. Underside *dull ochre*, forewing *blackish basally*, hind wing has dark smudges where upper side has pale spots. **Distribution:** Riverine Forest with grassy marshes from Swaziland to KwaZulu-Natal (Oribi Gorge), along the eastern littoral to Maputaland, and the lowveld of Mpumalanga and Limpopo Province. **Habitat:** Forest edges, wetlands. **Flight period:** Year-round, peak Jan–May. **Larval food:** *Saccharum* spp. and other Poaceae wetland grasses.

1A

1B

2A

2B

2C

3A

3B

3C

4A

4B

Genus *Gegenes*   Hottentot Skippers

AFRICA 4 SPP., SOUTH AFRICA 3

Small Skippers with characteristically short antennae distinguishing them from other small brown Skippers. Brown to yellow-ochre in colour, paler upper side spots in ♀. Flight not very fast or prolonged. ♂ ♂ form territories in open country, perching on prominent plants and darting out to challenge intruders. ♀ found more randomly. Both sexes found on flowers, ♂ on wet mud and fresh dung. Single egg laid on Poaceae; flattened, domed, yellow to pale green. Larva whitish green, with darker green dorsal lines; cream headshield with faint dark marks. Lives in shelter made from grass leaves held together with silken threads. Pupa also green, but with paler longitudinal lines; elongated, pointed at both ends.

1 Dark Hottentot Skipper   *Gegenes pumilio gambica*

Wingspan: ♂ 28–36 mm ♀ 33–37 mm. **Identification: 1A** ♂ upper side, **1B** ♀ upper side, **1C** ♂ underside, **1D** ♀ underside. Both sexes with upper side grey-brown, *lacking pale spots* in cell. ♀ has *whitish subapical spots* at the costa, *small white discal series of spots* on forewing. Underside of both sexes paler grey-brown than upper side, postdiscal series of faint whitish spots on both wings. Flight quite rapid. Usually found singly. ♂ territorial on hill tops as well as in flat country. ♀ flight more random. Fond of dry riverbeds. Both sexes on flowers. **Distribution:** Very widespread. Open woodland, Grassland, and Savanna and dry thorn belt savanna from E Cape coast (Kei River) to Swaziland and along eastern littoral to n KwaZulu-Natal, n Free State, Mpumalanga, Gauteng, Limpopo Province and e NW Province. **Habitat:** Forest edges, wetlands, flatlands, hill tops, gullies. **Flight period:** Year-round in warmer areas, peak Oct–Mar; in cooler areas, only Oct–Mar. **Larval food:** *Pennisetum clandestinum, Ehrharta* spp. and *Cynodon* spp.

2 Common Hottentot Skipper   *Gegenes niso niso*

Wingspan: ♂ 29–33 mm ♀ 29–35 mm. **Identification: 2A** ♂ upper side, **2B** ♀ upper side, **2C** ♂ underside. Sexes dimorphic. ♂ upper side *olive green*, grey-brown at margins. ♀ upper side has discal series of cream spots on *both wings*, on brown ground. Spots shifted distally from the rest of the series in areas M$_1$ and R$_5$. *Yellow-ochre* underside of both sexes conspicuous at rest, when wings closed. **Distribution:** Very common and widespread. From sea level to over 2 000 m, in Fynbos, Nama Karoo, Grassland, woodland and Savanna. From Saldanha area (W Cape), along littoral and seaward side of mountains through W Cape, E Cape, KwaZulu-Natal, Swaziland, n Free State, Mpumalanga, Gauteng, Limpopo Province and e NW Province. **Habitat:** Forest edges, wetlands, flatlands, hill tops, parks and gardens, mountains, coast. **Flight period:** Year-round in warmer areas, peak Oct–Mar; in cooler areas, only Oct–Mar. **Larval food:** *Pennisetum clandestinum, Ehrharta* spp. and *Cynodon* spp.

3 Marsh Hottentot Skipper or Latreille's Skipper   *Gegenes hottentota*

Wingspan: ♂ 31–34 mm ♀ 31–36 mm. **Identification: 3A** ♂ upper side, **3B** ♂ underside. ♂ forewing upper side has *strong black sex brand*, olive-ochreous scaling on basal half of upper side wings *more vivid* than in Common Hottentot Skipper (above). ♂ underside and both surfaces of ♀ identical to Common Hottentot Skipper than in common Hottentot Skipper (above), with which it flies. *Antennae generally slightly shorter.* Always in swamps and wet grassy river valleys. **Distribution:** Vleis at coastal Lowland and Riverine Forest edges, Savanna and Grassland from E Cape (Port St Johns) KwaZulu-Natal (Margate and Maputaland), to Gauteng (Honeydew, Pretoria), Limpopo Province (Modimolle), and Nelspruit, Lydenburg and Makande areas of Mpumalanga. **Habitat:** Forest edges, wetlands, flatlands, gullies. **Flight period:** Year-round in warmer areas, peak Apr–May. **Larval food:** No data, probably Poaceae grasses.

1A

1B

1C

1D

2A

2B

2C

3A

3B

Some frequently asked questions about butterflies

How long do butterflies live?

Many people believe that butterflies are short-lived, lasting just a few days at most. This is a fallacy. Even those that do not feed as adults live for about a week, and some of the more robust species (e.g. in the genus *Charaxes*) can live for several months. Distasteful species with aposematic coloration (and therefore shunned by predators), can live much longer. South American *Heliconius* species have been known to live for as long as a year.

Will a butterfly die if it loses the powder from its wings?

The 'powder' that comes off on your fingers when you handle a butterfly is in fact scales. Losing scales will do no harm nor impede flight. Severe damage to the wings is more serious: if the leading edge of the forewing is broken, a butterfly is no longer able to fly. However, damage to the hind wing seems not to affect the ability to fly agilely.

What is the difference between a butterfly and a moth?

Strictly speaking there is no difference, the distinction being somewhat artificial. Butterflies and moths are all members of the insect order, Lepidoptera. They all have scale-covered wings and bodies, and undergo complete metamorphosis. Currently two superfamilies – Papilionoidea ('true' butterflies) and Hesperioidea (skippers) – are considered to be butterflies, the other superfamilies within the order being moths. Some of the moth superfamilies differ more from one another than they do from butterflies!

To summarise the major 'accepted' differences between butterflies and moths.

- *Butterflies are day flying and moths are night flying.*
  Note: There are as many day-flying moths as there are butterflies, and some butterflies, particularly browns (Satyrinae) and skippers (Hesperiidae), fly at dusk or at night.
- *Moths have hairy bodies that are large in proportion to the wings; butterflies are slender and less hairy*.
  Note: Many skippers have large bodies and are hairy.
- *Moths are dull and brown whereas butterflies are brightly coloured.*
  Note: Most day-flying moths and many night-flying ones are as brightly coloured as the most brilliant butterflies. There are many sombre-coloured butterflies.
- *Moths sit with their wings flat over their backs; butterflies fold theirs vertically.*
  Note: Many skippers, and some nymphs (Nymphalinae) habitually rest with wings held flat. Some moths fold their wings vertically. But, no butterfly sits with its wings curled around its body, as do many moths.
- *Moths' fore- and hind wings are held together in flight by a frenulum; butterflies rely on the large overlap between fore- and hind wings.*
  Note: Some skippers have a frenulum.
- *Butterfly antennae usually end in a club and are straight, whereas moths' are usually filamentous, feathered or curved.*
  Note: Many butterfly antennae (e.g. skippers) are curved. Some butterflies have no clubs on their antennae. Many moths have clubbed antennae.

Butterfly foods

In the individual species accounts, butterfly foods are mentioned by scientific name only. This table provides **common names** for those foods with such names. *Note*: not all foods have common names.

SCIENTIFIC NAME	COMMON NAME	SCIENTIFIC NAME	COMMON NAME
Acacia ataxacantha	Flame Acacia	*Blighia unijugata*	Triangle Tops
A. brevispica	Prickly Acacia	*Boscia albitrunca*	Shepherd's Tree
A. burkei	Black Monkey Thorn	*B. oleoides*	Karoo Shepherd's Tree
A. caffra var. *tomentosa*	Hook Thorn	*Brachystegia spiciformis*	Msasa
A. erioloba	Camel Thorn	*Bridelia cathartica*	Knobby Bridelia
A. gerrardii	Red Thorn	*B. micrantha*	Mitzeerie
A. karroo	Sweet Thorn	*Burkea africana*	Wild Syringa
A. kirkii	Sweet Thorn	*Cadaba aphylla*	Leafless Cadaba
A. kraussiana	Sweet Thorn	*C. natalensis*	Mauve Cadaba
A. mellifera	Black Thorn	*C. termitaria*	Pink Cadaba
A. nigrescens	Knobthorn	*Calodendron capense*	Cape Chestnut
A. polyacantha	White Thorn	*Camponotus maculatus*	Spotted Sugar-ant
A. robusta	Ankle Thorn	*C. niveosetus*	Black Sugar-ant
A. saligna	Port Jackson Willow	*Canthium inerme*	Common Turkey-berry
A. schweinfurthi	River Climbing Acacia	*Capparis sepiaria*	Wild Caper Bush
A. sieberana	Paperbark Acacia	*C. tomentosa*	Woolly Caper Bush
A. tortilis	Umbrella Thorn	*Cassine tetragona*	Climbing Saffronwood
Acalypha glabrata	Forest False-nettle	*Catha edulis*	Bushman's Tea
Acridocarpus natalitius	Moth-fruit	*Celtis africana*	White Stinkwood
Adenia glauca	Bobbejaangif	*C. mildbraedii*	Natal White Stinkwood
A. gummifera	Slangklimop	*Chaetachme aristata*	Thorny Elm
Aeschynomene nodulosa	Small-leaved False-teeth Tree	*Chrysanthemoides monilifera*	Bush Tick-berry
Afzelia quanzensis	Pod Mahogany	*Chrysophyllum viridifolium*	Fluted Milkwood
Ageratum houstonianum	Floss Flower	*Citrus* spp.	Oranges, Lemons, Limes
Albizia adianthifolia	Natal Flat-crown	*Clausena anisata*	Horsewood
Allophylus africanus	False Currant	*Cleistochlamys kirkii*	Purple Cluster-pear
A. dregeanus	Simple-leaved Allophylus	*Clerodendron glabrum*	Cat's Whiskers
A. natalensis	Dune Allophylus	*Cola natalensis*	Common Cola
Annona senegalensis	Custard Apple	*Colophospermum mopane*	Mopane
Antirrhinum sp.	Snapdragons	*Colpoon compressum*	Cape Sumach
Artabotrys brachypetalus	Purple Hook-berry	*Combretum apiculatum*	Red Bushwillow
A. monteiroae	Red Hook-berry	*C. bracteosum*	Hiccup Nut
Asclepias fruticosa	Milkweed	*C. molle*	Velvet Bushwillow
Asclepias spp.	Milkweeds	*C. zeyheri*	Large-fruited Bushwillow
Azima tetracantha	Needle Bush	*Conyza canadensis*	Fleabane
Baphia racemosa	Natal Camwood	*Cotyledon orbiculata*	Pig's Ear
Barringtonia racemosa	Powder-puff Tree	*Croton gratissimus*	Lavender Croton
Bauhinia galpinii	Pride of de Kaap		

SCIENTIFIC NAME	COMMON NAME	SCIENTIFIC NAME	COMMON NAME
C. sylvaticus	Forest Croton	*Guibourtia conjugata*	Small False Mopane
Cryptocarya woodii	Wild Laurel	*Haplocoelum foliosum*	Northern Galla Plum
Cyanophyta	Blue-green Algae	*H. gallense*	Galla Plum
Cynodon dactylum	Couch Grass	*Hexalobus monopetalus*	Shakama Plum
Dalbergia armata	Thorny Rope	*Hibiscus tiliaceus*	Prickly Tree Hibiscus
D. melanoxylon	Zebrawood	*Hippobromus pauciflorus*	Basterperdepis
D. nitidula	Glossy Flat-bean	*Hyparrhenia hirta*	Common Thatching Grass
D. obovata	Climbing Flat-bean	*Hyperacanthus amoenus*	Spiny Gardenia
Deinbollia oblongifolia	Dune Soapberry	*Hypericum aethiopicum*	St John's Wort
Dichrostachys cinerea	African Christmas Tree	*Imperata cylindrica*	Cotton Wool Grass
Dioscorea cotinifolia	Wild Yam	*Kiggelaria africana*	Wild Peach
Diospyros austro-africana	Fire-sticks	*Lecaniodiscus fraxinifolius*	River Litchi
D. austro-africana var. microphylla	Fire-sticks	*Lobularia maritima*	Sweet Alyssum
D. lycioides	Blue Bush	*Lonchocarpus capassa*	Apple-leaf
D. mespiliformis	Jackalberry	*Mackaya bella*	River Bells
Dombeya burgessiae	Pink Dombeya	*Maerua angolensis*	Bead-bean
D. cymosa	Natal Dombeya	*M. cafra*	Bush Cherry
D. rotundifolia	Common Wild Pear	*M. juncea*	Bush Cherry
Dovyalis caffra	Kei Apple	*M. racemulosa*	Forest Bush Cherry
Dracaena hookeriana	Large-leaved Dragon Tree	*M. rosmarinoides*	Needle-leaved Bush Cherry
Drypetes gerrardii	Hairy Drypetes	*M. schinzii*	Ringwood Tree
Ekebergia capensis	Cape Ash	*Mangifera indica*	Mango
Elephantorrhiza burkei	Sumach Bean	*Manilkara discolor*	Forest Milkberry
Englerophytum magalismontanum	Stamvrug	*Maprounea africana*	Redskin
E. natalense	Natal Milkplum	*Margaritaria discoidea*	Common Pheasant-berry
Eragrostis aspera	Rough Love Grass	*Maytenus acuminata*	Silky Bark
Erythrococca berberidea	Prickly Red-berry	*M. heterophylla*	Common Spike-thorn
Erythroxylum emarginatum	Common Coca Tree	*M. senegalensis*	Red Spike-thorn
Euclea undulata	Common Guarri	*Medicago sativa*	Lucerne
Excoecaria bussei	Pawnbroker Tree	*Melia azedarach*	Syringa
Faidherbia albida	Ana Tree	*Melianthus major*	Kruidtjie-roer-my-nie
Ficus cordata	Namaqua Fig	*Milletia grandis*	Umzimbeet
F. ingens	Red-leaved Rock Fig	*M. sutherlandii*	Giant Umzimbeet
F. natalensis	Common Wild Fig	*Mimusops caffra*	Milkwood
F. pumila	Tickey Creeper	*M. obovata*	Red Milkwood
F. sur	Broom Cluster Fig	*M. zeyheri*	Milkwood
Gardenia volkensii	Transvaal Gardenia	*Monanthotaxis caffra*	Dwaba-berry
Grewia flava	Brandy Bush	*Monodora junodii*	Green-apple
G. flavescens	Rough-leaved Raisin	*Myrsine africana*	Cape Myrtle
G. monticola	Silver Raisin	*Obetia tenax*	Mountain Nettle
G. occidentalis	Cross Berry	*Ochna arborea*	Cape Plane
		O. holstii	Red ironwood
		O. natalitia	Natal Plane
		O. serrulata	Carnival Bush
		Ocimum canum	Wild Basil

SCIENTIFIC NAME	COMMON NAME	SCIENTIFIC NAME	COMMON NAME
Olax dissitiflora	Small Sourplum	*S.* brachypetala	Weeping Boer-Bean
Oricia swynnertonii	Twin-berry Tree	*Scutia* myrtina	Cat Thorn
Osyris lanceolata	Transvaal Sumach	*Securidaca* longipeduncularis	Violet Tree
Panicum deustum	Broad-leaved Panicum	*Securinega* virosa	White-berry Bush
P. maximum	Guinea grass	*Sesbania* sesban	River Bean
Pappea capensis	Jacket-plum	*Solanum* mauritianum	Bugweed
Parinari curatellifolia	Grey Apple	*Stenotaphrum* secundatum	Coastal Buffalo Grass
Passiflora edulis	Grenadilla	*Sterculia* quinqueloba	Large-leaved Star Chestnut
Peltephorum africanum	Weeping Wattle	*Strelitzia* nicolae	Natal Wild Banana
Pennisetum clandestinum	Kikuyu Grass	*Syzygium* cordatum	Umdoni/Waterberry
Persicaria attenuata africana	Snakeroot	*S.* guineense	Water Pear
Phoenix canariensis	Canary Palm	*Tamarindus* indica	Tamarind
P. dactylifera	Date Palm	*Teclea* natalensis	Natal Teclea
P. reclinata	Wild Date Palm	*Terminalia* sericea	Silver Cluster-leaf
Phylica paniculata	Common Hard-leaf	*Thamnocalamnus* tessellatus	Mountain Bamboo
Piliostigma thonningii	Camel Foot	*Trema* orientalis	Pigeonwood
Populus alba	White Poplar	*Tribulus* terrestris	Devil Thorn
Pouzolzia mixta	Soap Nettle	*Trichilia* dregeana	Mahogany
Protea caffra	Highveld Protea	*T.* emetica	Mahogany
P. cynaroides	King Protea	*Tricicleras* longipedunculatum	Rooihaarbossie
P. repens	Sugarbush	*Trifolium* africanum	Red Clover
P. roupelliae	Silver Protea	*Trilepisium* madagascariens	Bastard Fig
P. subvestita	Lipped Protea	*Trimeria* grandifolia	Mulberry-leaf Trimenia
P. welwitschii	Honey-scented Protea	*Triticum* sativum	Wheat
Prunus spp.	Peaches; Plums	*Tropaeolum* majus	Nasturtium
Pseudolachnostylis maprouneifolia	Kudu-berry	*Urera* cameroonensis	Climbing Nettle
Ptaeroxylon obliquum	Sneezewood	*U.* trinervis	Climbing Nettle
Pterocarpus angolensis	Kiaat	*Uvaria* caffra	Small Cluster-pear
P. brenanii	Large-leaved Bloodwood	*Vepris* lanceolata	White Ironwood
P. rotundifolius	Round-leaved Kiaat	*V.* reflexa	Bastard White Ironwood
Pycnostachys reticulata	Teasel	*Xanthocerces* zambesiaca	Nyala Tree
Rawsonia lucida	Forest Peach	*Xeroderris* stuhlmannii	Wing Pod
Rhamnus prinoides	Dogwood	*Ximenia* americana	Small Sourplum
Rhus longispina	Thorny Taaibos	*X.* caffra	Large Sourplum
R. undulata	Kuni-bush	*Xylotheca* kraussiana	African Dog Rose
R. zeyheri	Blue Taaibos	*Xymalos* monospora	Lemonwood
Ricinus communis	Castor Oil Plant	*Zanthoxylum* capense	Small Knobwood
Rumex lanceolatus	Dock	*Zea* mays	Maize
Saccharum officinarum	Sugar Cane	*Ziziphus* mucronata	Buffalo Thorn
Salvadora persica	Mustard Tree		
Sapium ellipticum	Jumping-seed Tree		
S. integerrimum	Duikerberry		
Schotia afra	Karoo Boer-Bean		

GLOSSARY

Abdomen The third and hindmost portion of an insect's body, carrying the digestive system, genitalia, and excretory organs. The softest and most vulnerable part of the body, visibly made up of segments (unlike head and thorax, which also consist of segments but these are not obvious).

Aberration Abnormal, rare mutant of a species, noticeably different in appearance from the norm. Includes excessively dark (melanistic) or abnormally light (albinistic) varieties. In many aberrations, markings normally appearing as rounded spots may be elongated into lines or streaks.

Aedeagus The sclerotised tube in male Lepidopteran genitalia through which the vesica or penis passes. The appearance of this structure can be useful in identification.

Alkaloid A physiologically active nitrogen-containing organic compound derived from plants, often poisonous to and used defensively against animals. The larvae and adults of some Lepidoptera can extract and store these substances, which, though harmless to themselves, are used as a defence against predators (e.g. Monarch butterflies). Also used as a feedstock for biochemical synthesis of sexual and warning pheromones.

Anal angle Angle between the outer and inner margins of the hind wing. The corresponding angle on the forewing is the inner angle.

Anal fold Portion of the hind wing that covers the abdomen of the resting insect. Of vital importance in butterfly's flight mechanism.

Anal margin Inner edge of hind wing closest to the abdomen.

Androconia Specialised wing scales in male butterflies, adapted to produce a scent or pheromone. Some males stimulate females to mate by 'dusting' them with pheromones produced by these scales. The scales may be grouped together in a definite patch, as in those of the male danaids.

Antennae Feelers or elongated sensory organs attached to the heads of insects. Long, flexible and stick-like in butterflies, pointing forwards with outer end usually thickened or clubbed. They are organs of touch, smell, and taste.

Apex Point on forewing where costa and outer margin meet.

Apical Area adjacent to the apex.

Apical angle Angle of the apex of the forewing.

Aposematic Advertising a warning by markings, coloration or behaviour, for example.

Basal In the wings, the part nearest the thorax.

Batesian mimicry Mimicry by a palatable species of an unpalatable model, which provides protection from predators. See Muellerian mimicry.

Bifid Divided into two parts.

Blind Specifically referring to eye spots or ocelli – lacking the pale 'pupil' inside the spot.

Camouflage See Cryptic colours, protective resemblance.

Caterpillar (= larva) The stage emerging from the egg of a butterfly or moth.

Cell (of wings) An open wing area bounded by veins. Situated at and near base of the wing and extending to centre of the wing.

Chitin Polysaccharide that forms the tough integument or exoskeleton that gives shape and support to an insect's body, and of which all the hard organs are made.

Chrysalis (= pupa) An insect's pupal or third development stage before complete metamorphosis.

Cilia In butterflies, the fine fringe of small hair-like scales along the outer edges of the wings.

Cline A character gradient; that is, a gradual

and essentially continuous change of character in a series of contiguous populations over considerable distances. An example in South Africa is the Burnished Opal *Chrysoritis chrysaor* (Lycaenidae).

Club The thickened or swollen apical end of the antenna.

Coccids Scale insects of the Order Homoptera, used as food by certain lycaenid larvae.

Colony A concentrated butterfly population living in a small area confined by microclimate, vegetation, presence of a host ant, or a combination of these and other factors.

Common names Vernacular names; these have no scientific significance.

Compound eyes Two large bulges on the side of the head of an adult butterfly or other insect, made up of many tiny facets called ommatidia, each of which is a separate lens focusing an image on the optic nerve. Like most insects, butterflies have poor visual acuity compared to mammals, but have extremely good motion sense. They have colour vision and can see in ultra-violet (UV) light. Many flowers have markings only visible in UV light and this is probably of significance to butterflies.

Costa Leading edge or front margin of fore- and hind wings.

Coxa First basal segment of an insect's leg, attached to the thorax.

Cremaster Hooks at the anal or hind end of the pupa for attachment to the pupal substrate – bark, leaves, twigs or rocks.

Cremastral hooks Microscopic hooks on the cremaster which attach it to the silk fibres of the cremastral pad.

Cremastral pad A pad of silk attached by the larva to the pupal substrate prior to pupation, and from which the pupa hangs.

Crepuscular Becoming active at twilight or before sunrise, as in certain hesperiids.

Cryptic colours Colours/patterns that conceal an insect or animal by matching it to the background.

Cubital veins Veins extending from the lower edge of the cell out to the distal margin.

Cuticle The non-cellular outer skin of insects, composed of chitin. This is cast off during moulting to accommodate increasing size.

Description In taxonomy, a brief formal statement of the characters of a taxon.

Dimorphism An organism that may exist as one of two different forms. This may be due to male/female differences (sexual dimorphism) or seasonal changes (seasonal dimorphism).

Disc The central area of the wing.

Discal cell The large central area of a wing, partly or completely bounded by veins.

Discocellular veins The short and weak transverse veins, which form the distal margin of the discal cell of the wing.

Distal Further from the centre of the body; outer part of the wing. (Opposite of distal is proximal.)

Diurnal Active in the day, or day-flying.

Dorsal The upper surface or back.

Endemic A natural inhabitant confined to a particular geographic area.

Eurytrope Able to utilise a wide range of habitat types.

Exoskeleton The chitinous external structural framework of an insect.

Eye spot The false 'eye' on the wing of an insect, or on the thorax of a caterpillar; usually ringed with contrasting colours and often with a dark, pupil-like centre. May be called an ocellus.

Falcate Sickle-shaped, as used to describe the apex of the wing when deeply excavated and extending beyond the level of the outer margin.

Family An assemblage of related genera. A taxonomic category ranking below an order and above a genus. Subamily and tribe may also be used between a family and a genus.

Femur The third segment of the leg (generally long and thick), which is connected proximally to the trochanter, and distally with the tibia.

Food plant The host plant on which butterfly and moth larvae feed.

Form Representative of a species that differs from the norm in some uniform character, and with which it interbreeds. Colour or shape variations may be constant. A form may be under genetic control in some species showing polymorphism or polymorphic mimics. Environmental influences produce seasonal forms. They are not recognised under the International Code of Zoological Nomenclature. Form names are used here only as an aid to identification.

Frass Solid larval excrement.

Fynbos The dominant vegetation type of the Cape Floristic Region – found in the southern and western parts of the Western Cape and Eastern Cape provinces. From the Dutch *fijnbosch*.

Genitalia The organs used for either copulation or oviposition; made of chitin and their shape is often typical to the species. Useful in distinguishing closely related butterfly species that are difficult to tell apart by their wing patterns.

Genus (pl. genera) A group within a family consisting of one or more closely related species.

Girdle The silken strand spun as a sling around the thorax of certain butterfly pupae to allow them to hang horizontally or head upwards.

Ground colour The predominant colour of the wing contrasted to that of the pattern.

Gynandromorph An individual insect having both male and female characteristics. A rare abnormality in the sex chromosomes resulting in the insect having a mosaic of male and female features, or more commonly where half the butterfly is male and the other female (a bilateral gynandromorph).

Habitat The favoured environment of a particular species.

Haemocoel The hollow interior of an insect's body, containing the internal organs and bathed in haemolymph.

Haemolymph The circulating body fluid of insects.

Hair pencil A dense tuft of specialised scale-hairs on the body or wings of male butterflies, displayed during courtship; may carry pheromones to attract or excite the female.

Haustellum The mobile distal part of the proboscis, used for sucking up liquids.

Head A butterfly's head contains the rudimentary brain and carries the major sense and feeding organs.

Hill-topping The habit of some male butterflies of frequenting higher areas, particularly during the hottest hours of the day. Hill-topping is a well-known butterfly behaviour, usually involved with mate location in species whose food plants, and hence individual adults, are widely scattered. Males compete for hill-top territories and females ascend the hills to find the dominant individuals. Hill tops therefore help to concentrate low-density species in small areas, and are of great help to the lepidopterist.

Holotype The single specimen selected by the author of the species as the 'type' or reference specimen. Can be used for the only known specimen at the time of description.

Honey gland A shallow slit or depression on the top of the seventh abdominal segment of a lycaenid larva, into which several glands secrete a fluid which attendant ants drink.

Host ant A species of ant allowing a butterfly larva to spend almost the whole, or part, of the immature stages in its nest.

Humeral vein A short vein arising from the

base of the hind wing and coursing towards the base of the costa; also known as the precostal spur.

Hyaline Clear; transparent, water-like in colour.

Hybrid The result of interbreeding between two species.

Imago (pl. Imagines) The adult or sexually developed insect.

Infuscated Darkened in colour, or with a black tinge.

Inner angle The tornus or anal angle.

Inner margin Same as the anal margin.

Instar The larval period between the hatching of the egg and first moult (first instar), and the period between each successive moult until pupation. There are usually four to six instars before pupation.

Integument The exoskeleton, or wall, of the insect body.

Irrorated Very finely speckled with tiny dots, lines or streaks.

Jassids Plant lice of the Order Homoptera, eaten by certain lycaenid larvae.

Karroid Karoo-like. Referring to the semi-arid central-southern region of South Africa, in the Cape provinces and Free State, called the Karoo.

Labial palpi Paired scale-covered finger-like sensory appendages arising from the insect labium, situated either side of the proboscis; those of butterflies have three segments. Used to clean the mouthparts, they also carry scent and taste organs.

Labium Fused mouthparts forming the posterior ventral wall of the mouth.

Larva (pl. larvae) = caterpillar. The sexually immature, feeding, developmental stage of an insect with complete metamorphosis.

Lateral Describing parts or features away from the midline, or on the side of an object.

Legs Butterflies have six legs, like all insects. The front legs of Nymphalidae and some Lycaenidae are atrophied and the butterflies

appear to have only four legs. The legs are jointed and consist of a coxa and trochanter (closely attached to the thorax and seldom visible in the field), femur (thigh), tibia (shin) and tarsus (foot). The foot is made up of several joints and ends in a two-pronged claw. Some butterflies carry additional taste organs on their feet. Butterfly larvae have six claw-like true legs immediately behind the head, used to grasp food; the fleshy buds used for walking are 'false legs', muscular protrusions of the abdominal segments equipped with bristles and sucker pads.

Lepidoptera The order of insects to which butterflies and moths belong. The four wings are covered with minute scales, hence the Greek derivation *lepis*, a scale; *pteron*, a wing.

Life-cycle The complete life-cycle of a butterfly or moth, including the egg, larval stages, pupa and imago.

Lunule A crescent-shaped marking or spot.

Malpighian tubules Tiny tubes that concentrate waste material from the haemolymph in an insect's body and transport it to the anus.

Marginal Describing features found on the outer margins of the wings.

Media The fourth main longitudinal vein (M) of the wing. The basal half of it is absent in butterflies.

Median The middle vein of the wing.

Melanism A colour aberration with a suffusion or replacement of wing or body colours with black or darkened colours. The opposite of albinism.

Membracid A member of the Membracidae, or leaf-hopper insects, on which some lycaenid larvae feed.

Metamorphosis The transformation from the larval to the adult state. Referred to as complete in the Lepidoptera, in which there is a non-feeding pupal stage. In insects such as grasshoppers it is referred to as incomplete because they develop through a series of nymphal instars that resemble the adult.

Metapopulation Series of small, independent colonies of butterflies or other organisms in an area, between which individuals may disperse and interbreed, or colonise new areas.

Micropyle Tiny hole at the top of an egg through which the fertilising sperm enters.

Mimic An organism superficially resembling another of a different species, so that one or other benefits.

Mimicry The resemblance of one species to another, occurring in the same area. See Batesian and Muellerian mimicry.

Model An organism that a mimic resembles.

Morphology The description and study of structural characteristics, particularly on the body surface.

Moult Changing of skin when the insect (larva in butterflies) has grown to the point where the old skin is restricting growth; new skin forms under the old skin and when it is ready the old skin splits and the larva, in a larger, looser skin, emerges.

Muellerian mimicry Form of mimicry in insects where both the model and the mimic are distasteful or poisonous to predators.

Myrmecophilous Living symbiotically with ants.

Nominate The first of two or more subspecies in any species to be named.

Ocellus (pl. ocelli) **1.** The small simple eye of an adult insect, not to be confused with the larger compound eye. Adult Lepidoptera have two, one behind each antenna. **2.** Alternative term for eye spot on the wing.

Onisciform Woodlouse-shaped, with a flattened body. Many lycaenid larvae have such an appearance.

Order The major taxonomical subdivision of a phylum (e.g. Insecta) into groups with similar basic characteristics. For example, all insects with wing scales are grouped in the Order Lepidoptera.

Osmeterium A fleshy extensible organ situated on the back of the prothorax of larvae of the family Papilionidae. Y-shaped, emitting a pungent smell, everted when the larva senses a threat.

Outer margin The distal or outer margin of a wing, also known as the termen.

Oviposition The act of egg laying.

Ovum (pl. ova) Insect eggs.

Palp or palpus (pl. palpi) One of a pair of segmented sensory organs of the maxilla and labium in insects. Palpi are relatively large processes, originating from below the head and curving forward in front of the face.

Parasite Any organism that grows, feeds or is sheltered on or in a different organism while contributing nothing to its host's survival. In fact, the wasps of flies whose larvae infest Lepidopteran larvae are strictly speaking parasitoids, since they kill their host – something a true parasite does not do.

Paratype Any specimen in a series from which a taxonomic description has been drawn up, other than the holotype.

Patrolling Mate-location behaviour in which male butterflies fly almost continually, often along a repetitive beat, in search of females.

Pheromone A chemical substance externally secreted by an individual which produces a response in another of the same species; or, in the case of myrmecophilous butterflies, a response to ants and vice versa.

Phytophagous Plant eating.

Polymorphism The occurrence of more than two forms in the same species.

Population A group of organisms of the same species living together in the same locality.

Postdiscal Descriptive of features occupying the area between discal and submarginal regions of the wing.

Proboscis The modified mouthparts of an insect; in Lepidoptera its distal end is prehensile. It takes the form of a long tubular organ attached to the crop and gullet. It is held under the head, between the lower parts of the labial palpi. It is usually kept coiled like a watch spring. Butterflies have a totally liquid diet and lack biting mouthparts. Some butterflies, such as the lycaenid genus *Thestor* (Skollies), gain all their nutrition as larvae and the adult proboscis, not being needed, is vestigial.

Process(es) A projection or protuberance.

Protective resemblance Cryptic colours or camouflage.

Proximal Nearest to the base or point of origin. The opposite of distal.

Pupa (= chrysalis, chrysalid). Non-feeding, post-larval stage of complete metamorphosis.

Race Subspecies.

Radius The third main longitudinal vein (R), usually with three to five branches in the forewing.

Savanna Open grassland with tall grasses and scattered trees or clumps of bushes.

Scales The microscopic plates (actually flattened hairs) attached, like shingles on a roof, to the wing surfaces of Lepidoptera, which, viewed as a whole, make up the colours and patterns on the wings. Pigments in these scales are responsible for the majority of colours (may fade over time). Iridescent colours are produced by thin film light interference caused by either a number of superimposed plates in the substance of the scale, or thin stacks of plates confined to the longitudinal ridges of the scale.

Seasonal dimorphism Two distinct colour and/or size forms in a species, whose appearance is dependent on the season. Intermediate forms may occur between the two seasonal extremes.

Segment Ring-like or tubular section of the insect body or its appendages.

Seta (pl. setae) Structure resembling a hair or bristle.

Sex brand Mark or patch on the wings of some male Lepidoptera, made up of androconial scales.

Sexual dimorphism Genetically controlled phenomenon where males and females of the same species have a strikingly different appearance (form, colour or pattern).

Species The primary biological unit. A population of interbreeding organisms alike in appearance and structure. They share a common mate recognition system, reproductively isolated from other similar insect/animal groups.

Species complex A group of closely related species within a genus, also known as a species group.

Specific name The second half of a binomial name; individual to each species within a genus.

Spermatheca A storage sac for sperm inside the female genitalia of an insect, opening into the vagina.

Sphragis A hardened secretion deposited by certain male butterflies around the genital opening of the female during mating.

Spiracles The external breathing holes of an insect, situated along the sides of the abdomen.

Striated Covered in striae, thin lines or bands.

Subapical Adjective describing features occupying the area of the wing immediately proximal to its apex.

Subcosta The second main longitudinal vein (S_c) of the wing.

Subcostal Describes features occupying the area of the wing immediately below the costa.

Subfamily A section of a family containing genera more closely related to one another than to other genera in the family.

Submarginal The area of the wing between the margin and the postdiscal area.

Submedian The area of the wing proximal to the centre or median portion.

Subspecies One or more taxonomically and geographically distinct populations or races of a species.

Superfamily A group of related families.

Symbiosis Whereby two or more individuals of different species live together, each benefiting from the relationship.

Sympatry The occurrence of two or more taxa (groups) having the same or overlapping geographical ranges.

Synonym One, two or more name/s applied to the same species. A name rendered obsolete by the taxonomic law of priority.

Tail A tail-like outgrowth along a vein from the outer margin of the hind wing. In some butterflies, an associated eye spot on the undersurface adjacent to tails may mimic a false head and antennae of a resting butterfly.

Tarsus (pl. tarsi) The most distal section of a leg or foot.

Taxon (pl. taxa) A taxonomic group that is sufficiently distinct to be worthy of being distinguished by a name and to be ranked in a definite category.

Taxonomy The arrangement of species and groups thereof into a system which exhibits their relationship to each other, and their places in a natural hierarchical classification.

Territoriality Behaviour in which an animal patrols and defends an area from others of the same species.

Tibia The fourth segment of the leg.

Thoracic legs The true jointed legs of a larva.

Thorax The second or intermediate region of the body, carrying the butterfly's means of locomotion; made up of three segments, the pro-, meso- and metathorax, each bearing a pair of legs. The meso- and metathorax of butterflies each bear a pair of wings. As the anchor for the flight and leg muscles, the thorax is the strongest and most rigid part of the body.

Tornus The posterior (bottom) angle of the wing between the anal margin (inner margin) and the outer margin (or termen).

Trachea The respiratory organs in insects. Branching tubes originating externally at the spiracles, spreading and branching throughout the body.

Tubercles Paired, eversible organs on the 8th abdominal segment of many lycaenid larvae, functioning in ant association.

Type The single specimen or any one of a series of specimens upon which a genus is founded, or selected as the type of a genus.

Type locality The locality at which the holotype was collected.

Venation The system of arrangement of the veins of an insect wing. The veins are neither true veins nor nerves. They are chitin-lined channels through which haemolymph and air can pass.

Warning coloration Conspicuous coloration patterns adopted by some insects to advertise their unpalatability to predators.

Wingspan The measurement of the length of the forewing from base to apex, or the greatest width of an insect measured across the forewings.

Bibliography

Clark GC & Dickson CGC. *Life Histories of the South African Lycaenid Butterflies*, Purnell, Cape Town, 1971

Henning SF. *The Charaxinae Butterflies of Africa*, Aloe Books, Johannesburg, 1989

Henning SF & GA. *South African Red Data Book – Butterflies*, CSIR, Pretoria, 1989

Henning SF & GA, Joannou JG & Woodhall SE.; *Living Butterflies of Southern Africa vol. 1*, Umdaus Press, Pretoria, 1997

Migdoll I. *Field Guide to the Butterflies of Southern Africa*, C Struik, Cape Town, 1987

Pringle E, Henning GA & Ball JB. *Pennington's Butterflies of Southern Africa*, 2nd ed., Struik Winchester, Cape Town, 1994

Williams MC. *Butterflies of Southern Africa, a Field Guide*, Southern Book Publishers, Halfway House, 1994

Williams MC. *Afrotropical Butterflies and Skippers*, Digital format encyclopaedia on compact disc (CD), privately published by Prof. M. C. Williams, 183 Van der Merwe Street, Rietondale 0084, Pretoria, 2003

Williams MC *et al* (eds). *Metamorphosis, Journal of the Lepidopterists' Society of Africa*, Florida, Johannesburg, vols 1–15, Woodhall SE (ed.), *A Practical Guide to Butterflies and Moths in Southern Africa*, Lepidopterists' Society of Southern Africa, Johannesburg, 1992

Author Steve Woodhall getting close to his subject.

List of Subscribers

Sponsor's Edition

Abri	**Gilbert, Tim**	**Marais, Johan**
Cockburn, Kevin & Stella	**Hammond, Dr Christopher A**	**McDermott, DL**
Coetzer, Bennie & André	**Hanni, Sonia**	**Staude, HS**
Dobson, Jeremy	**Haggett, David**	**Tooch, Harold**

Standard Edition

Abbott, John
ABC Bookshop
Abland (Pty) Ltd
Alexander, Graeme
Ashton, Peter J
Batchelor, David B
Beal family
Beukes, Prof Gerhard J
Blythe-Wood, Colin
Boolsen-Lotz, Melissa
Bouwer, Dr JJ
Bullen, Karen & Gerald
Carstensen, Norman
Clark, Max
Collins, S
Cooper, Mark & De Villiers, Kelly
Cottino, Debora Ann
Crosse, Neville & Charlotte
De Goede (FWD), Adrian Michael
Dobson, Jeremy & Chris
Du Randt, Francois & Ronelle
Duckworth's Dargle Delight,
   Machadodorp
Friedman, Russel, Bonnie &
   Gabriella
Gainsford, Kenneth
Gardiner, Dr Alan
Garvie, Owen & Wendy
Geertsema, Prof Henk
Goodall, Chris
Goodall, Mark
Greve, Jürgen & Anita
Grundlingh, Felicity I

Hammond, Dr Christopher A
Hanni, Marie
Hawkes, Peter G
Henning, Graham & Eileen
Hepburn, John K
Hermannsburg Nature Club
Hesketh, Richard
Hitchins, Peter & Stella
Horsten, Alison
Huggins, Peter & Van Dijk, Ineke
Hutson, Doug & Jane
Jeffery, RG
Juyn, N
Kloppers, JJ
Knight, RA
Kroon, DM
Kruger, John
Laidler, Dennis & Gigi
Lessing, Graham
Louw, Kirsten
Lubke, Prof Roy A
MacQuilkan, Peter – Managa Hills
Magagula, Dr Cebisile N
Mahlambi, Max
Marais, Johan
Martyn, Brett
Matthew, Mike & Anita
McBurnie, Heather K
McCann, Terry
McDermott, DL
McDermott, Phillip
McMaster, Cameron
Mey, Dr Wolfram

Morant, Patrick
Morton, Deryk
Morton, Doug & Terri
Mouton, Dr Jacques
Muller family
Murray, Bob & Jean
Niehaus, JP
Plowes, Allan
Podmore, Kevin & Glynis
Pretorius, Gerrit
Pringle, EL
Saunders, Chuck
Shankman, Allan
Sinclair-Smith, Dr C
Skelton, Geoff & Anne
Slotow, Dennis & Ansie
Steyn, Jannie & Juanita
Teasdale, Grant J
Toussaint, Dawn Cory
Trendler, Roy
University of Stellenbosch
Van der Jagt, Dick & Liz
Van der Sandt, Johan & Annatjie
Van Nierop, Pat
Van Zijl, Helm and Gillian
Viossat, Alexandre
Walton, Shaun
Watt, Ronnie
Wickham's Fancy, Machadodorp
Williams, Mark & Mathilde
Willis, Christopher & Carla
Zwiegelaar, Lyn & Johan

Index to common names

Index to scientific names

Male Saffron Sapphire *Iolaus pallene* resting on yellowed leaves of early spring bushveld trees; the butterfly's appearance is beautifully timed to take advantage of this camouflage.

Notes

Notes

Notes